PUBLIC ADMINISTRATION

Balancing Power and Accountability

SECOND EDITION

JEROME B. McKINNEY
AND
LAWRENCE C. HOWARD

Westport, Connecticut
London

To our parents and wives, Betty Howard and Mary Theresa McKinney, and
daughters, Katie and the late Melissan

Library of Congress Cataloging-in-Publication Data

McKinney, Jerome B.
  Public administration : balancing power and accountability /
Jerome B. McKinney and Lawrence C. Howard. — 2nd ed.
    p.   cm.
  Includes bibliographical references and index.
  ISBN 0–275–95564–8 (alk. paper). — ISBN 0–275–95565–6 (pbk. :
alk. paper)
    1. Public administration. I. Howard, Lawrence C. (Lawrence
Cabot), 1925–
JF1351.M25   1998
351—dc21   96–47619

British Library Cataloguing in Publication Data is available.

Library of Congress Catalog Card Number: 96–47619
ISBN: 0–275–95564–8
      0–275–95565–6 (pbk.)

First published in 1998

Praeger Publishers, 88 Post Road West, Westport, CT 06881
An imprint of Greenwood Publishing Group, Inc.

Printed in the United States of America

The paper used in this book complies with the
Permanent Paper Standard issued by the National
Information Standards Organization (Z39.48–1984).

P

Contents

Figures and Tables

FIGURES

TABLES

Preface

This text presents public administration as a tension between the necessary exercise of power and the search for accountability by public servants. Growing disillusionment about the behavior of some public administrators and frustration over the ineffective and ever-more expensive public programs make a new approach to the teaching of public management essential. Watergate and subsequent taxpayer revolts marked a turning point—public administration can no longer be taught apart from ethical and moral concerns. Today, downsizing and the pursuit of better government for less are the norm. We can no longer expect public budgets will continue to increase.

The authors have attempted to initiate a new approach. Our major focus is on middle- and low-level managers. These are the positions that most students of public administration will occupy for most of their professional careers. In the past, many public administration texts have had a bias toward upper-level officials and a Washington focus. We endeavor to modify that emphasis through recognition that most of administration is in field offices, in state and local government, and in cooperation with the private sector. Second, we focus on power and its potential for influencing the behavior of the bureaucracy. At many points in the text, we point out how middle- and lower-level managers are the key translators of policy objectives into program outputs in the delivery of services. We also point out that much of this power in the middle of bureaucracies is exercised without close and informed supervision and that much influence is applied beyond public view. Third, this leads us to attempt to relate theories about administration to the actual practice of administration. Numerous illustrations and cases depicting the applications of power are presented. Our text attempts to show that public administration occurs in a web of tension in which administrators, on the one hand, must husband and maintain power to permit needed actions. On the other hand, they must also enhance traditional responsiveness to elected superiors including programmatic accountability aimed at enabling people to function without dependency on government.

We have called for greater internalization of accountability, and in this sense the text assumes a moral stance, a commitment to reform in the practice of administration toward greater accountability. This is not simply a hope. Rather, it is the conclusion that greater responsiveness and increased enablement of citizens are cost-effective and that they will bring increased productivity and heightened recognition to the administrator who pursues this approach. We are fully aware that translating this call into performance will not be easily achieved and that a text with this intent will have to be supplemented by instructors similarly committed. We are encouraged, however, by a higher sense of accountability we have found in our students. A climate favorable to increased accountability exists. We seek to bring instructional materials in line with this healthy and hopeful development.

We have many to thank for help in this project. First must be the students and practitioners who have made up our classes and with whom the ideas in this text have been tested. We have also profited from critiques offered by Professors Robert T. Norman, the late Clifford C. Ham, and F. Burke Sheeran, and the assistance of Charles Coleman, George Nichols, Isaac Lowe, M. Sarmade, Carolina Rangel, and Hyman Weiss. We also owe thanks to Sheila Kelly and Willadean Baily for their secretarial help and to the Graduate School of Public and International Affairs.

Part I

Context of Administration

1

Ethical Foundations and Imperatives of Public Management

This chapter is divided into nine parts. Sections one and two discuss the definition and enduring themes of public sector ethics. Sections three through seven examine public and private sector ethics, showing how it can be used to promote accountability and how the application of ethical principles can be used to constrain administrative discretion and individual behavior. Section eight reviews the imperatives and parameters of a public service philosophy. Section nine outlines the organization of the book.

LEARNING OBJECTIVES

On completing this chapter, the reader should be able to:

- Obtain a clear understanding of the contrasting meaning of ethics and its enduring themes and concepts that guide public decision-makers.
- Explain the differences between the practice and standards of public and private ethics.
- Recognize how ethical principles can be effectively used to limit the exercise of discretion and enhance accountability.
- Understand the imperatives and utility of a carefully articulated and institutionalized public service philosophy.

Comments about public service ethics and unethical behavior in the public sector have been increasing over the past two decades. The increased emphasis on public service ethics can be attributed, in part, to the "goldfish bowl" or the open visibility in which public service is carried out. This approach allows the news media to readily see both positive and negative achievements. The proclivity of the news media to stress conflicts and unaccountable acts has created growing cynicism about public service. The constitutional system of checks and balances creates inevitable and continuing tension among the three branches of government, especially the legislative and the executive, that many citizens view as unhelpful and wasteful of public resources. Public events such as the Tonkin Gulf incident, Watergate, and the Iran-Contra scandal over the past thirty years have helped produce a high level of mistrust. These events reflect negatively on public service even though these actions are typically carried out by non-career public officials. Because these individuals carry the public mantle, they are expected to exhibit a model, moral leadership in pursuing the public interest. Aristotle said that people in government exercise a teaching function. Among other things, we see what they do and think is how we should act. Unfortunately, we learn from them when they do things that are underhanded or dishonest.[1]

Public administrators are constantly challenged by ethical decisions. Unclear delegated authority may involve choices between personal aspirations and organizational responsibilities. If the public interest is to be served, the public manager needs to have a clear moral framework that allows the administrator to sort through the options presented.

DEFINING ETHICS

Ethics is a moral compass. It is the study of and philosophy concerned with the morality of human conduct, emphasizing how to best determine right and wrong values in specific circumstances for a particular group, organization, region, or nation. Ethics involves the process of and search for moral standards that aid us in identifying and clarifying right and wrong actions.[2] To facilitate and promote consistent application of moral norms, basic standards or principles to guide right actions must be established. Ethics is thus the continuous pursuit of moral standards.

Despite the defined moral standards for action, numerous situations do not fit neatly within defined guidelines. The application of ethical norms involves consideration and deliberate thought prior to action. Should you shade the truth when presenting the results of a program for underprivileged children in order to continue it? Should you follow the orders of hierarchical officials when you know they are in conflict with organizational rules and practices?

The ideal applications of ethical norms preclude relativism, which says that there are no universal principles or rules to guide administrative action. Universal ethical principles do not permit differences among cultures in which operating norms and rules of conduct vary. For example, killing unwanted babies, burning witches, polygamy, incest, torture, and inhumane methods of punishment may be sanctioned in some societies while forbidden in others.[3]

MORAL PHILOSOPHY AS A GUIDE FOR
ADMINISTRATIVE ACTION

In many important actions, administrators must continuously determine which are right and which are wrong. To be consistent in choosing a particular course of action requires clearly defined criteria. In determining the criteria, one approach may be to rely on cost-effectiveness or the benefit principle. This means that the option to be pursued is the one that will achieve the desired results for the least cost. A second approach may be to apply universal moral principles or rules in deciding the course of action to be followed. A third approach may be *utilitarianism*. It holds that an action ought to be pursued whenever the greatest number of people will benefit. This approach does not adhere to universal principles; rather, each situation is determined to be moral or immoral on the basis of the calculation of the costs and benefits. The actor does not decide about right or wrong judgments in advance. The decision is rendered only after the harm that was done to individuals is compared with the assistance or benefits generated. The utilitarian perspective says that "actions themselves have no intrinsic values. They are simply means to attain things which do have value."[4]

The utilitarian view contrasts sharply with the concept known as *deontology*, which applies the principles of right and wrong on an a priori basis. This means that the principles can be applied without knowing the consequences of individual situations. Adherents to the deontological concept emphasize the importance of duties and responsibilities. The duty imperative demands that we do what is morally right and just without regard to the consequences.[5] Administrators who view themselves as adherents of the deontological approach are guided by internalized imperatives to which their organization subscribes. These attributes may include individual dignity, freedom, or respect for law and order.

APPLYING ETHICS AND MORALITY

It must be kept in mind that moral philosophy deals with applied ethics. It has become immensely popular over the last two decades. Ethics courses are now found in the curricula of many public affairs schools and programs. The Hastings Center in New York City and the Institute for Philosophy and Public Policy at the University of Maryland, College Park, Maryland and the Markkula Center for Applied Ethics at Santa Clara University in Santa Clara, California have been established. Yet it cannot be overstressed that morality cannot be effectively achieved unless it is socialized and internalized. Morality is thus a way of life. It is not a method of analysis. To treat morality as the study of abstract ethical reasoning may "*create* a moral vacuum rather than fill one" in public administration.[6]

Speaking from his many years of experience in the business community, one well-known observer expresses the view of many of his colleagues when he said that ethics is a learned pattern of behavior that cannot typically be taught to those over the age of ten. The belief is that ethics is one of those attributes with which one is born or is socialized by parents' teaching, priests or grade school teachers. It cannot be learned in college or graduate school unless the basic grounding has been laid and internalized.[7]

SOME ENDURING THEMES IN PUBLIC ETHICS

Though the commitment to and the concern for ethics in the public sector have gone through ebbs and flows, there are enduring themes that undergird public management. We emphasize the following: (1) citizenship, ethics, and democracy; (2) virtue, ethics, and the public interest; (3) ethics and the founding fathers' thoughts; and (4) ethics and administration.

Citizenship, Ethics, and Democracy

Public servants carrying out their administrative functions are also citizens who reflect the values of the broader American society and the community in which they live. Administrators are socialized to learn how to respond to the "deliberate will" of the people as reflected in publicly determined policies. At a minimum, democratic public servants have reverence for laws, commitment to participation, and tolerance and respect for others in the pursuit of the public interest. Generally, they must have commitment to the norms of political equality treating the least and most powerful alike; to political liberty, encouraging free expression; and to participation in helping to facilitate the formation and translation of policy into action. Public administration takes place in an environment in which democracy is understood as a kind of dialogue among people and their leaders.

Because of the strategic role administrators play in translating policies into specific goods and services for citizens, administrators have an important responsibility to provide quality information aimed at promoting effective dialogue not only among themselves and political leaders but also for ordinary citizens. This provides the opportunity to gain insightful exchange, analysis, and interpretation for all concerned.

Virtue, Ethics, and the Public Interest

In Socrates' view, happiness is impossible without moral virtue. Non-virtuous acts are unnatural and do more harm to those carrying out the acts than to the people they victimize. The conclusion suggests that unethical people are weak in character and intellect and are psychologically unhealthy. People engaged in vice lack the self-control and intellectual clarity required to live a happy life. To become virtuous, we must liberate ourselves from the addiction of perverted desires.[8] This can be achieved, Socrates said, mainly by learning and metaphysical truths that require years of long study to reveal moral virtue.

Aristotle's *Nicomachean Ethics* defines virtue "not according to the nature of actions but according to the disposition of the doer."[9] Virtue is developed in the same way as physical skills—by hard work, combining practice and habit. It is what the action achieves or produces that determines whether it helps and is thus ethical.

The Founding Fathers were likely influenced by John Locke, whom many had read and who articulated the need for virtuous public servants. Locke believed that a good reputation is an important attribute for public servants whose behavior should be influenced by public opinion. Opinion is important because it provides public servants with the opportunity to receive praise and esteem.[10] Locke believed that family influence was significant in shaping character and instilling virtue during the early childhood years. For Locke it was critical not only to provide civil law and religion but also to socialize children in the ways and standards of the community so that they internalize the practice of right and wrong and are constant in their efforts to uphold them. This orientation and socialization will act, in Locke's view, as a powerful force in minimizing the pursuit of self-interest.[11]

The virtue of public servants was clearly reflected in George Washington's criteria for selection only of those who had fitness of character to work in his administration. They were expected to be governed primarily by honor and esteem. James Madison and Alexander Hamilton expressed the view that public servants should possess appropriate attributes and traits. They were expected to be energetic and competent, firm, courageous, industrious, frugal, selfless, and virtuous. Public servants were expected to establish a model behavior and character that citizens could emulate. Delegates at the Constitutional Convention subscribed to the view that the character of public administrators was an important foundation for the fledgling United States.[12]

While natural virtue was recognized as an important ingredient for the promotion of the public interest, Hamilton and Madison believed that such norms could not alone ensure virtuous governors in the absence of political virtue. Corrective institutional and political arrangements had to be established to promote the public interest.[13] Today the prevailing view is that the bedrock for achieving public virtue is through the professionalization of the public service complemented by a code of ethics. The belief is that professionalization promotes the review and evaluation of members' behavior. The view is expressed that the promotion of professionalization promote is inevitable in a complex society. Yet it must be recognized that professional standards and democratic values inevitably create tension as professionals (middle- and lower-level managers) exercise enormous influence on policies.[14]

Ethics and Founding Thoughts

Delegates to the Constitutional Convention devoted considerable attention and deliberation to the character of citizens in the new government. Delegates believed that government would continually find enough citizens of character who would be sufficiently public-spirited and dedicated to effectively pursue the public interest.[15]

To obtain the best grounding and understanding to serve the public, the Founding Fathers felt that proper education was indispensable. Anti-Federalists were so strongly committed to the role of education that they advocated the establishment of schools or academies to educate prospective public servants in the ways of public virtue. These public servants would be imbued with a commitment to defend the government against all foes.[16]

On the Federalist side, Madison and Washington wished to see the establishment of a national university to educate and foster habits of public virtue and commitment to the public service. Thomas Jefferson, in his *Notes on the State of Virginia*, regarded his law that established the educational system in the state of Virginia as one of his most important contributions. He saw the need for public education as an important bulwark against despots.[17]

Jefferson articulated the view that "people will be happiest [in that government] whose laws are best and are best administered, and that laws will be wisely formed, and honestly administered in proportion as those who form and administer them are wise and honest." According to Jefferson, these are the citizens "whom nature had endowed with genius and virtue."[18]

To be eligible to carry out the public functions, students followed a progressively rigorous selection process after a defined program of study. From the advanced students only the best and the brightest were to be chosen after three years of additional study in science at William and Mary College before they began their public service.[19]

Ethics and Administration

Commitment to constitutional norms is of particular concern in the American system of government in view of the strong emphasis on individual interest, accountability to citizens, sovereignty issues, division of powers between the federal and state governments, and the system of checks and balances. In this regard Woodrow Wilson posed a series of questions in an 1887 essay:

The question for us is how shall our series of governments within governments be so administered it should always be to the interest of the public officer to serve, not only his superior alone but the community with the best efforts of his service and his talents and the soberest service of his conscience? How shall such service be made to his commonest interest by contributing abundantly to his substance, to his highest interest by furthering his ambition, and to his highest interest by advancing his honor and establishing his character?[20]

Hamilton believed that the federal constitutional system required a strong administrative system, unlike the weak one that the anti-Federalists advocated. In Hamilton's view, only strong and competent public administrators would receive the respect and public support necessary to "promote private and public morality by providing them with effective protection."[21]

The Constitution is the common and indispensable guide to all administrators. John Rohr suggests that ethical standards emanate from the Constitution, which all bureaucrats are required to defend. He notes the character-forming role of the U.S. Supreme Court, whose opinions and procedures keep us focused on fundamental and enduring principles, providing critical interpretations of American values. The Court's opinions directly affect administrative actions, often raising important questions while forcing us to reflect on basic values.[22] Additionally, public administrators are duty-bound to "maintain the constitutional balance of powers in support of individual liberty."[23]

According to Rohr, public administrators' critical role allows them to act as constitutional trustees, giving them great power and leverage to favor one branch of government over another. Administrators are forced "to think like judges as well as like legislators and executives because they are all three of these. In a regime of separation of powers, administrators must do the work of statesmen."[24]

The Constitution does not allow a politics-administration dichotomy. The Weberian neutral competent administrator who executes his or her duties without emotion or compassion, strictly following the orders of superiors, is inconsistent with the Founding Fathers' concept of the constitutional system. Administrators cannot and should not be guided only by superiors. Who did the Founders expect to provide guidance and evaluate public administrators' actions? In a democratic republic, the Founders believed that public opinion should play a role.

Though Woodrow Wilson believed that the government should be run by highly professionalized civil servants with significant discretion, he believed that administrators should always be mindful of public opinion but they should never be allowed to be meddlesome. He observed:

To whom is official trustworthiness to be disclosed, and by whom is it disclosed? Is the official to look to the public for his need of praise and his push of promotion, or only to his superior in office? Are the people to be called in to settle constitutional principles? The problem is: What part shall public opinion take in the conduct of administration?[25]

Wilson never intended the training of the highly professionalized civil service to be narrow, technical, and instrumental. He recognized the role politics plays in public administration. Thus, to be sensitive and responsive to the democratic environment in which they operate, public servants should follow a curriculum that includes constitutional principles, history, comparative government, politics, public law, and management.[26] It was in this context that Wilson stated:

The ideal focus is a civil service cultured and self-sufficient enough to act with a sense of vigor, and yet so immensely connected with the popular thought, by means of elections and constant public counsel, as to find arbitrariness or class spirit quite out of the question.[27]

OBSERVATION ON GOVERNMENT AND PRIVATE ETHICS

Like the public service, private sector actors are a microcosm of American society. The ethics of private sector participants are likely to differ from those of public administrators only to the extent that the context, opportunity, and the organizational culture and subculture differ according to experiences and ideologies.

The criteria for measuring success in the public sector often relate to qualitative goals and objectives such as improving personal security and educating citizens to their fullest capability. Undertakings in the private sector rely typically on quantitative indicators, such as the bottom line or profits. Thus, the teaching of ethics creates different expectations. While public sector administrators are willing to conform as best they can to particular norms or values such as fairness and equality, a private administrator "expects hard-headed decisive, pragmatic, issue oriented, goal directed" and bottom-line results.[28]

Truthfulness and credibility are critical to both sectors. Because the public sector operates in a goldfish bowl, under the watch of the media, unaccountable actions are more easily revealed. This allows for swift public reaction. These factors, combined with public administrators' norms and commitment to the public interest, act as a powerful restraining force to promote accountability.

Most public administrators view government as a powerful force for good and as an instrument for promoting the good life. Participants in the private sector adhere to a laissez faire ideology. Government is seen as having only a minimal role in business activity. The predominant cry has been to get the government off the private sector's back. Yet history has shown that businesses expected and were dependent on the king's navy to protect trade routes, soldiers to protect their factories, and the king's court to protect their contracts. Today, businesses rail against government influence but they fight hard to protect their subsidies. Invariably when there are economic imbalances, such as a recession, they are eager to blame government policies.

There is a pervasive view in America that it is somehow more virtuous to be associated with private undertakings than with public service activities. Private enterprise is viewed as efficient while government is not. The accepted belief is that the pursuit of materialism and profit engenders commitment to continuous growth and a spirit of adventure. Progress and growth promote service to the community and create greater commitment to social responsibility.[29]

Despite the fact that more than two-thirds of all businesses have adopted codes of ethics, there is no guarantee of moral probity; neither do these codes promote automatic social responsibility. In fact, a significant minority of corporations have been involved in illegal and unethical activities.[30] In a 1990 survey by *Business and Society Review*, 66 percent of business managers indicated that they will lie if they thought that they could gain from it. Additionally, 67 percent said that standards of honesty and morality are set aside when money is at stake.[31]

Public decisions involve the use of public resources and the exercise of coercive or police power. Frequently, government actions seek to resolve conflicts created by varied interest groups that seek to influence how scarce community resources will be divided among competing claimants. To promote accountability, public managers have to engage in a continuous balancing act to serve equally the haves and the have-nots. This is a very difficult struggle because of the continuing demand for greater efficiency in resource use. But this desire for efficiency and impartiality tends to favor the haves over the have-nots and tends to undermine the balance or social equity that administrators seek to maintain. This outcome is in direct conflict with those administrators who subscribe to John Rawls' view, which seeks to provide more equitable results to all clients. According to Rawls, "Each person is to have an equal right to the most extensive total system of equal liberties compatible with similar system of liberty for all."[32]

In the private sector, customers are individuals who desire service or products and have the required resources to pay for them (known as effective demand). Emphasis is put on efficiency of production and not solely on wants and needs, as may often be the case in the public sector. Prices are not set on a break-even basis to allow the maximum number of users to obtain the good or service, but at the maximum price the market will bear. Transactions are viewed as voluntary. The business agrees to supply a product or service with specified or expected quality at prices that yield maximum profit. There is no obligation to the customer to promote equity or liberty. Service to the community is donated and accepted as a civic act or exercise of social responsibility, beyond required expectations.

ADMINISTRATIVE DISCRETION AND ETHICAL PRINCIPLES

The magnitude and complexity of government make broad discretionary delegation of authority and power to middle- and lower-level managers (MLMs) a necessity. The legislature makes policies with general guidelines while the executive refines the guidelines. To operationalize the policies to fit the specific needs of the clientele, MLMs add greater operational details to facilitate meeting the needs. Given public administrators' commitment to equity, justice, rule of law and to professional standards, tensions are inevitably created. As previously stated, this tension forces administrators to engage in a continual balancing act between efficiency and responsiveness in pursuit of the public interest.

The reform movement drive that gave birth to modern public administration helped to cloud and create confusion about the policy role that public administrators play. The reforms demanded that administrators be strictly neutral in carrying out enacted policies or legislative mandates (this has come to be known as the neutral competence approach). Administrators are expected to carry out their policy functions without emotion or sympathy. The policy to be carried out is specifically set forth by the legislature. (This has come to be known as the policy-administration dichotomy.) This strict separation has typically been viewed as not only naive and impossible but improper even from the perspective of the Founding Fathers, as noted earlier.

Typically most ideas for programs emanate from administrators. While legislatures have dominant roles in approving policies and setting general discretionary guidelines to direct administrative actions, executive orders (the president issues policies, rules, and regulations that have the force and effect of laws, similar to legislative enactments) and specific administrative directives relating to program actions play a prominent role in guiding administrators. The degree of discretion that public managers should exercise in implementing legislative policies and the strictness of accountability to which they should be held for their actions have generated two contrasting perspectives. Herman Finer argued for the strict constructionist model while Carl Friedrich articulated the model that delegates greater discretion and thus trust to administrators.[33]

To Finer, administrative responsiveness means strict adherence to legislative mandates in the implementation of agency programs. The absence of discretion for administrators requires the legislature to pass minutely detailed laws that managers must follow if they are to be viewed as responsive to legislative intent.

In Friedrich's view, our complex society makes detailed legislative mandates impossible. We must be willing to trust administrators' commitment to the public interest to ensure responsiveness to the electorate. Because of the high percentage of professional public servants and socialized norms and the internalized sense of responsibility to democracy, the likelihood for accountability is greatly enhanced.

ETHICAL IMPERATIVES: A PUBLIC SERVICE PHILOSOPHY

A public service philosophy puts the focus on communitarian interest and the ties that bind. It emphasizes a collective interest that is consistent only with rational and enlightened self-interest that seek to be accountable to legislative pragmatic interest, producing the best for citizens in a responsive democratic society. The goal of public service is to assist in promoting civility as it finds the most economic and responsive ways of applying government resources to achieve publicly determined ends to enable citizens to realize their best potential in a good, just, and democratic society.[34]

Virtually every agency in government has codes of ethics. Most professional organizations such as the American Society for Public Administration (ASPA) and the International City Managers Association (ICMA) have well-articulated codes of ethics. While these are aids to promoting ethical organizations and professionals, they are not a substitute for an effectively socialized and internalized commitment to serve the public interest in pursuit of the greatest possible good.

The socialized norms that public philosophy espouses seek only the best for the public. To be worth the name of a public service philosophy, it must become a habit and a way of life that guides all decisions. This constitutes the essence of a public service that will be above reproach. The philosophy would promote the highest integrity, the greatest freedom, equity, trust and public confidence. This level of integrity and the pursuit of the best in the public interest will act as a powerful magnet in recruiting and retaining the best and the brightest in the public service.

The establishment of a public service philosophy is in keeping with the highest purpose and expectations of the Founding Fathers who wanted public servants to have "firmness, courage, endurance, industry, frugal living, strength and above all unremitting devotion to the weal of the public corporate self, the community of virtuous men. . . . [E]very man gives of himself totally to the good of the public as a whole."[35] This commitment will provide the under-girding for public servants to pursue and realize truly enlightened self-interest in which individual, organizational, and community interests are mutually and simultaneously realized.

Because of the strategic role that public administrators play in the making and implementation of policies that affect the liberty and well-being of Americans, public administrators can rightfully be called the guardians of democracy.[36] Thus it is critical that administrators be imbued with core democratic values and commitment to the preservation and maintenance of freedom on which the American democracy is built. In writing Publius No. 51, the Federalists recognized the importance of citizens who are entrusted with the operations of the government: "The aim of every political constitution is, or ought to be, first to obtain for rulers men who possess most wisdom to discern, and most virtue to pursue, the common good of the society; and in the next place, to take the most effectual precautions for keeping them virtuous whilst they continue to hold their public trust."[37]

Sustainability

To have maximum credibility, a public service philosophy should subscribe to the practice of sustainability. The application of sustainability involves linking goals and objectives with all programmatic activities' results (effectiveness). From the inception of a program, results must be linked to achievements that will have the impact intended on clients over time to accomplish transformation. That is, the clients, who have the capability for change, must be enabled to become independent of the program and thus become self-sustaining.

This commitment will likely be a powerful and influential incentive in preventing many programs from being initiated when the massive cost of the expected life of the program is revealed to the public and policymakers. The sustainability approach to conducting public programs will stop many undertakings before they are approved, based on the resources necessary to produce the anticipated sustainability results. This commitment will help stabilize and reduce new undertakings and budgetary outlays while promoting the maximum responsiveness of the public interest. This will be a rational and powerful weapon in the fight to balance the budget, while at the same time eliminating programs that cannot be funded to achieve the desired change and enablement.

In summary, the operation of a public service philosophy will at a minimum require adherents to:

1. Be totally committed to sustainability results as an operating norm and be prepared to leave their office far more capable of meeting the needs of clients and constituents than when they assumed office.
2. Recruit and advance the best-motivated and brightest minds, consistent with the Founding Fathers' expectations.
3. Be committed to structures not as an end or as a way of solving problems but to the results they propose to generate.
4. Develop the ability to balance demands of the legislature, executives, and citizens in pursuit of the ultimate prize—the enhancement of the public interest.
5. In decision-making, always ask how their decision will be viewed by the least powerful client.
6. Always pursue enlightened self-interest. That is, when their individual interest must be weighted against the public, they must make sure that both are mutually advanced with a bias toward the public interest.
7. Reinforce and complement compliance and integrity training.
8. Integrate ethical incentives in decision-making processes whenever possible, including promotional examinations and annual reviews.
9. At formal meetings commend subordinates for incorporating expressions of ethical concerns in daily operational activities at every level of the organization.[38]
10. Exhibit constant reverence for laws. As Abraham Lincoln said, it should "become the political religion of the nation." Said Theodore Roosevelt, "Our nation owes its strength, its stability and endurance to its principles."
11. Be committed to the "more-and-more hypothesis" in which delegation to subordinates is considered not a threat to the superior's authority but a mutually enhancing and enabling act.[39]
12. Accept goal succession (moving from one achievement to the next), not goal displacement (changing the goal to meet selfish interests) as the norm in which public servants seek to constantly achieve the end result or goal as quickly as possible. The objective is for public servants to work themselves out of a job so that they can move on to pursue new, unmet needs.
13. Internalize norms, attitudes, and practices essential to democratic governance.
14. Learn to resist special-interest pressures brought to bear on public servants in their policy-interpretating and implementing roles.
15. Recognize the critical role in converting legislative authorization into programs. Public servants have a primary duty to maintain accountability.
16. Pay greater attention to the way government programs affect citizens and seek ways to expand popular participation in government.
17. Better evaluate and analyze what is done so that the cost of government can be continuously kept down but still provide the required goods and services to the public at the time, place, manner, in the quantity and quality, and with sustainability impact to achieve client enablement and independence.

18. Be committed to continuously enhancing analytical and research skills.
19. Assist clientele and service recipients to be proactive in helping them to decide what the government's agenda will be.[40]
20. Promote best practice across all sectors and levels in the pursuit of maximum accountability and sustainability.
21. Encourage education and good citizenship about the public service.

MIDDLE- AND LOWER-LEVEL ADMINISTRATORS: CONCERNS ABOUT ETHICS AND ACCOUNTABILITY

The role of MLMs has grown in importance as their number has been reduced in continuing downsizing and decentralization efforts. Public administration theorists have charged that MLMs exercise power that is largely uncontrolled. There have also been public attacks against public servants for their lack of efficiency and responsiveness. These charges have been led by present and would-be politicians. This makes the commitment to public service all the more compelling, as it will be a powerful factor to refute these charges, when made for expedience.

Of the indictments against MLMs, the following represent a composite:

1. Career officials influence legislation in a partisan way by controlling the information available to legislatures. In determining broad policies, administrative staff is often said to be in advisory positions without direct policymaking authority. But administrators' training, experience, and access to data have made possible the acquisition of unofficial power far beyond the authority suggested by a staff designation. In a simple but vivid way James D. Carroll reflects the critical role of administrators in his syllogism:
   Administration is knowledge.
   Knowledge is power.
   Administration is power.[41]
2. Administrators have become effective lobbyists (the federal employees and their associations in Washington are good examples) working alone and in tandem with powerful interests. Even more broadly, argues John Rehfuss, administrative actions create in many ways our expectations about what government should and can do.[42]
3. Most of the policy surrounding a program is made from the choices surrounding implementation, and it is here that administrators are in charge.[43]
4. The practice of administrators has provided the basis for most theory in public administration. William Scott and David Hart argue that organizational survival has become the major basis of that theory.[44]
5. Loyalty to the agency supersedes upward accountability or commitment to clients. Public administrators are primarily motivated by self-interest, argue theorists such as Anthony Downs.[45]
6. Political tradition fosters conformity rather than conviction and group loyalty rather than individual accountability, borrowing from the language of the corporation.[46]
7. Control over who works for an agency is largely determined by that agency. The

internal norms of the agency are largely determined by who remains on the job, is promoted and disciplined.

8.   The rules and regulations determining who will benefit from legislation, when, and under what conditions are written, applied, and adjudicated by administrators. In most cities and in many states, the majority of policies are not committed to writing. Francis E. Rourke has labeled this practice of withholding information from the public as administrative secrecy.[47]

9.   Aside from internal review and infrequent audits, no assessment is normally made of what gets accomplished in government.[48] The federal Performance and Results Act is a structural attempt to address this issue.[49]

This volume continues the reassessment of public administration and the forces creating the tension between power and accountability experienced by middle- and low-level managers in implementing programs. There is general concern among citizens that they are denied a reasonable voice and the possibility of making a difference in governance.[50] The baffling and unfortunate reality is that public employees similarly have little confidence in people steering the rudder of public institution.[51] The average citizen is concerned that big government is and has been a negative influence on their lives.

Four of the last five presidents have run against "a bloated and unrepresentative bureaucracy." To achieve unified administrative policies Lyndon Johnson dictated the centralized, top-down decision-making approach called planning programming and budgeting (PPB). Richard Nixon sought to control bureaucracy by pushing legislation through Congress that would give him greater control over it. When this strategy failed he attempted to install loyalists in place of his initial appointees.

In contrast to Nixon, Jimmy Carter's style was centralized and personalized. He attempted to micromanage agencies by engaging in the details of their operations. If the best outcome was to be realized, Carter felt, he had to do it himself. Thus he minimized delegation of authority, which tends to engender mistrust and generate a problem of confidence.

To ensure that his political message got out to the public, as he wished, Ronald Reagan chose appointees who were personally and ideologically comfortable with his goals. Unlike Carter who left sub-Cabinet appointments to his Cabinet secretaries, Reagan's strategy required that he put his most doctrinaire loyalists in less visible and exposed positions to avoid their becoming potential "lightning rods for public criticism."[52] He was adroit in employing incentives such as invitations to state dinners and favorable budget decisions as powerful motivators. Because Reagan's appointees were both loyal and ideological he was able to decentralize authority, knowing the more he delegated to his subordinates the greater mutual trust he could expect. His appointees were also given to understand that the best way to maintain control and continuity of his policies was to minimize travel, especially abroad, and stay at home.

The foregoing suggests that elected executives tend to fear their inability to control career administrators to effectively implement their policies. Various styles have been employed to minimize deviations from policy agenda. These fears and tactics demonstrate convincingly that a career public philosophy can have a powerful impact in eliminating or minimizing policy implementation problems.

ORGANIZATION OF THE TEXT

Part I examines the ethical foundations and imperatives of public management and the critical links between administrative agencies and forces operating in the environment. Public administration is defined in the context of its practice, showing how the public and private are inter-related. The development and implication of public policies are examined, in particular, the tensions between legislative and executive branches, the process of policymaking and techniques of policy analysis. Emphasis is put on how policy is implemented.

In Part II, theory and practice are linked. This section evaluates public administrative theory, demonstrating the development of organization theory and its relationship to public management practice. The paradigm of traditional public administration theory is compared to that of organizational humanism, the new public administration, total quality management (TQM) and re-engineering, praxis and cultural hermeneutics. This discussion points to how the theory most in use in public organizations is validated in day-to-day practice.

In Part III, the functions of management are examined according to the major processes and practices. We explore how top-level administrators and MLMs perform the functions of planning, organizing, coordinating, and controlling. We then review decision-making, communication, and leadership processes, community relations, and the critical role of MLMs.

In Part IV, a look at the exercise of power through program implementation describes the controlling and support functions of personnel, financial management, and productivity. This section emphasizes monitoring and evaluating programs as well as their impact in terms of cost and benefits of goods and services, and the organization as an instrument in the delivering system. We are concerned not only with what is delivered but also with the effect it has on the lives of people. Two important areas are assessed: administrative and fiscal federalism in intergovernmental relations, and issues in international administration and development.

DISCUSSION QUESTIONS

1.   Describe the rationale for a public service philosophy.
2.   What is the difference between Socrates' and Aristotle's concepts of virtue?
3.   Discuss the Founding Fathers' commitment to a virtuous civil service.
4.   Define ethics. Is there a difference between ethics and morality?

5. Define the concept of sustainabilty and discuss the implication it has for managing public resources while obtaining responsiveness.

6. Why is Carl Frederich's idea of achieving responsiveness from public administrators more in line with the practice of policymaking and administration today?

7. Why is distrust of government a serious problem for public administration? Illustrate your answer by referring to a particular service government provides. What can administrators do to heighten popular confidence in government?

8. Who are the MLMs and why are they viewed as critical players promoting accountability in the delivery of goods and services?

NOTES

1. Sissela Bok, quoted in "What's Wrong: Hypocrisy, Betrayal and Greed Unsettle the Nation's Soul," *Time* (May 25, 1987).

2. Richard T. DeGorge, *Business Ethics* (New York: Macmillan, 1992), p. 12.

3. Gerald J. Williams, *Ethics in Modern Management* (Westport, Conn.: Quorum Books, 1992), p. 14.

4. DeGorge, *Business Ethics*, p. 40.

5. Thomas I. White, *Business Ethics: A Philosophical Reader* (New York: Macmillan, 1993) pp. 8–11.

6. Mark T. Lilla, "Ethos Ethics and Public Service," *Public Interest* 63 (Spring 1981): 3–17.

7. Felix G. Rohatyn, "Ethics in America's Money Culture," in *Ethics in American Business: A Special Report* (New York: Touche Ross & Co., 1988), p. 54.

8. "Socrates: Vice Harms the Doers," *Discovering Philosophy* Thomas White, (Englewood Cliffs; N.J.: Prentice-Hall, 1991), pp. 210–24.

9. *The Philosophy of Aristotle*, Renford Boubaugh, ed. (New York: New American Library, 1963), 1105a.

10. Robert H. Horwitz, "John Locke and the Preservation of Liberty: A Problem of Civic Education," in *Moral Foundations of the American Republic*, Robert H. Horwitz, ed., 2nd edn. (Charlottesville, Va.: University of Virginia Press, 1977), 139.

11. Ibid., pp. 139–41.

12. William D. Richardson and Lloyd G. Nigro, "Administrative Ethics and Founding Thoughts: Constitutional Correctives, Honor and Education," *Public Administration Review*, (September/October 1987): 368; and Forest McDonald, *Novus Ordo Seclorum: The Intellectual Origins of the Constitution* (Lawrence, Kan.: University of Kansas Press, 1985), p. 223.

13. Horwitz, "John Locke," pp. 132–33.

14. Frederick Mosher, "The Professional State," in *Public Administration: Politics and the People*, Dean L. Yarwood, ed. (White Plains, N.Y.: Longman, 1987), p. 198.

15. McDonald, *Novus Ordo Seclorum*, pp. 188–91.

16. Herbert J. Storing, What the Anti-Federalists Were For: The Political Thought of the Opponents of the Constitution (Chicago: University of Chicago Press, 1981), p. 21.

17. "Bill 79 of 1779 for more General Diffusion of Knowledge," in Thomas Jefferson and the Development of American Public Education, James B. Conant, ed. (Berkeley: University of California Press, 1962), pp. 88–93.

18. Lynton K. Caldwell, The American Theories of Hamilton and Jefferson: Their Contribution to the Thought on Public Administration (Chicago: University of Chicago Press, 1944), p. 110.

19. Thomas Jefferson, Notes on the State of Virginia, William Penden, ed. (New York: W.W. Norton, 1972), pp. 146–49.

20. Woodrow Wilson, "The Study of Public Administration" in Public Administration: Politics and the People, Dean L. Yarwood, ed. (White Plains, N.Y.: Longman, 1987) p. 29.

21. Storing, What the Anti-Federalists Were For, pp. 42–43.

22. John A. Rohr, Ethics for Bureaucrats: An Essay on Law and Values (New York: Marcel Dekker, 1978), pp. 59, 64–74.

23. Ibid., p. 185.

24. Ibid.

25. Wilson, "The Study of Administration," p. 26.

26. Dwight Waldo, "The Perdurability of the Politic-Administration Dichotomy: Woodrow Wilson and the Identity Crisis in Public Administration," in Politics and Administration: Woodrow Wilson and American Public Administration, Jack S. Rabin and James S. Bowman, eds. (New York: Marcel Dekker, 1984), p. 231.

27. Wilson "The Study of Administration," p. 27.

28. Robert C. Soloman, The New World of Business Ethics and Enterprise in the Global 1990s (Lanham: Littleford Adams, 1994), p. 16.

29. Francis X. Sutton, The American Business Creed (Cambridge, Mass.: Harvard University Press, 1956).

30. "How Lawless Are Big Corporations?" Fortune (December 1, 1980): 56–64.

31. Reported in Soloman, The New World of Business, p. 25.

32. John Rawls, A Theory of Justice (Cambridge, Mass.: Belknap Press of Harvard University Press, 1971), p. 302.

33. Carl J. Friedrich, "Public Policy and the Nature of Administrative Responsibility," Public Policy 1 (1940): 3–24; and Herman Finer, "Administrative Responsibility and Democratic Government," Public Administrative Review, 1 (Summer 1940): 335–50.

34. Jane Mansbridge, "Public Spirit in Political Systems" in Values and Public Policy, Henry J. Aaron et al., eds. (Washington, D.C.: Brookings Institution, 1994), pp. 146–64.

35. McDonald, Novus Ordo Seclorum, pp. 207-1.

36. Jerome B. McKinney, Risking a Nation: The U.S.-Japanese Trade Failure and the Need for Political and Economic Social Reformation (Lanham, Md.: University Press of America, 1995), Chap. 4.

37. Alexander Hamilton, James Madison and John Jay, The Federalist Papers (New York: New American Library, 1961), p. 350.

38. Carol W. Lewis, The Ethics Challenge in the Public Service (San Francisco: Jossey-Bass, 1991), p. 181.

39. Robert T. Golembiewski, *Men, Management and Morality: Toward a New Organizational Ethic* (New Brunswick, N.J.: Transaction Publishers, 1989), p. 212.

40. Mindy Lauer Schachter, *Reinventing Inventing Government* or *Reinventing Ourselves* (Albany, New York: State University of New York Press, 1997), p. 3.

41. James D. Carroll, "Service, Knowledge and Choice: The Future of Post-Industrial Administration", *Public Administration Review* 35, No. 6 (November/December, 1975): 578.

42. John Rehfuss, *Public Administration as Political Process* (New York: Charles Scribner's, 1993), p. 1.

43. Gordon Tullock, *The Politics of Bureaucracy* (Washington, D.C.: Public Affairs Press, 1973), pp. 180-81. Tullock argues that, given the absence of policies from above, inadequate communication and insufficient guidelines for implementation and policymaking by lower-level officials are not only inevitable but essential to effective decision-making.

44. William Scott and David K. Hart, "Administrative Crisis: The Neglect of Meta Physical Speculation," *Public Administration*, 33 (September-October 1973): 415–22.

45. Anthony Downs, *Inside Bureaucracy* (Boston: Little Brown 1967), p. 2.

46. Edward Weisband and Thomas M. Frack, *Resignation in Protest* (New York: Grossman Publishers, 1975), p. 2.

47. Francis E. Rourke, "A Symposium on Administrative Secrecy: A Comparative Perspective," *Public Administrative Review,* 35 (January-February 1975), pp. 1–43.

48. Alice Rivlin, *Systematic Thinking for Social Action* (Washington, D.C.: Brookings Institution, 1992), p. 1.

49. The Government Performance and Results Act of 1993 is an attempt to focus management attention on results.

50. David Matthews, "Putting the Public Back in Politics," *National Civic Review* 80 (Fall 1991): 349.

51. Gregory B. Lewis, "In Search of Machiavellian Milquetoasts: Comparing Attitudes of Bureaucrats and Ordinary People," *Public Administration Review* (March/April 1990): 224.

52. Robert Nathan, *The Administrative Presidency* (New York: Macmillan, 1983), p. 90.

2

The Environment and Setting
for Public Administration

This chapter is organized into three main sections. The first examines the setting of public administration; the second distinguishes the functions of top-, middle-, and lower-level managers and discusses the latter two, and the last analyzes the interdependence of power and accountability. The purpose of the chapter is to define the two key concepts used throughout the text, *power* and *accountability*, and to bring out the strategic role in public administration played by middle- and lower-level managers.

LEARNING OBJECTIVES

On completing this chapter the reader should be able to:

- State the importance and institutional setting of public administration.
- Identify the strategic role of middle- and lower-level managers in public administration.
- Critically evaluate the interdependence of power and accountability.

Organizations are essential to modern life. They are created to solve problems, but they mirror and are limited by culture, replicating "the kinds of available roles, skills, beliefs, values and institutions that shape the behavior of people."[1] Today, government is the single most important system of organization; it helps us to do those things we cannot do for ourselves, but it also tells us what we may not do. For example, it provides and maintains a system of highways; however, we may drive our cars on these highways only after first obtaining a driver's license. The tension between freedom and constraints forms the institutional setting for public administration.

The magnitude and variety of demands made on government and the resources, including specialized skills, required to meet these demands create the major challenges to public administration. To meet these challenges, complex resource delivery systems have developed, including a range of public organizations from the Liquor Control Board to the Department of Trans-portation in Pennsylvania. These organizations shape, change, and control individual citizens' behavior. Thus, the rationale for studying public administration is the interaction between people and organizations to achieve better living conditions (see Fig. 2.1).

WHAT IS PUBLIC ADMINISTRATION?

One observer defined administration as the "accomplishment of purpose through the organized effort of others." The manager of a business, for example, "carries out the corporation's purpose by building and modifying relationships through the efforts of men and women whom he recruits."[2] Administration in the public sector can be distinguished by a greater emphasis on people participating in their own governance. The determination of needs by the public makes one of the basic differences between a government agency and a private organization. These officials consider, bargain, and compromise to determine which of the demands presented will be satisfied and to what degree.

Narrowly defined, public administration encompasses all those activities that are concerned with implementing legislative mandates. It is the co-ordinated and cooperative management of materials and/or resources directed at achieving both the letter and intent of politically formulated programs. Public administration embodies the collective desires and needs of a community, which may consist of political constituents, agency clients, or the general public. In a democratic state, resources can be authoritatively allocated only by duly constituted representatives. In the private sector, a surplus resulting from operations of a business can be distributed to managers as bonuses, but public managers attempting to do the same things will likely find themselves, unless explicitly authorized by law or allowed in very exceptional cases, in prison for fraud, embezzlement, or both. It is the publicly determined purpose and the scrutiny of the way that purpose is pursued that make public administration

Fig. 2.1. Rationale for Studying Public Administration

Subject	Purpose	End Result
Knowledge about administration and organizations and Knowledge about people in their cultural settings	To assist To direct To understand To encourage participation To enable	To satisfy publicly determined needs in order to achieve the good life

public. We will have much more to say about defining public administration in operational terms in Chapter 4.

THE SETTING OF PUBLIC ADMINISTRATION IN THE UNITED STATES

Politics and Pluralism

Public administration is marked by a high degree of interest-group politics. The vast majority of public agencies exist as expressions of group or coalition pressure seeking to determine public policy (see Fig. 2.2). Pressure groups equate their interest with the public interest. At the national level, veterans support the Department of Veterans Affairs, men and women of business support the Commerce Department, and farmers support the Agriculture Department. In Pennsylvania, milk producers defend the Milk Marketing Board, which guarantees stable prices for their products while consumers generally protest. At the school district level, PTAs support or criticize school administrators. Administrators learn quickly that their interests and those of their constituents can be greatly enhanced through mutual support. Thus, administrators defend programs that expand the power and economic interests of constituents, while the latter in turn provide the power base that administrators must have to defend their agencies and their jobs.

In U.S. public administration, the organizations formed to carry out programs and/or activities come to be the recipients of loyalty. People do not give support to government in the abstract; in practice, loyalty is given to specific organizations and structures that are regarded as legitimate exercise of power. Reformers, clients, and constituents recognize that, until policy is implemented through administrative structures, it is no policy at all but wishful thinking, as we shall see in Chapter 3.

The Roots of Administration in the United States

The multiplicity of interests in community life in the United States is rooted in the values of free enterprise and individualism. These values developed out of a national heritage that fostered competition, individual risk taking, and a fear of centralized government for the tyranny it might bring. The system was designed to ensure responsibility and political accountability by providing (1) that elected officials would have the determining role regarding all administrative activities; and (2) that administrators would undertake only those programs initiated by the legislature and approved by the chief executive. The concepts of separation of powers and checks and balances were a response to these shared values. Separation of powers means the diffusion of responsibility among the three branches of government (legislative, executive, and judicial) so that each has a voice. Checks and balances mean that each branch can limit the exercise of power by another branch so that power in one is balanced by power in another. Thus, bargaining and compromise are at the root of administration as practiced in the United States.

Power is also divided between the state and the federal levels. Throughout the eighteenth and nineteenth centuries, executive power was kept fragmented, and most government was carried out at the state and local levels. In counties and cities, elected officials and independently appointed boards and commissions proliferated. It was assumed that these independent centers of power would check the growth of governmental authority and thus ensure individual liberty.

Fig. 2.2 Pluralist Politics in Administration

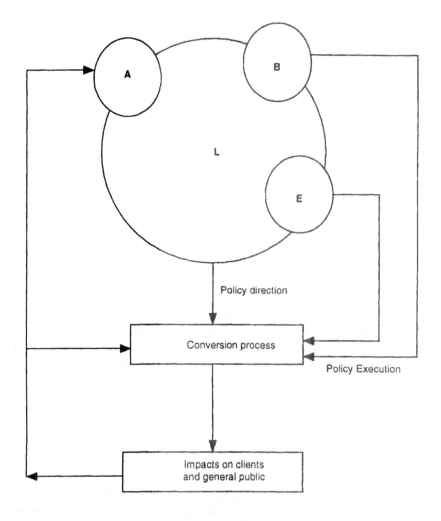

A- Agriculture   B-Business   L-Labor   E-Ethnic Groups

Restraints on government, as adopted by the framers of the Constitution and followed in varying degrees by all 50 states, include the following:

- A bicameral legislature consisting of two houses (except in the state of Nebraska), the lower with particular power in raising and spending money and the upper with considerable authority in confirming the executive's key appointed officials.
- Separate elections of the chief executive and the legislature.
- An independent judiciary holding review powers over both the administrative and legislative branches.
- A national government exercising only those powers expressly delegated to it or what these delegated powers imply.
- Executive veto power and the right of the legislature to override it with a two-thirds majority in both houses.
- Legislative right to review all major executive appointments.
- Legislative prerogative to review the actions of all branches and to impeach any government personnel for violating specified prohibitions.
- Taxes and budgets determined by the legislature but expenditures made by the executive.
- Executive control over administrative agencies but legislative right to review and conduct continuing oversight of all activities.

The diffusion of power among competing centers to maintain accountability was perhaps appropriate in the early years of the republic. In the last half-century, however, traditional patterns of separation of powers have proved inadequate, although the values of free enterprise and individualism have remained. Rising public expectations, global warfare, dwindling resources, and unemployment have produced a powerful and complex government in which the executive branch has emerged as dominant. Because of the magnitude of problems, executive power and administrative prerogatives have grown at all levels of government. The new checks and balances now tend to be *within* administrative practices, and they include more effective planning, better evaluations, and accountability.[3]

Experience in a number of administrative settings has shown that internal checks are often inadequate. Police boards and other peer review mechanisms have tended to be partial toward their members in punishing misconduct. Until remedies, such as citizen review commissions that have been adopted in a number of cities, for these actions become internalized norms, greater citizen participation on review boards and other review structures is essential if accountability is to be achieved.

Most problems can be defined only at higher levels of government, although program implementation to address them increasingly occurs in local offices of administrative structures. Pollution is a case in point. The drive to control pollution was at best minimal until the early 1970s, when the federal government began to provide leadership for a coordinated approach through the Environmental Protection Act. The administration of the act takes place largely in local communities but is backed up by state and national authority. The control of air pollution caused by the production of steel in Allegheny County in Western Pennsylvania provides a good example. There, local politicians wanted to relax the enforcement of air quality standards as applied to the Jones and Laughlin Steel Company, while the regional Environmental Protection Agency officials insisted that the company make greater efforts to provide clean air. The county officials said that they were not against clean air but they preferred that jobs not be sacrificed in the process.

Today most concerns that surface nationally (e.g., abortion, the environment, inflation) become executive problems. The executive can speak authoritatively and muster resources to attack problems swiftly and directly. The same thing is happening at the state and local levels. Lack of money to fund education becomes a problem for the governor, and potholes or lack of recreation in the city becomes the concern of the mayor.

TOP- AND LOWER-LEVEL MANAGEMENT PERSPECTIVES

We are all products of our environment and our experience. The way public administrators see their responsibilities and the amount of influence associated with their positions determine what they actually do in the bureaucracy.

Top-Level Administrators

Top-level administrators are executives. Like elected officials, they tend to serve from election to election. However, lower-level administrators are managers and generally have a longer tenure in their positions. According to Leonard White, top administrators are distinguished by their preoccupation with policy choices, their political roles, their representational functions, and their ultimate responsibility for program execution.[4] They are agency heads, program directors, and city managers, and have "been the traditional focus of public administration."[5] Most textbooks are written about high-level administrators giving the impression that young administrators will take initial jobs at or near the top policymaking levels.

Members of this group of public administrators lead far more glamorous lives than do their subordinates, and they are often in the news. When Allen Kennedy banned the artificial sweetener saccharine, his picture was flashed across every television screen and appeared in many newspapers. President Jimmy Carter's decision to recall General John Singlaub from South Korea held the news media's attention until the general was relieved of his duty. During the outbreak of Legionnaire's Disease in Philadelphia in 1975, the U.S. director of communicable diseases in Atlanta and the Pennsylvania secretary of health were in the public eye for almost three months. When Mayor Maynard Jackson of Atlanta dismissed the striking sanitary workers, we were all spectators as he said, "This is the most difficult thing that I have ever been forced to do as a public official." When the federal building was bombed in Oklahoma City, the president, the governor of the state and the U.S. attorney general were constantly in the media.

Many of us equate the actions of department heads or chief executives with everyday administration, but these should be more appropriately referred to as executive administration (executive in the sense that they are about high-level policy). The following are among the functions expected of top-level administrators:

1. Maintain relations with "several publics that affect and are affected by government."[6] This includes alliances inside and outside of government. (The Army Corps of Engineers is a good example. It is one of the most influential agencies because of its Rivers and Harbors Association, made up of Congress members and local elected officials around the country.) This is an important political role that pays dividends in the form of community, clientele, and constituency support.

2. Influence the determination of most major policies. This is especially important because the administrative branch is the initial source of most ideas that are ultimately transformed into law.

3. Maintain good relations with strategic legislators, especially those who sit on such powerful committees as those dealing with appropriations.

4. Maintain relations with interest groups such as business (Chambers of Commerce) and labor (AFL-CIO). At the national level, important appointments will normally not be made unless the business community (in the case of the Department of Commerce) and labor (in the case of the Labor Department) are consulted.

5. Lobby within the government structure to mobilize public support for particular issues. The Agricultural Extension Service maintains a nationwide network capable of exerting pressures whenever the situation demands. The Veterans Affairs Department has such a huge constituency that it can exert pressure on the national legislature in its own right.

6. Maintain control over the budget of the agency or section.

7. Control the power to organize, to determine functions, duties, and responsibilities, and to make decisions.

8. Set broad guidelines for allocating agency resources.

9. Manage conflicts, accepting them as normal and channeling them to constructive uses.

10. Manage change. This function mediates between the internal drive for organizational survival and external pressures to change the organization's rules and modes of service and/or product delivery.

Top-level administrators perform important functions and are engaged in a constant interactive give-and-take with MLMs on policy developments. They seldom, however, affect day-to-day policy implementation in the delivery of goods and services to constituents and individual clienteles. This is the area where middle- and lower-level mangers exercise dominance.

Walter Wright has written:

The accolades for good management are always showered on the president and his top vice presidents, whereas, in truth, it is the mid-management that actually produces the success. No matter how wise a policy is set at the top, it will not be carried out unless there is an industrious, highly motivated middle management dedicated to carrying it out. The key, then, to success is a personnel policy that minimizes the frustration of middle management officers.[7]

Middle- and Lower-Level Managers (MLMs)

The continued preoccupation with top-level executives and administrators in public administration literature has diverted attention from the main concerns of administration, the execution of public programs and the delivery of goods and services. It has to a large extent ignored those who actually carry programs out. We employ the term managers to focus attention on the individuals who actually control administrative operations.

MLMs are concerned with the implementation of day-to-day activities. They are the public servants who organize the delivery of the mail, direct rush-hour traffic, and control the caseload of probation officers. The functions they perform are government in action. Elected and appointed officials bear ultimate responsibility, but MLMs are the people who follow through to deliver goods and services.

Contrary to Osborn and Gaebler's claim that middle managers are obstacles to innovation and relentlessly seek to justify their existence, practicing managers say that these observations do not parallel reality.[8] Especially at the local levels of government MLMs' views are being expressed. MLMs are performing effective role in helping to achieve client accountability as opposed to being obsessed with steering to enhance individual objectives. These MLMs successfully perform four critical functions:

- Interpret and represent their work units involving an array of issues related to resource allocation, policy development, distribution of duties and community policing.
- Lend or receive assistance on inter- and intra-agency functions, such as community anti-drug efforts.
- Successful MLMs develop organizational relationships outside of work to facilitate cooperation to get things done that the agency cannot effectively do alone.
- Synthesize a variety of powerful influences which are impacting the agency, including demands from internal and external leaders while interpreting what good service means.[9]

"Middle managers play a critical role in ensuring a constancy of purpose in the midst of multiple sources of authority."[10] They interpret and transform policies and laws into concrete services for citizens. MLMs must continuously make tradeoffs between the demands for equality and efficiency. They must be able to develop a keen sense to know when to stick to rigid procedures and when to make the required and delicate indispensable exception that shows humanness and flexibility.

The rush to privatize and contract out public functions gives MLMs not less but unmatched discretion to determine what governing means after the go ahead authority has been granted. MLMs are free to negotiate contracts based on the general performa guidelines that have been approved. While there are numerous guidelines and rules that are established about carrying out functions and contracts, MLMs have considerable discretion in establishing performance standards that influence the service mix, the organizations that will be eligible to bid on the contracts and the kind of citizen participation that will be required.[11]

The major focus of this volume is on MLMs. This group constitutes the largest segment of managers at both the federal and local levels despite the widespread layoffs by the Clinton administration. The ranks of MLMs have been greatly increased by the baby boom that followed World War II, the Korean War and to a lesser extent the Vietnam War. Many of these managers are in their 40s and 50s and hope to move up the hierarchy—the lower-level managers to middle-level jobs and above, and the middle-level to the top. The number of high-level positions, however, is sharply limited, creating competition and tension within this large group of public managers.

The Middle Managers

These administrators are found between the top and lower levels of the organization. They are bureau chiefs and division heads or lieutenants in charge; they transmit "orders, decisions and guidance from the top down and communicate problems, viewpoints, complaints and suggestions from lower ranks to the top."[12] Because top officials are often so far removed from the everyday action of delivery goods and services, middle managers act for them by interpreting policies, motivating, coordinating, and building bonds of loyalty. This requires that middle managers know the laws, regulations, and procedures of their agencies and be able to handle both human and material resources.

Though middle managers sometimes assist top-level administrators in policy development, they are primarily concerned with achieving results within an established framework of policy. Although they can seldom speak for the agency and generally do not take full responsibility for what happens, they perform the substantive functions of public administration. (Middle mangers many times do get the blame when things to wrong.) Leonard D. White has enumerated these major functions: (1) program planning; (2) direction of operations; (3) establishment of standards; (4) enforcement of regulations; (5)

provision of personnel, supplies, equipment and good working conditions; and
(6) supervision of day-to-day operations.[13]

William G. Scott has described "the significant job" in government as a
juncture in a network of financial, material, informational, technical, and human
resources.[14] Middle managers occupy significant jobs because they supply these
networks with operational objectives, strategies for resource allocation,
standards of coordination, and program administration. If 100 miles of city
roads have been approved for resurfacing, it is the middle mangers who will
examine both the politics and the technical requirements and determine which
road will be improved and when.

Despite the vast authority they exercise, the names of middle managers
are seldom known, but they exercise great power with little public or political
supervision. As Scott puts it, "Today's significant jobs usually are buried so
deeply in the thickets of administrative systems that they are nearly invisible to
the people. . . . [T]he mass of citizens have little influence over significant job
administrators or over the decision processes they use."[15] How many know the
names of the contract officers who oversee the millions of dollars in Department
of Defense contract funds each month, or their counterparts in public works
departments in most large cities and counties in the country? Virtually no one
knows who heads the computer operations on which so many administrative
errors are blamed.

Lower-Level or Supervisory Managers

These administrators aid middle management. Sometimes known as first-
line supervisors (or foremen, in the private sector), they include all
administrators below the bureau chief level, such as section, unit, task, and
project leaders. Their functions are usually single or narrow. They direct the
work of others but exercise little discretion. They are heads of the typing pool,
road construction supervisors, or police sergeants. Lower-level supervisors are
the people who know best how to carry out specific tasks as set down by middle
management. They directly motivate the work groups to perform their tasks
within the framework of prescribed policies and procedures.

The typical supervisor has some technical and human relations skills and
must have a good understanding of the work done in his or her unit. Supervisors need not be experts, but they must have sufficient technical competence to
do the task they supervise. John M. Pfiffner indicated several attributes that we
should expect in first-line supervisors:

- liking for people
- emotional stability
- integrity
- courage and fortitude
- enthusiasm for the work

- high ethical standards
- curiosity and intellectual ability.[16]

Although this book will focus on MLMs, we will not exclude the view from the top, and have placed considerable emphasis on policy in such areas as privatization, problems confronting minorities, and international administration.

INTERDEPENDENCE OF POWER AND ACCOUNTABILITY IN PUBLIC AFFAIRS

Although many resources are often used to produce a public product, most of government's output is difficult to evaluate. There is no common yardstick, such as profits in the private sector. Top-level elected and appointed executives are most visible as they exercise power, and those at the lowest levels, the rank-and-file public servants, are held to some accountability by the clients they directly serve. It is in the middle ranges that accountability is a central problem, for here great power is exercised with low visibility.

A number of steps have been taken to improve MLM accountability. Most of the reforms that have been instituted since the 1970s concerning selection and promotion of personnel in a merit system have really been aimed at implementing managers (those responsible for carrying out the day-to-day functions as emphasized by the National Performance Review report known as the Al Gore Commission, or the NPR). When we speak of the movement of public administration toward professionalization from the 1960s to 1990s, we are referring to the establishment of standards of accountability that apply primarily to the middle levels. The continuing emphasis on reforming graduate programs in public administration addresses the knowledge and skills that are needed by managers.

And yet many are still apprehensive about the survival of values of limited government. Theodore Lowi, for example, views professionalism as a mixed blessing. It has brought authority, influence, and power, but these have not been balanced by accountability. Professionalism has been translated into a way for middle-level managers to hide behind the cloak of bureaucratic unity.[17] In cities and other local governments, nonpartisan elections and the manager movement are advanced as professionalizing approaches that will lead to the demise of the political machine. While these reforms have generally had this positive effect, they have also had the negative consequence of fragmenting and dispersing political leadership, leaving bureaucracies as the only potent organized force in the community. Professionalism has meant a high regard for efficiency and low toleration for corruption, but it has also created a new administrative machine. According to Lowi, this new machine exercises power arrogantly and without accountability.

ADMINISTRATIVE NORMS AS ADMINISTRATIVE POWER

At every level of government, but especially in the larger units and at the national level, the explosion of knowledge and the growing complexity of societal problems have forced the legislative branch to relinquish more and more of its policymaking function to the executive branch. This has increased the discretionary powers of administrators. As the providers of "significant information" and the major advisers to top-level management, middle managers have gained the most. Because most legislative policy ideas have their incubation at the administrative agencies, MLM administrators not only influence what the ultimate policy will be, through monopoly of the implementation process, they also shape the policies that give rise to the programs. The broad policy guidelines that legislatures (especially at the national level) enact as law leave administrators free to fill in the details, to make up rules and regulations around which the laws will be implemented.[18]

The results have not always been desirable. In separate studies, Jerome B. McKinney and John Gardner found considerable latitude in the discretion used by lower-level officials. Gardner compared two cities of similar size, Dallas and Boston, and found that, for every traffic ticket written in Boston, four were written in Dallas. McKinney, looking at employees in a state department of revenue, found that major policy on auditing returns was simply a codification of the informal practice of first-line supervisors. Pittsburgh police officers were angered by the city's policy to use a liaison in Traffic Court instead of having the officers appear. This policy deprived the officers of guaranteed overtime. In retaliation, the officers have allegedly exercised their discretion to write nearly 60 percent fewer traffic tickets.[19]

The operation of many administrative norms goes a long way toward increasing the power of MLM officials.

1.   The art of good management requires an ability to delegate authority to the lowest level in the organization at which competence and information are sufficient to accomplish a given objective.
2.   Once guidelines and policies have been set, higher-level management will rarely intervene in the activities of subordinates. This concept is known as the practice of "limited intervention." The most celebrated example was the free rein that John Collier was given in administering the Bureau of Indian Affairs. Despite the conflicts that he experienced with the press, particular members of the Congress, and his subordinates, neither President Franklin Delano Roosevelt nor Secretary of Interior Harold Ickes interfered with Collier's administration.[20]
3.   Middle- and lower-level administrators usually tell their supervisors what they want to hear. Subordinates tend to operate on the principle that only the good news is worth telling the boss or the "sovereign" (the term used by Gordon Tullock). Thus, the transmission of information is intentionally distorted.[21]
4.   Middle- and lower-level mangers operate on the principle of divide and rule.

From time to time they use their permanent career status and monopoly over information to play the executive branch against the legislative branch. President Jimmy Carter's cancellation of more than thirty dams and river projects drew the opposition of the Army Corps of Engineers. The Corps' powerful supporters in Congress forced the president to reconsider his decision. In Pittsburgh, former Mayor Pete Flaherty's reorganization of the Fire Department ignored the ideas of the firefighters. The latter took their case to the City Council, which promptly overturned the mayor's action.

The entire administrative environment is immersed in politics; it permeates every level of management. Because politics constitutes such an integral and potent element of administration, it can be asked: Whose interest is being safeguarded or disregarded? Do middle- and lower-level officials use their massive power to obtain the desirable ends of a democratic state? Have appropriate means been devised to ensure that the administrator's manipulative skills and self-aggrandizing drives for power are checked by institutional accountability to promote responsibility?

The drive for power in administration is perhaps more intense in the United States than in other Western countries because political parties have failed to provide responsible leadership. The fragmented parties at best give only minimal leadership on important policy issues, and they offer no guidance on crucial questions of implementation. Political parties are primarily concerned with electoral issues, leaving agencies to fend for themselves in the day-to-day operations of government. As noted earlier, this makes it necessary for agencies to establish a power base with clients and other attentive members of the public. For example, because the FBI (until recently) was supported by the general public and by policy associations around the country, it enjoyed considerable independence from legislators and elected administrators.[22]

Power permits administrators to control and stabilize their environment and to ensure organizational survival. But the greater the stability achieved, the more it tends to create inertia, circumscribing the agency's perspectives about the welfare and public interest of the wider community. Under these circumstances, the dominant constituency in an agency becomes its major focus and concern, and the public and other clients become the victims of insensitivity and unresponsiveness. Thus we see that the administor's drive for power necessarily runs counter to the general community's quest for accountability, creating inevitable tension.

As power adheres to administrators, giving them more leverage to resist change and perpetuate themselves and their organizations, it becomes more difficult to achieve accountability. This means, among other things, that those demanding accountability must apply more creative and forceful means in order to stimulate a response. Perhaps defining the concepts and applications of power and accountability will help us to keep the operation of these two important concepts in mind.

POWER

By power we mean the ability to induce others to perform tasks or carry out directives that they would not ordinarily do. Amos Hawley has noted that "every social act is an exercise of power, every social relationship is a power equation and every social group or system is an organization of power."[23] Power is the ability to bring about change in part or in whole in the face of resistance and opposition. Viewed from a more operational perspective, power is the potential for exercising influence and the basis for acquiring the legitimacy for authority. The Mellon family of Pittsburgh, with all their wealth (they control big banks and trusts), connections (access to relevant public and private officials), and persuasive ability, have all the attributes of power. Yet the Mellons will have no influence unless they use the resources that make up their basis of power. It is the actual application of power that constitutes influence. This means that we can have power without influence, but we cannot have influence without power. To have maximum leverage and impact, administrators must have both power and the ability to apply it.[24]

Type of Power

According to Leonard D. White, administrators exercise two basic types of power: (1) coercive, or the ability to compel compliance; and (2) non-coercive, or the securing of compliance through persuasion. Noncoercive power is less costly, more efficient, and more pleasant. It is normally used when there is some degree of agreement and voluntary consent. Coercive power remains in the background and is used only as a last resort. Accountable and responsive administrators know that the best compliance is achieved through voluntary means. It therefore behooves them, for example, to mail forms to taxpayers or supply them in convenient places, provide simple instructions, place tax assistants at strategic locations, and otherwise make it easy to comply with income tax law.

The bulk of administrative compliance is achieved through the application of noncoercive power. Usually it is enough for a citizen to be informed that he or she has violated a housing code, must attend school, or be inoculated for communicable disease. White offers nine ways in which noncoercive power may be applied:

1. The declaration of a public policy. The government announces that it is against national policy to waste our natural resources. Most American make sincere efforts to comply.
2. Declaration of a legal obligation with no sanction for noncompliance. A state may announce that it is illegal to discriminate in employment but provide no penalty for violators. In the background may lie the possibility of punishing violators, for example, through denying them public contracts. In practice, offending firms may know it is unlikely that the threat will be carried out.
3. The establishment of voluntary standards. Much of the regulation of commercial

activity is accomplished through the government's assembling the parties involved and encouraging them to regulate themselves.

4. Example setting by the government. The establishment of power-generating capability in the Tennessee Valley Authority projects showed how power could be brought to areas believed to be commercially unprofitable. The government also demonstrated how the generation of power could be associated with the development of new industries, like fishing and recreation.

5. Educational campaigns. Through newspapers, radio, and television, the government constantly informs the public of what it ought to do. The Extension Service of the U.S. Department of Agriculture, for example, continuously informs farmers of ways to improve their productivity.

6. Demonstration. This a more direct educational effort. The government conducts pilot projects to show how it expects the private sector to perform. Postal delivery and the operation of railroads are examples of demonstrations that have proved less then successful.

7. Mediation and conciliation. These methods are most familiar in labor disputes in which a government mediator attempts to assist management and labor in reaching an agreement. These methods are also used in other areas, such as in disputes between landlords and tenants.

8. The purchase of consent. Through the "soil bank," the government controls the amount of commodities put into the market by paying farmers to allow their fields to remain fallow. Government by contract is now extensively employed.

9. Compliance through publicity. This can be accomplished by praising those who do well (such as honoring agencies that increase their productivity) or by reporting failures in performance. Some states, for examples, have published the names of firms that pay below the minimum wage. Many cities post in restaurant windows the health and cleanliness ratings given by public health inspectors.

Restraints of Power

If the drive for administrative power is carried to its ultimate, there can be no "common good" or "general welfare." The ends of each administrator would be solely his or her own and would likely be in conflict with the ends of all others. From this perspective, administrators are seen as seekers of power willing to sacrifice the welfare of the community to attain it.[25]

Case Study 2A: Discretion and the Income Maintenance Workers

As an Income Maintenance Worker II employed by the Commonwealth of Pennsylvania, Department of Public Welfare, Allegheny County Board of Assistance, I exercise considerable power over the welfare recipients who make up my caseload. I am, to some degree, held accountable.

One of the most important aspects of my job is to determine the public welfare recipients' eligibility for public assistance. This usually involves a one-half hour to one-hour interview, during which the IMW II asks the recipient many questions designed to help determine whether he is still eligible for assistance. These questions are based on department rules and regulations. If the recipient is found ineligible, his assistance continues uninterrupted. A third situation that might occur is that he is found eligible but advised that the assistance he is currently receiving must be altered. For example, the amount of the recipient's biweekly check or the price he pays for food stamps could be increased or decreased based on his current circumstances or new department rules and regulations. A fourth possibility is that eligibility requirements may have changed and therefore, in order to remain eligible, the recipient must fulfill an new set of responsibilities. *Redetermination,* a word that covers these four circumstances, can be very disconcerting to a client. My finds may force the recipient to change his behavioral patterns.

Because recipients often find redetermination uncomfortable, they frequently do not keep the interview, which is scheduled either at their home or at the district office. Home interviews are preferred; a department maxim states that if you see a recipient in his home you can be fairly sure that he lives there. When a redetermination interview is not kept, this in itself constitutes grounds upon which assistance can be discontinued after ten days' notice is given by an official letter sent through the mail. In this "no show" instance, my discretionary authority is even greater.

There are still other points where I exercise considerable power. A recipient can request a clothing allowance if he starts vocational training or if he needs clothes in order to obtain employment. Such allowances can be provided under a policy titled *grant to decrease need.* A recipient can also request a moving allowance, which is provided if he is evicted or if verification is obtained that either his health or safety is in jeopardy. The IMW II exercises power in situations where special allowances are requested since he must obtain all verification and determine the legitimacy of the request.

Voluntary referrals (on the recipient's part) are made to the Commonwealth's Bureaus of Vocational Rehabilitation if the recipient has a handicap due to health problems and if he is the type of person who can be helped to become employable through rehabilitation and training. Many mandatory referrals are made to the Commonwealth's Bureau of Employment Security (the unemployment office). If the recipient fails to register, his assistance will be discontinued. The welfare worker exercises a high degree of discretion (power) when he categorizes recipients according to the degree of their health problems or degree of employability. The welfare worker makes these judgments.

Adapted from Report of Participant #25 Income Maintenance II, Dept. of Public Welfare, public Management, November 14, 1979.

Must the drive for administrative power be carried to its ultimate limit? Most often, it is not and should not be. Are there reasonable and practical means available to assist administrators in moderating their power and drives for survival of themselves and their organization? We believe that restraint can be applied to the misuses of administrative power if accountability can be achieved as discussed below. There is nothing inherently evil about power; it is the use to which it is put that makes it good or evil.

ACCOUNTABILITY

Administrators who consciously seek to promote the congruence of their actions with the preferences of the community, people, or groups whom they serve are said to be sensitive, responsive, and accountable. In its simplest form, accountability may be defined as any situation in which individuals who exercise power are expected to be constrained and in fact are reasonably constrained by external means (e.g., reversal of decisions, dismissal, and judicial review) and to a degree by internal norms (e.g., codes of ethics and professional training). Administrators must know, through established criteria, to whom and for what they are accountable. The holders of power are stewards performing tasks specified by those who have the authority to review their actions—based on codes, regulations, and guidelines[26]—and the ability to displace them. Participants who choose not be so constrained in the use of their power are said to be insensitive, unresponsive, and unaccountable.

Legislative oversight has also been a longstanding external means of control over administrators. The practice of calling administrators to explain their actions before legislative committees is a uniquely American invention for securing accountability. The legislature has a number of important controls available: (1) changing the enabling legislation; (2) action on budget requests; (3) investigations; (4) confirmation of appointments; and (5) audit and evaluation through agencies like the General Accounting Office at the national level.

But internal controls are also essential. Middle and lower managers must be imbued with the notion "that clients have a significant influence on service delivery" and feel "the ever present threat that client power can be called upon to serve as a curb whenever service (or other) bureaucracies become unresponsive."[27] To be most effective, accountability must be a learned pattern, a response to habit. This becomes obvious when it is realized that most unaccountable acts, such as unethical behavior, inefficiency, and inadequate initiative, are difficult to control simply by rules or other external means.

Responsive administrators, wishing to act accountably, should ask themselves the following questions:

1. Are the intended actions linked to desired outcomes?
2. Is the best technical knowledge being applied in providing the service at the time, place, and manner and in the quantity and quality desired to achieve sustainability?
3. Will the proposed actions benefit mainly *us* (administrators) or *them* (clients, constituents, and the general public)?
4. Of the many solutions being contemplated, which would the weakest client select?
5. How would the least powerful constituent judge our actions?
6. Are sound practices being instituted to minimize fraud, waste, and abuse?

SUMMARY

The exercise of power and accountability are inevitably interdependent. Unrestrained power creates unresponsiveness and inefficient delivery of goods

and services. But accountability normally cannot be achieved unless the desire
to be accountable has become internalized or those desiring accountability have
the power to compel the desired response. In this latter sense, power checks
power. In our earlier discussion, we showed that the typical public manager can
efficiently administer by establishing a power base. This administrative power,
however, will be used accountably only when clients, constituents, and the
general public possess power to counter it. As shown in Fig. 2.3., middle- and
lower-level managers are in charge, but they must answer to the top-level elected
or appointed executive, the legislature, clients, constituents, and the public at
large.

Fig. 2.3. Managers and Accountability

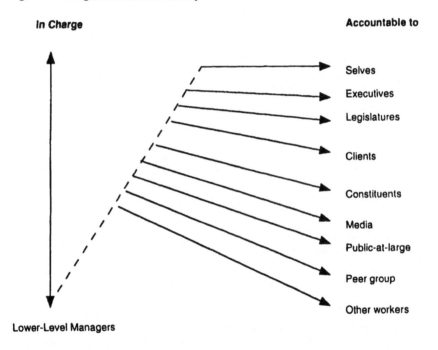

DISCUSSION QUESTIONS

1.   Why can we assert that Americans live in an organized society and that
     government is the most important system or organizations?
2.   Why is it necessary for administrators to establish continuing working
     relationships with interest groups operating in their field of interest?
3.   How have traditional approaches to check and balances been altered by
     administrative developments?
4.   What are the distinguishing characteristics that separate top-level executives from
     middle-level managers? Why does Scott refer to these managers as holding
     "significant jobs"?

5. Why are middle-level mangers said to be in charge of most of what government does?
6. In what way do middle-level managers act as the coordinating force among all levels of management?
7. What distinguishes a supervisor from a middle-level manager?
8. Why are power and accountability said to be interdependent?
9. Why are legislatures forced to delegate significant power to administrators?
10. What is it about a bureaucracy that forces the pursuit of power?
11. Why is it necessary to understand the difference between power and influence?
12. Distinguish between coercive and noncoercive power.
13. What are the major attributes of accountability?
14. What criteria or guide can administrators employ in achieving full exercise of power with accountability?

NOTES

1. Victor A. Thompson, *The Development of Modern Bureaucracy: Tools Out of People* (Morrison, N.J.: General Learning Press, 1974), p. 1.
2. "Effective Public Management: It Isn't the Same as Business Management," *Harvard Business Review* (March/April 1977): 132.
3. The adoption of the executive budget (centralized leadership for policy development and implementation) in many cities in the late 1880s marked a significant modification of the diffusion theory of power. See Chapter 15 for further discussion of this point.
4. Leonard White, *Introduction to the Study of Public Administration*, 4th edn. (New York: Macmillan, 1955), p. 58.
5. Richard L. Chapman and Frederic N. Cleveland, "The Changing Character of the Public Service and the Administration of the 1980s," *Public Administration Review* 33 (July/August 1973): 363.
6. John M. Pfiffner and Robert Presthus, *Public Administration*, 5th edn. (New York: Ronald Press, 1967), p. 142.
7. Walter B. Wright, "As You Were Saying," *Personnel Journal* (February 1973): 142.
8. David Osborn and Ted Gaebler, *Reinventing Government: How the Entrepreneurial Spirit is Transforming the Public Sector* (Reading, Mass.: Addison-Wesley Publishing Company, 1992), p. 265.
9. Douglas Morgan, Kelly G. Bacon, Charles D. Cameron and Robert Deis, "What Middle Managers Do In Local Government: Stewardship of the Public Trust and the Limits of Reinventing Government," *Pubic Administration Review* 56, No. 4 (July/August 1996): 360–61.
10. Ibid.
11. Ibid., p. 364.
12. Marshall Edward Dimock and Gladys O. Dimock, *Public Administration*, 4th edn. (New York: Holt, Rinehart and Winston, 1964), p. 350.
13. White, *Introduction to the Study of Public Administration*, 3rd edn. (New

York: Macmillan, 1950), pp. 89–102. Note that White views all managers below the top levels as middle level.

14.   William G. Scott, "The Theory of Significant People," *Public Administration Review* (July/August 1973): 310.

15.   Ibid.

16.   John M. Pfiffner, *Supervision of Personnel: Human Relations in the Management of Men* (Englewood Cliffs, N.J.: Prentice Hall, 1951).

17.   Theodore Lewis, "Machine Politics—Old and New," *The Public Interest* (Fall 1967): 86.

18.   John A. Gardner, "Policy Enforcement of Traffic Laws: A Comparative Analysis," in James Wilson, ed., *City Politics and Public Policy* (New York: Wiley and Sons, 1968), pp. 151–71; Jerome B. McKinney, "Influence of Lower Officials in Policy Making," Paper presented at the conference of the American Society for Public Administration, Denver, Colorado, April 1971.

19.   Johnna A. Pro. "Red Light on Traffic Tickets," *Pittsburgh Post Gazette* (May 22, 1996), pp. A1, A10.

20.   J. Lieper Freemen, *The Political Process: Executive-Bureau Legislation Committee Relations,* rev. edn. (New York: Random House, 1965).

21.   Gordon Tullock, *The Politics of Bureaucracy* (Washington, D.C.: Public Affairs Press, 1965); Anthony Downs, *Inside Bureaucracy* (Boston: Little, Brown, 1967).

22.   Norton Long, "Power and Administration," *Public Administration Review* (Autumn 1947); 257–64; Francis Rourke, *Bureaucracy, Politics, and Public Policy* (Boston: Little, Brown, 1969).

23.   Amos H. Hawley, "Community Power and Urban Renewal Success," *American Journal of Sociology* 68 (January 1963): 422. For an excellent discussion, see Robert Magill and Terry N. Clark, "Community Power and Decision-Making," *Social Services Review* (May 1975): 33–44; Terry N. Clark, *Community Power and Policy Output* (Beverly Hills, Calif.: Sage Publications, 1973); and S. K. Kenduka and Bernard Coughlin, "A Conceptualization of Social Action," *Social Services Review* (May/June 1975): 21.

24.   White, *Introduction*, 4th edn., pp. 467–70.

25.   Glen Tender, *Political Thinking* (Boston: Little, Brown, 1970), p. 129.

26.   Kenneth Kevnagham, "Responsible Public Bureaucracy: A Rationale and Framework for Analysis," *Canadian Public Administration* (Winter 1973): 573.

27.   Robert K. Yin and Douglas Yates, *Street-Level Governments* (Santa Monica, Calif.: Rand Corporation, 1974), p. 23.

3

Reinventing Government: Transforming Public Administration

This chapter is about rethinking and rediscovering public administration. Section one examines early reinventions, pointing out the continuity with ongoing efforts. In section two the new invigorated drive for entrepreneurialism in government is examined. Section three critically reviews the National Performance Review (NPR) report. In section four ideas for creating a responsive bureaucracy are briefly examined. Section five discusses the different ways of building public management into an effective learning organization. The sixth section reviews the problems and obstacles that public servants must face in executing their assignment. In the final section the MLMs' changing environment and their pursuit of accountability are briefly reviewed.

LEARNING OBJECTIVES

Upon completing this chapter, you should be able to:

- Understand the reinventions that preceded the current reinvention movement.
- Understand the opportunities and challenges for entrepreneurialism in the public sector.
- See how the proposed federal reinvention (NPR) will profoundly affect the distribution of power in the federal government.
- Recognize how public organizations can become effective learning instruments for change.
- Understand how satisfying the customer or clientele becomes the driving force for all organizational activities.
- Recognize the dynamics and problems with which managers must deal in the public sector.
- Understand the changing role of MLMs in the new reinvention environment.

Since the 1992 publication of David Osborne and Ted Graebler's

Reinventing Government, which argued for entrepreneurial and decentralized government, the view of many is that the reinvention focus is a new phenomenon. This could not be further from the truth. The emphasis on transforming government from a non-market to a more entrepreneurial instrument in delivering goods and services has had at least five antecedents in American history, focusing in various ways on the reinvention theme.[1]

REINVENTION: SOME PRIOR ATTEMPTS AND DEVELOPMENTS

The five reinvention-type developments include: (1) President Andrew Jackson's appeal for the common citizen administrators; (2) Abraham Lincoln and the Civil War aftermath; (3) Presidents Theodore Roosevelt's and Woodrow Wilson's reformist actions; (4) the Great Depression and President Franklin Delano Roosevelt's activist policies; and (5) Presidents Jimmy Carter's and Ronald Reagan's anti-Washington and anti-bureaucracy campaigns.

President Andrew Jackson, unlike his predecessors, felt that the powers of the presidency had to be applied more fully. He developed a direct line of contact with citizens, as reflected by the slogan, "Let the people rule." He was committed to the Constitution, state's rights, and retirement of the federal debt. He opposed direct taxes and loans and strongly supported the preservation of the Union. To promote his goals, he used the veto more liberally than any of his predecessors. He constantly challenged the Supreme Court and changed the relationship among the political parties, Congress, and the executive.

Abraham Lincoln, the Civil War, and its aftermath expanded the role of government to do more than merely protect the liberties and rights of citizens as anticipated by the Founding Fathers. He assumed an activist role that required a significant increase in federal employees. Lincoln viewed the Emancipation Proclamation as ushering in a "new birth of freedom." The role of government was greatly expanded in economic development throughout the nation, especially in the reconstruction of the South. Immigration was encouraged to expand and complement the labor force; land grants were used to develop the West, establish colleges, the rail system, and other important infrastructure.

The reformist activities of Theodore Roosevelt and the presidency of Woodrow Wilson may be characterized as the third reinvention period. Roosevelt used the power of the presidency to check and moderate the influence of monopolists, land speculators, and railroad barons. Congress was galvanized to pass laws to regulate railroads, protect the public from harmful foods and drugs, and preserve the virgin areas of U.S. forests and other environmental treasures. Roosevelt's vigorous and successful efforts against monopolistic practices earned him the nickname "Trust Buster."

At the first annual Convention on Good Government in 1884, Roosevelt supported efforts to streamline and transform the way government operates: budgeting and monitoring control to minimize the cost of government, building a wall between politics and daily administration (the politics–administration dichotomy), using professional managers to run government, and adopting the best scientific management as applied in business. The National Municipal League accepted the challenge later in 1913 to wage the fight in the states to give cities the opportunity to adopt the strong mayoral and professional manager system. The success of the league's efforts was evident by 1928, when approximately 324 cities had adopted the professional city manager system.[2]

Wilson continued Roosevelt's unfinished business by encouraging the passage of such regulatory acts as the Federal Reserve System (FRS), establishing the Federal Trade Commission (FTC), the direct election of U.S. senators (away from the control of state legislators), and the Nineteenth Amendment giving women the right to vote.

The Great Depression of the 1930s ushered in another period of reinvention. Events allowed Franklin Delano Roosevelt to take an extra-ordinarily activist role in government that came to be known as the New Deal. It allowed him to reform the currency, initiate public works to stimulate the economy, introduce unemployment assistance and old-age assistance, and aid to agriculture and the railroads; collect outstanding debts from World War I allies; reform the national debt and tariffs with trading partners; and mobilize the military to meet a fascist threat.

The fifth reinvention period began with Jimmy Carter's election in 1976. He entered the White House on an anti-Washington and anti-government theme. The forces that he helped unleash initiated the anti-tax revolt in California that led to Proposition 13 in 1978, which cut local property taxes by approximately 57 percent. The momentum led to similar efforts of differing magnitudes throughout the country.

The election of Ronald Reagan in 1980 gave renewed impetus to a groundswell that had been building about the role and efficacy of government. Reagan came to see government as the problem, not the solution. Yet he vastly expanded the military budget while failing to achieve domestic reductions in the budget. The actions created an unprecedented increase in the national debt that is a continuing source of major concern and conflict. Reagan also shifted many federal responsibilities to the state. The shift in attitude of the public about the proper role of government was given as a major reason. While the public was getting an adequate supply of services, it was unwilling to pay more taxes. Government was viewed as too big and unable to supply services effectively.

The slow pace of the economy sapped the government's ability to add and enhance goods and services without greater taxes, especially after the Arab oil embargoes of 1974 and 1978. Watergate and a number of scandals engendered the view that government was morally bankrupt and incapable of providing the dynamic and creative leadership required to redirect its accomplishments. This perception led to opposition to government's role in society, leading to demands for re-examination of the way government allocates its resources and the instruments employed to implement them.[3]

THE NEW ENTREPRENEURALISM IN GOVERNMENT

When David Osborne and Ted Gaebler articulated their reinvention cry for greater entrepreneuralism in government, it was preceded by a number of negative and anti-government developments that had been embedded in the consciousness of the American public. Despite these strongly held views, recent evidence suggests that public views may be due more to ideological reasons than to reality.[4] Thirty years ago, 76 percent of Americans believed that government could be trusted to do the right thing. Today this number has fallen to 30 percent. The general public belief is that 48 cents of every public dollar spent is wasted.

One observer notes that it is not lazy and incompetent employees who are undermining and creating obstacles to the system. Red tape and regulations suffocate and stifle creativity. At the national level, "the federal government is filled with good people trapped in a bad system; budget system, personnel, procurement system, financial system and information system."[5] These systems were designed for an environment that no longer exists and can no longer effectively serve the American public.

Federal agencies are monopolies and have few incentives to innovate and enhance the production and delivery of services. To add to this problem, Gore's National Performance Report claims that administrators have an operating pathology that seeks maximum risk-avoidance. To minimize the potential risk of poor program performance, elaborate systems have been developed to deter the possibility of scandals. This necessitates that monitoring systems be spelled out in minute detail. Thus employees are expected "to follow rules, pass the buck and keep their heads down."[6]

The imperative for reinvention emanated from a number of sources and developments, both national and international.

1.   The Reagan administration stimulated debate about what government should be required to undertake, how it should be undertaken, and who should have the responsibility to carry it out.
2.   The expansion of entitlement has occurred simultaneously with the public's unwillingness to pay additional taxes, creating a crisis as people demand more goods and services with less expenditure of funds.
3.   The collapse of Communism necessitated major shifts in Cold War priorities, resulting in a restructuring of federal programs.
4.   The new international economic order has generated new and increased competitive pressures in the global economy, technology, and the need to review the way public service undertakings are executed.

Osborne and Gaebler state that government's use of outmoded ways to conduct business can no longer be accepted. Citizens see in their living room, by means of television, how things are competitively done in the private sector compared with the monopolistic, single-vendor centralized public bureaucracies.[7] Osborne and Gaebler believe that government reinvention requires nothing less than complete change in the basic model of government. Stress must be put not on what government does but on how it does it. They catalog management innovations at the state and local levels of government. Among the principles the authors emphasize: (1) giving greater attention to in-house instead of outside delivery alternatives such as contracting out, public-private partnership, vouchers, and seed money; (2) empowering clientele governing councils' participation and management teams; (3) encouraging economic bidding and internal rivalry among units serving clients; (4) installing rational resource allocation and performance evaluation systems; (5) organizing all actions to focus on customer satisfaction; and (6) decentralizing authority, adopting participatory management, and labor-management cooperation.[8] Borrowing successful business practices is not good enough, however; government needs to reinvent itself to make its environment receptive to the "entrepreneurial spirit." This will facilitate new internal growth and the development of "performance-oriented organizational cultures."[9] Osborne and Gaebler say that government should "steer, not row" in the direction it wants to go, using clear guiding principles.[10]

The Privatization Movement

Proponents of the entrepreneurial drive in government say that its success has been outstanding in most countries where it has been tried. The privatization of British Telecom in Britain in 1984 was a major development. Since this event, approximately $328 billion of government-run operations worldwide have been privatized. *The Economist* noted: "The privatization advocates want to reduce the size of government to promote greater efficiency, to shrink budget deficits, create greater opportunities for the private sector and provide a greater number of choices in the consumption of public services."[11] To speed privatization in the U.S., President George Bush issued an executive order in May 1992 to remove many of the barriers impeding privatization of state- and city-owned infrastructures that were funded in part by federal assistance.

Criticism of the Reinvention Machine—NPR

The reinvention proponents tend to have a narrow focus: tinkering with management and changing structures. The innovation examples, typically local, that reinvention supporters highlight—such as Sunnyvale's long-range budgeting, and Visalia's mission-driven budget in California, or St. Paul's profit center in Minnesota have not been replicated elsewhere: "A real shift in American governance would require not merely managerial reinventions but sweeping disinventions. . . . But genuinely radical transformation in government cannot occur without radical transformations in policy, in the fundamental "what" of government as distinguished from the procedural "how."[12] Presidents Lyndon Johnson and Franklin Roosevelt are not remembered for their managerial feats but for their policies on expanding the scope of government.

These changes in scope and direction are due to policy changes rather than misguided management.[13]

The rush to the reinvention bandwagon and the Clinton administration's negative views on bureaucracy brought considerable positive public relations (about 10 percent in favorable opinion poll ratings). But the criticisms leveled at the bloated bureaucracy do not square with reality. Contrary to perception, the federal civilian workforce, at 2.1 million employees, is smaller today than it was in 1960. As then, nine out of ten workers live outside the Washington, D.C., area. The big growth in federal employees during the past thirty years has been the political appointees. Every program enacted since World War II has been administered by state and local governments, or contracted out to private providers and nonprofit organizations, sometime called the third sector.

Beside the structural and philosophical flaws and fuzziness of NPR, the Clinton administration wanted short-term success within two years from the sponsored innovation. The desire for quick wins was pursued without building a foundation that would have made success more likely. By emphasizing cost savings as a high point of his downsizing efforts, federal employees saw Clinton's actions as an attack on their jobs. An associated concern was how the layoffs would affect the capacity of government to carry out its required functions. Would the fast-paced drive to overhaul the administrative system leave the government lean and hollow, with reduced capacity, a cynical public, and a demoralized workforce willing to exercise less initiative?[14]

Lack of a Public Service Philosophy

The NPR framework lacks the glue to hold the reinvention ideas together. NPR empowers MLMs to make better decisions. It replaces the existing monopoly-based central control of management with greater competition and autonomy. Power is shifted from Congress to the bureaucracy. In the bureaucracy, power is shifted from the top to the bottom (MLMs). Without an internalized philosophy to guide government officials (MLMs), what is the restraining or mediating force to prevent MLMs from becoming fragmented quasi-autonomous operators who are unaccountable to democratically elected officials? How will public interest dominate over personal and private interests?

The NPR did not devise a system to keep the best and the brightest employees, especially those in whom large investments in time and money have been made. Thus, many of the best managers took the buyouts offered in the NPR downsizing plan. The implementation of the NPR plan allowed its short-term savings to turn into long-term losses as the required skills to maintain high-quality services was lost.

NPR did not attack the 3,000 political appointees at the top of the federal bureaucracy. These appointees act as layers between the president and the civil servants. The NPR team basically ignored the fact that the middle managers were its focus. The NPR team was preoccupied mainly with the pressure to cut jobs and produce savings. This single-minded orientation did not engender a positive attitude in a number of managers to embrace the offer to be empowered. Instead of becoming risk-takers, they tended to become risk avoiders as they were given no assurances that they would be rewarded for taking initiatives.

The reinventers gave virtually no priority to people and the tools they needed for improving government performance.[15] Little attention was paid to Levine and Kleeman's concern about the creeping "quiet crisis" that was eroding the capacity of government to do its job effectively.[16] The Volcker Commission expressed concern that paralleled Levine's. The commission warned that if the negative trends continued," America will soon be left with a government of the mediocre locked into careers of last resort or waiting for a chance to move on to other jobs."[17]

NPR: New Form of the Politics-Administration Dichotomy

In focusing on how government works rather than what government does, NPR introduces a new variant of the politics-administration dichotomy. Reporting requirements by Congress is viewed as intrusion. NPR adopts the ideology of the Progressives at the turn of the century. The Progressives were advocates of a non-political approach to municipal services. They believed in nonpartisan election and argued that the demand for government services could best be fulfilled by skilled professional managers.[18] NPR proposes an administration that provides goods and services to the American public (customers) without red tape and hierarchy. NPR requires a major shift in power from the top and staff officials to front-line managers (MLMs). These are the individuals to whom the discretionary power to interpret and implement the delivery of goods and services, are essentially devoid of politics.

The singular and overriding function of government is to maximize customer satisfaction. To achieve this objective, NPR ignores the complex set of social forces operating in the environment. These include reconciling a multitude of different values and interests (see Chapter 2), developing and regulating distributive and redistributive policies and the constraining and guiding constitutional values. Thus, public management is not simply a cost-effective pursuit of the maximization of customer satisfaction.

Since Congress' role is making law and policy, its role is political. Though both Congress and the president are accountable to the electorate for political and policy decisions, the Constitution confers the executive/administrative functions on the office of the president. Thus, Congress can make laws but not participate in their execution or the management function. This suggests that all those systems that have been erected to monitor personnel requirements, property management, procurement, analysis, and evaluation should be reduced or eliminated. These systems exercise political functions and are thus an inappropriate intrusion that has damaged the bureaucracy. Like Reagan and to some extent Carter, government is viewed as the problem and not the solution.[19] If the guidelines of NPR are carried out, the bureaucracy could become a responsive and effective instrument of presidential policy.

NPR is silent about the recommendation made by the Volcker Commission's view that the vitality and efficacy of the career public service require significant reinvestment. NPR sees front-line administrators as the only contributors who add value to service production.[20] Despite the expressed concern about political influence intruding into administration, presidential influence is greatly increased. While there has been more than 272,000 decrease in career middle level and staff managers, the 3,000 presidential political appointees are not affected. This increases the potential influence and direction of political officials as the ratio of political appointees to career officials rises. Additionally, NPR called for the abolishment of Office of Personnel Management (OPM) and transfer of its authority for recruiting, hiring, and promoting to the operating agencies. The decentralization of these functions brings into question the ability to operate a well-functioning civil service system when oversight for recruiting and promoting is removed. This becomes especially troublesome without an internalized public service philosophy. NPR proposes deregulation and decentralization of powers to front-line managers. The job for assessing effectiveness is moved totally from Congress to the president's, Office Management and Budget (OMB), and the customers. To make a smoothly operating machine, Congress must enact laws to transfer power to OMB to coordinate, consolidate, and simplify requirements. Congress is expected to pass legislation that is simple, explicit, and measurable. Once Congress has expressed its objectives, the administration should be totally on its own to implement the legislation.[21] NPR's underlying theory does not incorporate the concerns about excessive congressional delegation that might undermine the constitutional balance, carefully articulated by the Founding Fathers and addressed in Chapter 1.

In the final analysis NPR advances a strong case for the exercise of presidential leadership and responsibility, making it possible for government to take action in difficult situations. This would avoid the deadlock that occurs when government is divided and major actors are ideologically opposed, as with the Democrats and Republicans in disagreement over major policy issues such as a balanced budget and health issues. Interest groups and their interplay with politicians, the career officials and the Congress that help to produce acceptable compromises are minimized.

Despite the NPR demand for greater responsiveness and better delivery of results to satisfy customers, there are no ideas for enhancing the career public servants. No ideas are put forth for systematically rebuilding the public service, as was recommended by the Volcker Commission. The Senior Executive Service that was initiated by Carter to aid in revitalizing and providing capable and flexible officials to aid government decision-making is ignored.

NPR puts consumer sovereignty and satisfaction as the highest or greatest good, not liberty, justice or dignity. It sees government as a means for maximizing consumption. Government's role as referee in resolving conflicts, articulating the national mission, goals, laws, and charting the nation's future takes a back seat to customer satisfaction. NPR appeals to a culture of complaint and momentary self-gratification: "It reflects the reality of shared, economic needs that cannot be defined or realized by satisfying individual consumer desires. It converts citizens into a customer with little responsibility to the community. It de-emphasizes the future to satisfy the present."[22] The distinctive and unique role of government is minimized. Government is viewed as a giant department store, where rule of law, representative government, separation of powers, and individual liberty become unclear.

The NPR's adoption of Osborne and Gaebler's entrepreneurial leadership approach calls for freedom to spend money, change program priorities and organizational culture to accomplish particular policy ends. Paradoxically, as employees and clients are empowered, leaders are asked to delegate and decentralize authority and promote competition. However, these actions lead to disempowerment of the leaders. With no agreed public service philosophy and no guide for entrepreneurs, would these empowered managers promote the public interest? Charles T. Goodsell suggests that the drive for reinventing government cannot lose sight of certain basic principles that are the bedrock of American democracy. They include:

1.   Americans are sovereign of government, not the new proposed entrepreneurs.
2.   Public administration is a reflection of laws emanating from the Constitution in which due process is required and where equal opportunity for all is the enshrined goal.
3.   Flexibility of administrative action takes place only in the context of public accountability.
4.   Relaxation of financial constraints or rules does not mean the relinquishing of the stewardship of public funds.[23]

The NPR and its advocates say that changes are needed in public administration, that the rigidity that characterizes its operations is not conducive to creativity.[24] The current thinking and operating norms, they argue, do not create a fertile environment for entrepreneurs who can take innovative initiatives to channel resources to increase their value to the polity. In short, public managers need the leeway to create and add public value. Again, these advocates expect this new orientation to take root and sprout in public administration without changing the Constitution, laws, and philosophy of the public service. But before these types of changes can be made, we need to better understand how to create and internalize a more responsive public and learning bureaucracy.

CREATING A RESPONSIVE BUREAUCRACY

The changing nature of work has been a major impetus to rethink the structure of the traditional organization. Today, both technical and nontechnical work are more knowledge-based. Knowledge work requires information gathering and integration into larger systems. Unlike the traditional public organization, knowledge workers cannot be ordered about like assembly-line bolt turners or ditch diggers. The nature of the work allows the employees to learn more than their bosses. The knowledge worker of today involves "bringing everyone's native intelligence and collaborative abilities to bear on constantly changing ways of achieving shared goals."[25]

The bureaucratic environment has moved from the function-based work to project. Work is viewed not as taking place in a static state but as a series of problems providing opportunities to be seized. To maximize the opportunities and to make use of the widest number of skills in the shortest time possible, project teams are required. Teams learn collectively as the project move through stages of implementation. Since the bosses are external to the evolving processes, control is shifted from the traditional authority system to the project teams.[26]

The changed bureaucracy is moving from meaningless repetitive tasks to innovation and caring. Team work is replacing individual work. A multi-skilled emphasis is replacing the single-skilled. In the changing organization, the power of hierarchical bosses is giving way to the power of clientele and customers. Coordination from the top will give way to coordination among peers.[27]

HOW TO CHANGE PUBLIC MANAGEMENT

To initiate a process of transformation in public management, change must occur in the perception of how citizens view government and the way learning takes place in moving from existing ways of doing things to a more team oriented model if sustained change is to be realized. Despite its obvious real value such as in defense, social security and safety, citizens have profound distrust of government. They see it as an inefficient and ineffective instrument. A number of reasons can be given for the present attitude. The complexity and fast pace of society have often left government as the only visible and stable institution on which individuals can vent some of their frustrations and lay blame for policy failures.

The bureaucracy is a natural target for criticism as it is often seen, to be more preoccupied with perfecting rules and laws, over the past 150 years, to prevent and eradicate every possibility of abuse. The bureaucracy's single-minded focus on rule making, oversight, and enforcement has often lost sight of the main goal, the effective delivery of goods and services. As John Scully noted, "Our bureaucracies are rule factories, and our oversight and enforcement agencies spend most of their energy ascertaining whether employees are following the rules that are so complex that individuals of normal intelligence cannot possibly remember or follow them all."[28]

Given citizens' complaints about the lack of government responsiveness, public administration must accept the challenge as a strategic opportunity to change. Reactions to problems of the past are counter-productive, and officials (both administrative and elective) at all levels of the organization must collectively pursue and achieve better results or added value. This type of change and reorientation can only be achieved with a new leadership that has a vision of where employees and the organization needs to go. The leadership should:

1.   Articulate a clearly defined long-range process of change to which they are totally committed in spirit and in action.
2.   Enlist the support of subordinate leaders and all component agencies to the vision for change.
3.   Develop processes and mechanisms, over time, that facilitate and allow all participants to internalize the vision of change.
4.   Instill the understanding that the vision incorporates continuous change.
5.   Organizational members must learn together.
6.   Learning must be incremental and clearly understandable to promote innovation and to creatively cope with the transformation taking place.

Need for Cultural Learning and Change

If improvement is to be sustained and lasting, it must be influenced by the constant changes taking place. Enduring improvement demands continuous commitment to learning. All learning requires the introduction of something new. Thus, without learning something new, organizations cannot improve. This means seeing the model in a new light.[29] In organizations where there is an absence of learning, organizations and people will repeat the errors of the past. Learning organizations are those, Peter Sange noted, "where people continually expand their capacity to create the results they truly desire, where new and expansive patterns of thinkers are nurtured, where collective inspiration is set free and where people are continually learning how to learn together."[30]

David Garvin suggests that while definitions such as Peter Sange's are useful, they do not provide sufficient practical guide to managers. He suggests that emphasis be put on the special ability of an organization to create, acquire, and transfer knowledge, reflecting the new changes and insights in the behavior and practices of the people and the organization. The learning process is managed to ensure that the changes are instilled by design and not left to chance.[31]

Learning and change take place according to a prevailing paradigm, a pattern or way of thinking based on internalized cultural values and learned behaviors that guide organizational and individual decision-making. Paradigms must be useful and functional as they provide convenient and comfortable ways of thinking, organizing, and influencing decision making. Despite the guiding rule of paradigms in our daily lives, we are typically not conscious of their impact. Everything contrary to our operating paradigm is viewed as threatening. Scully notes: "Paradigms can be good or bad, depending on whether they are functioning to keep a particular culture in touch with reality and the people who live in them are well-served."[32]

If a paradigm shift is to occur in an effective organizational learning settings, four steps are suggested:

1.   There must be a shared learning of the leadership's vision and operating assumptions.
2.   The learning must take place incrementally and be clearly understandable.
3.   Once steps one and two are completed, the paradigm shift is achieved.
4.   The change must be taught to all of the employees of the old paradigm.

Practicing the new learned patterns is the sure way of promoting change. In those cases where key personnel are unwilling to adapt to the new learning environment, they may be "moved aside" where this is possible, or special accommodations may be made.[33]

Learning and the Bureaucratic Model

Bureaucracies function best when those at the top delegate authority and power to subordinates who are duty-bound to carry them out and report back to the top. Information flows only vertically, as shown in Fig. 3.1. Each bureaucracy operates as a self-contained unit.

As the size and complexity of the bureaucracy increase, as is the case in many government agencies, learning is nearly impossible. First, those wedded to the existing paradigm have distinctly unequal capability to change due to differences in "level and competence, unequal commitment to the old ways, and an unequal understanding of the need to change and commitment to that change."[34] Second, the separate mission in each bureaucracy is the drive for self-sufficiency and self-containment, which negates collective or lateral learning or cross-organizational lines. Laws and executive orders can be passed to deal with these problems but they will not have the desired effect because most key decision-makers are wedded to the old paradigm.[35]

Structure as the Inappropriate Solution

The response to most bureaucratic problems is to create new organizations and programs to cure the ills. For example in Allegheny County, Pennsylvania, a few county workers have been caught working in other pursuits, such as operating a tourist fishing boat on Lake Erie, when they are required to be at work. The county commissioners' solution was to create an inspector general. Here we have a behavioral problem that is being addressed by a structural response. Most often this approach does not work. Organizations often attempt to supplant existing programs with new ones, allowing the new agency to operate side by side with the old entrenched agency to serve the same clientele. While the new organization will add value, the conflict with the original organization is likely to lead to additional problems that impede the delivery of services to the original clientele. Thus the creation of the new structure disempowers those originally dealing with the problem, clouding their responsibility and incentives for solving the problem and hindering a long-term sustaining change.

Fig. 3.1. Hierarchy: Traditional Bureaucracy

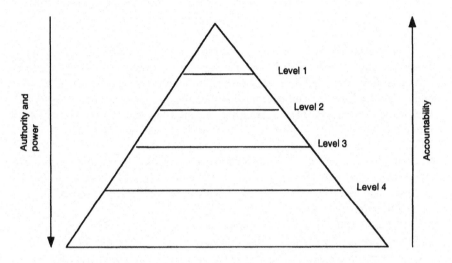

Introducing Learning and Change in Public Management

Important modifications must be successfully introduced if organizational learning is to become a way of life in public management, especially at the federal level. The following changes are needed to promote transformation from the old paradigm to the new:

1.   A clear statement of vision from the top down must be articulated.
2.   The changes should be incremental to permit them to be linked in a continuous learning building block.
3.   An extended time horizon of at least five years must be given to successfully institutionalize change.
4.   Support system, authority, and incentives must be developed to get key personnel to learn and work together to make things happen.
5.   New skills must be taught such as total quality management, team work, process analysis, communication, and leading skills.[36]

Unbridled Expectations and the Pharaoh Syndrome

Reinventing, re-engineering, and transforming government into learning organizations may be the appropriate response to the Pharaoh Syndrome, which top officials need to avoid in blaming public employees for their failure to meet public demands. Not infrequently, political officials set goals higher than what the resources allocated will allow subordinates to accomplish. Rather than informing their superiors about the unfeasibility of their expectations, directives are passed down to subordinates to achieve the target with less. This idea is derived from the plight of the Israelites, who "asked Pharaoh for more time to pray. Rather than address their need to pray, he reduced the amount of free time available to them by increasing their labor."[37] Pharaoh wanted to prevent the Israelites from reflecting on their life in Egypt as a way of stifling popular initiatives.[38]

The Pharaoh Syndrome brings to mind a tragic example that occurred in Western Pennsylvania. The secretary of a local borough received escalating demands for resources to meet various projects and favors sought by her commissioners. Every commissioner on the council knew the budget limits, yet they made demands far beyond what the budget allowed. The secretary always found sufficient funds to meet the mounting requests. No one knew or cared about the source of the funds. After extended periods, when the Internal Revenue Service and the Pennsylvania Department of Revenue did not receive withholding taxes, the borough secretary learned that she was about to be audited. Too avoid the investigation and its inevitable outcome, she committed suicide by asphyxiation.

Those in the Pharaoh Syndrome ask for results that cannot be satisfied, and the concept suggests that leaders do not seek to understand the real causes that give rise to demands. The assumption is that if enough pressure is applied to public employees, they can be whipped in line to produce more results with less, surpassing their resource limitations. These demands from the top have the potential of generating "mistrust, confrontation, demoralization and other dysfunctional behavior by employees," rather than cooperation, which often leads to greater effectiveness and efficiency. [39]

The application of the Pharaoh Syndrome extracts a price from the U.S. public service. Attacks on the public service "chisel away the trust that is one of the foundations of public sector productivity."[40] This observation does not suggest that public servants do not, from time to time, deserve criticism. The Pharaoh Syndrome draws attention to top officials' ways of avoiding future blame or trouble. It does not have the positive objective for enhancing performance or responsiveness to clientele.

Unlike the pharaoh, whose intent we could reasonably interpret, it is hard to discern motive and intent from the things participants do and say. Often citizens groups and the media are quick to characterize citizens' complaints as indicators of popular dissatisfaction when the reasons may be quite subtle. In fact, as we hear the outcry about mass dissatisfaction with government service, surveys of specific service delivery show very high degrees of public satisfaction.[41] Thus there might be those who are critical of public servants because they have personal objectives that may override legitimate criticism.

1.   The politician may wish to deflect criticism of his poor performance.

2.   The reporter's critical story may seek to enhance her paper's economic advantage while preserving her access to news leaks.
3.   One group may be promoting its objectives over that of the public interest.
4.   It may be an individual's attempt to "even up the score" with a public servant who refused to give him preferential treatment.
5.   A group or individual may wish to get an issue on the institutional agenda.[42]

Quick fixes are typically not the answer to complaints. Yet this may often be the tactic that top officials adopt to bring about change. Preferably a proactive approach should be followed that would pre-empt quick fixes. Approaches to emphasize should involve reinvention and re-engineering in which the learning organization institutionalizes the capacity to support positive achievements.[43]

MLMs AND THE CHANGING ENVIRONMENT AND ACCOUNTABILITY

The new emphasis on customer satisfaction forces managers to move away from narrow control and efficiency orientation. Emphasis is put on meeting customer expectations. Accountability is focused not on conformance to internal rules and administrative norms but on what, how much, when, and in what manner customers' demands are met.

The new entrepreneurialism demands that managers take far greater initiatives than in the past. Instead of being risk-avoiders, the new environment expects MLMs to be greater risk-takers. NPR's massive decentralization and deregulation give significantly enhanced powers to the MLMs. With this newly increased power, MLMs have fewer controls and far greater opportunities to exercise discretion. Can we expect MLMs to be sufficiently sensitive to the public interest with the greatly reduced controls and with no internalized public service philosophy to guide their actions?

Despite the large number of middle managers who have been eliminated from the public service, the power and influence of MLMs have not been reduced. On the contrary, the amount of authority to act has been increased while the controls, oversight, and monitoring requirements have been reduced. This gives MLMs greater opportunity to affect directly the lives of citizens. This means MLMs must develop a greater sense of balancing their personal needs with those of the public if responsiveness and accountability are to be maintained or enhanced.

DISCUSSION QUESTIONS

1.   How do the five reinvention periods prior to NPR compare with NPR?
2.   What constitutes a public entrepreneurial manager? What are the positive and negative implications of entrepreneurialism in public administration?

3.   Go to the governmental unit where you reside and obtain a list of entrepreneurial initiatives or projects that it has entered into during the last two years.
4.   Why is the NPR seen as an instrument to increase presidential power at the expense of Congress?
5.   In what way does the NPR reintroduce the policy-administration dichotomy?
6.   Discuss some of the ingredients that may help create a more responsive bureaucracy.
7.   What is a learning organization and why is it important to establish an organization that wishes to change?
8.   What is "the Pharaoh Syndrome?" In what way is it practiced in the U.S.?

NOTES

1.   John DiLulio, Gerald Garvy, and Donald Kettl, *Improving Government: An Owners Manual* (Washington, D.C.: The Brookings Institution, 1993).

2.   Dennis Judd, *The Politics of American Cities: Private Power and Public Policy* (Glenview, Ill.: Scott Foreman, 1988), pp. 95–109.

3.   *National Academy of Public Administration Report 1992* (Washington, D.C.: Academy of Public Administration).

4.   Craig W. Thomas, "Reorganizing Public Organizations: Alternatives, Objectives and Evidence," *Journal of Public Research and Theory* No. 4 (October 1993).

5.   Ibid, p. 2.

6.   Al Gore, "From Red Tape to Results: Creating a Government That Works Better and Costs Less: Executive Summary, Report of National Performance Review," *The Review* (Washington, D.C.: U.S. Government Printing Office, 1993).

7.   David Osborne in a speech to National Academy of Public Administration, June 1972, at the Jimmy Carter Presidential Library, Atlanta, Ga.

8.   David Osborne and Ted Gaebler, *Reinventing Government: How Entrepreneurial Spirit is Transforming the Public Sector* (Reading, Mass.: Addison-Wesley, 1992).

9.   Donald F. Kettl and John J. Dilulio Jr., eds., *Inside the Reinvention Machine: Appraising Governmental Reform* (Washington, D.C.: The Brookings Institution, 1995), p. 2.

10.   Osborne and Gaebler, *Reinventing Government*, p. 25.

11.   "Selling the State: Privatization," *The Economist* (August 21, 1993): 18.

12.   Louis Winnick, "Al Gore's Misguided Mission," *New York Times* (September 7, 1993): A-15.

13.   Ibid.

14.   Ibid., pp. 7, 12.

15.   Ibid., p. 18.

16.   Charles H. Levine and Rosslyn S. Kleeman, "The Quiet Crisis of the Civil Service: The Federal Personnel System at the Crossroads," in Patricia W. Ingraham, ed., *Agenda for Excellence* (Chatham, N.J.: Chatham House, 1992), p. 208.

17.   National Commission on the Public Service, *Leadership for America: Rebuilding the Public Service* (Washington, D.C.: Random House, 1989), p. 4. See also

Mark L. Goldstein, *America's Hollow Government: How Washington Has Failed the People* (Homewood, Ill.: Business One Irwin, 1992).

18. Richard Stillman, *The Rise of City Manager: A Public Professional in Local Government* (Albuquerque, N. M.: University of New Mexico Press, 1974).

19. John L. Palmer and Isabel V. Sawhill, eds., *The Reagan Record* (Cambridge, Mass.: Ballinger Publishing, 1984). See also National Commission on the Public Service, *Leadership for America*, pp. 17–19.

20. Albert Gore, *Creating Government That Works Better and Costs Less: Report of the National Performance Review* (Washington, D.C.: U.S. Government Printing Office, 1993), p. 71.

21. Ibid., p. 34.

22. Ibid., p. 36.

23. Charles T. Goodsell, "Reinventing Government or Rediscovering It," *Public Administration Review* 53, No. 1 (January/February 1993): 86–87.

24. Mark H. Moore, *Creating Public Value: Strategic Management in Government* (Cambridge, Mass.: Harvard University Press, 1995), p. 17.

25. Gilford Pinchot and Elizabeth Pinchot, *The End of Bureaucracy and the Rise of the Intelligent Organization* (San Francisco: Bennett-Koehler Publishers, 1993), p. 31.

26. Ibid., p. 4.

27. Ibid.

28. John P. Scully, "How to Really Change the Federal Government," *National Productivity Review*, 13 (Winter 1993/1994): 29.

29. David A. Garvin, "*Building a Learning Organization,*" *Harvard Business Review* (July/August 1993): 78–79.

30. Peter Sange, *The Fifth Discipline* (New York: Doubleday, 1990), p. 1.

31. Garvin, *Building a Learning Organization*, pp. 80–81.

32. Scully, "How to Really Change the Federal Government," p. 31.

33. Ibid., p. 32.

34. Ibid., p. 32.

35. Ibid.

36. Ibid., pp. 34–35.

37. Arie Halachmi, "The Pharaoh Syndrome and Challenge of Public-Sector Productivity," *National Productivity Review* 14, No. 1 (Winter 1994/95): 25.

38. Ibid., p. 27.

39. Ibid.

40. Ibid., p. 127.

41. Jerome McKinney, *Risking a Nation* (Lanham, Md.: University Press of America, 1995), Chap. 3. See also Charles T. Goodsell, *The Case for Bureaucracy* (Chatham, N.J.: Chatham Press, 1993).

42. Ibid., Goodsell, *The Care for Bureaucracy*, pp. 27–28.

43. Ibid., p. 28.

4

Administration in the
Context of Its Practice

This chapter comprises five sections. The first defines public administration in terms of the day-to-day actions of middle- and lower-level managers. This definition emphasizes the tension between power and accountability. The second section shows the large part of government that is carried out through private enterprise and points out how distinctions between what is public and what is private can be found only in relating actual practices to intended purposes. The third examines public and private management at the middle levels to show the importance of implementation in public administration as well as the high degree of manipulation inherent in normal public management. It shows the need for normative commitment to the public interest on the part of middle- and lower-level managers. The fourth section introduces a problem-solving approach to the difficulties that confront these managers. The chapter concludes by highlighting the tension between power and accountability.

LEARNING OBJECTIVES

On completing this chapter, the reader should be able to:

- Formulate and defend a definition of public administration in operational terms.
- Distinguish and interrelate public administration and private management.
- Explain the significance of public enterprises, government by contract, and the "third sector" of public affairs.
- Understand the inevitability of manipulation in the practice of administration.
- Apply a problem-solving approach to the analysis of public problems.

We have delayed an in-depth definition of public administration in order to present the need for a new approach. This approach defines accountable public administration as the congruence of administrative actions with the expressed or implied community intent, as articulated in legislative and other authoritative enactment.

Traditional definitions of public administration emphasize the work of upper-level elected executives and high-level appointed administrators. They reflect primarily the practices of the national government. Yet the greatest activity in public administration takes place in state and local government and in federal field operations. Definitions of public administration tend to be abstract and ignore the tension of government in action (the give-and-take involved in the day-to-day decisions and program implementation).

By defining public administration in terms of its practice, we seek to stress what most public managers do most of the time.

The case of "the threatened social worker" occurred in the routine exercise of a public function. It shows government and a private firm working together. It illustrates how, when confronted with a conflict between policy and the exigencies of a specific situation, middle managers are forced to act on the basis of their own assessments. The underlying political context of administration also is revealed in Thompson's fear of bad publicity. This case demonstrates the need for a new operational definition of public administration, one focusing on the practices of MLMs. An examination of traditional definitions clearly shows this need.

Case Study 4A: The Threatened Social Worker

John Briggs, a welfare worker in the Department of Public Assistance, walked into the interviewing area to see a client (a person receiving public assistance), as thousands of such workers do routinely every day. The client, Fred Brown, informed Briggs that he desperately needed a moving allowance and insisted that he be given it immediately. Briggs responded by referring to the *Manual of Regulations*. He pointed out that a moving allowance could be authorized only under one of two conditions: (1) to move furniture from one residence to another as a consequence of a verified eviction notice, or (2) if moving was made necessary as documented by a physician or a social agency because the present home was dangerous to health or safety. In either case, Briggs added, written documentation would have to be submitted and evaluated.

At this response, Brown became agitated. He immediately attempted to offer a story to meet the stated qualifications. Briggs listened but quickly concluded that the story was false. The more Brown talked, the more Briggs was convinced that there was no furniture to be moved. When Brown began to realize that his plea was having little effect, he became more insistent. "I know lots of people on welfare who come in here and get what they want," he said. "All they do is give you slick talk and you hand over the moving allowance. Over at Tim's Tavern, they brag about their gift of gab!" Briggs felt that Brown was becoming belligerent. As Brown spoke louder, Briggs began to feel threatened. Becoming apprehensive, Briggs broke away from the interview and left the office to advise his supervisor of the situation.

The assistant district supervisor, Marcia Thompson, quickly sized up the situation as Briggs explained what had happened. Together they returned to the interview area and again heard the emotional story. Although she disbelieved Brown's story, Thompson paid particular attention to his increasingly hostile behavior. By this time, Brown was demanding the allowance in a high-pitched voice.

The disorderly scene attracted the attention of the security guard. In recent years, particularly since the urban unrest of the late 1960s, guards have been stationed in welfare offices. They are, strictly speaking, not department employees but are under contract from a private security agency. Thompson noticed the guard coming to the scene. She was far from comforted by this development for she knew that the guards, who were paid only the minimum wage, were untrained and often difficult to restrain. It quickly came to mind, as the guard clutched his nightstick, that department regulations allowed guards only to restrain clients. Under no circumstances were they to injure them. She also remembered a recent incident in Philadelphia in which a supervisor was badly beaten by a client. The supervisor suffered a concussion and filed criminal charges only to find that the department itself had secured the client's release. The department then pressured the supervisor to drop the charges. Thompson knew well the Department maxim: "Never call the police!" Abruptly, she took action. She instructed the Authorization Section to prepare a check for the client at the minimal amount authorized for moving. She advised Brown that he would get his check immediately.

The incident prompted considerable discussion that afternoon in the agency. There was some disagreement about whether Brown's story was true. All agreed that he had acted in an emotional and threatening way. The case workers did not challenge Thompson's authority to act, for middle managers were authorized to deviate from the department's *Manual of Regulations* where the situation required such action. They did, however, strongly object to the way Brown had forced the award of allowance. They said this was a bad precedent, that it would only encourage other clients to threaten workers and undermine their ability to enforce regulations. Briggs, brooding at his desk, thought, "No manager in private business would be subjected to this kind of treatment."

TRADITIONAL DEFINITIONS OF PUBLIC ADMINISTRATION

In the early days of public administration instruction, 70 years ago, the field was defined in terms of managerial tasks clearly delineated in or derived from legal mandates. According to this view, the authority for the actions taken in the incident just described could be directly traced to a legislative enactment that set up the Department of Public Assistance, defined its mission, and outlined the duties and authority that case workers could exercise under the guidance of a director. Traditional definitions overlooked the fact that the criteria set forth in the *Manual of Regulations* were drawn up by MLMs and that it was an MLM (Thompson) who exercised the discretion to solve problems.

By the 1950s, this view of administrators as instruments within a legal framework was abandoned. As Gerald Caiden observed, definitions have emphasized policymaking and program execution.[1] Summarizing some of these definitions, which appeared in public administration textbooks between 1950 and 1995, public administration is:

- A cooperative effort in a public setting.
- The activities of the executive branch of the national, state, or local governments with the implementing functions of legislatures, courts, and special agencies.
- The rational maximization of public goals.
- A set of techniques or means, especially organizational and personnel practices and procedures essential to the effective carrying out of the work of government.
- A system of inputs from an environment converted into program outputs with an evaluative feedback.
- A response to changing ecological conditions that create demands that can be satisfied only by public action through government agencies or their agents.
- The need to develop capabilities (such as budgeting, personnel, and interpersonal skills) and understanding to provide effective and accountable operations.
- The major focus is on organization of government policies and program and the behavior of public officials who are accountable for their conduct.

These definitions help distinguish public administration from other disciplines (e.g., business administration or political science). However, they cannot be applied to such routine situations as that involving Thompson and Briggs. The bulk of administration occurs at lower levels in organizations, away from headquarters and far removed from the legislatures and the courts. The definitions do not address the drive by administrators to protect their interests in ensuring the survival of the agency. Both political factors and the details of administrative practice are glossed over, as is the discretionary power of MLMs. Furthermore, our case study illustrates how public and private units are interrelated in program execution. The guard was from a private security firm, and the agency was primarily a conduit, with money being channeled—depending on one's assessment—either to a private mover or a local bar. Finally, these definitions are too abstract; they do not bring out how much administration is a conversion process in which raw statements (publicly determined policies) are translated into programs and projects in which MLMs play the key roles in interpreting what will be authorized and denied in specific situations. A final shortcoming of these definitions is that they give too little attention to the impact of government on people or people on MLMs, such as bribes, the press, and so on. In particular, no attention is directed to the problems of nondelivery of goods and services and other situations in which the administrative system is itself the problem.

We are not suggesting that traditional definitions be abandoned but that they be subordinated to other considerations of day-to-day practice.

PUBLIC ADMINISTRATION: THE VIEW FROM THE MIDDLE

Our operational view requires us to sort through two approaches to the field. The first, the broad approach, is illustrated by Leonard D. White's definition: "Public administration consists of all these operations having for their purpose the fulfillment or enforcement of public policy."[2] Although this view is too all-encompassing for our needs, its stress on publicly determined policy is essential. A second approach goes to the opposite extreme: "Public administration is the study of government decision-making, the analysis of the policies themselves, the various inputs that have produced them, and the inputs necessary to produce alternative policies."[3] Here the emphasis is on operations, but the idea of responsibility to elected officials or responsiveness to the people being served is omitted. Our objective is to bring out what most administrators do most of the time in seeking to discover and achieve publicly determined purposes. This requires a focus on lower- and middle-management, where the strategic administrative acts take place.

PUBLIC ADMINISTRATION DEFINED

Public administration, seen as the accomplishment of purpose through the organized efforts of others, comprises activities required (1) to mobilize organizations and human resources (public and private); (2) to translate policy statements (publicly determined) into programs and projects; (3) to permit MLMs to translate ideas into actions that (4) ultimately enhance the lives of people. This definition emphasizes that administration:

- Occurs through both public and private organizational effort.
- Is the interaction of varying organizational norms and public processes.
- Essentially involves translating ideas into actions.
- Features MLMs, exercising discretionary power.
- Is publicly based upon the presence of accountability.
- Must ultimately be for the enhancement of the quality of human life.

Public administration so defined must be taught in a way in which power and accountability are interrelated to resolve the needs and wishes of people.

PUBLIC ADMINISTRATION AND PRIVATE MANAGEMENT

There is a longstanding debate on whether public administration and private management are separate operations or whether they are governed by the same set of principles. Once this discussion was largely confined to academics, but now the question has become of great practical concern to governments in Washington pledged to improve the management of government and to states and cities clamoring for greater efficiency and reduced costs for their programs. Many argue that better management in government will require the adoption of business methods. On the assumption that public and private managements have much to share, a new body of literature has developed around the idea of generic management. We enter that debate to demonstrate that, while legislative enactments can be carried out by both public and private agencies, it is the publicly determined (legislatively sanctioned will of the people) dimension that makes administration public. The critical distinctions are to be found in the purpose, irrespective of the organizational setting. Second, we wish to distinguish the public from the private way of doing administration. The ends of the business sector and the ends of government agencies can be readily distinguished, but many have argued that the means are the same. For example, it is said that the various techniques for collecting refuse or for building a bridge look essentially the same whether they are done by a sanitation department or a private refuse company. And they are much the same save for two important differences. First, the standard by which public management is judged is the public interest. Where private management is judged by the profit derived, the public interest (i.e., the "publicly determined" purpose) is in one way or another an expression of the legislature's desire to enhance the people that government is set up to serve. Thus, public administration must reflect a management style that enables people to do things better for themselves and not the level of profit that the administrator may achieve. Second, public administration must remain within the bounds for obtaining and maintaining accountability. The management style must be scrutinized in terms of both its congruence with intentions and its actual results in practice. Private management has neither of these fundamental constraints.

DISTINCTIONS BETWEEN THE PUBLIC AND PRIVATE SECTORS

Table 4.1 shows some of the major ways in which the public and private sectors differ.

Two illustrations show how the two sectors differ radically. The first is the classic story of the rise of IBM into a dominant position in the computer field. The second is taken from the experience of a director of a state department of public assistance.

The Computer Executive

It took IBM ten years to conceive and build the 360 series of computers. The effort began after Thomas Watson Jr. became chief executive officer in 1956, when IBM was predominantly a marketer and an assembler of computers. Watson brought about a revolutionary change in the organization, people, and purposes of IBM.

Table 4.1. Distinctions Between the Public and Private Sectors

Public	Private
1. MAJOR PURPOSE	
A. Provides nonprofit goods and services. B. Individual agencies survive based upon continuing legislative authorization. C. Decisions reflect client or constituent preferences.	A. Sells goods and services for a profit. B. Survival depends upon both profits and growth. C. Decisions are governed partly, at least, by market factors (consumer demands).
2. CONSTRAINTS	
A. Legal constraints permeate the entire administrative process. B. Administrators are sensitive to the political climate in which their agencies must operate. Solutions reached through compromise are standard.	A. Laws provide the outside limits of business activity. There is a large body of regulation, but compliance is secondary to profit-making. B. The market is the major constraining force. As long as customers are willing to buy, producers will endeavor to provide the quantity yielding the maximum profit.
3. FINANCIAL BASE	
A. Resources obtained through the ability to borrow and to tax. B. The budget process is fragmented and politicized.	A. Resources obtained from return on investments. B. Financial planning is integrated and related to income expectations.
4. MANAGING PERSONNEL	
A. The public service comprises persons selected through merit systems or by political appointment. The aim is to build a career service. Much of recruitment and the monitoring of promotions is handled by an independent regulatory commission. B. The idea prevails that government is staffed by less efficient personnel, although supporting evidence for this view is limited. C. Downsizing is used within the prescribed limits of the law to reduce costs to meet budget requirements.	A. The private workforce is generally selected on the basis of qualifications for a needed task, although nepotism is also common. There is usually little assurance of tenure. The promotion or separation of personnel is free of external rules and procedures. B. The idea prevails that business operates with efficiency and free from the influence of politics. What might be called waste in government is often hidden under labels of research and development. C. Downsizing is used to enhance profit objectives with minimal constraints—to meet the market competition.
5. MEASURES OF EFFECTIVENESS	
A. The legitimacy of the acts performed is a primary measure of effectiveness. Concerns with building consensus and reducing conflict rank ahead of assessment of the costs of providing a public good. The criteria for effectiveness are likely to be subjective.	A. Effectiveness is gauged by such measures as the ratio of net sales to working capital, profit per dollar of sales, and net return on capital. The social costs associated with making a profit are seldom assessed.

He began by formulating an integrated corporate strategy to achieve domination of the computer field. The promise of greater profits motivated the change. Drastic reorganization was achieved by diverting resources from sales to development, by entry into the manufacturing of components, and by promoting the concept of multiple users of a single computer. To speed the implementation process, Watson brought in a generation of aggressive, young, and talented managers committed to his "time-sharing" concept. He delegated unprecedented authority to this yeasty element. They reallocated and regrouped people and resources with singular dedication. Many old-timers who had been successful when the company was selling the computers made by other manufacturers were stripped of authority or dismissed. In its early stages, time-sharing commanded more than 25 percent of IBM's liquid assets. And as IBM's success widened, Watson took much greater risks by committing a large portion of the company's credit to the project.

In retrospect, the tempo was at a fever pitch, but it actually took from 1956 to 1966 for the innovations to gel. IBM did just what a well-managed corporation is supposed to do: It gained leadership in the industry and reaped unprecedented profits. Having succeeded, management was immune to challenges about Watson's methods. He and other top executives shared significantly in the profits, as did other selected employees and those holding the soaring IBM stock. Watson did not rest on these achievements but directed his new management into more diversified ventures. One was a project to provide security for information systems in public and private buildings.

The key role of the market and the profit motivation stand out. Top executives in private settings are free to radically deploy people and resources as they perceive market situations require. Top management operates on its own schedule. Most of the aggressive internal action is accomplished beyond scrutiny. Watson and his personally selected associates were able to plunge ahead, confident that success would bring them handsome personal rewards.

The Director of Public Assistance

The case of a public manager is strikingly different. Top-level managers in state government, like Frank Beale, the former director of the Pennsylvania Department of Public Assistance, often are recruited from private enterprise. Beale had been a manager and engineer at Westinghouse before entering government. Within one year he was moved from an advisory position to the directorship. The Department of Public Assistance was beset by problems: insufficient resources to provide benefits to those who were legally qualified; professional judgments that welfare programs really increased dependency; and widespread complaints that welfare workers degraded clients, violated personal privacy, and perpetuated demeaning stereotypes. In trying to change that image, Beale appeared as an outsider to most of his staff.

Beale decided to put the department on a business-like basis and introduced a radical departure in data gathering. Instead of having caseworkers personally prepare written reports on their clients, a computerized system was instituted. Not only did this make possible greater top-management control; it also gave promise of reducing the number of caseworkers required to manage welfare.

In a period of contracting budgets, Beale's methods won considerable favor, but his actions were restricted by limited delegation of power from the governor, a proliferation of laws from the state legislature, and growing pressures from the federal government to institute its own standards as a condition of further financial assistance. In two years in office, Beale was confronted with changing policies on eligibility requirements around family planning and formulas on benefits. A primary problem was the tendency of the legislature to be deadlocked on budget matters. Beale's response was to contract out an increasing number of departmental services, including the supply of security guards at area offices. Despite these unfavorable conditions and the goldfish-bowl environment, welfare programs have been conducted with greater efficiency.

The constraints under which public managers work are unmistakable. They must (1) accept goals set by organizations other than their own; (2) operate structures that can be changed only at great political cost; (3) work with people whose actions are largely beyond management's control; and (4) accomplish results in short time-frames and often in a state of crisis.

The vital differences between the private and public sectors are in purpose and accountability. If the market responds to what the private manager produces, the effort has been successful. In the public sector, however, managers attend not only to satisfying clientele demands but also to the process. The methods used are evaluated against the publicly determined purpose. To return to the case study of the threatened social worker, we ask if the supervisor, Thompson, acted accountably in paying a moving allowance to Brown. Hers was an act of public administration because the overriding concern was providing aid to those in need and not rigidly following regulations; because, given inadequate information and the necessity to act, the interests of the consumer should prevail; and because, ultimately, administrators are to be servants of the public even when it entails some discomfort.

THE CONVERGENCE OF THE PUBLIC AND PRIVATE SECTORS

Convergence of the public and private sectors help define public administration because many, and perhaps most, public programs are carried out by entities other than general-purpose governments (city, state, county, or federal). These hybrids illustrate how the public dimension can be delineated only by relating actual operations to publicly determined purposes. The first convergence covers governmentally constituted agencies that look like private businesses; we speak of public corporations and public utilities. The second area involves private activities that affect the public welfare to such an extent that government intervention and regulations are required to ensure that the public interest is given due consideration. These take the form of "business clothed in the public interest." Another convergence takes the form of social responsibility, whereby private businesses undertake expenditures for the public benefit. One of the major stimuli for the social responsibility concept has been the public's growing awareness of the tremendous impact private corporations have on the general welfare and the resulting pressure, both overt and subtle, for business to minimize negative associations and provide a positive image to the community.

PUBLIC CORPORATIONS

Public corporations are government-owned or government-aided business enterprises. The term includes a multitude of administrative devices, all enjoying a degree of freedom from direct political control and deriving their organizational character from large-scale private corporations with boards of directors, presidents, and managers. The conversion of programs from departmental management into public corporations occurred primarily during World War I and again during the Great Depression. The most prominent was the Reconstruction Finance Corporation, established in 1932. Other examples include the Tennessee Valley Authority, the Home Owner's Loan Corporation, the Federal Farm Mortgage Corporation, and the Federal National Mortgage Association. Perhaps the most extensive form of the public corporation is the "authority." Housing authorities and parking authorities are common in cities. The New York Port Authority, for example, was created by a New York-New Jersey interstate compact in 1921, and constructs and operates airport, bus, and highway systems and harbor facilities. The George Washington Bridge and the Holland Tunnel in New York City are monuments to its activity. Authorities constitute a large and rapidly expanding field in which public administrators are at work.

Why are public corporations created? Public corporations are public because their task cannot profitably be carried out by the private sector or because the amount of capital required cannot be raised solely by private sources. Another reason for establishing an entity with characteristics of a private corporation is that the typical governmental bureaucracy often does not provide the flexibility necessary to act quickly, effectively, and productively to meet community needs and desires. The history of the creation of public corporations has shown that many have been established to deal with emergencies and other pressing problems. The Federal Deposit Insurance Corporation was established at the time of numerous bank failures during the Depression. Parking authorities are established in central cities to help downtown businesses compete with suburban shopping centers and minimize the accelerating decline of cities.

The advantages of public corporations (also called districts, authorities, boards, or commissions) are in their political autonomy (freedom from legislative and other public controls); administrative autonomy (freedom from ordinary executive controls); autonomy in personnel (freedom from civil service requirements); and financial autonomy (freedom from the legislature's ordinary budgetary and auditing controls).

Public corporations look and operate like private businesses, and yet they are public. Since the Government Corporation Act of 1945, federal public corporations have been required to submit their financial statements to audit by the General Accounting Office (GAO) and to channel their budgets through the Office of Management and Budget (OMB). In cities that operate light and gas departments, these public utilities are established as self-sustaining entities, absorbing any profits or losses into the city's general fund. Public enterprises are public primarily because of their purpose and the political context in which they operate. The organization, operation, and political controversy around the Skybus in Allegheny County, Pennsylvania, clearly demonstrate this point.

Public corporations such as the Port Authority of Allegheny County operate like a business, but their reason for existence is publicly determined; that is, operating procedures are monitored in the public area through public processes, and they are directly affected by politics. Members on the commission board are appointed by the county commissioners.

As a microcosm of the community in which it is embedded, public corporations reflect its political environment. The Allegheny Port Authority's inability to obtain consensus on Skybus (see Study 4B) reflected the views of the different political perspectives and clientele concerns. Despite that the belief that a mass transit system was needed, the commissioners could not agree on the desired system and technology, resulting in the failure to implement a mass transit system for the county.

BUSINESS CLOTHED IN THE PUBLIC INTEREST

Midway between the government-business interface are corporations that are profit-making but whose operations affect the public to an extent requiring governmental intervention. The intervention is of two kinds: total government ownership (as in the case of state control of liquor stores) and government regulation (whereby government determines many of the rules). In the former case, the motivation for government ownership is to control a potentially harmful influence on the public, whereas in the latter case, the reason is to protect the public against unscrupulous actions by private corporations.

Government regulation occurs at all levels. At the federal level, numerous agencies control such activities as transportation, securities exchange, power, communications, commerce, and so on.

Case Study 4B: The Aborted Skybus

Westinghouse, the federal Mass Transit Authority, and Allegheny County, Pennsylvania agreed in early 1970 to demonstrate the use of a rubber-tire elevated vehicle with a fixed guidance system (no driver required) as an innovative means for moving people in public transit. This was to be a third alternative to existing heavy rail (subways and elevated trains) and surface modes (trolleys and buses). The Transit

Expressway Revenue Lines (TERL), system was dubbed Skybus and was to be operated by the Port Authority of Allegheny County.

The Port Authority developed an early action program containing four elements: (1) the Skybus; (2) an exclusive bus lane on selected streets; (3) the use of former rail lines by buses; and (4) extensive rehabilitation of existing bus and trolley equipment. The total cost for the package in 1973 was set at $295 million, $232 million of which was in the Skybus line.

Skybus almost immediately became embroiled in politics. The two Democratic county commissioners enthusiastically supported the early action program, but the minority commissioner was opposed. Some cities and smaller places in the county had reservations, but the mayor of Pittsburgh, Peter Flaherty, expressed adamant opposition. The Port Authority argued that the early action program was badly needed and would reduce transportation costs. The mayor countered that the program was yet another example of determination of the destiny of the people of Pittsburgh by the financial interests, all Republicans. The real beneficiaries of Skybus would not be the people of Pittsburgh, he argued, but only suburban residents, along with those investing in the project.

The mayor carried his opposition to the 1973 mayoral elections, conducting his campaign against absentee business interests and machine politics, and won re-election overwhelmingly. After more than six years of controversy, numerous expensive studies, and inconclusive litigation, the federal government threatened to withdraw all financial support.

The controversy was resolved through the establishment of a Transit Task Force, which included representatives from the city of Pittsburgh, the county, labor, and industry and was given authority to come up with a "workable program." By 1976 the task force recommended a program quite similar to the original early action program, but the Skybus had been replaced with a light rail-surface vehicle called the "Super-trolley," produced by Boeing Vetrol Company. Perhaps more important was Flaherty's decision to seek higher office.

The Skybus controversy cost the taxpayers $20 million in studies, promotion, legal expenses, and abortive construction. Offers of an additional $250 million in federal assistance were withdrawn. Over the seven-year struggle, the people of Allegheny County also suffered under an antiquated and inadequate transit system.

The Skybus issue demonstrates the problem of attempting to reach consensus over a sensitive issue that affects a multiplicity of interests. Because of the constant need for consultation and compromise, much time is exhausted. It can hardly be otherwise in the public sector, which demonstrates the need for public corporations. Because of the inability to reach consensus, the Pittsburgh region is basically without mass transit. This indecision is likely to have significant impact on the growth and revitalization of the area.

States regulate such practices as banking, insurance, milk prices, and so on. Local government commissions oversee rent control, planning agencies that must approve hospital and industrial expansion, and others. Regulated industries must adhere to prescribed standards of service, accounting methods, and financial practices, and in most instances their product or rate schedule is regulated. The activities are public to the extent that their operating procedures are scrutinized in terms of the publicly determined purpose for their existence.

Another form of regulation for private industries is the licensing requirements set up by many state governments. There are licensing requirements for such diverse activities as performing professional services (legal, medical), driving and maintaining motor vehicles, operating restaurants, hunting and fishing, and so on.

As in the case of government regulation, the primary objective is to ensure the public's convenience, safety, and welfare. A side benefit for states is the generation of revenue from the fees.

SOCIAL RESPONSIBILITY

A third example of the private-public mixture—this one as a publicization of private enterprise—is social responsibility. In this example, a private business or corporation expends private resources to improve the public good without expectation of an immediate profit. This can take many forms; an increasingly common practice is loaning executives to government without charge or carrying out a function of government (e.g., collecting taxes or providing services to the public). In some cities, local banks collect municipal taxes and keep the cities' financial records. A striking example is the distribution of government contraceptives in privately sold tea packages in India.

Other examples of the private sector's manifestation of social responsibility have not come about so willingly. Successful group-action lawsuits, as well as increasing governmental legislation, have caused many firms to take note of such environmental and social issues as measuring the effects of proposed actions in surrounding communities, hiring minority groups, providing financial information in greater depth to stockholders, and so on.

Such practices permit a firm to say that it is directly pursuing the public interest, but they fall short of being public administration because they are not subject to the strict accountability that we have just seen in businesses that are "clothed in the public interest." Again, we find what is public by viewing how the discharge of the service is carried out. The growing panoply of intertwined government and private activities promises to have continued implications for the welfare of citizens.

Profit Motive in Public Organizations

Turning to the government side of this coin, public organizations in which private profit is the dominant motive, the purpose-accountability distinction is maintained. An increasing number of public activities are judged on a cost-benefit basis. A particular bus route, for example, will be maintained or discontinued depending on the yield in fares. And yet a transit authority will be required to maintain some service, where it is badly needed, even though it is uneconomical. Ultimately, losses are made up from public funds, as evidence of the essential public character of the service.

A good example of cost-benefit analysis is found in the debates concerning the War on Poverty programs of the 1960s, created by the federal Office of Economic Opportunity (OEO). Many critics argued that the academic results of programs like Head Start (a program for preschoolers from disadvantaged homes) did not justify the expenditures. Defenders replied that the programs were also to combat the feelings of apathy and powerlessness that accompany poverty. One noted: "This meant designing political motivational activities to counter-condition long-range and inbred psychological attitudes of shiftlessness and withdrawal; to generate feelings of pride and involvement."[4] In short, in the operation of OEO there were overriding public-interest considerations for rendering people more able to exercise power on their own.

Republicization and Reprivatization

Increasingly, many tasks thought to be in the domain of government are also carried out by business. Examples include the provision of medical treatment, auto inspection, or the resurfacing of city streets, where the activities of public works departments and private asphalting firms are hard to distinguish until one closely examines accountability. Public services are provided in a fluid manner; we speak of republicization to describe the sequence of a public activity that is operated by government, is turned over to private hands, and then returns to the public sector, as in garbage collection. Reprivatization similarly denotes the private-to-public-to-private-sector sequence. As the nation proceeds into what is being called a "post-industrial society," the public and the private sectors are destined to become even more intertwined.

GOVERNMENT BY CONTRACT

While an analysis of public-private differences helps illustrate the crucial importance of purpose and accountability in public administration, we enter a far more complicated field when we examine government through the letting of contracts. Here, subtle distinctions must be sought in the ways in which public and private managers operate.

It is important to keep in mind that much of government is funded through a public budget item, but with the monies channeled to private firms. In the case study of the threatened social worker, the guard was supplied under private contract. Big federal agencies such as the departments of Defense, Housing and Urban Development (HUD) and Health and Human Services (HHS) (i.e., most of the federally budgeted money) carry out their functions almost exclusively by contract. In DHHS, for example, contract expenditures are seven times greater than the annual cost of full-time employees. As Daniel Guttman and Barry Willner point out, "Social Security and veterans benefits aside, the predominant activity of government [in Washington] is letting contracts, grants and subsidies to corporations for the purposes of performing governmental missions."[5] At the state and local levels, contracting out public services is huge and on the increase.

This is particularly true in areas of public works, where nearly half of local expenditures are made.

State and Local Contracting Out

James Mercer and others believe that "virtually every service or function performed by local government could be farmed out."[6] Services such as fire protection, prisons, police services, and parole programs have been contracted out. "For many privatization advocates, these examples suggests the ideal government: a mayor to administer contracts, a bookkeeper to pay the contractors."[7] Miranda, California, with a population of 41,000, has fifty-five workers to manage sixty contracted services. Lakewood, California, has 60,000 people with eight workers. One Dallas suburb has almost complete privatization as it has only one secretary to manage all of the contracted services. The three services most commonly contracted out are vehicle towing and storage, legal services, and street light operators.[8]

The reasons most often given for contracting out communities is the saving of money. The International City Managers Association (ICMA) survey revealed that 40 percent of local governments say that they saved 20 percent of outlays while another 40 percent say that they saved 10 percent to 19 percent.[9] In a Touche Ross 1989 study, 72 percent of respondents said that their opinions of contracted services were very favorable. Savings are attributable to eight main factors: (1) freedom from civil service rules; (2) flexibility to use pay-incentive systems; (3) greater control of hiring and firing; (4) use of greater number of part-time workers; (5) less absenteeism; (6) multitrained workers; (7) reduced wages; and (8) significantly reduced fringe benefits, especially retirement.[10]

It has been observed that "the cost-savings argument masks a genuine anti-government worker sentiment underlying the privatization prescription."[11] If nearly 50 percent of the total cost of state and local government comes from personnel, contracting out is a way to reduce the number of employees.[12] While some of the cost savings come from improved management, the largest portion comes not from enhanced workers' skills but from the flexibility to use workers and pay them less generous benefits. In John Donahue's view, the critical point seemed to escape many privatization advocates that "public versus private matters, but competition versus non-competition matters more."[13] In communities where competition for the provision of electric power exists, costs are reduced by an average of 11 percent.[14]

Contracting Out: Goal Definition as a Source of Problems

Goal definition is a weak point in federal and most government programs, making it difficult for managers to write specific and enforceable contracts. This imperfection is compounded by contractors' desire to avoid specific measurement indicators that they may find inconvenient to achieve. To overcome these problems, state and local governments often avoid output and impact measures. Instead, they concentrate on inputs such as consultant hours spent or number of persons served. Emphasis is typically put on input or process measures (things bought or hours worked).[15]

Because government puts stress on process measures, there is little or no opportunity to assess results. Thus, the impact of a contractor's achievement is typically not an objective. Given this reality contracting becomes a numbers game. When children are left at day-care centers we monitor the attendance numbers but not what happens to them during the day in terms of nutrition, or a nurturing learning environment. Donald Kettl has noted: "[T]hen there are precious few sources of information about what the government's alternatives might be: how contractors might operate differently and produce different results."[16]

Federal Contracting Out and A-76

In 1955 President Dwight D. Eisenhower developed formal policies regarding in-house or private production of goods and services to the federal government. The policy stated: "The federal government will not start or carry on any commercial activity to provide service or product for its own use if such product or service could be procured from private enterprise through ordinary business channels."[17] While minor modifications were made to A-76 policy during succeeding administrations, it remained the basic generalized policy until the Reagan administration.

Reagan established a more elaborate methodology for comparing costs. Each federal agency was required to undertake efficiency studies as one of the factors that were expected to be used in making cost comparisons between the in-house and outside contractors' proposals. Only the lowest bid would be accepted. Under the new guidelines, "federal workers performing tasks that could be contracted out were forced to bid for their own jobs."[18]

The implementation of the revised Reagan A-76 allowed only "inherently governmental service in nature" to be done without competitive bidding. The new review process allowed the selection of the government only when it could implement the function more efficiently. This practice brought government and the private sector in head-to-head competition with each other. The new process, known as the "most efficient organization" (MEO), became the main determinant in deciding whether the government service or the outside contractor would carry out the function.

The development of a performance work statement (PWS) was a critical precondition to the development of the in-house option (see Fig. 4.1). If the private sector could meet the criteria set in PWS at a cost 10 percent lower than the public service personnel proposal, it would get the bid.

Unfortunately, A-76 did not set any mechanisms to ensure that the promised savings were realized. The administration was willing to accept the assumption that market forces would continue to produce the best and cheapest price. This concept paralleled closely the Reagan administration's privatization agenda and its efforts to reduce the size of government.

Fig. 4.1. The A-76 Process

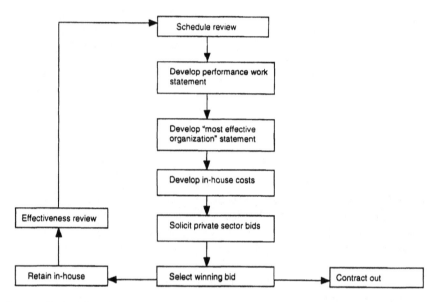

Source: Derived from General Accounting Office, *Federal Productivity: DOD's Experience in Contracting Out Commercially Available Activities*, GGD-89-6 (November 1988), p. 12.

While the basic concept of A-76 was simple, its implementation was difficult. Agencies' MLMs were expected to achieve specific goals that the Congress made fuzzy for a multitude of reasons.[19]   Because of the many fragments that MLMs had to piece together to make PWS and cost comparisons, the time to complete such estimates increased to two years. Perhaps one of the biggest obstacles was the poor quality of the government management information system. This problem was compounded by long delays in PWS and the virtual exemption of the military from A-76 in the 1988 and 1989 defense authorization act. Many of the outside contractors provided, some believe, intentionally low estimates so that they could get the contract and then raise their prices later, especially on cost-plus contracts. For example, the Northrop World Wide Aircraft Services contract proved to be $600,000 more than the government's in-house price. For maintenance at Fort Eustis, Virginia, Northrop underestimated cost at $6.4 million below its subsequent request for payment, allowing it to underbid government employees.

In contracting out libraries, the American Library Association warned of the potential problems inherent in the approach. Corporations did not see fit to contract out their libraries.   But despite objections from many sources—

including some industries' warning about the sensitive information over which contractors may gain leverage and control—libraries were contracted out.

The early concerns about contracting out the libraries were confirmed. The American Library Association found that contractors typically hired workers with inadequate experience, and gave them little training opportunity. Cost was kept down by high turnover.

About the Cost Savings

Most of the cost savings claimed by OMB could not be verified: "Despite the great effort to extol the cost savings from A-76, the best estimates of the annual cost to produce those savings in a single department had an error factor of 100 percent."[20] The GAO observed that no one really knew what A-76 review process costs were.[21]

While the intent of A-76 may be desirable, its implementation might have created more harm than good: "Good employees leave while others worry about keeping their jobs and do not do their job. While only a small percentage of employees lose their jobs, they all worry. Good businesses do not threaten people with the loss of their jobs if they do a good job."[22] Additionally, government workers believed that OMB intentionally turned the comparison criteria against them when it required a 35.75 percent wages benefit for government proposals instead of the 27.3 percent that was normally used.

Any complete definition of public administration must take into account these contract approaches to delivering public goods and services. Governments have turned to procuring services by contract for sound reasons: (1) Often the services can be provided more economically; (2) undesirable rigidities in civil service regulations are bypassed; (3) costs of maintaining a permanent work force (e.g., retirement and other fringe benefits) can be avoided; and (4) negative aspects of unionization are avoided.

There are also drawbacks to contracting out. First, the public jurisdiction relinquishes control, particularly in day-to-day operations. As we have seen, much of the public purpose is determined by relating operations to the legislature's intentions. Second, contracts prevent the development of in-house capability. The government unit becomes dependent for delivering its services on an entity that is largely motivated by profit. The private security guard in our hypothetical Department of Public Assistance, private bus and trolley companies, or privately operated liquor stores would find it difficult to keep the public interest ahead of profit.[23] Conflict of interest is a constant concern. Because of networking, contractors' lobbying tactics to restrict bids, and cozy relationships, overdependence on single source have been identified as problems. Typically there is lack of self-policing of market forces, especially in many local communities.

Equally serious is the problem of accountability. Even though the work conducted is wholly paid for out of public funds, there is no one place (or even a few places) where a list of employees or a record of the monitoring of the costs and benefits can be found. Information about management procedures is held by the private firms themselves (e.g., Booz Allen Hamilton, McKinsey & Co., and Arthur D. Little). And of primary importance, the objective of enabling people is lost as market criteria become controlling. Yet the portion of government conducted by contracts has grown so large that it now rivals the projects and programs carried on by public agencies. It is estimated that strictly private firms obtain over $20 billion annually for consulting and for system analysis, about half of it with the federal government. Accountability is made even more difficult when the contract is in the form of a grant from one level of government to another or from government to the "third sector," or not-for-profit, organizations.

Nonprofit Organizations and the "Third Sector"

The clearest definition of nonprofit agencies is that, like government, they are not allowed to sell stock, to earn a profit, or to make distributions to shareholders. They are, however, (1) governed by self-perpetuating boards; (2) able to finance growth out of "surplus" (generally computed as a percentage of the cost of a given contract); and (3) often structurally similar to firms in the private sector. Nonprofit organizations include numerous service agencies sponsored by such organizations as the United Way. Among them are day-care centers, programs related to criminal justice, and special projects in health care. These programs, together with the public service activities of universities and private foundations, constitute the "third sector."[24]   Because nonprofit organizations undertake activities the private sector does not find profitable and the public sector cannot effectively undertake, maintaining accountability becomes especially difficult. Nonprofit organizations:

- Survive on public support given directly or indirectly.
- Rely on volunteer help, particularly at the policymaking levels.
- Use a mix of private and public operating styles, depending on their origin.
- Maintain close ties with the "power structure" (business, labor, and political leaders) at the local level and are members of national associations that carry on education and lobbying in state capitols and in Washington.
- Carry on functions similar to those provided by government and in many cases even duplicate public services, existing because the demand for the service is not being met by government and it does not appear profitable enough for private investment.

Government by contract and the work of the third sector call to mind Woodrow Wilson's comment that the study of administration would make government more business-like.[25]

This discussion of the third sector and of government through public contracts and by private and quasi-private firms underlines the necessity of defining public administration operationally, with clear recognition that its practice in large measure occurs in conjunction with private business.

MLMs IN PUBLIC AND PRIVATE MANAGEMENT

From an operational viewpoint, the identifying distinctions between the public and private is less useful than emphasizing their interrelationships. In large-scale public and private organizations at the middle levels, the generic functions of management prevail (defining purpose and objectives, planning, organizing, directing, and controlling, along with a variety of analytical and problem-solving techniques). In middle- and lower-level positions, the salaries of public and private employees are comparable and modest. In both sectors, it is in middle management that the policy implementation, or day-to-day conversion of policy to program, occurs. In this implementation, we have suggested, MLMs of public organizations are caught between the policy intentions of elected executives and top-level career administrators and pressures to meet societal needs with methods open to public scrutiny. In the private sector, the squeeze on MLMs requires that they accommodate top-level executive drives for profit while minimizing the primary concern of lower-level personnel for security and improved working conditions. As Carl E. Lutrin and Allen K. Settle have commented, middle management in both sectors "is a cooperative group effort concerned with the means of survival in a difficult, sometimes hostile, environment."[26] But if MLMs are to play the critical role in the tension between power and accountability, they must be at home with strain and ambiguity.

THE IMPLEMENTATION OF POLICY

As compared with their studies of policy formulation, considerably less emphasis is given in traditional public-administration texts to policy implementation, though the literature in recent years has been growing. For details, one must turn to books on private management. Here we suggest that implementation is at the very heart of public administration. Why do we know so little about this vital process? The answer, according to Donald S. Van Meter and Carl Van Horn, is to be found in (1) naive assumptions that the nature of implementation is mundane; (2) a tendency to focus attention on known policymakers in Washington, the state capital, or City Hall, to the exclusion of unknown lower-level managers who actually convert policy into program; and (3) the complexity of implementation, in the requirement that attention be given to multiple actions carried over an extended period of time.[27] Consider a job-training program that may be created to provide viable employment for the disadvantaged so that they can be moved from the welfare rolls and become productive tax-paying citizens. Can we say that implementation is completed once the target population is identified, selected, trained, and placed? The answer is definitely yes. However, we do not know if the program is a success. The evaluation phase may continue indefinitely. We need to know (1) if the training matched participants' aptitude and skills; (2) if applicants were placed in jobs for which they were trained; (3) if the target population was the group that received training; and (4) if the training allowed individuals to be permanently removed from the welfare roll. From the time the program was initiated to the time we are able to know the status of participants who can be located, it may take months or years to make a final assessment of the success or failure of the program.

MANIPULATION IN ADMINISTRATION

As we have seen, MLMs, as implementors of policy, must comply with the directives of their superiors and satisfy the needs of the public. In their attempts to reconcile these demands, they must often resort to manipulation. We have seen illegal acts and the ruthless exercise of power in the Watergate affair, but much more pervasive and dangerous patterns of manipulation are built into the normal operations of agencies: (1) by top administrators in their efforts to get middle managers to respond to directives; (2) by MLMs who seek to rise in the hierarchy; and (3) by MLMs who seek to implement agency programs effectively. "Compliance," writes Amitai Etzioni, "is a universal in all social units."[28] It is a major element of the relationship between those who have power and those over whom they exercise it.

From the MLMs' perspective, compliance implies that the power is held by the upper levels of administration and that the lower-level officials translate directives into action. Upper-level managers seek compliance by exercise of three kinds of power: (1) coercion, or the threat of sanctions; (2) remuneration; and (3) normative power, or the offering of symbols of esteem or acceptance. At the receiving end, MLMs can react along the continuum of (1) alienation, or a negative response; (2) calculation, or a lower intensity of involvement; or (3) commitment, an intense and positive response. The compliance relationship is composed of the interaction of the superior and the subordinate.

In the quest for successful programs, higher-level administrators constantly seek to induce desired behaviors. When a continuing stream of inducements is required in a complex organization, manipulation becomes normal.

MLMs are also prone to manipulate their superiors. Responses that lack positive commitment are inherently manipulative. It is very common for top-level administrators to complain that their instructions have been misunderstood or deliberately distorted.

Any attempt to eradicate manipulation from organizational life thus involves the search for institutional ways to encourage the development of positive commitment. Of course, there is good and bad manipulation. Manipulation is bad when it is used for the self-aggrandizing interest of the manipulator, for it impinges not only on the rights of the manipulated but distorts the objectives of the publicly determined purpose. It is good when it is used to enhance the interests of all those affected by the administrative act. In the daily practice of administration, MLMs often must act according to their perception of where the public's interest lies. That is, we cannot expect to have specific rules and guidelines to guide every MLM act. The sheer number of procedures would make it futile. Thus, MLMs are forced to rely on codes of ethics, professional and internalized community norms. Conflict over value priorities is inevitable and will necessitate making a choice among them. This is close to what we have defined as the tension confronting the middle and lower managers: how to exercise authority with accountability to people.

In this chapter we have presented two cases: "the threatened social worker" and "the aborted Skybus." Each problem was chosen to emphasize the different dimension of public administration—the strategic role of MLMs, the political context in which public administration occurs, and the interaction between administrative theory and practice in accomplishing a publicly determined purpose.

The chapter began by defining public administration as the means required to realize publicly determined purposes. The interrelationship between the public and private sectors was stressed, and emphasis was placed on the crucial role of lower and middle managers. We conclude the chapter by examining problem-solving approaches to everyday public problems.

A PROBLEM-SOLVING APPROACH

Three elements are fundamental in the study of public administration. First, it is important to adopt an administrative way of thinking; too often, government operations are studied apart from the realities in which it operates. Second, the student must acquire considerable knowledge about the operations of government agencies, quite apart from any given problem under study. Finally, the focus of study should be a problem-solving approach that does not itself create new and bigger problems. We believe the case method is such an approach.

Thinking Administratively

Law students often find it most difficult to learn to "think legally." They must think how the law defines a type of problem, how it can be brought to the courts, and how this particular problem will be viewed by opposing lawyers, judges, and jurors. Lawyers must also think of legal precedents and of the legislature's original intentions. Similarly, public administrators must learn to "think administratively." That is, they must be able to clearly define the problems, determine the required information to analyze the problems, and examine the alternative solutions to the problems, recommending those that are best with a schedule for time-phase implementation. Fig. 4.2 shows five approaches the public manager may use in solving problems. (Despite the apparent adherence to a rational model as indicated in Fig. 4.2, in day-to-day practice, managers generally follow an incremental or satisfying approach. See

Chapter 11.) If the problem selected for solution is unemployment, the following explanations may be given:

1. *Conventional public administration.* A problem of unemployment is assumed to exist when people begin to apply for unemployment benefits above some average figure, for example 4 percent. Guidelines are set forth outlining who is eligible for benefits and the amount of benefits. As the number of people qualifying for benefits increases, it is automatically assumed that more people will sign up for unemployment benefits. A post-evaluation is made to assess what actions have been taken to meet the unemployment problem. Finally, a report on activities is put together. All of this represents a pragmatic response to the existing problem.

2. *Scientific method.* The theory is that only those persons looking for work are unemployed. The objective is to set up a system to identify the unemployed. A method would be to go out and count the unemployed. In any large government, this is a major problem; thus, a sample is taken. The data produced are interpreted to confirm or reject the theory and subsequently to determine the extent of the problem and kind of action that may be reasonably suggested to solve it. Depending on the interpretative analysis, counseling, training, and relocation programs may be attempted.

3. *Program planning.* Unemployment data are gathered and analyzed to determine what direction the government wants to take in solving the problem. A general plan on how to proceed in meeting the stated objective is drawn up for action. Subsequently, a specific number of steps aimed at achieving the plan are identified. Finally, the program is reviewed to determine its strengths and weaknesses.

4. *Management by objectives.* First, the specific unemployment problem must be identified. Second, the desired targets in terms of percentage unemployment—including target population or groups—must be identified. Third, the objectives are examined to determine if they adequately provide a solution to the stated unemployment objectives. Fourth, a schedule of means and procedures outlined to achieve the objectives is prepared. Fifth, the objectives are controlled to ensure adherence to the unemployment objectives.

5. *Administrative thinking.* The unemployment problem is identified and stated as objectively as possible. First, determine the problem that can be effectively dealt with. Second, identify relevant alternatives to solving the stated problem. Third, of the alternatives identified, select one that would produce the best (in terms of cost-benefit) or the most acceptable solution. Fourth, when the alternative selected does not produce an acceptable solution, continue the process until a desirable solution is found.

THE OPERATIONS OF GOVERNMENT

It is not enough to think administratively. Problem-solving within an administrative context must begin with a knowledge of laws, data, and the goals and functioning of a particular agency—and a feel for its impact on its clientele:

1. What is the statute or law governing the agency? Statutes can be read in Statutes at Large or in the U.S. Code. If the agency is established by an executive order of the president, it can be found in the Federal Register. In some states, there are parallel sources; for example, in Pennsylvania the Consolidated Pennsylvania Statutes and a special collection of state laws and executive actions. For cities, consult the city and county yearbooks.

2. Why was this agency set up in the first place? The deliberations on the floor of the House and Senate can be found in the *Congressional Record*. For details on the work of committees, see the hearings' reports published for each Congress. Only a few states and virtually no cities maintain comparable publications. The daily newspaper, however, generally contains useful background information.

3. What has this agency been doing? Most agencies publish reports on their operations along with other information relative to the area in which they are functioning. Consult the monthly catalog of U.S. government publications. For the states, see the monthly checklist of state publications.

4. What resources does the agency have? Financial details can be found in the budget of the U.S. government. Discussion of the expectations surrounding the budget can be found in the hearings conducted by the appropriation committees, which are issued as reports. The structure of the agency and the allocation of personnel can be found in the annual reports, as well as in the U.S. government organization manuals. States and cities issue budget and personnel information, but often it is not part of a regularly published series and must be specifically requested.

5. What are some of the major problems confronting the agency? For current items, consult the *New York Times* Index. For litigation in which the agency is involved, consult the *Index to Legal Periodicals*. For more detailed comments, consult the publications of the interest groups most concerned with the agency's operation (e.g., the American Automobile Association follows transportation or the National Welfare Rights Organization follows poverty-related issues).

Remember also (1) that the agency publishes much about itself; (2) most agencies have a legal and public information department to supply this kind of information; (3) the reference books mentioned above are available in libraries, the larger of which also have special government-documents sections staffed by specially trained librarians; and (4) the agency is in contact with the public and thus receives ongoing information about the success of programs.

USING THE PROBLEM-SOLVING APPROACH: THE CASE METHOD

This method of teaching is common in such fields as law, business, and social work. It was introduced into public administration before World War I, and it reached prominence as a teaching device in the 1950s with the appearance of *Public Administration and Policy Development: A Case Book*, edited by Harold Stein.[29] Cases are narratives of actual or hypothetical administrative situations that supply the reader with much of the information that would be available to the administrator confronted with the problem. Usually the cases are

Fig. 4.2. Public Administration and Problem-Solving Approaches

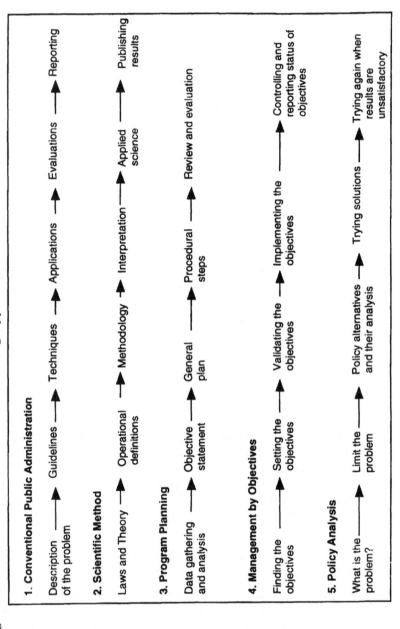

1. Conventional Public Administration

Description of the problem → Guidelines → Techniques → Applications → Evaluations → Reporting

2. Scientific Method

Laws and Theory → Operational definitions → Methodology → Interpretation → Applied science → Publishing results

3. Program Planning

Data gathering and analysis → Objective statement → General plan → Procedural steps → Review and evaluation

4. Management by Objectives

Finding the objectives → Setting the objectives → Validating the objectives → Implementing the objectives → Controlling and reporting status of objectives

5. Policy Analysis

What is the problem? → Limit the problem → Policy alternatives and their analysis → Trying solutions → Trying again when results are unsatisfactory written to reflect the dilemmas, lack of information, and other uncertainties that the administrator would face. In these simulations, the student is forced to make choices and decisions speedily and can then reflect on or discuss the nature of the problem, the information at hand, and the principles applied. To study a case, we need first to immerse ourselves in the facts and the values that are guiding their selection. The general approach to cases should take the following form:

1. Definition of the problem. Within the administrative context, the problem is related to difficulties in meeting objectives or to taking advantage of unanticipated opportunities.

2. Limiting the problem. Most problems relate to larger problems but must first be focused in terms of what this agency at this time, in terms of its mission and resources, can respond to.

3. Analysis of the causes. Some sources of the problem must be sought. Probably a variety of factors are involved. Some effort should be made to sort out a number of the most important factors.

4. Development of alternatives. Consider at least three approaches to the problem. Think through the implications of each and devise a test situation.

5. Evaluations of alternatives. As the test is conducted, better solutions can be identified. It is important that the solution goes to the basic problem and not simply to a symptom.

6. Selection of the most desirable alternative. Generally, in administrative settings, more than one alternative recommendation has to be made to superiors. Be sure that each alternative is sound in terms of relative costs or difficulty in putting the solution into effect.

7. Recommendation of a detailed plan of implementation. This should include a projection of the steps to be taken.

8. Provision of evaluation. The collection of data and the criteria for measuring results should be included in problem-solving. It is not helpful to engage in problem-solving without a way of knowing whether the problem has been solved.

9. Feedback process. Build in a means to obtain results to the problem. Beyond making sure that the results conform to expectations, the feedback exercise provides a means for evaluating the decision-making process itself.

The study of administrative situations can provide us with important simulated experience that can better prepare us for the job. We should keep in mind, however, that on-the-job situations are likely to be much more difficult to analyze than problem-solving devices suggested. It is difficult to sort out one situation from others that are closely related. Institutions have a history; a case does not. In this analysis, cases appear in isolation from the culture of the organization. The reader should not at first expect to be told there will be an opportunity to illuminate a process of analysis in which values are revealed. This book aims to make administrators think more in terms of public accountability, which is not possible without awareness of the process and the way administrators think about problems.

Benchmarking or Best Management Practices

Our problem solving approach parallels what the U.S. General Accounting Office (GAO) calls "Best [Management] Practice Methodology" for improving government operations. In identifying best practices among organizations, the benchmarking technique is often followed. Benchmarking involves: (1) assessment of how leading organizations perform a particular process; (2) comparison of your organization process with the one that is benchmarked; and (3) employing the information obtained to improve or to complete the organization's process(es). Benchmarking is, most often, carried out by personnel internal to the organization "who already have knowledge of the process under review."[30]

Ideally, the best practice's assessment will examine not only quantitative data such as costs, but also how other processes and aspects such as organizational culture might impact change. Six elements have been identified with the best practice approach. They require:

1. Gaining understanding of and documenting of the process to be improved.
2. Researching similar organizations or industry trends and literature, interviewing consultants, academics, and relevant interest groups.
3. Selecting similar organizations for review.
4. Collecting data from relevant organizations.
5. Analyzing barriers to change.
6. Making comparisons of processes to facilitate recommendations.[31]

BALANCING POWER AND ACCOUNTABILITY

The need to bring the exercise of power into greater balance with accountability underlies the search for a new approach to the study of administration. This new training must take into account the strategic position of MLMs and the heavy responsibility they bear in rendering the actions of government more sensitive to the people they serve. This new orientation must be based on a clearer understanding of the nature of power and the requirements of accountability and of how they must be brought into better balance. There must be power to act, but that power must be exercised with discipline; there must be accountability, but beyond checks, it must energize new sources of creativity in people.

DISCUSSION QUESTIONS

1. Give several examples of how middle- and lower-level management requires considerable policymaking in practice.
2. Identify examples of administration in legislatures that are comparable to administration in executive branch agencies.
3. To what extent is the practice of public administration an inherently normative undertaking?

4.   What are the advantages and disadvantages of defining public administration from the perspective of lower levels of management?
5.   Give an example of reprivatization.
6.   Why has this chapter put so much stress on understanding the practice of administration by looking at where the public and private sectors overlap?

NOTES

1.   Gerald E. Caiden, *The Dynamics of Public Administration* (New York: Holt, Rinehart and Winston, 1975).

2.   Leonard D. White, *Introduction to the Study of Public Administration*, 3rd edn. (New York: Macmillan Company, 1950), p. 3.

3.   William L. Morrow, *Public Administration: Policy and the Political System* (New York: Random House, 1975), p. 3.

4.   "A Sobering Look at State Stores," *Pittsburgh Renaissance* (September 1972), p. 5.

5.   Daniel Guttman and Barry Willner, *The Shadow Government* (New York: Pantheon Books, 1976).

6.   James L. Mercer, "Growing Opportunities in Public Service Contracting," *Harvard Business Review* 61 (March/April 1983): 178–88.

7.   Donald F. Kettl, *Sharing Power: Public Governance and Private Markets* (Washington, D.C.: Brookings Institute, 1993), p. 157.

8.   Ibid., pp. 158–59.

9.   Reported in Kettl's *Sharing Power*, p. 160, see also David Osborne and Ted Gaebler, *Reinventing Government: How the Entrepreneurial Spirit is Transforming the Public Sector from Schoolhouse to State House to the Pentagon* (Reading, Mass.: Addison-Wesley, 1992), p. 89.

10.   Kettl, *Sharing Power*, p. 161.

11.   John Donahue, *The Privatization: Public Ends and Private Means* (New York: Basic Books, 1989), p. 131.

12.   Ibid.

13.   Ibid., p. 78.

14.   Kettl, *Sharing Power*, p. 162.

15.   Ibid, pp. 172–74.

16.   Ibid., p. 174.

17.   Bureau of the Budget, "Policies Regarding In-House Production of Goods and Services," *Bulletin* 55-4 (1955).

18.   Kettl, *Sharing Power*, p. 43.

19.   U.S. House of Representatives, Committee on Post Office and Civil Service, "Contracting Out and its Impact on Federal Personnel and Operations," 101 Cong. 1 and 2 Sess. (Washington, D.C.: Government Printing Office, 1990), pp. 109–114.

20.   Kettl, *Sharing Power*, p. 56.

21.   General Accounting Office, "A-76 DOD's Reported Savings Figures Are Uncompleted and Inaccurate" (GGD-90-58, March 1990), p. 7.

22.   "Contracting Out and Its Impact on Federal Personnel and Operations," p. 103.

23. Michael A. Murray, "Comparing Public and Private Management: An Exploratory Essay," *Public Administration Review* 35, No. 4 (July-August, 1975), p. 367.

24. "Symposium on the Third Sector," *Public Administration Review* 35, No. 5 (September-October 1975).

25. Woodrow Wilson, "The Study of Administration," *Political Science Quarterly* (December 1941), pp. 481–506.

26. Carl E. Lutrin and Allen K. Settle, *American Public Administration: Concepts and Cases* (Palo Alto, Calif.: Mayfield Publishing, 1976), p. 4.

27. Donald S. Van Meter and Carl Van Horn, "Policy Implementation Process: A Conceptual Framework," *Administration and Society* 6, No. 4 (February 1975), pp. 450–451.

28. Amitai Etzioni, *A Comparative Analysis of Complex Organizations* (New York: The Free Press, 1975), p. 3.

29. Harold Stein, ed., *Public Administration and Policy Development: A Case Book* (New York: Harcourt Brace & World, 1952).

30. General Accounting Office (GAO), *Best Practices Methodology: A New Approach for Improving Government Operations* (Washington, D.C.: GOA/NSIAD-95-154, 1995), p. 1.

31. Ibid., pp. 1–2.

5

Public Administration and
Public Policy

In this chapter, we will highlight the role of middle- and lower-level managers and the tension they face in translating unclear instructions into programs that help people. Efforts will be made to link policy (theory) and management (practice) to show the critical role that policy implementors (administrators) play in carrying out policy intent. It is hoped that our focus on the interdependence of ideas and practice will lead public managers to become more accountable. This chapter is organized into five sections. The first provides an overview of the development of the policy concept. The different levels of policy are briefly outlined. The next section presents the policymaking process. The third examines the rationale and approaches to policy analysis, presenting two perspectives. One stresses the analytic method, while the other relies on accumulated experience. The fourth section examines the implementation of policy, emphasizing the important role of MLMs. The last section is a critique of policy and policy analysis.

LEARNING OBJECTIVES

- On completing this chapter, the reader should be able to present what is meant by policy in public administration.
- Describe what is generally involved in policy analysis.
- Identify the assumptions associated with rational comprehensive, and disjointed incrementalism approaches to policy analysis.
- Present and criticize the major steps in the policy process.
- Illustrate in some detail what is meant by administrative policy-making.
- Identify settings in which MLMs can act more accountably in the formulation and execution of public policy.

Public administration policy concerns have come center stage. We want to know more about the complex process through which plans are shaped and translated into action. "Governments," comment Ivan L. Richardson and Sidney

Baldwin, "are not great slot machines in which you insert your money, pull the handles and await the outcomes."[1]

Policy directs us to the great tasks facing government: devising a plan to ensure sufficient energy, ameliorating the plight of the elderly, reforming the criminal justice system, or providing a workable health care system. Policy defines the choices government makes to meet these problems.

Once, perhaps prior to World War II, Americans could look confidently ahead to inevitable progress, steady growth in the economy, and the rising influence of democratic ideals in the world. This has now changed. Increasingly, the questions center on how to maintain current standards of living, how to increase productivity in government, or how to clarify what we ought to be doing.

The public clamors for better policies because many governmental programs simply do not work. Old problems resist solutions while new problems continue to rise. Urban decay continues in older, once-vibrant cities such as New York, Pittsburgh, and Detroit, while such newer and seemingly insurmountable problems as crime, drug dependency, and teenage pregnancy demand solutions. There seems to be an unbridgeable gap between theories about how to solve public problems (legislation) and the practices of putting them into effect (implementation of programs). It is obvious that public policymaking and public administration need to be much better linked.

Until the 1960s, public administration was preoccupied with internal concerns—organizational functions and processes (i.e., plan, organize, staff, direct, coordinate, report, and budget, or POSDCORB).[2] The emphasis was on how things were done, how much was expended on costs of personnel, materials, and equipment, and how well expenditures conformed to appropriations.

The New Deal saw a shift of attention from management and legal concerns to the effect of key policy decisions and government programs on societal problems.[3] During these years, the Federal Deposit Insurance Corporation helped restore confidence in the banking system, and the Civilian Conservation Corps helped reduce youth unemployment.

The magnitude and complexity of problems and the public's demand for solutions provided the major reason for public administration's shift to policy orientation and policy analysis. Many people believe that only the national government can do something about the most crucial problems confronting society, such as the deterioration of the environment.

It is in this context that policymaking has come into prominence. The complexity of contemporary problems requires close coordination of public and private efforts to utilize scarce resources. Solutions are increasingly tested in qualitative terms. The central role of public administrators is to keep the public interest in view. In his book, *The Polity*, Norton E. Long writes: "Yet in any fair view of the facts of administrative life the establishment of policy consensus and the search for politically acceptable values [are] a highest priority of endeavor."[4]

No longer can we view administrators as neutral; they, as much as elected officials, must be held accountable for the results of governmental policies.

In schools of public administration, interest in policy is mounting. Some have begun to call themselves schools of public policy. Courses on policy analysis are recommended by the National Association of Schools of Public Affairs, which views this highly complex and controversial activity as one of the five areas in which public managers should be trained. Radically different approaches to the study of policy are now needed,[5] and many believe that policy analysis will eventually become the major thrust of public affairs education.

THE POLICY IDEA AND PERSPECTIVE

In democratic nations, the task of public policy formulation is normally dominated by individuals elected and authorized to act for the public. We refer to legislators or elected executives as policymakers and laws or city ordinances as policy statements. Yet a policy is not simply a statement of an objective. The concept of policy conveys the notion of a government taking action—for example, enforcing a county ordinance that calls for a reassessment of property every three years—rather than merely passing the law and stating an intention to enforce it. As we have shown, in pluralistic society elected officials do not monopolize the entirety of public policymaking, for there are multiple influences on policy decisions as we move from the formulation of a statement of intention to its execution. Neither is public policymaking a government monopoly. Individuals in the private sector affect public policy, as when a rise in steel or aluminum prices increases the costs of defense materials, road building, automobile manufacturing, farm equipment, and other materials or activities with the potential for creating inflation.

Public and private policy decisions differ considerably in terms of objectives. The latter are motivated by the desire for economic profit, fully supported by the nation's cultural norms. Public policymakers, on the other hand, are motivated by a different kind of profit—the possibility of maximizing votes. Legislators want to get elected and administrators want to expand their agencies, fend off attacks, or stabilize their environment. This means that public policymakers must take into account their constituencies, made up of a host of organizations and groups often in conflict with one another.[6]

COMPLEXITIES IN PUBLIC POLICY

It is difficult to conceptualize policy in a way that covers both objectives and achievement. Ira Sharkansky comes close when he notes, that public policy is an authoritatively and publicly determined course of action that achieves totally, partially, or not all a particular goal or purpose.[7] This view takes into account the fact that many policy outcomes vary greatly from or even conflict dramatically with the original intentions. In a democratic state, we think first of public policymaking as being what elected representatives do for the best interest of the people. Unfortunately, there are exceptions. It is not so much that political leaders wish to subvert the process, although that does happen on occasion. In big government, there are many points after the initial announcement of objectives at which elected officials lose control of what follows.

A second problem arises in the early stages of policymaking. A policy, seen as a statement of objectives as expressed in a law passed by Congress, a state legislature, or a city council, is usually a result of compromise. A majority articulates a policy, but to reach that consensus, opposing views must be taken into account. Take, for example, the policy on Equal Educational Opportunity:

Section 202(a). The Congress declares it to be the policy of the United States that:

1.   "all children enrolled in public schools are entitled to equal opportunity without regard to race, color, sex or national origin; and,
2.   the neighborhood is the appropriate basis for determining public schools' assignments."

The Equal Educational Opportunities Act of 1974 quoted above was intended to support school integration but it is unclear about the means that may be used to realize its intent. Section 202(a) significantly modifies the Act by restricting school assignments to a neighborhood basis. This reality is more the rule than the exception arising in those cases in which policy results from compromise on a highly disputed value, such as integration. When the law instructs so inadequately as this, bureaucrats must decide how to implement it. It is in filling in this legislative mandate that discretionary powers of MLMs, in concert with affected publics, play a large role in shaping and determining policy.

Public administration operates to satisfy public policy needs. Below are some recent definitions of policy:

1.   Policy is course setting. It involves decisions of the widest possible ramifications and the longest time perspectives in the life of the organization.[8]
2.   Policy is the direct output of policymaking.[9]
3.   Policy is the result of the interactions of governmental officials and groups.[10]
4.   Policy is the public response to the interest in improving the human condition.[11]
5.   Policy is "an indication of an intention, a guide to action, encompassing values which set priorities and relations between government and society."[12]
6.   Public policy is whatever government chooses to do or not to do.[13]

In a broad sense, all of these definitions present policy as a proposed course of action in which government does or does not do something specific. Raymond Bauer and Kenneth Gergin emphasize broad decisions, Yehezkel Dror stresses the outputs of decisions, and Charles Lindblom the interaction between private and public actors. Howard E. Freeman and Clarence C. Sherwood introduce the idea that policy aims toward improving the human condition. According to Robert Simmons et al., policy is a composite of many elements. To some degree, all of these definitions express what we mean by policy.

Our intention is not to concentrate simply on the broad view of policy but to highlight the strategic role of MLMs and to look at their day-to-day actions in government as they occur in the tension between imperfect instructions and the desire to produce favorable results in the lives of people. We are looking at formal policy as a preferred position (or choice) on how to meet a public problem. This choice is backed by the authority and resources of the state, normally expressed in a legally binding document such as legislation, judicial decision, executive orders, and administrative rules and regulations, and executed primarily by MLMs. Policy, in this context, is a set of values that guide action. The intent of this action is to benefit society.

The use of policy implies that we can improve an existing situation or prevent a bad one from occurring or becoming worse. Congress assumed its anti-hijacking law would discourage the crime, thus making air travelers feel more secure. When the federal government adopted the 55 mph speed limit during the 1970s, officials were attempting to conserve gasoline so as to lessen dependence on imported oil, thus strengthening the economy. As the price of oil fell and stabilized, the public found the 55 mph limit inconvenient when driving long distances, forcing Congress to increase it to 65 mph, particularly in Western states and rural areas. In simple terms, our definition of policy is what happens to people as a consequence of what the government does. This definition stresses actions that have been taken to implement a legally preferred public purpose.

EXAMPLES OF PUBLIC POLICY

Does the Fourth of July celebration, in which every unit of government is expected to participate, qualify as public policy? If Arab leaders read in the *New York Times* about prospective Israeli actions and respond by increasing their own combat readiness, does this reaction constitute policy? Is a federal or state constitutional convention a policymaking body? Are the contents of a constitution policy? Do the interpretation, clarification, and application of the U.S. Constitution by the Supreme Court constitute policy? Richard I. Hofferbert would say that all of these are indeed policy, which he defines as "purposeful action taken for the public."[14] Clear and specific indications of policy include road construction, city budgets, funding for schools, and welfare checks. These are "visible products of decisions taken by identifiable actors for public purposes."[15] Given these examples and definitions, we can say that the Republican Party's Contract With America is public policy? The answer is no. It should be viewed as proposals until they are enacted.

Policy often results not from a conscious mapping out of a rational course of action but from smaller, cumulative choices resulting from drift and inertia. Conscious policy determination seeks to minimize or eliminate policy arising in this latter manner.

INTERRELATIONSHIPS BETWEEN POLICY AND ADMINISTRATION

From a conceptual perspective, policymaking appears to differ from administration. Policymaking, as indicated in Fig. 5.1, involves the value choices about what government should do. Policy, in this view, is the controlling force that guides administrative action. Administration here relates to the decisions and rules made in pursuance of guiding policy. Administration is usually concerned with program implementation and is a function of MLMs. In practice, however, this theoretical difference largely disappears.

Though policy is intended to be a guiding force for administrative action, the search for administratively feasible policy statements limits available choices. It will do little good to promise what cannot be delivered. A second interrelationship arises because laws have to be written broadly and lawmakers cannot anticipate all of the special considerations that may arise in their implementation. The result is broad discretion by administrators to fill in policy details. For example, a library can be built "to bring the expanding world of knowledge to citizens." However, the realization of that aim may be largely a function of an administrator—the selection of books by a bibliographer. To provide another example, although Title XX of the federal Social Security Act of 1975 promises social services for low- to low-middle-income citizens and the disabled, the fate of the program rests largely with the quality of the services that become available. We can illustrate the policy–administration interrelationship by looking at the criteria (policies) that an intake clerk must utilize in passing on the eligibility and priority for the admission of a child to a day-care center. The clerk must determine:

- if parent is in the Work Incentive Program (WIP)
- if parent is working at least 20 hours a week
- if parent is in training (including college) leading to specific employment
- if parent is enrolled in General Education Development program
- if mother is disabled and needs someone to come for the child during the day
- if child is disabled and needs special programs and pre-education or just needs to be out of the house
- the child's level of socialization.

Fig. 5.1. The Policy Process

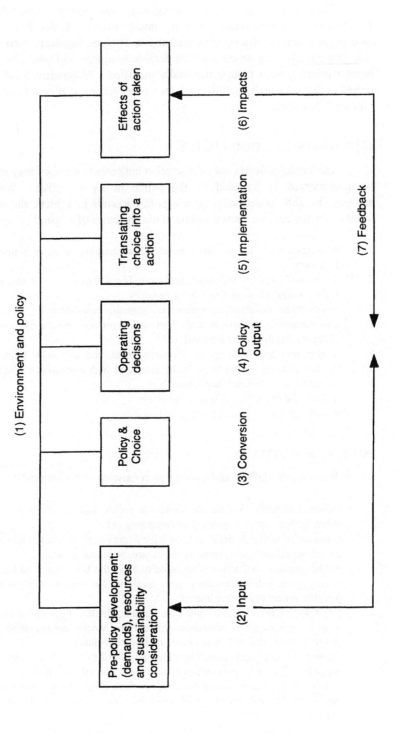

(1) Environment and policy

| Pre-policy development: (demands), resources and sustainability consideration | | Policy & Choice | Operating decisions | Translating choice into a action | | Effects of action taken |

(2) Input

(3) Conversion

(4) Policy output

(5) Implementation

(6) Impacts

(7) Feedback

These criteria are in descending order of priority. Eligibility determination is left almost totally up to the intake officer. At two Pittsburgh daycare centers, intake officers indicated that a fatigued applicant who comes in dragging a broken leg would get considerable sympathy and would be given the highest priority, even if only minimally qualified. "Alternatively, if someone comes in that maximally qualifies whom we dislike, we may rate them with low priority," they said.

IDENTIFYING A GOOD POLICY

The intake officer's use of discretion indicates that policy may not always be implemented as intended by the public policy objective. We should, however, be able to determine how a policy intends to achieve the objectives sought. To this end, we must understand the attributes of a "good policy":

1. It is responsive to perceived needs of contending interests (clienteles and customers).
2. It communicates the legislative intention. The authorization for action is clear, and the resources needed match the authority.
3. It is easily administered; compliance is reasonably cost-effective.
4. It is responsible and accountable. There is due process, and the rights and dignity of clients and the public are protected.
5. It takes into account long-run, short-run, local, and worldwide public interest.
6. Beyond allowing for outcomes to be compared with intentions, it should enable people to function more independently.
7. It should be free of fraud, waste, and abuse.
8. It indicates the full cost to achieve sustainability.

POLICY: A SUMMARY

We can now define public policy as consisting of six elements:

1. Preferred position. Values are inherent in policy, and the choice of a particular policy is made by a compromise of competing values.
2. Government action. Federal, state, and local units of government, including quasi-governmental units and private agencies, are the instruments.
3. Public purpose. All action is intended to be in the best interest of society. This quality gives policy legitimacy and represents the highest level of consensus possible among competing interests.
4. Legal documents. These include constitutions, charters, legal opinions, rules and regulations, contracts, memoranda, or less formal written documents such as "past practice" and verbal statements based on formal documents.
5. Decision for implementation. The authoritative order of the state is converted into programs initiated by government officials who execute the policy.
6. Results. Policy occurs as a consequence of these efforts. Some results are directly attributable to the broad social objectives and others are the products of implementing policies.

THE POLICYMAKING PROCESS

The public policymaking process in the United States is quite complex. All levels and branches of government (legislative, executive, administrative agencies, and the judiciary) make public policy. It involves an almost endless number of participants and institutions—powerful interests such as the National Rifle Association and Common Cause ("a government watchdog group") and weaker interests as the Temperance League. Participants make demands and express support in seeking to affect public policy goals.

Public administrators (principally through MLMs) exercise legitimate authority capable of making and enforcing public policy decisions; these are the agreements and compromises on values arrived at through the process of bargaining among groups, as shown in Fig. 5.1. The flow of events stresses the translation of policy statement into impacts. Fig. 5.1 illustrates seven components of the policy process model.

MLMs are the strategic actors in the conversion phase. Considerable attention has been given to (1) the social and economic problems that activate the system; (2) legislators and executives in their roles as decision-makers; and (3) the effects of what government does or fails to do. Surprisingly little attention has been given to policy as the implementation of public choices.[16] Implementation occurs after the goals and objectives have been decided on and after the resources have been committed. Therefore, the study of implementation examines those factors that contribute to the realization or non-realization of policy objectives.[17] These factors include public and private individuals and groups, all of whom are often in conflict.

First, America has been spending beyond its means, leaving the debt burden to be assumed by future generations. This clearly indicates the need to establish a balanced-budget policy. This conclusion is a result of defining the goal (value). America's continued massive deficit has the potential to choke off the opportunity for private sector borrowing that would enhance productivity, growth, and international competitiveness. The deficit will make it difficult to sell U.S. products overseas.

Second, policymakers must make choices between immediate consumption borrowing, such as to pay for welfare benefits, and investment borrowing, such as to enhance labor skills and to improve infrastructure development (e.g., building sewage plants, highways, and research and development) aimed at enhancing U.S. productivity and growth. These policy choices must be made in an environment in which the public is unwilling to pay more taxes.

Third, available alternatives include:

- Transferring many existing responsibilities to the states.
- Making cuts in major programs in areas such as welfare, education, Medicare, and Medicaid.

- Eliminating federal agencies such as the departments of Housing and Urban Development, Commerce, Energy, and Education.
- Reducing research and development grants to universities.

To achieve these objectives without destabilizing the economy, specific efforts must be mobilized, including:

- A drastic overhaul of welfare.
- Getting the public to expect less.
- Judiciously cutting programs to avoid jolts in the economy that produce harmful contraction and unemployment.
- Finding the right balance of borrowing for short-term consumption and for long-term investment and growth.

Finally, alternatives must be selected to best meet the objective. This is a complex stage because it involves the analysis of conflicting values and thus requires compromise.

POLICY LEVELS

In studying the policymaking process, it is important that we understand the different levels of policy as they are administered in a given agency. For example, both the state and federal governments operate internal revenue services. Fig. 5.2 depicts a simplified view of the various levels of policy that might occur in such an agency.

Quite clearly, the major decisions are made at the top. Yet from the point of view of the individual taxpayer—who walks into the office off the street, telephones, or writes a letter seeking relief for a particular problem—the minor and fundamental policies often become the most critical. The reality of a governmental policy is often experienced in terms of how long we sit in a reception room or wait for a written response to an inquiry.

Administrators must keep the following questions in mind: Do we have a clear perception of the level of policy that is being pursued? Have we sorted out the policy details to permit us to translate a solution of the problem into programs and procedures? Have we viewed the hierarchy of policy (see Fig. 5.3), including laws, judicial opinions, departmental regulations, guidelines, memoranda, and standard operating procedures, both written and verbal, and considered their interdependence?

COMPLEXITY AND FRAGMENTATION

Normally, there is no one point, actor, group, or body from which policy emanates.[18] The makers of public policy include bureaucrats, community

Fig. 5.2. The Effective Administration of the Tax Law

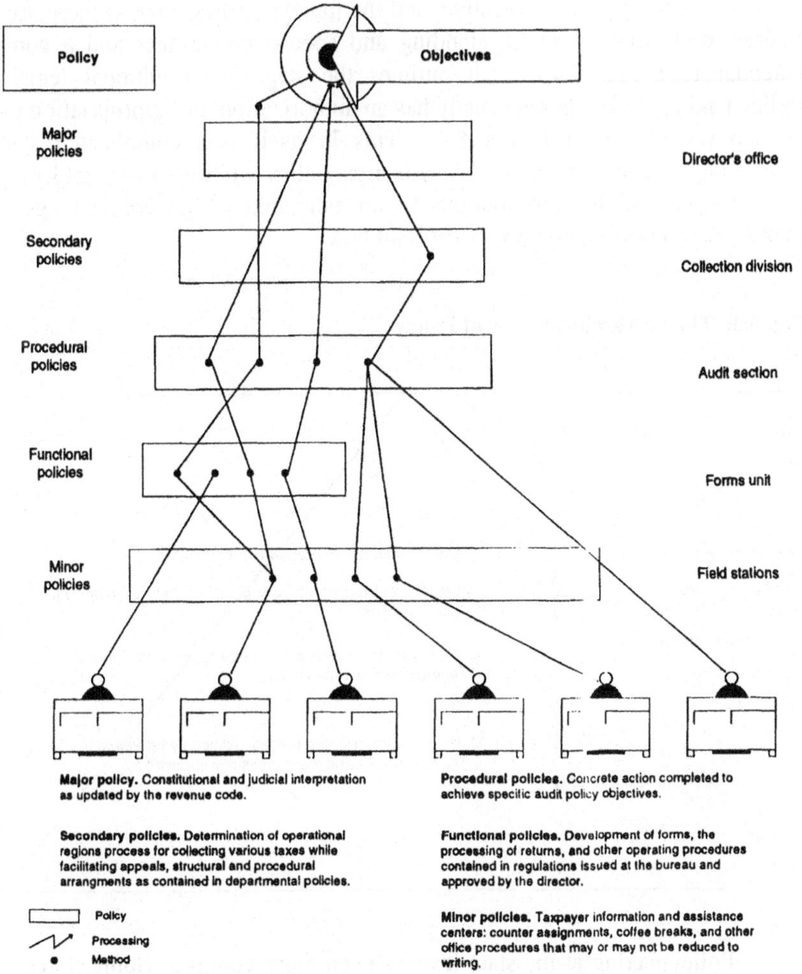

Policy

Objectives

Major policies — Director's office

Secondary policies — Collection division

Procedural policies — Audit section

Functional policies — Forms unit

Minor policies — Field stations

Major policy. Constitutional and judicial interpretation as updated by the revenue code.

Secondary policies. Determination of operational regions process for collecting various taxes while facilitating appeals, structural and procedural arrangments as contained in departmental policies.

☐ Policy
〰 Processing
● Method

Procedural policies. Concrete action completed to achieve specific audit policy objectives.

Functional policies. Development of forms, the processing of returns, and other operating procedures contained in regulations issued at the bureau and approved by the director.

Minor policies. Taxpayer information and assistance centers: counter assignments, coffee breaks, and other office procedures that may or may not be reduced to writing.

Source: Adapted from Theodore Haimann and William G. Scott, *Management in the Modern Organization* (Boston: Houghton Mifflin, 2nd edn. 1974, p. 105).

leaders, elected and appointed executives, the press, religious leaders, lobbyists, legislators, and such policy analysts as the Brookings Institution or the Rand Corporation.

Policy processes at city, county, or state levels are increasingly interconnected and overlap into the private sector. We have seen that many public functions are carried on outside of general-purpose government and in quasi-governmental structures, by contract, and by nonprofit organizations in the "third sector." We set these aside for a moment in order to describe traditional patterns.

In general-purpose government at the national level, there are three branches: Congress, the executive, and the judiciary. In Congress there are two houses, each with 15 or 20 standing and special committees and a complex calendar (see Fig. 5.4, which outlines the stages of traditional legislative policymaking). Legislation usually has an authorization and appropriation cycle, as partially shown in Figure 5.4. This in itself is a complicated system. According to *The New York Times*, energy policy—if we can be said to have one—consists of the contributions of an estimated 61 government agencies, making their coordination a very difficult task.[19]

Fig. 5.3. The Hierarchical Flow of Policy

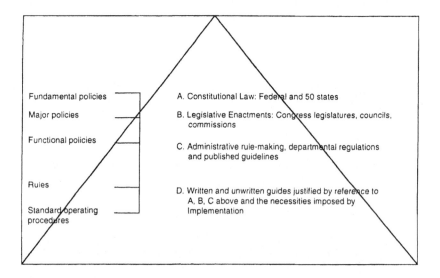

Policymaking at the state level is even more complex. Some states have 200 or 300 agencies and often elect numerous department heads. Moreover, governors tend to be weaker than presidents, and many state legislatures are leaderless and maintain totally inadequate records of their hearings and proceedings. The picture at the city and county level is one of considerable disarray:

[L]ocal legislatures are able to meet for only brief periods during the year. Their members hold full-time jobs elsewhere, receive very little compensation for being legislators, lack staff, and may have scant governmental experience themselves. Within these constraints the substantive knowledge and administrative skill they need for meeting their policy-making duties is frequently not available to them. For example, a typical county legislature does not, of itself, possess the time or technical resources needed to systematically evaluate budgetary proposals.[20]

Special districts, such as water or transportation authorities or health districts, proliferate at the substate level. Their policy decisions have major significance. Yet the operation of many of these entities is little known, as they function independently of the traditional governments.

Fig. 5.4. A Simplified Traditional View of the National Legislative Dominance of Policy Making

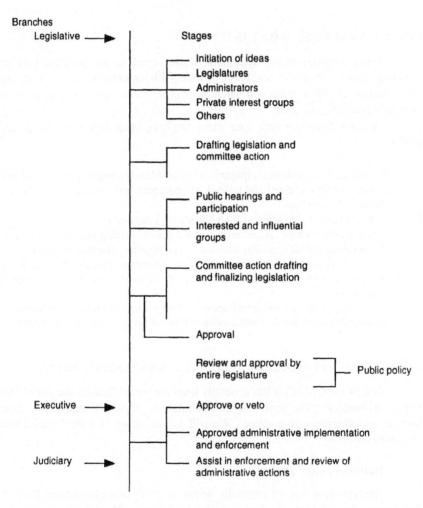

The policymaking system at any level does not operate in a linear fashion but rather as a network of ebbing and flowing interactive subsystems. Coalitions come and go with changing conditions, and forces tending toward entropy (the disorganization or unresponsiveness of the system), hypertrophy (exaggerated growth accentuating a particular aspect), and equilibrium can be observed.

Robert Simmons and others have spelled out the following as some of the factors that operate in this dynamic environment:[21]

- power arrangements;
- the historical context of the problem
- personalities and leadership style;
- conceptualizations and the way they get communicated; and
- organizational instruments.

POLICY ANALYSIS: WHAT IS IT?

Policy analysis is the systematic means used to aid policymakers in selecting sound options: "It involves a problem-solving approach, collection and interpretation of information and some attempt to predict the consequences of alternative courses of action."[22]

Norman Beckman sets four main attributes that characterizes policy analysis:

1. It is integrative and interdisciplinary. Each problem is complex and has multiple causes and effects, direct and indirect consequences, and involves the skills of a number of disciplines.
2. It is anticipatory. Its emphasis is on future policy decisions.
3. It is decision-oriented. Attention is directed toward existing problems and issues that are analyzed for feasibility and cost versus benefits. The analysis should help answer the following questions: Should government intervene to solve a problem? How? For how long? At what cost? Who will benefit? Is the solution satisfactory?
4. It is value-conscious and client-oriented. The preferences (cost or benefits) of participants are identified and considered in the analysis of each alternative.[23]

COMPETING APPROACHES TO POLICY ANALYSIS (MODELS)

The subject of policy has generally been presented through the use of two opposing models.   The first emphasizes analysis or theory and the second focuses on experience or practice. We will call attention to a third model that incorporates both.

Rational policy analysis

Analysis is a way to rationally arrive at preferable alternatives through techniques designed to (1) better define problems; (2) identify meaningful alternatives; (3) understand the framework of choice; (4) select the best alternative; and (5) follow the policy trail through the labyrinth of implementation. (See Fig. 5.5, in which a planning, programming, budgeting system, or PPBS, is applied to school management.) The recommended steps are:

Fig. 5.5. Rational Model Applied to Resource Allocation: PPBS School Management Context

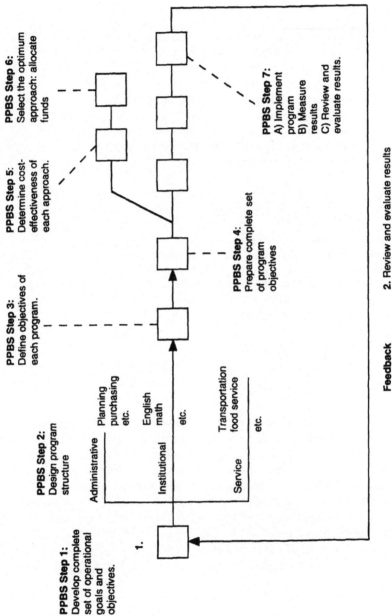

PPBS Step 1:
Develop complete set of operational goals and objectives.

PPBS Step 2:
Design program structure

Administrative
Planning purchasing etc.

Institutional
English math etc.

Service
Transportation food service etc.

PPBS Step 3:
Define objectives of each program.

PPBS Step 4:
Prepare complete set of program objectives

PPBS Step 5:
Determine cost-effectiveness of each approach.

PPBS Step 6:
Select the optimum approach: allocate funds

PPBS Step 7:
A) Implement program
B) Measure results
C) Review and evaluate results.

Feedback   2. Review and evaluate results

1. Redefine the policy issue and restrict it to what government can do.
2. Identify several relevant alternatives that represent the range of possible approaches.
3. Sub-optimize, or find some limited step that government can take that will bring about the desired good through minimizing the effort expended. (This implies having at hand a model of the problem.)
4. Give attention to objectives, priorities, and constraints of both legislative and executive decision-makers. Present them with alternatives, indicating their advantages and disadvantages. The policy analyst says, "if we follow course A, this will be the consequence; if course B, this alternative result."
5. Give attention to details of implementation, taking into account the fact that top administrators and MLMs select policies and operate their agencies in the light of the guidance they receive.

In rational policy analysis, the emphasis is on rational theory. William Dunn has presented a model in simple terms:

An individual who is making a rational choice typically participates in a mental process something like the following: The first available alternative leads to a particular result. The second available alternative leads to another result. The second result is more valuable than the first. Therefore the second course of action should be chosen. If we designate courses of actions as A (Alternatives) and results as O (Outcomes), the problem of choice can be diagrammed as follows:

$A_1 = O_2$

$A_2 = O_2$

$O_2 = O_1$ therefore choose A_2.[24]

This model contains the essential elements for a rational calculus: (1) an input is related to results; (2) the input-result sequences (or alternatives) are compared; and (3) a "value" choice is made based on a criterion.[25] Steps 1 and 2 are based on facts derived from previous study, while the third item reflects a value preference. This rational model, which can be elaborated on, placed in a system framework and supported by data, is what policy analysis entails.

Yehezkel Dror has elaborated this kind of analysis by identifying what he has called "metapolicy," or the policies that guide policymaking.[26] In simple terms, each level of policy is metapolicy (master or guiding policy) for successive lower levels. Figure 5.6 illustrates a specific example applying rational theory.

While analysis does provide guidance, it should be noted that it masks problems:

1. The choice would have been different had the outcomes related to the alternatives been different. The problem here is that we seldom know beforehand precisely what outcome a given input will produce.

2.   The actual situation is seldom as simple as the example.   Questions of expenditures enter: just how much does a unit of recruitment cost compared with a unit of training? There are problems of timing. Can recruitment be done in the short run?   Will training take a longer time and involve committing other resources?

3.   The suggestion implicit in both alternatives (A_1 and A_2) is that getting qualified minority and female applicants to the hiring office is the appropriate response to discrimination. The limited numbers of such groups already employed but in lower or dead-end positions may also be a critical factor.

4.   A combination of these two alternatives would probably yield a better result than either one alone.

5.   Several other alternatives need also to be taken in to account: A_3, the selection procedure (e.g., biased tests); A_4, the location of the job relative to the homes of minorities; A_5, the commitment of agency officials to the idea of equal employment opportunity.

6.   The conditions of change, the cost of securing information, and the relative ease or difficulty in administering the alternatives also must be considered.

Fig. 5.6. Alternatives for Meeting the Problem of Discrimination in Public Employment

A_1	Special recruitment of minority and women applicants.
O_1	Number of applicants increases by 25 percent up from 80 to 100.
A_2	Provide special training for minorities and women applicants.
O_2	Number of qualified applicants increases from 25 to 50 percent.

O_2 is better than O_1 (We get more qualified applicants through training than we do through expanding applications). Choose A_2.

Consider the complexities involved in attempting to accommodate some of these factors (see Fig. 5.7) in the rational calculation.

We can imagine that the data could be assembled. Regression analysis could also be used by examining experience to rank the alternatives on the basis of their composite scores on the effectiveness, cost, resistance, and ease of administration measures. The cost involved, however, would be substantial if we were trying to assemble data upon which to base a decision in the numerous installations where discrimination against minorities and women exists.

Analysis does bring together much information related to the problem but, on balance, it creates as many problems as it solves. Charles Lindblom and David Braybrooke have listed many difficulties associated with making rational judgments regarding policy:

1.   The selection of alternatives requires comprehension of all possible alter-
     natives—or at least assurance that the most important ones are included. Analysis
     seldom includes such an overview or the weighing of particular alternatives.
2.   Implied in the model is a value judgment, the choice, which governs selections.
     Thus, the calculations around alternatives are subordinate to an unexamined
     preference or prejudice.
3.   The recommended choice is presented as an intellectual exercise with scant
     attention to the political forces that might accompany that choice.
4.   Concerns related to tactics and strategy, formal and informal structures that might
     influence choices or existing conditions are omitted.
5.   It is assumed that each alternative is a solution to the problem at hand.   The
     implication is that we have in hand a model of how the problem evolves and that
     this intervention is a key to its solution.
6.   The rational calculus is poorly adapted to the dynamics of human organizations
     and the way problems interlock. [27]

Despite these many difficulties, it is still tempting to think that we have
the theory necessary to solve all of our problems by applying deductive methods.
Proponents of this view believe that solutions can be achieved with better data
and more sophisticated computer programs.

Fig. 5.7. Analyzing the Problem of Discrimination in Public Employment

		Effectiveness Measure		Cost per unit	Resistance Calculation	Ease of Administration	
A1	Recruitment	H-M-L		low-high	H-M-L	Easy-difficult
A2	Training	H-M-L		low-high	H-M-L	Easy-difficult
A3	Testing	H-M-L		low-high	H-M-L	Easy-difficult
A4	Location	Under two Over miles		low-high	H-M-L	Easy-difficult
A5	Committment	H-M-L		low-high	H-M-L	Easy-difficult

H-High	M-Medium	L-Low

Trial and Error: Incremental Decision-Making

A competitive model for policy stresses practice or experience.   This
approach is associated with Charles Lindblom and what he has called disjointed
incrementalism. "Disjointed" implies that, in practice, policymakers do not seek
the best alternative but instead respond to problems in a piecemeal, case-by-case,
disconnected way.   "Incrementalism" underscores what the proponents of

rational policy analysis failed to mention: Problem-solving occurs on the margins. Policymakers prefer to sharply limit alternatives to consequences that are generally known and differ only slightly (incrementally) from existing policies. This greatly reduces risks, providing greater certainty and continuity with past or existing policies.

The scope of change is small, but it is hoped that a series of small changes will accumulate. Disjointed incrementalism takes into account the status quo with which we must contend. To bring change about, lengthy series of small policy moves are pursued almost in an experimental way. Braybrooke and Lindblom explain that disjointed incrementalism is better described as moving away from known social ills than as moving toward a known and reasonably stable goal. A policy is directed at a problem; it is tried, altered, tried in its altered form, and altered again.[28] Federal policy in the field of medical assistance to older citizens provides a good example. The Kerr-Mills bill in the 1950s provided some aid to older Americans who were unable to pay their hospital bills. Then came Medicaid and Medicare in the late 1960s, which paid portions of older Americans' medical expenses in and outside the hospital. Now there is a drive to introduce total health care insurance to cover all Americans.

The following are additional characteristics of this strategy:

1. The "correct" sense of direction results from a mix of feedback and intuition.
2. Much of the direction of effort is based on operational discovery of what does not work.
3. Fundamental questions are eschewed in favor of practical solutions to small-scale and surface manifestations of the basic problems.
4. The calculus provides for trade-offs among a few closely related alternatives.
5. Any choice automatically contains assessments of cost, timeliness, and ease of administration.

Mixed Scanning: An Alternative Model

Amitai Etzioni has advanced an extensive critique of disjointed incrementalism.[29] It includes the following:

1. Incrementally based decisions of necessity reflect the interests of the most powerful, leaving unsatisfied the demands of the underprivileged and politically unorganized.
2. Individual and disjointed steps can be circular or cancel previous steps. Kenneth Boulding comments that, according to this approach, "we do stagger through history like a drunk, putting one disjointed incremental foot after another."[30]
3. Basic social innovations are avoided except in the long run.
4. The ideological preoccupation is with the inertia-prone, anti-innovation forces. One of the basic problems confronting government is to keep abreast of rapidly changing conditions that make innovation essential.

To meet these problems as well as the critique of rational comprehensive strategies, Etzioni combined the approaches into what he called mixed
scanning.[31] Assume we are about to set up a worldwide weather-observa-
tion system using weather satellites. The rationalist approach would seek an
exhaustive survey of weather conditions by using cameras capable of
detailed observations and by scheduling reviews of the entire sky as often as
possible.

This would yield an avalanche of detail, costly to analyze and likely to
overwhelm our capacities to act. Incrementalism would focus on those areas in
which particular patterns developed in the recent past and, perhaps, on a few
nearby regions; it would thus ignore all formations that might deserve attention if
they arose in unexpected areas.

A mixed-scanning strategy would include elements of both approaches by
employing two cameras: a broad-angle camera that would cover all parts of the
sky but not in great detail, and a second one that would zero in on those areas
revealed by the first camera to require a more in-depth examination.

The mixed-scanning approach requires us to identify a fundamental
direction, which then can be used as a guide for subsequent changes of an incremental nature. From the standpoint of structures, the wide-angle cameras tend to
be held by top-level choice-makers, while the MLMs are forced to deal with
details within that frame.

APPROACH TO FORMULATING NEW POLICIES

The opposing conceptual approaches of analysis and experience together
provide the format for the formal preparation of policy (i.e., legislative
recommendations). Beginning with the task forces used by the Lyndon Johnson
administration, a procedure was initiated to shape new ideas into "proposals" by
(1) a brief write-up of the idea; (2) a description of the problem; (3) determination of its relationship to ongoing programs; and (4) recommendations for
action. To this the Nixon administration added (5) analysis of the pros and cons
of the main alternatives as part of its normal "policy generating" format. Carter
expanded the format to include two additional steps: (6) estimates of the length
of time the federal government could be expected to carry on the function; and
(7) the "for" and "against" groups who might be expected to influence the
implementation of the proposed policy change. The next step is likely to be the
evaluation of policy initiatives' *sustainability*.

Techniques of analysis essentially involve projections of new approaches
aimed at modifying or replacing existing practices in meeting public problems.
The concept of mixed scanning incorporates this tension.

To further clarify the relationship between policy and public
administration, we must examine the policy-executing phase.

POLICY IMPLEMENTATION

Perhaps the biggest drawback in presenting the policy process as a system of environment to policymaking to policy execution-to policy evaluation is that it minimizes the major role of administrators in policymaking. Nevertheless, formulation by administrators in close consultation with powerful client groups is the normal procedure. Until the Kennedy administration, the president's legislative program was "formulated almost exclusively on the basis of proposals prepared by the departments and agencies and submitted to the president through the then Bureau of the Budget. . . . The departments and agencies carried most of the burden for policy innovation, drawing on their own experience and expertise and the inputs from their clientele groups for new ideas."[32] President-elect Kennedy, as part of his transition to office, commissioned 29 task forces, 24 of which reported prior to his inauguration. This approach, along with interagency task forces, somewhat changed the nearly exclusive role of administrators as policy initiators.

By now it must be clear that administrators also make policy as a consequence of the authority delegated to them from little-known and often ambiguous legislation; that policymaking is inherent in conversion; that functional and minor policies must be made to operationalize generalizations; and that policymaking authority accrues to administrators out of the complexity and fragmentation of federal grants-in-aid. Administrative policymaking can be reviewed under four headings: rule-making authority, the impact of structures or policy, the legislative–lower management alliance that has been labeled subgovernment, and "managerial" policies.

ADMINISTRATIVE RULE MAKING

The setting of general policy in the legislature occupies a limited period of time—a few days or months in preparing and passing legislation compared with the decades of life that many bills have once they become law. While the legislature in the short run lays down the broad outline of what is to be done, numerous lesser-level policies are required in the process of implementation. Conditions change, making adjustments mandatory. Issues requiring policy decisions are continually arising out of the experiences of execution. As Avery Leiserson and Fritz Morstein Marx noted nearly forty years ago, there are "two principal channels for policy formulation: one from the people through their elected representatives; the other from administrative officials to the chief executive."[33] The latter, administrative rule making, emphasizes administrators as policymakers.

THE IMPACT OF STRUCTURES ON POLICY

Graham Allison has articulated a second area in which there are administrative influences on policy. In his Cuban missile case study, he puts forth three models of decision-making: (1) rational, with-policy based on the results of logical analysis; (2) bureaucratic—the impact on policy produced by standard operating procedures and routines; and (3) political models—policy as the result of the interaction of contending forces.[34] Allison demonstrates how the bureaucratic model operates as definitively in policymaking as do the other models.

The effects of structure on policy include the following:

1.   It determines who in government can take the initiative.
2.   It defines formal responsibility.
3.   It shows where authority is vested.
4.   It points to the major contacts with the general public.
5.   It determines the points of access for interest groups.
6.   It is critical for evaluating interjurisdictional policy outcomes.

A given structure or procedure favors some groups and works to the disadvantage of others. If an individual or group makes demands on an agency that activates a procedure already in place, the response is likely to be prompt. If their demands, however, call for an organizational response not anticipated, delays can be expected. Bureaucracy tends to respond in terms of routines. Groups that assist in the evaluation of the agency or help it in monitoring or increasing its appropriation often establish routines that are particularly responsive to their interests. This gives the groups knowledge of the important contact points in the organization through which they can more easily obtain a response to the demands. The ordinary citizens who lack such contact or connections with administrative officials find it more difficult to satisfy their demands.

Legislative-Lower Management Alliances

Almost unreported in public administration literature are legislative-administrative links between MLMs and the administrative personnel who staff the offices of legislators and legislative committees. (Administration in legislatures is a widely expanding field, a literal army of employees.) This does not include legislative administrators at the federal or local levels. Legislative administrators perform a variety of tasks.[35]

The Constitution has provided for the separation of Congress and the president, but this is no bar against the commingling of their respective employees. On the congressional side, the staffs of the major committees (e.g., Defense or Foreign Affairs) make common cause with executive department personnel to exercise significant influence over the formulation of policy. Similarly, the policies determined in the executive branch are influenced by legislative staff members who use their links to administrators. So pervasive and powerful are these alliances that Randall Ripley and Grace Franklin have labeled them "sub-governments."[36] Fig. 5.8 describes this relationship.

Fig. 5.8. Sub-Government Policymaking

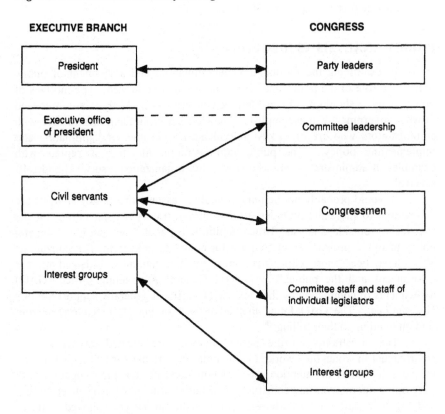

Managerial Policies

The type or group of policies that administrators make most generally relates to administrative practices. They include the procedures, methods, and standards designed to facilitate or make it possible to carry out the daily agency routine. While these guidelines are not law per se, they are derived from a composite of authorizations given to an agency to carry out the programs with which it has been charged. These intradepartmental regulations are generally compiled in an Administrative Procedures Series, or operations manual, and fall under the heading of managerial policies.

Managerial policies have the following characteristics:

1.   They function within major policies (see Fig. 5.1).
2.   They are narrow in scope. They focus primarily on processes or operations; for example, they tell what must be done before goods can be purchased, how letters are cleared before they are sent outside the agency, and what steps are necessary to accomplish a job.
3.   Managerial policies are incremental insofar as precedent (past actions) tends to control what will happen in the present.

4.   Because of the technical detail involved in managerial policies, they tend to emanate from the experience of MLMs.

POLICY ANALYSIS AS IDEOLOGY

In examining the formulation, determination, and assessment of public policy, the role of the policy analyst should not be overlooked. The motives of policy analysts should be of considerable concern to us. Analysts are interested in what government can accomplish. Their efforts bring them face to face with administrators who are often key individuals responsible for legitimating and implementing policy. The public administration literature is replete with examples of administrative preoccupation with organizational survival and self-survival.

It would probably not be unreasonable to assume that policy analysts are susceptible to the same attitudes as line administrators. Commenting on the motives of outside analysts, Bruce Smith notes that "the non-governmental policy analysts, in their ceaseless quest for contracts to keep their organizations alive, have been more guilty than most of flim flamming (misleading) the government and the public."[37] Federal General Accounting Office (GAO) assessments of contracting by the Defense Department generally support Smith's observations. The GAO found that advertised savings from contracting out seldom lived up to their billing.[38]

The constraints on the policy analysts are created largely by the environment in which they work: (1) the tight time frames for fact gathering and the constant focus of attention on choice-makers; (2) the preoccupation with developing alternatives and constructing scenarios with all of their uncertainties; and (3) their staff roles as advisers, close to the throne yet removed. But as government becomes increasingly a function of manipulating data, policy analysis has become ever more strategic. In the limited literature on policies, some of the stance of the analysts comes out; they project themselves as specialists stationed at central observation points, able to tell why a particular result has come about. There is a:

- Focus on political conflict and the personalities involved in order to produce the policy product.
- Focus on the most prominent and powerful interest groups and the impact they have on the process.
- Determination as to where leverage can best be applied in each stage of the process.
- Commitment to evaluation primarily in quantitative terms, with benefits and costs translated into dollars expended or saved.

This posture has made possible greater understanding about the way government is conducted, but it has added little to making government more directly accountable to people.

Fred A. Kramer has suggested that policy analysis is ideology, whether it is out of the tradition of rational-comprehensive calculations or muddling through experience. The criterion that has come to be used is maximization of returns. Even those who deny the validity of analysis tend to apply the same—primarily economic—analysis. This is what is meant by the ideological nature of policy analysis; it is the use of a narrow set of principles, a coherent system of beliefs used to organize and simplify the complexities of the world. The ideology in analysis is rooted in a commitment to the scientific method used either explicitly or implicitly: (1) the emphasis is on quantification, which is assumed to be value-free; (2) hard data tend to drive out any soft data; (3) there is a "seductive potential" in resorting to systems analysis[39]; (4) natural science rather than social science or humanistic theory is used; and (5) the analyst is insufficiently critical of his or her self-interest. While policy analysis should be the search for the public interest there is the hazard that the analyst will substitute his or her values for those of the people government is to serve. Analysis is always incomplete; it operates under conditions of uncertainty and ignores important aspects of a problem. In short, policy analysis has to be demystified and unmasked in order to reveal that it is the exercise of power with insufficient accountability. The analyst must be held accountable for the consequences of the analysis he or she performs or fails to perform.

In short, the policymaking process may be summarized as indicated in the following eight points:

1. An environment that stimulates government officials and receives the product of their work.
2. Pre-policy development: demands, resources, and sustainability consideration.
3. Consideration that carries stimuli from environment to the policymakers. This is the input point where the problem(s) is defined, based on the recognized needs, the accepted articulated demands and available resources. At this stage:

    - Interests from varied sources are articulated and aggregated.
    - Individual conditions are assessed.
    - Individual and group perceptions, values and desires are determined.
    - Community expectation (the wider interest) is assessed.
    - The agenda is formulated in terms of identified issues such as aid, the savings and loan crisis, or Iraq, and about which there is public disagreement over the preferred solution.
    - Sustainability requirements are incorporated at this stage if policymakers want to know the true costs and extended time duration of the proposed impact of the policy on the clientele.

These demands for action are aggregated and passed on to the conversion stage.

4. A conversion process consisting of the formal structures and procedures for government that transform demands and resources into public policy. This is a

critical point at which legitimacy is obtained both for the process and policy choice, emanating from that process. Particular consideration must be given to the inter-action of public and private actors:

- Public institutional leadership involving the executive, legislative, administrative agencies and judiciary.
- Stakeholder including clientele, relevant individuals, and interest groups.
- Organizing issues according to the systematic or popular agenda and the institutional agenda.[40] The systematic agenda is mainly for discussion, while the institutional agenda requires serious and active attention. Political timing often play an important role in enhancing the choices and issues reaching the institutional agenda. Examples of the factors influencing issues to be put on the institutional agenda include: (1) expert consensus, as in the case of the North American Free Trade Agreement (NAFTA) among Mexico, Canada, and the U.S., in which economists, business leaders, and foreign-policy specialists viewed NAFTA as being in the best long-term interest of the U.S.; (2) the willingness to resolve particular issues, as actors compare their strength and bargain with and among each other, ultimately forming power coalescence for policy choice.

5. Guiding operating decision (policies) that represents the formal goals, intentions, or statements of government.
6. The implementation of the policy (translation) as it is actually deliver goods and services to clients. Implementing agencies include departments, businesses, agencies, and private organizations (mainly by way of contracts).
7. The measurement of impact and benefits to target groups or clients. At this point an assessment is made to determine if sustainability—enabling or making clients better off and more independent than they were before the program was initiated—is being achieved.
8. The feedback of policy performance to the environment, which is transmitted back to the input stage as demand and support.

DISCUSSION QUESTIONS

1. Why can one say policy begins with compromise and ends with changes on the margin?
2. Give examples of major, secondary, functional, and minor policies. Add two examples of important policies that are communicated only verbally. How are all levels interdependent?
3. What lies behind the assertion that "policy is administration"?
4. Why does policy formulation necessitate translation or conversion?
5. Choose a problem area and show how Etzioni's mixed-scanning model might be employed.
6. What is the basis for the assertion that over time administrators are the primary formulators of policy?
7. Using the basic format of a "policy paper"—(1) statement of the problem; (2) background; (3) pros and cons of three major alternatives; (4) recommendation;

(5) expected need for government effort; and (6) groups "for" and "against" the implementation of the new idea—outline a suggestion for a policy change. Limit yourself to two typewritten pages, but indicate what additional detail might be included in an appendix.

8.   What is the institutional policy agenda and how does it differ from the systematic agenda?

NOTES

1.   Ivan L. Richardson and Sidney Baldwin, *Public Administration: Government in Action* (Columbus, Ohio: Charles E. Merrill Publishing, 1976), p. 121.

2.   POSDCORB is a word coined to reflect what administrators do: plan, organize, staff, direct, coordinate, report, and budget. We would add an E, for evaluate.

3.   Alan Schick, "Beyond Analysis," *Public Administration Review* (May/June 1977): 258–263.

4.   Norton E. Long, *The Polity* (Chicago: Rand McNally, 1963), p. 79.

5.   I. M. Mitroff and Louis R. Pondy, "On the Organization of Inquiry: A Comparison of Some Radically Different Approaches to Policy," *Public Administration Review* 34, No. 5 (September/October 1974): 471.

6.   Francis Rourke, *Bureaucracy, Politics and Public Policy* (Little Brown, 1969), Chap. 2.

7.   Ira Sharkansky, *Public Policy-Making in Government Agencies*, 3rd edn. (Chicago: Rand McNally, 1975), p. 4.

8.   Raymond Bauer and Kenneth Gergin, eds., *The Study of Policy Formation* (New York: The Free Press, 1968), p. 2.

9.   Yehezkel Dror, *Public Policy Making Re-Examined* (San Francisco: Chandler Publishing, 1968), p. 35.

10.   Charles Lindblom, *The Policy Making Process* (Englewood Cliffs, N.J.: Prentice-Hall, 1968), p. 4.

11.   Howard E. Freeman and Clarence C. Sherwood, *Social Research and Social Policy* (Englewood Cliffs, N.J.: Prentice-Hall, 1968), p. 2.

12.   Robert H. Simmons et al., "Policy Flow Analysis: A Conceptual Model for Comparative Public Policy Research," *The Western Political Quarterly* (September 1974): 465.

13.   Thomas Dye, *Understanding Public Policy*, 5th edn. (Englewood Cliffs, N.J.: Prentice Hall, 1984), p. 1.

14.   Richard I. Hofferbert, *The Study of Public Policy* (Indianapolis: Bobbs-Merrill, 1974), p. 34; see also Carl Frederick, *Man and His Government* (New York: McGraw-Hill, 1963), p. 7.

15.   Ibid., p. 4.

16.   This phase was the subject of a symposium on policy assistance. See Ross Clayton, Patrick Conklin and Raymond Shapek, "Policy Management Assistance—A Developing Dialogue," *Public Administration Review*, special issue (December 1975).

17.   Donald S. Van Meter and Carl E. Van Horn, "The Policy Implementation Process: A Conceptual Framework," *Administration and Society* (February 1975): 488; and Malcolm L. Goggin, Ann O.M. Bowman, James Lester, and Lawrence J. O'Toole Jr.,

Implementation Theory and Practice (Glenview, Ill.: Scott Foresman/Little-Brown Education, 1990).

18. The ideas that follow on fragmentation have been taken in part from George E. Berkeley, *The Craft of Public Administration* (Boston: Allyn and Bacon, 1975, chapter titled "The American Political System").

19. *The New York Times*, April 18, 1976, p. 29. Since this writing an Energy Department has been established.

20. Jerry C. Hillel and Patrick Lozito, "The Burgeoning Demands on Local Legislature," *Public Administration Review* (September-October 1975): 500.

21. Robert Simmons et al., "Policy Flow Analysis: A Conceptual Model for Comparative Public Policy Research," *The Western Political Quarterly* (September 1974): 460–67.

22. Jacob B. Ukeles, "Policy Analysis or Reality," *Public Administration Review* (May-June 1977): 223.

23. Norman Beckman, "Policy Analysis in Government: Alternatives to Muddling Through," *Public Administration Review* (May-June 1977): 221–22.

24. William Dunn, *Public Administration: Public Policy Analysis* (Pittsburgh: University of Pittsburgh School of General Studies, 1977).

25. Ibid.

26. Dror, *Public Policy Making*.

27. David Braybrooke and Charles Lindblom, *A Strategy of Decision* (New York: Glencoe Free Press, 1963), chap. 2.

28. Ibid., pp. 71–74.

29. Amitzi Etzoni, "Mixed Scanning: a 'Third' Approach to Decision-Making," *Public Administrative Review* 27, No. 5 (December 1967): 385–392.

30. Ibid.

31. Ibid., p. 389.

32. Norma C. Thomas and Harold L. Wolman, "The Presidency and Policy Formulation: The Task Force Service," *Public Administrative Review* (September-October 1969): 459.

33. Avery Leiserson and Fritz Morstein Marx, "The Formation of Administrative Policy," in Fritz Morstein Marx (ed.), *Elements of Public Administration Review*, 2nd edn. (Englewood Cliffs, N.J.: Prentice-Hall, 1959), p. 39.

34. Graham Allison, "Conceptual Models and the Cuban Missile Crisis," *American Political Science Review* LXIII, No. 3 (September 1969): 689–518.

35. Ibid., p. 498.

36. Randall Ripley and Grace Franklin, *Congress, The Bureaucracy and Public Policy* (Homewood, Ill.: Dorsey Press, 1976), Chap. 1.

37. Bruce L. R. Smith, "The Non-Governmental Policy Analysis Organization," *Pubilc Administration Review* (May/June 1977): 255.

38. For an excellent summary, see the U.S. General Accounting Office, *Federal Productivity: DOD's Experience in Contracting Out Commercially Available Activities*, GGD-89-6 (November 1988): 11–14.

39. Fred A. Kramer, "Policy Analysis as Ideology," *Public Administration Review* 35, No. 5 (September-October 1975): 509–517.

40. James E. Anderson, *Public Policy Making* (Boston: Houghton Mifflin, 1994), p. 91.

6

The External Environment
of Public Administration

If MLMs are to function optimally, they must know how to respond to pressures from the external environment. This chapter illustrates the constantly changing ecology of government, the often conflicting values that constitute its cultural setting, and the ways in which most public programs must adjust to political realities and fluctuating levels of resources. This knowledge will help MLMs relate to the forces and problems that have their source in the external environment. By understanding why organizations perform the way they do, MLMs will be able to change their own behavior in order to function more accountably.

LEARNING OBJECTIVES

On completing this chapter, the reader should have a greater appreciation for:

- The interdependency of public organizations and their environments.
- The manner in which basic values in U.S. society affect administrative practices.
- The ability to apply economic and political reasoning to accomplish organizational objectives.

Public organizations exist in a highly complex macro-environment that influences their purposes and modes of operation. This external environment consists of three major components: ecology, cultural setting, and political economy. Each directly affects MLMs. As we shall see, the ecology of the government largely determines what is to be done, the cultural setting identifies the preferred response to these demands, and the political economy defines how government officials exercise the power granted to them. The external environment is critically important to MLMs for three reasons: (1) it provides the demands and resources that activate and sustain the organization; (2) it sets the parameters within which organizational activities take place; and (3) it is one of the major places where organizational activities are judged.

A CHANGING ECOLOGY

In 1947, John M. Gaus used the concept of ecology (the interdependence of organisms in their environment) to describe the functioning of government. He wrote:

An ecological approach to public administration builds . . . quite literally from the ground up; from the elements of place—soils, climate, location, for example—to the people who live there—their numbers and ages and knowledge and the ways of physical and social technology by which, from the place and in relationship with one another, they get their living. It is within this setting that their instruments and practices of public housekeeping should be studied so that they may better understand what they are doing and appraise reasonably how they are doing and appraise reasonably how they are doing it.[1]

The ecological approach helps us to relate not only to rapid change but also to slow growth and retrogression. Additionally, as a model for relating public administration to its external environment, it is attractive because of its simplicity. It says in another way that public administration is best defined in terms of its practice. Table 6.1 gives examples of how six components channel authority and resources into public organizations.

The ecological concept helps explain administrative actions, but is does not show how the demands expressed affect MLMs.

First, the ecological approach stresses how programs are started as a response to articulated demands. It does not describe, for example, the continuing and critical problems relating to annual program refunding. Refunding has always been a crucial element in public management, and it is expected to take on even greater significance with the coming of target-base budgeting (establishment of a ceiling that may not be exceeded for 80 percent to 90 percent of the budget with requests for increments of the remainder being justified on a cost-benefit basis) and the reinvention of government movement that stresses program results, clientele/customer focus satisfaction and accountability. Also there is a strong anti-tax and spending bias. Thus, practicing managers (middle- and lower-level) are more concerned with ensuring resources for old programs than with launching new ones.

Second, the concept uncritically adopts the bias of growth. Incremental or yearly increases in existing programs are accepted as operating norms in virtually every government agency. Managers are taught to plan for increments, rather than decrements, and are given little guidance on how to respond to escalating demands in the face of declining resources.

Third, it implies that initiatives come primarily from the environment. This view is unrealistic and incomplete because most of the ideas for new directions come out of the experience of program execution.

Finally, it underplays the importance of structure and procedure. The structure of organizations largely determines how they respond to and exert pressures. For example, the U.S. Department of Agriculture keeps in close

Table 6.1: The Raw Materials of Politics

1. Population

   Many demands on government are traceable to population changes: growth, composition, and location. In 1790, the House of Representatives had one member for every 30,000 constituents (65 for the whole Congress). By the 1970s, the original membership had increased to 435, with each district containing 50,000 constituents. Now a population of over 200,000,000 growing by nearly 2,000,000 persons annually increases the difficulty of obtaining consensus about the specific citizen demands that government should attempt to satisfy.

   Our population is changing: it is growing older. In 1900, individuals over 65 years constituted approximately 5 percent of the population; in 1995 this figure has grown to nearly 13 percent. Programs of varying sorts must be adopted to meet the special needs of this group. From a predominant population of farmers, the United States has become urbanized, creating metropolitan areas with problems like crime, pollution, and urban decay.

2. Place

   Geography presents its own set of problems, and climate affects the kinds of services required in particular locations. For example, Pittsburgh, because of its three rivers, must carry on a large bridge-maintenance program while Columbus, Ohio, with a flat terrain and no rivers, does not have bridges. The quality of soil and availability of water and mineral resources affect the growth the development of a given location. Residents of the sparsely populated, resource-poor, mountainous city of Alamosa, Colorado, are likely to have different and perhaps fewer demands than will residents of New York City. Highly intensive water-use industries such as steel and aluminum are far more likely to locate along waterways.

   Prominent government regulations related to place include zoning, physical planning, and regional development. The national government has a highly controlled highway and waterway system.

3. Physical Technology

   Each major technological innovation greatly influences public actions. The automobile, television, and computers have transformed American life. A body of laws and regulations deals with the automobile. Motor vehicles may not be driven in many states without a license and valid insurance.

   The Federal Technology Assessment Act of 1972 created an office to assess the beneficial and adverse affects of technological innovations on society. Governments are besieged with demands to encourage and to discourage technology. In Pittsburgh, for example, air pollution has been associated with employment, while in Arizona employment is tied to clear air.

4. Social Technology

   Ivan Richardson and Sidney Baldwin have noted that "most of the significant innovations in public administration in the twentieth century have been technological; the merit system, based on a particular set of personnel management techniques; human relations methods, rooted in certain behavioral techniques; PPBS (planning, programming, budget, system), built on knowledge about the relationship between work, time, money and procedure; and organizational development, which is indebted to new knowledge about human behavior in complex organizational systems.

5. Wishes, Values, Objectives, Knowledge

   Government comes out of a people's world view. In the U.S., our commitment to individualism, private property, and the idea of democracy affects government. These attributes and values help us explain the differences in government in various parts of the country. They account for ways in which government in the U.S. differs from government in other countries, particularly those in which authoritarian ideologies prevail.

6. Power of Catastrophes

   Floods, fires, pests, drought, wars, depressions, and even the "best of times" call government into action and directly into varying missions. The tidal wave and hurricane that wrecked Galveston, Texas, in 1900 is said to have led to the commission form of government just as the cooperative effort between business and government in Pittsburgh, the so-called Pittsburgh Renaissance, is traced to the Johnstown flood of 1936. Catastrophes are ways of describing large-scale problems that are too big for people in their private capacity to handle; hence, they turn to government.

Sources: Table format adapted from Memorandum No. 2, in John M. Gaus's course, An Introduction to Public Administration, Harvard University (fall term, 1951–52); Ivan L. Richardson and Sidney Baldwin, *Public Administration, Government in Action* (Columbus, Ohio, Charles E. Merrill, 1976), p. 38.

contact with problems in every locality through its network of extension agents. When it needs to pressure Congress on pending legislation, it uses the network to solicit support from farmers across the country.

CULTURE AND ADMINISTRATION

Culture, like our changing ecology in the United States, is a major source of power for administrative organizations. But instead of arising from rapid change, the influences of culture on administration flow largely from continuity in values and institutions. Culture is the complex of knowledge, beliefs, laws, and customs in a society—literally, "what comes naturally" to a people. It is a key variable for explaining organizational behavior.

1. It influences how we perceive and interpret our environment.
2. It defines what is of value and what gives meaning to our lives.
3. It creates the means and the know-how to enable us to pursue our goals.
4. It defines the proper standard of behavior that organizations and individuals are expected to follow.[2]

American public administrators must understand their national culture and subculture. This knowledge can facilitate the execution of programs designed for citizens from different subcultures and help us to understand the practices that have come to be acceptable in government. In this section we will examine: (1) the value heritage of American public administration; (2) the practice of administration in the light of those values; and (3) the interplay of values and practice in lower management.

Novus Ordo Seclorum: The Heritage of American Public Administration

The cultural values that empower administration were examined in the bicentennial issue of *Public Administration Review*. Two articles deal with the heritage of public administration. The first, by Lyndon K. Caldwell, reviews the colonial period and early constitutions in the colonies, 1620–1800.[3] The second, by Barry D. Karl, discusses the century of administrative practice that followed.[4]

Novus Ordo Seclorum is the motto on the Great Seal of the United States. It means "a new order of the ages" and implies that this order has been established. As Caldwell states, "An American Public Administration has been a process of adapting the theories and practices implicit in this new political order to the radically changing circumstances of American Life."[5] Caldwell believes the values that the "new order" is presumed to have established are, while contradictory in many respects, "the fundamental beliefs that comprise the historical context of American public administration."[6]

What are these values?

1.   Sovereignty is vested exclusively in the entire people.
2.   An essential condition of human liberty is the specification and limitation of the powers of government.
3.   Individuals possess rights that government ought to observe and protect.
4.   The right to select one's political representatives by direct vote is a basic element of self-government.
5.   Democratic government implies popularly elected majorities.
6.   The legislature is the most democratic and representative branch of government but the one least able to fulfill its responsibilities.
7.   Equality is an accepted value.
8.   Desire for power is the greatest danger to a free society; therefore, public power must be divided.
9.   The strength of government lies in the virtue and responsible involvement of its citizens in public affairs.[7]

Administrative practice has been often at odds with the professed values of a free and responsible government. As Caldwell explains, principles in American politics are matched by qualifying or opposing principles; the values expressed are often liberal, but public institutions and administrative procedures reveal a conservative counterbalance.[8] Perhaps this is because the American Revolution was itself a conservative movement, although some of its principles were liberal and some indeed were radical.[9] As Alexis de Tocqueville said, Americans arrived at a state of democracy without having to endure a democratic revolution.[10] This paradox has greatly influenced our public administration heritage.

Instead of enhancing the "entire people," "human liberty," individual "rights," "self-government," and a "free society," the practice of colonial and early constitutional governments reveals the favoring of a narrow and privileged minority. The most prominent group denied public benefits were blacks, who— whether slave or free—in 1790 were a larger percentage of the U.S. population than they were in 1977. Women also had second-class status. These two groups and other minorities who were similarly denied their "natural rights" constituted the majority of people in the U.S. 1776–1800. And yet to recall this fact only makes clearer how the paradox of promising freedom but withholding it in practice is a reasonably accurate picture of the American heritage.

A second example of the liberal-conservative paradox is provided by contrasting the amendments to the U.S. Constitution with the practice of government of the time. The Fourth Amendment (prohibiting unreasonable searches by government) and the Eighth (forbidding cruel and unusual punishments) imply a limitation on the executive, and the Ninth Amendment (limiting the coverage of powers enumerated in the Constitution) makes that explicit. In fact, however, as Caldwell records, "the issue of power was treated realistically by the Philadelphia Convention of 1787; the delegates neither discounted the dangers of power in office nor naively assumed that it could be legislated out of existence.[11]

The paradox of *Novus Ordo Seclorum* is still unresolved. Federalist and democratic ideals of government and administration still compete with each other for ascendancy, neither having been able to command the full confidence of the people. In this balance, indeed, we may discover the essence of the system of administration in the U.S.: power versus control, experts versus laypersons, nation versus state, executive leadership versus legislative supremacy, law versus discretion, direction versus freedom. As Caldwell stated, "Hamilton is our great teacher of the organization and administration of public power; Jefferson, our chief expositor of its control. "[12] Despite unprecedented power exercised by administrators, a deference to popular and limited government remains. This was evident in the 1977 Inaugural Address of Jimmy Carter as the 39th president of the United States, three overriding themes seem clear. First, the Preamble to the Constitution commits the government to "establish justice, insure domestic tranquility, provide for the common defence, promote the general Welfare, and secure the Blessings of Liberty." Second, these ideals, as expressed in the basic policies that guide government, are to be articulated by the people's elected representatives, especially the chief executive. Third, these ideals remain intact. Popular government is alive and well; hence, the quiet return of Gerald Ford, Jimmy Carter, and George Bush to the status of private citizen. *Novus Ordo Seclorum* commits public administration to the quest for a better society for the people as a whole, and it institutionalizes popular "revolution" as a civil process.

ADMINISTRATION: A CENTURY OF PRACTICE

Historian Barry D. Karl has presented a second view of the cultural heritage of public administration. It is both unfamiliar and unflattering.[13] To appreciate his revisionism, we must review the standard version of U.S. administrative history.

The official beginning of the field of public administration dates from Woodrow Wilson's 1887 essay "The Study of Administration" and its call for order out of what was regarded as the shambles of the Reconstruction period.[14] Public administration is said to be rooted in reform, in the early commitment to the merit system and to more efficient forms of local government, and in ideas of scientific management based on the nation's industrial experience. The high point of success came in 1937, when President Franklin Delano Roosevelt followed the suggestions of administrative theorists on ways to restructure the federal government. An interlude followed in a search for empirical foundations, which gave way to an eclecticism that turned to a growing commitment to professionalism: standardized preservice training, adherence to norms generated by practitioners, and the appearance of public administration interest groups and the assertion that customary practices are neutral and therefore should be above criticism.

Against this view of public administration as reformist, indigenously

American, and benign, Karl paints a contrasting picture: "All in all, historians have tended to present the history of public administration in terms which satisfied the practicing ideologies of the field, and those terms are clear: that it was essentially a methodological field posing no threat to the traditional political structure."[15] Karl believes, instead, that the practice of administration shows resistance to reform, and that its origins are not with Wilson in the 1880s but with elitist opposition to Andrew Jackson a half-century earlier. Wilson's essay merely confirmed an administrative theory that had already rejected the democratic model of governance implicit in Jackson's presidency. Neither, in Karl's view, has there been much attention to social reform since. At the turn of the century, when city managers and executive budgets were introduced, administrative theory supported a Victorian elitism that combined an intense concern for the betterment of the community with the protection of special interests. Even in 1937, reform was accomplished by accommodating its detractors. Theodore J. Lowi testifies to this tendency:

American reform movements, committed to democratic compromise, have all tended to institutionalize defeated oppositions in the administrative structures the reforms succeed in creating. The result is often to sustain in a new administrative structure, at a level of acceptably reduced hostility, the old opposition, and give that opposition a lifeline to continuity[16]

Karl does not believe that U.S. public administration is a native product. Its deepest roots, he points out, are British or European. At least since the middle of the 19th century, Americans have venerated the administrative systems of Germany; Max Weber, the German sociologist, still towers over any U.S-born theorist. In fact, the first generation of public administration scholarship reflects an emigré mentality. This imported model, once in place, has never been seriously challenged, and the elitist theory has been fully incorporated into administrative practices.

As to whether professional (the pursuit of generally accepted practices) American public administration is benign, Karl recalls the tendency of presidents under fire for official excesses to invoke the Lincoln version of morality, or the primacy of national security:

In terms of administrative history, the Lincoln presidency is perhaps the one crucial episode most neglected by serious administrative analysis. It is possibly a good bit more embarrassing as a model of the presidency than those presidents who reach for it for support seem to know. No presidency since Lincoln's has managed to reach such levels of unconstitutionality. Lincoln took steps to solidify the war confrontation without calling Congress into session or waiting for its regular date of assembly. He spent money from the Treasury without proper authorization. No presidential encroachment of the rights of citizens has yet touched Lincoln's watermark: the suspension of habeas corpus; and Lincoln's use of military forces to assure his re-election in 1864 makes the hanky-panky of CREEP (Committee to Reelect President Nixon) appear even more childish. . . . History contains many justifications of extra-legal behavior by public officials and the ground is always the same: that their sense of national need required it.[17]

According to Karl, Harry Truman, Lyndon Johnson, and Richard Nixon are only some of the public servants who have acted beyond the bounds of popular government. This professionalism in the name of national security at the top is repeated lower down the bureaucracy in the effort to legitimize administration. Professional administrators seek to avoid the wastefulness of ignorance, wrong guesses, and impulsive imagination, and to routinize behavior to make it more effective. This means the continuing search for "technical advice capable of removing the necessity for judgment."[18] Lowi notes: "The chief defect of professionalism, in all fields, is the tendency of the profession to insist upon its own standard of judgment, its certification and its own forms of punishment and to become increasingly protective of its membership against external criticism."[19]

When this not benign, not fully Americanized professionalism, with its ambivalence about reform, is taken as one piece, what is, for Karl, the central theme of a century of public administration stands out: "The continuing problems of relating effective management to popular democracy."[20] The promised new order of liberty is not yet fully established in practice, which is to say our heritage is a paradox.

For those who yearn most for the fruits of liberty because they are systematically denied to them, and for those who strive for equal opportunity in public employment—especially in positions of influence—Caldwell's and Karl's perspectives show why the promised new order has not been established. Blacks and women have bitterly experienced a democratic ideology ruthlessly administered to deny them freedom. To get the fuller picture of the "unfinished order" and the hazards of administrative coaptation, we must examine the day-to-day practices of management at the lower levels.

Lower-Level Officials: Theory and Practice

It should now be clear (1) that the external environment is dynamic and hence, continuing adjustments are required; (2) that the guiding values are a complex composite of the unresolved tension between popular needs and administrative response; and (3) that MLMs work under inherently elitist executives who are resistant to reform, strongly influenced by British and German models, and motivated by the desire to be "professional." In many respects, administration at the MLM level is an effort to achieve equilibrium among these forces.

To get a better look at empowerment and implementation, we will first examine the origin of organizations, how administrative units must continually use power to exist, and finally how those who are unable to affect power in a major way view it. This further extends the implicit elitism, resistance to reform, and Germanic influence on administrative practice although popular government is still venerated.

How Government Organizations Originate

This is the title of a chapter in *Public Administration* (1962), a textbook by Herbert A. Simon, Donald W. Smithburg, and Victor A. Thompson.[21] The authors suggest that much can be learned about patterns in organizations, particularly their methods of operating, structures, program emphasis, and staffing, by inquiring into their birth and early stages of development.

The original flow of power to an organization has its roots in a perceived problem transformed into a public concern. The pressures that come to bear in the enactment of a law, which gives authority for a new agency, determine (1) where the function will be in government; (2) the organization that will be given the responsibility; and (3) the mix of activities that will be performed.

The influence of a problem on organizational structure is best illustrated by a clientele agency, such as the bureaus of Veterans Affairs or Indian Affairs. The functions most often delegated to a clientele agency are of a service character: They include research and exchange of information, formulation of standards, and regulatory activities designed to benefit the clients themselves. At the state level, the milk marketing boards of public utilities commissions have the dual purpose of serving the agency's clients as well as the general public.

The process of origination sheds much light on what the organization does:

1.   It identifies the interests that prompt public action.
2.   It clarifies the appropriate solutions.
3.   It reveals the range and the depth of the intended response.
4.   It distinguishes between the authority to be exercised by the legislative body as distinct from the executive.

Agencies and Interest Groups

It is well to underline the special relationships between agencies and interest groups. "A striking feature of American politics," points out V.O. Key Jr., "is the extent to which political parties are supplemented by private associations formed to influence public policy."[22] Key indicated that these pressure groups fill the gaps in the political system by manipulating public opinion, persuading legislators, influencing committee hearings, and relating to administrators. Interest groups maintain a continuous relationship with administrative agencies, especially where delegation permits administrators to act as quasi-legislators. The Federal Administrative Procedures Act of 1946 requires that federal agencies allow interested persons to present arguments prior to rule changes.

The exercise of influence is not one-way. Once an agency is set up, its managers seek out interest groups because such groups are likely to have information and expertise that the agency needs. Generally, an informal relationship emerges in which the agency solicits interest-group support and in return responds to the demands of the groups. "The groups and agency directly served," points out Francis E. Rourke, "provide the most natural basis of such political support and it is with these interest groups that agencies ordinarily establish the firmest alliances."[23] Such groups have often been responsible for the establishment of the agency in the first place. Thereafter, the agency and the group are bound together by deep ties that may be economic, political, or social. The agency usually carries on activities that advance the material welfare of members of the groups. The group in turn may often provide political support and private employment opportunities for employees of the agency. It is sometimes said that the private employment-to-public position-to-private employment sequence constitutes a "revolving door practice." Though this practice is frowned on, it continues.

Tactics of Survival

The environmental influences that first shape an organization continue throughout its life. To maintain their external support, agencies will cultivate the favor of those holding power wherever they can be found, and will "sometimes sacrifice elements in the program that attract the most effective political opposition."[24] It is common for agencies to make do with a poor law rather than seek changes that will reopen the uncertainties of the legislative process. They will work with dissident client groups and try to dissipate opposition by including critics on advisory committees, by seeking the formal or informal clearance of appointments and promotions to key positions, and by exchanging information and expertise with influential client groups. With the general public, the agency strives to present a positive picture of its program and carefully trains its personnel who meet the public on a day-to-day basis. Norton Long comments:

The lifeblood of administration is power. Subordinates cannot depend on the formal chain of command to deliver enough political power to permit them to do their jobs. Accordingly, they must supplement the resources available through the hierarchy with those they can muster on their own or accept the consequences in frustration—a course itself not without danger.[25]

Hence, organizations continually must adjust to their political and social environment, attempting to minimize conflict while maximizing support in an effort to establish a sustaining equilibrium.

Unfortunately, at the level of middle management, promoting the tactics of survival commands as much time as the pursuit of the agency's mission. This can result in goal displacement, as when an agency established to regulate a particular industry becomes, through its efforts to survive, in effect a promoter of that industry. In describing how socialist parties originally arise as forces of change but over time become impediments to it, Robert Michels came up with the "iron law of oligarchy." It describes how small group elites in large-scale organizations always seize control, displacing official goals with unofficial ones aimed at perpetualizing their power.[26]

The External Environment: The View From the Powerless

The inner-city environment has changed. Middle-class whites have abandoned the city for the suburbs, leaving behind growing percentages (often large majorities) of lower-class blacks, the elderly, and the poor. These are the new clients of urban bureaucracies, and it should be no surprise to find these bureaucracies under attack in the inner cities of the U.S., where the organization's exchanges with the environment are in the delivery or nondelivery of police protection, welfare payments, public health programs, and training for employment and education. All of these areas are sources of conflict between public agencies and inner-city residents. "It is understandable," write Virginia B. Ermer and John H. Strange, "that frustrations over the general failure of the society should center on that point within the overall structure where it seems as though rules, regulations and red tape convert promising policies and programs into burdensome, discriminatory and even humiliating experiences for citizens."[27] These authors believe that "the devotion of administrators to the middle class ideals of efficiency and economy, professionalism, civil-service reform and centralization has resulted in urban bureaucracies that are conservative, static and far removed from large segments of the urban population."[28]

To substantiate this disturbing view of MLMs in action, Ermer and Strange assembled excerpts from black activists and respected urban commentators, writers such as Stokely Carmichael, Charles V. Hamilton, Claude Brown, Peter Rossi, Eldridge Cleaver, Michael Lipsky, Imamu Amiri Baraka, Paul Jacobs, Bobby Seale, and Sherry Amstein. Two reinforcing conclusions emerge: the hostile response of the powerless to urban bureaucracies and the defensive posture of MLMs.

From the perspective of urban blacks, several themes are evident: (1) they know they are held in low esteem by white officials; (2) they reject the poor quality of service they receive; and (3) displeasure with this poor quality has extended to a distrust of the entire governmental system. When Ermer and Strange expanded their perspective to include the nonblack poor in cities, they found a generalized urban pathology: (1) original goals of serving were effectively displaced by narrow and bureaucratic self-serving goals; (2) program distortions, questionable on grounds of morality or efficiency but consistent with class and race distinctions; and (3) the deliberate use of bureaucracies as a medium for the middle class to maintain its advantaged position vis-à-vis the lower classes.[29] Ermer and Strange conclude: "At issue is the humanization and democratization of bureaucracy—a concern not only of the poor blacks but of all Americans."[30]

Although Ermer and Strange concluded that professionalization and unionization are closely associated with efforts by urban, white, and middle-class bureaucracies to maintain their positions despite the radical transformation of their clienteles,[31] public managers are not wholly insensitive to the needs of their lower-class urban clients in such areas as education, housing, and welfare. In reviewing the literature on this subject, Ermer and Strange noted these themes:

1. The general acknowledgment by lower managers of program failure. Resources are seldom sufficient for the tasks to be performed: "Large caseloads, demeaning clientele investigations and an incredible panoply of formal rules further contribute to the dependent, impersonal nature of the situation."
2. A recognition that racism persists in bureaucracies although it clearly varies with programs and with specific individuals. In addition, there are important occasions on which the public agency supports powerless groups against the attacks by other powerful groups.
3. Bureaucratic's acknowledgment that they do not deliver to black and poor communities the services to which they are entitled. Many managers believe that this cannot be done under existing circumstances.
4. The realization that fiscal and program controls require packaging of service in an unacceptable way.[32]

Alienation

The picture that emerges from this look at the external environment and the flow of power and authority is of MLMs in tension. This view is reiterated by Michael P. Smith when he writes of the "paradoxical factors which contribute to man's (clients and administration) growing sense of bureaucratic alienation within the context of the massive urban public service bureaucracies."[33] The theme is an old one, he reminds us: John Stuart Mill's fear of routinized and hierarchical decision-making, Marx's appeal to the alienated worker, and more contemporary calls for I-thou relationships by Martin Buber. The pervasive feelings of anxiety and estrangement, the confusion of goals, the generalized feelings of powerlessness, and a diminished sense of personal efficacy combine to produce alienation. Smith adds that as the bureaucracy's resources are mobilized, so are its potentially harmful tendencies. Its specialization of functions, while necessary when dealing with complex problems, tends to foster the fragmented or excessively specialized personality. Its hierarchical chain of command and multiple layers of supervision tend to produce dependency on the part of subordinates and unorganized clients. Bureaucracy's spirit of official impersonality and its routinized procedures, although designed to promote fairness in administration, also discourage warm interpersonal relationships.[34]

The condition of the delivery system has produced a popular demand for reform and for new approaches. It has been suggested that public administrators should be trained differently, that more participation in management is needed. Surely changes are needed, but they cannot rest entirely on transactions at the bottom. They must include a different perspective on the whole system of empowerment, which, we have seen, includes a consistent pattern of paradox.

To promote greater responsiveness and accountability to citizens the last three presidents, especially Reagan and Clinton, have attempted to privatize and contract out, decentralize federal administrative structures, and devolve responsibilities from federal to state and local governments. President Clinton continued many of the Reagan initiatives such as massively downsizing government and embracing the government reinvention movement which strongly advocates entrepreneurialism as a means of responding to citizens' demands while reducing costs (see Chapter 3). U.S. state and local governments and countries around the world have attempted to emulate aspects, particularly privatizations, of U.S. reinvention initiatives.

POLITICAL ECONOMY

Political economy represents a third way of looking at the impact of the external environment of public organizations. Ecology produces demands; culture determines the type and quality of response that government will make; and political economy identifies the strategy—that is, how, when, and in what manner these demands will be satisfied. The political economy perspective allows us to view public organizations in terms of the power government officials exercise.

This section is divided into three main areas: (1) the meaning of political economy; (2) a discussion of public organizations and an analogy with the marketplace; and (3) an examination of the central role that MLMs play in the political economy approach.

The Meaning and Setting of Political Economy

Let us divide political economy into two separate parts. The first part, political, refers to the power that public organizations exercise in obtaining citizen's compliance with community objectives. It indicates how power is distributed and who has a legitimate right to exercise it. The people, through their elected representatives, determine what power can be exercised and in what form; it is from this source (legislative authorizations) that administrators draw their guidance.

Politics plays a large role in public management. Legislative authorizations (policy outputs) are reached after consideration of a multitude of demands made on government (its ecology) in the context of conflicting choices (cultural setting). Administrators are attentive to the external political environment, for if they wish to further their own and organizational interest, they must mobilize and maintain support for their agencies.

The second part, economy, refers to the rational management of public resources. Through the power of the state, administrators are charged with the responsibility of collecting taxes, levying user charges, and borrowing in order to educate, construct roads, build dams, and provide health systems to achieve identified public purposes efficiently and effectively. Rational economic analysis of government has become increasingly important. At the national level, the Council of Economic Advisers provides advice to the president on how to efficiently generate revenue and how to best allocate scarce national resources to achieve national objectives. Public organizations employ productivity measures such as cost-benefit analysis to achieve greater economy and efficiency.

Public Organizations and the Market Analogy

Political economy helps us to understand the application of economic reasoning to political decision-making in public bureaucracies, which emphasizes hierarchy and the superior–subordinate relationship while minimizing the role that power plays and ignoring the exchange that takes place. This exchange is not unlike those in the marketplace, where firms are required to (1) attract needed resources; (2) convert these resources into products, services, and ideas; and (3) distribute the outputs to various consumers. Exchange is the central operating instrument that permits producers to provide the highest quantity of products for the maximum profit possible and for consumers to pay the lowest price for the best product.

Fig. 6.1 shows that participants seek utility maximization (the greatest benefit for lowest expenditure). Demands arise from consumers' desires and expectations, and producers respond to satisfy them with goods and services. "It is not from the benevolence of the butcher, the brewer or the baker, that we expect our dinner," wrote Adam Smith in *The Wealth of Nations* (1776), "but from their regard to their own interest." Where the market is functioning optimally, both the private interest and the public welfare are simultaneously achieved or enhanced.

Government may use its right or power to intervene in the market when the satisfactions of consumers or the profit of producers is adversely affected and may impair the general welfare. Intervention may also occur if some segment of the society is inadequately served through the mechanics of the market. By means of legislative acts, government may regulate the private market, acting sometimes as referee (as when the Federal Power Commission sets the guidelines for competition among private producers of natural gas) and other times as direct competitor with private firms (as when it operates liquor stores, provides health care and education, and borrows money in the open market). It can be seen from Fig. 6.1 that the criteria for intervention reflect the desire to maximize voter support.

This exchange in the private economy has its direct counterpart in the public economy. Here, exchange results from the interaction between supply (tax resources available to the legislature for appropriation) and demand (expressed by citizens, clients, and interest groups). The latter attempt to gain the greatest return (utility maximization) for their taxes, while the legislature attempts to levy taxes and appropriate resources so as to best meet expressed demands (voter maximization). These competing forces of supply and demand in the public sector often operate with low visibility, but the intensity may be as great as or greater than that among private firms. Legislators must fiercely compete with the private sector to obtain available tax dollars to meet articulated needs and demands on government. In addition, state and local governments actively compete with each other to gain a bigger share of the federal dollar. Florida and Massachusetts are rivals for the federal money to research solar energy, and the city of Pittsburgh competes with other cities to obtain federal money to set up model housing projects and develop cutting edge high technology firms.

Fig. 6.1. Political Economy

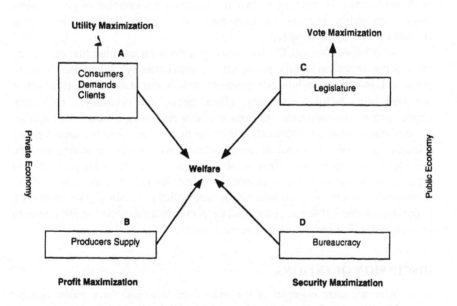

The delivery options that government employs in responding to citizens' needs often directly affect competition. The government may itself operate programs or provide grants and contracts. In attempting to meet health care needs, the government operates public health programs, finances hospitals, underwrites private health delivery systems in many forms, and is one of the major providers of health insurance. Many of these approaches are in direct competition with each other.

Competition also takes place among the bureaus themselves, in the form of protecting or expanding policy space, or sphere of influence. Bureaus must continuously cultivate support from the groups (clients, constituents, and relevant individuals) in their environment to ensure a source of support, especially in struggles to increase budget appropriations. The struggle for bureau expansion simultaneously furthers the interest of individuals in these agencies in helping them to maximize their personal security.

Market controls in the public economy are carried out through appropriation and review processes, through monitoring contracts or subsidies, and through such instruments as independent audits, post-evaluation techniques, and systems of inspections.

Political Economy and MLMs

The political economy approach emphasizes the use of political and economic reasoning in the management of resources. It draws attention to the acts of managers within bureaus. We have examined three motivations for administrative action: security maximization, expansion of policy space, and professionalism. To the degree that the bureaucrat's exercise of power veers away from public purpose to meet personal or professional needs, public accountability may be impaired.

It is hoped that MLMs will employ a decision calculus that will bring security maximization and the public interest into harmony. When one listens to public administrators on how our government is or ought to be run, three terms are most often heard: efficiency, effectiveness, and economy. Efficiency implies getting the maximum use from available resources, effectiveness implies actually doing what was intended, and economy implies using the least amount resources possible. The goal of the calculation is to select the alternative that provides the optimum mix. This involves balancing the drive for personal and organizational survival with a reasonable identification with the goals of the community. Much of the balance of this volume is about the increasing opportunities that MLMs have to exercise power and the need for the power to be balanced with a commitment to accountability.

DISCUSSION QUESTIONS

1.   What are some examples of the major "raw materials" for a public agency? Identify a specific agency in this community, and rank these raw materials as to their importance for day-to-day operations.
2.   What are the major ways that public organizations are given power from the environment?
3.   Illustrate why a combination of constitutional ideals and practices that are less than ideal provides a guide for administrative action.
4.   How do you account for the existence of "standard" and "revisionist" versions of the history of public administration? How does this square with the Caldwell view of the American heritage?
5.   What are some of the major "value" questions of concern to administrators at lower levels?

6.   What is the empowerment out of which the administrative cycle begins?
7.   What do we mean by the political economy of administration?

NOTES

1.   John M. Gaus, *Reflections on Public Administration* (Tuscaloosa: University of Alabama Press, 1947), pp. 8-9. Gaus's "ecology" offers, in a broad sense, collective demands and responses including the attitudes of mind behind the demands.

2.   Don Hellriegel and John W. Slocum Jr., *Management: A Contingency Approach* (Reading, Mass.: Addison-Wesley Publishing, 1974), p. 18.

3.   Lyndon K. Caldwell, "Novus Ordo Seclorum," *Public Administration Review* (September-October 1976):   476–83.   Caldwell has written other articles on administrative history, including "Thomas Jefferson and Public Administration," *Public Administration Review* Vol. 3 (Summer 1943): 240; and Alexander Hamilton: Advocate of Executive Leadership," *Public Administration Review* (Spring 1944):   113–17.

4.   Barry D. Karl, "Public Administration and American History: A Century of Professionalism," *Public Administration Review* (September-October 1976): 489–94.

5.   Caldwell, "Novus Ordo," p. 476.

6.   Ibid., p. 482.

7.   Adapted from ibid., pp. 482–84.

8.   Ibid., p. 485.

9.   Louis Hartz, *The Liberal Tradition in America: An Interpretation of American Political Thought Since the Revolution* (New York: Harcourt, Brace, 1955), pp. 2–4.

10.   Ibid., p. 5.

11.   Leonard D. White, *Introduction to the Study of Public Administration*, 3rd edn. (New York: Macmillan, 1950), p. 14.   White's reference in the quote is to Lyndon K. Caldwell.

12.   Lyndon Caldwell, quoted in Leonard White, *Introduction to Public Administration*, p. 15.

13.   Karl, "Public Administration and American History," pp. 490–94.

14.   Reprinted in *Political Science Quarterly* (December 1941).

15.   Karl, "Public Administration and American History," p. 490.

16.   Theodore J. Lowi, "Machine Politics—Old and New," *The Public Interest* (Fall 1967): 83–92.

17.   Karl, "Public Administration and American History," p. 500.

18.   Ibid.

19.   Ibid., p. 499.

20.   Ibid.

21.   Herbert A. Simon, Donald W. Smithburg, and Victor A. Thompson, *Public Administration* (New York: Alfred A. Knopf, 1962), pp. 25–55.

22.   V. O. Key Jr., *Politics, Parties and Pressure Groups*, 4th edn. (New York: Thomas Y. Cromwell, 1958), p. 76.

23.   Francis E. Rourke, *Bureaucracy, Politics and Public Policy* (Boston: Little, Brown, 1969), pp. 14–15.

24.   Simon, Smithburg, and Thompson, *Public Administration*, p. 389.

25. Norton Long, "Power and Administration," *Pubic Administration Review* (Summer 1949): 758.

26. Robert Michels, *Political Parties* (Glencoe, Ill.: Free Press, 1949), p. 65.

27. Virginia B. Ermer and John H. Strange (eds.) *Blacks and Bureaucracy: Readings in the Problems and Politics of Change* (New York: Thomas Y. Crowel, 1972), p. 2.

28. Ibid.

29. Ibid., pp. 155–223.

30. Ibid., p. 4.

31. Ibid., p. 52.

32. Ibid., pp. 51–125; and Michael P. Smith, "Alienation and Bureaucracy: The Role of Participatory Administration." *Public Administration Review* (November-December 1971): 651.

33. Smith, "Alienation and Bureaucracy," p. 657.

34. Ibid., pp. 659–60.

Part II

Linking Practice and Theory

7

Organization Theory and Management Practice

This chapter presents a broad overview of the major organization theories that have influenced administrative practice. Theorists are divided into two major groups: (1) those who conceive of organizations in formal, closed, or mechanistic terms generally referred to as the formal or classical school; and (2) the organizational humanist, who see public agencies largely in terms of people.

The chapter begins with some discussion of the idea of theory and how it is used in public administration. Next, those theories that stress the power of upper-level administrators and the push for power and productivity are presented. Third, opposing theories of human relations and organization development are assessed to bring out concerns for adjusting organizations to people, both those within organizations and the clients they serve. Finally, a framework for assessing theory as it relates to practice, and practice as it relates to theory, is presented as a guide to channeling organizational power in the direction of greater accountability. It is hoped that this exposure to theory will help the student to understand the consequences of administrative practice.

LEARNING OBJECTIVES

On completing this chapter, the reader should be able to:

- Present the functions served by theory and show how theory permeates public agency practices.
- Distinguish between theories that emphasize power and those that focus on participation.
- Separate practices following from the theory serving upper-level administrators from those guiding middle- and lower-level managers.
- Account for the crisis in contemporary administrative theory.
- Critically evaluate the difference between the "new public administration" and "scientific management".

- Learn how TQM and re-engineering operate to enhance organizational humanism in achieving accountability.
- Understand the meaning and uses of praxis and cultural hermeneutics in organization theory.
- Indicate how organization theories facilitate or impeded the achievement of accountability.

Organization theory provides an interpretive framework that helps us to conceptualize the structure, work, and function of public agencies. Over the past half-century, various theories have been offered to explain why agencies operate the way they do. The theory that has most guided administrative practices is a rational and mechanistic approach described as bureaucratic theory. The essence of this theory is that organizations should pursue economy and efficiency through a division of labor, the avoidance of duplication, the grouping of tasks by function, and, above all, a hierarchical structure. This orthodoxy reflects a top-down view of power and stresses the strategic role of top administrators.

While bureaucratic orthodoxy rests heavily on the thought of Max Weber, it first appeared in Woodrow Wilson's classic essay, "The Study of Administration," in 1887. In the 1920s it reappeared as "principles of administration" in the first public administration textbooks. During the 1940s these "principles" were attacked for being only "proverbs" that could not bear up under close analysis.[1] They re-emerge, however, in the early 1950s, supported by a scientific rationality. And while this new foundation of bureaucratic theory in empirical study was eroded somewhat in the 1960s, it remains influential today, largely because it best describes the practice of public administration and the commitment to professionalism.

In the last 25 or 30 years, however, public administration theory has been in a state of crisis. One reason for this is the failure of the field to develop any coherent and comprehensive set of propositions to explain and predict organizational behavior. In the absence of its own theory, public administration has drawn ideas from many sources, particularly from newer ideas in social psychology, to supplement traditional themes taken from economics and engineering. This lack of theory affects administrative practices, which, unguided by any theory, have become eclectic, fragmented, and expedient, providing us with little purposeful guide in the administration of public policies. There has been as well a growing national outcry that government is unresponsive to human needs. Finally in the 1970s, a younger group of organization theorists began asserting that the traditional preoccupation with economy (now rendered as productivity) and efficiency (now including effectiveness) should be balanced by concerns for equity and social justice. Some contemporary writers have even sought to base their organization theory on the needs and desires of the clients rather than on the administrators and the organizations themselves. This trend calls for a re-evaluation of traditional organization theory in the direction of accountability.

THE IMPORTANCE OF THEORY

To theorize is to make abstractions of reality and to reflect on experience. The word "theory" is derived from the Greek word *theoros*, which referred to beholding an event and then reflecting on its meaning. *Theoros* was the practice of sending a representative from the Greek city-state to behold holy celebrations conducted in honor of the gods. The observer had to abandon personal views in order to understand what the gods had in mind. The observer was to grasp the ultimate rational principles and thus know the nature of reality. Theory in modern times has maintained much of this concern with grasping the meaning of events. We can say that theory is:

- a way of saying something meaningful about experience
- an ordering of otherwise disjointed events
- a search for the essential meaning of occurrences
- a way to fill in gaps in what is known
- the highlighting of what is crucial though not self-evident
- the foundation on which predictions can be made
- the basis for further theorizing.

In these many ways, theory is a guide to action and an aid in the solution of problems.

In public organizations, theory should inform practice, and administrative practices should generate theory. Unfortunately, in public administration there has been only limited theoretical research in the sense of producing if-then statements (i.e., the experimental testing of hypotheses). Instead, most of what is regarded as theory is really descriptions of normative statements, prescriptions of what ought to be. Neither have the practices of administration been probed for the implicit theory they utilize. As we point out throughout this volume, most of the crucial decision-making, problem-solving, and converting of ideas to practice occurs in the middle levels of management, but theory addressing linkages between top-level policymaking and implementation by operators is almost nonexistent.

A second weakness in public administration theory is the absence of a metatheory, a theory about theories. We have not thought much about these components of a theory: (1) the relationship between hypothesis testing and theory-making; (2) the impact of intellectual disciplines and research methods on findings; (3) the bias associated with the interests of the theorists and the research enterprises of which they are a part; and (4) the interdependency of theory and action. Metatheory is theory about unarticulated assumptions and interests as a way to improve our ability to formulate more useful theory:

1.   *Theory genesis.* Theory develops out of specific needs and practices relevant to a
       particular time and place. Political, economic, and cultural factors influence the
       hypotheses that are selected for testing. Furthermore, theories not only grow out
       of social reality, they also outlive the needs that produce them.

2.   *Tools for theory building.* Theories differ in what they emphasize, depending on the academic discipline involved.   Political scientists tend to concentrate on power relationships, while anthropologists note patterns of behavior and cultural values.   Engineers tend to see systems and structures, while economists are preoccupied with utility and costs. Some disciplines, like behavioral psychology, utilize laboratory experiments, while others, like sociology, collect data through questionnaires.   In each case, the technique employed largely determines the information that can be collected.

3.   *The research enterprise.* Theorists are also people.   They have needs and aspirations, and they are involved in organizations that finance, publish, or utilize their results. They are affected in what they are able to study and report by these social relations.   External pressures intrude on the research.   Large research organizations (e.g., the Chamber of Commerce or the American Medical Association) are sensitive to the theoretical positions their researchers adopt.

4.   *The interest bias.*   Theory derived through the natural sciences generates information designed to permit predictions; social science disciplines measure group feelings and seek to facilitate intergroup understanding; and those theories that arise from the humanities raise ethical questions and attempt to stimulate action to better the human conditions.

5.   *Theory and application.* Most critical in public affairs is the way that theory finally gets used. Public organizations are studied so that they may be changed. This gives high priority to the study of the change process itself.

Theory is of critical importance in public affairs because the administrative process is the link between ideas and implementation.   If there are to be better results for the people government seeks to serve, public administrators will have to have a theory that utilizes and balances the insights of all of the academic disciplines.

CONVENTIONAL MECHANISTIC THEORY

This approach refers to a school of thought that developed over several centuries and reached its high point in the 1930s. It is best exemplified in the writings of Max Weber on bureaucracy[2]; Luther Gulick's essay, "Notes on the Theory of Organization"[3]; and James D. Mooney and Alan C. Reiley's *Principles of Organization.*[4] Other exponents of this school include Henri Fayol and Woodrow Wilson. These theorists view organization theory as problem-centered and aimed essentially at the development of rational thinking that will produce a   maximum of human satisfaction. The common thread that runs through the writing of these theorists is a concern with economy, efficiency, and executive control. The organization is an indispensable means to achieve four objectives that may be referred to as the cornerstones of this theory: division of labor, hierarchy of authority, structure (a logical arrangement of positions in an organization), and span of control.

In the formal sense, structure (organization) permits individuals to relate to each other in a regularized and predictable manner. It identifies superior–subordinate relationships, indicating authority exercised, who (how many) does what, and who reports to whom. It serves as a network of coordinating instruments connecting and identifying positions throughout the organization from the highest level (the head of the agency) to the lowest official in the organization providing direction to the hierarchy.

Of the four cornerstones, division of labor ranks as the most important. The other three are directly dependent on it. The hierarchy of authority is the vertical network through which legitimate compliance is obtained. The idea of a span of control assumes that only a specified number of subordinates can be effectively supervised by a superior. Thus, it determines how the organization is shaped. A short span will produce a tall structure (more bosses or supervisors would be needed), while a wide span will give a flat structure (fewer bosses or supervisors will be needed).

In this chapter's discussion of theories, we will analyze the writers in terms of (1) their concept of the nature of man; (2) their view of power; (3) their concept of leadership (administrators) and followers (MLMs); and (4) their concern for accountability.

MAX WEBER

Much of the thinking of modern sociology can be traced to Max Weber (1864–1920). Though he is best known for his contribution to sociology, Weber was also a pioneer in administrative thought. He wrote in the fields of religion, history, economics, and sociology and concentrated much of his efforts in the study of bureaucracy. Weber saw bureaucracy as the instrument which socialized people to adopt more rational modes of behavior. He saw history as the transition from tradition domination to the new order where people embraced the domination of rational principles and rational laws.

Weber attempted to examine bureaucracy (all large-scale organization) to determine the rational relationship between bureaucratic structures and their goals. He concluded that there were three types of power exercised in organizations, paralleling each distinct type of social order:

1. *Traditional.* People accept commands as justified because they conform to the folkways and pattern of how things have always been done.
2. *Charismatic.* People accept a superior's commands as justified because of the force of his or her personality.
3. *Rational-legal.* People accept the superior's commands as justified because they view the abstract rules on which they are based as efficient and legitimate.

The unfolding of history brought an end to tradition and charisma, replacing them with bureaucracy. According to Weber, people are more disposed to comply when they view power as legitimate. At this point, it becomes authority. Weber recommends that organizational relationships be structured on the rational-legal basis because this is the only form of organization that has a systematic division of labor, specialization, and stability and is free from political and other irrelevant personal relationships.

Though Weber viewed the rational bureaucracy as a most desirable type of organization, he was concerned that it would not survive unless means were devised to preserve it. Thus, his rational-legal ideal bureaucracy is designed to maintain its autonomy by providing safeguards against internal and external pressures. Weber requires that rational bureaucratic structure contain the following attributes or elements:

1. Official duties and jurisdictional areas are clearly defined by law or administrative regulations.
2. Rational division of labor determines the distribution of functions and activities in the organization.
3. The principle of hierarchy provides the criteria for the exercise of authority. This requires that each lower office be under the control and supervision of a higher one.
4. Positions are awarded on the basis of professional qualification and competence obtained through expert training. Recruitment and selection are based on examination and/or educational certification.
5. Administrative actions are based on written documents known as "files," which are maintained in their original form.
6. Separation of ownership of the means of production and administration is enforced. That is, staff members are not expected to own any of the property required to carry out the functions and duties of the organization.[5]

Weber's system is based on a highly differentiated basis in which compensation and privileges are based on one's position in the hierarchy. Each office constitutes a career or vocation to which an individual is committed for a long period. Advancement within the hierarchy of the personnel system is based on seniority or examination.[6]

In Weber's view, the rational-legal bureaucracy is the best means to achieve maximum efficiency in the undertaking of any large-scale activity. Efficiency in organizations can only be ensured if rational standards exemplified by detachment, impersonality, and strict impartiality are observed. Personnel are expected to execute their duties with neither affection nor enthusiasm.[7]

Two Models of Bureaucracy: Machine Bureaucracy

Standardization is the key concept that characterizes all machine bureaucracies such as the tax collection offices, health regulating offices, fire protection, and standardization of work processes, which are used as the chief means to obtain coordination and control.

The machine bureaucracy's functions and tasks are routinized based on formal rules and regulations. Tasks are grouped according to functional departments, centralized authority, chain of command and structure that clearly defines line functions (carrying out the mission for which the organization is created to implement) and staff functions (assist the line indirectly in carrying out the mission of the organization). Rules and regulations are pervasive throughout the organizational structure.

In the machine bureaucracy, related specialties such as research and development, personnel, and finance are grouped together under functional officials. Each official controls his or her functional specialty and in turn is accountable to the department or headquarters which provides overall coordination.

Strengths of the machine bureaucracy include the following:

1. They carry out standardized activities in a very efficient manner.
2. They provide for economies of scale, minimizing personnel and equipment duplication.
3. They provide opportunities for people with similar expertise to communicate with each other, creating more satisfied employees.
4. They reduce cost by allowing managers with less skill and talent to be employed in the middle and lower levels of the organization.
5. They reduce the need for management to exercise discretion due to standardization and centralized decision-making, minimizing the need for experienced decision-makers.

Weaknesses in the machine bureaucracy include the following:

1. They encourage specializations, leading to narrow perspectives, creating conflicts among subunits.
2. They foster preoccupation with conformance to rules, leading to rigidity.
3. They promote efficiency only if decisions are highly routinized based on familiar, programmed decision rules.

The machine bureaucracy should be used by relatively large organizations with stable environments and technology that can be readily standardized. This would include organizations such as the U.S. Postal Service, in which employees can be specifically assigned to sort letters, packages, delivering mail and collecting mail from mail boxes. Efficiency is virtually ensured as long as the technology is routine and the environment remains stable. Machine bureaucracy such as the post office does not effectively adapt to change.

Professional Bureaucracy

This type of bureaucracy allows highly trained experts to be hired to operate as an efficient group or core. Professional bureaucracy combines standardization and professionalization. Because of the knowledge explosion and the complex job requirements, undergraduate and graduate degrees are necessary to enable professionals to produce the goods and services needed. Organizations found in this category include universities, social welfare agencies, museums, libraries, hospitals, and school districts.

The power in the professional bureaucracy resides with the operating core because of the critical skills that the organization requires. The professionals have a very high degree of autonomy through the operation of the decentralized style. This model allows professionals to exercise maximum discretion to apply their expertise. Typically, there is a support staff whose activities are aimed at assisting the operating core professionals.

One strength of the professional bureaucracy is that because of their expertise, these professionals can perform highly specialized tasks with efficiency, paralleling that of the machine bureaucracy. While management would like to apply the machine model, the need for expertise and professional skills demands autonomy to perform work effectively, forcing management to delegate significant power to professionals.

A weakness of the professional bureaucracy is the same as in the machine bureaucracy. Conflicts among subunits are always a threat. Subunits tend to have a narrow focus in pursuing their objectives over those of the organization. Like the machine bureaucracy, the professional bureaucracy is addicted to short-run conformity. Because of professional standards and codes of ethical practices that have been internalized in professional bureaucrats' training, some find it difficult to adjust to rigid standards in carrying out their duties.

The professional bureaucracy could typically work well in large and complex stable environments where there is routine technology. These complex and stable environments need the special skills that are learned only in formal education and extended training.

Nature of Workers

Weber believed that strict adherence to his ideal bureaucracy would achieve precision, speed, unambiguity, knowledge of the files, continuity, discretion, unity, strict subordination, reduction of friction and material costs. Organization is seen more as a machine without passion or emotion, operating according to calculable rules and without regard for persons. Efficient activities can take place only in the formal setting; deviations (informal activities) from the rational-legal model would be viewed as idiosyncratic. Recent theorists have disagreed, however. Chester Bernard believes that informal relations may be indeed aid the survival of both the individual and the organization.[8] Similarly, Peter Blau found in his 1955 study that informal relations can have very positive outcomes for both the individual and the productivity of the agency.[9] Weber views people more as a means than as ends. The rational-legal bureaucratic system is designed to eliminate or severely minimize the exercise of discretion. To permit discretion would inevitably lead to dysfunctional activities and reduce the organization's efficiency, its ultimate objective. Weber's regimented system is based on a pessimistic and distrustful view of humans. In the ideal bureaucracy, structure and conformity are given total primacy over the thinking human.

View of Power

In Weber's rational-legal system, legitimate power is preferable to traditional and charismatic power because it permits greater congruence with abstract rules that people view as being more legitimate. Once people view power as legitimate, it becomes authority (institutionalized power). Power in the organizational context becomes synonymous with what is legally sanctioned. Because only those at the apex of the organization have legitimate authority, power is exercised only at one point in the organization. Because bureaucratic structures have a tendency to endure and survive, especially in the public sector, bureaucracy is an instrument of power for those who control it.

Leaders and Followers

In Weber's ideal bureaucratic system, superiors are assumed to be the most competent and have the right to give orders to their subordinates (MLMs). Sitting at the apex of the organization, the administrator can exert leadership on subordinates at every level and position throughout the entire organization by rigid adherence to the chain of command.

Followers (MLMs) are merely cogs in a wheel. Their decisions are determined more by impersonal procedural rules than by an analytical situational and problem-solving approach. Because there is a rule to meet every situation, every problem has a ready-made solution based on available criteria and information supplied by the bureaucratic system. Weber's rational-legal bureaucracy may be likened to perfect competition in the capitalist marketplace. No one seller or buyer can affect the price given for services or for goods produced. MLMs are part of an inexorable machine operating under impersonal rules. All participants are affected by it, but none can influence it.

Concern for Accountability

The rational-legal bureaucratic approach seeks to realize economy and efficiency (as maximum productivity) in the use of organizational resources. The assumption is made that society is better off whenever productivity is maximized. A number of concerns arise with respect to this assumption: (1) We do not know who is receiving the services or goods that are being produced; (2) we have no idea if the products or services being produced are the ones that are needed; (3) we are given no criteria for comparing the planned objectives with actual accomplishments (effectiveness); and (4) we are also given to assume that productivity in the use of human resources is maximized where strict rules are employed in the accomplishment or organizational tasks and activities.

If all of these concerns could be resolved in favor of Weber, his system would indeed achieve a high degree of accountability (responsiveness to the recipients of the goods and services). But Weber's view that a comprehensive set of rules can alone promote the most efficient accomplishment of objectives cannot be supported, especially in a rapidly changing social and technological environment. To attempt to make rules to anticipate even a minor number of possible exceptions will submerge us in a sea of red tape.

Weber's belief that total objectivity will prevail in the hierarchy fails to recognize that the hierarchy itself may be a barrier to efficiency and productivity. Subordinates may manipulate the information they exchange with superiors. They may also withhold or manage the information so as to reflect positively on themselves and ensure their continued advancement in the hierarchy.

In summary, the concern for productivity is at least an effort to minimize the use of resources. It is accountability in the very narrow sense. However, Weber fails to recognize responsiveness and effectiveness. Additionally, his assumptions about maximum efficiency through the rigid enforcement of rules are simplistic.

FREDERICK TAYLOR AND SCIENTIFIC MANAGEMENT

Frederick W. Taylor's scientific approach to management contrasts sharply with the seat-of-the-pants practices that help to build many large U.S. corporations. Taylor (1856–1915) moved the "hunch approach," the experimentation, and the trial and error approach to a systematized and standardized method. The following characterized Taylor's approach:

- management given the exclusive prerogative overall aspects of the work place
- selection of best implements and working conditions
- enforced cooperation
- provision of teachers to train each person in new, simpler ways.[10]

In Taylor's view, workers were not productive because they did not know the best way to carry out tasks. Thus, this critical function of producing more could not be left to them. Staff members steeped in scientific management were best suited to plan ahead to get the work economically done by effective division of labor.[11]

To achieve the desired cooperation, control, and great productivity increases, Taylor introduced economic incentives by way of piecework. Once standards have been set, the worker could increase his or her pay by exceeding the predetermined scientific standard. Thus, the drive for greater pay could become a powerful motivation for the workers to cooperate to produce more, Taylor believed.

Taylor was a zealot in his pursuit of efficiency. In his view, management's lack of commitment, ignorance, laziness, and group pressure were critical factors that produced generalized inefficiency, precluding managers from finding that one best way to get tasks done.

To find the optimum method to achieve efficiency, a complete understanding of every task, movement, and the timing of each act was absolutely essential: "The development of a science . . . involves the establishment of many rules, laws and formulas which replaces judgments of the individual workman and which can be effectively used only after having been systematically recorded. . . . [E]very single act of every worker could be reduced to a science."[12]

Known as the father of scientific management, Taylor, a mechanical engineer, was a production specialist, business executive, and consultant. His approach to management is still widely practiced today in production-oriented public organizations and in business. Even today, people are still discovering many of the ideas and suggestions that he put forth more than a half-century ago. Taylor was one of the major forces behind the economy and efficiency movements in public administration. He applied the scientific method to find solutions to problems in the factory, replacing trial-and error approaches then in existence. Among Taylor's many contributions, three stand out: (1) He applied the analytical and scientific approach to improving production methods; (2) he popularized the view that management could be systematically organized as a body of knowledge that could be taught and learned; (3) he introduced the concept of functional supervision (which was resisted). [13] Taylor thought that if a worker performed four or five jobs, he or she should report to the particular supervisor who was in the best position to give him or her guidance. This meant in effect that the worker would have a number of bosses. Although the idea was tried in a number of places, it was quickly abandoned as impractical due in part to criticism about its violating the principle of one boss or unity of command.

Taylor isolated three main underlying principles of scientific management, all of which required a mental revolution on the part of management and worker: (1) the development of an approved science; (2) the scientific education and development of workers and managers; and (3) intimate, friendly cooperation between management and workers. He felt scientific management would be impossible unless these three principles were accepted.

Taylor believed, as noted above, there was one best way to perform any activity and that the secret to finding this method lay in job analysis and time and motion studies. To this end, he suggested five methods: (1) Study carefully the workers' body movements to discover the one best method for performing an activity in the shortest time possible; (2) standardize tools, based on the specific requirements of a given job or activity; (3) select and train each worker for the job for which he or she is best suited; (4) abandon the principle of unity of command and adopt functional supervision, as noted above; (5) pay workers according to their individual output.

Taylor's Pursuit of a Revolution

Taylor truly believed that the triumph of his method would eliminate or minimize management's abuse of labor and bring harmony between labor and management instead of the bloody conflicts and the potential class struggle that was ever-present during his time. He believed that the achievement of his scientific management would "create a mental revolution and a revolution of the spirit."[14] The realization of these pursuits would inevitably lead to brotherhood and world peace.

In Taylor's time, the U.S. had to compete with countries such as Germany and Britain that had a well-established artisan class and highly developed system of apprenticeship. These artisans were capable of producing products with uniformly high quality. The U.S. had few well-trained artisans. Thus, the products of U.S. factories were not comparable with their competitors. While goods that Taylor's scientific methods produced could not match the quality of U.S. competitors, U.S. producers were able to produce goods in far greater quantity, permitting the goods to be less expensive. This allowed the U.S. to gain, over time, a significant comparative advantage.

Despite the economic success of Taylor's scientific method, the institutionalization of his method has impeded the development of organization theory. Taylor's piecework, excessive specialization, great reliance on money incentives, strict adherence to managerial prerogative, and hierarchical chain of command retarded the vertical and lateral communication flow across different departments of the organization. They also impeded the natural development of teamwork and project management.

Nature of Workers

In Taylor's view, humans are rational economic beings; thus, the best way to motivate them is through economic incentives. He believed that, given time and the appropriate research, virtually all functions could be routinized and performed by people with the accuracy of a machine. The objective is to find that one way. In Taylor's view, people can be manipulated by pay incentives and cooperative relationships into greater productivity. Humans are organic automatons that can be programmed to achieve optimum productivity, he believed. Best results can be achieved by fitting people to machines.

View of Power

According to Taylor, power flows in only one direction—from the top down through the hierarchy. Taylor felt that management should seek cooperation; but when it is not forthcoming, it should apply its power to obtain it: "It is only through enforced standardization of methods and enforced cooperation, that this faster work can be assured. And the duty of enforcing the adaptation of standards is management's alone." [15] Taylor believed that neither unions (collective bargaining) nor negotiations must be allowed to determine working conditions or working hours. These decisions were to be the prerogative of management.

Leaders and Followers

For Taylor, as well as for Weber, the people at the apex of the organization make the important decisions. But unlike Weber, Taylor spoke of leadership role in a complementary sense. The generalist managers make decisions to affect policy in the organization as a whole, but specialists provide the necessary technical information required to make the best decisions. Thus, the vast majority of the specialized activities performed in an organization are carried out by MLMs within the context of prescribed policy. Additionally, Taylor's emphasis on close supervision requires the supervisor to play a large role in achieving the organization's goal of efficiency and productivity.

Concern for Accountability

Like Weber, Taylor adopted a narrow view of accountability; it is achieving efficiency. Efficiency became virtually an end in itself. Necessary questions, such as whether the right product or service is being produced at the right time, place, and in the quantity and quality desired, were not asked.

THE OTHER FORCE OF SCIENTIFIC MANAGEMENT: CLARENCE BERTRAND THOMPSON

Clarence Bertrand Thompson (1882-1969) served as an apprentice of Frederick W. Taylor from 1911 until Taylor's death in 1915. During this period it was Thompson who more than any of Taylor's disciples most forcefully articulated the ideas and concepts that have come to be known as scientific management. Thompson's work transcended Taylor's fixation on production with his lack of emphasis on distribution, worker welfare and societal betterment.

Despite the fact that Thompson's *Scientific Management* (1914)[16] and his *Theory and Practice of Scientific Management* (1917)[17] are virtually unknown in management science, they contain the core of what was to become organizational behavior, and more recently, simulation of computerized human thinking that has been popularized by Herbert Simon. Peter Drucker has put Taylor in a lofty position. Drucker asserts that Taylor, not Karl Marx, deserves to be in the trinity with Charles Darwin and Sigmund Freud as the most important forces that shaped the thought and practice of the modern world. Thompson's contribution significantly helped to make scientific management what it has become; but, he has been overshadowed and virtually forgotten.[18] Yet Thompson's ideas have been influential in undergirding modern industrial democracy.

Thompson's parents lived in Boston from the 1860s to 1870s, moving to Colorado during the early 1880s where Clarence Thompson was born in 1882. Thompson traces his family ancestry to Jerome Bonaparte, Napoleon's younger brother, and to his offspring of a Virginia planter, Indian and black slave.

In 1900 at the age of 18, Thompson received his LLB degree from the University of Southern California. In 1908 he completed his AB degree from Harvard. During his senior year he published his first book, *The Church and the Wage Earners,* in which he called upon the religious community to support the economic and social aspirations of working people.[19]   Thompson saw wage earners as the central actors in the emerging industrialization of American society and argued that churches should support more equal distribution of increasing profits in order to aid in bringing together owners and directors of the business on one hand and wage earners on the other. This achievement would promote greater cooperation in the workplace and enhanced parity of the industrial rewards, allowing business to act as a major force in enhancing society. This would enable the churches to gain relevance for working people and ease the threat of what looked to him, at the time, as an impending class warfare.

Harvard School of Business published its first book length on scientific management in 1914. It was Thompson's *Scientific Management,* a collection of significant scientific articles describing the Taylor system of management, consisting of a series of articles that appeared in professional journals in 1913. Taylor was most impressed by one of the collections that Thompson wrote. Of this collection Taylor wrote: "Your article on the literature of scientific management . . . is the most thorough of its kind yet published."[20]

Another of Thompson's outstanding contributions on scientific management was also published in 1914, almost simultaneously with his Harvard Business School *Scientific Management.* Thompson wrote an article in the British publication *The Sociological Review*[21] in response to the opposing views by well known British industrialists, sociologists and economists of Taylor's *Principles of Scientific Management* (1911).[22]   The arguments the British opponents made against scientific management have come to be standard textbook negative views about Taylor's "one best way". Among the criticisms levied against scientific management five stand out:

- it is a driving system
- its emphasis on specialization creates worker monotony
- it tends to be a debilitating force on workers' initiative, skill, and judgment
- it does not promote equitable distribution of wealth
- its operation is incompatible with organized labor.

When Taylor was invited to respond to these criticisms, he deferred the reply to Thompson whom he felt was more than equal to the task of expounding and clarifying the concerns that were raised. Thompson dismissed the criticisms. He noted that the British commentators' views of scientific management were unsupported by the facts. In Thompson's view, "results in scientific management are attained not by doing the same thing faster, but by doing a different thing to achieve the same end."[23]   The criticisms relating to monotony creating fatigue can be easily remedied by regulating the hours of work and rest. With respect to specialization, far from promoting monotony, it actually enhances interest. Typically specialized operations are complicated requiring more rather than less interest on the part of the worker. At the heart of scientific management was the aim to achieve high wages and shorter working hours which is the best antidote to monotony, as it provided greater opportunity for leisure and the cultivation of other interests.[24]

Perhaps the most definitive work ever published on scientific management was Thompson's *The Theory and Practice of Scientific Management* (1917).[25] While many of the ideas contained in this volume were discussed in Thompson's 1914 *Scientific Management,* he felt that he had amassed sufficient practical experience in applying the Taylor principles that allowed him to make useful and reliable generalizations. In this volume Thompson explicitly adopts a praxiological approach in which theory is derived and validated from actual practice. Derived theory is then tested as part of an ongoing process that allows the theory to move towards becoming fundamental laws. This theorizing, testing, and validating approach sets Thompson apart from other management theorists of the time. He viewed the process of validating theory through rigorous testing as an inevitable and continuing process that leads ultimately to the improvement of the human condition.

By 1925 Thompson had become world renowned for his expertise and scholarship of scientific management methods. He had introduced the Taylor Method in France, Germany, Italy and translated major management works into French. He spent a year in the Philippines where he successfully applied the Taylor Method to 7000 acres of the Calami Sugar Cane Plantation and Processing Plant. On invitation from the British Army, he attempted to organize a business school in Shanghai, China, based on the Harvard Model. Thompson advised the allied powers on how to greatly increase the production of materials required for World War I. He was employed by the French Weapons' Ministry to improve the management of the shell loading facilities and to instruct technical officers to the avant garde methods of scientific management. One of the French officers and an apprentice wrote:

The arrival of Thompson caused quite a stir—more so because over and above his technical knowledge he had acquired a culture and an intellectual curiosity that were both uncommonly deep and diversified."[26]

CONTRASTING TAYLOR WITH THOMPSON

Thompson was interested not only in the technical achievements of scientific management but also in bringing management and labor together while Taylor pursued a narrow focus, promoting efficiency, productivity and profits. In Thompson's view these objectives were important but they were insufficient to produce the best outcome for all concerned. He believed that greater attention had to be given to the distributive component of the efficiency equation if distributive justice and social equity is to be realized.

For Taylor efficiency and profit provided a pie that is large enough for all participants to obtain a reasonable share of the productive system. Labor's share was automatically determined by the value that management gave to labor's inputs. To Thompson the value of labor's inputs was not clearly self evident as Taylor claimed. According to Thompson, a fair day's pay for labor could not be easily determined. It was something that needed greater reflection and joint consideration between management and labor if the best approximation of the true value of labor inputs into the production equation is to be fairly rewarded.

Thompson was a renaissance man. Unable to practice law after completing his LLB degree, Thompson became a unitarian minister. The totality of Thompson's experience as a world traveler, consultant, lecturer and scholar, embracing chemistry, biology, law, sociology, philosophy, divinity, accounting, economics, metallurgy and an accomplished reader in literature, allowing him to develop a cosmopolitan world view that sharply contrasts with that of his mentor, Taylor. This is evident in the writing and research of the two scientific management proponents. While Taylor developed the basic paradigm that revolutionized the way activities were done in the work place, his writing and research were confined to the area of scientific management techniques. Taylor's preoccupation with increasing the organization's efficiency and productivity allowed him to totally endorse top management's prerogative in decision-making. This perspective shows his unquestioned embrace of the mechanistic model of organization.

Thompson's multi-disciplinary training and humanistic orientation allowed him to develop an outlook that view decisions as emerging from an interplay between management and workers. It is this interplay that gives meaning and validity to the decision making process and the resulting decision outcomes. The process involves a bottom-up approach in which practice modifies theory and vice versa, paralleling the modern organization concept of praxis, discussed later in this chapter.

In Thompson's view, workers are pivotal to an organization's success. It is thus important for management to realize that some employees work with their hands while others do so with their heads (the knowledge worker). The success of the process depends on the context and linkage, similar to what today is called organizational learning.

To be most effective Thompson stresses that the relationship between management and workers be characterized by a balanced interplay, very suggestive of total quality management and reengineering. His call that we study and understand the context of the workplace and the decision making environment predates Herbert Simon's call for the use of behavioral methods in studying organizations. To Thompson, effective scientific management had to continually improve the worker, his tools and must seek to make the production process a truly collaborative effort between management and workers. This is essential if quality products are to be produced.

At the Harvard Business School, Thompson sought to incorporate his powerful idea of humanism that was so pervasive both in his writing and consulting practice. He believed that his model of Scientific Management was a powerful instrument capable of achieving efficiency and harmony between workers and managers. This was a system in which profits should be used to foster distributive justice and social equity.

Unlike Taylor who confined his practice and consulting to private organizations, Thompson worked extensively in both the private and public sectors. From his visible job as Secretary of Boston's Chamber of Industrial Relations in 1909, Thompson consulted with numerous private organizations and with many prominent public sector officials. For his assistance to the French government he was given their highest medal of valor. Finally, though Thompson was Taylor's most powerful disciple, as Taylor duly acknowledged, Thompson's accomplished scholarly achievement and cosmopolitan world view allowed him to transcend Taylor's narrow technical focus.

Nature of Man

Like Taylor, Thompson saw people as rational, reflecting his life long commitment to teaching and consulting. He also has a higher regard for those who applied themselves to community uplift rather than profit making, reflecting his ethical orientation. In later life, however, Thompson wondered about some correctable basic flaws in the genetic make up of people which is reflected in his post World War II work in cancer research.

View of Power

Unlike classical theorists, Thompson was not upper management oriented. Power was more fluid, arising out of productive interrelationships between management and workers. Thompson's persisting progressivism led him to see the use of power as empowering others.

Leaders and Followers

Leadership goes to those who are creative, committed and skilled, typically producing the highest quality product at the least cost.

Accountability

Increasing productivity, Thompson believed, generated additional resources and freed up workers to devote time to personal and community development. Scientific management was to be held to account not only for its use of resources but also for distributive justice.

LUTHER GULICK AND LYNDALL URWICK:
THE PRINCIPLES AND PROVERBS

Gulick (1891–1993) and Urwick (1892–1983) are synthesizers who fill in many of the details left unarticulated by Weber, and they provide a more polished theoretical framework to accommodate Taylor's views. Where Weber stresses the ideal form of bureaucracy and Taylor stresses scientific techniques of management and work, Gulick and Urwick formulate principles of formal organizations. From these efforts came the seven principles (with the acronym POSDCORB) that have had enduring influence in public management.[27]

POSDCORB is an attempt to define the principal responsibilities of an executive:

1. *Planning* involves working out broad outlines, indicating the things that need to be done and the methods necessary for achieving them.
2. *Organizing* concerns the establishment of a formal structure of authority in which work subdivisions are organized, defined, and coordinated for the defined objective.
3. *Staffing* includes the personnel function of recruiting and training the staff and maintaining favorable work conditions.
4. *Directing* combines the activities of the enterprise and decision-making based on specific orders and instructions.
5. *Coordinating* aims at relating and integrating the various parts of the organization.
6. *Reporting* requires keeping the executive and those to whom he or she is accountable (including subordinates) informed of enterprise activities through records, research, and inspection.
7. *Budgeting* requires fiscal planning, accounting, and capital.[28]

Gulick and Urwick's principles are concerned primarily with the structure of formal organization and the need for organizational division of labor. This division provides the means whereby functions can be broken down into more specialized activities, permitting workers to become more skilled in executing their jobs.

In Gulick's view, division of labor should be such that homogeneity (the grouping of similar functions) can be achieved. According to Gulick, "the normal method of interdepartmental co-ordination is hierarchical in operation."[29] It can be facilitated if work is grouped and identified according to one or more of the following determinants:

- *Major purpose*—used to describe such activities as maintaining streets and highways, providing education, and conducting public health services.
- *Process*, which identifies such specialized functions as accounting, engineering, medicine, or surveying.
- *Persons or things*, designed to deal with or serve parks, forests, the poor, automobiles, or veterans.

- *Place*, referring to areas where service is provided, such as Central High School, Baltimore, or Region Four.[30]

The principle of unity of command permits each individual in an organization to serve one master. While this principle may lead to excessive rigidity and confusion, Gulick believes that the violation of unity of command can produce inefficiencies and problems of accountability.[31]

The determinants are not based on empirical data. They are prescriptive, indicating what ought to be. A particular organization obviously may be affected by many factors, such as the cultural environment, the personalities involved, and political considerations.

Urwick believed that the scalar principle, or hierarchy, is indispensable to functioning organizations; without it, "authority will break down."[32] Authority confers power on the office holder to require actions of subordinates. The operation of the chain of command establishes clear lines of authority through the organization as suggested in Fig. 7.1, in which A directs B, C, D, and E; B directs L, M, N, and O; L directs, P, Q, R, and S; and so on in all organizations. The manager at each level is directly accountable for the actions of all of his or her subordinates.

Fig. 7.1. The Operating Hierarchy

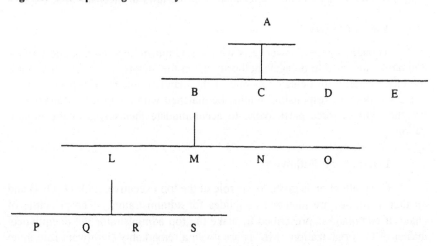

According to Gulick and Urwick, bureaucracy operates independently of people. It is the position that is the basis of authority, not the person who occupies it. Since the organization is set up to run automatically like a machine, everyone must be committed to the organizational operating norms and requirements. In essence, individuals are viewed as cogs to serve the functions and purpose of the machine.

The theory of Urwick and Gulick is also viewed as the process approach. Management is seen as a process of getting things done with the cooperation of organized groups. Managers perform the functions of planning, leading, and controlling, or the expanded POSCDORB.

In summary, Gulick and Urwick set forth seven principles to facilitate the operation of division of labor: (1) unity of command, or reporting to only one superior; (2) fitting people to the organization's structure; (3) provision for adequate staff; (4) use of only one top executive, which leads to unity of responsibility; (5) knowledge on how to delegate; (6) matching responsibility with authority; and (7) adherence to a limited span of control (limiting delegation to a small number of subordinates whom the supervisor can adequately supervise and control). [33]

Nature of People

Individuals are seen as passive beings who must be molded by the ordered and efficient force of the organization. As in the views of Weber and Taylor, the organization of Gulick and Urwick can exhibit no emotion toward its workers. They must be treated like machines and fitted to the organization to maximize the goal of efficiency. According to Urwick, "the idea that the organization should be built up around its individual idiosyncrasies, rather than that individuals should be adapted to the requirement of the sound principles of organization, is as foolish as attempting to design an engine to accord with the whims of one's maiden aunt rather than with the laws of mechanical science."[34]

View of Power

Though supreme power rests with top administrators, Gulick and Urwick emphasize the need to delegate authority down the hierarchy. In fact, they view the lack of ability to delegate as one of the major problems of top executives. All delegations of responsibility must be matched with authority. Management has the right to force participants to accommodate themselves to the organization.

Leaders and Followers

Great attention is given to the role of the top executive. POSDCORB and all that it implies are intended as guides for administrators. The principle of chain of command is prescribed to make the top administrator the unequivocal master of the organization. MLMs are given a remarkably significant role in an organizational system that is dominated from the top, for delegating to MLMs is one of Gulick and Urwick's central principles.

Concern for Accountability

These authors hold a narrow view of accountability. Attention is focused on internal operations of the organization to ensure control, subordination, conformity, and effective division of labor, all of which must be pursued to achieve the greatest goal of the organization—efficiency. No effort is made to go beyond this narrow view of accountability. Gulick and Urwick's total pre-occupation is finding that one best way to manage an organization. There is no responsiveness either to the workers in the organization or to the recipients of its goods and services.

THE INTEGRATIONIST MODEL

The integrationist model represents a combination of the ideas of the conventional mechanistic writers. It is a centralized model of organization in which authority and responsibility devolve from a single chief executive and his or her assistants, who are directly accountable to him or her. The most popular form for organization of departments is by major purpose, so that the general public can readily identify the goods or services the agency is providing.

Coordination takes place from the top by means of communication lines running throughout the organization: "Within the organization this system ensures control by the official at the top, while citizens' control is enhanced by centering responsibility in a single head. Staff units and such elements as a reasonable span of control and clear-cut assignments of authority and functions assist the head in directing the organization."[35]

The dominant position and popularity that the integrationist model enjoys today did not come about overnight but evolved over a relatively long period. The administrative organization for problem-solving in the U.S has reflected three dominant themes or values: representativeness, neutral competence, and executive leadership.[36] Representativeness is consistent with the cultural values of dispersion of power and checks and balances, which are embodied in the U.S. Constitution and reproduced at all levels of government. It is exemplified in the practices of electing officials, rotating officeholders, and administering by boards and commissions popularized by President Andrew Jackson. However, the abuses and problems attendant with this approach gave rise to a reform movement that culminated in the demand for neutral competence (a merit system) and the development of the civil service.

The expectations of proponents of a neutral competent civil service did not materialize, leading to the demand for strong executive leadership. Reformers believed that democratic government must be strong and efficient, responsible and accountable. Though this view is inconsistent with the demo-cratic norms of wide representation and checks and balances, the reformers felt that the concentration of power in the chief executive would facilitate the use of expertise and promote "true democracy" (one that is responsive and responsible) and "true efficiency" (the best use of resources, both human and material). Because citizens would know "where the buck stopped," they could more readily hold public officials accountable for the performance of their duties.[37]

In summary, the integrationist model has the following general character-istics:

- A traditional hierarchy complemented by such elements as unity of command and chain of command.
- The grouping of like administrative activities and functions into a small number of administrative units or departments.
- A small span of control that permits the executive to give personal attention to department heads.
- The centering of authority to appoint and remove department heads.
- Boards that are permitted to act only in advisory roles.
- The provision of staff to assist the executive in directing the administrative departments.
- The maintenance of neutral competence for personnel administration.
- The executive budget as a powerful coordinating force for the chief executive.[38]

SYSTEMS THEORY

The most recent phase of mechanistic or bureaucratic theory is systems theory. A system is the grouping together of functionally related parts that are conceptually separated from their environment in order to achieve a unified whole (purpose). Examples of systems are an automobile engine, the market system, and the educational system. Systems concepts are devised to help us order the interrelationships of activities or events that we seek to direct or control. Systems are highly rational means to achieve predetermined ends. The idea of open systems was the theoretical possibility that systems (and hence governmental programs) could be self-correcting, that they could learn from their mistakes. As is pointed out below, that theoretical possibility has yet to be realized, and the openness of systems remains highly circumscribed.

In studying organizations from a systems perspective, individual parts are viewed as highly interdependent; that is, the way one unit of an organization operates affects the functioning of other units. In large organizations, the job of managers is to be constantly aware of the performance of all parts and to direct or redirect them toward organizational objectives. The organization became a dynamic machine with the manager as the engineer, and this need to control the parts of the machine has generated systems theory.

Systems approaches have been in use in government for more than three decades. The most influential theoretical writing that promoted the use of systems theory, particularly in public administration, was by political scientist David Easton. His classic article, "An Approach to the Analysis of Political Systems," greatly influenced the way organizations were perceived in political science. [39] Major applications of systems theory were undertaken by the U.S. Defense Department in the early 1960s in connection with weapons systems and approaches to a global strategy. By 1970, the systems approach appeared as the organizational framework for a public administration textbook by Ira Sharkansky.[40]

Closed Systems

Fig. 7.2 presents the essential elements of an administrative system—a typical example of a closed system. In this model, organizations are seen as conceptually isolated from their environments, from their clients, and from the larger community. Even legislatures, which authorize and fund public agencies, are presented simply as an input. The key control agency is the "black box," reminiscent of the switch or control. Here the process of conversion takes place and conventional administrative practices (essentially, the integrationist model) are used to process inputs into outputs. The organization becomes a mechanism that is inward-looking and the criterion of efficiency in satisfying terms predominates.

Fig. 7.2. A Closed System Model

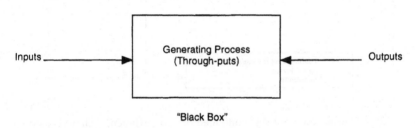

"Black Box"

Open Systems

Increasing complexity in government and the rapidity of change in society rendered closed systems theory inadequate for the tasks governments face. Consequently, a new theory on open systems has been formulated. It is diagrammed in Fig. 7.3.

Open systems are outward-looking. Organizations are seen as instruments of the communities they serve. An operating assumption of the open system is that effective achievement of an organization's mission requires that continuous due recognition be given to the relationships between internal components of the system and the external environment.

The central concerns in systems theory have been about how systems can be made to maintain themselves, to prevent the loss of needed energy, and to avoid stultifying routines. Critics of systems theory, however, worry about their tendency to take charge of government—to give citizens "what they need" without democratic consultation.

Open systems (see Fig. 7.3) operate in a dynamic interactive way with its environment. Chester Bernard first introduced the concept in the 1930s. The systems approach suggests that organizations are made up of "interdependent factors, including groups, attitudes, motives, formal structure, interactions, goals, status and authority."[41] The manager is charged with the responsibility of coordinating all internal parts of the organization so that the organizational goals are maximally achieved. If, for example, the purchasing department does not obtain enough material of the appropriate quality, service delivery to clients may be impeded or halted.

Fig. 7.3. Open Systems

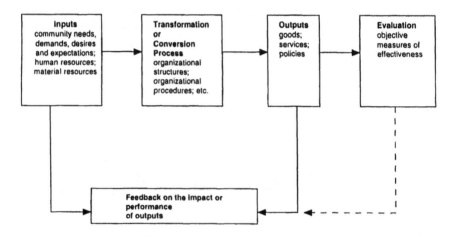

Organizations are not self-contained or self-sufficient. They rely on their environment for life-sustaining resources (inputs) and as outlets for the goods and services (outputs) that they produce. The stability and survival of organizations depend on a multitude of external clients and constituents. To succeed, management must be constantly aware of the dynamic forces operating in the environment and the constraints they impose.

CONTINGENCY APPROACH

Proponents of the contingency approach sought to reconcile the rational mechanistic model and the human relations model, indicating that the external environment influences the appropriate type of management practices relevant for designing the organization. The success of such an organization is dependent on the fit between the organization and its operating environment; the greater the congruence between the two, the more likely the success or effectiveness of the organization.

The operating premise of contingency theory is that organizations are systems consisting of interrelated parts. The relevant organizational design can be determined only by examining the specific environment in which each organization is found. The contingency approach allows the manager to select the most relevant factors in aiding the organization to design alternatives to best achieve its goal.

There is no one best way of managing. Contingency management suggests different situations and conditions require different management approaches. It has been used as a useful concept to integrate management theory, instead of relying on simplistic principles of management. Early theorists such as Frederick Taylor and Max Weber provided principles of management and organization, which they assumed to be universally applicable. As experience and research accumulated, it became evident that there are many exceptions to these principles. For example, division of labor has been proven to be helpful in carrying out a number of tasks. However, in some situations, the application of the division of labor principle can become too specialized. Chapter 11 shows that worker productivity can be increased by expanding rather than narrowing job tasks. In some decisions, the contingency approach is the preferred style of leadership, while in other situations it is not.

Since systems theory incorporates the integrationist model, it accepts individuals largely as passive and as incidental elements in the production of organizational output.

Power is evident in: (1) energizing power (authorizations); (2) power to transform or convert; (3) program power; and (4) power to make needed adjustments. Of these, the conversions power is most important because at this point the information from all parts of the system are integrated.

Hierarchy is manifested throughout the systems approach. The system is set up in government by top-level officials. In the conversion system, MLMs play the key roles. Operators collect information in the field, which is then fed back to leaders for them to determine if changes should be made.

In theory, accountability entails making output congruent with energizing input (policies). In practice, however, systems tend to function in ways that allow systems to maintain themselves.

ORGANIZATIONAL HUMANISM

The rise of an interest in the people within organizations was largely due to disenchantment with classical mechanistic organization theories, the increasing strength of and pressure from labor unions, and the fundamental reappraisal made necessary by the Great Depression. The classical theorists gave little attention to industrial workers and nonsalaried personnel in government. In the U.S., the plentiful supply of immigrant labor and the lack of concern shown by organization theorists for the laboring class, among other factors, encouraged management to look at the work force as another resource, like the machines that were fast replacing them. Management viewed workers as docile. They could permit workers to endure hardship in the work place because of the large supply of labor. During this period managers practiced a two-sided ideology, maximizing the democratic values of liberty and equality for themselves but minimizing them for the workers. Through the state police and the courts, management forced workers and nonsalaried personnel to submit to arbitrary authority and excessively long working hours. The right of workers to organize was highly restricted or prohibited. At the same time, managers enjoyed the "privilege of voluntary action and association for themselves, while imposing upon all subordinates the duty of obedience and the obligation to serve their employers to the best of their ability."[42]

Management actions were consistent with the prevailing view of Social Darwinism (a theory of the survival of the fittest). In this view, those who amassed riches brought success both to the nation and to themselves. Great wealth was a reward for those who had proved themselves in the struggle for survival.[43] The president of the National Association of Manufacturers felt that labor was not willing to accept its place and was bent on using unacceptable means. He noted: "Organized labor knows but one law and that is the law of physical force—the law of the Huns and Vandals, the law of the savage. All of its purposes are accomplished either by actual force or by threat of force."[44] Views such as these were the cause of much violence between management and labor; moreover, they ensured a major source of continuing tension and friction. The dislocation and deep uncertainties occasioned by the 1929 stock market crash and labor's persistence in demanding recognition and better working conditions played a major role in curbing management's authoritarian and paternalistic attitude toward workers. This helped to usher in a change in attitude, exemplified by greater concern and acceptance of the human element in management.

This new emphasis gave particular attention to the behavior of individuals and the functioning of small groups. The behavioral sciences were employed in the study of public organizations as a reaction to the natural sciences' (economics and engineering) preoccupation with mechanistic and bureaucratic theories. Concerns with structures and processes had prevented the study of the ways in which people relate to each other in organizations. By the time that "scientific approaches" to management finally discovered the individual, organizational humanists were focusing their attention on the study of the organic behavior of organizations as a whole and their interactions with their environment. From original concerns with human relations, the movement has turned toward the study of planned change, or what is now called organizational development (OD). A normative prescription has also appeared: the view that organizations should help their employees to mature psychologically by providing them with "meaningful" work and allowing them to work enthusiastically to achieve organizational goals. Finally, a "new public administration" paradigm has emerged, in which organizational humanists have called for public organizations to be guided by the goals of equity and social justice as well as by present concerns for economy and efficiency.

CHARACTERISTICS AND DEVELOPMENT OF THE SCHOOL

The human relations approach has been given such names as neoclassical theory, the informal approach, the open model, and collegial and organic theory.

A number of writers and practitioners have been included under these labels, among them Elton Mayo, John Dewey, Kurt Levin, F. J. Roethlisberger, Mary Parker Follett, and Chester I. Bernard.[45]

The emphasis of the human relations school was on interpersonal communications and collective decision-making. Two important assumptions guided its thinking and practice: (1) that there is a direct correlation between the level of satisfaction in an organization and the level of efficiency and productivity achieved; and (2) that productivity is also affected by the extent to which the work and organizational structure are successful in accommodating the social needs of employees. A greater understanding of these assumptions required the study of philosophy, psychology, sociology, economics, and political science. These concerns led to greater attention to conflict management and the discovery of informal organizations (organizations arising to meet the social and emotional needs of individuals that the formal organization fails to recognize) operating in the work place.

Mary Parker Follett

While she did not break with the classical organization theory of Luther Gulick, Lyndall Urwick or Henry Foyol, the writings of Mary Parker Follett (1868–1933) showed her recognition of differing psychological and physiological needs of workers.[46] She drew particular attention to control and order-giving during an age in which the prerogative of the boss was unquestioned. In her view, the leader should always attempt to anticipate the impact of control and orders given to the worker to ensure that the response will be positive.

The controlling process involves data collection related to the activity or job to ascertain how the job will be implemented. This control is referred to as fact control, that is, decisions rendered on the basis of fact. In this situation it is not the manager that is controlling the outcome. Rather, the weight and force of the facts in the situation drive the decision. As facts play the major role in determining control, they permit individuals to better adjust to and accommodate controlling decisions. An important concern is the coordination of "reciprocal relations" to facilitate the accomplishment of the goals of the organization.[47]

Order-giving, like control, is a reciprocal act in which respect for the individual, the dignity of the work and the skills or ability required to do the work should be carefully considered. The order-giver cannot use only formal authority. He or she must have a clear understanding of the psychological context of the order's recipient if a positive response to the order is to be realized.

Follett felt that conflict resolution within an organization is an important concern that deserves highest consideration. She proposed three approaches to the resolution of conflict: domination, balance of power, and integration.

Resolution through domination involves the high-handed use of superior force to obtain compliance. This approach is employed by the conventional mechanistic theorists. In Follett's view, this approach is unacceptable for resolving conflict because it represses behavior instead of promoting cooperation.

In the balance-of-power situation, there is no dominant participant or holder of power. The agency head may have hierarchical or formal power, but the MLM may have expert knowledge about the decision. Resolution of the conflict is accomplished through bargaining and compromise. Neither participant is satisfied with the outcome: the agency head feels that he or she was forced to bend to suit the wishes of the MLM, while the latter feels that his or her counsel was not given the weight it deserved. Under these circumstances, the problem is resolved but its cause remains.

Integration is the preferred approach because it allows participants to engage in mutual give-and-take until a meeting of minds results, producing a healthy and cooperative attitude in both parties. It is conducive to keeping channels of communication open and to building mutual trust.

The Hawthorne Studies

The participants in these studies were psychology professors from Harvard Business School.[48] Their contractual agreement with Western Electric Company at the Hawthorne Works in Cicero, Illinois, was to determine the ideal workplace and physical conditions in which productivity could best be enhanced. Contrary to the expectations of the researchers, the six-year study (1924–30) revealed that nonphysical conditions play a decisive role in the productive activities and outputs of the participating employees.

The Hawthorne studies generated the most important contribution to human resource management up to that time, and perhaps since. The studies demonstrated that workers are not machines and scientific management's emphasis on the "one best way" to work had to be tempered to recognize the impact of group behavior. When the studies were begun in 1924, they aimed to examine the effect of various illumination levels on worker productivity; control and experimental groups were set up. The control group worked under constant light intensity. While the experimental group was subject to varying intensities of illumination, the researchers expected individual outputs would vary with the intensity of the light. As the intensity of light was increased in the experimental group, output went up for both groups. Surprisingly, as intensity dropped in the experimental group, productivity continued to rise for both groups. Productivity in the experimental group dropped only when the intensity of the light fell to a moonlight glow.

It was not until the Hawthorne studies that Follett's ideas on cooperation and problem-solving were experimentally tested. The studies were conducted by a Harvard professor, George Elton Mayo (1880–1949), and his colleagues to determine the effect of the amount of light in the working area of the factory, the length of the working day, and the number of rest breaks on the level of productivity. The original hypothesis was that increased illumination would result in higher production. For the experiment, a group of young women assembling telephone equipment was selected and placed in a special room under close supervision.

At each degree of increase in illumination, production correspondingly increased. When the tests were completed, the women were returned to their former poorly lighted workbenches, working their usual long day without breaks or other benefits.

Though production fell, the researchers were surprised to find that output was still far higher than under the original pre-experimental conditions. This finding forced Mayo and his colleagues to put forth a new hypothesis: that social relations between the workers and their knowledge that they were participating in a company-conducted experiment were the main factors affecting productivity and quality of work. Tests in succeeding experiments offer the following findings:

1.   Social relations significantly influence the individual worker's productivity.
2.   Workers do not respond predominantly to economic incentives and technical changes in working conditions.
3.   Informal groups arise and exercise influence quite independently of management's control.

The researchers found that workers tended to respond favorably when they believed that people were trying to help them. This type of behavior, in which individuals show greater job satisfaction and improved productivity, is now widely known in the social sciences as the "Hawthorne Effect."

The informal group norms, as they were labeled, were discovered to be actually setting production levels by branding those who did more than the group prescribed as "rate busters" and those who did less as "chiselers." The researchers found that employees would sacrifice greater production (and correspondingly greater pay on a piecework basis) rather than risk the displeasure or ostracism of their fellow workers. On closer study, it was documented that most workers seemed to conform to informal group norms quite independently of management's knowledge or wishes. This was the beginning of organization theory arising from knowledge of the behavior of individuals in groups.

The conclusion drawn from the Hawthorne studies was that behavior and sentiments are closely related. More important, group influences significantly affect individual behavior. Particularly important is the role played by the social organization of the work place. Each factory work unit developed its own culture that could not be readily observed or analyzed. Additionally, that the group's standards determined individual worker output, and money was less important in determining output than group standards, group security and group sentiments.

The Hawthorne study helped advocates of the human relations movement to make a strong commitment to management practices that were more humane. Advocates uniformly believed that a satisfied worker was a productive worker. Among the names associated with the post-Hawthorne human relations movement included Dale Carnegie, Abraham Maslow and Douglas McGregor. The views of these proponents were shaped more by personal philosophies than by empirical research.

Dale Carnegie has been overlooked by most scholars, yet his ideas have had an enormous impact on management practices. In the 1920s to 1950s, millions read his book *How To Win Friends and Influence People.*[49] Tens of thousands of managers and aspiring managers participated in his seminars and listened to his speeches. In Carnegie's view, success requires winning the cooperation of others. Success is dependent on the following: (1) creating an atmosphere that makes others feel important by generating sincere appreciation of their efforts; (2) creating a good first impression; (3) winning over people by allowing them to do the talking, demonstrating sympathetic support, and never indicating to a person that he or she is wrong; and (4) winning over people by praising particular traits of theirs and always giving an offender the opportunity to save face.[50]

Douglas McGregor is widely known for his formulation of Theory X and Theory Y assumptions about people and human nature. These assumptions are discussed in Chapter 11. Theory X is a negative view of people who lack ambition, positive work habits, and responsibility and who need to be closely supervised to work effectively. Theory Y presents a positive view of people who are self-directed, willing to accept responsibility, and find work pleasurable. In McGregor's view, Theory Y best captures reality for workers and should guide management practice.[51]

Chester I. Bernard

Bernard (1886–1961) was a practitioner and a theorist who has had profound influence on the theory and management of organizations. He wrote his celebrated *The Functions of the Executives* (1938) as an amalgam of concepts of organizations and his experience as executive with New Jersey Bell Telephone Company. He de-emphasized the authoritarian top-down model that characterizes classical organization theory. Instead, he stressed the importance of cooperation, the group over the individual, morality and leadership in informal organizations.

Bernard's 1938 book, which examined the exercise of authority in organizations, followed closely on the Hawthorne findings. He found that when top administrators issued orders that were either impossible to carry out or were viewed by subordinates as exceeding the administrator's authority, these orders were simply not obeyed.[52]

Bernard believed that authority, like the pursuit of all endeavors in the organization, is a cooperative act. Its exercise is a two-way street. Top administrators could employ their formal authority to influence MLMs, but at some point the MLMs had to be willing to be influenced. Bernard wrote of a "zone of indifference" (which Herbert Simon later renamed a zone of acceptance) to suggest that managers would be well advised to limit their orders to what they were sure subordinates would find acceptable. From the tested hypothesis followed the observation that only those orders that would be obeyed should be issued.

Bernard required that management develop an inducement and contribution system that allowed employees to maintain a level of contributions (inputs or work and loyalty) to the organization while the organization provided inducement (output or wages, prestige, etc.) to employees. If the inducement-contribution equilibrium does not provide sufficient satisfaction, employees will restrict their level of contribution. In extreme cases, where the level of satisfaction falls below an acceptable point, the individual may leave the organization. Bernard's work indicated that the factors motivating worker behavior are far more complex than conventional mechanistic theorists believed.

Human-Centered Organization

The human relations theorists such as Follett and Bernard recognized that there were not only independent sources of power, but that there were underlying motivating factors that must be considered. Theorists thus turned their attention to how this power can be best channeled and the motivating factors best understood and effectively applied to achieve organizational goals. Many of the ideas associated with the psychological humanist Abraham H. Maslow have been found to be useful in explaining worker motivation.[53] Maslow set forth a hierarchy of needs, illustrated in Fig. 7.4.

The fundamental physiological needs for food, warmth, shelter, and sexual fulfillment are at the base of the hierarchy. These tend to take precedence over other needs because they relate to physical survival. The next level of needs pertains to a feeling of safety from physical and emotional injury, such as

Fig. 7.4. Maslow's Hierarchy of Needs

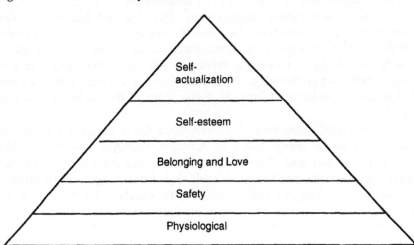

Self-actualization

Self-esteem

Belonging and Love

Safety

Physiological

having a secure job and a steady income. As these are achieved, the individual focuses attention on the need for friendship, belonging, and love. The need for esteem refers to achievement, recognition, and fame. The final need, at the top of the hierarchy, is for self-actualization, or the fullest use of the individual's creative abilities.

The significance of the hierarchy of needs lies in understanding the motivating factors for individuals. Once a particular level of needs has been satisfied, different or higher types of motivators are required if the organizational goals are to be achieved. This means that the manager must be constantly aware of workers' changing wants. According to Maslow, humans are a perpetually wanting animal.[54]

While Douglas McGregor[55] recognized the need to operationalize Maslow's theories regarding people's needs and wants in organizations, his efforts were confined to continued theorizing about the nature of people. McGregor proposed Theory X and Theory Y to explain undesirable and desirable ways of affecting working behavior (see Chapter 11).

Other theorists, such as Chris Argyris, Frederick Herzberg, and Rensis Likert continued writing on and experimenting with the factors affecting motivation or mastering the hierarchy of needs. Herzberg developed concepts dealing with "motivators" that could be directly correlated with job satisfaction. The factors affecting motivation fall into two categories. The first ("hygiene" factors, consisting of company policy and administration, salary, supervision, interpersonal relations, and working conditions) describe ways in which the workers relate to their working environment. Because the hygiene factors (due to mismanagement) seldom motivate workers, Herzberg called them "dissatisfiers." The second category, relating to "intrinsic" factors such as recognition, the nature of the work, responsibility, and promotion or advancement, are known as the "satisfiers" and are directly job-related. These motivating factors promote an enduring sense of motivation because they provide an opportunity for growth and self-actualization.[56]

The research carried out by Likert,[57] Herzberg, and Argyris in testing hypotheses about motivations has almost universally reported a positive correlation with participative, or democratic, decision-making. Such decision-making contributes to meaningful work and job satisfaction, which in turn promote better job performance. Despite these claims, a review of the literature by Edward E. Lawler and Lyman W. Porter indicates that the reverse may be true.[58]

The reward system for higher performance that is viewed as a dissatisfier may indeed be the critical factor in increasing employee satisfaction. The conclusion was thus made that management may find it more useful to identify better reward systems than to agonize itself about maximizing the satisfaction of its employees. Finally, the basic criticism of the Herzberg theory is that it has not always been replicated by research because it is too general and ignores differences between individual expectations. Additionally, it has usually been impossible to distinguish differences between dissatisfiers and motivators, because the same factors are mentioned in both categories.[59] Despite these verification problems, the work of Maslow has had a continuing impact.

ORGANIZATION DEVELOPMENT

OD looks at the human side of organizations in their attempts to bring people, structures and technology into harmony to better realize their goals. OD stresses techniques to change people and the quality of interpersonal work relationships to enhance the organization's ability to adapt to new technologies, challenges, and opportunities. OD is carried out through planned effort and an organization-wide approach, directed from the top, and planned interventions aimed at increasing organizational effectiveness and health.[60] This includes structuring the environment so that management and employees can use their skills and abilities to their maximum potential.

An accepted view is that OD can be successful if its efforts are long range in perspective. It allows OD to enhance the organization's problem-solving ability and self-renewal processes while engendering collaborative organizational culture and changes.[61] OD's organization-wide changes allow the operating dynamic forces to be unleashed so that the functioning organization will develop efficiency and the ability to renew itself.

In Kurt Levin's view, successful change typically involves a three-step change process (see Fig. 7.5).[62] This change requires unfreezing the status quo, changing to the new state, and refreezing the achieved change to give permanence. Since the status quo is viewed as an equilibrium state, movement away from this equilibrium requires unfreezing.[63]

Fig. 7.5. A View of the Change Process

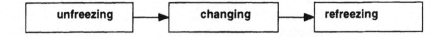

The initiating effort of OD begins with management's recognition that organizational performance can and should be improved. Typically OD efforts involve the following phases: (1) diagnosis; (2) strategy planning; (3) education, and (4) evaluation.

Diagnosis involves gathering and analyzing information about an organization to determine the areas that require improvement. The desired information is normally gathered from employees by means of questionnaires or attitude surveys. Strategic planning involves the development of a plan to carry out the organizational improvements based on the data collected. The planning step pinpoints specific problem areas and the steps required to resolve them.

Education provides the opportunity to share diagnostic information with the affected workers, assisting them to become convinced of the need for change. The evaluation phase collects data to assess the impact of OD in achieving the organization's purposes.

Process Consultation

This OD technique requires the use of an outside consultant who helps management "to perceive, understand, and act upon a process event" with which the manager must deal.[64] These might involve work flow, informal relationships among unit members, and formal communications channels. The consultant provides management with ideas and insights about what is happening around and within him or her and among other workers. The consultant is not expected to solve the manager's problem. Ideally, the consultant becomes a coach to aid the manager in diagnosing the problems that need improvement. In those cases where the consultant is unable to aid the manager in solving identified problems, the consultant typically helps to locate an expert with the requisite technical knowledge.

OD is based on the premise that change is a relatively straightforward thing that can be accomplished. In reality an organization's culture is built on generally stable and permanent characteristics, which tends to make the culture exceedingly resistant to change. Culture takes extended periods to form, and once established or institutionalized, it becomes entrenched.[65]

While human relation theorists focused on adjusting the organization to the individual, organization development (OD) is concerned with top-directed, planned, organization-wide change that employs knowledge of the behavioral sciences to achieve effectiveness and productivity. In Warren G. Bennis' view, OD seeks to change beliefs, attitudes, values, and the structure of the organization to facilitate adaptation to the fast-changing and highly complex environments with which we must contend.[66] Typically, organizations employ outside consultants to assist in planning and implementing the desired changes.

Though OD in many ways overlaps the human relations field, its overall emphasis is on rational planning and systemic analysis. At the same time, OD must be set apart from such subareas as sensitivity training and operations research. While the former tends to be passive, allowing the outcome to emerge rather than initiating action to make things happen, the latter relies on neutral, mechanistic, and predominantly value-free instruments. OD humanizes operations and rationalizes human sensitivities. The following are some of the operating premises of OD:

1.   A person develops a concept of self and for the most part behaves in a way consistent with this concept.
2.   By dispelling the tenuous base of existing norms and giving participants a common view based on new data, the environment in which action will take place can be influenced.

3. When there is no threat to the self-structure, inconsistent experiences may be perceived, examined, and used as a basis for change.

4. Personal growth is aided through honest, caring, and nonmanipulative relationships.

5. Positive change comes naturally when a group feels a common identity and an ability to influence its environment.

6. People are more likely to change if they participate in exploring the reasons for change and the ways to achieve it.

7. Participation in decision-making increases group cooperation toward attaining organizational goals.

8. Increasing participation enhances satisfaction. and satisfaction is reflected in increased work effort.

9. Successful change includes "unfreezing" (if necessary) present attitudes and their accompanying ways of performing, introducing change, and then freezing group life at the new level. [67]

These hypotheses reveal the normative and value-laden quality of the OD movement. OD advocates exhibit an almost missionary zeal in their belief that bureaucracies can become democratic. Human development is presented as a desirable end that justifies reforming the bureaucratic value system that has undergirded public organizations. Larry Kirkhart and Orion F. White Jr. have identified "technicism" as one of these destructive values (i.e., "the rise to predominance of mechanistic process over substance, the reign of routine, the tendency to set policy by viewing technical capability as opportunity, the pervasive systemization and control of human existence").[68] Critics of organizational humanism, however, see statements such as this as "a thin veneer [that] barely veils the strong ideological orientation of organization humanists."[69]

OD techniques have undergone an evolution. Most early OD training took place in a laboratory at Bethel, Maine. Through a group dynamics procedure labeled "action training and research" (ATR), participants were shown how they were perceived by others and helped to use this information as a basis for making personal changes. Some of the early techniques, popularly known as "T-groups" or "sensitivity training," were criticized for the extreme measures used to shock participants into a recognition of their hidden biases.

Later developments, called "laboratory training," took the form of strategies for bringing about organizational change. The essential features were: (1) a systematic analysis (by trainers or consultants) to identify organizational problems; (2) the sharing of these data with a team from the organization (a mixture of upper-, middle-, and lower-level personnel); and (3) the preparation of a plan for joint action to overcome the identified problems. The action research rests conceptually on three questions:

1. Where are we (the organization) now?

2. Where do we want to be?

3. How do we get from where we are to where we want to be?

OD next moved from external laboratories to "team building" within organizations as it came to be understood that both the organizational setting and biases within the individual had to be taken into account. Through team building, OD involved five major phases, all carried out in the organization to achieve planned change:

1. *Initiating phase.* Identifying expectations, demonstrating that data gathering is "safe," beginning the process of group interaction, and explaining the role of the trainer (catalyst, resource person, and interpreter).
2. *Diagnostic phase.* Efforts to expand mutual openness of individuals in group.
3. *Prescriptive phase.* Attention to the problems the group wants to work on (problems related to individuals, groups, or situations), introduction of the problem-solving process (formulation, focusing of needed data, development of options, testing of options, selection of a preferred option).
4. *Team and implementation phase.* Determination of who does what, when, with whom; for what expected payoff; and how to know it got done.
5. *Team assessment phase.* Establishment of criteria of evaluation, introduction of evaluation process, and development of new concerns.

OD, which flourished in both government and private firms in the late 1960s and early 1970s, has come under attack. The following are typical charges:

1. OD is really a method for providing the controlling elites in organizations an opportunity to manipulate members. It regards people as means to achieve an organizational end.
2. OD is limited by the survey technique. Trainer-consultants may be able to count how many people in an organization report that they hold particular opinions about problems, but this information is only tangentially related to the forces that can produce change.
3. OD's concern for increased efficiency requires the movement to apply conventional criteria that are organizationally defined. What is needed is an evaluational criterion that does not rely on institutional interests.
4. OD needs to deal with people as they are instead of holding the implicit view that participants must be transformed into a healthier state.
5. OD trainers themselves legitimize one of the most basic barriers in organizations—pay differentials. OD trainers tend to be highly paid and to work only after achieving approval of top administrators.
6. While OD may achieve some good results within the organization, it does not address the reality that the organization is itself in a force field (there are always factors arrayed for and against each problem) that remains unchanged.

The most pointed challenge to the OD movement has been directed against its fundamental ideas: (1) that people desire personal fulfillment on the job; and (2) that personal goals and organizational goals can be made compatible. H. Roy Kaplan and Curt Tausky argue that the bulk of the research does not support these hypotheses. Instead, they report:

1.   It is only at the level of first-line supervision that collegial models (i.e., participation) have been tested, and here the incentive of increased material rewards is more dominant than that of increased participation.

2.   Worker control over the pace. quality, and design of tasks has been virtually untried. From what is known, only a person like a research chemist has the setting in which it is possible for these controls to be exercised.

3.   Participation through representation does not necessarily produce increased worker satisfaction.

4.   Measured increases in worker satisfaction have not brought increased work effort.

5.   Organizational goals and worker self-interest remain incompatible in most researched instances. [70]

Kaplan and Tausky conclude that the best we can hope for at this stage of research on organizational humanism is a healthy pluralism of approaches rather than the ideological commitment to creating "healthy" organizations and "self-actualized" people.

THE NEW PUBLIC ADMINISTRATION

The most recent manifestation of organizational humanist theory has been labeled the "new public administration" (NPA) to signify its radical departure from conventional and scientific views of administration. While NPA is not easily defined, the thrust of the movement has been toward the creation of a new organization and administrative theory. "Simply put," noted H. George Frederickson, "new public administration seeks to change those policies and structures that systematically inhibit social equity."[71]

The origins of the NPA can be traced to a meeting called by Dwight Waldo at the Minnowbrook Conference Center in upper New York state in 1968. Mostly younger administrative theorists were invited to discuss "Public Administration in a Time of Turbulence." At the time, social unrest was shaking the nation in the form of urban rioting and an increased militancy on college campuses. Opposition to the Vietnam War, demands by minority groups for equal opportunity, and a growing concern about the polluting of the physical environment were producing national alarm.

The NPA writers reflected on these concerns, which they saw as traceable to undesirable public administration practices. The following were specifically criticized:

- the unresponsiveness of government to social ills
- the misuse of authority by administrators, growing out of the tendency for professionals in government to cling to power
- the undue emphasis on efficiency and productivity without regard to societal outcomes
- a preoccupation with the preservation of the status quo
- an emphasis on rationality to the exclusion of other human characteristics

- diminishing accountability to client groups
- an elitism inherent in merit employment systems
- the dehumanizing impact of administrative norms on workers and client groups.

Frederickson summarized the concerns:

Conventional or classic Public Administration seeks to answer either of these questions: (1) How can we offer more or better services with available resources (efficiency)? or (2) How can we maintain our level of services while spending less money (economy)? New Public Administration adds this question: Does this service enhance social equity?[72]

It was not until 1974 that the concept of social equity was spelled out for readers of the public administration literature.[73] In that year, John Rawls's *A Theory of Justice* was offered as a rigorous philosophical statement drawn from his two principles of justice.[74] While NPA theorists hailed the Rawls formulations, perhaps because they were difficult to understand, they failed to catch on. What did have an impact was a simpler view that was adopted in city after city by administrators seeking greater participation by minority groups in local government. The essential ingredients of the equity ethic, according to Frederickson, were:

- The recognition that administrative value-neutrality is improbable, perhaps impossible, and certainly not desirable.
- That a public service is a general public good that can be well or badly performed.
- That however well or badly performed, generally provided public services vary in their impact on recipients.
- That variations in the impact of public services tend to mirror social, economic, and political status (that is, higher-quality services go to those with higher status).
- That the public administrator is morally obligated to counter this tendency.
- That equity in the delivery of services, so far as it is calculable, should be one of the standards by which the goodness of public service is judged.
- That variations from equity should always be in the direction of providing more and better services to those in lower social, economic, and political circumstances.
- That the isolation of administrators and public agencies from either political or administrative responsibility is not equity enhancing.[75]

Similarly, William H. Lucy, Dennis Gilbert, and Guthrie S. Burkhead have spelled out what equity in the distribution of services should include:

1.   Equal treatment for all service recipients should be.the norm.
2.   Deviations from that norm should follow after specific justification.
3.   Part of that justification should be a minimum or floor for each service below
       which quality and quantity of service should not dip. [76]

The NPA's critique contains three themes (1) that public administration theory was at best "scientistic" (i.e., it was labeled scientific but in actuality it was not based on empirical research); (2) that while conventional public administration theorists objected to the value judgments in organizational humanism, this was only because they sought to protect their own values and preferences, which favored the ascendancy of administrators over both elected officials and clients[77]; and (3) conventional public administration theorizing was largely irrelevant to the major concerns of the nation—maintaining social solidarity, solving human problems, protecting the environment, and promoting popular confidence in government.

For nearly a quarter-century, challenged NPA theorists, public administration in both the bureaucratic and organizational humanism schools had unwittingly and unsuccessfully tried to employ scientific methods. For bureaucratic theorists, this meant borrowing from economics and engineering (cost-benefit analysis, computer modeling, operations research); for organizational humanists it involved reliance on the behavioral sciences, especially experimental psychology, which eschews values and concentrates on the measurement of behavior. The quantitative method, argued NPA theorists, was dominating public administration almost as a fetish.

The NPA critique joined a larger philosophical debate on the overuse of logical and empirical methods and the underreliance on values and ethics. This debate was crystallized in Thomas Kuhn's *Structures of Scientific Revolutions,* which popularized the idea of paradigms.[78] A paradigm refers to a tradition, style, or approach for looking at problems along with particular methods for problem-solving. By studying the history of scientific movements, Kuhn found that paradigms evolved through a cycle: They had a beginning and a period of dominance, and then they were superseded. The ideas of Copernicus, for example, were superseded by those of Newton, which in turn gave way to those of Einstein. All of this was translated into the debate over public administration theory: Classical theory (Max Weber et al.) had given way to scientific theory (Herbert Simon et al.), and now the new public administration was superseding the scientific outlook. Textbooks on public administration linked conventional public administration theory with scientific rationality and logical empiricism (the empiricism of Hegel, Comte, and Kant) and the NPA with phenomenology (the science of perceptions) and existentialism (the call for action to change the human condition). Kuhn argued that historically, schools or paradigms were superseded when they were unable to solve problems or answer urgent questions. NPA above all was a call for action to meet human problems in a new way.

The program of NPA can be summarized as follows:

1.   Administrators are to be proactive. They should be advocates of those clients who have the greatest needs.
2.   Administration should be relevant to societal needs. In theory and practice it should give primary attention to the major problems confronting society.
3.   Administrators should strive to deliver services in a manner that enhances the dignity and self-worth of the people being served.
4.   They should work to help clients build their own capacities so they will no longer require help, or to bring them in as major participants, particularly in the policymaking inside public agencies.

But mainly NPA argued that the idea of equity should be added to the conventional concerns with economy (now labeled productivity) and efficiency (now translated to include effectiveness).

The ideas of NPA have been severely challenged in the literature. It has been argued that these ideas are not new, that the attack on science has not been well conceived and has been overstated, and that NPA creates as many problems as it solves. But it is now established that the traditional emphasis on "who gets what out of the system" has been supplemented by a normative dimension of "who ought to get what."[79]

STIMULATING INNOVATION AND CHANGE

In Chapter 3 we focused on building a response and learning about public bureaucracy and its adaptation to change. This section briefly examines the importance of anticipating change and designing organizations to meet the needs in the changed environment. The layoffs and changes taking place in government and private organizations are required to maintain viability in a fast-changing environment. Organizations that wish to maintain flexibility must know how to foster innovation and master the art of change. Two people who have played important roles are Rosabeth Moss Kanter and consultant and lecturer Tom Peters.

Kanter's ideas are found in her book, *The Change Masters*, in which she explains the results of her research on more than 100 U.S. companies.[80] She discusses how U.S. corporations can develop the capability to create a renaissance among people and organizations. To achieve this result, organizations must develop and fine-tune the art of anticipating the need for and channeling the efforts to productive change. One of the important findings of Kanter's research is that innovations appear to be closely related to structure. Bureaucracies tend to be less innovative, while other types of organizations that are more flexible and adaptive have structures that are more innovative.

In a more aggressive approach, Tom Peters argues that the old guidelines for managing do not fit the new changed paradigm.[81] The stable and predictable world that the guidelines represent does not fit the reality of today. The fast pace of change of the present environment is unprecedented. In the private sector new competitors are constantly emerging while old ones are quickly disappearing through mergers, acquisitions or the inability to adapt to change and innovation. In the public sector, demands and wishes of the public is changing faster than officials can recognize or meet. This incongruence between public expectations and the response of public officials is a significant factor in the current expression of dissatisfaction.

Peters states that continuous innovation in computers, tele-communications, and the new international economic order has created chaos. The winners in this new environment will be organizations that have been able to learn to cope and thrive. A successful organization must emphasize world-class quality and service, enhance responsiveness, flexibility, and continuous innovation and improvement.

PRAXIS AS A LEARNING AND HUMANIZING FACTOR

The Concept of Praxis

Praxis is seen as a way of bringing theory and practice together. Praxis suggests actions or a deed that is carried out to produce a desired end. It is through praxis that people are aided to achieve their potential. Praxis helps a free people develop disciplined and ethical values and behavior directed at enhancing the actions of public life. Praxis emphasizes people's enablement and liberation as it leads people to greater pursuit and realization of their potential.

Praxiology directs attention to the roles that people play in organizations and the efficiency with which actions are discharged in realizing the purposes being sought. Praxis is necessary if theory is to emerge. Praxis, to operate optimally, requires constant interdependence between theory and practice.

Since praxis directs public servants to commit themselves to liberating and enabling all citizens, it may be asked why there is an indifferent attitude toward the public by public service officials, especially from the perspective of the poor, the powerless, and minorities. The praxis concept suggests that the interdependence of theory and practice leads to a focus on mechanistic theory or accountability upward to political officials and top administrators and not responsiveness and sustainability to clients and constituents. Emphasis is put on control and efficiency. NPR proponents say that this is why the attempt is made to shift managers' attention from their internal focus on accountability and conformance to rules and processes laid down by top officials. We propose a philosophy of the public service because of the lack of a people-oriented theory that could guide the action of public managers. This absence of praxis-based theory fosters action that is devoid of ethical and historical meaning. This allows managers to develop an institutionalized tendency to carry out programs that create people's dependency rather than their transformation and enablement.

Praxis relates to people's struggle for liberation. Experience constitutes the practice that leads to liberation (theory). Praxis is particularly a preoccupation of the poor, who despite their poverty can glimpse the good life. For citizens in the Greek city-states, praxis was the acting out of what a free and ethical people do in the *polis*. The objective of citizens of the *polis* was freedom, directly linked to the appropriate constitution.

Cultural Hermeneutics

Cultural hermeneutics comprises a set of principles that are used for interpreting the ways of understanding meaning, especially of classical texts. It is the systematic approach that seeks to understand forms of communication. Hermeneutics allows people to read and obtain an accurate and clear understanding of written and oral communication. This is an indispensable skill in government, yet only minimal attention is given to developing this vital skill in public servants.

Hermeneutics comes from the Greek word *hermeneuein,* meaning to make clear. Those versed in hermeneutics have an ability to grasp the underlying or hidden meaning in written communication. To gain this insight, the interpreter has to engage in both a dialogue or participation in the written text. The aim is to provide a meaning that parallels the original intent. This requires that the interpreter immerse himself or herself in the cultural context of the original writing to learn precisely what is being conveyed. In so doing, the interpreter can create a dialogue with the text in order to grasp the meaning of the culture that could not be obtained simply by reading the words in the text. The study of hermeneutics thus bridges the gap between one cultural setting with another.

Hermeneutics is closely linked to praxis. While praxis releases the human potential, hermeneutics seeks to aid the release process as it improves communication. It does so by illuminating and helping us to reflect and obtain insights on our condition. The understanding that we obtain from the past makes it possible for us to realize an enhanced future. Hermeneutics thus allows us to reveal who we are and what we can become. This interrelationship between theory and practice allows us to enhance our human fulfillment.

ORGANIZATIONAL HUMANISM: A SUMMARY

Nature of Workers

Human relations theory and its related subfield, organizational development, and to some extent NPA reflect an abiding faith in the malleability and trust in individuals (workers). From this perspective, these theorists have a lot in common with Jean-Jacques Rousseau, who believed unfailingly in human cooperativeness, trustworthiness, and dignity. There is no debate about the possibility of motivating people to perform effectively. Rather, it is a matter of finding the right motivators, such as Bernard's inducement–contribution equilibrium, the Hawthorne studies' show of care for the individual's interest, or Maslow's hierarchy of needs.

A number of summarizing observations may be made about human nature according to the organizational humanism theorists:

1. Carl Rogers' propositions on the nature of man are at the core of organizational humanism:
    a. Every individual exists in a continually changing world of its experiences.
    b. The organism has one basic tendency—to actualize, maintain, and to enhance.[82]
2. The organization is viewed as an organism rather than an atomistic mode.
3. The organization is operated for a moral purpose, as articulated by Bernard and implied by the others.
4. Individuals are willing and eager to assume responsibility.
5. There is continual conflict and mutual adjustment in the organization.
6. People do not resist change; they resist being changed.
7. Participation (democratic involvement) tends to be more productive for organizations.

View of Power

Power is seen as operating from multiple centers. For Bernard it is more a bottom-up approach because the ultimate ability to accept or reject orders lies with the person who must respond. Especially for the OD advocates, power is seen as drawing more from norms and as supported by the group. Thus, power is a shared experience rather than a unilateral one. The strategic source of power is monopolized by no one in the organization, not even the chief executive, allowing for greater diffusion and decentralization of power.

Leaders and Followers

The role of leader, especially in the OD process, is that of consultant and facilitator. There is less competition and more collegiality. Leadership and authority are viewed as emergent factors rather than incumbent and permanent. Leadership emanating from formal structure is replaced by a free-floating functional type that varies with the needs of the group. There is a confluence of interest between superior and subordinates. In this context the focus is more on the group (MLMs). Unlike the mechanistic focus at the top, the greatest concern is given to the needs of leaders in the group.

In human relations, especially in the OD context, it is hard to understand how top managers can be neutral when they are responsible for determining the organizational structure. It is top management who decides if there will be planned change and how much. Accordingly, leadership from the group or by the group can occur only within the guidelines or parameters laid down by those at the top. Thus, as noted above, some questions that have focused critical attention on the human relations field.

Concern for Accountability

Loyalty is given to the group and ultimately to the organization as a whole. Participants exercise collective responsibility in that they are expected to participate in accomplishing the organizational goal according to their competence and skills. Additionally, the organization is assumed to be pursuing a moral end; to the extent that its objectives are achieved, the community benefits. The concern of NPA for accountability is its greatest strength. The concern is first focused on how the organization treats its employees, but also how organizational resources are used to promote social equity (clients and constituents).

TOTAL QUALITY MANAGEMENT (TQM): NATURE AND THEORY

The Quality Movement

The total quality management (TQM) orientation and practice contrast sharply with mechanistic organization theory. The philosophy, and cultural and learning changes that TQM requires demand a profound transformation in the way workers carry out the functions of organizations. The birth of TQM in America during the 1980s forced organizations to rethink and modify their commitment to Frederick Taylor's scientific management and administrative management advocates such as Gulick and Urwick to move away from the focus on top management functions: planning, organizing, staffing, directing, and controlling. The new emphasis is on decentralization, teamwork, continuous process improvement, and workers' empowerment. All are directed toward promoting the satisfaction of the customer and clients, with attention to the provision of appropriate resource allocation, assignment of people to quality projects, provision of appropriate training for project participants, and institutionalization of a structure and environment to enhance quality and to maintain achieved gain.

TQM is a philosophy, a set of principles, tools, and procedures that provide guidelines for maximizing the achievement of an organization's goals in meeting expectations of customers and clients. TQM requires commitment from the top and participation from all employees in the organization. In an organization, the internal customers and external customers are equally important. In a school system, the ultimate external customers are the parent and the students. The internal customers would consist of the math teacher, the librarian and management team.

TQM is a continuous process, a never-ending journey. TQM provides an integrated management system, continually improving all processes to ensure that the best outcomes are realized. Employees are viewed as an indispensable resource that must be continuously enhanced. The highest quality is produced when things are done right the first time. This allows unnecessary steps to be removed from the work situation. Every organization continuously controls and improves ways to meet and exceed customers' expectations. To be flexible and maximally responsive, TQM takes place in a dynamic context in which strategic planning is used to promote a future orientation.

Because TQM is about organizational learning, change, and transformation, management must act as a positive force in facilitating the creation of a new culture. In this new environment challenges are seen as opportunities, and conflicts are channeled into means of producing constructive outcomes. The team approach is used to reconcile differing perspectives.

The TQM philosophy inverts the traditional management pyramid and brings workers closer to the external customers, as shown in Fig. 7.6. The application of these principles requires six supporting elements.[83]

- leadership
- education and training
- communications
- supportive environment and structure
- reward, recognition and measurement.

TQM fosters creativity, teamwork, and the empowerment of workers. The TQM leader is a coach, mentor, trainer, and supporter of workers or colleagues. The leader focuses attention on shared vision and strategy to aid the achievement of team goals.

THREE MAJOR PROPONENTS OF TQM

While TQM proponents such as Philip Crosby, Armand V. Feigenbaum, Shigeo Shingo, and Genichi Taguchi have made important contributions, we will limit our brief review to the late W. Edward Deming, J. M. Juran, and Kaoru Ishikawa.

J. M. Juran

During the 1950s, Juran (1900–   ) advised the Japanese in ways of improving the quality of their products and restructuring their industries to compete in world markets. Juran believes that 80 percent of all organizational problems are inherent in the system. These systemic problems are controllable only by management. To know whether management or the worker controls the problem requires the answers to three questions: (1) Do clearly defined standards exist that permit workers to know what to do? (2) Can workers measure their progress against that standard? (3) Do the workers have the authority to initiate change to achieve the standard? If the response to any of the questions is "no," the problem is controllable by management. If management wants to enhance workers' ability to promote improvement, management must solve the problems. To facilitate the achievement of management quality, the Juran trilogy is applied:

1. Quality planning identifies customers, their expectations and desired product or service, and the process necessary to produce and deliver them with the

appropriate attributes. The process is complete only when the required knowledge can be effectively transformed to the producing arm or responsibility center of the organization.

2.   Quality control is the examination of the customers' requirements against the attributes of the product produced.

3.   Quality improvement is the established way to ensure continuous achievement to promote continuous improvement.

W. Edwards Deming

Deming (1900–1994) was a statistician who gained fame for his training of Japanese engineers in the 1950s and is credited as the father of the Japanese quality revolution after World War II. It was not until Deming's NBC television program, "If Japan Can Why Can't We?" on June 26, 1980, that his visibility rose in the U.S. According to Deming, 95 percent of all quality problems are due to imperfections in the system and are management's responsibility and not workers'. Management's intervention is required to fix the system's problems.

Workers are directly responsible for special problems over which they have control; for example, the workers in the state unemployment service may be incorrectly calculating benefits for employed workers. Once this mistake is recognized, the worker can easily correct the problem. However, if the eligibility policy for unemployment allows inappropriate people to qualify, only the policymakers or the legislature can correct the common, systemwide problem by redesigning the policy. Thus, workers control special problems while management controls common problems.

In Deming's view, the major focus of TQM is on processes and people and how they are effectively trained and motivated to minimize variation. To realize this objective, management must have a clear view of its responsibilities to the agency, employees, and clients. This is an important factor because quality is rooted in management's understanding of how power affects variation. Since all systems are subject to some degree of variation, it is critical that management learn how to manage it. The failure to control variation will inevitably lead to inconsistency, which will damage both product and quality, generating unpredictable loss to the agency.[84]

Management must turn away from its reliance on the balance sheet, as is done in the private sector, or line-item budget, as is the case in the public sector. To achieve maximum success, management must be process-obsessed and have the ability to harness the know-how of employees' initiative to aid the fine-tuning of the organization and thereby achieve higher standards.[85]

Management leadership has a profound impact on the success of TQM. It is important that management gives total support to the TQM effort if maximum output and the highest quality is to be obtained. To this end Deming offered fourteen imperatives for management.

1.   Create constancy of purpose to ensure continuous improvement of product and service. Management's commitment is required to create and redesign

products, services, materials, job skills, training, and investments in research and education.

2 and 3.   Commit totally to the new philosophy and cease dependence on inspection. Eliminate or minimize errors before they occur.

4.   Emphasize the minimization of total cost and avoid awarding business on the basis of price alone. Reduce or minimize cost by dealing with a single supplier. Develop long-term relationships between purchaser and supplier to enhance mutual interest.

5.   Improve constantly and forever every process for planning, production, and service.

6.   Develop continuous on-the-job training.

7 and 8.   Teach and promote effective leadership. Foster innovations among the staff so that they may become less task-oriented. Drive out fear and build trust to make the environment conducive to innovation.

9.   Eliminate barriers between staff areas and promote cooperation with teams and groups.

10.   Avoid slogans, exhortations, and targets. Slogans often ignore the fact that most problems are created by the system. Exhortations generate frustration and resentment.

11.   Eliminate numerical quotas and numerical goals. Preoccupation with quantitative goals prevents an understanding of the real problems; it is an attempt to manage without knowledge. Since improvement is often incremental, management may need to accept new changes to improve productivity.

12.   Remove barriers that rob people of their workmanship, including the annual performance rating and the merit system.

13.   Encourage a vigorous program of education and self-improvement for everyone.

14.   Everyone in the organization must be energized to achieve transformation.

Deming formulated a systematic approach to problem-solving, the plan, do, check, and action, or PDCA cycle. As these planning steps are completed, the planning cycle continues. While specific control (SPC) emphasizes management's responsibility for dealing with common variability problems or errors, PDCA stresses the critical role that management must play if an organization's goals are to be achieved.

TQM PROCESS

Our conceptualization of the TQM process is shown in Fig. 7.6. The schema is presented in five phases:

1.   *The research and diagnostic phase* identified output, customer requirements and satisfaction, cost of quality, participants, and process parameters.

2.   *The analysis phase* tries to understand the variations in terms of common causes, special causes and capability. In this phase, new ideas are developed and tested to address the root causes.

3.   *The solution phase* identifies the planned improvements.

Fig. 7.6. TQM Continuous Process Improvement

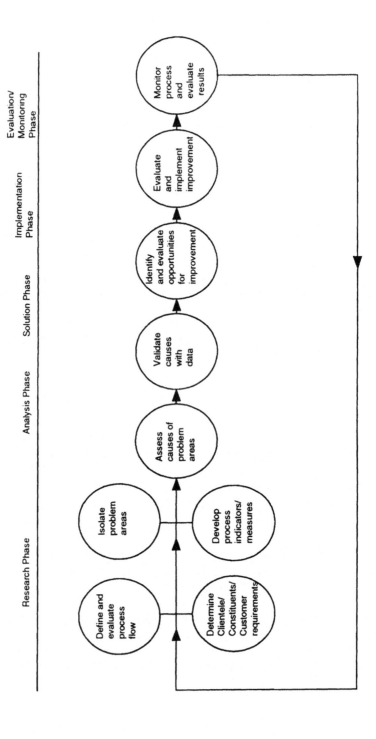

4.   *The implementation phase* initiates the system and documents changes, evaluates system performance, and rewards participants.
5.   *The monitoring phase* ensures that improvements are maintained and recycled to phase one.

Kaoru Ishikawa

Ishikawa's approach focuses on quality control that involves:

1.   Determining the requirements of the clients and customers.
2.   Knowing the buying intentions of customers.
3.   Knowing the cost as a precondition to defining quality.
4.   Developing the ability to anticipate potential defects and complaints.
5.   Maintaining quality by taking appropriate controlling action.
6.   Producing quality without the need for inspection.

Ishikawa identifies the preconditions required to produce quality assurance as:

1.   Quality is produced by design and at each process and not by inspection.
2.   Eliminate quality control by inspection.
3.   Emphasize the prevention of errors.
4.   Incorporate total quality control at the development stage of each new product.
5.   Understand the basic underlying cause of quality failure and not the symptom.
6.   An agency's quality system's efficiency is realized when the customers and clients express satisfaction and confidence in the product or service.[86]

Re-engineering

While TQM is a continuous process of incremental improvements, re-engineering can be viewed as an initiating phase in the TQM process. Re-engineering starts from scratch and questions conventional wisdom and standard operating procedures. It rethinks and challenges everything that is ordinarily done to best accomplish the organizational goals. The objective of TQM is the radical redesign and transformation of the work process to bring about major improvements in the key performance measures as they relate to quality, cost, service, and the delivery or response time. Re-engineering is intended to dovetail into the organization's strategy or strategic planning.[87]

Like TQM, re-engineering employs the team concept, draws from different disciplines, and pools expertise in studying existing processes. Greatest emphasis is put on maintaining and redesigning activities that add value to the organizations while eliminating those that are not contributing value. For example, if 60 percent of the existing budget meetings can be dropped without affecting the quality and cost of the budget, the meetings should be eliminated. To achieve the most from re-engineering, a five-step process is suggested.

1.   Allow one individual to control the process. Where there is more than one unit contributing to a major process, consolidate the review control to one manager

(process ownership) who has authority to examine the chain of events from the point of initiation of the production or service to the customers.

2.   Map the process to facilitate a clear identification of the key processes.

3.   Identify and eliminate existing and emerging trouble spots in the system.

4.   Be committed to completing the re-engineering goals in the shortest time possible. Avoid exhaustion from the preparation of data, charts, and reports that generate little change.

5.   Incorporate re-engineering into the TQM process and be ready to begin the process at any time in the future when the potential payoff for adding value to the organization processes is recognized.

Nature of Workers

TQM and re-engineering are committed to the "more and more" hypothesis, which suggests strong confidence and mutual trust between all levels of management. Teamwork characterizes all interactions in a continuous pursuit to maximize mutually agreed goals and objectives. Management is seen as a positive force for change as it views workers as vital assets and resource investments that must be continuously enhanced. TQM emphasizes creativity, and empowerment of workers or colleagues.

View of Power

TQM inverts the traditional management pyramid and brings the operating line workers closer to the clients they serve. Power is exercised from the bottom up. It is seen as operating in a collegial context, as a collective and consensual instrument to enhance the interests of all.

The leader operates more as a dispenser of information, a facilitator, colleague, coach, and builder of consensus. The team approach is used to promote cooperation and coordination. Decisions are driven predominately by the collectively determined priorities of participants in the organization.

View of Accountability

TQM is characterized by a ceaseless pursuit of the highest quality goods and services to internal and external customers at the least cost possible. All activities are driven by the desire to maximize satisfaction of the recipients of goods and services.

CONCLUSION

The mechanistic classical theory provides little opportunity for human discretion. It emphasizes rules and procedures aimed at promoting predict-ability, precision, and speed. The operation of the system requires strict subordi-nation and a rigid hierarchy. For Weber, rules were created to cover all situations. For Taylor, there was the one best way to perform a job. Despite Thompson's commitment to scientific management, he emphasized distributive justice and harmony in the workplace. The administrative theorists, Gulick and Urwick, suggested that each organizational problem must be handled in the right order if the best results are to be achieved.

The efficient achievement of the organization's goals is the highest pursuit, one in which the workers or civil servants are seen as inert instruments to be used as the organizational situation (objective) dictates. Leaders obtain their power from the hierarchy and have a right to expect obedience from subordinates. The basic assumption is thus made that authority and power flow down and the strict obedience of subordinates to organizational rules and procedures keeps them subservient and accountable to the top. Though Taylor recognized the importance of expertise in MLMs and indicated the need for partnership, he did not develop a theory of the influential role of MLMs.

The mechanistic classical school assumed accountability was automatic. The goals of the organization were seen not as satisfying clients' expectations. Whatever was produced was adequate and acceptable, as long as it was done efficiently according to prescribed procedures.

Organizational humanism arose to meet the problems created by the practice of the mechanistic classical school. While the latter saw workers as free from friction and emotions and the actions of organizations as calculable and predictable, organizational humanism saw organizational decisions as having unanticipated consequences, and workers' feelings, ideas, and perceptions as important in achieving the organization's goal. It emphasized finding ways to fit the organization to people—both the MLM and the operators. The assumption was made that human resources in organizations can be developed to achieve satisfaction for the workers while simultaneously promoting high productivity of goods and services.

Paradoxically, like the mechanistic theorists, organizational humanists (1) stress economy and efficiency as a goal (maximally achieving organizational goals); (2) assume a rational organizational model (though worker motivation was viewed as more important and elusive among the humanists); (3) view organization hierarchically (top management knows how the organization's structure and people should be manipulated to achieve the organizational goals); and (4) promote minimal concern for accountability for goods and services to the external community (except for the NPA, which espouses a more equitable distribution of public goods).

Despite the objectives pursued by organizational humanism, there has been continued unionization, due, among other things, to a feeling of alienation and manipulation. Additionally, the government has found it necessary to initiate affirmative action to assist women and minorities to obtain a more equitable treatment in government jobs. These and other developments help to indicate the divergence between theory and practice, demonstrating a need for a better conceptualization of theory to explain how organizations do indeed behave.

The new public administration arose to redirect the emphasis of the mechanistic and humanistic schools from their preoccupation with economy and efficiency toward greater participation in agency decision-making and equity in the distribution of goods and services. Unfortunately, the NPA theory was not built on a rigorous empirical base, and it was discarded before any attempt was made to operationalize it. Thus, we still need to develop a theory that would explain: the mounting problems in public agencies; the best way to identify and harness power; and a means to meet the mounting alienation that people have toward government.

DISCUSSION QUESTIONS

1. Why is traditional organization theory known as the theory without people?
2. Why are traditional organizational principles still widely practiced despite continuing attacks?
3. What is the human relations school in organization theory?
4. Discuss the objectives and implications of the new public administration.
5. How does a "theorist" concept of the nature of workers affect organization theory?
6. Describe the major features of Frederick Taylor's scientific management. In what way might it be said that Taylor's scientific management was intended to be a means for social revolution?
7. Why is it said that successful organizations must be adaptable to constant change in order to survive in the new economic environment?
8. What is TQM and what utility does it have for modern public management?
9. What is the difference between TQM and re-engineering?
10. Discuss the utility of the concepts of praxis and hermeneutics. What lessons or insights might we learn from the application of these concepts?

NOTES

1. This criticism charted that traditional principles of organization theory are not based on empirical evidence but on values of the theorists.
2. Max Weber, *Essays on Sociology,* translated by H. H. Gerth and C. Wright Mills (New York: Oxford University Press, 1946).
3. In Luther Gulick and Lyndall Urwick (eds.), *Papers on Science of Administration* (N.Y.: Institute of Public Administration, 1937) pp. 1–45.
4. James D. Mooney and Alan C. Reiley, *Principles of Organization* (New York: Harper & Row, 1939).
5. Max Weber, *The Theory of Social and Economic Organization*, edited by Talcott Parsons, translated by A. M. Henderson and Talcott Parsons (New York: Oxford University Press, 1947), pp. 329–30.
6. Weber, *Essays on Sociology*, p. 199.
7. Peter Blau and Marshall Myer, *Bureaucracy in Modern Society*, 2nd edn. (New York: Random House, 1971), pp. 19–20.
8. Chester I. Bernard, *The Functions of the Executive* (Cambridge, Mass.: Harvard University Press, 1938), p.127.
9. Peter Blau, *Dynamics of Bureaucracy* (Chicago: University of Chicago Press, 1955).

10. Frederick W. Taylor, *Principles of Scientific Management* (New York: Harper and Brothers Publishers, 1911), p. 83.

11. Ibid., p. 38.

12. Ibid., p. 29.

13. Frederick W. Taylor, *Shop Management* (New York: Harper & Row, 1911).

14. David Schuman and Dick Olufs III, *Public Administration in the United States* (Lexington, Mass.: D. C. Heath, 1988), p. 72.

15. Frederick W. Taylor, "The Principles of Scientific Management," in *Classics in Management*, Harwood F. Merrill, ed. (New York: American Management Association, 1960), p. 78.

16. Clarence Bertrand Thompson, *Scientific Management* (Cambridge, Mass.: Harvard University Press, 1914).

17. Clarence Bertrand, *Theory and Practice of Scientific Management* (Chicago, Ill.: A.W. Shaw, 1917).

18. George F. Will, reviewing Robert Kangel's, *The One Best Way, Frederick Winslow Taylor and the Enigma of Efficiency* (New York: Viking, 1997) in *New York Times Book Review* (June 15, 1997)

19. Clarence Bertrand Thompson, *The Church and the Wage Earners* (New York: Scribbner, 1910).

20. Clarence Bertrand Thompson, "The Literature of Scientific Management," *Quarterly Journal of Economics* (May 28, 1914): 506–57.

21. Clarence Bertrand Thompson, "The Case for Scientific Management," *Sociological Review*, 12 No. 4 (October, 1914): 315.

22. Frederick W. Taylor, *Principles of Scientific Management* (New York: Harper and Rcw, 1911).

23. Thompson, "The Case for Scientific Management," p. 316.

24. Ibid. pp. 316–17.

25. Clarence Bertrand Thompson, *The Theory of Practice of Scientific Management* (Boston, MA: Houghton, Mifflin, 1917).

26. Paul Planus, "My Acquaintance with the American Who Introduced Scientific Management in France," *Enterprise* No. 441 (February 22, 1964).

27. Gulick's principles were drawn from Henri Fayol's list of five (planning, organization, command, coordination, and control). See Henri Fayol, *General and Industrial Management*, translated by Constance Storrs (London: Isaac Pitman Sons Ltd., 1940), pp. 43–110.

28. Gulick and Urwick, *Papers*, p. 13.

29. Ibid., p. 35.

30. Ibid., p. 15.

31. Ibid., p. 9.

32. Lyndall F. Urwick, *The Elements of Administration* (New York: Harper and Brothers. 1943), p. 118.

33. Ibid., pp. 34–39, 51–52.

34. Quoted in Dwight Waldo, *The Administrative State* (New York: Ronald Press, 1948), p. 174.

35. John M. Pfiffner and Robert Presthus, *Public Administration*, 5th edn. (New York: Ronald Press, 1967), p. 179.

36. Herbert Kaufman, "Emerging Conflicts in the Doctrines of Public Administration," *American Political Science Review* (December 1956): 1057.

37. For an excellent discussion of this topic, see Dwight Waldo, "Public Administration," in *International Encyclopedia of the Social Sciences*, Edward L. Sills. ed., (New York: Macmillan, 1968): 147.

38. Pfiffner and Presthus, *Public Administration*, pp. 184-85.

39. David Easton, in *World Politics*, Vol. 9 (April 1957), pp. 383-400. See also *A Framework for Political Analysis* (Englewood Cliffs, N.J.: Prentice-Hall, 1965); and *A Systems Analysis of Political Life* (New York: Wiley, 1965).

40. Ira Sharkansky, *Public Administration: Policy-Making in Government Agencies* (Chicago: Rand McNally, 1970).

41. Kenyon B. DeGreene, *Sociotechnical Systems: Factors in Analysis of Design and Management* (Englewood Cliffs, N.J.: Prentice-Hall, 1973), p. 13.

42. Reinhard Bendix, *Work and Authority in Industry* (New York: John Wiley & Sons, 1956), p. xxi.

43. Ibid., p. 250.

44. Ibid., p. 260.

45. Because of the large number of people in this school, there will be only minimal discussion of specific individuals.

46. Henry C. Metcalf and L. Urwick (eds.), *Constructive Conflicts in Dynamic Administration: The Collected Papers of Mary Parker Follett*, (New York: Harper & Brothers, 1940), chap. 4; and Harvey M. Fox, "Mary Parker Follett: The Enduring Contribution," *Public Administration* (November-December 1968): 520-529.

47. Mary Parker Follett, "The Giving of Orders," in *Classics on Organizational Behavior*, J. Steven Ott, ed. (Pacific Grove, Calif.: Brooks/Cole Publishing, 1989), pp. 255-64.

48. George C. Homans, "The Western Electric Researches," in *Human Factors in Management*, rev. edn., (New York: Harper & Row, 1951); and F. J. Roethlisberger and William Dickson, *Management and the Worker* (Cambridge, Mass.: Harvard University Press, 1972).

49. Dale Carnegie, *How To Win Friends and Influence People* (New York: Simon & Schuster, 1936).

50. Daniel A. Wren, *The Evolution of Management Thought*, 3rd edn. (New York: John Wiley & Sons, 1987), p. 422.

51. Douglas McGregor, *The Human Side of Enterprise* (New York: McGraw-Hill, 1960).

52. Bernard, *The Functions of the Executive*, Chaps. 10-12.

53. Abraham Maslow, *Motivation and Personality*, 2nd edn. (New York: Harper & Row, 1970), pp. 35-58.

54. Abraham H. Maslow, "A Theory of Human Motivation," *Psychological Review* (July 1943): 370.

55. Warren E. Bennis and Edgar H. Schein, with collaboration of Caroline McGregor, *Leadership and Motivation: Essays of Douglas McGregor* (Cambridge, Mass., MIT Press, 1960), Chap. 1.

56. Frederick Herzberg, Bernard Mausner, and Barbara Snyderman, *The Motivation to Work* (New York: John Wiley & Sons, 1959).

57. Rensis Likert, *New Patterns of Management* (New York: McGraw-Hill, 1961).

58. Edward E. Lawler and Lyman W. Porter, "The Effects of Performance on Job Satisfaction," *Industrial Relations* (October 1967); and Herbert A. Simon, "Organization Man: Rational or Self-Actualizing," *Public Administrative Review* (July-August 1973): 346-53.

59. Marvin D. Dunnette, John P. Campbell and Milton D. Hakal, "Factors Contributing to Job Satisfaction and Job Dissatisfaction in Six Occupational Groups," *Organizational Behavior and Human Performance* 2, No. 2 (May 1967): 143–74.

60. Richard Beckhord, *Organizational Development: Strategies and Model* (Reading, Mass.: Addison-Wesley Publishing, 1969): pp. 10–11.

61. Wendell French and Cecil H. Bell Jr., *Organization Development* (Englewood Cliffs, N.J.: Prentice-Hall, 1969).

62. See Wendell L. French and Cecil H. Bell Jr., *Organizational Development: Behavioral Science Interventions for Organization Improvement* (Englewood Cliffs, N.J.: Prentice-Hall, 1990).

63. Kurt Lewin, *Field Theory in Social Science* (New York: Harper & Row, 1951).

64. Edgar H. Schein, *Process Consultation: Its Role in Organizational Development* (Reading, Mass.: Addison-Wesley Publishing, 1969), p. 9.

65. Thomas H. Fitzgerald, "Can Change in Organizational Culture Really Be Managed?" *Organizational Dynamics* (Autumn 1988): 5–15.

66. Warren G. Bennis, *Organizational Development: Its Nature, Origins, and Prospects* (Reading, Mass.: Addison-Wesley Publishing, 1969), p. 2.

67. Beckhord, *Organizational Development* (Addison-Wesley Publishing, 1969).

68. Larry Kirkhart and Orion F. White Jr., "The Future of Organization Development," *Public Administration Review* (March-April 1974): p. 129.

69. H. Roy Kaplan and Curt Tausky, "Humanism in Organizations: A Critical Appraisal," *Public Administration Review* (March-April 1977): 174.

70. Ibid., pp. 171–80.

71. H. George Frederickson, "Toward a New Public Administration," in *Toward A New Public Administration*, Frank Marini, ed. (Scranton, Pa.: Chandler, 1971), p. 312.

72. Ibid., p. 313.

73. "Symposium on Social Equity and Public Administration," George Frederickson, ed., *Public Administration Review* (January-February 1974): 1–51.

74. John Rawls, *A Theory of Justice* (Cambridge, Mass.: Belknap Press, 1971). Rawls's two principles are:

> *First Principle*: Each person is to have an equal right to the most extensive total system of equal basic liberties compatible with a similar system of liberty for all. *Second Principle*: Social and economic inequalities are to be arranged so that they are both: (a) to the greatest benefit of the least advantaged, consistent with the just savings principle, and (b) attached to offices and positions open to all under conditions of fair equality of productivity.

Conditions in the first principle must always be met before the second can be effectively fulfilled. Thus no organization has the right to deny a person his basic liberties except as outlined in the priority rules attached to the principles.

75. Ibid., p. 141.

76. William H. Lucy, Dennis Gilbert, and Guthrie S. Burkhead, "Equity in Local Service Distribution," *Public Administration Review* (November-December 1977): 687.

77. In one critique, Orion White noted that public administration theory implicitly projects administrators as adults and the people they serve as children. See his "The Dialectical Organization: An Alternative to Bureaucracy," *Public Administration Review* (January-February 1969): 31–33.

78. Thomas Kuhn, *Structures of Scientific Revolutions* (Chicago: University of Chicago Press, 1962).

79. Alan K. Campbell, "Approaches to Defining, Measuring, and Achieving Equity in the Public Service," *Public Administration Review* (September-October 1976): 556.

80. Rosabeth Moss Kanter, *The Change Masters: Innovation for Productivity in the American Corporation* (New York: Simon and Schuster, 1983).

81. Tom Peters, *Thriving on Chaos* (New York: Alfred Knopf), 1988.

82. Carl Rogers, *Client-Center Therapy* (Boston, Mass.: Houghton Mifflin, 1951), pp. 483–87.

83. Arthur R. Tenner and Irving J. Detore, *Total Quality Management* (Reading, Mass.: Addison-Wesley Publishing, 1992).

84. Andrea Gabor, *The Man Who Discovered Quality* (New York: Times Book Random-House, 1992), p. 5.

85. Ibid., p. 7.

86. Kaoru Ishikawa, *What is Total Quality Control?* (Englewood Cliffs, N.J.: Prentice Hall, 1995).

87. Andrew J. Dubrin, *Reengineering Survival Guide* (Cincinnati, Ohio: Thompson Executive Press, 1995), pp. 3–4.

Part III

Processes and Practices

8

Planning in Public Management

This chapter discusses public sector planning in the narrow sense. We are not concerned with planning in relation to environment or social or economic goals; our focus is on planning in public agencies as it occurs in the intermediate level, among MLMs. We will emphasize what is appropriately called "planning as an administrative process."[1] This takes place inside the agency as the "development of a sound organization, the method of staffing organizations, the procedures and practices to be followed, and the direction and coordination of operation."[2] Administrative planning may also be labeled program planning or organization and method management. We also emphasize that when public planning is intended to be a guide to action, it becomes involved in the policymaking process.

First, the chapter examines the planning done by top or upper-level administrators. Second, we discuss the critical role and function of the MLM's in successful administrative planning and review commonly used methods. Finally, we offer a critique of planning, focusing on the difficulty and necessity of maintaining accountability to the public.

LEARNING OBJECTIVES

On completing this chapter, the reader should be able to:

- Defend a definition of planning and distinguish the differences between administrative and other types of planning.
- Distinguish between the planning done by top administrators and that done by MLMs and understand the relationship between them.
- Identify the problems inherent in planning, especially the need to relate long-range and short-range plans.
- Design a simple short-range planning system.

In the United States, especially in the public sector, discussions of planning have been characterized by ideological concerns. Public planning efforts are seen as a prelude to totalitarianism or Communist collectivism. Most people would define governmental planning as intervention into economic affairs at the national level, to control such things as health care, natural gas prices, inflation, and air and water pollution. Opponents believe such intervention is inimical to a free democratic and capitalist society, in which the individual decision-maker and business firms (operating in the marketplace through the price mechanism) should determine what happens.

The public's (especially private business managers') apprehensions about public sector planning contrast sharply with the highly developed planning that takes place in individual businesses. A Marxist economist visiting the U.S. would be bewildered to find that business managers are continuously warning of the dangers of a planned economy yet engage in extensive planning themselves. In terms of setting priorities of time and money, private sector economic planning in the U.S. surpasses even public sector planning in the former Soviet Union. In the U.S., planning is decentralized (done by the individual corporations) and short range in perspective, but it is a critical feature of the great industrial, interdependent society in which we live.[3]

The ideological perspective that dominates most discussions of planning will be of only minor concern to us. First, these debates focus on macro-economics or broad societal public policy determination. This type of planning (commonly known as comprehensive or strategic planning) is reserved normally for legislative officials, elected executives, and top-level administrators in governmental agencies. Second, the ideas exchanged are not intended to and do not generally provide operational guides to MLMs who must implement policy. Our focus will be mainly on the planning that takes place inside public agencies concerned with the functional requirements necessary to produce and deliver goods and services to the community.

Planning requires that we do something in the present if we hope to affect the future. Virtually all organizations, from the family and social clubs to public organizations, are manifestations of a human desire to maintain permanence despite the passing of time and possibility of uncertainty. But planning is not a natural phenomenon that we do automatically. The pressures of everyday work force us to concentrate on the present, forget the past, and let the passage of time solve tomorrow's problems. Organizations that permit managers to develop this syndrome cannot expect to achieve their goals. This is especially important for public agencies, which are subject to many unpredictable variables (changing political forces, both legislative and executive, shifting power among competing interest groups and clients, and other ecological factors) so that changes often come either suddenly and with little warning or almost imperceptibly. Planning provides insights, allowing the successful manager to master such changes, while the unsuccessful manager is abandoned to the whims and vagaries of unforeseen problems.

Planning as a public function has had an uneven history in the United States. Alexander Hamilton's fiscal program for President Washington, which advocated national planning under governmental leadership, is generally given as the first example. Actually, this kind of economic planning was not taken seriously again until the National Resources Planning Board was established in 1933.

Planning as a continuous activity is most familiar at local levels, where it generally takes the form of physical planning of cities, for example, determining where business districts end and residential areas begin and how many stories businesses and apartment buildings may have. Physical planning had its beginning before the 1880s but took on added impetus in the 1950s with the coming of metropolitan planning, particularly in the New York region. During the Lyndon Baines Johnson administration, many resources were made available in social and human service areas such as health, education, and personnel. During the early years of the Nixon administration, most of these programs were terminated, although a number of planning agencies (planning for the country as a whole) still exist, such as the Council of Economic Advisers, and the National Security Council.

WHAT IS PLANNING?

Planning is a supreme function in the management of organizations. It involves, first, conceiving of a range of meaningful goals and developing alternative choices for action to achieve these goals. The provision of alternatives and the projection of means require significant input by MLMs. Second, planning involves a systematic procedure for the reduction of many alternatives to an approved course of action (a legislative function). Planning determines not only goals but also the sequential order in which they are pursued, the need for coordination (see Fig. 8.1), and the standards for maintaining control. The latter is critically dependent on and presupposes planning. After all, control is the instrument employed to ensure that activities or events conform to plans. Planning requires that we determine the correct path to map out precisely where we wish to go, because as someone has said, "If we don't know where we are going, any road will take us there." By the same reasoning we can also say, "If we don't know where we are going, no road will take us there."

Definitions of planning are numerous. Each of the following contains part of what is meant by planning.

1. Planning is the establishment of objectives and the assessment of limitations—that is, thought before action.
2. It identifies specific objectives for concrete action and the means by which they may be undertaken.
3. It identifies, in the broad generic sense, objectives that a governmental unit or agency determines that it will pursue at some specified time in the future. A set of decisions is developed to facilitate actions directed at achieving the publicly determined goals and objectives, using the best means possible.
4. It facilitates the coordination of an organization's activities in achieving defined and agreed goals and objectives.
5. It makes things happen that would not otherwise occur.

6.   It attempts to anticipate future events and thus reduces the impact of change.
7.   It minimizes waste and redundancy.
8.   It means obtaining a vision of the future and looking back to structure present events to conform with that vision.
9.   It relates to proposals for the future evaluation of alternative proposals and the methods by which such proposals may be realized.[4]
10.   It sets standards to facilitate control.
11.   It is a disciplined process that forces policy decision-makers to reflect and act rationally when selecting actions to maximize benefits and minimize costs.

These definitions emphasize three main aspects: (1) the future; (2) alternatives; and (3) rational choices. This is in the tradition of science, or what we have come to call the bureaucratic model—the concern for a process that is impersonal or neutral, a scientific approach.

Fig. 8.1. Comparing Planned and Unplanned Organizations

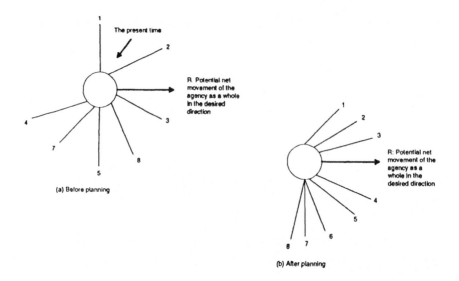

Source: Adapted from Herbert G. Hicks, *The Management of Organizations* (NY: McGraw-Hill, 1967), pp. 21–22.

The process view of planning may easily be illustrated. In taking a trip to the Smithsonian Institution in Washington, D.C., we may use a road map indicating which of the available routes we should follow, keeping in mind the allotted time, weather conditions, and facilities available along the way. Planning begins with the decision to take the trip to achieve the objectives of visiting the Smithsonian. It continues throughout the trip, involving the buying of gasoline, the determination of which of the available restaurants we will use along the way, where we will park our car, and which displays we will see at the Smithsonian after we arrive.

Personnel at all levels, but especially MLMs, should be aware of the advantages and disadvantages of planning. The attributes of a good plan were summarized by Henri Fayol:

1. It is based on clearly defined objectives stated in a concise manner.
2. It covers all actions that are required for the plan to be fulfilled.
3. It is flexible so that it can be adjusted to meet unexpected conditions.
4. It contains contingency plans to cover areas that are most uncertain.
5. It allows for frequent feasibility checks.
6. It has been properly disseminated to all who are committed by the plan.
7. The resources made available match the tasks assigned.
8. It is reduced to writing.

Fayol summarized these features when he wrote: "Unity, continuity, flexibility, precision, such are the broad features of a good plan of action."[5] When planning is done effectively, it produces many benefits that help to make the job of managing easier:[6]

1. It is an orderly way to institute desired change.
2. It is a useful way of clarifying goals.
3. It is a stimulus to creative thinking.
4. It provides a tool for evaluation.
5. It focuses resources on objectives.
6. It permits managers to provide confident and aggressive leadership.

Most of the benefits to be gained from planning will be dissipated if due recognition is not given to the constraints and limitations that are inherent in the planning function. This is especially true when the plans are not continuously compared with the problems that are often encountered in the process of implementation (at the MLM level). The following are among the limiting factors:

1. Information about the future is frequently incomplete and inaccurate. Thus, constant updating is required.
2. Considerable investment in time and resources is required.
3. People tend to have greater regard for the present than for the future.
4. It can result in rigid procedures.
5. It faces resistance from line administrators, especially when close consultation is not maintained.
6. As it becomes sophisticated, it multiplies rules and can become incomprehensible.[7]

THE NEED FOR AND COMPLEXITY OF PLANNING

Modern technology has made planning an inevitable requirement. It has narrowed specialization, greatly increasing the need for continued division of labor, which in turn generates the need for coordination (an aspect of administrative planning). Specialization divides the work activity into smaller segments to concentrate greater expertise and knowledge and thereby obtain more effective and superior solutions to problems. It was not uncommon only a few years ago for us to take our car to the neighborhood garage and get whatever was wrong fixed. Now this process may involve a host of other shops and garages.

Technology has lengthened the lead time between the conception of an idea and its implementation. Building a highway requires not only engineering specifications but social, economic, political, and environmental impact statements, all of which may take months or years to complete, depending on the interests operating in the environment. It took the British and the French, for example, more than a decade and billions of dollars from the beginning of the development of the passenger supersonic aircraft until the first successful flight.

It takes greater investment (due to inflation and rising costs) to conduct virtually every activity now than previously. Because investments are larger, management must be in a position to cancel or modify programs to minimize service delay, human suffering, and monetary losses. Planners must keep this in mind so that managers will be able to develop contingent responses that will allow programs to be followed smoothly.

Well-conceived planning helps direct the stream of interdepartmental or intersectional activities toward the main objective of the agency, and agency decisions are constantly measured against this goal. Well-planned activities give rise to efficient and coordinated efforts because they concentrate on achieving the best way of organizing and performing activities.

Instead of piecemeal activities, agency efforts are jointly directed toward achieving the maximum results. More important, as noted above, without planning there can be no control. Subordinates' accomplishments can be monitored effectively only if there is a plan against which their actions can be measured.

Planning is a major and critical instrument that provides greater rationality and order to organizations than would otherwise be present. It "permits a manager to act with initiative and to create situations to the organization's advantage."[8] The effectiveness of planning lies in increased coordination, closing the gap between independent action and the potential net movements of the whole agency.

PLANNING: THE ROLE OF TOP ADMINISTRATOR

According to Harlan Cleveland, executives operate in a world of continuing uncertainty. Even the contingencies in which they invest much effort seldom, if ever, occur as anticipated:

The executive's work often consists in meeting a series of unforeseeable obstacles on the road to an objective which can clearly be specified only when he is close to reaching it. He tries to imagine the unforeseen by posing contingencies and asking how his organization system would adjust if they arose. But the planned-for contingency never happens; something else happens instead. The planning does not produce a usable plan, but something more precious: people better trained to analyze the unpredicted and to winnow out for the decision makers the choices that would be too costly to judge or postpone. [9]

To ensure that administrators will have enough time to plan effectively, Holden et al. suggest three preconditions:

1. Development of a sound plan of organization for realizing the agency's goals and objectives. This permits responsibility to be clearly delineated and facilitates clear pursuit of the agency mission.
2. Selection of the best available qualified personnel for all key positions.
3. Provision of effective methods for controlling the agency's activity.[10]

In public and private agencies, the master functions (planning, organizing, coordinating, and controlling) are performed mainly by top-level administrators who are responsible for visualizing, initiating, and achieving future objectives. Top managers are concerned with strategic planning or comprehensive planning—planning for the overall agency.

There are, however, significant differences in the way the top administrators in the public and private sectors are expected to operate and discharge their responsibilities. Every planning act by public administrators must be traceable directly or indirectly to some legislative authorization. We have shown (Chapter 5) that authorizations represent a multitude of compromises among many groups and different factions even in the legislation itself. Because the legislature, for political reasons, can easily undo even the best-conceived plan, public administrators must be ever mindful of relevant legislative members, important interest groups, and clients. Successful planning dictates that formal and informal approval of seemingly trivial changes in proposals be obtained as a normal part of administration. This means that part of top public administrators' planning time is involved in maintaining and building external alliances among relevant interest groups, clients, and legislators. Viewed in this context, most top administrators' time is taken up with planning. In spite of this reality, administrators have little impact on operations, which, as we will see below, are dominated by MLMs.

Administrators pursue and emphasize overall objectives of the agency consistent with legislative authorization and in harmony with relevant interest groups, negotiating where the agency will go (policy) and the resources that will be needed to realize its mission. They must choose a set of specific programs so that they can reach specific goals. Success is dependent on at least four steps: (1) clarification of goals; (2) thorough evaluation of the situation; (3) selection of a course of action after weighing relevant alternatives; and (4) determination of the best means.

The preceding discussion suggests that top administrators carry on planning in the external and internal environment of the agency. Often the chief executive officer (for example, former FBI Director J. Edgar Hoover, Robert Moses of the New York City Parks Department, or Allegheny County Coroner Cyril Wecht) comes to symbolize his or her agency.

The two most common types of plans in public management are *long range* and *short range*. Strategic and contingency planning are sometimes used to realize short- and long-range plans. Depending on their purpose, plans are referred to as strategic single-use or standing plans. Fig. 8.2 presents a scheme of long-range planning. Alternative one is selected while alternative two and three are rejected because they sunk costs, representing the status quo that will not produce the changes desired.

Top-level planning functions are exhibited primarily in the left-hand column. Executives or top administrators dominate this area. Long-range planning normally covers a span of three years or more, but this period is only a convention because what may be long range depends greatly on the context. In the case of farmers, who face highly competitive markets and are subject to natural disasters, such as floods and tornadoes, long-range plans may be no more than two years. In the fashion design industry, which operates in a relentlessly competitive environment, long-range plans may not extend over six months. The degree of uncertainty is the crucial variable that determines the time span of plans.

Fig. 8.2. Long-Range Planning Sequence

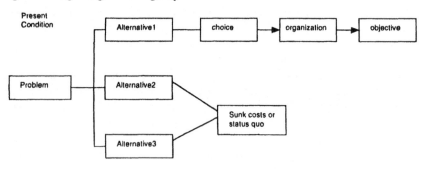

LONG RANGE PLANNING

The following questions and steps will serve as important guides. In attempting to plan successfully and accountably, administrators must respond not only to their visions of the future but also to articulated client and constituency needs:

1.   *What must we do?* The preparation of the stated goals.
2.   *Where are we now?* The internal assessment of present operations and trends.
3.   *How are others similarly situated?* Comparisons with alternative approaches being taken by the agency.
4.   *What are the alternatives open to us?* The review of the range of feasible operations for the agency.
5.   *Which course should we follow?* The decision to make a commitment of resources.
6.   *Who will do what, when?* The schedule of key events.
7.   *How will we know how well we are doing?* The arrangements for feedback and evaluation.

Long-range planning, if properly executed, will produce guidelines for managerial planning (Fig. 8.2). The process begins to directly involve the MLM in step 4, as the resources of the agency are committed.

Additionally, steps 6 and 7 require follow-up short-range planning. In the case of road cleaning, it is the MLM who will determine where the streets will be cleaned and the individuals who will be assigned to specific streets; and MLMs determine how well the streets have been cleaned. Step 6 requires that responsibility and resources assigned to a specific unit in the organization, indicating when group X or client Z will get what service and at what cost. Step 7 compares what was accomplished with what was planned.

Strategic Planning

Strategic planning is a "coalition of the willing."[11] It is the strategy or means of carrying out a policy. Administrators look closely at the alternatives and costs associated with the choice that must be made. To assist in the decision-making process, the consequences of each available approach are usually simulated. In the public sector, this typically involves simulating the power and influence of the various groups and the available resources (potential legislative appropriation to the agency). Steps in this process include (see Fig. 8.3): (1) Establishing a vision, mission, and goals; (2) internal and external environmental assessment of threats and opportunities; (3) clarifying strategic directions[12] by reviewing the mission, goals, and objectives, and strategic issues; (4) foster commitment and cooperation among critical constituencies, enhancing maximum benefit while minimizing liabilities; (5) evaluate and adapt plans; (6) establish a clearly defined implementation process; (7) evaluate performance; (8) review strategies and strategic process. Three criteria are used to assess the issues in step 3. They are the potential impact of the action, the likelihood that the action will occur within a specified time frame and that the successful outcome will be compatible with the organization's capability and culture.

Strategic planning is not a substitute for critical thinking and leadership. Strategic planning is not synonymous with the creation of an organizational strategy. To become overly obsessed with it can create a myopia that can blind the organization to unplanned opportunities and useful sources of information that provide insight for effective action.[13]   The U.S. General Accounting Office review of U.S. Agency for International Development (AID) indicated that AID failed to follow goal planning practices and proposed that the agency adopt strategic plans (see Fig. 8.4) to improve its productivity and effectiveness.

Fig. 8.3. Strategic Management

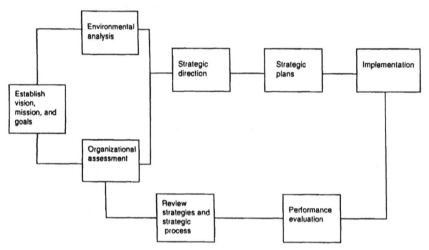

Source: Adapted from Lynne Hall, *Strategic Management and the United Way* (Alexandria, VA: United Way of America, 1995), p. 95.

Contingency Planning

Contingency planning commonly refers to actions taken to meet situations that cannot be specifically planned for because of their unpredictability. Yet a reasonable estimate of the problem, cost, and the general action that may be taken can be held in reserve. For example, the typical government unit in a snow-belt area budgets for snow removal, but the snow does not fall uniformly every year. The government unit must have plans to get extra money, personnel, and equipment to deal with excessive snowfall when it comes, as was the case in the winters of 1990 and 1995–96.

Standing and Single-Use Plans

Standing plans are concerned with continuing or ongoing policies and standard operating procedures. They are used again and again. These include plans for recruitment of personnel, purchasing, or evaluation. In contrast, single-use plans are for one-time events. Normally they are designed to achieve specific objectives covering a short period of time. Projects, budgets, and programs are common examples. During World War II, the Normandy beachhead was to be stormed only once.

Fig. 8.4. Proposed Strategic Management Framework for AID

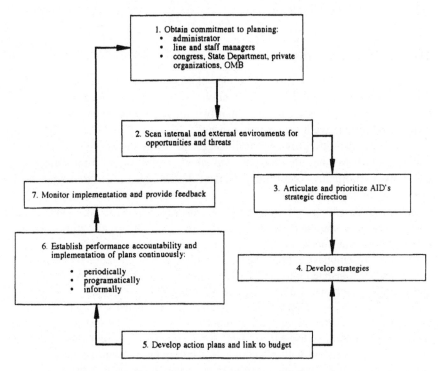

Source: Adapted from U.S. General Accounting Office, *AID Management: Strategic Planning Can Help AID Face Current Challenges* (Washington, D.C. GAO NSAID-92-100, March, 1992), pp. 22.

SHORT-RANGE PLANNING

Short-range planning is concerned predominantly with events occurring within one year or less and fits into the scope of a long-range plan as a phase of its execution. The results of short-range planning tend to be translated into numerical goals. While top management dominates long-range planning, MLMs reign supreme in short-range planning. Short-range planning involves the same seven questions noted above for long-range planning, although greater emphasis is placed on the tactics and means to implement programs or activities.

If we view planning as a vertical ladder or hierarchy, the further we move down the organization, the shorter the planning time frame becomes. Focus is given to immediate tasks to be done or specific assignments to be carried out. For example, how can the excessive snowfall be expeditiously removed while minimizing the inconvenience to the public and holding the line on cost?

In government, the most common short-range planning takes place in the preparation of the annual budget. A budget is not only a final plan; it is also a plan of work in that all activities that are undertaken must be authorized and indicated in dollars and cents.

THE MLM AND PLANNING

Though administrative planning plays an important role in MLM activities, writers on public administration seldom give it more than passing mention. This emphasis contrasts sharply with textbooks on private management, which often give it considerable space.

MLM planning provides the linkage and continuity so vital to effective planning. MLMs are the funnels and chief providers of information and alternatives (normally requiring technical knowledge and familiarity with operation) to top-level planners. Top management typically consults middle managers in deciding on organizational strategy and mission. While top administrators comprehensively plan for the overall organization, MLMs translate these plans into programs and services to meet client needs.

MLMs emphasize procedures, techniques, and operational concerns— how plans are translated into action. The focus is on immediate tasks to be done and specific assignments to be completed. The MLMs' organizational sphere of influence covers a large area of the organization concerned with administrative planning, implementation, and, very important, control. The last relates to the primary responsibility that MLMs bear for keeping results (delivery of goods and services) consistent with planning. Not infrequently, what top management has set forth in the plans and what interest groups have initially acquiesced in cannot be realized because of later interest-group demands, shifting alliances, insufficient appropriations, or changes in priorities after an election or an emergency (such as a flood) that requires at least temporary redeployment of resources. This means that the policy that has been hammered out at the top may have to be adjusted, not by the administrators, but by MLMs based on what they think is practical and consistent with goals. This gives MLMs leeway to modify or even redirect plans.

PROGRAM PLANNING

There are a number of tools available to assist MLMs in accomplishing the organizational plans. Perhaps the most widely used are program planning (also commonly known as programming), management by objectives (MBO), and program evaluation and review techniques (PERT).

Sound program planning or analysis is one of the techniques most widely used by MLMs. It provides the critical link between planning and implementation. Essentially, it involves identifying the best program and activities required to effectively accomplish the goals and objectives set forth by top administrators. For example, when plans for higher education are worked out, the goals for industrial development decided, or a highway department concludes that it will resurface 100 miles of rural roads, more specific plans can be drawn up indicating how the program can be achieved. It is the MLM who will decide the order in which rural roads are to be resurfaced and the necessary steps required to resurface them, the time that each step will take, and how the staff will be deployed. Detailed attention will be given to the necessary technical skills, the activities required to realize the goals, and any legal ramifications. The program planning involves the following steps:

- Dividing activities into steps necessary to achieve the objective.
- Noting the relationship between each of the steps, especially any required sequence.
- Deciding who will be responsible for each step.
- Estimating the time required for each step.
- Assigning dates for the completion of each step.
- Rechecking to see that allocations of resources match assignments.

MANAGEMENT BY OBJECTIVES (MBO)

MBO originated in the business sector and was practiced mainly by businesses but found its way into the public sector with the Nixon administration in the early 1970s.[14] On April 18, 1973, President Nixon wrote a letter to 21 federal agencies calling for the adoption of the MBO approach in carrying out programs. MBO is used to establish realizable, quantifiable goals that individuals or groups agree to accomplish within a specified period. The typical approach permits subordinates to prepare a set of concrete objectives that are consistent with the agency's goals and the administrative plans.[15] There are a number of characteristics of which we should be aware:

1. Goals are jointly set by MLMs and administrators.
2. The participative style of management is emphasized; that is, the subordinates gain greater control, and there is greater freedom of choice and greater responsibility for the work performed.
3. Both superiors and subordinates know the criteria on which subsequent assessment is made.
4. MBO increases job satisfaction.
5. Objectives are concretely defined and quantified where possible, such as the number of miles of roads to be resurfaced in a month.

The MBO system makes a number of positive contributions but also produces a number of unintended consequences to which MLMs must give consideration if they wish to effectively implement goals and objectives as planned. Table 8.1 shows eight of the outstanding advantages and problems associated with the use of MBO.

Table 8.1. MBO Advantages and Problems

Advantages	Problems
1. Harmonizes upper-level goals and lower-level objectives	1. This style of management (cooperative) tends to restructure the authority system.
2. Has potential for saving resources by minimizing misdirectives.	2. Leads proponents to believe that goals can be neatly broken down into segmented objectives.
3. Enhances motivation of MLMs through greater participation	3. Qualitative aspects of programs tend to be neglected.
4. Reduces direct control and supervision.	4. Requires significant investment in time, personnel involvement, and training.
5. Provides a greater objective basis for evaluation.	5. Requires considerable amount of paperwork.
6. Minimizes emphasis on organizational maintenance.	6. Oversimplifies the ease of measuring performance.
7. Facilitates the periodic review of progress toward objectives and provides feedback.	7. Risk-aversion creates strong pressures to set comfortable or easy objectives.
8. Encourages the achievement of objectives with reinforced performance rewards.	8. Objective-oriented management with set parameters may discourage finding optimal solutions.

PROGRAM EVALUATION AND REVIEW TECHNIQUE (PERT)

PERT is another device used by MLMs in implementing agency goals. The concept was jointly developed in the 1950s by the Navy and Booz-Allen-Hamilton to assist in the planning and development of the Polaris missile. PERT is designed to aid in planning and controlling costs and time by (1) focusing management's attention on key aspects of program development; (2) alerting MLMs to potential problems that may hinder achievement of program goals; (3) facilitating evaluation of programming; (4) providing management with a prompt mechanical reporting device; and (5) improving the quality of management decision-making.

PERT is an attempt to quantify program planning and control. It differs from other systems in that it seeks to systematize and mechanize the planning and control process, using computers, gant charts, and network flow plans. The last-named is the most fundamental tool in the PERT approach. As Fig. 8.5 shows, the network is composed of a series of related events or required stages, represented by arrows. An event may be produced by one or several interrelated activities, represented by arrows that connect the various events and denote the time consumed in performing that phase of the program. As far as possible, only significant accomplishments (such as administrative, intellectual, or hardware) should be represented and related to the degree of complexity involved. As Fig. 8.5 shows, some events can occur simultaneously while others must occur in

Fig. 8.5. YouthBuild Pittsburgh's HUD Grant Implementation Flow Plan

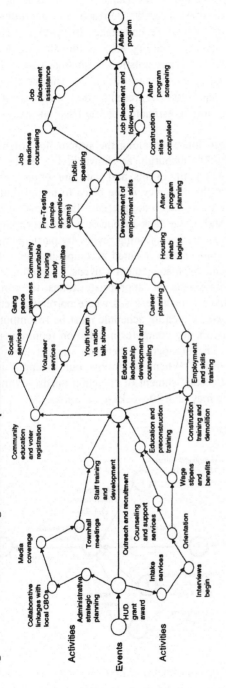

3 Months

Percent or number of:
1. Trainees in attendance
2. Trainees selected
3. CBOs participating
4. Social services provided
5. Wages and benefits
6. Applicant inquires
7. Performance reviews

6 Months

Percent or number of:
1. Trainees in attendance
2. Hours of classroom instruction
3. Hours of construction activities
4. Hours of leadership development
5. Trainees registered to vote
6. Hours of community services
7. Local media coverage
8. Hours of youth conferences attended
9. Performance reviews

9 Months

Percent or number of:
1. Trainees in attendance
2. Trainees passing Pre-test exams
3. Hours of public speaking engagements
4. Houses ready for rehab
5. Resources needed for after program
6. Performance reviews

12 Months

Percent or number of:
1. Trainees graduating
2. Job placements
3. GEDs awarded
4. Houses completed
5. Other rehab projects
6. After program participants
7. College or vocational enrollees
8. Stipends
9. On-going after program services needed
10. Hours spent on follow up activies
11. Performance reviews

Source: Adapted from Jeffery Perkins Jr. for YouthBuild Pittsburgh, Inc., May 5, 1995.

sequence. For example, intake, orientation, construction, and media coverage can all occur at the same time, but obtaining the Department of Housing and Urban Development (HUD) grant must precede outreach and recruitment.

Estimations of time between events are undertaken by MLMs. Three estimates are given with the associated cost (see Fig. 8.6): optimistic completion time, most likely completion time, and pessimistic completion time. The optimistic time is based on minimal problems and difficulties; the most likely time assumes normal development and represents the most accurate approximation; and the pessimistic time is estimated on the basis of maximum difficulties.[16]

The critical path (the longest time span along the system flow plan) to complete the objective in YouthBuild Pittsburgh, as shown in Fig. 8.5, is 30 months. In determining the critical path, events and data are organized in sequence. The terminating point in the sequence is the place to begin plotting the critical path, going backward until we reach the present. In the case of Fig. 8.5, we start with job placement and move back to outreach and recruitment.

After the PERT schedule is created, continuing review by participants is necessary to ensure that progress conforms to planned accomplishments. The time interval for reports will depend on management's needs. Timeliness of reports permits management to intervene at appropriate times to correct deviation from the planned objectives. In those cases where corrective action cannot put the project back on course, the entire schedule must be recomputed.

Fig. 8.6 shows a PERT network for computer installation requirements. Each letter represents an event. The numbers in between suggest the time required from one event to another. When we follow our example into operation, point A can represent the establishment of computer needs. Point B represents recruitment of staff which may take 20 weeks to 28 weeks.

Fig. 8.6. PERT Computer Installation

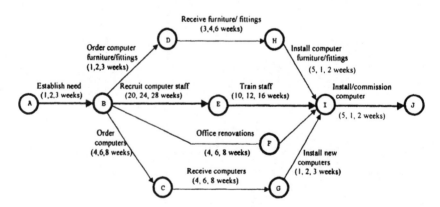

The example given of PERT is a reasonably simple one; many procedures involve several operations taking place simultaneously. For example, in our

YouthBuild Pittsburgh illustration, besides the scheduling of outreach and recruitment, education leadership development and counseling, and development of employment skills, we must find job placement and make follow-up review.

As a management tool, PERT forces management to focus greater attention on planning control and coordination. PERT facilitates greater participation between MLMs and administrators mainly because PERT systems emphasize a bottom-up approach. The people who will eventually have to implement the plan are the ones responsible for putting the estimates and schedules together. This atmosphere acts as a catalyst for better teamwork and communication, commitment, and intelligent planning.

As is evident from this examination of MLM short-range planning tools, MLMs exercise most important roles. They ultimately decide how, when, and to what degree planned organizational goals will be implemented. Administrators are dependent on MLMs to provide information to initiate comprehensive planning, to implement the plans, and to set up systems to motivate and control the progress of the plans to conform to objectives.

A CRITIQUE OF PLANNING: THE PROBLEM OF ACCOUNTABILITY

We have examined planning at the level of upper administration as viewed by lower-level management. We conclude with a few observations about planning in general.

There is a highly rational dimension to planning that sets in once the goals for planning are articulated. Goals inevitably encompass value judgments, and in the public sector, as we have seen, they are formed in the political process through compromise involving a multitude of interests. Planning, to reach these goals, can never be better than these compromised goals. That does not mean the planners should reduce their efforts because the goal is ambiguous, incompletely formulated, or unclear but rather that planning must proceed within the constraints of complexity characterizing the goals themselves. Harlan Cleveland emphasizes this when he characterizes planning as "improvisation on a general theme." The critical point is that all planners, and particularly MLMs, must internalize a sense of public accountability. MLMs must be cognizant that planning is undertaken to meet human needs. This means, among other things, that due care must be given to the public's input. These inputs may be made in a variety of ways, such as requiring citizens on boards that are open to the public, providing for citizens groups to be heard before final decisions are taken, and allowing citizens an opportunity to appeal adverse decisions. MLMs must recognize that the achievement of the public interest inconsistent with their own. They must resist the temptation to substitute their own bureaucratic interests or their self-interest for the goals as articulated by responsible elected officials or the needs of people that are embodied in plans. This puts an enormous burden on MLMs as they are charged with converting these often (sometimes intentionally) unclear signals into effective action.

Planning is looking into the future. Because no one can see the future with a crystal ball, the accuracy of forecasts and the premises derived from them are one of planning's limitations. Meaningful public input becomes an important ingredient in a process that represents policy and value judgment about what the future will be.

DISCUSSION QUESTIONS

1.   Why does planning in the United States constitute such an important role in the private sector but a less prominent one in the public sector?
2.   Why may planning be considered a universal requirement for exercising effective leadership in public management?
3.   Discuss the role and functions of top-level administrators in planning.
4.   Describe the practical insight that a manager can obtain from understanding the different types of planning.
5.   Discuss the power and influence that the MLM may exercise in carrying out his or her responsibilities.
6.   Discuss some of the means available to MLMs in the planning process to promote accountability.

NOTES

1.   C. E. Summer, "The Future Role of the Corporate Planning," *California Management Review* (July 1953): 22–41.
2.   Herbert A. Simon et al., *Public Administration* (New York: Alfred A. Knopf, 1962), pp. 423–24.
3.   Henri Fayol, "Planning," in *Management: A Handbook of Readings,* Harold Cans and Carl O'Donnel, eds. (New York: McGraw-Hill, 1972).
4.   Simon et al., *Public Administration,* pp. 440–41, lists the principal types of resistance: (1) inertia—people resist departing from old ways; (2) mores and beliefs—any plan that goes against cultural values will be resisted; (3) personal self-interest—if there is no apparent incentive, compliance is unlikely; (4) resistance to irrational proposals—people must see and accept the reason for a planned change; (5) resistance to subordination—people resent being told what they must do.
5.   Herbert Hicks, *The Management of Organizations* (New York: McGraw-Hill, 1967), p. 203.
6.   Fayol, "Planning" in *Management Handbook of Readings,* Harold Cans and Carl O'Donnel, eds. 1972.
7.   Donald C. Stone, "Planning as an Administrative Process," in *Administration,* Albert Lepisky, ed. (New York: Alfred A. Knopf, 1955) p. 527.
8.   Leonard D. White, *Introduction to the Study of Public Administration,* 3rd edn. (New York: Macmillan, 1950), p. 235: "Organization and methods work (often referred to as O and M) may be broadly defined as the improvement of all aspects of

transacting business with special emphasis upon procedures and relationships. The object is to secure the most complete utilization of available resources, physical and human, or conversely, to eliminate so far as possible what and loss of effort."

9.   Harlan Cleveland, *The Future Executive* (New York: Harper & Row, 1972), p.78.

10.   Paul E. Holden, et al., *Top Management Organization and Control* (New York: McGraw-Hill, 1951).

11.   Harlan Cleveland, *Birth of a New World: An Open Moment for International Leadership* (San Francisco: Jossey-Bass, 1993).

12.   In Vietnam the Air Force used strategic bombing to soften up the enemy garrison area. The Navy was assigned tactical or close support bombing for the troops in action. On occasion the boundaries overlapped, and American bombs fell on American troops.

13.   John M. Bryson, *Strategic Planning for Public and Nonprofit Organizations*, rev. edn. (San Francisco: Jossey Bass, 1995).

14.   Peter F. Drucker, *The Practice of Management* (New York: Harper & Row, 1954).

15.   F. Burke Sheeran, *Management Essentials for Public Works Administrators* (Chicago: American Public Works Association, 1976), p. 359.

16.   The formula for determining activity time is computed as follows: O = optimistic completion time, M = most likely completion time, and P = pessimistic completion time.

$$\frac{O + 4M + P}{6} = Activity\,Time$$

9

Organizing, Coordinating, and Controlling the Internal Environment of Management

Organizing, coordinating, and controlling functions have a symbiotic relationship in that organization is dependent on coordination to produce synergy and the integration of goals and objectives, while controlling is required to ensure that they are realized. This interrelationship suggests the importance of these critical functions.

This chapter has five main purposes. It shows how structures affect mission in public agencies and how they have particular implications for accountability. Organizing is known as the activity done at the top, largely by administrators, to achieve agencies' goals and objectives. The reorganizing that takes place later occurs mainly as the responsibility of the MLMs, who adjust the stated mission to available resources and constraints at the operating level. Next the chapter underscores the importance of coordination, showing the constant need to pull together existing, new, or terminated services as regulations change. Last, the chapter shows how MLMs employ controlling to regulate behavior to achieve goals.

The first section discusses the internal environment, stressing organization as an administrative function performed by top administrators, reorganizing as a function of MLMs, and organization in the context of power and accountability. The second section examines coordination in the internal environment, stressing the characteristics of coordination in government, types of coordination by the upper levels of administration, coordinating as employed by MLMs, and the relationship between coordination and authority. The third section explores controlling and the internal environment, examining the role of top administrators in establishing controls, the ways that power, authority, and influence are interrelated, typical control systems used in public agencies, the process of controlling by MLMs and a review of controlling and accountability in achieving program goals.

LEARNING OBJECTIVES

On completing this chapter, the reader should be able to:

- Distinguish and relate the organizing functions carried out by top-level administrators and the reorganizing done by MLMs.
- Understand how organizations overlap at the operational level.
- Describe how organizational structures may impede or facilitate the delivery of goods and services to people.
- Work through a simple organizational problem.
- Distinguish between upper- and lower-level coordination and know how they are interrelated.
- Identify essential guidelines for coordination and be able to apply them.
- Illustrate how coordination embodies accountability.
- Distinguish between a controlling system and controlling done by MLMs.
- Illustrate how power, authority, and influence are interrelated in the controlling process.
- Describe some typical controlling problems and ways they can be handled.
- Relate controlling to accountability (obtaining congruence between stated objectives and actual outcomes).

The organizing and reorganizing of public agencies are ongoing concerns at every level of government. Each new president, governor, or mayor commonly begins office with a proposal for a new structure or procedure to make government more effective. Task forces on government reorganization, for example, have been established by each president since Harry Truman. President Nixon attempted to make the reorganization of the federal bureaucracy a top priority of his administration. His plan to create four new Cabinet departments (Natural Resources, Human Resources, Economic Affairs, and Community Development) was defeated, but he did succeed in strengthening the regional structures of major departments, simplifying work procedures and reducing paperwork, consolidating grant programs, and promoting the idea that government should be brought closer to the people. President Carter initiated organizational efforts, particularly proposals that created a Department of Energy, reduced the size and authority of the executive office, increased the flow of program authority to states and cities, and reorganized the civil service in the Civil Service Reform Act of 1978. Carter divided the former Department of Health, Education, and Welfare into two new departments, Education, and Health and Human Resources. President Reagan installed Cabinet secretaries in the Departments of Education and Energy to dismantle them. Dismantling was not achieved because the secretaries were won over by the MLMs.

Although structural changes ordered by presidents command public attention, equally dramatic reorganizations have occurred in Congress and in state and local governments. In 1974, Congress reorganized its procedures for handling the federal budget in the Budget and Impoundment Act of 1974. These structural changes gave the legislators greater control of expenditures and correspondingly reduced the power of the presidency. The powerful Office of Management and Budget (OMB), which is an arm of the president, no longer has a monopoly on budgetary analysis and policy recommendation. The Congressional Budget Office, established in 1974, provides the legislature with the information and analysis to challenge OMB.

Although most state executive and legislative branches have undergone some form of reorganization since World War II, no state government is now regarded as adequately structured to meet the demands created by federal moves to decentralize national programs. There is some validity to the facetious comment that our three-level federalism leaves the national government with the money, the states with the legal powers, and the local government with the problems. As the keystone in the arch of federalism, the states carry on much of their reorganizing efforts to ward off or minimize federal encroachment and to better coordinate the actions by local units. Some examples of local reorganizing are seen in the strengthening of county governments through home rule, as in Colorado; in city–county consolidations, as illustrated by the merger of the city of Columbus and Muscogee County in Georgia; or in the creation of regional corporations, as in the case of the Twin Cities, Minnesota, Metropolitan Council, which performs both coordinating and line functions for local governments in the region, and the Allegheny County Compact 21, which is aimed at restructuring county government and reducing fragmentation among municipalities. Americans are preoccupied with organizing and reorganizing government. When there is a major public problem, the natural inclination is to seek a solution through a new or altered public structure or program procedure. (For example, the energy crisis initiated the creation of the Department of Energy.)

THE IDEA OF ORGANIZING

Organizing is the act of marshaling power for a purpose. The move to establish a council of governments for metropolitan areas is prompted by the need to bring together county, city, township, and borough governments in a region to accomplish a purpose individual governments could not do alone. Establishment of a transit system or implementation of a common air-quality-control standard are examples of what can be accomplished by joint effort. Organizing tends to deal with an overall approach to more effectively achieving public objectives, such as restructuring an agency or one of its major bureaus, linking agencies in a new way, or establishing new intergovernmental structures.

Organizing often requires considerable power. The creation of a new Energy Department or a merit-oriented county personnel system can be accomplished only through managing diverse interests and overcoming traditional ways of operating. Organizing is thus most likely to occur soon after a landslide election or following the arousal of public opinion in the wake of some well-publicized scandal. The recommendation to change the internal machinery of the House of Representatives came after it was revealed in 1976 that Congressman Wayne Hays had a mistress on his public payroll. In the aftermath, Democratic leaders named a commission on administrative review, consisting of both members and outsiders, to suggest better ways to run the House. A scandal in the House of Representatives post office brought reorganization in its internal controls. Organizing, then, is putting together the structural means to accomplish goals.

The Organizers

Authorization to organize a public sector function or agency rests with the legislature. The real roots of the power to organize, however, are in the demands made on legislators by interest groups and by changing environmental circumstances. When an interest group such as organized labor or a women's group brings pressure to bear on Congress or a state legislature, it usually suggests specific structures along with its call for new policy initiatives. As public concern over insufficient energy resources mounted, many states considered separating the energy function from public utility commissions. As they consider such demands, legislators often consult high-level administrators as to the feasibility of suggested structural arrangements. If the topic takes on technical dimensions, top-level administrators in turn may consult MLMs for a more operational view of what a particular structural change might entail.

TYPES OF ORGANIZATIONS

There are a number of ways to organize public structures, but the following are most prominent.

By Major Purpose

The provision of medical care, education, or tax collection can form the basis for structures. A school system may be organized around the levels of elementary, middle, and secondary schools; a medical care organization may be broken down into emergency, clinical, hospital, and long-term care units.

Organizations structured around purpose are easily understood by the general public. Because they tend to contain a full range of employees, from operators to professionals, they tend to have a low average employee cost. A major disadvantage is the difficulty of separating one purpose from another. For example, a health department may attempt to organize the delivery of health care, but clearly the water, sanitation, and parks and recreation departments are also involved in health matters.

By Process

The steps in construction, handling a claim, or the completion of performance review can be the basis for setting up an organizational structure. Process organizations bring together common technical skills (e.g., engineers, lawyers, or accountants). The advantage of such specialized departments is their concentration of expertise. By grouping all accountants in a single department, a wider range of services can be provided than when they are in separate departments. Specialized process departments are better able to recruit talented personnel seeking to use their professional skills.

Unfortunately, the general public has little understanding of what departments organized on the basis of process do. On a per capita basis, the personnel are usually costly because process departments tend to have high concentrations of professionals. Another disadvantage is that a process approach tends to undercut the need for technical support to be closely related to the general operations of an agency.

By the Clientele Served

Government units directed exclusively toward the elderly or veterans are examples of clientele-organized units. The Bureau of Indian Affairs was set up to provide an integrated approach to government–Indian relationships. It was argued that the bureau would be, in effect, an advocate for Indians inside government. To some extent most clientele units take this posture. The Indian population, however, has increasingly viewed the bureau as a force for maintaining, rather than changing, in their favor, the status quo.

The disadvantages of clientele units arise out of their client focus. Indians are also veterans, disabled, and farmers. It is hard for a single department to adequately meet these diverse needs. If one clientele group gains some advantage through special representation, it prompts other groups to seek a similar advantage.

By Place

Government units can be organized around place (e.g., the states, cities, or Appalachia). The chief advantages of an area approach are (1) convenience for public access; (2) a greater capacity to adjust programs to local conditions; and (3) quicker responding time—for example, neighborhood police or fire departments can reach the scene of a problem more quickly.

Disadvantages arise from difficulty in maintaining a uniform quality of the service offered. In addition, more influential citizens tend to receive better services for their communities. Coordination is also a problem, and most community needs cannot be met on a strictly community basis.

Thus, organization cannot be neatly delineated. Medical care, for example, may be organized as a process, aimed at a particular clientele, and offered on an area basis, all within the same agency. Whatever the organizational structure, a focus on purpose, process, clientele, or place—or a department with several of these emphases—should be seen primarily as a way in which structure is a manifestation of power used to achieve an objective.

ORGANIZING AT THE TOP

Administrators attempt to anticipate how particular structures will affect purpose. Three major aspects should be considered in the organizing process. The first is to set up a structure that will function, making sure that structures mesh closely with their mission. Second, attempts must be made to reduce friction within the organization and among related organizations. The proposed structure must facilitate the work to be done and not be impeded by its own procedures. As Robert T. Golembiewski and Frank K. Gibson have said, "Top level management is preoccupied with developing and maintaining a social institution that gives organic meaning and continuity to technical procedures, formal policy and proper procedures."[1] Third, as Fig. 9.1 shows, adjustments

Fig. 9.1. Top-Level Organizing Concerns

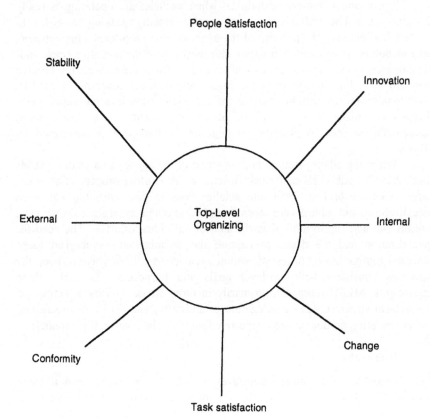

must be made to competing groups inside and outside the organization, giving recognition to stability versus the need for change; conformity of effort versus creativity; and task satisfaction versus people satisfaction.

As MLMs look to the organizing done at the top, they should ask these questions: Does the structure reflect the purpose of the agency? Can the organization be understood by those who work in it? Have allowances been made for adjustment to changing conditions? In short, they should seek to understand the top administrator's organizational philosophy priorities, and values that have been built into structures. John M. Gaus et al. defined the organizing task to encompass these concerns:

Organization is the arrangement of personnel for facilitating the accomplishment of some agreed purpose through the allocation of functions and responsibilities. It is the relating of efforts and capacities of individuals and groups engaged upon a common task in such a way as to secure the desired objective with the least friction and most satisfaction to those for whom the task is done and those engaged in the enterprise.[2]

REORGANIZING BY MLMS

The changes that are undertaken when agencies are operating is really reorganizing, and here MLMs play a major role. Broadly speaking, the task is to create a link between the purpose of the agency, which top-level administrators have embodied in an overall structure, and the work of the operators (rank-and-file employees) who deliver goods and services. These links inevitably involve reorganizing. Fig. 9.2 presents the major reorganizing concerns of MLMs. Traditionally, reorganization refers to the infrequent occasions on which major changes are made in the structure of an organization. In this chapter, reorganizing is used to describe an ongoing function that is performed by MLMs.

While top administrators think in terms of the agency as a whole, MLMs concentrate on sub-goals and work structures. A twofold process is at work: Large tasks are broken down into smaller ones to gain advantages through specialization, and subtasks are carefully linked to obtain synergistic effects (i.e., a result that adds up to more than the sum of individual efforts). The need for specialization and the desire to capture the organization's synergism make continual reorganization necessary within agencies as MLMs strive to keep the outcomes consistent with top-level goals and purposes. To make these adjustments, MLMs reorganize primarily in three areas: (1) by affecting the hierarchical structure; (2) by delegation of authority; and (3) by distinguishing and interrelating producing and supportive functions (line and staff personnel).

Hierarchy

Probably the most controversial—and yet most prominent—organizational feature is the hierarchy or pyramid of power. Robert Presthus has defined the principle of hierarchy "as a system for ranking positions along a descending scale from the top to the bottom of the organization. . . . Each person [is] under the control of the person immediately above . . . [and at] the same time . . . superior to the person directly below."[3] The organization chart displayed by most public agencies is a graphic reproduction of the hierarchy of authority.

Fig. 9.2. Organizational Concerns of Administrators and MLMs

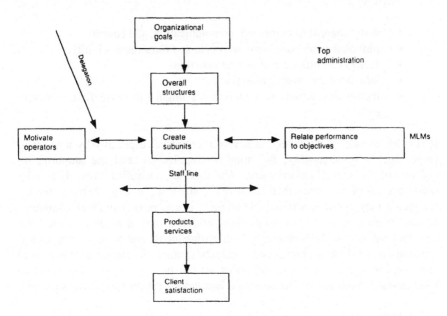

Hierarchy is controversial because it sets forth who is over whom. With each ascending step in the pyramid goes increasing formal power and benefits, a higher salary, larger offices, special parking places, and additional support personnel. Superiors not only sign formal memoranda; their views also set the parameters for what gets said or listened to in an organization. As it is said in the military, "With rank goes privilege." Because hierarchy reflects the formal power distribution in an organization, its structuring and restructuring are a major concern of MLMs. They must constantly relate the authority associated with a position to achieve the organization's purpose.

There are several hierarchies within an organization. At the middle levels two are of particular importance: ascribed authority figures, usually middle managers, and professionals, who are highly skilled personnel. In a medical agency, for example, an ascribed manager may be at the top of the organization chart, but operating physicians and their supportive personnel, who are shown as reporting to the manager, will insist that they are guided by independent professional standards. A continuing struggle is likely to occur between these two hierarchies. Over the long run, ascribed managers tend to prevail through the repeated decisions they make on organizational and logistical matters—the use of resources, timing in the delivery of services, and reporting procedures. Managers dominate reorganizing because they effect many changes in the process of program implementation through administrative rules and procedures.

The hierarchy performs a variety of functions and, as the list below suggests, in many ways the embodiment of what is meant by organizing.

Hierarchy:

- is the channel of command, communication, and control
- pinpoints where decisions are made and fixes responsibility
- fosters compliance and applies sanctions
- integrates the organizational effort
- legitimizes actions that individuals might otherwise find reprehensible.

Hierarchy, as one might expect, is severely criticized, especially by those who emphasize its impersonality, the mindless regulations, and the authoritarian ordering of the internal environment. And there are identified costs. Hierarchy reinforces ascribed rather than achieved leadership; it can obstruct needed change; it may produce internal oligarchies; it can restrict internal communication; it often insulates top levels from criticism; and it tends to curtail the contributions that might be made by both professionals and ordinary employees. Illustrations of these problems come quickly to mind in relation to the general discontent many civil servants feel about actions by their "boss." The point to keep in mind, however, is that ascribed hierarchies reflect the power structure.

Delegation

Delegating authority provides one of the most common ways in which the internal operations of agencies are reorganized. Delegation occurs when a superior in a hierarchy grants to a subordinate the authority to act in his or her behalf.

The power and authority that MLMs exercise in the ascribed hierarchy come from delegation. Typically, legislation vests the legal authority in an agency to a chief executive officer (i.e., to a department secretary or agency manager). These top administrators in turn parcel out authority to their immediate subordinates, the middle managers, who in turn delegate some of the power they have received to the supervisors who report to them. In broad terms, delegation is reorganizing the authority to confer, resolve, originate, and, above all, to decide in an agency.

Top administrators are under considerable pressure to delegate some of their authority The primary tasks at the top are the maintenance of external relations, assuring, that resources will continue to flow to the agency, and looking to the overall consequences of agency action. Due to lack of both time and expertise, top administrators are forced to delegate the authority to manage internal operations on a day-to-day basis. The principle governing decentralized administration is that authority to act and decide should be pushed down the hierarchy to the point where the flow of information is most likely to result in the most reliable decision. Generally this means delegation to MLMs who understand the policy objectives articulated at the top and are in direct contact with operators in work groups.

Ultimate responsibility cannot be delegated, so a grant of power or authority is always incomplete. To improve the effectiveness of delegation, MLMs should attend to the following principles. Delegation:

- must make clear who is being asked to do what
- must be based on the power to delegate as well as the power to carry out the task
- must be accompanied by additional communication about the delegation, especially to those the newly empowered person will be directing.

Those who delegate must also be expected to establish some form of reporting and to have some means of making sure that the delegated power has been accepted.

Delegation is an important reorganizing task for several reasons. First, unresponsive organizations, or organizations that cannot make timely decisions, are likely to be over-centralized, requiring decisions to be referred to the top. Second, through delegation, superiors are unburdened and subordinates are given a chance to improve their administrative and decision-making skills. If subordinates remain only messengers for the presumed will of those at the top, they are less able to develop their own leadership abilities. Finally, subordinates must be given some power if they are to be responsible. When delegation of the authority to decide is accompanied by the resources to implement decisions, the ingredients are in place for achieving both accountability and high morale, responsibility can be better fixed, and a better opportunity is afforded to meet client demands.

Delegating Continuum

Robert Golembiewski provided two models for explaining the way managers behave in approaching the delegation task.[4] On the one hand, the manager may operate on the "more-or-less hypothesis." In this situation, the zero-sum approach operates. The manager is fearful that delegation leads to dissipation of authority and power. There is considerable distrust of subordinates who recognize the situation and reciprocate with equal distrust of the superior. Thus, the less authority that is delegated, the greater the power that the superior retains. This model typifies the mechanistic approach and theory X approach to managing.

On the other hand, the manager may practice the "more-and-more hypothesis." This model typically operates in an environment of mutual good will and trust. The manager views delegation as a positive and constructive action. The delegation of power involves sharing and mutually enhancing superior and subordinate relationships. Delegation generates reciprocal trust and confidence. The subordinates attempt to achieve the best in their use of delegated powers to demonstrate their worthiness of the delegation. By so doing, subordinates increase the power and prestige of the managers, making them more disposed to delegate even more authority and power. This model parallels the human-centered organization theory, the total quality management (TQM) approach, and theory Y.

Case Study 9A: The New Administrative Assistant

The organizational structure at the top level of the day care center council is the source of power and accountability. In this case we can see changes in these two forces in what we call the pre- and post-administrative assistant eras. The original top level of the council is represented below:

a

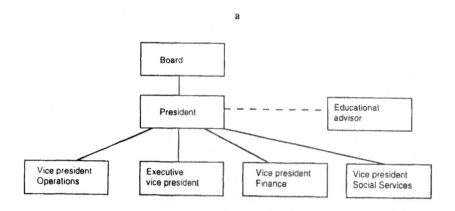

Within the structure, ultimate power rested with the president, but responsibility was delegated to middle managers, the various department heads. Each department was responsible for a well-defined area within the administration of the council. The vice president for operations controlled the day-to-day operation of 43 day care center sites and operated the student data system. The vice president for finance controlled the fiscal department, budget personnel, and procurement processes. The executive vice president was responsible for the day care centers operating in the northwest territory, made up of 12 rural sites. The vice president for social services controlled parent-involvement programs and managed the training, evaluation, and counseling. Each of these persons had power over his or her department as long as he or she remained accountable to the president. Each was expected to produce certain results. The operations director was to monitor day care operations and teacher loads through monthly reports. The fiscal director was to control costs, generate new revenue sources, and produce regular financial reports.

The organizational structure worked well, but, from the viewpoint of one of the department heads, all of this was shattered with the addition of only one new person—the administrative assistant. The current organization structure is represented below:

b

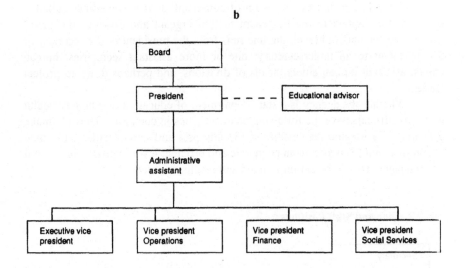

The reason the president gave for adding this new position was to reduce some of her administrative burden. This reduction has been achieved, but at the cost of sacrificing much of the clarity of responsibility, power, and accountability that existed before. The new person has taken it upon himself to garner some of the authority within other departments at the council. For instance, he has taken the personnel function from fiscal and the evaluation area from operations. He has sought to channel most information meant for the president into his office.

As a consequence, communication lines have been broken, authority has been questioned, and power has been shifted, all through a change in structure. Accountability has also been clouded. Because the administrative assistant is an arm of the president, he periodically gets involved in changing objectives of the departments over the objections of department heads. Who then becomes responsible for the results?

Needless to say, some of the department heads find the shift in structure distressing and at points dangerous for the organization. Change is always resisted. Time will show whether this new position is worth the frustration and discontent that it has so far engendered.

LINE AND STAFF PERSONNEL

A third reorganizing condition within agencies arises from the way in which line and staff personnel are related. Fig. 9.3 shows line and staff functions. The manner in which line personnel relate to staff personnel is largely determined by MLMs.

Line Positions

Line personnel form the delivery system; they are the individuals who directly carry out the organization's mission. In a police department, for example, the line positions—or chain of command, as it is sometimes called— run from the captain to the lieutenant to the sergeant and down to the patrol officer. At the national level, the line runs from the president or the secretary of a department to an undersecretary, one or more assistant secretaries, bureau chiefs, assistant bureau chiefs, heads of divisions, and perhaps down to project leaders.

Whether the agency is a state department of education or a county health unit, line officials have the following characteristics in common: They (1) make decisions; (2) assume responsibility; (3) interpret and defend policy; (4) plan operations; and (5) maintain an economic and efficient level of production. Good line managers tend to be action-minded and results-oriented.

Fig. 9.3. Line and Staff Positions

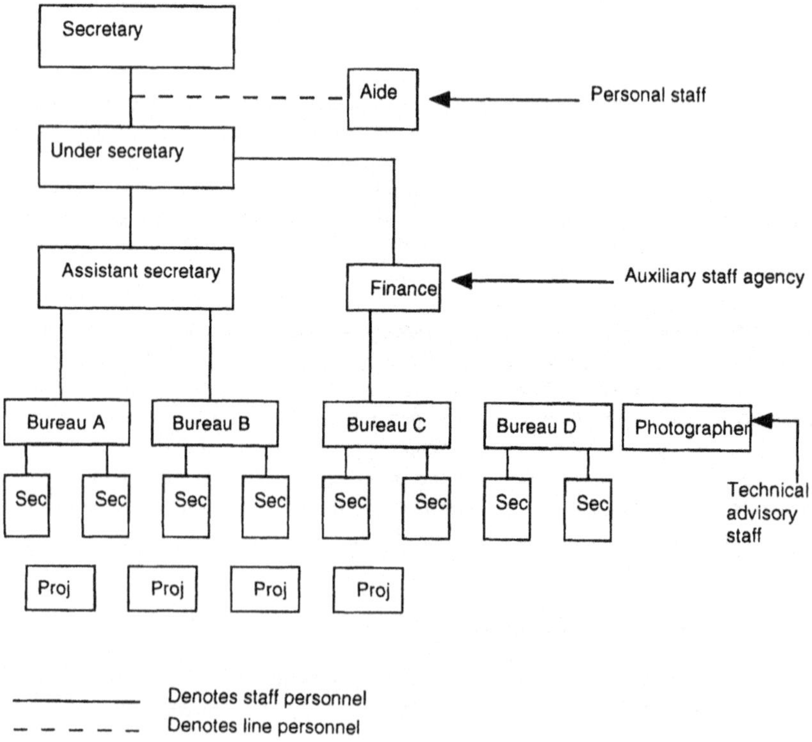

Staff Positions

Staff positions appear after an organization grows in size and complexity, and the work load of line personnel increases beyond a manageable capacity. Because of this overload, new positions are created to help line personnel do their jobs more effectively. Staff positions, as illustrated in Fig. 9.3, may be of three varieties: (1) advisory (including the general staff, as found in the military or very large organizations); (2) personal staff aides; and (3) auxiliary staff agencies.

Advisory staff positions require special education or training (e.g., in law, accounting, engineering). Typically, advisory staff hold university degrees and regard themselves as professionals. They often are younger than line officials, are likely to begin their government service at the middle levels, and tend to have little operating experience. They often are regarded by line personnel as preoccupied with theory, as people who make recommendations but do not bear the burden of their execution. Advisory staff supply the organization with valuable information about legal requirements, costs, and other technical services; typically, they are budget analysts or management specialists. A first-rate specialist has a passion for detail and tends to think in terms of future costs and benefits. The power they exercise comes from the strength of their advice in support of the achievement of the organization's mission. MLMs are constantly adjusting and readjusting this tension between theoretical knowledge and operational experience.

Individuals whose staff positions provide direct support to the unit head are personal aides. These positions often bear the title of assistant or administrative assistant and the individuals are usually selected primarily on the basis of their personal loyalty to the unit head. They may perform tasks from running errands through complex data gathering. Their continual access to the unit head provides the basis for their influence. Generally, assistants should exercise care in using the informal power they have.

The case study of the new administrative assistant illustrates problems that arise when an administrative assistant begins to assume direct line authority and as a consequence significantly reorganizes the agency.

Organization units that are not directly in the line of direct implementation of the agency's mission are auxiliary staff agencies. Yet these agencies carry on more than an advisory or personal support function. Examples of these units are personnel, accounting, or purchasing. Staff agencies have a mission of their own, and they service the organization as a whole. Each produces an identifiable product and exercises a functional authority over part of the work that the line units perform. The personnel unit is charged with recruiting and maintaining the work force, and a purchasing unit develops and manages the procurement procedure. These functions tend to appear in any large public organization, irrespective of the mission.

MLMs must carefully analyze and constantly monitor the inter-relationships of line and staff functions. In tuning these adjustments, an effective reorganization is taking place, as power in the internal environment is being reallocated. F. Burke Sheeran has listed ten ways to improve and strengthen line–staff relations:

1. Select competent staff. It is a mistake to think that only reasonable intelligence is needed for staff work.
2. Clarify authority and responsibility. The boundaries of functional authority must be specified and monitored.
3. Bring staff and line personnel together early in the planning process. Too often staff personnel handle planning and line personnel are subsequently informed.
4. Strengthen communication between line and staff. Frequent and informal communication can overcome inherent tendencies for conflicts to arise.
5. Include a service attitude among staff personnel. Remember that it is the line personnel who are carrying out the mission, and staff is auxiliary.
6. Insist that line personnel make use of staff expertise. Line personnel's failure to make use of staff expertise is the major weakness in line-staff relationships.
7. Managers should make proper use of staff. A typical error is for the manager to use line personnel for advisory roles and advisory personnel in line responsibilities.
8. Evaluate the performance of both staff and line managers. This will require evaluating the relationship between the two categories.
9. Insist that line personnel carry out staff recommendations when they have accepted them.
10. Rotate managers between line and staff positions or attach them to a line or staff organization when possible.[5]

ORGANIZATIONAL OVERLAYS AT THE OPERATIONAL LEVEL

In examining day-to-day operations, much organizing can be observed in the informal groups, channels of communication, and concentrations of power that come to exist despite formal arrangements. It is common for many operational structures to exist at the same time. John M. Pfiffner and Frank P. Sherwood have referred to these as organization overlays.[6] Fig. 9.4 presents four examples.

1. *Job-task pyramid* refers to the relations between individuals in the organization that evolve as specific tasks are performed.
2. *Sociometric structures* are those on-the-job social relationships that are based on personal preferences.
3. *Decision overlays* are those influenced patterns that emerge in an organization as a consequence of decision styles of individuals. Sometimes these focus on persons with specific skills.
4. *Communication overlay* refers to the people who are talking to each other. Such overlays become particularly important when one is left out of the informal patterns of communication.
5. *Network of influence* refers to the recognition of the actual path of the formal and informal operation of power in organization.

Fig. 9.4. Organizational Overlays

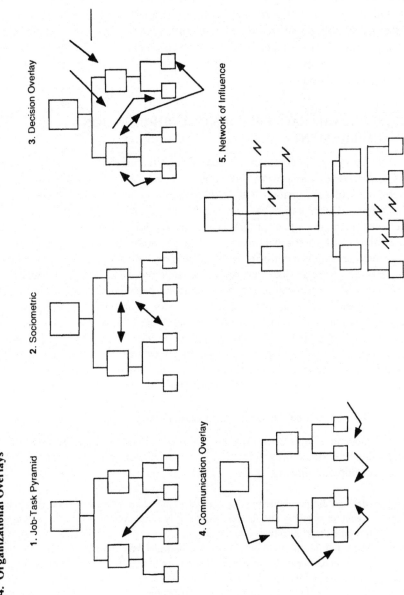

1. Job-Task Pyramid

2. Sociometric

3. Decision Overlay

4. Communication Overlay

5. Network of Influence

If we put these four informal structures on top of the organization chart and adjust it according to what we have said about hierarchy, delegation, and line–staff functions, we will begin to comprehend the complexity of organizing in public agencies. If accountability is to be achieved, MLMs must pay close attention to both the overall organizing done by top-level administrators and the overlays on formal structures that agency personnel establish on an informal basis in day-to-day operations. These are part of the environment in which coordination takes place.

GENERAL CHARACTERISTICS OF COORDINATION IN GOVERNMENT

To grasp the complicated idea of coordination, it is necessary to realize its pervasiveness in government operations and to understand some of the definitions of coordination that have appeared in recent public administration literature. Coordination, as we shall see, involves both establishing links between elements of a program and overcoming diverging or conflicting procedures and criteria within a single agency and/or between agencies that can frustrate the achievement of program objectives. As a first step, all functioning organizations require that everyone knows precisely what he or she is charged to do. In public organizations this is a constant problem as most policies suffer from vagueness, due to laws that are imprecise, unclear goals and objectives, ambiguous court decisions, and unanticipated factors that arise after the policy has been formulated. The checks and balances and pluralistic (multiple competing interests and political factors) environments in which U.S. public administration takes place create chaotic communications, making it difficult to achieve the consensus that is vital for coordination.

The Need for Coordination in Government

Coordination is a requirement of government at all levels, between levels, and within individual programs. The following factors show why administrators must develop coordinating skills:

1. Most public programs require good working relations between a legislative and executive branch. The former says what is to be done and the latter attempts to translate these objectives into results.
2. Many public programs involve more than one level of government. A county health department, for example, typically is funded by federal or state programs but carries out its work at the local level.
3. A typical government program involves more than one unit of the executive branch. Personnel, financing, and evaluating functions are almost always superimposed on program operations.
4. Within a single program are technical and nontechnical operations that must be brought together. Road construction, for example, requires highly trained engineers and manual laborers.

In the operations of private enterprise, we do not always have these links between levels and functions to coordinate.

Coordination also comes into play as a consequence of starting a program. Recall that we spoke of organization as a process in which tasks are divided or subdivided to obtain the benefits of specialization. To obtain program unity, coordination then follows as the links that permit the effective reassembly of the parts.

Coordination: Some Recent Definitions

The subject of coordination in public administration literature reveals a growing appreciation of its complexity. Below are definitions that have appeared in public administration textbooks since 1955. Coordination attempts:

- to bring about the consistent and harmonious action of persons toward a common end[7]
- to adjust the parts to each other, and the movement and operation of parts in time so that each makes its maximum contribution to the product as a whole[8]
- to combine the action of a number of muscles in a complex movement and in administration the harmonious combination of actions of agents or functions toward a given objective[9]
- the process of understanding, unifying, harmonizing, and integrating managerial functions, actions, and operations[10]

Note the emphasis: people to ends, parts to each other, harmonious combinations, and a unifying and integrating process. These definitions reflect a growing appreciation of the complexity of the coordinating function. Two key functions can be singled out for further illustration: establishing links and overcoming divergent administrative procedures within an organization.

Links

The major links that coordination bridges are between human operations and program objectives. Link-building is the preoccupation of MLMs. Largely this is accomplished by increasing the effective communication of information within the organization. Links have to be constantly pursued because of these common conditions:

1. Executives are often pushed for time and overlook the divisive implications of orders they give or actions they take.
2. Instructions from top management are often given in haste—over the telephone, in personal conversations, or embedded in memoranda—and fail to communicate what is expected.
3. Work specializations tend to become ends in themselves, preventing operators from seeing how their efforts fit into the overall objective.

Managers must constantly provide the links between what people do in the organization and what they are expected to do in achieving stated objectives. It cannot be taken for granted that the statement of mission or a hierarchy will automatically result in coordination.

Perhaps the most common task in an organization is responding to a letter or memorandum. This example can be used to illustrate how diverse efforts must be brought together. The substance of the answer may involve the expertise of a single line department, but getting the answer prepared and sent may necessitate relating (1) research on what should be said; (2) editorial clearance on how the answer is to be stated; (3) clerical processes for producing the letter or memo, filing, and distributing copies; (4) securing of the appropriate signature (a ritual in itself); and (5) arrangement for any follow-up. Coordination is the linking of these processes, and it often requires the talents of a ringmaster rather than those of a performer. Marshall Edward Dimock and Gladys Ogden Dimock had MLMs in mind when they noted, "Energy and performance depend as much on the linkages involved in the total operation as they do on the energy contributed by each component part."[11]

BRINGING TOGETHER DIVERGENT PROCEDURES

A particularly difficult coordinating task is to overcome conflicting procedures within an organization. It is well known that "administrative distance" (analogous to the "social distance" that separates people due to class or race differences) separates program components occasioned by differing procedures.

In almost every organization of any degree of complexity, internal procedures develop to meet differing objectives. For example, busy administrators may be seen only by appointment, reimbursements for travel expenditures may require valid receipts, or equipment must be reserved in advance. Such arrangements, developed to meet specific needs, can interfere with the operation of a particular project, becoming minor or major obstacles in the achievement of specific goals. Comstock Glaser offers this more detailed example:

To show how this "administrative distance" applies to an everyday problem, let us take the case of a construction superintendent on a highway project who finds that he needs an additional steam shovel. The purchase of this engine is an administrative problem of some importance, particularly as there are salesmen with good political connections in the "offing." The simplest way in which the superintendent could get his steam shovel would be to go out and buy it. However, the rules of all public agencies and most private concerns require that materials (except minor items) be purchased through established channels, the reasoning: (1) to make sure that supplies bought are for reasonable and legitimate needs, (2) to see that they are appropriate for the uses to which they will be put, (3) to prevent "rake-offs," and (4) to secure the lowest prices through centralized purchasing and competitive bidding. So the superintendent, instead of buying the shovel, fills out a requisition stating exactly what he wants, accompanied by a memorandum explaining why.   The requisition is approved by the District Superintendent, and probably by certain other officers, and forwarded to the purchasing agent. This official has the specification prepared or checked by a consulting engineer and then advertises for bids. Then he buys the shovel and has it delivered to the project. All these administrative steps and the consequent moves take time and cost money, both directly and indirectly, by holding up work on the project. Whether this results in a net gain or loss depends on a number of intangible factors including individual quotients of honesty and ability. One superintendent could perhaps buy machinery as effectively as the procurement officer, still another might spend twice as much and not get the right thing. But whatever the channels are for purchasing (or any other sequence), they should operate with the fewest and shortest moves for the necessary administrative operations.[12]

This example of making an equipment purchase—a very common occurrence in government—illustrates the need for coordination growing out of diverging procedures within an agency. The main objective of the procurement unit of the highway department is sound purchases, and these must be coordinated with the overall departmental objective of building roads. In all these processes, MLMs play key roles.

Administrative distance can also arise among agencies, creating tensions and resulting in further difficulties in coordination. Consider, for example, the administrative distance that occurs when an auditor from the General Accounting Office appears. Auditors often bring their own criteria for evaluating performance, criteria that do not always agree with the standards the agency has been using. Auditors also tend to look to the authorizing legislation to determine an agency's mission, while the agency itself has had to translate a variety of unclear authorizations into programs and projects. And when the audit is completed, administrators are expected to use the evaluation as a means for improving agency operations. To overcome administrative distance, coordination often requires the use of political as well as administrative skills.

We must keep in mind that coordination refers to selective applications of power and influence that, when properly applied, result in program outcomes that closely approximate what was planned. Mary Parker Follett conceptualizes coordination arising in precisely that way as occurring "in the situation." She describes it as a process of integrating the efforts of many people in an organization toward the achievement of a wholeness. She legitimized the use of power to achieve accountability in government or in a specific program, for diverse resources must be forcefully brought together to realize objectives.[13] The power to coordinate is a major instrument in making accountability possible.

COORDINATION BY TOP-LEVEL ADMINISTRATORS

While coordination preoccupies administrators and managers at every level, those at the top approach the problem with unique concerns and rely on particular methods. In general, top-level administrators coordinate the affairs of the agency in its external environment and set up the structures to obtain coordination within the agency. We turn first to what administrators do beyond the agency and then to internal agency coordination, particularly to the use of committees.

External Coordination

Three areas of government operations make coordination by top-level administrators essential: the constitutional requirements for checks and balances, the need for inter-agency coordination, and the working of the federal system. As Edwin Corwin has pointed out, the U.S. Constitution did not antici-pate the president as the monopolizer of program execution; instead, it was expected that the Congress would play a major administrative role.[14] Congress participates in administration by granting administrators the power to conduct each program, by confirming the appointment of top-level administrators, by authorizing the structures through which programs are to be carried out, by appropriating the needed money on an annual basis, and by conducting investi-gations, called "legislative oversight." These are highly important administrative functions. In fact, the existence of administration presupposes a legislative link.

The U.S. Constitution, as ratified in 1789, provided that government would be limited—especially the federal government. Most of the power to govern was reserved for the states or the people. And to further contain the powers enumerated for the federal government to perform, a system of checks and balances was established. Congress was to authorize, the executive was to execute, and the courts were to adjudicate (settle disputes). Thus, each branch could check the other two. But in addition some judicial power (e.g., the right to rule on administrative matters) is given to administrators; some executive power (e.g., the right to write rules) is shared by courts and administrators. This means, for our purposes, that top-level administrators inevitably become involved in coordination as part of the checks and balances system.

In state and local governments, similar legislative-judicial, executive-administrative links can be seen. Over the last 175 years, however, and particularly during the last 60 years, power at all levels of government has steadily gravitated to the executive branch. This has meant that top-level administrators have had to increase the time spent on coordination in the external environment, in maintaining smooth relationships with legislatures, other executive agencies, and interest groups.

In the field of foreign policy, for example, the president must bring together diplomatic, economic, cultural, and intelligence information in the attempts to create policy with a particular country. At any major embassy abroad, the U.S. ambassador will chair a "country team" composed of these elements to assist him or her in presenting a coordinated U.S. policy to that country. The president, in turn, must make certain that Congress is fully informed of the range of initiatives being undertaken throughout the world.

To coordinate external security, the president uses the Joint Chiefs of Staff to bring together Army, Navy, and Air Force approaches to defense. The president also uses the National Security Council to broaden participation in policymaking beyond the military branches, including the economic dimensions of foreign policy, and in other national resources that affect security.

These examples are intended to show that much of the coordination that is done by top-level administrators occurs outside specific agencies in linking together several agencies that must be coordinated in order for an objective to be reached. The enormity of the president's coordinating task was expressed in President Nixon's March 25, 1971, message to the Congress on reorganization:

[T]he power to achieve goals and to solve problems is exceedingly fragmented and broadly scattered throughout the federal establishment. In addressing almost any of the great challenges of our time the federal government finds itself speaking through a wide variety of offices and bureaus, departments, and agencies. Often these units trip over one another as they move to meet a common problem. Sometimes they step on one another's toes. Frequently, they behave like a series of fragmented fiefdoms—unable to focus federal resources or energies in a way which produces any concentrated impact.

Internal Coordination

Top-level coordination within an agency necessitates the use of still other devices. Probably the most fundamental is the hierarchy itself. Its central purpose is to link the top with the bottom of the organization and to settle any disputes over what is intended. Coordination is primarily worked out at higher positions in the hierarchy. A department head usually makes coordination the major responsibility of one or more of his or her deputies. A related technique is to coordinate through the adroit delegation of authority. For example, line agencies are required to obtain clearance from a staff unit before certain actions can be taken. Before a bill can be introduced in the Pennsylvania state legislature, it must have a "fiscal note" attached by the Appropriations Committee (i.e., the financial obligation must be stated before the legislation is passed).

The Role of Committees

Probably the most pervasive device for coordination is the committee. Committees can have both external and internal functions. In many agencies, committees are mandated by statute to ensure that interest groups will be consulted. Far more important is the use of committees within the organization.

A committee may be defined as a group of people (usually no more than can sit around a table) that makes decisions or presents viewpoints within the context of an established set of rules. Cyril O'Donnell defines a committee as "two or more persons appointed by their immediate supervisor for the purpose of acting or advising their supervisor on a subject that is not clearly within the competence of any one of them."[15]

In general, the proper function of a committee meeting in which a top-level administer consults with staff are:

- To give members a sense of the unity and interconnectedness of the organization's work.
- To learn from the chief executive about new programs and developments affecting the work.
- To solicit and enlist the thought and cooperation of staff and line officials.
- To give lower-level officials a chance to bring to the attention of the boss other matters they find of general importance.[16]

The most common agency committee is the staff committee. The head of the agency, at stated intervals, calls together the principal unit heads and advisers to discuss current problems and iron out difficulties in the interest of coordination. A large State Department of Agriculture has as many as 100 intra-bureau committees. The Office of Personnel Management traditionally holds ABCD staff conferences. An A conference brings together the bureau heads and other first-rank officials. Statements from each person are then solicited as to how they understand their duties and responsibilities. Overlapping duties, ambiguous assignments, vagueness of responsibility, and outright gaps or conflicts come into the open. With the main decision-makers in the same room, coordination is hammered out, duties are agreed, and the policies are put in writing. In the following weeks, a B conference repeats the process at the bureau level; then C conferences at the division level; and finally D conferences at the office level. This procedure provides coordination from a broad through a narrowing specificity. In the process, a feeling of participation is engendered.

In general, the staff committee can be a forum for reducing friction and achieving coordination. Defenders of committees say: (1) They make better decisions than individuals because they draw from a wider base; (2) they provide an efficient means of securing acceptance; (3) they tend to reduce paperwork; and (4) they are valuable when the problem has diverse elements and the best solution is a compromise.

Detractors see committees as slow-working and expensive, producing only limited results. Once authorized in an agency, they tend to multiply. (Within the Danforth Foundation, a careful study of the costs associated with committee meetings to review grant requests brought out that the cost of the review associated with an individual grant ranged from several hundred to several thousand dollars. As a result, a small grant authority that did not require the full review was given to executive officers.) Other critics point out that committees tend to become sounding boards for dominant personalities, who use them mainly as a stage. Committees, it is said, gravitate to the lowest common denominator and are devices usually resorted to as a delaying tactic. Despite these criticisms, committees are prominent features of government life. MLMs should study them as part of the top level's coordinating efforts. Critical attention must be given to committee size and personality types, and, above all, the committee creator must know what outcome is desired and how the committee can best be used as a conciliating and facilitating instrument.

In summary, as MLMs look to the coordinating efforts of upper-level administrators, they should take into account how their individual units are politically and administratively related to the overall organization. They should become aware of the functions of committee meetings and of the ways to operate effectively in them. Top-level coordination will bring good results:

- when it clarifies lines of authority, makes the allocation of functions clearer, and removes unintended overlapping or duplication
- when it is accompanied by increased delegation
- when it is used to allow participation among those who are called together to execute programs
- when incentives are offered to encourage cooperation.

COORDINATION AND MLMs

MLMs are strategically located to carry out the coordination functions. Coordination in the process of implementing policy defines much of what they do. The necessity for coordination depends on the manner in which policies come to an agency. A legislative policy is most often a compromise, arrived at by bargaining, in which the goals are often unclear or even unstated. Yet top-level administrators must find ways to act decisively in converting policy into programs, Frequently, what key legislators were able to achieve in the legislative process they demand as an administrative result. One of the prime functions of legislatures is to oversee the way administrators translate broad statements into specific action. Thus, to be held accountable, administrators must be clear on goals so that they can instruct operations. Coordination often requires MLMs to accept inconsistent objectives, as coordination is a technique of drawing together conflicting skills and interests and directing them toward a common end. To accomplish this, many of the same techniques used by upper management are employed, such as delegation, linking devices, and the use of committees; but some techniques unique to MLMs are also employed.

We have spoken of how top managers delegate some of their authority as a means of linking program efforts. The other side of distributing power and authority is receiving the power to act, and this is largely the authorization given to MLMs. In the middle levels, this authority is used to create links between policy and operations. In the federal Veterans Affairs, there is a practice of the Monday morning "hot line" to regional directors, a conference call that allows all 10 regional directors to hear via phone at one time the top VA administrator's immediate concerns, particularly plans for implementing policy in a uniform way throughout the nation. At the regional office in Pittsburgh, the director has major middle managers as a group listen in on this conversation so they too can hear the instructions from the administrator and the interaction between him and regional directors. Coordination is the objective, and when the call ends, the Pittsburgh director solicits input from the middle managers on what the "hot line" call requires of them individually and in connection with each other. When these MLMs return to their individual units, they informally re-enact this process with operators. Then in the context of translating policy into operations, MLMs take into account group interests, individual concerns, and the myriad internal and external pressures that characterize execution. When we speak of techniques like MBO (management by objective) or PERT (program evaluation and review technique), we really mean steps taken by MLMs to promote coordination, as these techniques require breaking policy objectives into smaller, workable units and adjusting resources and people as conditions require to achieve the desired outcome.

Coordination Through Monitoring Contracts

Many projects in public works, human services, housing, health care, and job power development are implemented through contractual agreements with private agencies. MLMs are frequently cast in the role of contract officers, and those in these important roles must have basic familiarity with the following:

1. *Contract contents*: scope of services statements, which reflect the project objectives (see Fig. 9.5); requirements for monitoring and evaluation; grant disbursement schedule; agreement on records, reports, and inspections; subcontractor agreements and property ownership; and personnel agreement on any training or employment restrictions (e.g., Equal Employment Opportunity Commission requirements).
2. *Contracting process*: legal drafting of the document; internal review of the provisions; selecting a contractor; the competitive bidding process; further negotiation on details; community or client review, if required; approval process, usually involving more than one layer of government; and contract compliance.

In all phases of contracting, the establishment of links between objectives and means is the primary concern. Contract monitoring is a particularly important method of coordination in which MLMs play important roles. Often no one in government except the monitoring officer is aware of what is actually being received for expenditures made. From the MLMs' perspective, contracting has become a prominent feature of the internal environment. It demands competence in administrative and technical skills to adequately supervise in the public interest.

As the contract proceeds, MLMs must:

*   Act as a focal point for the project in government.
*   Ensure compliance with the contract (on-site visits, meetings, review and evaluation reports).

- Provide needed assistance from various aspects of the agency in the areas of information, space, approvals, and problems around the flow of resources.
- Expand contact with potential users and then actual users of the product of the project.
- Carry on the report, especially final evaluations for the agency as a whole.

Fig. 9.5. Project Work Program/Neighborhood Medical Clinic

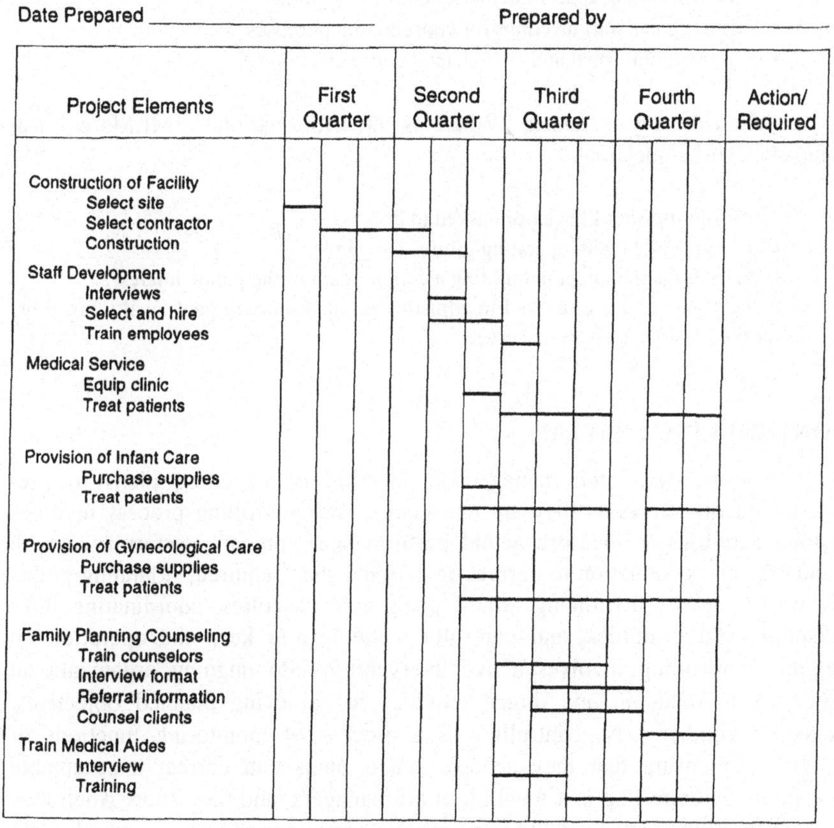

Date Prepared _____   Prepared by _____

Project Elements	First Quarter	Second Quarter	Third Quarter	Fourth Quarter	Action/ Required

Construction of Facility
   Select site
   Select contractor
   Construction					

Staff Development
   Interviews
   Select and hire
   Train employees					

Medical Service
   Equip clinic
   Treat patients					

Provision of Infant Care
   Purchase supplies
   Treat patients					

Provision of Gynecological Care
   Purchase supplies
   Treat patients					

Family Planning Counseling
   Train counselors
   Interview format
   Referral information
   Counsel clients					

Train Medical Aides
   Interview
   Training					

By way of summarizing the tasks of coordinating from the MLM perspective, the following are guidelines[17]:

1. Middle managers are expected to sell coordination to lower managers.
2. Coordination should be pursued strenuously and on a daily basis, despite its time-consuming features.

3.   Coordination must take place both laterally and vertically in the organization and
      will often extend outward to similar programs, with middle and lower managers
      acting in ambassadorial roles.
4.   The committee device is an increasingly useful means for bringing places and
      action together, and often on the work site.
5.   Coordination is the other side of delegation; it relates the product to the original
      planning.
6.   Contracting, while it puts work responsibilities on others, increases the
      coordination and control functions within the agency.
7.   Coordination may be strengthened in the following ways
      • identify and assign special coordination functions to specific individuals
      • establish policies and procedures that pinpoint coordination responsibilities
      • clarify cloudy areas of authority and responsibility
      • use regular staff meetings for coordinating purposes
      • promote informal and cross-lateral communication.[18]

       When the cry is raised, "Where is the coordination?" MLMs can ask
themselves these questions:

1.   Am I sold on what I have been asked to do?
2.   Have I consulted with operating groups enough?
3.   Have I invested enough in building a commitment to the public interest?
4.   Is the balance I have reached in adjusting group loyalty to goal loyalty favorable
      for the clients we all are to serve?

CONTROLLING SYSTEMS

       Controlling is the management function of adjusting plans to pre-
determined objectives as they are executed. The controlling process involves
distinct activities to measure actual performance, compare performance with
standards, and take action to correct deviations when required. Planning points
the way to goals, organizing relates goals and structures, coordinating links
personnel and resources, and controlling attempts to keep the operation on
target. Controlling involves active intervention into ongoing organizational
processes to maintain and direct activities in achieving planned objectives.
Stated in another way, controlling is a process of monitoring functions or
activities to ensure that they achieve stated plans and correct unacceptable
deviations. Controlling is a function of all managers, and they know when they
are performing well only when actual performance is compared with
predetermined or desired standards. The success of any control system is
determined by the degree of congruence between planned and achieved
objectives, also known as the control accountability gap.[19] Control is critically
important. It is the final link in the management process, making sure that
activities are achieved as planned. Control provides the continuing link between
planning and delegating responsibilities. The operating assumption is that there

will not necessarily be automatic execution of assigned activities. The saying, "The best-laid plans of mice and men oft go awry," sums up much of what we mean by managing.

In measuring performance four typical sources of information are often used: (1) personal observation based on familiarity with the activity; (2) statistical reports such as computer data, graphs, and charts; (3) oral reports by means of conferences, one-to-one exchanges, or telephone discussions; and (4) written reports involving more comprehensive and concise information.

To control is to exercise power. Much of what is done in organizations is subject to rules and regulations and informal constraints. We think first of upper-level officials, who set the objectives, deploy resources, are responsible for carrying out evaluations, and can make the changes they desire. These upper-level officials set up the lines of authority and apply the organizational rewards and discipline. The essence of this view of controlling as the exercise of raw power is reflected in the sign that used to sit on President Truman's desk: "The buck stops here!" This was a graphic reminder that the chief executive—and no one else—was in charge of the federal government. Truman's dismissal of the World War II hero Douglas MacArthur from his position as commander of U.S. troops in Korea dramatized the president's control, even over the military. MacArthur carried his disagreement with the president over U.S. policy in China to a joint session of Congress. In the end, however, the general lost, and we remember primarily his words to Congress: "Old soldiers never die; they just fade away."

Ultimate control in a democracy rests with the people. Through periodic elections, representatives and executives are chosen and given authority to determine what people can and cannot do. Truman ousted MacArthur because in this country military leaders take orders from elected officials. Some of the power exercised by government restricts what citizens can do, while other applications are aimed at helping people do what would be difficult without public support. The important point to keep in mind is that the people grant power to government in order that it be used in the public interest.

CONTROL SYSTEMS

A small group of appointed top administrators, typically department secretaries (e.g., the secretary of the Department of Health and Human Services), directors of major agencies (e.g., the Federal Trade Commission), and commissioners (e.g., the FTC or the Federal Communications Commission) are given authority by elected officials to act in their behalf, including the right to exercise the power to compel compliance to their orders. The regulations these officials and administrators issue have almost the effect of laws passed by the legislature, and they are backed up by the military force of the state. Broadly speaking, elected and appointed officials use their punitive powers only through prescribed procedures, and they justify their action as being in the public interest. The comptroller-general of the United States, for example, exercises power indirectly through prescribed accounting procedures and through carrying out audits of agency performance on behalf of Congress. The ultimate coercive power to punish or to fire is used primarily as a threat to bolster a variety of control systems. Perhaps the most important controls in organizations are the general administrative systems:

1.   *Planned delegation.* Control through selecting and strategically placing authority in the delivery system.
2.   *Control over communication.* Channeling correspondence, policy questions, and information on personnel and financial matters for clearance and approval at the highest levels.
3.   *Preparation and enforcement of a manual of operations.* Specifying the duties and responsibilities of each structure and position in the organization.
4.   *Periodic reporting and inspection.* Controls arising from knowledge that the work performed will be evaluated.

POWER, AUTHORITY, AND INFLUENCE

Controlling, a modest application of power, occurs continuously inside government and is directed at the specific acts of personnel. The concern is less with requiring compliance than with adjusting inputs into a program in order to obtain desired results. The thermostat that regulates the temperature of a room provides an analogy for what we mean by controlling. The thermostat is not the source of cool or warm air but is only the regulating point. When the temperature in the room varies from the setting, the thermostat activates either the furnace or cooling mechanism to bring the room back to the desired temperature. As we have said, controlling is a regulating intervention to achieve conformity with a predetermined standard.

The control systems set up by top administrators serve as the backup for the controlling done by MLMs. In the process, however, attention moves from the system to the people implementing the program. The regulation of interventions with operators tends to be highly personalized and takes on the quality of improving communication and exerting leadership rather than of applying threats. Top-level administrators recognize the need for these extended controlling activities. They realize that objectives are presented in fairly general terms and that they must be translated by MLMs into specific actions. While top administrators retain the right to review what is done, they allow subordinates considerable leeway in controlling how objectives will be reached. As orders are handed down the hierarchy, they are expanded and made more specific. The Department of Defense may establish the policy of maintaining a missile capacity to balance the threat offered by foreign launching sites, but that will necessitate vast detail at every level, from the office of the secretary down to instructions given to the technician first class. The subgoals and specific actions become the policy because they more closely determine the final outcome.

Henri Fayol defined control as follows:

Control is the examination of results. To control is to make sure that all operations at all times are carried out in accordance with the plan adopted—with the orders given and with the principles laid down. Control compares, discusses, and criticizes: it tends to stimulate planning and strengthen organization, to increase the efficiency of command and to facilitate coordination. [20]

TOP-LEVEL CONTROL PROBLEMS

Top level managers' major functions involve the building of the agency's image, interacting with elected officials, networking with relevant external groups to build and maintain agency support, and maintaining effective relationships with other agencies that might impact operations. This political posture best describes the approach to controlling taken by top officials and administrators. Part of the politics of control takes place in the external environment in which the agency operates, and part occurs within the organization (see Fig. 9.6). Both aspects are important yet quite distinct from the controlling in the middle levels of government agencies.

External Controls

The basic control system for an agency is embedded in authorizing statutes. These give the purpose of the agency, detail the power of top administrators, and determine what authority can be delegated. Top administrators abstract from the legislative history of authorizing statutes the power configuration intended. They also maintain liaisons with legislators and interest groups critically involved with their agencies in order to obtain additional clues as to what kinds and what range of power have been authorized. Top administrators must also look at other agencies that affect their operations, especially at budget, finance, and evaluation units that operate government-wide controls. They attempt to monopolize the information about power relations from external sources.

CONTROLS IN THE INTERNAL ENVIRONMENT

The controls within agencies reflect the need for a small group of top administrators to initiate actions and then to control the organization once it is in motion. This requires a careful calculation of how and where to apply the power that has been legislatively granted.

The basic controls available to top managers have been identified by Anthony Downs:

- an official set of orders

- a calculation of the time required for subordinates to act
- selective evaluation of performance
- determination of what action is required to bring intentions and outcomes into better congruence
- the decision to do nothing, to correct behavior, or to modify previous goals
- the issuance of a new set of orders (if appropriate) in response to the decision about action.[21]

Several principles can be derived from this basic top-level control system. They suggest the nature of top-management controls and their limits. Top administrators tend to:

- ground their orders in legislative authority
- check out proposed directives in advance with subordinates to minimize the possibility that unanticipated resistance will occur
- keep the number of orders issued to an absolute minimum
- make known the measures or standards that will be used to evaluate performance
- select only a small portion of all activity for review, primarily what is controversial and highly visible.

Discipline

Top managers can use discipline to enforce compliance. The positive side of discipline comes through promotions, preferential assignments, and publicizing favorable performance reviews. Government personnel are generally looking for higher-status jobs and increased compensation, and top officials can capitalize on these desires to achieve preferred behavior.

The negative side of discipline—the imposition of punishments—has evolved from a rough and ready exercise of power into a more formal procedure, particularly where merit systems are in place. A further restraint is involved when an agency is unionized. Disciplinary action may be defined as an application of penalties in order to achieve future compliance. It is in this sense an important control device used by top administrators.

Disciplinary action usually becomes necessary for one of the following reasons:

- inattention to duty exhibited in tardiness, carelessness, breakage of property, or inefficiency
- insubordination through infraction of rules or displays of hostility against supervisors
- intoxication, the use of unlawful drugs, or immoral behavior
- insufficient integrity (violations of codes of ethics, excessive indebtedness, soliciting or accepting a bribe)

- inappropriate residence or moonlighting
- "conduct unbecoming an officer"—a catch-all category.

This is not an exhaustive list, and MLMs (to whom they apply) learn through experience what lies behind these general prohibitions laid down by top administrators. Every person in government is controlled by this type of restriction on behavior. It should be kept in mind, however, that the maintenance of discipline will not in itself bring about the achievement of the organization's objectives.

Moreover, behind infractions often lie other conditions: (1) boredom with routine tasks, (2) frustrations arising from dead-end jobs; (3) the need to assert personal freedom; (4) personality conflicts; (5) resistance to discriminatory practices; or (6) disagreement over assignments. This suggests that the causes of undesired behavior must be sought beyond the behavior itself. Nevertheless, here are some broad guidelines for a reasonable disciplinary system applied by top management:

1. Acts, not the individual, should be viewed as unacceptable.
2. The attitude should prevail that all employees, including past offenders, are willing to conform to reasonable standards that have been adequately communicated.
3. Following the confirmation of an infraction, sanctions should be promptly applied.
4. Generally, discipline should be administered in private.
5. The facts should be ascertained objectively, and both sides of the story should always be heard.
6. Consistency and flexibility should be balanced so that discipline is evenly applied while taking into account extenuating circumstances, the intent, past record of the offender, and previous penalties for similar offenses.
7. The penalty should contain a constructive dimension; hence, counseling is an essential element for future compliance.
8. There should be some built-in method for systematic follow-up.[22]

Applying discipline is difficult. Many managers hesitate to penalize other people directly. Others punish subordinates without hesitation, almost as if it is an obligation. In general, however, most of the uses of discipline as a control mechanism by top administrators must adhere to the rule of anticipated reaction: "The authority of sanction rests on the behavior responses that are induced by the possibility that sanctions may be applied."[23]

Top-Level Control Problems

As Weber has pointed out, controlling that is dependent on coercive power presents many problems in regard to: (1) requiring compliance to improper goals; (2) the use of inappropriate indicators; (3) resentment and rejection of controls by operators; (4) precipitous reaction to infractions; (5) the

Fig. 9.6. Administrative Control Process

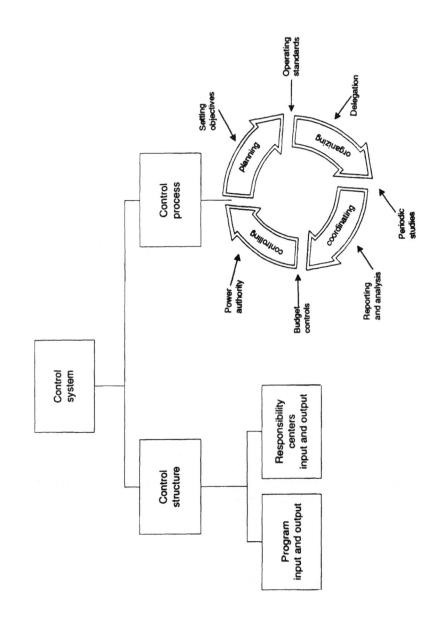

excessive cost of conditioning; and (6) distortion of upward-flowing information. The following case study illustrates all of these problems.

Case Study 9B: Changes in the Bureau of Employment Security Procedures Brought Unintended Consequences.

A bureau of employment security (BES), which is a state agency charged with providing job leads for unemployed applicants, experienced a change in management with the election of a new governor for the state. The new director observed the existing work procedures and decided that a new set of controls would be necessary to meet agency goals of "a job referral for every registered unemployed person and a special concern for the hard-to-place long-term unemployed" (those out of work for more than 15 weeks).

Under the previous management, the office procedures called for the unemployed to register at BES regional offices, where they were interviewed by employment specialists. Each office had six specialists who interviewed on a first-come, first-served basis and matched applicants to jobs in a common job bank. Interviewers had high morale and willingly provided information about new job leads. Some specialization developed within the group based on the type of job and the kinds of employers. One interviewer, for example, became particularly effective in placing people in service jobs in higher education, while another tended to specialize in training opportunities in health-related professions.

The new administrator was motivated to institute changes when he observed that long lines tended to form at BES centers, with the apparent bottleneck being the inter-view stage. To meet this problem, he required that information be gathered on the number of interviews completed by interviewer per hour. The new control was issued at as BES was faced with the possibility of a cut in its budget and therefore a reduction in personnel.

The new procedure had the effect of reducing the waiting lines, a result that led the new administrator to express satisfaction with the change. However, within a short time the lines returned, and they contained a much higher percentage of persons who had been through the process than was the case before. On closer inspection, it appeared that the number of interviews had increased, but the quality of each one had declined, and a lower percentage of persons referred were actually placed. There was also a noticeable increase in complaints from business firms about inappropriate candidates being sent to their employment offices.

The new administrator, concerned about these developments, instituted a second control that measured the number of interviews completed but added data on the number of placements. The revised control improved the quality of the interviews but also caused fierce competition among the interviewers. Instead of the cooperative informal relationship, interviewers now refused to share job information. One particularly insecure interviewer was accused of copying job information from a co-worker's desk during the lunch break, an incident that led to the practice by all interviewers of keeping their job information locked in their desks. A more serious problem emerged when inter-viewers discovered that easier placement could be made of minorities whose appearance was middle class or of women who were young and attractive. This advantage led one interviewer to use a personal friendship with the intake clerk to get a higher percentage of persons fitting this description referred to him. In the monthly summaries of placements, the central headquarters at the state capital noticed that while overall placements were up, the mix of the group contained higher percentages of persons than before of those easiest to place. The director of BES received a call from a state senator complaining of BES's failure to place the hard-core unemployed and its overemphasis on putting minorities and women on jobs for which they were overqualified.

The new administrator, by this time in charge for more than a year, was called to the office of the governor to explain why the agency's basic objectives were not being met.

CONTROLLING AT THE MIDDLE AND LOWER LEVELS

Middle- and lower-level managers control by focusing attention on results. They take administratively defined goals, plans, and standards and check them against performance. Where they find outcomes match intentions, they allow operations to proceed—even though they have involved unanticipated means. Where they find unacceptable outcomes—even when the prescribed means have been used—they *consider* intervening to make corrections. We say "consider" because MLMs must take into account their ability to overcome the resistance of operators to change. Wherever people are involved, management must be concerned with subordinates' reactions to controls. Fig. 9.7 illustrates the major steps MLMs follow in the controlling process.

MLMs are well placed to achieve effective controlling. They are familiar with the needed skills and can make fine distinctions about quality. They enjoy a permanent status in the organization and, as such, participate actively in both formal and informal groups. Moreover, MLMs know the policy intent and can see the actual program results. These are enormous advantages growing out of their proximity to delivery systems. But perhaps the most critical knowledge that MLMs possess concerns the necessity for supplementing traditional power and authority control systems with controlling based on influence (the ability to apply power). We stress this dimension of managerial controlling because it provides a key for relating controlling to accountability.

MLM CONTROLLING METHODS

MLMs work within the administrative control system. They use the threat of power or authority as a way of maximizing influence. The planning, organizing, and coordinating systems of upper management are reinterpreted within the internal environment, as shown in Fig. 9.8.

Information is collected from all stages of the implementation process, from scheduling through the evaluation of work performance. Some of these data are in the form of reports, some come from direct observation, and still others result from trying to personally carry out the plans top administration has suggested. Quantitative and qualitative information is collected and blended to form the basis of the decision to intervene or to let operations continue as they

Fig. 9.7. Four Steps in Controlling Operations in Process

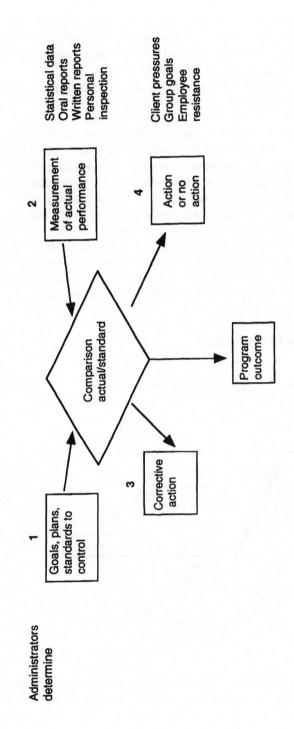

Source: Adapted from Robert Albanese, *Management: Towards Accountability for Performance* (Homewood, Ill.: Richard D. Irwin, 1975), p. 187.

are. Some of the intervention takes the form of reporting to top administration information that can be helpful in rethinking plans or modifying objectives. The following example illustrates the kind of corrective interventions MLMs are called on to make relative to top-level administrators:

A taxing division was instructed to collect all delinquent accounts. The unit was losing $100,000 per month through a failure to properly scrutinize tax rolls and to get bills out on time. A new procedure was established to attack this problem at a cost of $30,000 per month. Subsequent reports revealed that the control system was resulting in the collection of $40,000 per month from the accounts in arrears. The top administration insisted that the collection of delinquent accounts be expanded, but the manager noted that a doubling of the effort (the expenditure of an additional $30,000) would probably still leave some accounts outstanding. He said the accounts easiest to collect had responded but that those still outstanding would be more difficult to collect. He estimated that the second $30,000 might recover only $10,000 in additional payments. The manager asked how much top administration wished to spend to reach the goal of collecting delinquent accounts. If the top administrators' emphasis is on collection efficiency, they will not spend the additional resources.

Fig. 9.8. Managerial Controlling

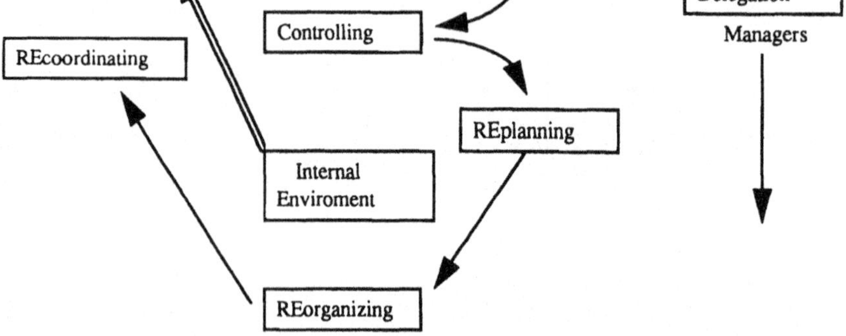

By being close to the operation, MLMs are able to report what the control systems yield, and they can offer suggestions as to when controls need to be modified. In public sector service agencies, where there is no market mechanism, managers often have a virtual monopoly on cost and benefit data. This means their interventions with upper administrative personnel often have great impact.

MLMs also have to intervene to change the behavior of operators. At times, this takes the form simply of activating the disciplinary mechanism by passing information about infractions to upper levels with recommendations for action. More common is the utilization of less formal forms of discipline— giving an operator an unfavorable performance evaluation, reassigning the poor performer to a less desirable job or location, reducing authority, or denying minor privileges. These informal means of controlling can generally be applied quickly and thus make possible corrections before a problem gets out of hand. Even more likely is that the manager will seek out the conditions that are giving rise to the undesirable behavior. Because many of the reasons for poor perform- ance have to do with operator dissatisfaction, controlling most often takes the form of motivating procedures.

THE EXERCISE OF INFLUENCE

MLMs employ influence in recognition of the fact that power is not a zero-sum game. They have learned from experience that every situation does not have to be a win-lose proposition, with one person gaining power because another loses it. MLMs seek to establish the kind of relationships in which the power of both management and operators can be enhanced. In day-to-day operations, there are numerous examples of how this can happen. When a police officer controls an intersection, it does not mean simply that the officer's orders must be followed; it also means that motorists, through submitting to the control, can get through the intersection more quickly and safely. Because the control opens up the possibility of more desirable freedoms, it is more willingly accepted.

To get a better understanding of ways to be influential, MLMs devote considerable attention to small-group behavior. MLMs' interest in small groups is in the first instance pragmatic, from the desire to understand how they work in order to influence how operators perform. At a deeper level, MLMs recognize that only the shared values of a social collective can legitimate the power or influence of a superior: The bureaucratic superior whose managerial practices further the interests of subordinates creates a condition that justifies the exercise of controls. It is this pursuit of legitimacy that directs the MLMs' attention to the group.

IMPROVING CONTROLS

We have suggested that managerial controlling contains elements of an art and is clearly not yet a science. Controlling involves making comparisons about the congruence of intentions and results in order to stimulate discussion, promote better planning, and encourage operators to organizational goals. Controlling of this type grows out of the situation and is likely to have some of the following characteristics:

1.   It should be as simple as possible.
2.   It must produce timely and reliable data.
3.   It should be understood as useful to both superiors and subordinates.
4.   It should be based on known and accepted costs.
5.   It should focus on exceptional rather than routine behavior. This rewards micro-management as deviations are brought to upper management's attention only when they exceed permitted levels.
6.   It should stimulate self-regulating systems.
7.   It should be flexible to take advantage of opportunities.
8.   It should have selective controls; that is, management should identify strategic control points where the greatest harm or impairment of results can occur.
9.   If should have multiple criteria. That is, when feasible, more than one measure should be used to assess performance. This will minimize the manipulation of one measure to allow a manager to look good. Additionally, it provides a more objective basis for evaluation.

ORGANIZING, COORDINATING, AND CONTROLLING: POWER ACCOUNTABILITY AND MLMs

Organizing

The purpose of organizing at top levels is to relate structures to mission; in the middle levels, reorganizing brings formal structures into harmony within the organization. Organizational overlays emerge as people work out their own ways of relating to each other. At every level the struggle is over power and how to obtain desired results with accountability. In the internal environment of organizations, only MLMs have the potential of bringing power and account-ability into balance through organizing and reorganizing. They function in the day-to-day operational roles in the hierarchy; power to achieve overall results is delegated to them and they orchestrate the line and staff relationships, know the operational overlays, and can see how structures relate to the effects that programs have on people.

Coordinating

Coordination is fundamentally the exercise of power that brings organizational actions into harmony with program objectives. MLMs typically face difficulties in their pursuit of accountability, particularly in bringing together organizational goals and the goals of employees who have differing perspectives about how to best realize them.

In a democratic society such as the U.S., policy outcomes are seldom crystal-clear for the simple reason that amorphous objectives such as justice, enhanced freedom, or increased security are sought. These imprecise and fluctuating societal objectives established by ambiguous legislation reappear in less-than-clear restatements of policy by top-level administrators. It is in the middle ranges of organizations that power is welded to translate ideas into action, that accountability is achieved or lost. MLMs must sort through poorly defined functions, unclear delegation, and overlapping authority to hammer out directives that operations' personnel can understand and use for guidance. Unanticipated events inevitably occur, but MLMs must handle them by applying their understanding of accountability. MLMs must select from broad policy statements and act to produce results consistent with policy goals.

Controlling

Our discussion of controlling focused on applied power (influence) as the ability to impose one's will on others despite resistance. While this type of power is typically monopolized by administrators and officials, constraints in organizations operate to counter this enforcement. We must recognize the key role that persuasion plays in program implementation and the strategic role of MLMs. Productive outcomes can be maximized, most often, when creative ways are found to merge voluntary compliance with organizational demands. In the long run, controls are best executed by operators (not administrators), who make continuous corrections to keep predetermined objectives in tune with results. The interdependence of controllers and the controlled gives MLMs unique opportunities to demonstrate how objectives and methods, theory and practice complement each other. The end result of all the controlling is accountability, in which planned objectives coincide with achievement.

DISCUSSION QUESTIONS

1. Why is so much attention given to government reorganization plans by newly elected administrators, although much more significant reorganizing occurs within agencies?
2. What relationship does organizing have to the legislatively defined mission?
3. What are the advantages and disadvantages of an organization based on purpose compared with one based on clientele?
4. Support the assertion: Top administrators organize, but middle managers reorganize.
5. Why are delegation and the interrelationship of line and staff function important ways for reorganization within the internal environment of an agency?
6. Why are MLMs in a strategic position to use reorganizing to balance power and accountability?
7. Can we achieve effective coordination in an organization in which the policy goals have not been well articulated?
8. One writer has said that coordination is the chief instrument that keeps an organization from fragmenting. Discuss the merits of this view.
9. What means do top administrators use to achieve better coordination, both inside and outside the organization?

10.   What instruments do MLMs employ in effective coordination? How are they
       alike and different from those used by top administrators?
11.   What implications does coordination have for power and accountability in a
       public agency?
12.   Why is power related to influence? Show specifically why it is too narrow a view
       to see control as simply a way of policing the organization.
13.   What likely effect stems from too rapid intervention in instituting controls?
14.   Why do quantitative measures tend to dominate evaluations?
15.   What are the basic techniques used in controlling?
16.   Why does the need to use discipline also suggest a need to look into the causes of
       undesirable behavior?
17.   What is the relationship between small-group forms and the legitimate exercise of
       power by MLMs?

NOTES

1.   Robert T. Golembiewski and Frank K. Gibson, eds., *Managerial Behavior
and Organizational Demands: Management as a Linking of Levels of Interaction*
(Chicago: Rand McNally, 1967), p. 317.
2.   John M. Gaus, Leonard D. White, and Marshall E. Dimock, *The Frontiers of
Public Administration* (Chicago: University of Chicago Press, 1936), pp. 66–67.
3.   Robert Presthus, *The Organizational Society: An Analysis and a Theory*
(New York: Vintage, 1962), pp. 31–33.
4.   Robert T. Golembiewski, *Man, Management and Morality* (New Brunswick,
N.J.: Transaction Books, 1993).
5.   F. Burke Sheeran, *Management Essentials for Public Works Administration*
(Chicago: American Public Works Association, 1976), pp. 202-204.
6.   John M. Pfiffner and Frank Sherwood, *Administrative Organization*
(Englewood, N.J.: Prentice-Hall, 1960), pp. 17–29.
7.   Leonard D. White, *Introduction to the Study of Public Administration* (New
York: Macmillan, 1950), p. 210.
8.   Ibid., 4th edn. (New York: Macmillan, 1955), p. 38.
9.   Marshall Edward Dimock and Gladys Ogden Dimock, *Public Administration*
(New York: Holt, Rinehart, and Winston, 1969), p. 403.
10. Sheeran, *Management Essentials*, p. 177.
11. Dimock and Dimock, *Public Administration*, p. 404.
12. Comstock Glaser, *Administrative Procedures: A Practical Handbook for the
Administrative Analyst* (Washington, D.C.: America Council on Public Affairs, 1941),
pp. 41–42.
13. Henry Metcalf and L. Urwick, eds., *Collected Papers of Mary Parker Follett*
(New York: Harper and Row Brothers, 1940), pp. 96–97.
14. Corwin
15. Cyril O'Donnell, "Ground Rules for Using Committee," in *Management: A
Book of Readings*, Harold Koontz and Cyril O'Donnell, eds. (New York: McGraw Hill,
1972), p. 381.
16. Ibid., pp. 381–82, and Neil J. Smelser, *Effective Committee Service*
(Newbury Park, California: Sage Publications, 1993), pp. 1–3.

17. Adapted from Dimock and Dimock, *Public Administration*, p. 407.

18. Drawn from F. Burke Sheeran, *Management Essentials*, p. 13.

19. Kenneth A. Merchant, "The Control Function of Management," *Sloan Management Review* (Summer 1982): 43–55.

20. Henri Fayol, "Administrative Theory in the State," in *Papers on the Science of Administration*, Luther Bulick and L. Urwick, eds. (New York: Institute of Public Administration, Columbia University Press, 1947), pp. 99–114.

21. Anthony Downs, *Inside Bureaucracy* (Boston: Little, Brown, 1967), p. 144.

22. Edwin B. Flippo, *Management: A Behavioral Approach*, 2nd. edn. (Boston: Allyn and Bacon, 1970), p. 442.

23. Herbert Simon et al., *Public Administration* (New York: Macmillan, 1953), p. 196.

10

Decision-Making and Communication as Basic Management Activities

This chapter focuses mainly on internal decision-making and communication as they occur at all levels in public organizations. The first section explores the nature and process of public sector decision-making. In the second, the vital role of communication is examined. A third section compares the functions of top administrators with those of MLMs. Finally, decision-making and communication are examined in relation to the exercise of power and accountability.

LEARNING OBJECTIVES

- Know the elements that go into management decision-making.
- Understand the constraints under which the public decision-maker operates.
- Be able to relate deciding and communicating to exercising leadership and to distinguish between the decision-making and communicating functions in public organizations.
- Distinguish the roles of top administrators and MLMs in decision-making.
- Understand how decision-making, communication, and information play an important role in the deciding process.
- Recognize the use and importance of committees in public sector decision-making.
- Appreciate the potential that decision-making has for promoting greater accountability.

When we refer to decision-making and communication as basic management activities, we mean the energizing ways in which executives, administrators, and managers act to bring about desired change. Typically in some organizations, the top administrators solicit inputs from aides, staff, and wherever else possible and then prudently select a course of action. This requires that decision-makers constantly determine what is to be done, who will do it, when, where, and (frequently) how. The decision-maker should possess experience, judgment, and creativity. Additionally, in Herbert Simon's view, it is not enough to simply make decisions; an organization must provide the means to promote and ensure correct decision-making.[1] Finally, whatever is decided has no impact until it is communicated.

The effective direction of core management functions (planning, organizing, coordinating, and controlling) requires decision-making and communication. Management is a decision-making process; communication is the medium through which choices are made among alternative means in accomplishing specified objectives. The Royal Bank of Canada views its organization from a decision-making perspective: "The management principle is readily stated: the manager is paid to find and define the problem, analyze it, develop alternative solutions, decide upon the best solution, and convert this decision into effective action."[2]

In the typical agency, individual choices constitute one of many elements in a web of relationships that form the basis for collective action in responding to problematic situations. Prudent and successful decisions require that we understand the overall effect before initiating a response to any given situation.[3]

THE NATURE AND PROCESS OF PUBLIC
SECTOR DECISION-MAKING

Decision-making falls within the province of all levels of management, though it is generally assumed to be reserved to individuals fairly high in the administrative hierarchy. This assumption fits our cultural belief that each organization has someone in charge who makes the real decisions and exercises the responsibility. For example, Fred Smith (a client) went into a local welfare agency to avail himself of the service to which he believed he was entitled. On being told that he no longer qualified, he demanded an explanation, which he got and promptly rejected. He insisted on seeing the person in charge. The assistant director responded, giving the same unacceptable explanation. The assistant director called the director, who came and gave the same explanation. Though Mr. Smith was still not entirely placated, he thanked the director for his time, shook his hand, and left.

In attempting to meet and resolve different types of problems, two schools of thought have developed. One holds that decisions are mainly the product of intuitive and creative elements. In this view, decision-making is largely an art. The Cuban missile crisis provides a good example. President Kennedy had to decide whether to bomb, invade, or blockade Cuba when the Soviet missiles were discovered. There was no single way in which he came to his decision. Instead, the president was forced to consider a multitude of information and proposals, some of which overlapped and conflicted.

Graham Allison writes that the competing proposals for determining the decision (output) of the president were greatly affected by "large organizations functioning according to standard operating patterns of behavior."[4]   Each participant (the military, the presidential security adviser, the United Nations ambassador, and the others) in decision-making desired an outcome that was consistent with his or her own views. For example, the military officials wanted strong military action, while the ambassador wanted a resolution through diplomatic channels. From all of these conflicting pressures and viewpoints, the president made a decision.

Those who view decision-making as a rational process represent the opposing school, associated largely with the work of Herbert A. Simon. These theorists believe that decisions can be reduced not only to a rational process but to computer programs, capable of making decisions with the range and depth similar to that supplied by human thought. Our alarm clock provides an example. When the alarm goes off, we wake up; the decision has been made mechanically. Decisions of this sort are common in cases involving hiring on the basis of a cutoff score or expanding a particular service based on increased demand. Decisions made in this way are also referred to as programmed decisions. MLMs typically make these types of decisions.

Programmed Decisions

Most problems that confront us are repetitive, permitting well-defined search and choice procedures to be used each time they occur. These programmed decisions, as Simon calls them, are made by habits of response, standard operating procedures, clerical routines, and organizational arrangements.[5] In the typical purchasing department, a drop in inventory to a given level sets off a routine procedure for replenishing the stock. An amount to be ordered is determined, a purchase order is initiated and sent to a vendor, and copies of the ordered inventory are simultaneously transmitted to other recipients, such as the receiving office and accounts payable.

We stated above that decision-making in the typical organization is a collective response to problematic situations.   In the modern organization, specialization and the division of labor have been carried to such a point that most individuals participate in only a small routine part of any decision. Consider the individual attempting to obtain a driver's license. As many as four or more participants (giving the written examination, examining eyesight, administering the driver's test, photographing the applicant, collecting license fees) may be involved.

William Gore and J. W. Dyson have observed: "Programmed or routine decisions embody a high degree of agreement on what is to be accomplished and how and what resources are required to obtain these ends through these means. Above all, routine decisions give predictable consequences for known inputs."[6] Programmed decisions allow the manager to fall back on a systematic rule, procedure, or policy that establishes clear parameters for decision-making.

Nonprogrammed Decisions

These decisions represent the other end of the spectrum and do not lend themselves to a routine response. Almost by definition, nonprogrammed decisions are unstructured. Problems are often new and poorly defined, making it difficult to tell what factors are applicable in obtaining a desired solution. The search for solutions is far more difficult and thus more expensive because there is normally "an absence of rational problem solving strategies."[7]

In public agencies, nonprogrammed decisions most often fall in the province of top administrators due to the cost, uncertainty, and the need for committing the organization and obtaining coordination and control. In the 1960s, the occupation of university administration buildings and other facilities by irate students required administrators to make nonprogrammed decisions. Such decisions were very taxing and costly; no one knew how to handle these novel and potentially explosive situations.

President Clinton's election promise to bring security and confidence to the American public qualifies as a nonprogrammed decision. Despite the president's success in creating jobs and economic prosperity, the feeling of insecurity and anxiety is high and rising. The president must contend with a situation in which the economy is near full employment yet very profitable businesses and governments are laying off thousands of people.

CONSTRAINTS

There are limits and constraints on all decision-makers, and in the public sector, additional constraints come into play. They include the following:

- agency rules, structures, procedures and precedents
- administrators' social backgrounds, values, and skills
- the political relationships that the agency and administrators can effect and maintain with political parties, relevant individuals, clients, interest groups, and other government units in their environment
- the kind of relationship that can be maintained with legislative officials, chief executives, and the courts.

In public sector management, understanding of the constraints noted above is important because they affect the quality of decisions.

Steps in the Decision-Making Process

All administrators view their efforts as serving some meaningful end. Thus, the purpose must be articulated at the beginning of the decision-making process. If decision-makers wish to accomplish their purposes, they need to establish a consistent and logical process that will produce the most acceptable outcome.

1.   Correct diagnosis of the problem(s). Problems may appear internally in the organization in the form of absence of teamwork, conflicting authority, vague or ambiguous assignments, bottlenecks, poor work distribution, insufficient delegation, and unclear responsibility. One way of identifying the problem is by using critical factor analysis, which is the search for the key element, that when changed, will trigger the desired results. Finding such an element usually leads to a breakthrough in defining the problem and is a direct aid to decision-making. It is important to recognize that some problems should not be solved:

    A. A small problem, the solution of which will create bigger problems. Discharging a low performer could produce costly grievance procedure or litigation.
    B. A problem that is annoying but not fundamentally important. It might be inadvisable to punish tardiness by an employee who otherwise performs well on the job.
    C. A short-range problem for which long-range implications have not been assessed. In the 1970s, Westinghouse rushed to sell nuclear power plants without taking into account the future price of uranium. Westinghouse promised to supply millions of pounds of uranium at a moderate price as an inducement to potential purchasers of power plants. When the uranium prices rocketed, the company was almost destroyed. Westinghouse committed a similar mistake in the 1980s. It rushed into real estate business to produce immediate profits without considering the cyclical and long term nature of the real estate market. When the market fell dramatically, Westinghouse experienced massive losses, again driving it to near bankruptcy.
    D. A problem whose solution has spill-over consequences far beyond the original problem. To provide hydroelectric power for short-range needs, a dam is built. In the long run, however, it may create unforeseen negative ecological effects. (e.g., soil erosion and harm to plant life).

    Thus, it is helpful to set down the problem in writing, to divide it into manageable parts, and to assess its positive and negative aspects. Questions such as who, when, what, why, and how help us to understand obstacles that create the problem or prevent goals from being achieved.
    In general, decision-makers tend to spend too little time determining what the problem is and too much time, too early, reaching for a solution. It is important to remember the aphorism: "If we don't know where we are going, any road will take us there."

2.   Collecting data and identifying decision criteria. To aid in illuminating the problem(s) and to avoid reinventing the wheel, we need to assemble information that may be in reports or other agencies' experiences and interview other relevant participants. We identify decision criteria that will be important in solving the problem. We want to define what is relevant in the decision and apply it (see Table 10.1).

3.   Identify alternatives from doing nothing to a range of plausible solutions (see Fig. 10.1). This process permits the comparison of alternatives with each other and with inaction. For example, if a local government unit receives a federal grant for specified purposes, opportunities to make expenditures for other

purposes are automatically eliminated. Local administrators, by way of contrast, like grants that give them maximum discretion because these allow them to select where allocations are to be made.

4.   *Analyze critically, exhaustively and compare alternatives*, assessing advantages and disadvantages, making sure that appropriate alternatives are considered when the choice is to be made.

5.   *Select and recommend the alternative to be considered.* These four steps in the so-called rational decision-making process are expanded in Fig. 10.2. Note first that rational decision-making processes are regarded as the desired approach; that is, administrators are discouraged from making arbitrary choices.

But, note in Fig. 10.2 that the criterion for selecting suitable alternatives and for choosing among them is selected without analysis. Thus, what appears to be a rational process only disguises the underlying arbitrariness.

6.   *Implementing the alternative.* This step is concerned with putting the decision into action. This requires conveying the selected choice to those affected and obtaining their commitment. Quite often, as we discuss in this chapter, a committee or group can aid the manager in achieving commitment. The operating view is that if individuals are expected to carry out a decision in which they participate, they are more likely to fully support the outcome.

Table 10.1. Criteria and Weight of Prioritizing Garbage Removal

Criteria	Weight
Budget Removal	10
Accountability	8
Technology update	7
Repairs	6
Performance	5
Convenience	3
Training	1

Chester I. Bernard (1938)[8] and Herbert A. Simon (1957)[9] were among the early writers who questioned the inadequacy of the rational model of decision-making in organizations. These observers found that, instead of an exhaustive search for alternatives, there was, typically, a preferred alternative based on an undisclosed criterion. R. M. Cyert and Simon (1958) went even further in their critiques of the rational model: (1) Search was not begun until a significant change or crisis took place in the organization; (2) the proposed solution was not found by examining all alternatives, but reflected a preferred action determined long before the problem arose; and (3) contrary to accepted views, an internal cost-benefit analysis of the consequences of alternatives was seldom done and most often there was no explicit justification for making the "most favorable" choice. [10]

Fig. 10.1. Decision Alternatives

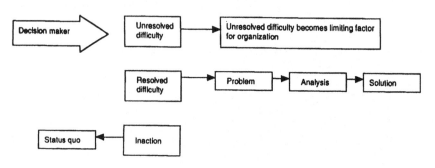

Source: Adapted from Billy J. Hodge and Herbert J. Johnson, *Management and Organization Behavior* (New York: John Wiley, 1970), p. 333.

Further Barriers to Rational Choice

Rational decision-making is based on a number of assumptions that often do not hold true in government agencies:

- that the problem is clear and unambiguous
- that there is an awareness of problems and alternatives and consequences are known
- that preferences are clear
- that there is an information base containing data about possible effects on the agency and its environment that would arise from alternative courses of action
- that there is a capability to adapt, modify, or adjust to changes that come in the wake of the decision
- that personnel have the freedom to abandon goals and policies to which they were formally committed
- that decisions are made consciously to achieve optimum outcomes.

Still other factors militate against perfect rationality (e.g., perceptual distortion, fear, and anxiety). Perhaps the most influential cause of departure from the rational course of action is time. In business decision-making, the common cliché "time is money" provides a rationale for managers to set aside the search for perfect rationality in order to get on with the task at hand.[11] This suggests that occasionally being irrational is perfectly rational![12] To make the point more generally, behind rationality lie other unarticulated criteria.

The rational decision-making approach oversimplifies the difficulties faced by decision-makers, especially in public organizations. In these organizations, political demands and realities may require that certain goals be pursued and others avoided. This is a continuing problem in public sector organizations, which are required to be responsive to elective officials.

Fig. 10.2. Rational Decision-Making

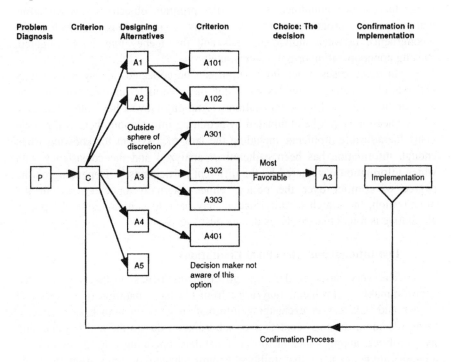

Confirmation Process

Lack of Awareness of Problems and Alternatives

The assumption is made that decision-makers (1) know the problem; (2) know that they must make decisions; (3) have alternatives; and (4) have explicit criteria for making decisions. The decision-making process, however, seldom if ever proceeds this neatly. The routine or programmed way in which most decisions are made and the pressure to make them preclude taking time to search for alternatives or for the implications of choices for future problems. The Bay of Pigs fiasco during the early days of the Kennedy administration provides a good example. The pressure to act created a momentum of its own, obscuring the alternative of not acting, and ultimately forced the administration to choose from the poor alternatives promising action.[13]

Alternatives typically are considered only in those cases where crises and stresses create great anxiety.[14] The search for alternatives usually ceases once a satisfactory choice is identified. Thus, the creativity typical in the non-programmed decision-making approach is the exception to the rule. Time inevitably limits the search and directs attention toward a satisfactory outcome rather than an optimal one.

Lack of Information

Inadequate information is a continuing limiting factor in rational decision-making. This can be an especially sensitive problem in public agencies in which there is a commitment to particular program objectives. When information on the program or project options is meticulously collected, the incongruence between individual goals and the agency may be highlighted, causing noncooperation or political disputes.

In many cases, when information can be collected, it may not be fully understood or decision-makers may not have enough time to consider the number of issues and their implications. Anthony Downs has noted that even where uncertainty can be eliminated by acquiring information, there still remain many ineradicable problems, including the lack of a system for knowing when enough information has been gathered or analyzed and the consistency with which information is gathered by the different participants.[15] Depending on the degree of conflict over the policy, either internally or externally in the organization, the search for information may have to continue until the policy alternative is found that produces the greatest acceptance.

Institutional and Structural Limitations

The very basis of the U.S. government creates obstacles to rational decision-making. Problems may arise from (1) the separation of powers and checks and balances in exchanging information between branches of government; (2) administrators' control over subordinates due to the merit system and party politics, among other factors; (3) standard operating procedures in most administrative agencies that militate against change or innovation; and (4) empire building and competition for control and expansion of policy space between administrators in positions of authority.

Sunk Cost

The concept of sunk cost holds that decisions or policies made in the past limit adaptation to future situations, due mainly to inertia and the tendency to cling to existing commitments. Thus, once we have made a sizable investment in a course of action, such as a career, we find it difficult to shift to a new one even though the prospects may be more promising. This pattern of decision-making may characterize even a national government, as many believe has been the case in Britain's labor movement and the modernization of critical industries particularly during the 1970s to mid-1980s. Planning aims to reduce uncertainty and make the future more predictable. For this reason, decisions or policies that prove satisfactory provide reason for their own continuation.

Elective and administrative officials often find that their predecessors have taken actions or established procedures that commit them to a further course of action that cannot easily be changed without the appearance of awkwardness, political expediency, or irreverence. For example, only a few months before President Eisenhower left office, he initiated a break in relations with Castro's Cuba that tied the hands of successor presidents.

Virtually every executive coming into office, especially at state and national levels, promises to "cut the fat" out of the budget or trim the bureaucracy, but such promises are soon modified (President Carter's reform of the federal civil service in 1978 may or may not be an exception to this). Powerful interest groups, clients' commitments to programs and personnel, and the budget routines limit the administrators' options to change the course of action without significant difficulties.

Prevalence of Other Decision Models

Because the rational decision-making model cannot be easily used in most administrative decision-making situations, other models, such as the incremental, satisficing, and mixed-scanning approaches have been widely used. While the rational model assumes an optimum outcome, these approaches represent compromises and are mixtures of rational methods, experience, and intuitive aspects.

Incrementalism. In this approach, decisions or policies are made that differ only slightly from existing ones. The expectations of all relevant participants, such as legislators, interest groups, and constituents, are taken into consideration. No attempt is made to identify the full range of alternatives and their consequences or to calculate the cost-benefit ratio of prospective decisions.[16] Incrementalism takes a conservative view by accepting existing programs (sunk costs) and tacitly agreeing to continue them by making small increases or decreases periodically. Essentially, the past becomes the present and the present becomes the future.

A major goal of incrementalism is to obtain consensus. This objective is so important that we may, while observing administrators discharging their duties, view the pursuit of agreement as an end in itself. This requires that administrators have or develop the fine art of bargaining. They must be able to achieve compromises and accommodate divergent interests within and between agencies, interest groups, and relevant individuals who might be able to affect the fortunes of the agency, positively or negatively.

The main characteristics of incrementalism may be summarized as:

1. The focus is on decisions or policies that differ only slightly from present ones.
2. Because of uncertainty about the consequences of new programs, decision-makers normally accept the legitimacy of previous policies or programs, whether or not they have proven their worth.
3. Innovation or radical change is the exception to the rule because great investment has been made in existing programs (sunk costs).
4. Because of political expediency and the small increases or decreases, consensus is more easily obtained.
5. The lack of agreement about fundamental societal values makes it easy for administrators to make decisions.

Satisficing. This operating norm for decision making should be viewed in the context of bounded rationality.[17] In bounded rationality, decision-makers develop simplified models that capture the essential features of problematic situations without including all of their complexities. Given the information limitations and constraints inherent in the organization, decision-makers attempt to act rationally within the parameters of the simplified model. This is known as a "satisficing decision". It is a variant of incrementalism in that it does not seek an optimum solution to identified problems. Instead, a search for information is continued until an alternative is found that meets the minimum satisfaction level. No further choices are considered. In commenting on the concept, Simon wrote: "While economic man maximizes—selects the best alternatives from among those available to him—his/her cousin, whom we shall call administrative man, satisfices—looks for a course of action that is satisfactory or good enough."[18]

Satisficing permits criteria or general guidelines to be established in advance of the search for alternatives. Thus, search is carried to the point where the information suggests that the alternative will provide an acceptable solution to the perceived difficulties.

Mixed-scanning. This approach to decision-making is a recent development. Amitai Etzioni advances it as a critique and complement to the widely accepted incremental model. Etzioni argues that the incremental model simply does not provide sufficient guidance for fundamental or unique decisions that establish the foundation and set basic direction for later events, and that fundamental decision-making occurs far more often than incremental advocates like to admit.[19] When such decisions have to be made, the examination of details alone will not reveal the information that is needed to gain insight into the overall problem.

The mixed-scanning model holds that in order to meet an unfolding problem, many decisions, both short range (incremental detail) and long range (overall perspective), are needed. For example, the U.S. energy crisis that began in 1973 has been forcing public policymakers into major, fundamental decisions aimed at changing the pattern of U.S. transportation and life in general. Though President Carter indicated in his first major address on the energy problem in April 1977 that Americans would have to make significant sacrifices, the changes that were initiated were small incremental steps. The speed limit on federal highways was reduced to 55 miles per hour and has since been increased to 65 miles per hour as the urgency of the energy problem faded.

Automobile gas mileage was raised over a ten-year period and mass transit systems were given more generous subsidies. Universities restructured their curricula to reflect the new emphases. These incremental events indicated that the fundamental decision had been made. For example, in response to the AIDS crisis during the 1980s, President Reagan allocated a small amount of resources to conduct research. As the problem became more severe during the late 1980s, President Bush significantly increased the budget for research and prevention of the disease. Meanwhile a number of drug companies began to accelerate their research and the federal Food and Drug Administration eased regulations to permit some experimental AIDS drugs to be tried on selected patients before giving final approval. With the Clinton presidency, resources for prevention greatly increased.

According to Etzioni, fundamental decision-making must guide incremental decisions, or society will experience greater problems due to lack of direction. In summarizing the comparative gains to be obtained from mixed scanning, Etzioni noted:

In the explanation of mixed-scanning it is essential to differentiate fundamental decisions from incremental ones. Fundamental decisions are made by exploring the main alternatives the actor sees in view of his conception of his goals, but unlike what rationalism would indicate details and specifications are omitted so that an overview is feasible. Incremental decisions are made within the context set by fundamental decisions and fundamental reviews.[20]

With the mixed-scanning approach, the decision-maker scans the entire organization on a regular basis, making no attempt to absorb all of the information generated. Decisions continue to be made incrementally as long as the scanning turns up no significant deviations from expectations. When such deviations do occur, the decision-maker makes an in-depth examination of the problem so that basic decisions may be made if the problem demands it.

The "Garbage Can" Model.[21] In the mid-1970s, astute decision-makers observed that the traditional explanation provided for decisions characterized by pervasive ambiguity was incomplete. When organizations are faced with "goals that are unclear, technologies that are imperfectly understood, histories that are difficult to interpret, and participants who wander in an out," the organizational choice process is described as the "garbage can" model.[22]

The garbage can theory helps us to understand that choice does not conform to predictable, conventional theories. Because traditional theories are not effective in explaining decisions of ambiguity and uncertainty, the more flexible garbage can model fills an important gap. This model seeks to make sense of the constant flux of people, problems, and solutions. Thus, with randomly operating factors, decision outcome is much more a product of chance than of rationality. In important ways the garbage can model reminds us to take note of Herbert Simon's concept of bonded rationality. Given the decision-making context of contemporary public organizations, the garbage can model may provide useful insights.

GROUP OR COMMITTEE DECISION-MAKING

Most public and private organizations use group decision-making, such as in committees, task forces, commissions, review panels, and study teams, particularly in cases that are expected to have far-reaching impact on the community organizational activities, and personnel. Recent studies suggest that managers typically spend more than 40 percent of their time in meetings formulating problems, identifying solutions, and articulating means for the implementation of the solution.[23]

Advantages and Disadvantages of Group Decision-Making

Individual and group methods of decision-making have strengths and weaknesses. Neither is applicable in all circumstances. The following are some of the advantages for the group or committee approach.

1. It typically provides more complete information. The axiom that two heads are better than one has some truth. The group adds diversity of experience and seasoned perspectives that the individual is not capable of providing alone.
2. It creates opportunity for generating more alternatives due to the group's diversity and experience.
3. It promotes greater potential for participating members to accept the proposed solution.
4. It enhances legitimacy, which is important in a democratic society that is committed to particular ideals.

There are also disadvantages associated with the group approach to decision-making:

1. It consumes a great deal of time.
2. It carries the risk of minority domination because of rank, knowledge, verbal skills, and assertiveness.
3. It creates pressure to conform as group members wishing to be accepted may become willing followers.
4. It produces ambiguous responsibility as no one individual is in charge of producing the outcome.

Decision-Making by Committee

Decision-making by committee is not a different approach, but a technique or tool that is available to the decision-maker. As a technique it is very widely used, but little discussion and few empirical studies can be found in public management literature. The ability to assign the right committee to the appropriate decision-making situation is a skill that may be indispensable to the effective public decision-maker.

"A camel is a racehorse designed by a committee." This popular saying expresses the perceived inadequacies of the committee. Yet committees are alive and operating everywhere because they provide wide experience and varied knowledge, mutual support, and an ability to absorb antagonism. Though committees are slower than individuals and less decisive than the best individual, they often produce more accurate decisions.[24]

Risk-Taking in Committees

It is generally believed that committee decisions tend to be conservative, but laboratory experiments indicate that following discussion of problems, group decisions tend to entail more risk than those made by individuals.[25] However, findings have indicated that the shift of the group depends on where members originally stood. A conservative group tends to move to the conservative end of the scale and a less conservative group to the "riskier" end.[26] This indicates that committee decisions reinforce prevailing cultural norms.

In large organizations, committees are found useful for such purposes as exchanging views and information, generating ideas and alternatives, recommending a course of action, facilitating coordination, and solving and making binding decisions. In the public sector, committees are formed for a multitude of reasons: (1) To obtain expert and specialized opinions on new technology; (2) to ensure involvement and greater participation (the organization needs to vest power for important functions in more than one person so as to spread authority and to avoid mistakes); and (3) to make unpopular decisions so that responsibility for unpopular actions may be diffused. They can also help cool off hot heads in crises. The leader of a committee is a facilitator who must employ problem-solving ability and avoid using persuasion as a means of reaching a decision.[27] The leader must emphasize a search for ideas and exchange of opinions, aim for group participation, keep members informed of where they are and what is expected, and suggest alternatives. The leader should attempt to avoid selling opinions, showing bias, and defending predetermined positions, refuting and criticizing, and allowing two-person discussions to absorb large portions of the meeting. The leader must give precedence to members' ideas over his or her own, listen without giving premature judgment, and put no one on the defensive.

Appointment to Committees

This is a very important administrative role and can become an art. The right mix of individuals is strategic and can often determine what the outcome will be. Strong-willed persons can change the mandate or objectives for which the committee has been created. Individuals should not be kept off committees simply because they do not agree with the administrator's policies. The committee may well be the means to air opposition. Additionally, it provides constructive counterpoints to proposals that may otherwise be accepted uncritically.

Types of Committees

Three basic types of committees are found in public management.

1.   *Instrumental committee.* This type of committee is essentially a facilitating device. It is composed of representatives from the interest that needs to be

accommodated, both in the process of deciding and in implementation. A classic example is provided by the Tennessee Valley Authority. When it faced opposition from local interests, the TVA instituted a practice of representing these varying viewpoints on boards. This technique is also illustrated in the increasing practice by utilities of including consumer representatives on their boards. The instrumental committee facilitates the efficient and effective operation of the agency. Its work is closely related to the concept known as coaptation, participation in decision-making by symbolic involvement.

2.   *Problem-solving committee.* Decision-makers, on occasion, give a mandate and delegate authority to a committee to find a solution. Administrators agree to accept and implement the outcome. The committee, in effect, acts instead of the decision-maker. The nature of the problem (such as one requiring a higher degree of compromise) may be the determining factor in setting up this type of committee. In working out air-pollution standards, joint government–industry committees balanced the demands of unions and other groups to save as many jobs as possible, the desire of industry to keep costs down, and environmentalists' insistence on maximum reduction of pollution in the shortest time possible. Arbitration is another example of this type of committee.

3.   *Prohibitive procrastination (PP) committee.* This committee is set up to prevent or stall for as long as possible the reaching of a decision. The PP committee and the instrumental committee are the most widely used in government. In crisis situations, such as when riots have occurred, it is not uncommon to find such a commission (e.g., the Kerner Commission on Civil Disorder set up by President Johnson, President Nixon's commissions on campus unrest and pornography, President Reagan's Peter Grace Commission, or President Clinton's Commission on Gays in the Military). The PP committee is sometimes referred to as a substitute for thought and action.

Techniques for Enhancing Group Decision-Making

A number of techniques may be used to aid consensus and decision outcomes:

1.   *Brainstorming* is one simple approach that has been used to minimize the pressure for conformity and to promote alternatives. It encourages the generation of alternatives without criticism. A brainstorming session takes place in a small group whose leader clearly states the problem in language understood by all. Members identify as many alternatives as possible without criticism until all alternatives have been recorded.

2.   *Nominal group techniques* restrict the exchange of ideas during the decision-making process. All group members must be present. However, members are required to explore their ideas independently through the following steps:

   A.   All members meet as a group but writes down their ideas independently.
   B.   The silent period ends as each member presents one idea to the group, until all ideas have presented, typically on a flip chart or a chalk board. Discussion is allowed only when all ideas have been presented.
   C.   The group evaluates each idea.

    D.   Group members then are required to independently rank each idea. The final decision is reached based on the highest aggregate ranking.

3.   *The Delphi technique* is similar to the nominal group technique but is more time-consuming and complex. It does not, however, require each member's physical presence. Members are never allowed to meet face to face. The Delphi technique involves the following steps:

    A.   After the problem is identified, participants are expected to identify potential solutions by means of a carefully constructed questionnaire.
    B.   Members complete the questionnaire.
    C.   The questionnaire results are centrally tabulated and reproduced.
    D.   Copies are sent to each participant.
    E.   Members are required to review the results and again indicate their solution. Often the results produce new solutions or cause changes in the original position. Steps (D) and (E) are repeated.[28]

COMMUNICATION: ITS VITAL ROLE

Successful communication occurs only when the transference and understanding of meaning has taken place. The philosophical question is often posed: If a tree falls in the forest and no one hears it, does it make any noise? In a communicative context, it must be answered negatively.

Communication Process

A prerequisite for communication is the expression of purpose as a message to be delivered from the source (the sender) to the receiver in symbolic form (encoding) and sent by means of some medium (channel) to the receiver.[29] The receiver translates the sender's message (called decoding), completing the transfer of meaning from one individual to another (see Fig. 10.3).

At any point in the process noise or disturbances may interfere with the transmission of the message, as shown in Fig. 10.3. Examples of noise may include inattention by the receiver, background sounds or voices, telephone static, and illegible print or writing. Additionally, sources initiating the message may affect the encoding by their skill, attitudes, knowledge, and culture.

Non-Verbal Communication

Much of the most important communication is not written or spoken, but is nonverbal. A green light, the size and trappings of subordinate's office in relation to the top executive, the intonation of one's voice, and emphasis on words and phrases can be important ways of communicating. Nonverbal communication may be referred to as the ability to read people or to interpret nonverbal communication.

Decision-making is never complete until the person to whom it is directed receives it and interprets it as intended: "The communication of information is the life stream of any organization."[30] Decisions are not meaningful events in and of themselves, to be effective they must be communicated to others. Those communicated with must also carry out the tasks and understand the implications of the decisions. When decision-making is viewed in this manner, it is a process for achieving action; it necessarily involves communication from superior to subordinates and includes upward and laterally-oriented communication because it requires the cooperative efforts of many people. The communication surrounding decisions is not limited to formal channels; it extends to the rank and file in public agencies and the informal channels that they use to carry out their everyday activities.

Fig. 10.3. The Communication Process

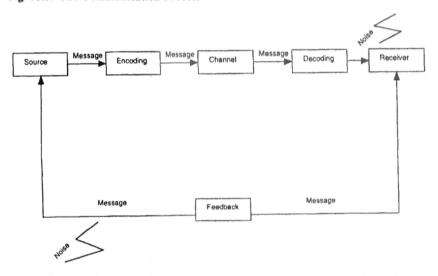

Because of the crucial role of communication in decision-making and in carrying out an organization's mission, it is important to understand how a communication network operates and the elements that contribute to an effective system. It is through the communication system that plans, decisions, policies, and information flow in public agencies. As noted above, communication links all levels of management in three main ways: formally, informally, and laterally.

Formal Communication

Formal communication operates according to the hierarchical model of organization, in which authority and orders flow down and information flows up. The hierarchy is used as a reductive information network. Each step in the communication chain acts as a screening point to decide how information will flow up.[31] This becomes necessary because subordinates find it impossible to transmit all of the details available to them. To keep the communication of information to a reasonable volume, subordinates must synthesize and summarize the facts available to them. This means that facts tend to be substituted for judgments. Where the chain of the communication is very long, each level of the hierarchy takes the information from lower echelons (often unidentified judgments) as its facts. This continued substitution has been referred to as the "absorption of uncertainty."[32] The reverse happens in the downward flow of information.

To minimize the distortion transmitted up the hierarchy, the administrator must devise means such as multiple and overlapping responsibilities and sources of information to counter what is coming through the regular channel. Arthur M. Schlesinger Jr. concluded that this approach worked with a high degree of success with President Franklin D. Roosevelt. The president from time to time arbitrated disputes between Cabinet members and subordinates over conflicting program goals, and by doing so he was able to obtain first-hand alternative sources of information.[33]

The operation of the formal hierarchy gives considerable power to MLMs. Because they control the information flowing up, they can decide what will be transmitted. When information enters the organization that MLMs wish to shield from superiors, they can easily screen it out.

Informal Communication

Informal communication becomes necessary whenever the formal channels fail to provide for communication needs deemed necessary by the agency participants. Typically, it includes channels of communications that are not outlined in the official rules and regulations and manuals of the agency. Though management sometimes regards informal channels as competition to the formal ones, it would be unwise to discourage them. The fact that informal channels have speed and believability helps to improve efficiency rather than hinder it.

Lateral Communication

Lateral communication takes place among employees at approximately the same level in an organization or among employees of different levels who do not report to each other in the superior–subordinate relationship. Traditionally, it is viewed as part of the informal organization that the designers of the formal organization failed to anticipate. Though lateral relations take place mainly to fill social needs, Conrad Arensberg believes that many are work-oriented. These include:

- Controls involving work flow among individuals in different hierarchies who need to collaborate to get the work done.

- Staff and line relationships in which cooperation is critical to accomplishing an organization's missions.
- Appeals of MLMs to persons in higher management other than their superiors to modify decisions.[34]

Lateral communication provides a number of benefits: (1) It helps to build communication links with peers and to facilitate the exchange of ideas and communication among individuals in similar specialties (for example, accountants, engineers, and computer programmers, all with highly technical language); and (2) it promotes greater coordination and permits direct communication without forcing a shift of the formal lines of the hierarchy. Lateral communication requires special skills because the number of officials outside the line of authority in the hierarchy increases as the number of different specialties are included. Thus, more personalities are involved, requiring more effort to maintain cooperative relationships.

Bypassing the chain of command is frowned on in theory, but speed and productivity, among other advantages, require that this action sometimes take place. Where such bypassing does occur, it is customary to inform the regular chain to ensure that all affected persons are aware. Because the practice of exchanging outside the channel occurs with some frequency, agencies may want to establish standardized ways for handling bypassing. Leonard Sayles and George Strauss suggest that top management may (1) give higher supervisors advance notice before relaying messages to lower levels, (2) urge the immediate supervisor to add a few words to supplement the formal message, and (3) encourage subordinates to ask questions concerning these materials to their immediate boss. "[35]

Feedback

Fig. 10.3 shows that the feedback loop occupies a strategic role in the communication process. The feedback system may be formal or informal. Whatever the mechanism, it is important that the system operate to keep critical decision-makers aware of the feedback. Because public administration constantly demands the accountability of top administrators for activities in an agency, it is critical that the organization have effective feedback channels so that they can be on top of clients' and constituents' problems. This is not always an easy goal to realize, as noted later in this chapter.

There are a number of ways of promoting and encouraging feedback, such as by: (1) encouraging and engaging individuals in conversations with subordinates both by top officials and by supervisors, known as the open-door policy; (2) instituting employee opinion surveys; and (3) employing public satisfaction surveys about the quality of service, as is done by the U.S. Postal Service and many cities (e.g., Dallas, Texas).

A major problem with the feedback system is the built-in reluctance and incapacity of organizations to transmit bad news quickly to the appropriate officials at the top of the organization. Good news is often communicated speedily up and across the organization, but bad news lingers in areas the subordinates control, where they tend to be suppressed. Few subordinates like to be the bearer of bad news to their supervisor. This problem is exacerbated by the management-by-exception operating principle in most organizations, in which subordinates take care of ordinary problems and bring only major or unmanageable problems to the supervisor. This operating discretion gives MLMs considerable opportunity to filter feedback. Thus they tend to report or exchange only what is pleasant.

Overcoming Barriers to Communication

To minimize the problem in communication, the public administrator must recognize and overcome the barriers before they occur. The following are some suggested ideas:

1. Employ the feedback loop effectively by making sure that the receiver understands what is intended. When a message is transmitted, the sender should require more than a "yes" or "no" response from the receiver to the question, "Do you understand what I said?"
2. Messages should be made clear, simple, and understandable.
3. Be an active listener. Since listening is a passive activity, it takes considerable concentration and effort to listen. It is said that we can speak an average of 150 words per minute but we have a capacity to listen at the rate of 1,000 words per minute.
4. Avoid emotion when communicating, which can cloud and distort the transfer of meaning.
5. Create an environment of trust and confidence between superior and subordinate, as with the democratic style of leadership that encourages subordinates' exchange and communication.

Remember that positive feedback tends to be more readily and accurately perceived, typically because people tend to hear good news and block out the bad.[36] This does not mean that MLMs should not convey bad feedback, but they should study the situation to discuss how it might be communicated to minimize resistance.[37] Keep the negative feedback on a descriptive basis—job related, and not judgmental—and never criticize a subordinate personally.[38] Make the interval between the behavior and the negative feedback as short as possible.[39] Negative feedback should be directed toward something over which the individual has control.[40] For example, a manager should not criticize a subordinate because his bus was late, but because he left work early.

Communication Must Have Clarity

In 1995, the Democratic commissioner of Allegheny County, Pennsylvania, Mike Dawida, and his running mate had a big lead in the polls. Dawida was asked if he needed the black vote to get elected. He unhesitatingly said to a reporter he did not. African-Americans took this to mean that their votes were inconsequential and unneeded. What Dawida was trying to convey, but never clarified during the interview, was that he could win the seat if he did not get the black votes but he certainly wanted them to vote for him and his running mate. Dawida's lack of clarity cost him the majority commissioner position as blacks voted overwhelmingly for Republicans. It was the first time the Democrats lost the Allegheny County majority commissioner seat in almost 100 years, a defeat of extraordinary proportions.

Consensual Communication

This goal that decision-makers should strive to achieve is equivalent to the concept of collective accountability. When a position or policy is arrived at, often with give-and-take, all participants are expected to speak with one voice. In the Japanese model of management, consensus decision is not something to be strived for; it is an operating philosophy.

TOP ADMINISTRATORS AND MLMS

In traditional administrative theory, top administrators are the most competent and informed individuals in an organization and should make its overall policies. The policies are then passed down the hierarchy and at each successive level are "spelled out in increasing detail and transformed into operating instructions."[41] While the top administrator indeed does make the important decisions in public organizations, his or her power to pursue a course of action unilaterally is severely limited. Among the constraints are: (1) limited time; (2) the need to consult with subordinates; (3) the necessity to compromise conflicting views of interest groups, clients, and constituents; (4) temporary tenure as a political appointee; (5) minimal to total lack of expertise; and (6) the continuing drive for legislative support to maintain the agency's appropriation. The administrator's effectiveness lies in his or her ability to obtain agreement among individuals with differing demands who control the agency's resources. Perhaps top management's most potent instrument for influencing decision-making is the power to appoint the committees that play a major role in public sector decision-making. This can be an important way to win acceptance of predetermined conclusions.

Of the constraints listed above, the fifth most affects the role of MLMs. The complexity of modern life requires administrators to abdicate many key decisions to professional and technical personnel who are better trained to make such decisions.[42] This is especially true in the public sector, where generalists normally populate the top. The major concerns of the administrator tend to be political and strategic, as contrasted with the mainly technical orientation of specialized subordinates.[43] The typical administrator makes choices from recommendations based on information organized by specialists who have examined several alternatives, supplied supporting evidence, and outlined the probable consequences. At any time, these MLMs have the ability to withhold or manipulate this information as it passes up the hierarchy. Because they control the quality of information that enters the base of the hierarchy, MLMs exercise an especially crucial role in decision-making.

The power and influence that MLMs exercise is derived not from formal grants but from expertise, giving advice, lateral relations, responding to unanticipated consequences, and the design and operation of the formal hierarchical organization. Thus, formal control mechanisms (aimed at limiting the power of MLMs) will not only significantly increase the cost of operating but are likely to be ineffective because: (1) such mechanisms will require more controllers and thus produce more red tape; (2) they are likely to create poor morale and decrease the quality of performance and productivity; (3) areas over which control is being sought are highly discretionary (e.g., the form and mode of communication); (4) unanticipated consequences cannot be predicted; (5) close and rigid supervision is antithetical to American democratic and cultural norms; (6) MLMs are usually a permanent part of the bureaucracy while top management is not; and (7) decisions made at the top represent the collective judgment of many, which acts as a controlling force in the use of power and the exercise of influence. All of this means that accountability for decisions in public organizations rests in great part on the shoulders of MLMs. They are the ones who provide continuity in administration. Unless they can see how their interests and that of the public mesh, they are likely to act contrary to it. As noted before, the responsible exercise of power requires a learned pattern that eventually becomes a way of life and an operating philosophy.

POWER AND ACCOUNTABILITY

In examining the various decision-making models, we found no one model that could predictably provide the optimum outcome in social decision-making. The rational economic model, which is widely admired, has limited applicability in public decisions. The best model is thus often not the most rational but the one that best permits decision-makers to reach consensus and compromise. This means that public sector managers are constrained by many factors, such as need for participation, and/or consultation with many groups operating in the internal and external environments, and the many institutional processes, such as the budgetary one, that they must learn to understand and operate. The prevalence of committees in public decision-making also provides continuing communication between the organization and its environment.

The areas of greatest concern, where power may be exercised and accountability is difficult to obtain, involve rules, regulations, and procedures applied by MLMs making mainly routine programmed decisions, and involve the MLM's ability to screen information or communication going up the hierarchy, creating the possibility of "absorption of uncertainty." Because of the reductive process that takes place as information travels up the hierarchy, MLMs exercise significant opportunities to substitute their views.

Finally, the bargaining environment in which public decision-making takes place ensures that checks and balances can significantly influence what decisions will be made. There are limits, however, to how well bargaining can control the quality of decisions and their implementation. These are areas where the MLM reigns supreme.

DISCUSSION QUESTIONS

1. Why are communication and decision-making inseparably linked in organizations?
2. Why is the traditional rational economic model of decision-making so widely admired and yet so little applied in public decision-making?
3. Identify and discuss important powers of and constraints on top administrators in public sector management.
4. Discuss why MLMs play a major role in effecting accountability in public management.
5. What is the garbage can decision-making mold? Discuss how and in what situations it might be employed in the public sector.
6. Discuss the critical role of feedback in decision-making and why its neglect can lead to unsatisfactory results.
7. Under what conditions may group decision-making be superior to individual decision-making?

NOTES

1.   Herbert A. Simon, *Administrative Behavior* (New York: Macmillan, 1st edn. 1947), p. 1.
2.   *Royal Bank of Canada Monthly Newsletter* (January 1963).
3.   William Gore and J. W. Dyson, eds., *The Making of Decisions* (London: Free Press of Glencoe, 1964), p. 1, Chap. 11
4.   Graham T. Allison, *Essence of Decisions, Explaining the Cuban Missile Crisis* (Boston: Little, Brown, 1971), p. 67.
5.   Herbert A. Simon, *The New Science of Management Decisions* (New York: Harper & Row, 1960), p. 5.
6.   Gore and Dyson, *Making of Decisions*, p. 2.
7.   Ibid., p. 3.
8.   Chester I. Bernard, *The Functions of the Executive* (Cambridge, Mass.: Harvard University Press, 1938).
9.   Herbert A. Simon, *Models of Man* (New York: John Wiley and Sons, 1957).
10.   R. M. Cyert, W. R. Dill and F. G. March, "The Role of Expectations in Business Decision Making," *Administrative Science Quarterly* (September 1958): 307–40.
11.   See, for example, C. H. Jones, "The Money Value of Time," *Harvard Business Review* (July-August 1968): 94–101.
12.   S. Kadon, "Rationality and Irrationality in Business Leadership," *Journal of Business Policy* (July 1972): 39–44.

13. Theodore Sorensen, *Kennedy* (New York: Harper & Row, 1965); and Arthur M. Schlesinger Jr., *A Thousand Days* (Boston: Houghton Mifflin, 1965).

14. S. G. Winter, "Satisficing, Selection, and Innovative Remnant," *Quarterly Journal of Economics* (May 1971): 237–61.

15. Anthony Downs, *Inside Bureaucracy* (Boston: Little, Brown, 1967), p. 3.

16. Charles Lindblom, "The Science of Muddling Through," *Public Administration Review* (Spring 1959): 79–88.

17. Neil Mck. Agnew and John L. Brown, "Bounded Rationality: Fallible Decisions in Unbounded Decision Space," *Behavioral Science* (July 1986): 148–61.

18. Herbert A. Simon, *Administrative Behavior,* 1st edn. (New York: Free Press, 1947), p. 1.

19. Amitai Etzioni, "Mixed-Scanning: A Third Approach to Decision Making," *Public Administration Review* (December 1967): 387–88.

20. Ibid., p. 388.

21. Michael D. Caher, James G. March, and John P. Olsen, "People, Problems, Solutions and the Ambiguity of Relevance," in *Ambiguity and Choice in Organizations,* James March and John P. Olson, eds. (Bergen, Norway: Universitetsforlaget, 1976).

22. Ibid., Preface, pp. 8, pp. 24–37.

23. "This Meeting Will Come to Order," *Time* 126, No. 24, (December 16, 1985, p. 50); and Neil S. Smelser, *Effective Committee Service: Survival Skills for Scholars* (Newbury Park, Calif.: Sage Publications, 1993).

24. Ross A. Webber, "The Relation of Group Performance to the Age of Members of Homogeneous Groups," *Academy of Management Journal* (October 1974): 570–74.

25. Ibid., p. 574.

26. E. B. Ebesen and R. S. Bowers, "Proportion of Risky to Conservative Arguments in a Group Discussion and Choice Shift," *Journal of Personality and Social Psychology* (October 1974): 316–27.

27. G. M. Price, "How to be a Better Meeting Chairman," *Harvard Business Review* (January-February 1969): 98–108.

28. Andre L. Delberg, A. H. Van de Ven, and D. H. Gustafson, *Group Techniques for Program Planning: A Guide to Nominal and Delphi Processes* (Glenview, Ill.: Scott Foresman, 1975).

29. David K. Berlo, *The Process of Communication* (New York: Holt, Rinehart & Winston, 1960), pp. 30–32.

30. Craig C. Lindburg, "Administration Receives a Scheme for Analysis," in *The Making of Decisions,* William Gore and S. W. Dyson, eds. (London: Free Press of Glencoe, 1964), p. 27.

31. Herbert A. Simon, Donald W. Smithburg and Victor A. Thompson, *Public Administration* (New York: Alfred A. Knopf, 1958). p. 245.

32. George Petti, *The Future of American Intelligence* (Washington, D.C.: Infantry Journal Press, 1966), p. 8.

33. Arthur M. Schlesinger Jr., *The Coming of the New Deal* (Boston: Houghton Mifflin, 1958), p. 55.

34. Conrad Arensberg, "Behavior and Organization Industrial Studies," in *Social Psychology at the Crossroads,* John Robinson and Mugifer Sherif. eds. (New York: Harper & Row, 1951).

35. Leonard R. Sayles and George Strauss, *Human Behavior in Organizations* (Englewood Cliffs, N.J.: Prentice-Hall, 1966), p. 350.

36. Cyril R. Mill, "Feedback: The Art of Giving and Receiving Help," in *The Reading Book for Human Relations Training*, Larry Porter and Cyril R. Mills, eds. (Bethel, Maine: NTL Institute for Applied Behavioral Science, 1976) pp. 18–19.

37. Ibid., p. 19.

38. Kathleen S. Venderber and Randolph F. Vanderber, *Inter-Act: Using Interpersonal Communication Skills*, 4th edn. (Belmont, Calif.: Wadsworth, 1986).

39. Lyle E. Bourne Jr. and C. Victor Bunderson, "Effects of Delay of Information Feedback and Length of Feedback Interval on Concept Identification," *Journal of Experimental Psychology* (January 1963): 1–5.

40. Mill, "Feedback," pp. 18–19.

41. Peter F. Drucker, "Long-Range Planning, Challenge to Management Science," *Management Science* (April 1959): 242.

42. John M. Pfiffner and Robert Presthus, *Public Administration* (New York: Ronald Press, 1967), p. 108.

43. Ibid., pp. 109–10.

11

Leadership in Public Management

This chapter attempts to explore the theories, art, and processes of leadership as practiced in public sector organizations. Six sections are included. The first examines the various ways in which leadership has been studied and practiced. The second briefly discusses the three basic styles of leadership. In the third section, the context of leadership in public management is reviewed. The fourth section explores the role of top management in leading. The fifth examines the role of MLMs. Finally, we explore the application of power and accountability in the leadership function in public management.

LEARNING OBJECTIVES

On completing this chapter, the reader should be able to:

- Distinguish the ways in which leadership has been studied and practiced.
- Appreciate the crucial role the leader plays in making things happen in organizations.
- Understand the role of top-level administrators in leading.
- Understand the role of MLMs in exercising leadership in public organizations.
- Recognize the different styles of leadership found in practice.
- Understand the context in which leadership takes place in public organizations.

In 1950 Leonard D. White observed: "The life and spirit of an organization do not spring from its structure. Quality depends on the motivations that energize (or paralyze) staff. They derive in large measure from the character of the leadership."[1] The effective functioning of social units requires leadership—the art of persuasion in which the leader or the team induces a group to pursue the objectives of the leader and/or his followers.[2]

By focusing on leadership in this chapter we do not mean to suggest that leadership in an organization is a compartmentalized phenomenon. Indeed, leadership is pervasive in every act of management.

The person who can mesh divergent and conflicting forces, recognize and create opportunities, use the influence and moral basis of his or her position, and employ the minimal amount of resources to maximally achieve publicly desired ends is in great demand everywhere. The social milieu and context of the leader are very important: "Leaders cannot be thought of as apart from the historic context in which they arise, the setting in which they function (e.g., elective political office), and the system over which they preside (e.g. a particular city or state)."[3]

Despite the obvious importance of leadership, the concept has been difficult to understand and the skill even harder to develop. When the average person thinks of leadership the most common association is usually to charisma, from the Greek word meaning divine right. In this view, leadership is regarded as a gift of influence over the behavior of others. Some of us have this gift and others simply do not. In the middle 1960s, John M. Pfiffner and Robert Presthus defined leadership by putting the emphasis on the leaders, who employ the "art of coordinating and motivating individuals to achieve desired ends."[4] Harland Cleveland defined public leadership more as brokerage and bargaining, operating in a highly complex web of tension in which control is loose, power is diffused, and centers of decision are plural.[5]   In the 1970s, H. George Frederickson emphasized that leadership is in a stage of transition from the individual to the group (see Table 11.1).[6] The coming of total quality management (TQM) has highlighted the need for greater reliance on the team and group leadership.

Table 11.1. The Evolving State of Leadership

From	Transition	To
1. Leadership by authority from the top down	1. Leadership by consent, authority from the group.	1. Leadership for change facilitation, authority in the group.
2. Regimented work environments.	2. Consultative work environment.	2. Democratic work environment.
3. We know what ought to be done; the problem is discovering how to do it well.	3. Seeks to develop commitment to goals to get action.	3. Seek to develop commitment to sensible action in order to achieve sensible overall objectives.
4. We know what is done; the problem is discovering how well it was done.	4. We know how to do things; the problem is discovering how to determine what ought to be done.	4. We know better what ought to be done, but we must also know how to stop part of what we have been doing.

Leadership occurs as a collective or group process. It is a cohesive force that holds the group intact, an accommodating factor that makes it possible for members to live together and to pursue a common goal. However, effective group behavior does not automatically produce purposeful action. There must be a cohesive and guiding force that helps to maintain membership and facilitate purposeful group interaction.[7]

THE STUDY OF LEADERSHIP: CHANGING FORMS

Though leadership has been viewed as an indispensable factor in the management of organizations, it is a dynamic and elusive phenomenon. In the words of Warren G. Bennis: "Of all the hazy and confounding ideas in social psychology, leadership theory undoubtedly contends for top nomination. . . . More has been written and less is known about leadership than any other topic in the behavioral sciences."[8] Generally, the discussion and practice of leadership has involved three aspects: (1) attributes related to or emanating directly from the leader; (2) conditions created from interpersonal and group influence; and (3) conditions determined largely by environmental and situational factors.

THE LEADER'S ATTRIBUTES

Leadership was traditionally presented in terms of the traits that the leader possessed and the ways that they influenced the achievements of organizational goals. For centuries, writers examined the lineage of great personalities in search of the qualities that all successful leaders shared. A number of factors turned up: Leaders were generally taller than followers; they had greater retention ability than the average person; saints lived longer than the average peasant during the Middle Ages. In varying degrees this approach was carried over into the writing of public administration. Leonard D. White in the 1950s spoke of leaders' command of symbols, skills in inventing policies and plans, courage in deciding, and what he called the leaders' "touch—an elusive quality intuitive in nature."[9] He used Alexander Hamilton as a prototype, pointing to Hamilton's restless energy, high ambition, and thirst to be at the center of events. Leadership in this mode involves:

1. *Single-mindedness* sufficient to sustain striving for the fulfillment of a goal. One thinks of George Allen, former coach of the Washington Redskins football team, or the late Vincent Lombardi of the Green Bay Packers.
2. *Basic intelligence*, which is not necessarily an esoteric intellectual gift but a demonstrated ability to think. One of the objectives of early public administration courses was to teach the student to "think administratively."
3. *Physical energy*. No one without an abundance of energy can ever be a leader.
4. *Personality balance*. Without sacrificing integrity of purpose, the leader must relate personal needs to the organization's goals. General Eisenhower is credited with having these qualities in his "crusade in Europe" but lacking them in the presidency.

5. *Self-confidence.* Without losing sensitivity and empathy for others, the leader must present an image of assurance, the capacity to deal fairly with others, self-control, and decisiveness.
6. *Character and integrity.* Leadership is also associated with striving for higher purpose or the public interest. President Kennedy's call illustrates this theme: "Ask not what your country can do for you, but what you can do for your country."

The theory of leadership that stresses personal characteristics has largely fallen into disuse. "Fifty years of study," comments Eugene E. Jennings, "have failed to produce one personality trait or set of qualities that can be used to discriminate leaders from non-leaders."[10] Nonetheless, the trait theory remains important. The absence of supporting research has not deterred the continual use of traits in the selection of leaders. The most prominent example is elections, which often are referendums on personality traits. Often the traits used as criteria bear little relation to the real requirements for being a leader. Harland Cleveland summarizes what is perhaps the best thinking today on leadership traits:

The most obvious trait is physical energy [and beyond] a set of attitudes and aptitudes more intellectual, more reflective, than the executives of the past: they will show a talent for consensus and a tolerance for ambiguity; they will have a penchant for unwarranted optimism; and they will find private joy in public responsibility.[11]

Personality and behavioral traits vary with the level of leadership in public organizations. Fig. 11.1 summarizes this difference.

Figure 11.1. Leadership Traits

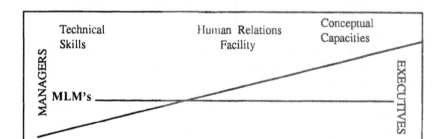

At the lower levels of leadership, technical skills predominate; at the upper levels, conceptual capacities predominate. Personnel at all levels, however, must have a facility for good human relations. Over time, an executive who once might have been competent in the details of operations loses this capacity as he or she becomes increasingly preoccupied with a more abstract overall concern for the entire organization. Middle-level managers play particularly important leadership roles over time precisely because they must balance the conceptual with the technical requirements in the process of program implementation.

THE GROUP BASIS OF LEADERSHIP

While the traitists tended to look at the organization as consisting of leaders without people, the human relations theorists emphasized people almost without leaders. This alternative look at leadership took cognizance of the workers' feelings, beliefs, perceptions, and ideas. The major assumption at the outset was that greater leadership could be accomplished through fulfilling certain socio-psychological needs of workers. Ideas of efficiency, deeply embedded in the trait approach, were balanced with a new emphasis on organizational stability and the building of a sense of community at the work place. In the middle 1950s, group theorists generally identified five key differences between the group and trait approaches (see Table 11.2).

Table 11.2. Trait and Group Leadership Approaches

Trait Approach	Group Approach
1. Decision-making centralized with administrator	1. Wide participation in the decision-making
2. Interactions reflect a person's position in the hierarchy	2. Face-to-face group interactions
3. Authority is the basis of integration in the organization	3. Mutual confidence is the primary force in the organization
4. Communication channeled through formal organization structures	4. Inter-group and intra-group communication encouraged
5. Control of operation for the sake of performance	5. Growth for members of the organization is recognized as a priority objective

As the group approach to leadership became accepted, the leader's role became primarily one of helping the group to clarify and achieve its goals. One important consequence of this change was a shift in emphasis or even displacement of organizational goals for the group's. Another was an almost unnoticed shift of leadership from executives to managerial and supervisory levels. The downward thrust is illustrated by efforts to use action research (sensitivity approaches such as encounter groups in which individuals at different levels in the organization are allowed to openly exhibit their conflicts and latent frustrations, forcing participants to deal with each other's concerns) to effect change in organizations. In the late 1960s, this often degenerated into amateur counseling or permissiveness. The group approach (1) produced a functional leadership that varied with group needs; (2) recognized the latent power—over time—of group norms to transform externally introduced rules; and (3) transformed the leader into coordinator, partly leading and partly led.

The group approach to leadership is based on a theory of motivation. One pole views work as a means of obtaining a livelihood while the other views the job as an opportunity for growth and development. F. Scott Myers has outlined these factors, which he calls maintenance and personal growth needs, respectively (see Table 11.3).[12]

Motivation research has proved difficult to relate to leadership. First, Frederick Herzberg urged that maintenance and personal growth factors be seen as two separate and unconnected poles or categories (maintenance or high-end extrinsic factors and motivation or intrinsic factors). Improvement in wages or tenure (maintenance factors), for example, should not be related to needs for personal growth, such as recognition, achievement, or responsibility (motivators). The successful leader should build in as many motivators as possible while giving due recognition to the maintenance factors.[13]

Table 11.3. Maintenance and Growth Needs

Maintenance Needs	Personal Growth Needs
1. Economic. Wages and fringe benefits.	1. Growth. Sense of improvement in the capacity to perform.
2. Security. Tenure and comfort with the assignment.	2. Achievement. Feeling that something worthwhile is being accomplished.
3. Status. Some reasonably satisfying recognition.	3. Responsibility. Doing more as a way of accepting more fully the organization's goals.
4. Social. Informal as well as formal relationships on the job.	4. Recognition. Both the internalized positive assessment of one's own work and the expression by others of a job being well done.
5. Physical. A reasonably pleasant and safe working environment.	5. Esteem. This quality derives form Abraham Maslow's hierarchy: physiological needs, safety needs, love or social needs, and self-actualization.
6. Orientation. Some sense of a role in performing a purposeful task.	

Second, maintenance needs in government, for all practical purposes, are determined by legislatures. That is, they have little directly to do with leadership. Instead of a leader being able to appeal to some work ethic as a means of motivating workers, the public service is charged with nurturing an avoidance ethic (the incentive and performance appraisal systems of the Civil Service Reform Act of 1978 modified this somewhat with a new emphasis on performance evaluation). This kind of criticism tends to shift attention from material incentives and disincentives to personal growth factors.

Third, measuring growth has proved difficult. Growth is largely abstract and unmeasurable unless other criteria are postulated. As for achievement and responsibility, evidence mounts that not everyone seeks them. Moreover, management from the bottom up has generally not worked in many situations. The work of Rensis Likert seems to be an exception. In research spanning nearly 25 years, Likert appears to have found that a "participative" form of management, which he labels System 4, has long-range potential for contributing to organizational effectiveness.[14] The Likert model is a transorganizational "linking" approach, as Fig. 11.2 suggests. As Frederick C. Thayer has put it, "The Likert design attempts to transform vertical span of control relationship into a network of nonhierarchical small groups."[15] We will have more to say about Likert momentarily, for his emphasis on high levels of trust and intimate interaction between superiors and subordinates makes his work most applicable to leadership at lower and middle levels. But with this exception, motivation theory offers little in the way of empirical results that can help us in understanding the leadership phenomenon.

Perhaps the least verification can be found for Maslow's self-actualization hypothesis. The self-actualizing model suggests that a relationship exists between work performance and the satisfaction of personal growth needs, and this assumption is at the core of the human relations approach. When Frank K. Gibson and Clyde E. Teasley reviewed this hypothesis from the perspective of public organization, they found the following:

1. There are few studies that have attempted to test the theory of the hierarchy of needs, and those that have been done fail to establish its existence.

2. Many studies have shown no correlation between job satisfaction and performance.

3. Where participation has been sustained as a motivational factor, the studies have not controlled for attitudinal differences. Considerable evidence suggests that supportive or benevolent attitudes are related to increased performance even when these attitudes are held by nonparticipative leaders.

4. Generally, the quality of the research in the humanistic field has been low: There are usually no control groups, and the mere existence of a statistical correlation does not justify the linking of the variables.[16]

To sum up, the subject of leaders' attention to the growth needs of followers enjoys a prominent place in the literature, even though there is little confirmed empirical validation. Participation is advanced as what ought to be, even though there is very limited support for this position. Second, we lack a model of motivation on which to base generalizations. Third, because participation has entered the organizational culture—as a part in the value system—it has become a factor, nonetheless, that must be understood. The fact that the names of Argyris, Bennis, Herzberg, Maslow, McGregor, and Likert are associated with the idea gives it status.[17] Finally, a deeper reason is that the assertion of leadership over others—in our culture—carries with it an unspoken covenant to be in the best interests of the led. The present focus on TQM and the reinvention of efforts in government that stress clientele and customer satisfaction are indicators of this cultural norm.

Fig. 11.2. The Linking Pin

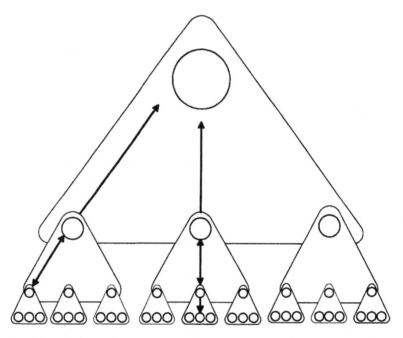

The arrows indicate the linking pin function.

Source: Adapted from Rensis Likert, *New Patterns of Management* (New York: McGraw-Hill, 1961), p. 113.

THE SITUATIONAL APPROACH TO LEADERSHIP

A third approach, following the trait and human relations groups, is that of the situational theorists. This approach maintains that the situation dictates the qualities of leadership and that each situation calls for a different leadership capacity. Rather than adjusting the organization to fit the leader, here the leader adjusts to the organizational requirements.   Among the situational variables identified are (1) expectations of followers; (2) technology associated with the task to be performed; (3) pressures of schedules and the delivery environment; (4) degrees of required interpersonal contact; and (5) various stages of the organization's development. Gordon L. Lippitt and Warren H. Schmidt have identified six stages of organizational development that call for different kinds of leadership:

- creation of a new organization
- survival of a continuing system
- attainment of stability
- gaining reputation and prestige
- achieving uniqueness and adaptability
- contributing to society.[18]

It is obvious that each condition calls for different qualities—and for a different order of relationships with groups within an organization. The analysis also brings out the significance of extra-organizational factors from the environment.

The leader, in the situational approach, is at best a coordinator of internal and external pressures. We have already noted the role of informal groups within organizations and the impact of interest groups on public agencies. We believe that the Lippitt and Schmidt approach applies to executives dealing with the overall configuration of the agency rather than with its administrative dimensions. Again, the data of situational theories are more a priori than empirical. The point to underscore is that situational leadership presupposes a value criterion to determine which situation to respond to. Below, several models are examined.

Contingency Theories

As the research in leadership progressed, it became clear that the ability to predict successful leadership is far more complex than simply isolating specific traits or desirable behaviors. Failure to replicate consistent results about leadership led to new interest in situational influencing factors. Fred Fiedler's contingency model research has been one of the most comprehensive studies undertaken on leadership. In Fiedler's view, effective group performance is dependent on the match between the leader's style of interaction with subordinates and the degree to which the situation provides the opportunity for the leader to exercise control. To assess these situational factors, Fiedler developed an instrument called least-preferred co-worker (LPC) questionnaire (see Table 11.4). To aid in predicting the proper style of leadership for a specific situation, Fiedler developed three additional criteria that can be manipulated to produce desired behavior or outcome: (1) leader-member relation, which reflects the degree to which members of the group trust and like the leader and are willing to follow his or her guidance; (2) task structure indicated by the degree of the detailed standards or operating procedures; and

Table. 11.4. Fiedler's Least-Preferred Co-Worker Scale

Pleasant	8	7	6	5	4	3	2	1	Unpleasant
Friendly	8	7	6	5	4	3	2	1	Unfriendly
Rejecting	8	7	6	5	4	3	2	1	Accepting
Helpful	8	7	6	5	4	3	2	1	Frustrating
Unenthusiastic	8	7	6	5	4	3	2	1	Enthusiastic
Tense	8	7	6	5	4	3	2	1	Relaxed
Distant	8	7	6	5	4	3	2	1	Close
Cold	8	7	6	5	4	3	2	1	Warm
Cooperative	8	7	6	5	4	3	2	1	Uncooperative
Supportive	8	7	6	5	4	3	2	1	Hostile
Boring	8	7	6	5	4	3	2	1	Interesting
Quarrelsome	8	7	6	5	4	3	2	1	Harmonious
Self-assured	8	7	6	5	4	3	2	1	Hesitant
Efficient	8	7	6	5	4	3	2	1	Inefficient
Gloomy	8	7	6	5	4	3	2	1	Cheerful
Open	8	7	6	5	4	3	2	1	Guarded

Source: Adapted from Fred E. Fiedler and Martin M. Chemers, *Leadership and Effective Management* (Glenview, Ill.: Scott Foresman, 1976).

(3) position of power, which refers to the authority (institutionalized power) of the office or position such as the power to fire, hire, and promote. Fig. 11.3 shows the leadership style (high or low LPC) in three dimensions of the group. Using the results of Fig. 11.3, Fiedler has shown that the best leadership style depends on how favorable the particular situation is for the leader. The task group leader works best in very unfavorable and very favorable situations. When a permissive or non-directive situation and task of some difficulty exist, the high-LPC leader achieves greater success. While Fielder's model does possess aspects of the trait theory, given the simple psychological test, his model goes far beyond the trait and behavioral approach as he isolates situations and links them with individual personalities. From these links he predicts leadership effectiveness as a function of the two.

Fig. 11.3. Continuum of Leadership Styles

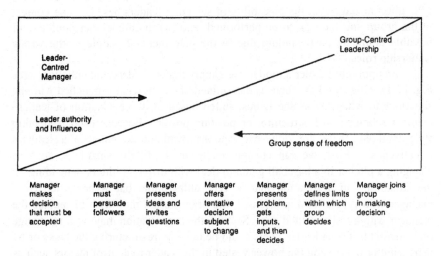

Source: Adapted from Roger Tannenbaum and Warren H. Schmidt, "How to Change the Leadership Pattern", *Harvard Business Review* (March-April 1958): pp. 96.

Fiedler carried out many years of research in an attempt to find the type of leadership that is best suited to specific situations.[19] As noted above, the least preferred co-worker (LPC) scale was developed as a key variable in his model. Simply stated, an individual is asked to rate the attributes of the person he or she least prefers to work with. A high score (meaning that most attributes were rated on the positive end of the scale) indicates a person sees both good and bad in fellow co-workers. A manager with a high LPC score is more human relations-oriented and is ready to allow for differences in others. A low LPC score indicates a lack of concern for one's co-worker. Such a person has a tendency to reject those with whom he or she cannot work. His or her primary emphasis is on getting the job done, regardless of the likes or dislikes (personal or otherwise) of co-workers.

Fiedler sees the LPC is an index of motivation hierarchy. That is, given a task to do, and depending on the situation, a person with a high LPC score prefers to get to know fellow workers and only secondarily to get the task done. The reverse would hold for the person with a low LPC score.

It has been found that leaders with low LPC scores were more successful in terms of performance in situations that were either very favorable (the task is structured) or highly unfavorable (the leader is not liked). By contrast, the high-scoring leaders perform most successfully in favorable and moderately favorable situations.

Finally, the LPC approach suggests some interesting observations: (1) There is at least one empirically tested leadership concept with considerable potential; (2) contrary to prevailing beliefs, hard-driving taskmasters can be as effective as human relations-oriented managers under varying conditions; (3) LPC gives management the possibility of selecting leaders based on the context of the group and the task to be performed; and (4) the model can minimize or possibly eliminate costly failure due to the placement of people in the wrong leadership roles.

In applying Fiedler's model, we simply match leaders and situations (see Fig. 11.4). Once the LPC focus is determined, the individual is matched with the situations to which he or she is best suited based on the evaluation of leader–member relations, task structure, or position power. Because each leadership style is fixed, there are only two options available to enhance a leader's effectiveness. First, we can change the leader to fit the situations, such as changing a pitcher in a baseball game to deal with different hitters depending on the situation. In a situation that is very unfavorable but is being led by a manager who is relationship-oriented, the organization may wish to replace the manager with a task-oriented one. Second, the organization may wish to change the situation to fit the leader. This could be done by restructuring the tasks or by increasing or decreasing the power vested in the leader to control factors such as salary, promotions, or disciplinary actions. This would increase the leader's power position.

There are a number of advantages to Fiedler's approach. The organiza-tion can change the makeup of the group to accommodate the existing manager. Technical and nontechnical individuals can be hired without regard to leadership style. That is, the group dimension can be altered to fit the person. We can change the shape of the hole, rather than attempting to change the shape of the peg. On the whole, Fiedler's model has been reviewed favorably, and there is much evidence to support his model.[20] One remaining problem relates to the logic underlying the LPC, which is still not well understood. Studies have shown that respondents' scores are not always stable.[21] Additionally, it is difficult to assess the quality of leader–member relations, the degree of task structure, and the position power of the leader.[22]

Fig. 11.4. Assessing Effective Leadership Styles Varying with the Situation

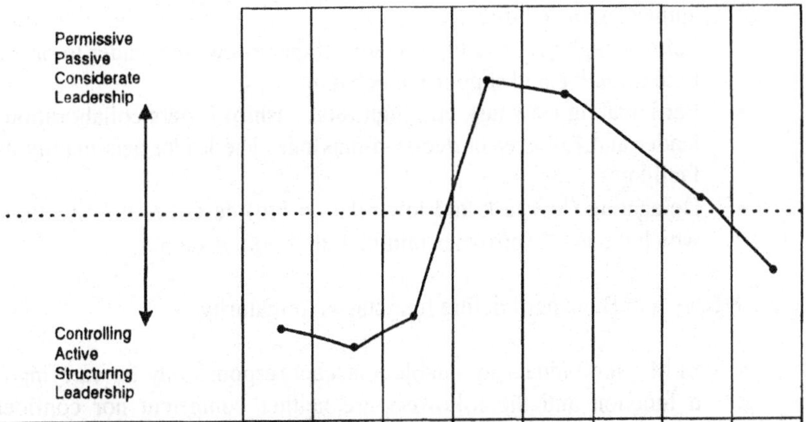

	Permissive Passive Considerate Leadership ↑ ... Controlling Active Structuring Leadership								
Leader-Member Relations	Good	Good	Good	Good	Poor	Poor	Poor	Poor
Task Structures	Structured		Unstructured		Structured		Unstructured	
Leader Position Power	Strong	Weak	Strong	Weak	Strong	Weak	Strong	Weak

Source: Adapted from F. E. Fiedler, "Engineer the Job to Fit the Manager," *Harvard Business Review*, 43:5 (1965): p. 115–22.

The Hershey-Blanchard Situational or Contingency Theory

The situational leadership theory focuses on followers' maturity. Many large corporations and the U.S. military employ this approach even though it is still in its early stages of development.[23] The theory's proponents (Paul Hersey and Kenneth Blanchard) articulate the view that successful leadership is achieved by employing appropriate leadership, which is significantly dependent on the level of the followers' maturity.

Hersey and Blanchard define maturity as the ability and willingness of individuals to accept responsibility for guiding and directing behavior. Maturity has two important components: job maturity and psychological maturity. Individuals who possess job maturity have the knowledge, skills, experience, and ability to carry out their job without the assistance of others. Psychological maturity indicates that individuals have the willingness and motivation to perform expected functions. Because of the intrinsic motivation of these individuals, they can execute their tasks without external encouragement.[24]

Hersey and Blanchard employ Fiedler's two leadership dimensions of task and relationships behavior. To refine Fiedler's contingency model, Hersey and Blanchard assess both as high or low and then combine with four leadership styles:

- Telling (high task and low relationships) involves the leader's indicating when, how, and where to perform tasks. This style is authoritative and directive.
- Selling (high task and high relationships) allows the leader to provide both directive and supportive behavior.
- Participating (low task and high relationship) fosters collaboration of leader and follower in decision-making. The leader acts mainly as a facilitator.
- Delegating (low task and low relationship) describes the situation in which the leader provides minimal direction or support.

Hersey and Blanchard define four stages of maturity:

- In M1, individuals are unable to accept responsibility for carrying out a function and the followers are neither competent nor confident.
- In M2, individuals are unable but willing to take responsibility for carrying out the required tasks because they are motivated but lack the required skills.
- In M3, individuals are able but unwilling to comply with the wishes of the leader.
- In M4, individuals are both willing and able to comply with the wishes of the leader.

The Hersey-Blanchard theory suggests that as maturity levels rise, the leader decreases both control over activity and relationship behavior. Because individuals in the M1 level lack the skills and the will to perform their tasks, the leader is expected to provide clear and specific direction. The M2 stage requires both high-task and high-relationship behavior to compensate for the individual's lack of ability while the high relationship behavior attempts to psychologically induce followers to embrace the leader's wishes. In M3, problems of motivation are overcome with supportive, nondirective participative style. Finally, in M4, the capability and willingness of the individual require the leader to be only minimally involved.

Unlike the Fiedler contingency model, which has been widely researched, the Hersey-Blanchard theory has been given minimal attention.[25] The studies have not been comprehensive. To date, evidence provides partial support for the theory, especially in the case of the follower with low maturity (M1).[26]

Path-Goal Theory of Leadership

The path-goal theory of leadership holds that it is in the interests of the leader to increase pay-offs to subordinates for work-related goal attainment.[27] The leader should make the path to the pay-off easier and increase the opportunities for satisfaction in pursuit of the goal. The effectiveness of that path depends on the situation. This theory attempts to define the relationship between the leader's behavior, and the subordinate's performance and work activities. Subordinates find the leader's behavior acceptable to the extent that it is viewed as a source of satisfaction and as a step toward future satisfaction. The leader's behavior acts as a positive influence on subordinates when they see the link between the satisfaction of their needs and successful performance, providing guidance, support, and reward.

In the Path-Goal theory, the leader's behavior is categorized in four main types:

- *Role classification leadership* provides subordinates with information to let them know what is expected of them. The leader provides guidance about what should be done and how, scheduling and coordinating work among subordinates and maintaining clearly defined performance standards.
- *Supportive leadership* is practiced by having a friendly, approachable leader who is interested in providing a pleasant work environment.
- *Participative leadership* consults with subordinates, seeking their input into the decision-making process.
- *Autocratic leadership* is a directive approach in which orders are given and are to be carried out without questions.

Under each of the leadership behaviors, subordinates' achievements depend on each subordinate's satisfaction and the structure of the work tasks. Role clarification produces high levels of satisfaction and performance for subordinates engaged in unstructured tasks. Supportive leadership is the most desirable approach as it provides for the highest level of satisfaction for those who are carrying out highly structured tasks. The participative leader promotes greater performance and satisfaction for subordinates in well-defined tasks. Finally, autocratic leadership behavior negatively affects satisfaction and performance in both structured and unstructured tasks.

These three approaches—personal traits, group factors, and situations—constitute present theories about leadership.

The ethical dimensions of leadership, which have received little or passing mention in the literature, deserve a brief mention at this point. Robert T. Golembiewski provides an exception to the prevailing trend in the writing of his *Men, Management, and Morality*. Golembiewski notes: "Men can be free within wide limits in organizations, but almost everywhere they are in unnecessary and effective bondage."[28] He suggests that leadership aims to approximate the values of the Judeo-Christian ethic could be incorporated into the attributes that provide a sound basis for moral management. Such management would enable individuals in the organization to exercise greater control over their lives and permit them to recognize their mutuality of interests, motivating improved individual and organizational performance.

THE THREE STYLES OF LEADERSHIP

After discussing the varying forms of leadership, we are now able to look at leadership styles. Style may be defined as predictable behavior patterns that are observed and/or ascribed to the leader. Three styles are normally discussed: authoritarian, democratic, and free-rein. Both the authoritarian (or coercive) style and the democratic (or permissive) style were put forth by Douglas McGregor, an early disciple of the human relations school, as Theory X and Theory Y.[29] The theories are based on the view that a leader's actions in managing are guided substantially by his or her operating assumptions about human nature.

AUTHORITARIAN STYLE—THEORY X

This approach assumes that most people dislike work and seek to avoid it if they can. Leaders who accept this view feel their subordinates must be coerced, controlled, and constantly threatened with punishment. They believe followers prefer to be directed, are lazy, dislike responsibility, and prefer security to psychological independence. Because most workers lack creativity and a sense of responsibility, management must provide very close supervision if organizational goals are to be achieved. Additionally, rewards to motivate workers must be confined to the lower order of Maslow's scale of the hierarchy of need.

DEMOCRATIC STYLE—THEORY Y

Under the Theory Y assumption, followers are viewed in a positive light. They naturally find work enjoyable and creative. Theory Y requires that rewards beyond salary and physical surroundings be provided.[30] Management must include the psychological rewards that are derived from undertaking and completing activities in a congenial work environment. In this context, followers welcome responsibility and the opportunity for self-expression and participation. Workers like to exercise initiative and to have control over their own destiny. Close supervision or coercion results in anger and resistance.

Theory Y suggests a leadership that willingly exercises power and accountability. This approach provides greater freedom to both sides. It allows workers to undertake their tasks with trust and confidence and frees administrators to pursue other objectives that will improve productivity in the organization.

FREE-REIN OR INDIVIDUAL

This approach is sometimes referred to as the abdicative approach because of the near-total autonomy that is permitted. It allows a worker or participant (group or individual) to carry out tasks with minimal participation by the leader. Because of the higher degree of personal accountability and responsibility that it requires, the free-rein style has been confined to highly skilled work, such as research, teaching, and the like.

IDENTIFYING APPROPRIATE LEADERSHIP STYLE

Robert Tannenbaum and Warren H. Schmidt have presented a range of possibilities (see Fig. 11.3) representing a decision-making continuum from the authoritarian to the permissive or democratic style. Seven different decision-making styles are shown. Rensis Likert constructed a continuum of four styles (exploitative authoritative, benevolent authoritative, consultative, and participative), later referred to as Systems 1-4, respectively.[31] The continuum represents job-centered style (authoritative, lack of trust, and close supervision) on one end and employee-centered (participative, mutuality and trust, and collective decision-making) on the other end.

Likert tested managers to see where they fell along his continuum while noting the level of productivity achieved by each style of management. He found that productivity improved steadily as the management style moved closer toward the participative group (System 4) and decreased toward the task-centered style (System 1).

Although the participative approach still commands wide acceptance, it has come under criticism. John Morse and J. W. Losch believe it is meaningless and perhaps counter-productive to talk about a desirable leadership approach without knowing the context of the situation. They state: "An effective organization must be designed to fit its task and its people, not to satisfy some universal 'theory.'"[32] Fred Fiedler's contingency model of leadership, discussed above, shows empirically that generalizing about leadership style in the abstract provides little practical guidance. The problem is not whether to be job-centered or employee-centered but when to apply which pattern. The Fiedler and Chemers findings indicate that we must fit leaders to the jobs that take advantage of their particular competencies, and not expect each leader to be effective in all or even most situations.[33]

Finally, McGregor, the major exponent of Theory Y and participative management, had some reflective views on the style of management. On leaving his post as president of Antioch College (known for its highly participative life), he noted: "It took a couple of years but I finally began to realize that a leader can't avoid the exercise of authority any more than he can avoid the responsibility for what happens to his organization."[34]

LEADERSHIP IN THE PUBLIC MANAGEMENT ENVIRONMENT

The "charismatic" type of leadership about which Weber wrote is virtually impossible to operate in a bureaucratic environment.[35] In the bureaucratic setting, leadership is based more on professional skills (expertise) and the ability to employ the appropriate manipulation. The leader must take due cognizance of the merit system, which protects permanent subordinates against removal for capricious reasons. Even legitimate actions against a subordinate require procedural due process (that is, the subordinate is given the opportunity to exhaust the rules and remedies of the organization and/or civil service commission), and this process can extend for a long period before the disciplinary action can be taken. Especially at the federal and state levels, management must interact with interest groups, legislative officials, and the courts. The bicameral legislature, the budget process, and the requirement for public hearings and participation before new or modified policies are implemented provide the public with many opportunity for access to the bureaucracy. It can thus be seen that top administration leadership is based not on command but on compromise.

As leaders, top public executives have five main functions: (1) policy and administration; (2) formal authority role; (3) maintenance of external relationships; (4) overall direction of internal operations; and (5) direction of the control system. This model of executive leadership relies on the U.S. presidency as a prototype.[36]

DUAL FUNCTIONS: POLICY AND ADMINISTRATION

Executives participate both in broad policy determination (politics) and in implementation (administration). They continually exercise discretion by interpreting the laws and statutes, giving them the meaning that they will take over time. Yet the predominant role of the administrator is more that of a generalist (interacting with other executives and external groups) and less that of an administrative specialist. As the administrator concentrates more on the generalist activities, he or she gives up the specialist role. Thus, the more one moves up the hierarchy in public management, the more administrators' roles become political. This dual role distinguishes the public executive from counterparts in business or higher education. There are no boards in public agencies to set policies as there are in private business or universities. Government administration combines the policy initiative and administration in a single official, the chief executive officer or the top administrator.

Authority Figure

Executives hold the legitimate power in an agency to mete out rewards and punishment, and they can determine the agency's direction. An executive leader has long been judged by how effectively he or she uses authority and power to bring about the actions desired by organizations, personnel, clients, constituents, or citizens at large. At the national level, Theodore Roosevelt, Woodrow Wilson, Franklin D. Roosevelt, Lyndon Johnson, and Ronald Reagan are considered effective executives because they knew how to apply power to accomplish the things they wanted to happen. U. S. Grant, William McKinley, Warren G. Harding, and Calvin Coolidge are not highly regarded as leaders because they did not succeed in applying power imaginatively.

External Relationship

Top administrators spend much of their time cultivating and maintaining external relations with the news media, political parties, legislatures, groups, and individuals to obtain support for the agency's mission. They wish to be seen as doers seeking to maximize responsiveness and accountability to the public. To the extent to which an administrator achieves this public support for agency policies, he or she is said to be effective.

Internal Direction

Due to each unit's need to obtain greater portions of scarce resources of money and power, most bureaucracies develop fragmenting tendencies. It is not uncommon to find specialists who believe their expertise should afford them special recognition. This, among other factors, makes it necessary for administrators to channel conflicting skills and interests into constructive uses that will contribute toward the organizational goals. This is an important activity that we refer to as coordination. As Chester Barnard wrote: "The executive art is nine-tenths inducing those who have authority to use it in taking pertinent action."[37] He believes that coordination attained through leadership is a vital factor in organizational survival.

Controlling Role

Operating through the chain of command, executives concentrate on strategic control points. Because top administrators are generalists with temporary tenure, and thus have few if any ideas about how informal control norms (such as peer group pressures) are operating in the agency, the budget often becomes the only means through which they can exercise effective control and promote coordination. Reliance on the budget mechanism has led to excessive emphasis on specific items such as personnel, supplies, equipment, and cost.

In large agencies the top administrators and executives often find it necessary to develop machinery to bring about program and policy coordination. We typically find committees on personnel, budget, organization, and so on.

The role of top administrators can be summarized as follows: (1) defining and redefining the organization's purpose; (2) guiding the organization toward the achievement of its mission; (3) representing the organization in the larger public and private environments; (4) providing a generalist view of program implementation; and (5) assuming the responsibility for expanding the available resources.

MLMS AND THEIR LEADERSHIP ROLES

It is at the MLM level in an agency that leadership most directly affects the core functions of management—planning, organizing, coordinating, and controlling. Through exercising these core functions, MLMs facilitate the conversion of objectives hammered out at top administrative levels into organizational outputs (goods and services).

Most of the leadership in organizations takes place between middle managers and supervisors on the one hand and supervisors and the rank-and-file workers on the other. This requires MLMs to have the ability to influence behavior of others in a group. Leadership is aimed at inducing others not only to perform the desired tasks but to carry them out as well as possible.

From what source do MLMs draw their influence? They enjoy the delegated activity of the hierarchy through the chain of command, and it is they who must implement organizational policies. As Barnard has noted, influence depends ultimately on the follower.[38] It is the follower's decision to respond that determines if the process of order-giving will succeed. In Likert's view, "An individual's reaction to any situation is always a function not of the absolute character of the intervention, but his perception of it. It is how he sees things that counts, not objective reality."[39] The leader must continually assess the subjective perceptions of the led.

MLMs must constantly be concerned with (1) what will satisfy the needs of the followers; (2) the kind and strength of motivational stimuli that will induce desired behavior; and (3) the importance of the need satisfied compared with other needs. These requirements mean that MLMs must be part-time psychologists who know their followers well if they hope to assess such motivating abstract needs as love, prestige, security, and power. MLMs must be able to view conflicts in organizations not as challenges, but as opportunities to channel conflicts to bring about constructive ends.

From the above, it is obvious that MLMs occupy crucial roles: (1) They have a monopoly on expertise; (2) their permanent role in the bureaucracy permits them to maintain leadership continuity in the public sector and to build up stable relationships; (3) they exercise the greatest control over the agency's personnel; and (4) they have the greatest understanding of the motivating factors necessary to achieve the organizational goals.

MLMs have the potential to affect the mission of the agency. Formal checks on their exercise of power are tenuous at best and at worst impossible. MLMs will act accountably only if they have internalized patterns of responsibility over extended periods of time.

POWER AND ACCOUNTABILITY

To the typical citizen, organizational leaders consist only of top administrators. These are the individuals who have a high level of visibility. When things go wrong in the agency, it is not the MLM but the top administrators who must take the blame. There is a degree of control over top administrative decisions because of the bargaining and compromise that take place at the upper levels of the hierarchy. But top management has not developed ways to control MLMs other than through formal checks, such as holding the line on the cost of personnel, supplies, and equipment. Top managers lack the expertise to directly check the nature and content of MLM performance, and the need to maintain external relations takes up more of their time. Again, we see the difficulty of achieving accountability within public organizations if the use of power is not guided by a clear understanding of the mutual self-interest for all concerned with the output and impact of the agency for the public intent.

DISCUSSION QUESTIONS

1. Why has the way in which people view leadership changed over the years?
2. Why has the Theory Y approach to leadership come under severe attack?
3. Outline and discuss the leadership role of the top-level administrator in public management.
4. Discuss the leadership role that MLMs can play in promoting accountability in public management.
5. In what way will the development in situational leadership be most useful in avoiding the selection of inappropriate leaders?

NOTES

1. Leonard D. White, *Introduction to the Study of Public Administration*, 3rd edn. (New York: Macmillan, 1950), p. 185.
2. John Gardner, *On Leadership* (New York: Fall Press, 1990), p. 1.
3. Ibid.
4. John M. Pfiffner and Robert Presthus, *Public Administration* (New York: Ronald Press, 1967), p. 88.
5. Harland Cleveland, *The Future Executive* (New York: Harper & Row, 1972), p. 7.
6. H. George Frederickson, "Public Administration in the 1970s," *Public Administration Review* (September-October, 1976): 570.
7. Marshall Edward Dimock, ed., *Administrative Vitality* (New York: Harper & Brothers, 1959), Chap. 12, pp. 175–98.
8. Warren G. Bennis, "Leadership Theory and Administrative Behavior: The Problem of Authority." *Administrative Science Quarterly* (June-March 1959–60): 260.

9. White, *Introduction*, p. 186.

10. Eugene E. Jennings, "The Anatomy of Leadership," *Management of Personnel Quarterly* (Autumn 1961): 1.

11. Cleveland, *Future Executive*, p. 77.

12. F. Scott Myers, *Every Employee a Manager* (New York: McGraw-Hill, 1970), pp. 11–14.

13. Frederick Herzberg, Bernard Mausner, and Barbara Snyderman, *The Motivation to Work* (New York: John Wiley, 1959); and Frederick Herzberg, *The Managerial Choice: To Be Efficient or To Be Human*, rev. edn. (Salt Lake City: Olympus, 1982).

14. Rensis Likert, *New Patterns of Management* (New York: McGraw-Hill, 1961), p. 103.

15. Frederick C. Thayer, *An End to Hierarchy* (New York: Franklin Watts, 1973), p. 24.

16. Frank K. Gibson and Clyde E. Teasley, "The Humanistic Model of Organization Motivation: A Review of Research Support," *Public Administration Review* (January-February 1973): 89–96.

17. Chris Argyris, *Personality and Organization* (New York: Harper & Brothers, 1957); Warren Bennis, *Changing Organizations* (New York: McGraw-Hill, 1966); Frederick B Herzberg, et al., *Motivation to Work*; Abraham Maslow, *Motivation and Personality* (New York: Harper & Row, 1954); Douglas McGregor, *The Human Side of Enterprise* (New York: McGraw-Hill, 1960); and Rensis Likert, *The Human Organization* (New York: McGraw-Hill, 1967).

18. Gordon L. Lippitt and Warren H. Schmidt, "Crises in Developing Organizations," *Harvard Business Review* (November-December 1967): 103.

19. F. E. Fiedler and M. M. Chermers, *Leadership and Effective Management* (Glenview, Ill.: Scott Foresman, 1974), Chap. 5.

20. Lawrence H. Peters, D. D. Hartke, and J. T. Pholman, "Fiedler's Contingency Theory of Leadership: An Application of the Meta-Analysis Procedure of Schmidt and Hunter," *Psychological Bulletin* (March 1985): 274–85.

21. For example, see Robert W. Rice, "Psychometric Properties of the Esteem for the Least Preferred Co-Worker (LPC) Scale," *Academy of Management Review* (January 1978): 106–18; and Chester A. Schriesheim, B. D. Bannister and W. H. Money, "Psychometric Properties of the LPC Scale: An Extension of Rice Review," *Academy of Management Review* (April 1979): 287–90.

22. Edgar H. Schein, *Organizational Psychology*, 3rd edn. (Englewood Cliffs, N.J.: Prentice-Hall 1980), pp. 116–17; and Boris Kabanoff, "A Critique of Leader Match and Its Implications for Leadership Research," *Personnel Psychology* (Winter 1981): 749–64.

23. Paul Hersey and Kenneth A. Blanchard, "So You Want to Know Your Leadership Style?" *Training and Development Journal* (February 1974): pp. 1–15; and Paul Hersey and Kenneth Blanchard, *Management of Organizational Behavior: Utilizing Human Resources*, 4th edn. (Englewood Cliffs, N.J.: Prentice-Hall, 1984): 150–61.

24. Hersey and Blanchard, *Management of Organizational Behavior*, p. 71.

25. R. K. Hambleton and R. Gumpert, "The Validity of Hersey and Blanchard's Theory of Leader Effectiveness," *Group and Organization Studies* (June 1982): 225–42;

Claud Z. Graeff, "The Situational Leadership Theory: A Critical View," *Academy of Management Review* (April 1983): 285–91; Warren Blank, John R. Weitzel, and Stephen C. Green, "Situational Leadership Theory: A Test of Underlying Assumptions," paper presented at the National Academy of Management Conference, Chicago, August 1986; and Robert P. Vecchio, "Situational Leadership Theory: An Examination of a Prescriptive Theory," *Journal of Applied Psychology* (August 1987): 444–51.

26. Vecchio, "Situational Leadership Theory," pp. 444–51.

27. Janet Falk and Erick R. Wendler, "Dimensionality of Leader-Subordinate Interactions: A Path-Goal Investigation," *Organizational Behavior and Human Performance* (October 1982): 241–64.

28. Robert T. Golembiewski, *Men, Management, and Morality* (New Brunswick, N.J.: Transaction Publishers, 1989), p. 7

29. McGregor, *Human Side of Enterprise*.

30. W. F. Whyte, ed., *Money and Motivation* (New York: Harper & Row, 1955).

31. Likert, *New Patterns of Management*.

32. John Morse and Jay W. Losch, "Beyond Theory Y," *Harvard Business Review* (May-June 1970): 1.

33. Fiedler and Charmers, *Leadership and Effective Management*, Chap. 5.

34. Douglas McGregor, *Leadership and Motivation* (Cambridge, Mass.: MIT Press, 1966), p. 6.

35. H. H. Gerth and C. Wright Mills, eds., *From Max Weber: Essays in Sociology*, (Fairlawn, N.J.: Oxford University Press, 1946), pp. 51–55, 245–48.

36. John A. Vieg, "The Chief Executive," in Fritz Morstein Marx, ed., *Elements of Public Administration*, 2nd edn. (Englewood Cliffs, N.J.: Prentice-Hall, 1959), Chap. 8.

37. Chester I. Barnard, *The Functions of the Executive* (Cambridge, Mass.: Harvard University Press, 1938), p. 283.

38. Ibid., Chap. 12.

39. Rensis Likert, "A Motivational Approach to the Modified Theory of Organization and Management," in Mason Haire Jr., ed., *Modern Organization Theory* (New York: John Wiley & Sons, 1959), p. 161.

12

Community Relations
in Public Management

This chapter examines how public managers shape opinions and mobilize support in order to carry out an agency's mission. Five main sections have been included. The first discusses the nature of public relations in a bureaucracy. The second section examines secrecy and publicity, the tactics employed by public managers to influence public attitudes toward specific programs. In the third section, the role and perspective of top administrators are studied. The fourth section describes the role of MLMs. Finally, we discuss public relations and power and accountability in public management.

LEARNING OBJECTIVES

On completing this chapter, the reader should be able to:

- Understand the nature and meaning of public relations.
- Understand how administrators influence policy outcomes.
- Appreciate the power that public officials exercise through publicity.
- Examine the perspective and role of top administrators in public relations.
- Recognize the important role MLMs play in public relations.

Though public relations as a career or field of study is a recent development, it has been practiced for many centuries. Generals have written memoirs, politicians have written speeches, and religious leaders have evangelized. For example, Caesar wrote about his campaign in Gaul, Saint Paul preached the gospel, and Marco Polo gave a detailed account of his travels in the East.[1] The practice of many U.S. presidents of "going public," a strategy whereby a president promotes himself and his policies "by appealing directly to the American public for support," is a potent means for enhancing public relations.[2] President Teddy Roosevelt used his "bully pulpit" to advocate his appeals for Progressive reforms. President Woodrow Wilson employed the tactic on his "ill-fated whistle-stop tour of the country" in support of the ratification of the League of Nations Treaty.[3] President Franklin D. Roosevelt provides another example with his fireside chats aimed at keeping his congressional opponents at bay and reminding them of his New Deal mandate. President Carter practiced it with a modicum of success to galvanize support for his energy policies. Finally, President Reagan went public with spectacular success in getting his tax cuts and spending policies through a Congress dominated by Democrats.

Both in Britain and later in the United States, community public relations has taken on major importance in the practice of public management. Public relations was performed as an ancillary activity to other professional interests. Seldom did it produce more than a modicum of income for its participants. Early writers attempted to influence public policy through the media by tracts, pamphlets, or political cartoons. In Britain, publicists used tracts to bring attention to the shocking working conditions in the factory. The muckrakers did the same in the United States to initiate reform of the massive corruption of public officials that was evident following the Civil War. By 1910, public relations had become an indispensable instrument for conducting administration in public and private organizations. One observer has noted, "Public relations seek to locate centers of political, social, economic, and intellectual power and apply effective leverage on them."[4]

Most people think of public relations in government as the activities of agency employees who are attached to some unit such as a public information office. While this definition may be useful for locating a formal place for the public relations duties, it does not give us an adequate picture of the range and variety of an agency's contacts with its many publics. It's not uncommon to find personnel conducting public relations under misleading and innocuous titles such as "special assistant," "assistant to the director," and the like.

In a typical government agency, public relations is "performed by both a special group of employees and by the agency as a whole."[5] To examine this full range of "agency-public communication,"[6] we will adopt Richard L. Kolbe's broad definition of public relations: "Those are agency communications or censorships which may be construed as having some effect on policy or opinion."[7] This definition is not intended to encompass messages or information flowing through the regular hierarchical chain of command in the organization. The focus is on communications that are intended for the general public, the legislature, the news media, and relevant individuals in the agency environment and that are meant to modify attitudes on behalf of the agency.

Though most agencies practice public relations, many will deny it. It is thus difficult to obtain accurate information about its true extent. Says Kolbe: "Administrators have tended to hide public relations activities, to be secretive about a function which has subjected them to much past criticism."[8] Because administrators are supposed to be neutral implementors of legislative intent, they have been reluctant to admit that they are creating an atmosphere aimed at directly influencing decision-makers, the public, or special groups toward a favorable position on some predetermined agency policy. The secretary of the

Department of Energy was recently criticized for conducting surveys to determine how its services and image were viewed by the press and the public.

In many ways, public relations is at the heart of modern democratic governance. Free government cannot survive without the voluntary support of a large number of its citizens. For the government to remain aware of what citizens are thinking requires constant feedback. V. O. Key Jr. said: "Governments must concern themselves with the opinions of their citizens, if only to provide a basis for repression of disaffection."[9]

Many programs' achievements have been realized because of the influence and consequences of public relations. In a way, everyone in an organization is involved in public relations: "Publicity and communications are much more fundamental than image building; they lie at the heart of program achievement."[10]

In many communities and at the national level of government, there are many watchdog organizations such as Ralph Nader's consumer group, better-government associations, and economy leagues that keep a watchful eye on government and have developed the expertise to adroitly use public relations to counter government public relations objectives. The city of Tarpon Springs, Florida, saw its desire to prioritize the local Helen Ellis Memorial Hospital thwarted by a local citizens group's skillful use of public relations.

The city officials had been communicating with the community about the $20 million that could be obtained by selling the hospital. The city commissioners promised that they would earmark the funds received from the sale of the hospital to reduce future tax increases. The public's initial enthusiasm for the hospital's privatization was overwhelming, at almost 60 percent.

To counter the city hall publicity machine, Ketchum Public Relations firm in Pittsburgh, Pennsylvania, was hired by the local citizens group. With the aid of Ketchum's targeting surveys, the citizens were able to mobilize and coordinate a massive grassroot support around a "Save Helen Ellis Committee." The city redoubled its effort, including direct mail and public appearances. City officials were unable to persuade the citizens that the benefits of selling the hospital outweighed the cost of keeping it. Thus, the city's early lead in the public opinion polls was dramatically reversed on Election Day when the matter was put on the ballot to settle the issue by referendum. By a margin of nearly three to one, the referendum was rejected.[11]

Information is generally viewed as a good thing that agencies should most definitely exchange with individuals and the public. It allows us to know what is occurring in an agency and provides one of the bases for accountability. Propaganda, on the other hand, is invariably associated with evil. To many Americans, public relations is often less an activity of information dissemination than an instrument for persuasion.[12] Indeed, public relations may operate at two levels in a government agency: (1) at the political level, aimed at maintaining, consolidating, and extending political influence, shaping opinion, and building support for present and future policies; (2) at the administrative level, falling in the province of official information services. With respect to administrative public relations, J. A. R. Pimlot has noted: "Public relations is indispensable to the efficient administration of many programs which cannot be carried out unless the public is adequately informed and, in some cases, persuaded to cooperate."[13]

It is not easy to draw the line between propaganda and information because the mandates of many agencies are imprecisely worded. For example, the statute creating the Office of Education in 1867 stated the agency was to "diffuse such information as shall aid the people of the United States in the establishment and maintenance of efficient school systems and otherwise to promote the cause of education." The scope of the wording is so broad that it includes a vast number of tangentially related activities. Perhaps a main guideline determining the kind and extent of information and/or persuasion to be provided could be based on the public acceptance of the program being undertaken. For example, a public appeal for citizens to contribute to the Easter Seal or cancer societies or to protect their children against measles will likely meet with no opposition.

BUREAUCRATIC TACTICS AND PUBLIC RELATIONS

Separation of powers is an institutional norm legally sanctioned by the Constitution. At both state and national levels on occasion one political party controls the executive branch while another controls the legislature. This promotes legislative and bureaucratic autonomy. But a policy that can galvanize people and retain their support requires the building of coalitions both inside and outside the bureaucracy, especially with the legislature.[14] Bureaucrats are thus constantly involved in creating and dissolving coalitions, or what Morton Halperin has called "the games bureaucrats play," in order to achieve policy outcomes they desire and inhibit the development of those they dislike.[15]

Those Anthony Downs labels "climbers" and Robert Presthus terms "upward mobiles" have a real stake in being on the right side.[16] These individuals find that supporting the right policy commitments—those popular in the eyes of relevant public—carries high rewards. It can mean speedy advancement up the ladder in the bureaucracy. Leon Segal indicates that it is no accident that the military services are engaged in constant rivalries. Many of these struggles can be traced to the desire for career advancements.[17] One of the most widespread examples of public officials "jumping on the bandwagon" of public opinion is their new-found zeal for reducing government spending—a course broadly associated with Proposition 13 and, more recently, with privatization and budget cutbacks as a means of reinventing government to promote client satisfaction, balancing the budget, and promoting the prioritization of goals and objectives.

There is an operating assumption on the part of bureaucrats that decisions can be affected if those responsible for making them are provided with the "right type" of information. This implies that whoever is making the decisions will act rationally. Because decision-makers do not have all of the information, an "uncertainty gap" exists. The bureaucrat who has access to information and favors a particular side can use the press to "plant" news, forcing the decision-makers to take due recognition. Perhaps the most pervasive effort at using the press is the presidential press conference. Increasingly, administrators at all levels of government have press conferences and appear on radio and television in advocacy roles. Most top-level administrators also systematically monitor the news. Especially at the federal level, newspaper stories that even remotely touch on the agency's mission will almost never be overlooked. Federal officials constantly monitor the press to learn information and public opinion relating to their external environment.[18] They also take the initiative in the press. For example, John Kenneth Galbraith, former ambassador to India, has observed, "I found it easier to bring my views to bear on the president of the United States by way of the *Washington Post* and its Delhi correspondent than by way of the State Department."[19]

Segal describes several tactics often used by bureaucrats:[20]

1. *Trial balloons.* A prospective policy is leaked to the press to test the reaction of legislators or other important groups and individuals before the proposal is put into effect. The feedback obtained can be used to allow the policy to go forward or to modify it if the analyzed information dictates it.
2. *Issuing a "hunting license"* A top executive, such as the president, governor, or mayor, gives subordinates the power to speak on his or her behalf. In this way the executive can allow the prestige of his or her office to be used by subordinates to persuade reluctant colleagues to go along. All of this is done without the executive's having to risk direct public commitment and possible open defiance. It allows executives the opportunity to retract or amend what has been exchanged.
3. *Eliciting commitment from above.* Here, a series of officials attempts to elicit commitment to some course of action by getting the top executive to make his or her position publicly known. The former ambassador to Saigon, Henry Cabot Lodge, kept up a flood of "inspired" stories to the press in an effort to get President Kennedy to pressure the Diem regime to initiate reforms. In Lodge's view, "The leak is the prerogative of the ambassador. It is one of the many weapons for doing the job."[21]
4. *Announcing a decision.* Bureaucrats attempt to get publicity for decisions by planting questions for reporters to ask at a news conference, thus necessitating that a chief executive or top official announce his or her decision.
5. *Promulgating an action as though it were authorized.* When only the chief executive has the power and legal right to authorize an action, a powerful senior official may promulgate policy on his or her own initiative as though it were the decision of the executive, hoping that the publicity will make it too difficult to countermand. General Douglas MacArthur is credited with this type of action. When the United States was hesitant in its peace negotiations following World War II, MacArthur called a press conference announcing, "The time has now approached that we must talk peace with Japan."[22]

The environment in which the agency operates provides an opportunity for the agency to exhibit an exemplary image. Employees must (1) be responsive, replying promptly and considerately to inquiries and requests for information; (2) exhibit a sense of mission and dedication; and (3) express enthusiasm, commitment, and pride in the agency's accomplishments when providing services. These attributes are important to both public and private companies. At Southwestern Bell (SBC), employees are expected to be model citizens, to pay their bills on time, volunteer for civic activities, and avoid conflict with authorities. In Southwestern Bell's view, each of its employees is an ambassador of good will to the community. What they do reflects directly or indirectly on the company. It is important for personnel in public agencies to recognize that these expectations by top management apply equally in government.

Among the many organizations and activities that an agency may be expected to become involved with are: (1) local professional clubs such as the Kiwanis; (2) community campaigns such as the United Way drive; (3) knowing and maintaining contacts with local business leaders and newspapers; (4) permitting groups to use its building for meetings; (5) giving demonstrations and holding open houses to explain agency mission and operations; and (6) exchanging speakers with different local agencies (see the discussion on social responsibility above).

As noted previously, the information officer is but one of many who conduct public relations in most agencies. The officer is, however, most knowledgeable and often is a main source of formal information to many groups. This means that he or she can be a valuable aid to the agency and should be kept thoroughly informed on policy development and program changes in the agency.

SECRECY AND PUBLICITY

William Rudder, former assistant secretary of public affairs in the U.S. Department of Commerce, commented: "Government . . . has a responsibility to send information which articulates policy and conveys material concerning rules, regulations, and limitations to constituencies." Information at all levels of government should be looked on as the necessary means to create an informed public that can make intelligent decisions about government programs.[23]

The critical role that free access to information plays in a democracy has been recognized from America's earliest days. Patrick Henry believed that information was indispensable to the liberty of a free people. He wrote that government officials must be prevented from "covering with the veil of secrecy the common routine of business, for the liberties of the people never were, or never will be, secure when the transactions of their rulers may be concealed from them."[24] Henry did maintain that the right to know had to be modified in cases relating to "military operations on affairs of such great consequence, the immediate promulgation of which might defeat the interest of the community."[25] Today most states have "sunshine laws" that require public organizations to conduct meetings (except executive sessions) that are open to the press and public.

New nations emerging from a colonial period have been especially cognizant of the importance of information. Most have ministries or departments of information that are headed by cabinet-level officers. These ministries are responsible for nation-building and are in charge of informing the people of what the government is doing and why and encouraging them to increase their own contributions to society.

BUREAUCREATIC SECRECY AND CORRUPTION

The demand for openness continues to have wide appeal in American society. Many advocates of openness subscribe to the views espoused by Woodrow Wilson, who equated secrecy with impropriety and publicity as a means to keep democracy pure and accountable.[26] Advocates of openness point to events such as the Bay of Pigs in 1961, the war in Vietnam, Watergate, and the Iran-Contra scandal to support their argument.

Though such events have given the public reason to suspect secrecy, the general view comes closer to Patrick Henry's, requiring that we strike a balance. Military secrets, sensitive negotiations, and personal confidential records may be properly kept secret. Yet the undisputable fact remains that a free people cannot govern themselves if "government agencies can deny access to information bearing on the issues the public is supposed to decide."[27] Secrecy grants to administrators several opportunities repugnant to democracy: (1) to cover up mistakes; (2) to conceal misbehavior; (3) to make policy without consultation; (4) to allow officeholders or officials to escape accountability for their actions; and (5) to undermine the rationality of governmental decisions.[28]

FREEDOM OF INFORMATION ACT

This act was passed in 1966 in response to what many saw as a growing trend of secrecy in the federal government. Many states passed similar laws, but our discussion here will be confined to the federal act of 1966. The act gives all persons the judicially enforceable right to see the records of all federal agencies, except to the extent that the records may be covered by an exemption. The applicant need not give a reason for his or her request. The following are the main exemptions: (1) classified defense records; (2) tax returns; (3) trade secrets; (4) government employee advice; (5) personnel medical files; (6) investigating files for law enforcement; (7) bank examination records; and (8) certain geological information relating to minerals.

Even though records may be exempted, agencies are legally free to grant access voluntarily. According to Robert L. Salochin, this practice has been occurring with increasing frequency.[29] In addition, the House Committee on

Government Operations noted in 1972 that while the Freedom of Information Act provided citizens with greater access, many impediments were introduced in the course of administration. There was excessive classification of documents "to avoid administrative mistakes, waste of funds, or political embarrassment."[30] Nicholas Henry has classified the various means bureaucrats have used to thwart access to public documents:

- *The contamination tactic,* in which potentially embarrassing unclassified information is exempt from the act.
- *The specificity tactic,* in which an agency will delay responding to requests for files on the basis that the requests were not sufficiently specific.
- *The search fee tactic,* in which the agency imposes an arbitrarily high fee for gathering the solicited information.
- *The trade secrets tactic,* in which an exemption pertaining to a trade secret (which is legally exempt under the act) is extended by the agency to all other information provided by the manufacturer.[31]

In 1974, Congress made several significant modifications to the Freedom of Information Act, giving the courts the initial right to review classification decisions.[32] These amendments included (1) initial review of exemptions by the court; (2) a requirement that agencies publish and distribute indexes of the classified documents, identifying their general nature (e.g., policy statements, administrative manuals, etc.)[33]; (3) the issuing of a uniform and reasonable schedule of charges for searching and duplication; (4) giving the information within ten working days and, in case of rejection, providing for an appeal to the agency head to be heard within twenty working days from the date of receipt; (5) assessment of costs in those cases where the complainant "substantially prevails"; and (6) reporting of personnel to the Civil Service Commission (now Office of Personnel Management) for disciplinary action where withholding was based on arbitrary and capricious actions. The amendments were vetoed by President Gerald Ford because of their potential danger to national security, diplomatic relationships, and the right to privacy relating to investigative files.

EXECUTIVE PRIVILEGE

Under executive privilege, the president can claim a constitutional power to withhold information concerning his office and the executive establishment generally from the other two branches of government. There was little concern about the use or misuse of this power until recently in public administration or in the teaching of basic U.S. government. Presidents from time to time have invoked the executive privilege doctrine, but none claimed the vast discretionary powers asserted by President Nixon.

A development in the area was the publication of a book by Raoul

Berger, who refutes the claims of proponents of a long-standing practice of executive privilege.[34] In his view, there is not a thread of evidence to support its constitutional existence. The doctrine originated in 1958 with the Eisenhower presidency. Despite Berger's contention, the Supreme Court has upheld the existence of the doctrine of executive privilege. In *Nixon vs. the United States*, although President Nixon's claim of unlimited presidential privilege of immunity from judicial process was overruled by a Supreme Court vote of 8-0, the court noted the following: (1) Certain circumstances (e.g., involving military, diplomatic, or sensitive national security secrets) require deference from the court; (2) an undifferentiated or unspecified claim for privilege on the basis of the public interest is unacceptable; (3) the court could afford sufficient protection to permit inspection of the communication in question; (4) justice requires that evidence relevant to a criminal trial be disclosed; (5) the existence of executive privilege is based on the separation of powers. [35]

THE ROLE OF TOP ADMINISTRATORS IN PUBLIC RELATIONS

Public relations is ideally designed to aid top administrators in achieving the mission of the agency. The fact that each agency exists in a pluralistic environment (many groups competing to exercise power and influence) carries great significance in the U.S. public administration setting. Administrators cannot expect to obtain power from the chief executive or the political party, particularly at the national and state level, to carry out their mission. Unlike in Britain, once administrators are put in their positions, they are expected to fend for themselves. This means that they must fight to maintain and expand their policy space (the areas over which they exercise power and influence).

The very premises on which administrators operate demand that they assiduously cultivate good working relationships with their clients, constituents, legislatures, interest groups, and the general public. Administrators constantly strive to keep their names and programs in the public eye. As politically astute practitioners, administrators know that most publics are fickle. Out of sight and hearing may be tantamount to being out of mind. In the public sector, the lack of a common yardstick for measuring success, such as profits in the private sector, creates a continuing problem.[36] Thus, it is not enough for an agency to effectively deliver goods and services; the public must constantly be told and reminded of this fact. In this context, public relations becomes strategic for the survival, growth, and prestige of the agency and the future careers of its administrators.

With such high stakes riding on the image of an agency, there is great potential for good or ill in the use of public relations. In most agencies, the tendency is to rigidly control whatever information reaches the public. When a news person enters an agency, his or her presence is often reported to top administrators in record time. Henry Scharer, former information director of the U.S. Department of Commerce, doubts that administrators wish to make much information available to the public. He noted: "The truth of the matter is that despite increasing acceptance of 'let the people know,' too many government officials are fearful that information exchange with the public, unless closely controlled, will reflect adversely on the agency."[37] In this atmosphere, even the formal public information officer is looked on with suspicion.

William Rudder, also a former information officer, has expressed concern about the way top officials manage information. Their view of the public's "right to know" is determined too often by expediency. As an information officer, Rudder came to feel that "the less light shed on any given subject the better. The less real public debate, the less said until something is a fait accompli—the less chance there is of something going wrong. The fewer the number of variables, the more certain the outcome."[38]

Too often top officials believe that they can manipulate information to gain the desired public support or to neutralize controversy. It is understandable that top officials wish to accomplish their jobs with minimum difficulties, but this view contravenes the democratic process. Public relations is a powerful tool that can be used to obtain political advantages. It is another means that administrators have at their disposal in their battle to maintain and expand their agency's basis of power. Yet if used without sufficient institutional and cultural controls, this power could impede the democratic process and ultimately impinge on the freedom of the people it is intended to serve.

MLMS AND PUBLIC RELATIONS

The formal public relations area is regarded with such suspicion that it is one of the most closely controlled functions of MLMs in public organizations. What public relations officers do or fail to do tends to have high visibility. Top administrators can get feedback about the agency's image by talking to people outside the agency, by reading the newspaper, or by watching television.[39] All of these factors act as regulating mechanisms.

Much insecurity accompanies the formal position of the public information officer. Among the reasons are (1) the profession's high visibility; (2) its newness and relatively undefined nature; (3) its lack of legitimacy; and (4) its employment as a ready-made scapegoat for agency program failures. According to Scharer:

The importance of the career information officer in the government hierarchy has escalated in recent years, but he has not yet achieved the level of recognition and authority that his work merits or his interest of the government and the public require. His ascent up the ladder of the bureaucracy has been slippery and fraught with hazard; his present perch is not secure and there is always the possibility of a backslide to oblivion.[40]

It is important to remember that formal information units and the employees attached to them are not the only people conducting public relations for any agency. All employees are potential public relations ambassadors. Thus, MLMs concerned about the direction of the agency policies can be important sources of leaks to the press. Because MLMs have a virtual monopoly on information, their support is vital. To forget this fact can create real problems for an agency's press relations and, obviously, for its image. All of this can adversely affect the agency's bargaining position in obtaining resources and expanding its policy space.

Again, we see the crucial role that MLMs play in affecting the image and power of an agency. Though MLMs in their formal public relations positions operate in a highly controlled environment, their colleagues in the line positions elsewhere in the organization can affect public relations through unauthorized releases. These acts can serve as checks on top administrators' exercise of power. However, they leave MLMs subject mainly to their own self-control as opposed to formal institutionalized control.

PUBLIC RELATIONS: POWER AND ACCOUNTABILITY

Administrators have devised two main means to ensure that information and/or propaganda is effectively disseminated. These are secrecy, or with-holding of information, and publicity, which conditions public attitudes. Public relations has emerged as a one-way street rather than the two-way street it should be, although the Freedom of Information Act was passed to help to redress this imbalance.

Top administrators feel that the amendments to the act have created too great a burden. Proponents, such as Ralph Nader, feel that the act still does not provide citizens with the unfettered access to public information that will enable them to intelligently judge the actions of public officials.

Perhaps some qualification must be made on this general conclusion in light of the passage of the Civil Service Reform Act of 1978, which encourages lower-level public workers to "blow the whistle" (i.e., report to the press and media on the wrongdoings or incompetencies of their peers or superiors). After more than a decade, there has not been an increase in whistle-blowing on the scale expected as the fear of subtle retaliation has acted as a retarding factor.

There is no doubt that the rise of publicity has brought with it great potential to affect attitudes toward government. Fortunately, the pluralistic environment (competing centers of power) in which U.S. administration operates, with its checks and counter-checks, acts as one important restraining factor. Francis Rourke believes that dispersion and fragmentation of power act as a major barrier against excesses: "The existence of competing centers of power with society serves to guarantee that official pronouncements will not go uncontested, if there is any question of their accuracy on matters of fact or interpretation, and it insures that efforts to conceal information will be subject to frequent challenge."[41]

DISCUSSION QUESTIONS

1. Why has public relations become an important factor in contemporary public administration?
2. Discuss some of the means available to an administrator to affect policy outcomes.
3. Why is secrecy frowned on in democratic societies? What guidelines would you suggest to ensure a high degree of accountability?
4. How do pluralistic forces serve as an important check on the use of publicity in U.S. public administration?
5. What is "going public" and what role has it played in federal initiatives and policymaking?
6. How might citizens use public relations to make government more responsive to their needs? Identify at least two examples.

NOTES

1. Robert O. Carlson, "Public Relations," *International Encyclopedia of Social Sciences* (New York: Free Press, 1977), pp. 209–10.

2. Samuel Kernell, *Going Public: New Strategies of Presidential Leadership* (Washington, D.C.: Congressional Quarterly Press, 1986), p. 2.

3. Ibid., p. 2.

4. Ibid., p. 213.

5. Richard Lee Kolbe, *Public Relations and American Administration* (Ann Arbor, Mich.: University Microfilms, 1973), p. 1.

6. Ibid.

7. Ibid., p. 7.

8. Ibid., p. 30.

9. V. O. Key Jr., *Public Opinion and American Democracy* (New York: Alfred A. Knopf, 1961), p. 3.

10. William A. Gilbert, "Public Relations in Society" in *Public Relations, Local Government* (Washington, D.C.: International City Management Association, 1975), p. 13.

11. Pete Pierce and Lloyd Corder, "Ketchum If You Can," *Profiles in Health Care Marketing* (March/April 1996): 1–6.

12. Ibid.

13. J. A. R. Pimlott, *Public Relations and American Democracy* (Princeton, N.J.: Princeton University Press, 1951), p. 194.

14. Leon V. Segal, "Bureaucratic Objectives and Tactical Uses of the Press," *Public Administrative Review* (July-August 1975): 113.

15. Morton Halperin, "Why Bureaucrats Play Games," *Foreign Policy* (Spring 1971): 70–90.

16. Anthony Downs, *Inside Bureaucracy* (Boston: Little, Brown, 1967); and Robert Presthus, *The Organizational Society: An Analysis and a Theory* (New York: Vintage Press, 1965).

17. Segal, "Bureaucratic Objectives," p. 113.

18. Ibid.

19. John Kenneth Galbraith, "Affidavit Filed in U.S. v. Ellsberg," quoted in the *Washington Post* (June 26, 1972), p. A-15.

20. Segal, "Bureaucratic Objectives," p. 117.

21. Clark Mollenhoff, *Washington Cover-Up* (New York: Doubleday, 1962), p. 116.

22. Martin E. Weinstein, *Japan's Post-War Defense Policy, 1947–1968* (New York: Columbia University Press, 1971), p. 14.

23. William Rudder, "Information as Two-Way Communication," in *The Voice of Government*, Ray Eldon Hierbert and Carlton E. Spitzer, eds., (New York: John Wiley and Sons, 1968), p. 77.

24. Quoted in Wilber J. Cohen, "Communication in a Democratic Society," *The Voice of Government*, Ray Eldon Hierbert and Carlton E. Spitzer, eds. (New York: John Wiley and Sons, 1968), p. 13.

25. Ibid.

26. Francis Rourke, "Administrative Secrecy: A Comparative Perspective," *Public Administrative Review* (January-February 1975): 1.

27. Ibid.

28. Ibid., p. 2.

29. Robert L. Salochin, "The Freedom of Information Act: A Government Perspective," *Public Administration Review* (January-February 1975): 12.

30. U.S. Congress, House Committee on Government Operations, *Administration of the Freedom of Information Act* (Washington, D.C.: Government Printing Office, 1972), p. 8.

31. Nicholas Henry, *Administration of Public Affairs* (Englewood Cliffs, N.J.: Prentice-Hall, 1975), p. 92.

32. Public Law 93-502, 93rd Congress, A.R. 12471 and Freedom of Information Act Amendments, 93rd Congress, 2nd Session, House of Representatives, Report No. 93-1380.

33. In those cases where the agencies decide not to publish the indexes, they are required to duplicate them on request for a reasonable cost.

34. Raoul Berger, *Congress Executive Privilege: A Constitutional Myth* (Cambridge, Mass.: Harvard University Press, 1974), especially Chapters 7 and 10.

35. 418 U.S. 683 (1974).

36. Francis Rourke, *Secrecy and Publicity* (Baltimore: Johns Hopkins Press, 1966), p. 210.

37. Henry Scharer, "Information in the Hierarchy," in *The Voice of Government*, Ray Eldon Hierbert and Carlton E. Spitzer, eds. (New York: John Wiley and Sons, 1968), p. 69.

38. "Information," p. 78.

39. Scharer, "Information in the Hierarchy," p. 69.

40. Ibid., p. 71.

41. Rourke, *Secrecy and Publicity*, p. 216.

Part IV

Supporting and Controlling Functions

13

Personnel: The Administration and Management of Human Resources

In this chapter, we take up first the functions performed by managers in the personnel process. We then turn to the evolution of personnel systems in government. Third, we address five contemporary issues: the drive by managers for greater productivity, the demand by workers for their civil and political rights, the rise of public sector unionism, the struggle in government over affirmative action, and the 1978 civil service reform. The chapter concludes by examining the key roles of MLMs in relating the human resources movement to the need for a better balance between power and accountability in government.

LEARNING OBJECTIVES

On completing this chapter, the reader should be able to:

- Describe the role and function of personnel in government.
- Explain why the merit system has come to be the dominant ideal in public personnel systems and why it is under attack.
- Analyze the major controversies in the personnel field, particularly around unionization, affirmative action, productivity, and merit.
- Review the evolving comparable-worth application.
- Indicate how the human resource function in personnel management strengthens the role of MLMs and provides an opportunity for greater accountability.

The personnel function encompasses the processes through which managers work with people to achieve organizational goals. The traditional functions include recruitment, examination, certification, position classification, pay policy, assignment of duties and job supervision, training (especially in service) and promotion, service records, and removal; safety plans, relations with professionals and union organizations, and morale; prestige, discipline, and the means for creating a career service.

The personnel functions can be understood as a continuum with activities associated with recruiting and placing a satisfactory work force (personnel administration) on one end and the efforts to develop human resources, enhance job satisfaction and productivity of public employees and relate public sector employment to the pursuit of societal goals (management of human resource) on the other. At one pole, where top-level personnel prevail, is the administration of a system; at the other, where MLMs are much more in evidence, is the development of the capacities of people. The personnel function involves the search for ways to bring power and accountability into better balance, or, in the language of this chapter, to coordinate personnel administration and the management of human resources.

The sheer number of positions and diversity of job classifications in government distinguish public from private personnel systems. One person in six in the country's labor force is a public employee, and there are seven times as many in state and local governments as in the federal service. The most important difference between the public and private systems, however, is that public employment occurs in a political context. The top officials who set major policies in government are elected, and their close associates, the top administrators, are selected by them on the basis of political considerations. A second major difference is the role played by independent civil service commissions in the recruitment and regulations of public employees. The major concern of these systems has been to eliminate the awarding of lower-level jobs on the basis of patronage by establishing merit systems in which jobs are obtained on the basis of competitive examinations. Merit systems have come under criticism; as one observer noted: "One person's merit is another person's favoritism. One person's excellence is another person's unreasonable require-ment."[1]

Criticism of the administrators became very severe during the mid-1970s. There were accusations that the system was too preoccupied with protecting the jobs of public employees and thus interfered with demands for higher productivity and that it was too procedure-oriented. Technique had triumphed over purpose. The system was incapable of supplying the quality staffing that agencies required. Discontent was voiced by professionals in government; by employees protected by union contracts; by minorities and women, who felt that the system discriminated against them unfairly; and by the public, which expects that human resources should be utilized by government for achieving social ends.

As a response to many of these concerns, changes were initiated at the federal level in a number of states to correct some of the problems, particularly at the upper levels. In 1978, Congress replaced the U.S. Civil Service Commission with the Office of Personnel Management (OPM). The Civil Service Reform Act (CSRA) sought to make it easier for the president to remove incompetent employees from the public service and to grant bonuses to other employees whose work is judged outstanding. The legislation allowed super grades and administrators in comparable pay levels to become part of the roughly 7,000 senior executive service (SES) as a means of obtaining greater control of lower-level personnel. Approximately 99 percent of the administrators eligible for the SES initially joined it.

The criticism that gave rise to the CSRA in 1978 and the 1993 criticism made by the National Performance Report (NPR) are of particular concern to MLMs. First, they are preeminently the products of merit systems as they generally are members neither of professions nor of unions. Second, overcoming the criticism of the civil service system depends largely on MLMs' ability to make public servants more accountable to their superiors and to the people. This search for accountability provides the theme for this chapter.

THE PERSONNEL PROCESS

The personnel process begins with a community demand and a labor supply as inputs. A legislative body authorizes a program and appropriate resources. A designated public agency then converts these resources into an agency program or project to be performed in specific organizational structures using specified techniques. Under the civil service rules in many states and cities, personnel subsystems (personnel planning, selection, placement, etc.) are employed as throughputs to facilitate the performance of specific tasks. The outputs are goods and services that can be measured in quantitative and qualitative terms. Fig. 13.1 presents the public personnel process.

There is also a "people" dimension of the personnel process. The inputs are societal values (work ethic, expectations about personal growth, and views of the rights of the individual and society). People also bring to jobs in government personal skills, varying levels of motivation, and attitudes about their work. Many employees participate actively in on-the-job informal groups that produce norms about work and a system of rewards and sanctions to develop conformity.

Through unions or associations, employees interact with the personnel subsystems to affect the quality of the work environment. The outputs, in addition to those defined by the organization, are the workers' sense of an increased capacity and, of primary importance, the achievement of societal goals. The end of personnel administration is to accountably achieve publicly determined ends. To take a closer look at the personnel process, we will first examine recruitment and selection before looking at the system as a whole.

Because there is considerable unemployment and an abundant supply of college graduates aggressively seeking employment, we might think that recruitment would not be a problem for the public service at this time. The government, moreover, has become a desirable employer, with competitive salaries and fringe benefits. Yet the recruitment of desirable candidates for public jobs has grown increasingly difficult. The relentless, and many times undue, criticism of the public service, and the publicized mass layoffs promised by President Clinton and the NPR created an image problem about the desirability of a public service career, especially for the best and brightest.

Fig. 13.1. Public Personnel Process

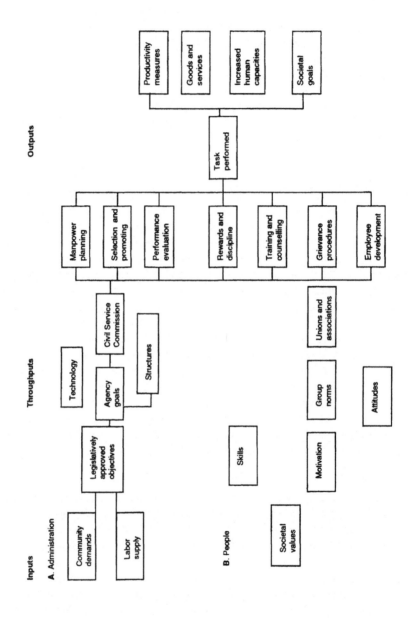

Public agencies face competition from business, industry, education, and non-profit organizations. Competition is particularly keen in occupations such as engineering and accounting, where high technical competence is required. In the federal and state governments, pressures to reduce the work force have resulted in a much more intensive search to best fill the limited number of jobs available. Recruitment has also become more difficult because of increased demand for opportunities by minorities and women, traditionally excluded from the better-paying jobs in government. Since the passage of the Civil Rights Act of 1964 and its subsequent amendments, public employers at all levels have been forced to re-examine their recruitment and placement processes to eliminate discriminatory practices. More recently, the government has become an employer of last resort when the private sector is unable to utilize human resources.[2] This situation is in sharp contrast to Japan, where the best and the brightest see government service as a most prestigious and desirable profession.[3] Recruitment begins with a precise determination of the skills required for specific jobs and an assessment of how many individuals will be needed. These steps are part of personnel planning. There are two ways in which a person can be brought into public employment: through a merit procedure or through a patronage appointment. Both systems are of major importance in the personnel process.

MERIT RECRUITMENT

From the earliest days of the Republic, the general criteria for selection of civil servants were laid down by George Washington. He sought individuals who had "fitness of character" and who possessed especially great competence and integrity. While this approach produced an outstanding and a relatively stable civil workforce, positions went mainly to a few wealthy, educated individuals. This gave the public service a significant hue of elitism.

The merit system encompasses 94 percent of all federal employees, both general and special merit, such as the FBI, the Foreign Service or public health. Tradition holds that there should be equal opportunity for all qualified citizens who aspire to public service. A corollary to this view is the doctrine that the most efficient way to make selections is through a competitive examination formally administered by a civil service system. Applicants are not required to enter the civil service only at the lowest grade. The civil service is open permitting lateral entry; that is, it allows administrators to move from one department to another. Extensions of the merit tradition are the principles that promotions should be made on the basis of merit and that every person selected for entrance into the public service should be able to aspire to a professional career. Thus, while the merit system began with a focus on recruitment, it has come to be much more concerned with providing for careers in government and ensuring fair pay, adequate fringe benefits (particularly provisions for retirement), the promotion of performance criteria, freedom from partisan interference (neutrality), protection of employees from unfair treatment by superiors, and the steady raising of the status of the public employee through improved training and the efforts of professional societies like the American Society for Public Administration. The objectives of the merit system in recruitment are:

- adequate publicity about job openings
- genuine opportunity for interested persons to apply
- realistic and fairly applied standards
- ranking of candidates based on relevant qualifications
- public knowledge of the results of the process
- an improvement of the public's image of the civil servant.

Probably the most controversial restriction on open recruitment through the merit system is the preference given to veterans, a policy that permits those who served in the military and certain of their close relatives to automatically receive a bonus of five points (ten if they have a service-connected disability) on their examination scores. This policy recently has been challenged as discriminatory against women, who participate in the military to a lesser extent than do men.

Many other challenges to the merit system arise out of sharp disagreement over what is a fair method for selecting candidates, whether examinations are culturally biased and unrelated to job requirements, and whether civil service examiners (who make a career of correcting examinations) have the necessary on-the-job experiences to make the fine distinctions that often separate one candidate from the other by a single point. While recruitment campaigns try to aggressively seek qualified applicants and ensure that the government is getting a chance to examine the right people for specific jobs, civil service commissions pursue this objective with imperfect knowledge of what the jobs will be, with often drastically limited resources for conducting searches, and with a body of merit doctrine for appeal and review of disciplinary actions against civil servants that has created the popular feeling that public employees, once on the job, cannot be removed.

It is useful to summarize a merit system operating principle as it is generally accepted in the U.S. federal system. The principle involves the following:

- Recruitment from all segments of society and selection and advancement on the basis of ability, knowledge, and skills under fair and open competition.
- Fair and equitable treatment in all personnel management matters, without regard to politics, race, color, religion, national origin, sex, marital status, age, or disability and with proper regard for individual privacy and constitutional rights.
- Equal pay for work of equal value, considering both national and

local rates paid by private employers, with incentives and recognition for excellent performance.

- High standards of integrity, conduct, and concern for the pubic interest.
- Efficient and effective use of the federal workforce.
- Retention of employees who perform well, correcting the performance of those whose work is inadequate, and separation of those who cannot or will not meet required standards.
- Improved performance through effective education and training.
- Protection of employees from arbitrary action, personal favoritism, or political coercion.
- Protection of employees against reprisal for lawful disclosures of information.[4]

PATRONAGE HIRING

Recruiting under the patronage system occurs at all levels. Appointments to executive positions (for example, department heads, commissioners, judges, and prosecuting attorneys) come largely through the patronage system. In professional jobs, such as those held by physicians or accountants, where the technical qualifications are determined by an educational institution or certifying board placement often depends on political recommendations. Finally, jobs at the lowest pay and status, particularly part-time employment such as summer jobs, are traditionally filled through patronage.

Appointments based on political consideration have a firm base in democratic government. Political appointments at the level of department heads are seen as means for putting into effect the policy choices decided in elections. Legitimization for political positions in the middle levels of organizations is traceable to the administration of President Dwight D. Eisenhower. His Republican administration took office in 1952 following twenty years of unbroken Democratic Party rule. To be able to carry out his electoral mandate, Eisenhower felt the need to put his own people into key middle-management positions. To accomplish this, a separate listing, called Schedule C, was devised to contain the names of individuals who might be appointed because of their competence to do the job and their commitment to the president's point of view. Schedule C selections made by President Carter when he took office in 1977 numbered some 2,200 positions. Today there are more than 2,500 presidential appointees, compared with an average of just over 100 in most advanced democracies such as Britain and Germany. Schedule A positions are those for which examinations are impractical because of the complexity involved and discretion that must be exercised. Schedule B employees are often appointed on the basis of noncompetitive examination. For example, tax specialists for Treasury Department positions are given such an examination to determine if they are qualified. The Schedule C appointments are of a policymaking or confidential character, such as upper-ranking staff assistants or secretaries to policymaking officials.

As discussed in Chapter 1, President Reagan, more so than any previous president, required a "loyalty test" and strong commitment to his administration's ideology as a precondition to being hired as a political administrator. Because four and a half times more federal officials were prosecuted and convicted during the Reagan presidency than during the previous eight years, the view has been expressed that the problems probably resulted from excessive pressure to toe the political line.[5]

At the local level of government, political appointment is even more pervasive than at the federal level. There is a strong belief that this practice is likely to decline in view of the U.S. Supreme Court ruling in *Rutan vs. Republican Party of Illinois*, 497, U.S., 62 (1990). In this case the court ruled that party affiliation could not be a factor in hiring, promoting, or transferring the majority of Illinois's 60,000 gubernatorial appointees.[6]

Political appointments to lower-level jobs have been resisted because of a history of abuse in what has been labeled "the spoils system." Public administration literature puts great emphasis on the need to develop a professional public service rather than one tied to political organizations, citing past abuses by "machine politics." At the federal level, this type of political appointment for lower-level positions has been almost entirely eliminated. In state government, there is less acceptance of the merit principle. In the Commonwealth of Pennsylvania, 30 percent to 40 percent of the jobs are not in a merit system but are handled through the governor's patronage secretary. At local levels of government, the picture is also mixed. Large cities are generally moving toward merit systems, but rural areas and urban counties still maintain a predominant patronage approach.

Arguments for and against patronage systems persist. There is little correlation between merit systems and the quality of workforces. Some jurisdictions have been able to assemble excellent workforces using patronage, and some merit systems have shown a lack of responsiveness to electoral candidates. There is little doubt, however, that merit employees have achieved security in their jobs while patronage employees come and go as administrations change. This has prompted most employees, once on the job, to seek to be included on a merit list or to join a union as a means to seek job security. The prevailing opinion in merit/patronage discussions is that the public service should be made up of competent people who are at the same time responsive to elected officials, which suggests some combination of merit and patronage systems. Fig. 13.2 presents the steps in the employment process and compares the merit and patronage systems.

THE EVOLVING PUBLIC PERSONNEL SYSTEMS

The personnel system in federal, state, and local governments began as an

adaptation of European practices, went through an elitist period followed by a
popular phase, and then evolved into a merit system in the period between the
enactment of the Civil Service Act of 1883 (also known as the Pendleton Act)

Fig. 13.2. Steps in the Employment Process

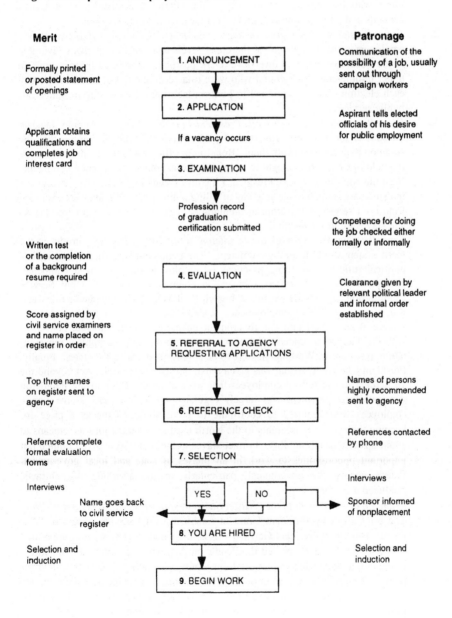

and World War II. In the last 25 years, as we noted at the outset of the chapter, merit systems have come under attack. The following is a brief history of American public personnel systems.

1. *From the early colonial period to independence.* Public employees, who were few in number in colonial days, were drawn from the privileged classes and from those who had a financial interest in the chartered companies. Indentured servants and African slaves supplied what we now call public works.

2. *From President Washington through President John Quincy Adams.* Public employees were "gentlemen" at the upper levels and generally persons favorable to the Federalist cause. Lower-level clerk positions were filled by men with an upper middle-class background who were rotated in and out of government with each election. Slaves continued to perform laborious, unhealthful, or dangerous public services.

3. *From President Jackson through President Lincoln.* President Andrew Jackson introduced the idea that government jobs should be made so simple that the common man could perform them. Rotation in office was advocated, but because the field of candidates thought to be qualified was limited, he depended on people from the educated classes. President Lincoln exceeded all other chief executives in using partisan patronage as a way of filling public jobs. Women were excluded from civil service, but European immigrants began to compete with free blacks and slaves for lower-level jobs.

4. *From the Civil War through the Pendleton Act of 1883.* The Act introduced the merit system to the federal government. The Pendleton Act sought to eliminate political influence in hiring practices by employing only the most competent personnel. The Act created a bipartisan commission, the U.S. Civil Service Commission, within the executive branch to develop and implement rules and procedures for federal employment. Lateral entry (opportunity to enter the service at any level) into the government positions was encouraged, consistent with the Jacksonian concern for openness. To promote geographical representation, positions in Washington were to be apportioned among the states. Finally, President Chester A. Arthur was given the authority to extend the Act beyond the 10 percent of the federal employees that were covered. Prior to the Pendleton Act, public employment was largely regulated by legislatures. Some public employees were required to contribute to political campaigns as a price for keeping their jobs. Immigrants in the North used government jobs as a means to attain upward social mobility. Former slaves in the South were given limited but important opportunities to work in all phases of state and local government. Frauds against the government, particularly in the awarding of contracts, produced a cry for reform.

5. *From the establishment of the civil service system to the Civil Rights Act of 1964.* The brief effort by President Grant to establish a civil service system in 1871 failed. But when President Garfield was assassinated in 1881 by a disappointed office seeker, Congress passed the Pendleton Act, which established competitive examinations, protected employees from removal for political reasons, called for public servants to be neutral in political campaigns, and enumerated the principle that the public service was open to all. In the early 1960s, women achieved the right to equal pay, unions the right to organize, and minorities the policy that

discrimination in public jobs was illegal. Since then, union and affirmative action pressures have multiplied. Until the late 1970s, employees increasingly called for full political and civil rights, and personnel administration appeared to be evolving toward a human resource development approach. For a number of reasons, including politics, the tide against affirmative action has been gaining momentum. This was especially true during the Reagan years and to a lesser extent during the Clinton administration. President Clinton's layoffs, decentralization, downsizing, deregulation, and privatization efforts spelled out in NPR added pressure against affirmative action and human resource management in the federal system.

6.   *From President Johnson's Civil Act of 1964 to President Carter's Civil Service Reform Act of 1978.* The Civil Service Reform Act of 1978 (CSRA) is a major effort of the Carter administration to bring greater coordination and order to the federal personnel management system that had haphazardly developed over the decades. There was no basic agreement on the principles that were necessary to guide the evolution and development of the system. Responsibility for various aspects of the federal personnel management were parceled out among the president, Congress, the courts, the Civil Service Commission, and a number of other government agencies. Advocates of the CSRA claimed that, in its zeal to promote political neutrality, it created a maze of detailed regulations relating to recruiting, testing, classifying, and releasing employees producing technical overkill, excessive protection of employees, lack of management flexibility, lack of creative incentive to promote efficiency and leading to discrimination in pay to minorities and women. To remove these problems and restore the merit principle, the CSRA attempted to correct the contradictory role of the Civil Service Commission. It divided the commission's function by creating a new Office of Personnel Management (OPM) to direct policy leadership and the Merit System Protection Board (MSPB) to deal with investigations and appeals.

The MSPB is an independent, quasi-judicial agency in the executive branch. It is given the authority to safeguard the federal merit system and civilian employees against unfair personnel action. It hears and decides employee appeals of actions and determines if they are consistent with the merit system principles. Actions may include suspensions, reduction-in-grade and removal of an employee. Based on its authority, the MSPB can order corrective and disciplinary action of an agency or employee whenever it deems it appropriate. From time to time it conducts studies of merit systems to determine whether prohibited actions are being practiced. Prohibited actions include the following:

- Discrimination against an applicant or employee.
- Using official authority to force or coerce political actions, demanding political contributions or to retaliate for refusal.
- Knowingly deceive or obstruct an individual regarding his or her right to compete for federal employment.
- Giving preferential treatment to an applicant or employee not authorized by law.
- Appointing, employing, or promoting relatives.

OPM is the president's principle agent for managing the federal workforce while the Merit System Protection Board operates as the "watchdog" of the personnel system. As noted, it hears and resolves complaints while attempting to protect whistle blowers from potential reprisals.

The CSRA created a Senior Executive Service (SES), very similar to the idea proposed by the Hoover Commission report about 25 years earlier. The service is comprised of 7000 senior members of the permanent civil service who are allowed more flexible assignments and transfer practices, not possible under the previous civil service rules. Finally the CSRA sought to tie pay and performance for SES and those in the managerial ranks below them.

CSRA attempted to make federal personnel administration politically responsive. This was directly recognized with the establishment of the SES who could be flexibly assigned, removed, use money as an incentive, or carrot and stick to motivate them.

COMPETING PERSONNEL SYSTEMS

While the above history charts the general course of development, it should be kept in mind that there are many of personnel systems in the public service. Every branch of government—executive, legislative, and judicial (at federal, state, and local levels)—has its own personnel system. In addition, public employees in educational institutions are organized separately from those in other executive departments, with the public schools and higher education constituting entirely separate systems. This multiplicity of systems alone is bewildering.

Within the executive branch public work force alone, there are four distinguishable groups of personnel systems operating side by side, each with its own distinct values and allegiances: (1) the patronage system, where selection is based on a combination of competence and political loyalty; (2) a unionized system, where many personnel actions are determined through labor-management negotiations; (3) the professional service, where recruitment is based largely on education and experience; and (4) the classified merit system, where entry and advancement require an examination process. The complexity of this system—and the resulting lack of overall attention to human resources in government—is one of the reasons demands have arisen for reform.

Until the early 1960s, the federal civil service was highly regarded. Most states and many large cities followed the lead of the federal government in establishing centralized personnel agencies. In the last two decades, however, criticism of both federal and state civil service systems has accumulated.

PROTECTIONISM AND PROFESSIONALIZATION

First, the merit system has been accused of promoting protectionism for employees. Two related developments have fueled the charge that civil service systems overprotect public employees to an extent inappropriate in democratic government. The first is the zealous manner in which civil service systems have attempted to root out patronage. While the eradication of hazing, the practice of requiring employees to contribute to a superior's political campaign or personal fortune, is widely supported, concerns have arisen when the fight against patronage tended to undermine the exercise of discipline. Employees were quick to charge that acts of discipline by their superiors were politically motivated and to seek protection through the elaborate civil service appeal procedure. The demotion or firing of a public employee became so difficult that it became a common practice to transfer or even to promote (if that meant his or her movement to some other department) an undesirable employee rather than to attempt a disciplinary procedure. This condition produced charges that public employees were nonproductive and that government contained an excess of marginal employees.

The second development is the drive by professional associations and schools of public administration to "professionalize" the field. By professionalization is meant the creation of an education and training program (preservice and in-service) that will enhance the knowledge, skills, values, and behavior of public employees. Those entering and moving up in the service are presumed to have this body of knowledge and skills. The movement has been spearheaded by the National Association of Schools of Public Affairs and Administration (NASPAA) through its committee on standards. Critics of the professionalization movement have charged that academic institutions are too far removed from the operations of government to be the judges of what public employment requires. Such institutions might consider themselves professional schools, but they should not be equated, say, with schools of medicine, which have a much closer relationship with patients and hospitals. Underlying this criticism is the charge that public administration theory is itself in disarray and that without valid theory it is difficult to prescribe good practice. Nonetheless, NASPAA has pressed on with the establishment of standards (though less rigid than original prescriptions), and its lobby urges that the graduates of the schools that measure up should be given preference in government. As a corollary concern, as top-level administrators increased their insistence that the performance of public employees be upgraded, they have also called for agency managers to play a larger role in personnel administration. This concern has taken the form of a direct attack on civil service commissions and CSRA.

The Municipal Manpower Commission and the National Civil Service League have called for personnel management to be made an integral part of the executive function. They argue that personnel systems should be measured not by the number of personnel transactions (for example, examinations) they complete but in terms of how they contribute to better government. The implication is that personnel systems conducted under the control of top administrators would be less protective of poor performers. As we point out below, these concerns have become part of a reformed federal civil service system.

CONTEMPORARY PUBLIC PERSONNEL ISSUES

The cost and level of efficiency of government have become national issues made prominent in NPR's attempt to reinvent government. As growth in public employment has leveled off, and as cries for greater productivity in government have become more insistent, the managers of public personnel systems have found themselves increasingly on the defensive. We will examine contemporary criticism of the merit and civil service systems in this context.

The Demand for Greater Productivity

The complaints of upper-level administrators against the civil service system reflect the increasing desire of managers to control the workforce. Managers want to utilize their skills in planning, organizing, coordinating, and controlling; they want to exercise leadership and to make the key decisions in translating objectives into outcomes. Managers object to the procedures required by independent commissions that claim to be representing the interests of the general public and employees as well as serving management.

The following are some specific complaints by top administrators:

1. The civil service recruitment system supplies employees that are inappropriate and made available too slowly to meet production demands.
2. Where promotions are to be made, discretion must be in the hands of the administrators, and they should look for guidance to their elected superiors and not to a centralized system.
3. When layoffs become necessary, they must be carried out in close coordination with the redesign of jobs, the introduction of automated equipment, and the broader use of contracting out, if reductions in costs are to be achieved. Such decisions about who should be let go have to be made within the agency.
4. Tenure should be based only on desirable performance. Lengthy procedures must not contravene the personnel judgments that managers must make if they are to carry out the legislation they are charged with implementing.
5. The measurement of success on the job is complex and includes at least the nature of the task, the group situation, the environment, and leadership characteristics. All of these form a symbiotic system that cannot be understood from the distance of the centralized personnel system.
6. Instead of a regulatory approach to personnel, administrators prefer management by objective (MBO)—that is, arrangements made by managers with operators at the outset of a work period (usually annually) about what operators are expected to do in a specified time. Periodically, managers would consult with operators to determine the progress made against agreed work plans. Alternatively, a TQM team approach may be encouraged and implemented.
7. There is need for greater accountability and satisfaction both for internal clients (recipients of immediate outputs) and external clients (final customers or recipients of products or services).
8. There is greater need to develop teamwork in achieving agency objectives.
9. There is need to cut out the large number of controlling individuals who have

been hired to minimize scandal and corruption. The result has been excessive bureaucratic red tape and control.

CONSTITUTIONAL RIGHTS TO PUBLIC EMPLOYEES

Beginning with the case of *Gilmore vs. James*, the federal courts have eroded away the tradition that working for the government was a privilege voluntarily accepted and, hence, public employees had few constitutional rights that needed to be respected. In the *Gilmore* case, the court said "a state [or the federal government] cannot condition an individual's privilege of public employment on his non-participation in conduct which under the Constitution is protected from direct interference."[7]

This decision, and others that have followed it, have cast doubt on the so-called doctrine of privilege, which justified the policing of off-the-job behavior of public employees. Civil service commissions in the past have required exemplary conduct: scandal-free private lives, no excessive debts, no memberships in controversial organizations, discretion in speech—particularly if it reflected unfavorably on their place of employment—and absolutely no involvement in politics at any level. This has now been replaced by the doctrine of substantial interest, which holds that the discharge of a person from government cannot violate an employee's basic constitutional rights unless the government demonstrates the necessity for this action. In *Board of Regents vs. Roth*, the courts went on to suggest that a discharged employee had the right to know the reason for his or her firing and could demand the procedural right to challenge this reasoning through counsel in a hearing.[8]

This line of decisions has completely transformed the constitutional position of public employees, creating a new context in which personnel administration is conducted. While the rights of employees must be pursued on a case-by-case basis, the following are the outlines of the new direction, in which the courts are playing larger roles in personnel administration:

1. Within broad limits, the public employee, like the ordinary citizen, has the right to freedom of speech. This means that he or she cannot be punished for criticizing superiors. For the government to take actions against such utterances, it will have to demonstrate some compelling reason why the speech should be curtailed.

2. Generally, a public employee can join controversial groups without facing automatic disciplining, as in the past. This can include membership in such organizations as Common Cause or the NAACP, which may be openly critical of the employing agency's policies. Again, should the government desire to discipline a person for such a membership, it would have to be justified if litigation resulted.

3. When an employee is removed or disciplined and this results in an impairment of his or her reputation, or makes it difficult for the employee to take advantage of other employment, a hearing may well be in order in which superior and subordinate would face each other under adversarial circumstances.

4.   Unlike in the past, civil service systems have to use much greater care in penalizing employees whose lifestyle may not be condoned. For example, a person discovered to be homosexual cannot be automatically discharged, or a police officer found to be living with a man or woman cannot be summarily disciplined without proof of the alleged act, that it was in fact immoral—both in general and in connection with the employee's reputation—and that it had an ascertainable and deleterious effect on the efficiency of his or her service.

5.   While the Hatch Act (which forbids public employees from taking an active part in political party activities and campaigns) is constitutional, this prohibition does not extend to nonpartisan activity.[9] Public servants are to remain nonpartisan, but this does not require them to be apolitical.

The implications of these decisions, while still incomplete, suggest that public personnel administrators will have far less policing and punishing authority to regulate employee behavior and will have to turn to other means of inducing compliance.

PUBLIC SECTOR UNIONISM

Because the public service has been thought of as a unique profession, employees perhaps saw it as more of a calling consistent with their ideology and philosophy. It was seldom thought that public service employees would find it necessary to unionize. As we discuss below, the confluence of a number of events helped to change this view. Of the approximately 17 percent of government workers who are unionized, 6 percent work for the federal government and 10 percent work for state and local governments. Unions represent 37 percent of all government workers, representing about a 6 percent decline since the early 1980s.[10]

Beginning in the 1960s, public jobs came under collective bargaining pressure. Public employees began to organize more as a consequence of their sense of power than out of any specific grievances. Executive Order 10988, issued by President John F. Kennedy in 1961, opened the door by giving federal employees the right to bargain collectively. The states soon followed with similar authorizations.

While public sector unionism declined during the early 1980s, the upward climb continued since that period. In the last 25 years, union memberships have soared and the subjects over which bilateral (union and top management) decisions are made have greatly expanded. Currently, one-third of the public workforce is unionized, as against only one-quarter of private sector employees. This staggering growth is due mainly to two factors: (1) The labor movement began after 1960 to shift its attention to service occupations and, hence, primarily to government; and (2) public employees had an accumulation of exploitable grievances against both their agencies and the civil service systems. High on this list were a growing sense of impersonality in government, a feeling that they were being treated as "hired hands," and the belief that, banded together, they could exert considerable pressure to change agency policies.

In 1970, 200,000 Postal Service employees went on strike, and the government bargained with the union (the salary agreements were later ratified by Congress). This example was not lost on other unions and the general public, and it has prompted concerns about (1) the right of public employees to strike; (2) how productivity might be undercut by unionization; (3) the growing political power held by public sector unions; and (4) the conflict between seniority and efforts to achieve equal employment opportunity in government.

Under President Jimmy Carter's Reorganization Plan No. 2, the Federal Labor Relations Authority was created as an independent agency. Its functions were later incorporated into the CSRA. The CSRA attempted to clarify the role of organized labor in the federal government. While federal employees were given the right to organize, they were prohibited from striking and engaging in a work slowdown. The Federal Labor Authority (FLRA) was given the opportunity to use its powers in 1981 when officers of the Professional Association of Air Traffic Controllers (PATCO) authorized a strike. The FLRA decertified PATCO, eliminating the union, and dismissed most of its members.

Should Public Employees Be Permitted To Strike?

Increasingly, the question is an academic one, for public sector strikes are occurring. States like Pennsylvania have authorized a limited right to strike. In public education, particularly, teachers strike with great frequency. Through local government "sick-outs" (where employees en masse call in that they are ill) and slow-downs, collective resistance to the orders of superiors has become quite common. Table 13.1 shows some of the arguments on both sides of the issue.

Productivity

The demand that top management bargain with the union over salaries and working conditions, the unions say, is nothing more than the interested parties working out problems in a bilateral fashion. From the perspective of the American Federation of State, County and Municipal Employees, labor and management simply have different approaches toward responding to the needs of the same demanding public.

Some attention has gone into productivity bargaining, by which is meant an agreement that wage increases will be tied to corresponding increases in productivity. While this approach is appealing in the abstract, it has been difficult to implement because costs are difficult to identify and measure in order to show increases or decreases in productivity.

Demand for Recognition

Public employees demand (1) to be treated with dignity and to participate bilaterally in making personnel-related decisions; (2) support for the expertise of the public workforce (they resist the growing tendency for managers to turn to outside contractors to implement many programs); and (3) that promotions be related more to seniority, with those longest in feeder positions being generally promoted when vacancies occur.

The impact of public sector unionism on personnel systems has been profound. Increasingly, grievance procedures are policed by the unions. The dollar value of the settlements, in wages and fringe benefits became a factor in the 1970s in helping to undermine the financial solvency of cities. There has been, however, a significant decline in political and judicial support for affirmative action as the application and practice of the principle have become quite controversial.

Table 13.1. Pros and Cons on the Right to Strike

Against the Right to Strike	For the Right to Strike
1. It interrupts essential services.	1. Strikes are essential if the parties are to bargain seriously.
2. The state is sovereign and to allow a strike undermines that sovereignty.	2. Much of government service is not essential, and if these functions can sustain strikes in the private sector, then why not in the public arena?
3. Unions are already too strong, and the elected officials they bargain with have to stand for re-election.	3. Unions insist that they are as responsible and as public-interest minded as employers.
4. Only the legislature can raise taxes, but strikes force elected officials to reach agreements that necessitate the raising of additional revenue.	4. If not given the right to strike, it is likely that aggrieved employees will strike anyway.
5. Unions should be restricted because government one day may face the devastating effects of a "general strike."	5. The right to strike gives unions bargaining power. A denial of the right weakens the union's ability to bargain effectively.
6. Working conditions won by unions in bilateral negotiations serve to undermine the whole merit idea.	

AFFIRMATIVE ACTION

A final major issue generating debate in the personnel field comes from the drive by minorities and women to achieve equal employment opportunity in public jobs. Through protest, legislation, and continuing litigation, governments at all levels have been forced to initiate affirmative action plans—that is, to take steps to eliminate employment barriers and to compensate for the effects of past discriminatory practices. Various forms of affirmative action have been consistently sustained by the courts because of continuing evidence of systemic discrimination: the existence of employment practices that have the effect, intended or unintended, of excluding from the workforce minorities, women, and other groups protected under civil rights legislation.

The pressure for affirmative action began in the early 1960s at about the same time that the drive toward public sector unionism was getting under way. It has followed essentially the same course, initially resisted as undercutting merit, then embraced as the essence of merit, and currently claimed as the rights of all—with white males seeking to halt preferential hiring as a denial of their equal opportunity for employment. In the course of this protracted struggle, major changes have been wrought in the personnel function.

To grasp the complexities of affirmative action it is necessary to (1) review how public personnel practice has evolved from a discriminatory posture; (2) understand why the subject is of key importance in personnel administration; and (3) assess current trends in defining the parameters of equal opportunity.

From Discrimination to Equal Employment Opportunity

Systematic discrimination by government against minorities and women is of long-standing concern. It can be traced to the slavery system, where laws prevented blacks and custom prevented women from holding public jobs. Slaves performed much of what is now called public works: They constructed roads, harbors, and bridges; they served in the military; and they maintained sanitation systems. Yet they were neither regarded nor paid as public employees. For the first 200 years of the nation's history, the government firmly enforced an employment policy that made discrimination mandatory.

The first breakthrough into public employment for minorities and women came with the Reconstruction périod following the Civil War. For the first time, blacks and some women entered the public service, primarily in state and local government. Most of these advances occurred in the South, but after little more than a decade the gains were lost with the removal of federal troops in 1876 and the enactment of "Jim Crow" laws in the South. At the national level, the employment of blacks in Washington, D.C., continued to grow slowly, and by the turn of the century their representation in the federal services was proportional to their representation in the population. Women made less progress during this period, perhaps due to the persistence of Victorian chauvinism. With the administrations of William Howard Taft and Woodrow Wilson, however, the policy of restricting the number of blacks in government and segregating those who were employed returned as the national personnel policy. Blacks were prevented from working alongside whites, they could not use the same lunchrooms or toilet facilities, and they were restricted to the lowest-paying public jobs. A condescending protectionism for women forced them into low-level clerical jobs. State and local governments throughout the country followed these practices of systematic discrimination.

From the 1930s to 1961, the policy of the government at all levels supported discriminatory practices in public employment. The rule of three (which allowed appointing officers to select from the three highest scorers on a civil service exam), coupled with the requirement that applicants include a photograph, permitted systematic discrimination. With the threatened protest march on Washington by 100,000 blacks seeking equal employment opportunity, led by A. Philip Randolph in 1941, the federal government reluctantly took the first steps toward ending the denial of employment opportunity to minorities. In Executive Order 8802, President Franklin D. Roosevelt declared that federal policy no longer condoned employment discrimination.

The policy for the period from 1941 to 1960 remained reactive. Employment discrimination was condemned, but little initiative was taken beyond recognition that the problem existed. With the Kennedy administration, a proactive posture was assumed. Through Executive Order 10925, the federal government committed itself to taking affirmative action to root out employment discrimination. The passage of the Civil Rights Act of 1964 added congressional support and established the U.S. Equal Employment Opportunity Commission to administer the government's nondiscrimination policy.

Importance of Affirmative Action to the Personnel Function

The law against discrimination is clear and unequivocal. Title VII of the Civil Rights Act of 1964 as amended states: "Discrimination because of race, color, religion, sex, age, handicap, or national origin in all employment practices including hiring, firing, layoffs, promotion, wages, training, disciplinary action and other terms, privileges, conditions of benefits of employment is prohibited."

The Civil Rights Act of 1964 was passed to protect the rights of racial minorities. Subsequent amendments, executive orders, and administrative regulations extended comparable rights to women, those with Spanish surnames, members of religious groups, those between ages 40 and 65, the physically disabled, and ethnic minorities. Collectively, this group constitutes well over 80 percent of all Americans. In addition, equal employment opportunity reaches beyond ending discrimination toward a goal of diversifying governmental profiles, and it counters the inherent elitism in merit systems (the meritocracy) with the values of a representative public service.

In the late 1990s, the problem is not so much that there are fewer minorities and women in government than whites, although in some city, state, and federal departments that is the case. Blacks constitute 11 percent to 12 percent of the nation's population and have 16 percent of the federal public jobs; women make up 51 percent of the population (40 percent of the workforce) but hold 34 percent of the federal public jobs. A 1973 study showed that black groups made up 18.2 percent of all public employees at the state and local levels. A 1976 survey of 31 of the 50 largest cities concluded that women in the workforce were not employed in top-level jobs to the extent that their numbers would suggest. These overall figures obscure the fact that the employment of women and minorities in government is unevenly distributed across job categories.

The central problem that affirmative action addresses is the concentration of women and minorities in lower-paying, limited-status, and dead-end positions. White males monopolize the positions of power and influence in government. Table 13.2 presents this problem at the level of the federal government, which is by far the most committed to affirmative action. It indicates how poorly minorities and women are represented in the higher levels of the civil service.

Table 13.3 shows myths about women that further illustrate the problem.

A similar set of myths persist about minorities; stereotypes are developed in the attempt to justify discriminatory patterns. Black women, moreover, suffer from both racial and sex-related discrimination. The persistence of patterns that deny equal employment opportunity reflects a larger failure on the part of management to promote an ethical and supportive work environment and to incorporate a human resource development perspective into personnel practices.

Table 13.2. Percentage of Minorities and Women in Selected Federal Pay Grade Ranges

Pay Grades	Minorities	Pay Grades	Women
GS 1-4	28.5	GS 1-6	46.6
5-8	21.1	7-12	23.4
9-11	10.8	13-18	4.5
13-18	6.0		

There are other compelling reasons for equal opportunity programs. For example, minorities and women:

1. Have greater difficulty in entering government at the middle ranges. In career-ladder jobs, they usually have to begin at the bottom.
2. Are largely limited to certain occupations. For example, nearly 40 percent of sanitation work is done by nonwhites, and 7 percent of white-collar women workers are in clerical occupations.
3. Seldom supervise men and have made little progress in moving into managerial positions. They are underrepresented in intellectually demanding jobs. Although 11 percent of all males in the labor force are managers, only 4 percent of all women and less than 1 percent of minorities have similar positions.
4. Work primarily in central cities, at state capitals, or in Washington. That is, the farther removed women and minorities are from headquarters, the fewer are the opportunities available to them.
5. Have upper-level jobs primarily limited to agencies where the clientele is composed largely of women or minorities.
6. Are required by informal pressures to conform to a white and male cultural standard in the conduct of their work.

Table 13.3. Myths and Realities About Work and Women*

Myth	Reality
1. A woman's place is in the home.	1. Homemaking is no longer a full-time job for most women, and half of all women between 28 and 64 are in the workforce.
2. Women work for pin money.	2. Single women average 45 years in the workforce. Half of all working women work because of a pressing economic need.
3. Women have a higher turnover rate.	3. Those off the job for illness or injury average 2.2 per 100 males per month and 2.6 per 100 females, with this difference disappearing when equivalent jobs are compared.
4. Women won't relocate.	4. This is inapplicable to single women, and, increasingly, family patterns are adjusting to life styles that accommodate greater female mobility.
5. Women are not suited for certain kinds of work.	5. There is little evidence to support a difference in manual dexterity. Few jobs require strength and male/female strength profiles largely overlap.
6. Women don't want responsibility on the job.	6. When given the opportunity, women cope with responsibility.
7. Women should not work in unpleasant circumstances.	7. Where there is danger, training is the key, not discrimination.
8. Women take jobs away from men.	8. Most unemployed men are out of work for lack of skill, poor health, or because of the structure of employment.
9. Women prefer male supervisors and men won't work for women.	9. Most supervisor–subordinate conflict is accounted for by reasons other than sex. There is much evidence of successful women supervisors.
10. Women don't want to be promoted.	10. The desire for promotion is tied most closely with the chance for promotion. With equal opportunities there is a corresponding desire for promotion among men and women.

* Data for this chart have been drawn from materials from sources that could not be located by the authors.

7.   Must have better qualifications, more education, and more experience than white males similarly situated to compete successfully for jobs.

Discriminatory practices may exist at virtually every point in the employment process, and these are closely associated with undesirable personnel practices:

1.   *Recruitment.* The passive approach to recruitment or the limiting of efforts to a few prestigious schools must be replaced by a broader search to make sure that all qualified candidates are given an opportunity to apply. Some agencies are now recruiting for the first time at predominantly black and women's institutions.

2.   *Announcements.* Historically, the government has relied on word-of-mouth to make it known that jobs are available. In many jurisdictions, this remains the primary way people learn of vacancies, particularly at middle levels. Because white males predominate at middle-management levels, they tend to monopolize this kind of information. Affirmative action requires that more equitable methods be designed and used to get the best candidates.

3.   *Application forms.* Application forms formerly contained questions that were designed to identify sex and race (including the requirement to submit photographs) as a means for permitting selecting officers to exercise their biases. All such questions and requirements must now be justified as being directly job-related if they are included on the application forms.

        Except for specific job-related reasons, the following categories of information are illegal pre-employment inquiries: country of birth, age, religion, race, organizational affiliation, marital status, and dependent children.

4.   *Testing.* Tests that have been validated only with a white and middle-class population, or that are not shown to be job-related, can no longer be used as a way of excluding women and minorities.

5.   *Interviews.* What has been said about illegal questions on applications extends to interviews. Examples of questions that now must be avoided include:

- Do you mind working with people from other racial groups?
- Will you be taking holidays based on your religious views?
- Do you have to miss work at certain times of the month?
- Is your income supplemental to the household?
- Do you plan to have children in the near future?
- Will your spouse mind if you have to travel on business trips?
- Did you ever receive public assistance?
- Do you enjoy a good Polish joke?
- Are you willing to work for someone younger than you?
- How will you take care of your children while you are working?

All of these discriminatory practices in the recruitment process are illegal because they seriously undercut the employment opportunities of minorities and women. They are also inept management practices. Recruitment should be active, not passive; application forms should be designed to meet the requirements of the job and not to sort out applicants based on social classifications; tests should be validated; and interviewing should address areas relevant to the job to be performed. Selection processes should allow the government to choose from the widest field of qualified candidates. The demand for affirmative action arises increasingly out of the necessity to have greatly improved personnel.

Issues of Quotas and Reverse Discrimination

Litigation has proceeded in two spheres of equal opportunity. The first engages the issue of what constitutes discrimination, and the second deals with quotas, particularly as they relate to public service jobs.

Discrimination once required an overt act, the employer's intention to limit the job opportunities of minorities or women. Until very recently, for example, local fire departments simply would not hire women firefighters. With the *Griggs vs. Duke Power Company* decision, the Supreme Court held that the absence of discriminatory intent does not redeem unemployment procedures that produce unequal results.[11] Employment tests, for example, that minorities or women fail at significantly higher rates than do white males indicate that Title VII has been abridged. In such cases, the burden of proof shifts to the employer to show the necessity for the test in the conduct of the agency's operation. As Chief Justice Warren Berger put it, "The Act [Title VII] prescribes not only overt discrimination but also practices that are fair in form, but discriminatory in operation."[12]

The *Griggs* decision cast a cloud over the open competitive examinations that provide the cornerstone of the civil service system. By implication, it also challenged the validity of academic credentials (e.g., *requirements* that applicants have a high school diploma). *Griggs* forced personnel administrators to defend the validity of their selection procedures. Many practices have since appeared questionable, including all tests that do in fact weed out minorities and women and tests that have no validation. If the test does not predict reliably who will later do well on the job, its uses are in doubt. Validation that is done on white males cannot be used as predictors of how minorities and females may fare. Criteria for "success on the job" must now be spelled out. Beyond efficiency ratings, public sector agencies will have to develop defensible measures of success.

When the selection process produces an adverse impact, it is incumbent upon the agency to demonstrate job-relatedness. If the screening process cannot show a specific relation to job performance, it has to be excluded as a valid criterion for employment selection decisions. The demise of the Professional and Administrative Career Examination (PACE) is an example of a test that could not pass the job-relatedness criterion.

Washington vs. Davis, weakened this position. This case established that some intention to discriminate will have to be "at least inferred from the totality of relevant facts."[13] This has not, however, absolved personnel departments from pushing tests without much knowledge of what the results mean. With the meritocracy idea changing and coming under close scrutiny, attention has shifted to making public resources more representative.

The need to provide public service jobs has raised the issue of affirmative action in a more general way. Black joblessness has become a major national concern and priority. Acknowledging this concern in 1976, Congress passed the Local Public Works Act of 1976 (Public Law 94-447 as amended in 1977), in which 10 percent of the $4 billion appropriated was to be set aside for minority contractors. The purpose of the bill was to create jobs through publicly financed construction, and the amount set aside was to ensure that a portion of these newly created jobs would go to unemployed blacks. The opponents of this type of affirmative action were quick to label this "reverse discrimination," an imposition of invidious "quotas." They have carried this attack on affirmative action to the courts.

A year later the U.S. Supreme Court ruled in the *United Steelworkers of America-AFL-CIO-CLC vs. Weber et al.*, 443, U.S., 193 (1979), upholding a training program that accepted black workers over white workers despite the latter's seniority. The apparent critical factor in this case was that the private organization voluntarily initiated a program to eliminate discrimination, and it did not require the termination of white workers. In 1984, in a very similar case of *Firefighters Local Union 1784 vs. Carl W. Stott et al.*, 467, U.S., 561 (1983), the court ruled that a lower court could not require the discharge or layoff of senior workers in favor of a minority with less seniority simply to preserve a racial percentage. Two decisions rendered in 1987—*United States vs. Paradise*, 480, U.S., 149 (1987) and *Johnson vs. Transportation in Santa Clara County California Agency*, 480, U.S., 616 (1987) echoed essentially the same ruling as in *Firefighters Local Union 1784 vs. Stott*. The view seems to be that no broad interpretation of affirmative action will be permitted. Each case will be decided on its specific merits and context. The Civil Rights Act of 1991 appears to have adapted the conclusion of the *Johnson and U.S. vs. Paradise* cases, indicating that race, color, religion, sex, or national origin cannot be used as a legal ground to make employment decisions. While the act does seem to support affirmative action programs, or selection for hiring and promotion, there is a need to wait for more interpretations of the act in the future.

The most celebrated case that contested affirmative action by labeling it an unconstitutional quota was *The University of California at Davis vs. Allan Bakke*, 438, U.S., 265 (1978).[14] The case involved Bakke's failure to be admitted to the Davis Medical School through its Special Admissions Program, in which 16 positions (out of 100 in each class) were reserved for "disadvantaged racial minorities." Bakke's position, which was staunchly supported by many liberal organizations, urged that to set to one side 16 positions is to establish a quota for minorities that restricts to that degree (by 16 percent) the opportunities of whites. Such a practice, asserted Bakke supporters (subsequently endorsed by the California Supreme Court), is in violation of the equal-protection clause of the U.S. Constitution. The opposing view argued that Davis had the right to set criteria for admission to the medical school on factors other than scores on written tests. They insisted that the Davis mission was, in part, to provide medical care to people who needed it but were not getting it. Minorities, particularly low-income blacks, had an undeniable need for more care, and history had demonstrated that minority physicians were far more responsive to that need.

On the surface, this litigation threatened the nationwide effort to open up our most selective education institutions to more than a token number of those who are not white. Indirectly, however, and far more consequentially, the *Bakke* case threatened the constitutionality of all forms of affirmative action aimed explicitly at helping to overcome the nation's discriminatory barriers confronting minorities and women. At bottom, the issue seems to be whether the public service is to search for "the best"—assuming an unbiased method of making that choice can be found—or to use public employment as an instrument for achieving social justice.

The *Bakke* decision was handed down in 1978 by a sharply divided Supreme Court that issued six separate opinions. The majority position affirmed the essence of both claims: (1) It was ordered that Alan Bakke be admitted to Davis (essentially, that reverse discrimination through the application of unconstitutional and rigid quotas could not be condoned) and (2) that at the same time, however, valid admission criteria could be used to make choices among applicants on a basis other than test scores (essentially, that affirmative action efforts to overcome prior discrimination would be approved). While the conflict between quotas and affirmative action was not fully resolved, it appeared that governments would be required to work affirmatively to overcome long-standing discriminatory patterns against minorities and women—a requirement reiterated in the Civil Service Reform Act of 1978.

In the *Paradise* case, the court reaffirmed the idea that "race-conscious relief" must be narrowly tailored to the problem it is supposed to solve.[15]

CIVIL SERVICE REFORM ACT OF 1978

Criticisms of the merit system and the U.S. Civil Service Commission were made plank issues in Jimmy Carter's 1976 presidential campaign. He promised to reform the federal civil service and to make it more easily understood by people, more responsive to executive leadership, and more efficient. In 1977, he initiated the Personnel Management Project, in which some 1,500 persons (mostly careerists) undertook nearly a year-long study of what should be reformed in the federal personnel system. The results of this study produced two reorganization plans and the president's proposal for reform. With substantial congressional modification, Carter's proposal became law on October 13, 1978, as the Civil Service Reform Act of 1978.

Unexpectedly, the first act of reform was to remove the U.S. Civil Service Commission's authority to enforce laws prohibiting discrimination in employment by federal agencies. That authority, which the Civil Service Commission had exercised since 1964, was given to the U.S. Equal Employment Opportunity Commission (EEOC). The president acknowledged, in Reorganization Plan No. 1 of 1978, that the Civil Service Commission had been ineffective in promoting equal employment opportunity for minorities and women.

President Carter's Reorganization Plan No. 2 called for replacing the Civil Service Commission with an Office of Personnel Management (OPM), which would be the president's personnel arm, and a Merit Systems Protection Board (MSPB), which would hear cases involving alleged merit violations. This dramatic change was justified by reference to the breakdown in merit performance appraisals. Because only a tiny fraction of federal employees had received anything other than favorable appraisals over the years, the service had acquired the reputation for protecting incompetents. By this reorganization, the president signaled his intention to base all annual salary increases, beyond a minimum cost-of-living adjustment, on merit performance.

The passage of the Civil Service Reform Act of 1978 contained many new provisions which are broadly reviewed below:

1. *Title I. Merit System Principles and Prohibited Personnel Practices.* Merit principles are: (1) recruitment, selection, and advancement conducted toward achieving a workforce drawn from all segments of society to ensure equal employment opportunity; (2) fair and equitable treatment in all aspects of personnel management without regard to political affiliation, race, color, religion, national origin, sex, marital status, age, or disability and with proper regard for employees' privacy and constitutional rights; (3) equal pay for work of equal value, modified by incentives for excellence in performance; (4) high standards of integrity by employees, including a concern for the public interest; (5) efficiency and effectiveness in work to be the basis for retention in the service but with training available for employees to improve themselves; (6) protection for employees against political pressures and encouragement for them to make public (whistle-blowing) intra-agency violations of law, mismanagement, or abuse of authority.

    Parallel merit principles are prohibited personnel practices: (1) acts of discrimination; (2) intervention on behalf of an employee under consideration; (3) coercion for political reasons; (4) illegal influencing of any phase of the employment process; (5) nepotism in an agency; (6) exercising reprisal against a "whistle-blower."

2. *Title II. The Federal Personnel System.* The OPM and the MSPB are given statutory basis and authorization is granted for the delegation of personnel management authority to line agencies. The MSPB with its independent Special Counsel beyond hearing appeals serves as a "watchdog" of OPM to ensure that merit principles are maintained and that prohibited practices do not occur.

    A system of performance appraisals is established to serve as the basis of salary increases along with safeguards and appeal rights for those judged to have unacceptable performance.

3. *Title III. Staffing.* Several staffing innovations are authorized including: (1) a volunteer service made up of students who can be given on-the-job experience

without pay: (2) aids to expand opportunities for the disabled; (3) a minority recruitment program to overcome underrepresentation; that is, minority employment below determined levels of their availability. The EEOC is to provide the guidelines for underrepresentation and monitor recruitment results; (4) a temporary ceiling is placed on the number of federal employees not to be exceeded by using contracts, but also not to be a bar to expanding the number of students or disadvantaged youth in government.

4. *Title IV. Senior Executive Service (SES).* A senior service is created to replace the former supergrades. Members of the SES may receive an annual bonus for outstanding performance or other financial awards for distinguished or meritorious service. They are also subject to removal from the SES for unsatisfactory performance.

5. *Title V. Merit Pay.* The principle of pay for performance is established for employees generally with incentive awards and cash payments for useful suggestions available to managers and lower-level employees.

6. *Title V. Research and Demonstration.* The OPM, and to some extent the MSPB, are authorized to initiate research and demonstration projects toward improving the efficiency and effectiveness of the public service.

7. *Title VII. Federal Service Labor-Management Relations.* Congress gave statutory recognition to the right of employees to organize and bargain collectively. Formerly, this right existed only by executive order. A Federal Labor Relations Authority is established to provide leadership in promoting collective bargaining, and to hold hearings on complaints of unfair labor practices. Management rights and the rights and duties of labor organizations are spelled out in detail.

Although passage of the Civil Service Reform Act was regarded as a major legislative accomplishment of the Carter administration, the new system was expected to immediately face difficult implementation problems. In the first place, Congress made many changes to the president's proposals: reducing the leadership role of the OPM, committing the service to equal employment opportunity goals to be monitored by the EEOC, granting increased authority to employee unions, and mandating annual reports of personnel operations to Congress.

Among the duties and functions performed by OPM include:

- External relations, comprising general counsel, congressional relations, and public affairs.
- Internal management, consisting of functions including internal evaluation, equal opportunity, and personnel.
- Labor management relations such as labor liaison and policy leadership.
- Policy analysis, focusing on areas such as interagency advisory groups, policy issues, and research and development.
- Affirmative action such as Hispanic, federal, women, and handicapped.

- Agency relations, including compliance and evaluation, human resources, natural resources, energy, and science.
- Intergovernmental personnel programs, comprising functions such as the presidential management internship programs, merit standards, and faculty fellows.
- Executive personnel and management development, overseeing functions such as the senior executive service, federal Executive Institute, and federal executive development.
- Staffing services including duties such as recruiting, entry and promotional information, test scoring, downsizing efforts, investigations, and student employment programs.
- Compensation, including pay/classification incentive and performance pay guidelines, comparability surveys, and actuarial studies.
- Workforce effectiveness and development, including occupational health, employee relations, performance evaluation, and incentive awards.

Critics of the reform have expressed skepticism about the performance appraisal system, which they doubt can be correlated with increased productivity. Despite these concerns, the Civil Service Reform Act of 1978 was a significant step toward improving the efficiency of government, as it attempted to strike a better balance between management rights and employee protection.

Despite the establishment of the MSPB that was intended to be the bulwark for the protection of civil servants, fears about its ability to protect employees have been raised. The former Executive Director of the Civil Service Commission expressed the view that the legal separation for assessing civil servants' effectiveness and legal compliance still informally reside in OPM which is dominated by political appointees. Without the existence of a bipartisan commission, the MSPB is apt to use the inspection reports put together by the politically controlled OPM.[16]

There is criticism pertaining to CSRA operating theory about human nature. According to Professor Frederick Thayer, CSRA is a clear thinking path of theory.[17] In order for servants to gain, they must take away from fellow servants. Participants are motivated by greed (fear) and fear (punishment). This approach is in sharp contrast to modern management which is characterized by trust, collegiality and teamwork. The CSRA's emphasis on extrinsic motivation is not likely to produce constructive outcomes in the long run.

Comparable Worth

Affirmative action focuses on comparable worth, in which men and women holding jobs that are not identical but demand similar skills and training should receive equal pay. Assume another context in which women teachers dominate elementary teaching. Teacher certification requires at least four years of college and postgraduate and continuing-education training. In contrast, plumbers are paid a great deal more than most teachers with far less training and education. Should the teachers' salaries be increased to meet the average salary of the plumber? In these two cases we have two issues: (1) The first case relates to the call for equal pay for equal work and (2) the second relates to the idea of equal pay for comparable work. The basis for the comparable-worth argument can be traced to Title VII of the Civil Rights Act of 1964 in which discrimination related to sex is forbidden. Additionally, in the Equal Pay Act of 1963, the legal basis for equal pay for equal work language states "on jobs the performance of which requires equal skills, effort and responsibility, and which are performed under similar conditions, should be equally rewarded." These two acts are often considered together but it is usually the Title VII of the Civil Rights Act of 1964 that is used to redress past discrimination practices.

When a women believes that she has been discriminated against because of sex, she must demonstrate to the court that the work she is performing is similar to the work performed by her male counterparts. To the extent that her contention can be proven, the agency is required to show how it is exempted under the Equal Pay Act. This may be done by demonstrating the differences accrued for one or all of the following reasons: (1) the application of the seniority principle; (2) the apparent application of a merit system; (3) earnings based on productivity or a factor unrelated to sex.

A notable case that brought great interest in the comparable-worth debate was the *American Federation of State, County and Municipal Employees (AFSCME) vs. State of Washington.* In 1983 a federal district court held that the state had violated Title VII of the Civil Rights Act for discriminating against its employees on the basis of sex. The state was ordered to award back pay to 15,500 employees in female-dominated positions. Additionally, the state was ordered to speed up the implementation of its comparable-worth plan. A year later, in 1984, the Ninth Circuit Court seemingly took an opposite view in *Spaulding vs. University of Washington,* holding that the university did not violate Title VII despite the fact that it paid workers in its nursing facility (mainly women) lower salaries than workers in male-dominated departments.

In 1985, in an appeal of the 1983 *AFSCME vs. State of Washington* to the Ninth Circuit Court overturned the lower court decision and held that the state did not have to award back pay to 15,500 employees. The court noted that the state was not obligated "to eliminate an economic inequality which it did not create." Subsequently the case was settled out of court involving 60,000 state employees at a cost of $570 million.

The law in comparable worth is still evolving.

PERSONNEL AS HUMAN RESOURCE DEVELOPMENT: THE STRATEGIC ROLE OF MLMS

The rise of unionism, the merit system, the increasing emphasis on finding the best person for the job, affirmative action requirements, and the mounting intervention of the courts into personnel issues have clearly demonstrated the need for fundamental reforms. One of the current emphases is on the development of human resources.

Human Resource Development

What has traditionally been called manpower management has been broadened to include the activities of human resource development (training, motivating systems, development of affirmative action, etc.). These activities have focused on "on the job" workers and have been directed at obtaining the right people for the job at the right time. An early emphasis was put on more aggressive recruitment for both entry and mid-level positions, but it soon became clear that equal attention had to be given to releasing underutilized talent already in the agencies. Human resource development now generally covers the following activities:

1. Planning and forecasting the skills an agency will require and closely monitoring these assessments in the light of changing external conditions and demands.
2. Aggressive recruitment to get a larger share of the best qualified people coupled with efforts to make the public service more attractive.
3. Career planning for each employee (from entry to retirement) in order to use personal abilities to the fullest, thus benefiting both the worker and the organization.
4. Conducting sophisticated training and supervisory practices that will increase skills and add to the worker's motivation to use his or her talents for program ends.
5. Utilization of "organizational development" techniques (planned organizational change using behavioral science techniques) to improve the human climate of public agencies.
6. Management of the total work force (in-house and contract services) as a single resource to be altered in its mix, expanded, or contracted as conditions require.

Increased attention to these concerns has projected personnel administrators more into line-decision roles in top management and has focused attention on the external environment. More recent pressures in the human resources development field have come from increased governmental concerns about the skills necessary to perform effectively in the technologically oriented economy. For instance, training programs have to take into account where jobs will occur and the skills required to perform these jobs. Moreover, the combined civilian workforce of federal, state, and local governments contains approximately 13.5 million persons, or over 16 percent of the total labor force.

Training for government employees remains controversial. Only in recent years has the federal government developed formal training facilities—the Federal Executive Institute, at Charlottesville, Virginia, for "supergrades" and the regional Executive Seminar Centers for middle-level personnel. The bulk of training, particularly at state and local levels, is on the job. It is widely believed that only job-related training is relevant, and broader learning experiences are difficult to justify. Controversy also continues around the content of training, who should get it and for how long, and where the training ought to be conducted. It is worth noting that the Civil Service Reform Act gave high priority to training as integrally related to a productive merit system.

Government is increasingly viewed as an important training ground and the employer of last resort for those who are unable to find employment elsewhere. Most white-collar training is for administrative, professional, technical, or clerical positions; and the government workforce contains about twice as many white-collar jobs as does the private sector. These developments have given personnel administrators the opportunity to play important roles in present and potential resolutions of inequalities found in U.S. society.

STRATEGIC ROLE OF MLMS

The representation of minority groups in government employment has recently become a public concern, but few people have been aware of the strategic role that MLMs can play. MLMs have a major voice in and responsibility for a wide number of actions that have far-reaching effects on the personnel function:

1. Once laws relating to personnel are passed, responsibility for putting them in rules and procedures fall on MLMs. Where the law is vague and unclear, their interpretations, with minimal review, become policy. Where tests are required, they are the ones who construct and administer them.
2. MLMs conduct on-the-job training.
3. Evaluation guidelines for assessing employee performance are carried out at the MLM level.
4. MLMs are responsible for conducting, monitoring, and follow-up reporting on agency-promulgated procedures and regulations.

MLMs' potential for affecting agency personnel policy is thus considerable. This potential lies not in their intricate connections with politicians and interest groups, but in the subtle ways in which they can make changes in the interpretation, implementation, and the evolution of the laws.

DISCUSSION QUESTIONS

1. What are the differences between a merit and a patronage personnel system?
2. What is affirmative action and what are the pros and cons regarding it?
3. How has the rise of collective bargaining affected the public personnel system?
4. Identify the main impediments to political actions by federal civil servants. What are the arguments against these impediments?

NOTES

1.   David T. Stanley, "Whose Merit? How Much?" *Public Administration Review* (September-October 1974): 425.
2.   See the Volcker Commission Report, *Leadership for America: Rebuilding the Public Service* (Lexington, Mass.: Lexington Books, 1989).
3.   Jerome B. McKinney, *Risking a Nation* (Lanham, Md: University Press of America, 1995), Chap. 3.
4.   General Accounting Office, *The Public Service: Issues Affecting Its Quality, Effectiveness, Integrity and Stewardship* (GGD-90-103 Washington, D.C.: General Accounting Office, 1990), p. 15.
5.   Reported in Nicholas Henry, *Public Administration,* 6th edn. (Englewood Cliffs, N.J.: Prentice-Hall, 1995), p. 229.
6.   See Jeffrey L. Katz, "The Slow Death of Political Patronage," *Governing* (April 1991): 58.
7.   274 F. Supp. 75 (1967), p. 91. For greater detail on this topic, see David H. Rosenbloom, "Public Personnel Administration and the Constitution: An Emergent Approach," *Public Administration Review* (January-February 1975): 52–59.
8.   33 L.Ed.2d 548, 577 (1972).
9.   *United Public Workers of America vs. Mitchell*, 330, U.S., 75 (1947).
10.   U.S. Bureau of Census, *Statistical Abstract of the United States*, 1992, p. 422, Table 672.
11.   91 S.Ct. 849 (1971).
12.   Ibid., p. 853.
13.   426 U.S. 229.
14.   *Regents of the University of California vs. Bakke*, 438, U.S., 265, 387 (1978).
15.   John Nalbandian, "The U.S. Supreme Court's 'Consensus' on Affirmative Action," *Public Administrative Review* 49 (January-February 1989): 39.
16.   Bernard Rosen, "Merit and the President's Plan for Changing the Civil Service," *Public Administration Review*, 38 (July/August 1978): 301–304.
17.   Frederick Thayer, "The President's Management 'Reform'" Theory X Triumphant," *Public Administration Review*, 38 (July/August 1978): 309–314.

14

Financial Management

This chapter, which examines the importance and critical role of financial management in public administration, is divided into five sections The first section examines the organization involved in carrying out financial administration. The second discusses revenue raising, or how public funds are obtained. The third evaluates the budget as an instrument for program and policy determination. In the fourth section, the role of the elective and appointive administrators is briefly reviewed. Finally, the crucial role of MLMs in administering controls and maintaining accountability is explored.

LEARNING OBJECTIVES

On completing this chapter, the reader should be able to:

- Organize and sort out the financial functions.
- Understand the critical role that finance plays in the administration of public organizations.
- Realize the importance of determining the role that politics plays in revenue raising and budgeting.
- Defend the meaning of budgeting.
- Clearly distinguish the major types of budget systems in practice today.
- Understand the role and functions of elective and appointive administrators in financial administration.
- Appreciate the important role of the MLM in administering financial controls and maintaining accountability in public organizations.
- Understand the role of the federal chief financial officer (CFO).
- Understand political, economic, and social implications of the national debt.

Financial management is as old as government. It is a critical management function that fuels the engine of public administration, and it is the only function that touches every employee in an organization. Despite the omnipresence of finance, its study is often avoided by students of government. Typical apprehension relates to fear in working with statistics, accounting, and, to a lesser degree, economics. There is often little understanding of how much politics and value judgments pervade the raising and expenditure of public revenue.

In broad terms, financial administration consists of three main concerns: (1) determining fiscal policies, a process in which community or political leaders identify the general programs and authorize appropriations to get them implemented (problems such as employment, taxation, inflation, revenue raising, and borrowing or deficit financing); (2) ensuring accountability, so that public funds are spent honestly and wisely for the purpose duly authorized by the public at large; and (3) providing the required organizational structures and controls to effectively carry out the fiscal duties and responsibilities.[1] In short, it is the process by which a government unit obtains money and the methods employed to effectively control how this money is spent in accomplishing public ends. The major components of the process are taxation (revenue raising), budgeting, accounting, treasury management, purchasing, and auditing. The two most pervasive financial activities are budgeting and accounting. A sound financial management system requires that:

- Tax levies and other charges be collected as economically as possible.
- Money be spent in such a way that it meets the demands of competing claimants and yet maximizes the public interest.
- Programs be executed in an efficient and cost-effective manner.
- Safeguards be provided to ensure that community resources are lawfully used to accomplish public ends.

The financial function permeates every phase of management, as shown in Fig. 14.1. Recognition of the interrelation of everyday management and financial administration is helping it to be viewed, as it should be, within a broader perspective.

The traditional preoccupation of financial administration with control (ensuring that things are done according to laws, rules, and procedures) and with how agencies can most efficiently and honestly conduct their internal administration has been changing at all levels of government, as the discussion in this chapter will demonstrate. Activities such as accounting, purchasing, auditing, and treasury management are still important, but new technology (e.g., computers) and improved training have pushed these concerns into the background, especially at the levels of federal, state, and large local units of government. At the national level, financial management is fully understood only when viewed in a larger setting. Questions related to purchasing and accounting procedures have more relevance as they are linked with national fiscal policy concerning such issues as employment, price stability, and economic growth.   As we move down the levels of the federal system, the financial management perspective narrows, especially in small units of government, where concentration is mainly on narrow accounting controls.

Fig. 14.1. Critical Role of Financial Management

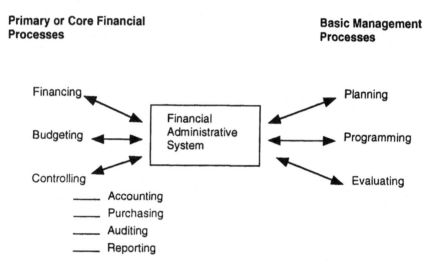

Primary or Core Financial Processes

Financing

Budgeting

Controlling
    _____ Accounting
    _____ Purchasing
    _____ Auditing
    _____ Reporting

Financial Administrative System

Basic Management Processes

Planning

Programming

Evaluating

ORGANIZING FOR FINANCIAL ADMINISTRATION

A continuing concern in the U.S. has been to devise ways to structure financial organizations.   The cultural norms of checks and balances and separation of powers have had significant impact on American models of financial administration. It has long been accepted that honest government can best be achieved by dividing powers among independent officers. This view has led to the election of many fiscal officers at state and local levels, but rarely has this method produced competent and innovative individuals; more often, it has produced decentralized, fragmented, and uncoordinated financial systems.

The financial management process consists of the following components:

1.   *Planning* identifies the goals and objectives that a government unit or agency determines that it will pursue at some specified time in the future.
2.   *Programming* identifies and selects the activities that will achieve the plans outlined in terms of stated goals and objectives.
3.   *Financing* involves securing and raising funds (creating a pool of financial resources) necessary to carry out identified programs and activities.
4.   *Budgeting* requires that plans (long or short range), policies, and priorities be reduced to specific courses of action and that the level of funding be specifically identified within a defined period of time such as the work plan for a one-year period.

5. *Controlling* attempts to ensure that programs and activities are carried out as planned, programmed, and budgeted and that activities are executed according to established work plans. This phase subsumes the accounting function, measuring the activities in monetary terms, recording, ordering, reporting, and analyzing information about financial resources.

6. *Evaluating* measures, tests, and judges the appropriateness, utility, and congruence between the stated and achieved goals. It attempts to assess the extent to which programs and activities that have been properly planned, programmed, budgeted, implemented, and controlled have achieved the stated goals and objectives.

In local governments the decentralized structures vary but are generally characterized by a number of individuals in a governmental agency, headed by an officer either elected or appointed, carrying out the finance activities. Most often one or more individuals other than the chief executive are given supervisory powers over the financial officers but insufficient powers to effect any measurable degree of integration or coordination.[2]

The Chief Financial Officer

The Chief Financial Officers Act (CFO) was passed in 1990 to bring about integration of the financial activities in the federal government. To oversee the financial functions, a deputy director of management reports directly to the Office of Management and Budget (OMB).

There are 23 CFOs that have been established in federal agencies. The CFOs carry a title equivalent to assistant secretary for management and are required to "develop financial management plans and provide annual progress reports to agency heads and Congress. Based on CFO reports, Inspector General (IGs), Treasury Department, and GAO, program managers and private sector inputs," OMB produces a five-year government-wide financial management status report plan.[3]

Three important contributions emanate from the execution of the CFO Act: (1) ongoing improvement and linking of the financial functions with program activities; (2) making audited statements and audit results available to program decision-makers; and (3) carrying out timely audits (though some of the functions of CFOs parallel the IGs, the act attempts to promote complementarity between the two offices).

Even at the national level, in terms of the classical organizational structure, there is decentralization of financial administration. For example, the secretary of the Treasury is responsible for estimating and projecting revenues while the director of the Office of Management and Budget is responsible for estimating and projecting expenditures. Determination of interest rates and the supply of money is vested in the Federal Reserve Board, an independent agency.

Though the decentralized finance model still exists in a number of government units, since the 1880s the pressures of reformers in advocating greater executive control and coordination, the complexity of modern public management, and citizens' demands for swift and more accountable and effective government action have seen a move toward unified or centralized financial structures. A centralized finance organization is one that concentrates the powers to direct and supervise financial officials and all financial activities of the government in one individual, normally appointed by the chief executive officer. Such an organization in a large city conforms to the National Municipal League's recommended model based on the "Model City Charter."[4] The financial functions are centered in a director of finance who is accountable to the city manager. The only function that is excluded is the external audit, which is the direct responsibility of the legislature. Fig. 14.2 shows a typical organization chart for financial management in a large city.

The importance of the budget as an instrument of policy, which will be discussed later, is emphasized when the budget activities are operated as a separate division and the staff is responsible directly to the chief executive, as in the case of the Office of Management and Budget and the cities of Chicago and Fort Worth, Texas.

Integration facilitates more efficient management because the raising and allocation of revenue give rise to major policy issues—who pays what and how much, who gets what, when, and how much. To effectively deal with policy concerns, minimize divided responsibility, and ensure policy execution, financial activities must be planned as an integrated whole.

Lennox L. Moak and Albert M. Hillhouse have suggested three major objectives that should be considered in organizing for financial administration: (1) the establishment of standards of effective leadership; (2) efficiency in the use of resources; and (3) accountability to citizens.[5] When the emphasis is put on effective leadership, due cognizance should be given to the following guidelines:

- A requirement that staff be provided to aid the chief executive in planning financial matters.
- Provision of effective controls to obtain compliance with authorized plans.
- A system of checks and balances to maintain administrative integrity.
- Provision of control over and technical assistance for operating managers.

In pursuing the goal of efficiency the organization should also:

- Provide for specialization and division of labor.
- Group related financial activities together.
- Establish a monitoring and control system.
- Set up "responsibility centers" to permit comparisons between actual performance and predetermined standards.

Fig. 14.2. United Municipal Finance Organization

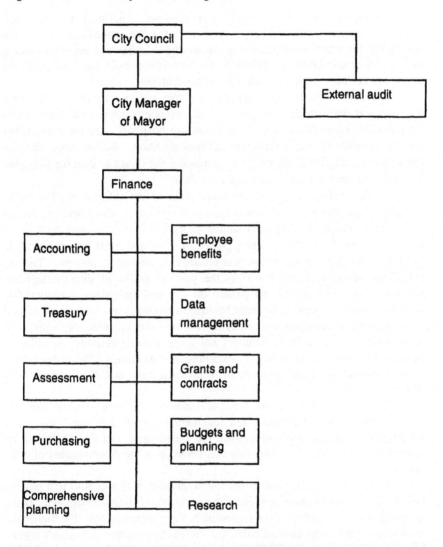

To make the system accountable to the public, the organization must be structured to receive and to respond to citizens' concerns and demands by:

- Providing clear lines of authority to facilitate identification of officers.
- Placing responsibility for and requiring integrated financial reporting.
- Providing an independent post-auditor.
- Giving citizens an opportunity to appeal or seek relief from arbitrary financial rules and regulations.

PUBLIC REVENUE RAISING

Public revenue comes largely from taxation. The most important tax, largely pre-empted by the federal government, is the personal income tax. At the state level, the major sources of revenue are the sales tax and the state income tax. Counties and cities rely primarily on the property tax. Fig. 14.3 gives the major sources of revenue for each level of government.

Revenue sources tend generally to have stable patterns. With some exceptions at the local level of government, revenue is not normally earmarked for particular expenditures such as education or hospitals. For these and other reasons, revenue raising attracts less political attention. Additionally, administrative and political officials prefer to emphasize the things or benefits they give to voters and not what they take away from them.

Undoubtedly, the approval of Proposition 13 in California in 1978 marks a distinct departure from the noncontroversial context in which revenue raising takes place. Proposition 13 (and similar proposals in other states) aims to set legal limits on the revenue raising-power of state and local governments; in California, the local property tax was reduced by almost 50 percent. The so-called tax revolts reflect action on the part of voters to directly legislate accountability. The anti-tax revolt and the demand for greater accountability have forced governments to be more hesitant in raising taxes. They have helped to focus greater attention on satisfying clients' and citizens' demands. The reinvention movement in government has been a direct response to citizens' demand for greater accountability. Vice President Al Gore's NPR at the federal level is attempting to get government to produce more and better results with less.

The setting of the level, type, and amount of taxes involves intricate statistical analysis, but political and judgmental aspects are overriding. The predominance of the qualitative over the quantitative can be illustrated by reference to several critical questions that come up in the determination of a tax policy.

In formulating a tax policy the initial question is that of who will pay the tax. Citizens want to know how fairly the tax burden is being distributed. Is the tax progressive, proportional, or regressive? For progressive tax, the higher the income, the greater the amount collected. When low-income individuals contribute a larger percentage of their income to taxes than do those earning higher salaries, the tax is said to be regressive. For example, a sales tax on necessities such as food is regressive because everyone, regardless of level of income, has to buy food. On the other hand, if the tax is on luxuries, which are primarily purchased by high-income groups, it is more progressive. Where everyone is required to pay the same rate of taxes at any level of income, the tax is said to be proportional. Fig. 14.4 illustrates the three different types of tax rates.

Progressive tax policies have come to be a basic tenet of democratic societies, for they promote greater equity. The choices surrounding who will bear what relative burden thus constitute one political dimension of taxes.

Fig. 14.3. Federal, State, and Local Revenue (percentage of revenue provided)

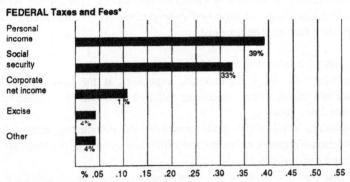

Source: The Budget of the United States Government (Washington, D.C.: Office of Management
and Budget, 1997).
* The federal revenue obtained from borrowing was excluded.

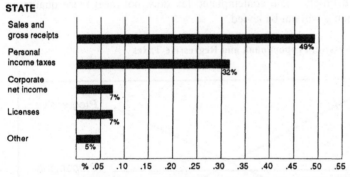

Source: Statistical Abstract of the United States (Washington, D.C.: U.S. Bureau of Statistics,
1995), National Data Book, Table 490.

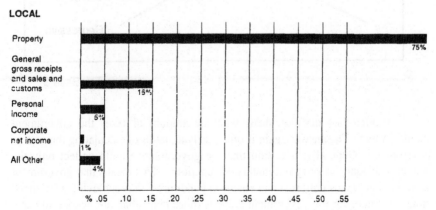

Source: Government Finance (Washington, D.C.: U.S. Department of Commerce, 1990-91),
Summary 7, Table 6.

A second example of the key role of value judgments in making tax policies occurs in response to the questions of when government should enact a new tax and what guidelines or criteria should be considered. The answer goes beyond the simple calculation of proposed expenditures to take into account a number of important factors. The tax must:

- Be equitable (as noted above).
- Contribute to fiscal stabilization, especially at the national level (promote steady prices, minimize inflation, and maintain consumer demand as a whole).
- Encourage productivity and growth while minimizing economic distortions (promote economy and efficiency as well as maintain and expand consumer demand).
- Be simple to administer (e.g., by withholding from payroll checks, as is the case with the income tax).

Note that there are many critical value judgments about what is fair, productive, and timely. If a contemplated tax does not meet these qualitative criteria, it probably will not be levied.

Fig. 14.4. Progressive, Proportional, and Regressive Taxes

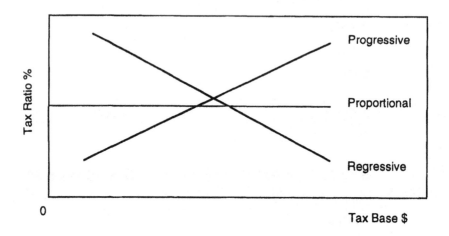

Another key question deals with the amount of taxes the government should collect. The answer again is only partly a matter of calculating the cost of government. Generally, it is said that the government should collect only the amount necessary to carry out mandated functions. This means that government should collect taxes until revenue equals expenditures, thus achieving a balanced budget. Whenever the government collects more taxes than are needed to carry out mandated functions, the excess is taken from the private sector, thereby transferring expenditures from the private individuals to the government. The determination of when and to what extent this should be done depends on judgments about the kind of society we are seeking to build. Table 14.1 broadly compares allocations and objectives of the public and private sectors.

Revenue raising has long been used to gain and maintain political power. The successful career of Peter Flaherty, the former mayor of Pittsburgh, was built on his ability to convey to the residents the idea that he could increase expenditures and yet decrease taxes on wage earners and property. The reductions were minuscule, but they carried potent symbolic impact, enhancing the mayor's ability to gain votes and the belief that he was acting in the public interest. Additionally, Mayor Flaherty often overestimated expenditures while underestimating revenue, thus producing a yearly built-in surplus and political acclaim for his responsible fiscal management.

Table 14.1. Revenue Sources and Allocation in the Public and Private Sectors

Objective and Allocation	Public	Private
Resource allocation	The public economy	The private economy
The means for allocation	The budget	The market
The process for allocation	The political process	The pricing process
Ultimate objective	Meeting people's needs and wants	Meeting private needs and wants

In some jurisdictions, such as the state of Maryland, where the responsibility for estimating taxes was once, until recently, divorced from the Office of the Chief Executive because of state law, the official estimating the taxes was able to use his tax-estimating power to compete with and embarrass the governor. If the governor permitted state agencies to base their budgets on these figures, deficits occurred, creating the damaging image of gubernatorial fiscal irresponsibility.

It should now be evident that revenue raising is a political activity. It is not surprising, therefore, to find that Article 1, Section 8 of the U.S. Constitution expressly gives Congress control over the nation's purse strings. (Congress has the power to collect taxes, to pay debts, and provide for the common defense and general welfare of the United States.) The Constitution further states that "no money will be drawn from the Treasury, but in consequences of appropriation made by law." As we shall see, the determination of taxes and budgeting is deeply immersed in conflict and compromise.

BUDGETING: THE POLICY AND EXPENDITURE PLAN

The idea of modern budgeting grew out of the social and political necessity for sharing power. In exacting the 12th article of the Magna Carta in

1215—"no scrutage or revenue shall be imposed in the kingdom unless by the common Council of the Realm"—the English aristocracy, obtained an important leverage.[6] The original right of the sovereign to exact from all of his subjects had enabled the king to exercise absolute power vis-à-vis other members of the royal establishment. Because finance represented a strategic resource that was vital to the sovereign's administration, establishing a collective and recognized procedure for obtaining resources provided the barons with the means to exact accountability.[7] (They obtained from the king the right to say no to his raising of revenue.)

The development of the budget concept and philosophy was the product of the institutionalization of rules and processes wrested from sovereigns excessively jealous of their prerogatives. The budget in time became the formal instrument guaranteeing accountability and the vehicle for sharing power in the modern democratic state.

Budgeting at first had a narrow meaning. For a long time, the word was used to refer to a leather bag "in which the king's treasurer or finance minister [the chancellor of the exchequer] carried the document explaining the country's needs and resources when he went to parliament."[8] Over time, the budget came to refer not only to the bag but to its contents—the government's financial plan, with supporting statements and accounts.

Because of modern government's pervasiveness in almost every activity of human endeavor, the budget intimately affects our lives, our perspectives, and our fortunes. The actions of the government, mainly through its coercive ability to levy taxes and its right to spend and distribute services, may significantly affect our freedoms, depending on the extent to which it uses its allocative and distributive authority to correct social and economic maladjustments in society.

Budgets involve two sides of the same coin: revenue and expenditure. They aid decisions on revenue and debt policies that allocate expected income among competing public programs. Budgets thus become an instrument for answering the politically sensitive questions indicated earlier: Who will be taxed how much and in what way? A budget links financial resources and human behavior to accomplish policy objectives. It is a legal, political, economic, and social document (see box below). It represents a collective compromise among choices.[9] It is a plan to spend money for specified purposes that takes into account competing claims as to how the money will be spent. A budget expresses the community's preferences in allocating scarce resources. As an economic document, it reflects the allocation of those resources among alternative uses, effectively balancing the needs against resources. The purposes to which expenditures are put may determine if we can find or keep our jobs or if some businesses will make a profit and how much.

As a political and social document, the budget represents the decision-maker's preferences (in monetary terms) as to "who gets what the government has to give." It is political because it is a contest over whose preferences will prevail. All of those whose preferences (influence) count will be represented by an amount. An analysis of these amounts tells us which groups received what benefits or subsidies for welfare, day care, medical relief, or tax relief for senior citizens. When the budget is formulated, it settles, at least for a year, disputes over what programs will be funded and which clients will benefit.

Component Instruments of the Budget

Planning instrument coordinates community resources in an expenditure plan indicating what programs or activities will take place and at what levels.

Political instrument involves competing interests attempting to use the budget to direct public policy favorable to their interests.

Legal instrument authoritatively grants the right, responsibilities, powers, and administrative guidelines that regulate the budget format, timing, and process.

Social instrument used as a vehicle to grant and deny privileges and distribute burdens and benefits to individuals and businesses.

Economic instrument holds powerful potential for affecting the growth and productive capacity of the community and its citizens.

Finally, a good budget is a device to:

- Indicate a specific policy direction for a specific period of time.
- Explicate the proposed expenditure of projected revenue.
- Identify the level of service produced by the projected revenue.
- Serve as control on expenditure.
- Communicate the objectives and standards of performance expected.
- Motivate employees to achieve objectives in their organizational units.
- Monitor and assess the performance of constituent units and programs in providing continuing feedback information on their progress.
- Provide information regarding the impact of a specified level of service on a target population.

As noted earlier, in the United States the strongly held belief in checks and balances, separation of powers, and decentralized and limited government did not permit the budget to develop as an effective executive coordinating instrument. Thus, the idea that the chief elected official (mayor, governor, or president) should prepare the budget is relatively new. Prior to 1910, no level of government gave the budget-making responsibility to the executive. The 1880s reform movement, which sought to overcome corruption in government, advocated restraints on expenditures in order to eliminate waste and misuse of taxpayers' money. Reformers felt that control could be achieved only through making a specific person accountable. State and local governments took the lead, and it was not until the Budgeting Act of 1921 that the national government adopted an integrated budgeting system. (The United States was the last of the major modern industrialized states to make this change.)

THE BUDGETING PROCESS

Budgeting is a dynamic and ongoing process. It is typically viewed as having five phases: (1) planning and priority setting; (2) preparation based on guidelines; (3) legislative review of agency requests and appropriations; (4) execution of approved programs; and (5) post-audit and review of agency expenditures. Each of these phases occurs in a regularly established framework of deadlines, reports, hearings, policy reviews, and work experience and is deeply immersed in politics, as the daily newspapers make vividly clear. Fig. 14.5 conceptualizes the dynamics that take place in budgetmaking.

Fig. 14.5. Budgeting Resource Allocations

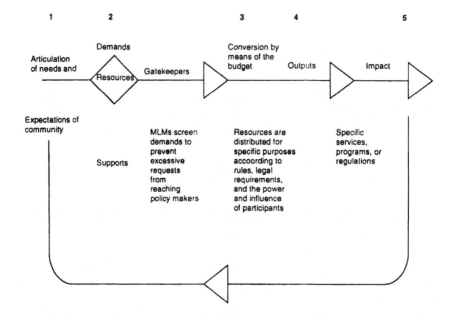

From left to right in Fig. 14.5, five activities are taking place.

1. The community, made up of the general public, clients, constituents, and other relevant groups, expresses its desires about what it wishes government to do or not do.
2. The gatekeepers, or MLMs, receive these requests, compare them with the resources available, and accept, modify, or reject them, based on their perceptions and consultation with top policymakers (executive and/or legislative officials).
3. Policymakers examine the available resources and assess the power and influence of interest groups. Through compromise, the policymakers decide how the resources will be distributed, based on a balance between the maximum number of votes they will get at the next election and what they feel is in the public interest.
4. The decisions regarding allocation of resources become the policy output identifying specific services, programs, or regulations.
5. The impact (benefit and costs) of these services, programs, and regulations on the target population is assessed and fed back into the system.

Most of the push and pull that takes place in budget making centers on maintaining what is. These dynamics are only secondarily concerned with significant changes and innovations. Budgets are like icebergs; the largest portion is beneath the surface. At the national level, the president and Congress do not have a free hand in budget making, for nearly 75 percent of the annual outlay is controlled as a consequence of previous commitments. There are many multiyear commitments that were made to individual programs in the past (e.g., Social Security payments or veterans' benefits) and payments for prior year contracts (for defense or public works, interest payments on the national debts, and general revenue-sharing commitments). This uncontrollable part of the budget has risen from slightly over 50 percent of its total in 1967 to nearly 75 percent in 1996.

At the federal level, an executive budget cycle is as follows:

Spring: Agencies evaluate program issues and policy issues are identified. Planning figures and projections for the coming year are made.

June: Preliminary plans are presented to the president. The Treasury Department projects estimated receipts. The Council of Economic Advisors forecasts the economy.

August: The president, through the Office of Management and Budget, projects budget and fiscal policy. A tentative ceiling on spending is established. The president identifies overall budget objectives.

September-December: OMB reviews agency requests. Final adjustment of receipts and outlays is made.

November: President submits current services budget.

January: President transmits budget to Congress.

The federal budget cycle for the legislature is set forth in the Congressional Budget and Impoundment Act of 1974:

On or before:	Action to be completed:
November 10	President submits current services budget.
15th day after Congress meets	President submits his budget.
March 15	Committees and joint committee submit reports to budget committees.
April 1	Congressional Budget Office submits report to budget committees.
April 15	Budget committees report first concurrent resolution on the budget to their houses.
May 15	Committees report bills and resolutions authorizing new budget authority.
May 15	Congress completes action on first concurrent resolution on the budget.
7th day after Labor Day	Congress completes action on bills and resolutions providing new budget authority and new spending authority.
September 15	Congress completes action on second required concurrent resolution on the budget.
September 25	Congress completes action on reconciliation bill or resolution, or both, implementing second required concurrent resolution.
October 1	Fiscal year begins.[10]

Until the establishment of the Congressional Budget Office (CBO), under the Congressional Budget and Impoundment Act of 1974, uncertainty and chaos surrounded the congressional budget process. The creation of the CBO was an attempt to bring greater rationality into the federal budgetary and fiscal policymaking process through the legislative branch. Before 1974, neither the House of Representatives nor the Senate had any coordinating committee responsible for considering the president's budget proposals as a whole. Budget decisions were fragmented. The executive budget—painstakingly put together—was broken up and parcelled out to the many committees dealing with specific parts. There was no process for considering the total impact that isolated individual actions would have on the economy: "No systematic procedure existed for resolving conflicts among authorizing, appropriations and tax committees on the basis of conscious congressional decisions related to the national goals and priorities."[11] The Congressional Budget and Impoundment Act created a budget committee in both the House and the Senate and charged them with developing overall targets for fiscal policy as well as priorities among budget programs.

The CBO has given Congress a versatile technical staff to aid it in assessing the president's executive budget. Congress can now examine the premises on which the president's budget is built, give its own assessment of the state of the economy, and set its own targets regarding such matters as inflation and unemployment. The act attempts to promote such reforms as controlling "back door spending" by requiring annual appropriations for new loan authority and a number of entitlements. It also limits the president's ability to impound appropriated funds. Finally, it charges the CBO to undertake planning to give Congress a five-year projection of budget expenditures.

TYPES OF BUDGETS

Five general types of budgets are found in use today: traditional or incremental, performance, program, program-planning-budgeting system (PPBS), and zero-base budgeting (ZBB). These five types represent a progression in the techniques of public budgeting. In recent years, rationality has been the overriding concern of academicians and practitioners in financial administration. This is especially true of PPBS and ZBB, both of which were initiated to meet the dissatisfactions with traditional incremental budgeting, which focuses on specific objectives or expenditures with little systematic regard for programmatic priorities and results.

Traditional Incremental Budgeting

Budget changes are made only in small increments at a time. The focus of the decision rule (rules of thumb, benchmarks, or criteria for easily making decisions) is on marginal changes from existing expenditures to proposed expenditures. When an initial amount is given for a program or activity, it becomes the base from which "fair share" increases or decreases will be made. Only the difference between the current year's budget and the proposed budget needs justification. This approach permits policy to continue indefinitely without scrutiny; the past becomes the present and future becomes the projection of the present. The incremental budget is almost totally input- and detail-oriented, emphasizing line items (salaries, equipment, supplies, etc.). This approach tells how much government spends and what it buys but not why. Early budgeting traditionally was aimed at close control, avoiding theft, securing comprehensive and accurate financial statements of expenditures, and preventing various administrative abuses. Because most top administrators obtained their jobs on the basis of political or party affiliation and have limited tenure, line-item budgets provide important means to control MLMs. These have been among the major reasons for the enduring and widespread acceptance of traditional incremental budgeting.

Performance Budgeting

As in incremental budgeting, the existing organization is accepted as a given. Unlike in PPBS and ZBB, no attempt is made at restructuring the organization. The major emphasis is on activities performed. For example, if we are given the program Code Enforcement, the activities would include licensing, building inspection, and so on. Activity identification permits work measurement and workload standards to be determined. The work measurement for building inspection might be the number of inspections made at a specific unit cost and the workload would be a fixed number of units that should have been inspected over a given period of time. Output is expressed almost solely in terms of the work (measurement) units produced: "Thus the selection of the appropriate work unit is a crucial step in measuring performance."[12]

The development of performance budgeting typically involves five main steps:

1.   The work activities (e.g., making inspections, patrolling residential areas, and conducting interviews) must be identified.
2.   The work or output units (e.g., the quantifiable units of things done such as number of inspections made, hours of patrol, and number of interviews conducted) must be identified.
3.   The input units (e.g., miles for traveling and hours for patrolling) must be specified.
4.   The cost per work unit or input unit (cost of resources divided by volume or level of activities) must be established.
5.   The cost per work or output unit is multiplied by the projected workload for the year. If we take the activity of police patrolling and assume that the work units are hours, unit cost is $15.50 and total volume of work is 34,000 hours, total expenditure is calculated as follows:

Activity	Work Unit	Unit Cost	Units Completed	Expenditure
Patrolling	Hours	$15.50	34,000	$527,000

Performance budgeting focuses on the major activities or functions of an agency or government unit. It is concerned with the character and relative performance of work to be done rather than on things to be acquired. Emphasis is put upon workload, outputs (number of miles of road paved, tons of garbage removed, etc.), efficiency or cost of producing a unit of output, minimizing costs, and maximizing output. Thus, work standards must be agreed in advance to match workers' skills with required activities and to facilitate measurement and provide for recordkeeping. The performance budget permits one government unit to compare its accomplishments with those of others undertaking similar functions. However, there are no mechanics for analyzing budget proposals in terms of objectives or ends to be obtained (e.g., safe streets or impacts).

Performance budgeting was designed to focus attention on the performance of the work to be done rather than on things to be acquired. It is output-oriented, organized around objectives or programs to be achieved. Stress is put on programs for which money was allocated. As a principal aid to management, its main emphasis is assessing the efficiency of operating units or the programs government carries out or wants to do. Finally, it is intended to provide greatest assistance to MLMs.

Program Budgeting

Program determination sets the framework in which measurement can be undertaken, as in the above example of code enforcement. Program budgeting embraces a number of performing units or activities. It is useful for reviewing decision-making at or above the departmental level (administrators). It facilitates control of the budget and review by the chief executive and the legislature.

Program budgeting is one step toward the PPBS because it includes one of the main objectives of that system: the examination of program results or output. The approach emphasizes management's perspective rather than the accountant's. The program budget says to the voter, "You indicated a need for a park in this location and this is what it will cost. This is the time it will take to build."[13] However, this approach differs from PPBS mainly because it does not systematically consider alternatives and their long-term cost implication. Additionally, there is little evaluation of output in terms of accomplishment or impact.

Program-Planning-Budgeting System (PPBS)

In this approach, objectives and resources and their interrelationships are taken into account to achieve a coherent whole. Three major concepts underlie the PPBS approach:

- Development in each agency of an analytical capability to examine in depth both agency objectives and the various programs to meet these objectives.
- Formulation of a multiyear (at least five-year) planning and programming process coupled with a sophisticated management information system.
- Creation of an improved budgetary mechanism that can facilitate broad program decisions, translate them into more refined decisions in a budgetary context, and present the results for executive and legislative action.

The PPBS approach is premised on such questions as:

1. What are the basic goals and objectives being sought?
2. What are the alternative means for achieving the stated goals and objectives?
3. What are the comprehensive costs (present, future, and full) of each alternative, in financial and nonfinancial terms?
4. What are the benefits to be achieved from each alternative and how effective will each be in achieving the stated goals and objectives?

PPBS attempts to orient governmental budget-making toward rational planning. The budget is used as a vehicle (1) to set the agenda and goals of government; (2) to decide what will be done; (3) to conceptualize and design programs to achieve these goals; and (4) to devise tools to measure these accomplishments.   Once goals and objectives have been identified, PPBS attempts to allocate resources to achieve the best output, given the resource constraints. Fig. 14.6 shows a simplified schematic model of PPBS.

Priority setting is one of PPBS's greatest assets. As Fig. 14.6 shows, it provides line managers and division supervisors with information that can be used to effectively allocate resources among a number of competing claimants.

Figure 14.6. PPBS Budgeting Model

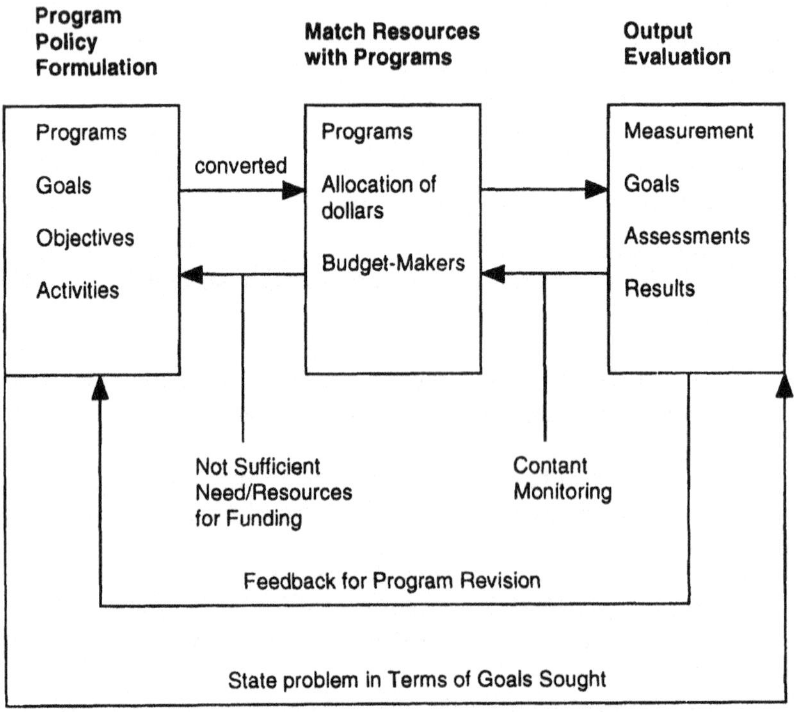

Program Policy Formulation	Match Resources with Programs	Output Evaluation
Programs Goals Objectives Activities	Programs Allocation of dollars Budget-Makers	Measurement Goals Assessments Results

converted

Not Sufficient Need/Resources for Funding

Contant Monitoring

Feedback for Program Revision

State problem in Terms of Goals Sought

Opponents of PPBS hold that this attempt to put the budgeting process on a rational basis has created inevitable problems:

1.   PPBS minimizes politics, on which budgeting greatly depends.
2.   It shifts the emphasis from the line-item control orientation to the program level (for example, from supplies, labor, etc. to total cost for a program).
3.   The sophisticated techniques for pricing services and products will inevitably initiate the decline of the legislator and the generalist administrator to the detriment of public budgeting and the democratic process. The process will eventually become the province of systems analysts, cost-benefit technicians, and mathematical specialists.
4.   Decision-making is "top down" rather than "bottom up" (by MLMs).

Zero-Base Budgeting (ZBB)

Because of considerable dissatisfaction with PPBS, especially at the national level, ZBB has risen to prominence as a tool for allocating scarce public resources. It is hoped that many of the criticisms associated with PPBS will be obviated by this approach. ZBB requires that every item in a proposed budget be justified and approved. Each administrator must demonstrate why he or she should spend money. Moreover, ZBB requires that all decisions be evaluated and ranked in order of importance based on systematic analysis.

While PPBS is concerned with the life span of a program, ZBB is short-term or tactically oriented. It concentrates on one fiscal year at a time. Though it is viewed as a budget system, it should be understood mainly as a rational aid in budget formulation. ZBB operates on the assumption that every cost item included in the budget must be justified each year. Each administrator is assumed to start from $0. This forces administrators to defend every operation under their control. They are expected to evaluate each function in terms of cost and merit of alternative solutions and then to rank each of them with a dollar value.

Several important aspects of the functions and processes of ZBB are:

1. Goals and objectives are clearly set forth.
2. The cost centers or units (known as the decision package) that will perform the activities are identified.
3. The decision-unit managers identify the purposes or goals of each component of work activity(known as the decision   package), indicating alternative ways of achieving them (e.g., contracting out, performing it in-house, or merging the activity with another department); set forth different levels of services, including the minimum level; set the level of service necessary to prevent impairing the integrity of the program or activity; and specify the cost and the benefits related with each level of service.
4. Decision-unit managers rank the packages, as shown in Fig. 14.7, and send them up to the next level, ultimately to the top executive (president, mayor, city manager, etc.).

Because of the appeal of the theoretical presentation of ZBB, it is important to call attention to some of the realities of ZBB systems in practice:

- The pure form of ZBB (as offered above in our discussion) does not exist in practice.
- Implementation appears extraordinarily difficult.
- Instead of the expected zero base, levels of around 80 percent tend to be the starting point.
- Annual review of all programs at a given level of government has also proved too demanding.
- The comparison of levels of spending is customary instead of the

promised examination of alternative ways of achieving program objectives.

- The system for ranking priorities permits a high degree of political judgment to enter the decision-making process.

Figure 14.7. The ZBB Process: An Overview

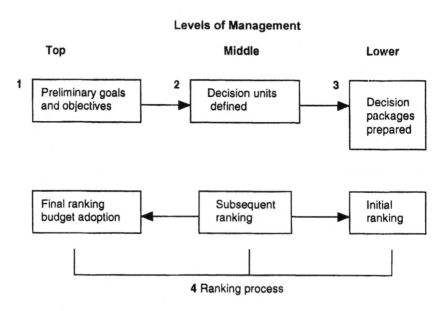

Levels of Management

Top   Middle   Lower

1 Preliminary goals   2 Decision units   3 Decision
   and objectives   defined   packages
                                                prepared

Final ranking   Subsequent   Initial
budget adoption   ranking   ranking

4 Ranking process

Many of the problems that confronted the adoption and practice of PPBS are being faced by ZBB. The latter has many of the attributes of PPBS (for example, it requires highly trained staff capable of performing system analysis, cost-benefit analysis, cost-effectiveness analysis, etc.). The political reality that budgets are compromises of differing values has not sufficiently been recognized. To date, no ZBB system has structured an incentive system to induce MLMs to effectively adopt and operate it.[14] Because of the time constraints and skill required to operate ZBB effectively, few jurisdictions still practices it. Many jurisdictions have reverted to incremental/line-item budget. Some have adopted target-based budgeting (TBB).[15]

Target-Based Budgeting (TBB)

A number of local governments including, Tampa, Florida, Cincinnati, Ohio, and Rochester, New York, have adopted target-based budgeting. Though the first mention of TBB appeared in a 1982 article about its positive application in Cincinnati, only a few articles on it have appeared in the literature.[16] The pressures brought on by the recession during the early 1980s played an important role in producing revenue shortfalls. The event forced budget makers to look for ways to control deficits while maintaining a degree of rationality in budget decision-making. TBB was seen as the instrument to achieve this objective.

TBB requires that budget priorities be made within resource constraints. This process facilitates the collection of information that permits the analysis of target-based funding levels as opposed to the entire budget, as in the case in ZBB: "TBB's executive role in budgets and budget making provides direction earlier in the process rather than later."[17]

TBB decisions are revenue-driven and are required to be made at the lowest level in the organization. At the outset, estimates of revenue inflow are made for the coming fiscal year. These expectations allow the budget official to establish limits on the amounts that departments or responsibility centers may request. Prior to submission of requests to the budget office, requests must be divided into two parts: (1) activities that are permitted within the targeted amount allowed (both for current operating and capital expenditures) that will be funded; and (2) needs that cannot be accommodated within the allowable target but that the responsibility center still desires and new requests. To meet unfunded and new requests (including political priorities), a pool of funds is held in reserve.[18]

The initial target amount for responsibility is not fixed and may change. The stability of the target amounts depend on continuous revenue projections, changed priorities and political expediency. Whatever the total revenue, an amount to permit add-backs is taken out to meet demands for new or expanded activities and to accommodate political priorities.[19] When revenue forecasts fall below levels that permit reasonable add-back amounts and allocation to other priorities, the base budgets in the responsibility centers are cut to permit the generation of the necessary reserve.

There are some arguments for TBB: It does not require rigid budgeting structures. Attention is not focused on the entire budget but on the priorities at the margin. Simplicity characterizes TBB, which allows priority changes without significant analysis. It has been called a zero-based budgeting without a lot of extra work. Despite the central direction of TBB, it allows for autonomy and decentralized decision-making in responsibility centers. The lump-sum targets that the responsibility center managers are given allow them to make tradeoffs between programs and between line-items. The central coordinating role of TBB forces managers to focus on popular high-priority areas such as drugs and crime.

And there are arguments against TBB. There is no link between intended results and budgetary allocations. TBB is totally revenue-driven. Because TBB operates top-down, it forces responsibility managers to accept the target determined by the top. There is a built-in bias for managers to make overall conservative and unwanted revenue estimates. This can lead to premature staff and service cuts that may be politically embarrassing. Assigned targets often involve across-the-board cuts. Because responsibility managers are expected to find resources to meet emerging and unforeseen events such as snow storms or floods, TBB forces them to engage in creative budget padding. The sensitivity of TBB to political priorities carries a negative political potential.

CAPITAL BUDGETS

There has always been a distinction between capital and current operating expenditure budgets. Both types of budgets are used widely in the state and local governments, while the federal government has yet to adopt a capital budget. The current expenditure budget includes all proposed items that are funded for the current fiscal year. It is a budget that contains recurrent expenditures required for use in everyday activities to control and monitor such items as labor, materials, and travel.

Capital budgets contains the programs and cost of large outlays that generate benefits for a number of years. This typically include expenditures for undertakings for infrastructure such as sewage systems, water systems, highways, tunnels, bridges, schools, hospitals, public housing and correctional institutions. Though the federal government does not officially have a capital budget system, it does make numerous capital purchases for domestic and particularly for military purposes, such as bomber fleets, submarines, and Coast Guard centers.

While budgeting for capital expenditures is similar in many ways to the current budget, it has some major differences. Especially at the state and local levels, long-term bonds tend to be the usual way of financing large outlays. The rationale that is given for long-term financing of capital projects is based on the reality that the benefits generated from the outlays will accrue to succeeding generations. Thus it is not unreasonable for them to participate in paying for them.

It is considered irresponsible to engage in long-term borrowing to finance current expenditures. This practice is not only frowned on at the local government level, it typically is forbidden. In contrast, the federal government regularly engages in borrowing to finance current consumption.

Because capital projects normally involves large investments, they are very appealing to politicians who seek to get such projects located in their districts. To minimize this possibility of "pork barrel" (obtaining expenditures that have mainly political benefits and very minimal economic pay-offs) a carefully planned system should be established for identifying, prioritizing, ranking, and selecting projects.[20] To facilitate this process, many government units have established a comprehensive improvement program (CIP). The CIP contains an inventory of projects for several years based on the inputs of many agencies and knowledgeable officials. As each year approaches, the closest year is removed and operationalized into the current budget year and an additional year of projected expenditures is added.

BALANCING THE FEDERAL BUDGET

Concern about the federal deficit (the shortfall between what the government spends and what it takes in) did not rise until the 1980s. The deficit is equal to the total of what government owes in treasury bonds, bills, and notes to American citizens and institutions such as financial, insurance companies, corporations, foreign individuals, foreign governments and banks, and to the federal government itself, as in the Social Security trust fund. Unlike the federal government and states, a balanced budget is not an issue at the local levels, as state constitutions and laws prohibit it. The states that were incurring deficits during the late 1970s and early 1980s have eliminated them. At the federal level, no acceptable solution has been found.

THE POLITICS OF DEFICIT MANAGEMENT

The deficit issue took center stage during the presidential election of 1992 and it played a major role during the 1996 presidential election. In 1994 the Republican's Contract With America emphasized their strong commitment to a balanced budget and played an important role in their winning the majority leadership in the U.S. House of Representatives and the Senate.

Because the deficit has been under control except in periods of war and major economic periods of dislocation such as the Great Depression, political leaders have dealt separately with the spending and the revenue sides of the budget. It was not until the 1974 Budget and Impoundment Act which directed Congress to consider the budget as a whole, that the revenue side and the spending side were formally linked. The act does not allow Congress to take individual action on taxing bills until both houses have agreed to spending and taxing targets. At the same time, Congress is required to specify the surplus or deficit that is appropriate in light of the economic conditions. Congress could not adjourn until it had reconciled overall spending and taxing targets.

Despite the formal requirement of the Budget and Impoundment Act, conservatives were worried that the reconciliation procedures were not working to achieve the intended objectives. In 1985 the Balanced Budget and Emergency Deficit Control Act (popularly known as the Gramm-Rudman-Hollings Bill after the sponsors, Senator Phil Gramm of Texas, Senator Warren Rudman from New Hampshire, and Senator Fritz Hollings of South Carolina). The act specified the amount that the budget would be cut over a six-year period in order to balance it by 1991. If the targeted cuts could not be met, automatic cuts were required, half in defense and half in non-military areas, excluding Social Security. Due to Congress's inability to reach targets, a bill was enacted in 1987 postponing the balanced budget until 1993. Even these amended goals could not be met.

When the threat of automatic budget cuts became eminent in 1990, to avoid cuts in cherished programs, President Bush and the Democratic Congress suspended the automatic cuts until 1994. The 1990 agreement replaced what were previously deficit targets with specific spending limits and mandated cuts in defense and domestic spending. This legislation, like the previous ones, did not work.

When President Clinton took office in 1992, he proposed a five percent down payment on the deficit of $500 billion by cutting expenditures and raising taxes. The fight over the deficit continued in 1996. The Republican-controlled Congress proposed a five-year budget-balancing plan, while the president offered a seven-year plan. With the inability to reach a compromise between the two plans, a stalemate developed over the passage of the 1995–96 budget. Finally in July, 1997, President Clinton and the Republicans agreed to balance the budget by the year 2002. The agreement is based on the assumption that the current prosperity will continue.

Until the post-World War II period, most modern governments ran deficits only in exceptional circumstances, for wars and economic downturns. Such debts were quickly retired after the problems subsided. Surpluses were generated to permit the elimination of debts. This norm changed in most industrial countries as deficits grew in relative size to the gross domestic product or gross money value of goods and services produced. The increase in the U.S. occurred because of increasing expenditures on social programs, welfare, and military expenditures. Political leaders spent more to meet the demands of citizens while failing to require the citizens to pay more taxes.[21]

The federal debt is estimated to be over $5 trillion. In terms of the GDP the deficit has been doubling every ten years for the last forty years. In fact, a greater deficit was incurred during the last fifteen years than during the previous history of the country. The most dramatic growth, approximately $200 billion yearly, occurred during the 1980s. In the 1980s, the rapid increase in the deficit reversed the long gradual decrease in the size of the national debt relative to GDP since the 1920s.

NATIONAL DEBT: TWO PERSPECTIVES

Despite the rising debt, there are strongly opposed views about its implication. Those expressing concern typically articulate the following.

- The national debt relative to GDP is increasing at the fastest rate in America's peacetime history.
- The rise in the national debt during the 1980s paralleled a period of U.S. economic deterioration and was related to the stagnation of private investment. This was caused by government's borrowing for the national debt, which crowded out private investors and kept interest rates high.
- Approximately 30 percent to 40 percent of U.S. debt is now funded from abroad, reducing American control over the economy.
- Borrowed funds have not been spent prudently (e.g., on education,

research and development, infrastructure, and to aid long-term economic growth). Debt funds have been squandered on such non-productive activities as the military, subsidies, bailouts, and failed social programs.

- The holders of the national debt are mainly large banks, financial institutions and wealthy individuals, contributing to increasing inequality in the U.S. [22]

Others are more sanguine about the debt and argue that opponents greatly exaggerate the threat. They put forth the following points:

- If we use the accounting method of private businesses, the national debt will be significantly lower as the government does not recognize assets such as land, building equipment, and natural resources in calculating the national debt.
- The national debt today is no higher relative to the GDP than it was during the late 1940s and early 1950s.
- There is no evidence to suggest "crowding out" has taken place in modern capitalist countries many major nations have large relative national debt, yet they have had no problems maintaining required investment, productivity, and growth during the 1980s. There always is a large quantity of money available for business and individuals to borrow. Unfortunately, businesses did not use it productively.
- More than 80 percent of the interest paid on the national debt goes to Americans.
- Government deficit is required most of the time to spur economic activity when labor and productive capacity are being employed at less than full capacity. U.S. long-term growth and international competitiveness are directly dependent on the deficit to advance critical programs such as education, research, and infrastructure to strengthen the U.S. economy.
- Reduction of the national debt should not be a focal point of U.S. public policy in bad economic times, as this would exacerbate the problem, increasing unemployment and depressing overall economic activity.
- Fred Thayer says that repaid retirement of the debt has typically caused economic instability throughout American history. [23]
- As a percentage of GDP, the nation's debt was smaller in 1994 than among the other Group of Seven nations (Japan, Germany, Canada, France, Britain, and Italy). [24]

CONTROLLING EXPENDITURES

When the budget is returned to the executive, program management and the administrative phase of financial management begin. At this stage, the major focus is on control, which is accomplished through accounting, Treasury management, purchasing, and auditing.

Accounting

This is the most pervasive activity of the control functions; it provides a link between the money that is appropriated and where and how it is used. Appropriated funds are usually recorded and classified on the basis of a code of accounts that may be structured to identify the fund, organizational unit, program, activity, or object of expenditure. The uniform classification of revenue and expenditure permits budget administration, reporting, and post-auditing because it facilitates standard terminology. Every dollar appropriated must be recorded in one of these coded accounts before any expenditure is made; managers pre-audit to see if appropriated amounts are enough to cover expense. It is from these reports that unit cost, performance cost reports, and variance analysis are obtained. Effective budget execution "is based on accurate accounting information respecting the progress of commitment, expenditures, revenue collections, the treasury's cost position and borrowing."[25]

Variance analysis (the difference between budgeted amounts and the actual expenditure) is a key control device used by accounting officials. Normally the amount budgeted is accepted as standard. Table 14.2 shows a simplified version of the variance report.

Table 14.2. Variance Report

City Department: Streets and Roads

Activity	Item	Budgeted Cost	Actual Cost	Variance	Remarks
Street Cleaning	Personnel	$10,500	$10,000	$200 (UF)	Due to overtime
Inspection	Materials	$ 3,200	$ 3,150	$ 50 (F)	Due to increased price
Inspection	Supplies	$ 500	$ 650	$150 (UF)	Due to increased price
	TOTAL	$14,200	$13,800	400 (F)	

F = Favorable
UF = Unfavorable

In summary, the accounting function includes the following main purposes:

- To maintain and strengthen the day-to-day direction of operations.
- To reduce waste and inefficiency.
- To ensure that resources are used in accordance with legislative intent.

Treasury

At the national level, the Treasury function consists mainly of revenue collection, fiscal policy determination, and management of the public debt. At the state and local levels, the function consists mainly of four activities:

- Acceptance and deposit of money.
- Overseeing the custody of funds and the management of the government's portfolio.
- Ensuring proper disbursement of government money.
- Investment of available funds.

The Treasury functions once were completely enmeshed in politics; political groups vied for the power to determine which banks would receive government deposits. For long periods, a few state governments received no interest on their deposits, with this income going to the treasurer. This kind of patronage has now largely ended, with public money being placed in banks on the basis of the services that these institutions, through competitive bidding, offer.

Some political overtones mark the non-revenue-raising tasks performed by treasurers. Some governments have surplus funds that must be invested in short-term notes or certificates. Increasingly, governments also must negotiate short- and long-term loans. In both activities, an element of judgment permits possible political influence.

The assessment and collection of taxes, which once were performed by the treasurer, are now carried out by separate administrative units. This does not mean that politics has been eliminated; rather, it has become more refined and moved to a lower level. The assessment and collection of taxes are the most significant revenue functions that the Treasury performs today in state and local jurisdictions.

Purchasing

Unlike the Treasury functions, purchasing and supply management has increased in importance during the last 25 years. More than half of all public revenue goes toward purchasing supplies and services. The purchasing function can be abused if proper controls and efficient management practices are not successfully implemented. On the other hand, effective procurement can be a significant instrument for enhancing the effectiveness of government service. In addition, it has the potential for reducing costs and effecting savings in all facets of government. The ideal purchasing system is one that obtains goods and services in the right quantity and quality at the time and place and in the manner desired.

In recent years, the trend has been toward centralizing the purchasing function in order to (1) take advantage of bulk purchases; (2) employ competent and qualified personnel; (3) standardize specifications and improve inspection and testing; (4) fix responsibility for irregularities; (5) enhance the financial control system; (6) improve contacts with vendors; and (7) reduce administrative cost and stimulate competitive bidding. At the federal level, the General Services Administration (GSA) regulates the policies and procedures on federal purchases and supply management.

In recent years selected government units and nonprofit organizations, especially medical-related organizations, have been experimenting with just-in-time (JIT) inventories. The approach was developed and popularized in Japan. It permits the organization to order items only as they are needed. The system minimizes storage costs and record keeping and maintains up-to-date inventories.

Auditing

The final control over public expenditures occurs through the audit. Auditors, therefore, are not merely keepers of books and accounts; their main duties are to examine accounts and books of others and to relate expenditures to program outcomes. There are two types of auditors: internal auditors, who look at the daily operations and examine proposed expenditures, and outside ones (usually post auditors), who examine the records after the fact through selected samples of expenditure documents as they relate to program objectives.[26]

The audit function has expanded and taken on added significance in recent years. In the General Accounting Office's (GAO) Audit Guide to State and Local Governments, the comptroller required that the audit of a program, function, activity, or organization include (1) an examination of financial transactions and reports, including an evaluation of compliance with applicable laws and regulations; (2) a review of the efficiency and economy in the use of resources; and (3) a determination of whether the desired results were effectively achieved. The auditing of this range of concerns requires not only traditional accounting but extensive evaluation techniques such as operations research and systems analysis.

As an arm of Congress, the GAO has been used increasingly to aid that body in evaluating governmental programs and organizations. Beginning in 1950, the GAO was given responsibility for setting up accounting and internal control systems throughout the federal government. This authority was expanded by the Congressional Budget and Impoundment Control Act of 1974, which reiterated that GAO's primary function is to assist Congress in evaluating federal programs.

Through its own initiatives, including public relations and its very effective analysis of public programs, GAO has become one of the most acclaimed and feared agencies in the federal government as well as a model that state and local governments, to varying degrees, attempt to copy. Because of its dominant role in public program evaluation, "it is becoming a resource for information about the state of the art in analysis and evaluation."[27]

Though the GAO is considered a neutral agency, it can show its political side, intentionally or unintentionally. In the 1976 presidential debates, the GAO released prior to the foreign policy debate a sensitive report critical of President Ford's handling of the Mayaguez incident. This event illustrates the inevitable political consequences associated with the selection of agencies for audit and the release or withholding of findings.

ADMINISTRATORS AND FINANCIAL ADMINISTRATION

Much of the reform movement attempting to make government accountable to the people has focused on modifying the American cultural belief that multiplying checks and balances ensure honesty and effectiveness. This approach led to highly fragmented executive leadership. Recently, the greatest effort and resources have been directed at pulling together the dispersed financial functions and creating a centralized organization for financial administration. As a result, the powers of the disparate offices have been consolidated in the hands of one executive or administrator (in the case of the city manager). Advocates of the unified financial model believe that it allows greater accountability precisely because it centers responsibility in the hands of a specific individual whom citizens can hold responsible for what is or is not achieved.

The cornerstone of the unified financial model is the executive budget, which has come to be a most powerful instrument for maintaining a high degree of coordination in the face of counter-forces striving for autonomy in public organizations. At all levels of government, the budget is unparalleled in the control that it exercises over agencies. This is especially significant in view of the fact that more than 75 percent of executive recommendations at the state and federal levels of government and more than 90 percent at the local levels are accepted with minimal changes by the legislature.[28] The budget has become the administrator's chief means for (1) identifying the community's needs and problems; (2) establishing a system of priorities for dealing with them; (3) pulling resources together from within and from other sources, federal, state, or both; (4) matching available resources and allocating them on the basis of established priorities; (5) instituting a system of control to ensure that budget priorities are realized; (6) attempting to gain the "biggest bang for the buck" (by establishing performance and cost-reduction criteria whenever possible); and (7) helping to change and direct or redirect the mission of the agency more with the going trend—that is, where the federal and state governments are putting their money or resources. (This is especially important for nonprofit organizations.)

If administrators strive to realize all of the above goals, especially the first six, accountability to the community can be assured. As we have seen, however, much of what administrators do is affected by the many interest groups operating in the environment. Administrators do not operate in a vacuum. They must constantly weigh and compromise and, it is hoped, act in such a way that benefits accrue to all parties. This is never an easy task because the administrator almost always has an interest in obtaining votes (if elected) or maintaining security (if appointed). He or she must keep the public interest in mind while satisfying advocates' interests. As Robert Finley, a former town manager of Mount Lebanon, Pennsylvania, has said, the administrator must strive to "satisfy the disgruntled without disgruntling the satisfied."

MLMS: FINANCIAL ADMINISTRATION AND ACCOUNTABILITY

If the goals of top management are to be achieved effectively, or at all, the participation of the MLM is essential. As we look back, it is clear that MLMs play critical roles at every phase of the financial management system. In the preparation of revenue estimates, top management depends on information generated by technicians or operating officials who do the actual forecasting. The strategic people who scrutinize what gets in—and what expenditures are approved—are budget analysts. Similarly, management of investments, the operation of purchasing systems, and the host of accountants and auditors are MLMs. MLMs constitute two distinct groups in financial administration—both line and staff positions. They are staff in the planning and preparation and line in the implementation of programs. As staff personnel, they are responsible for providing the planning options administrators consider in developing the mission and direction of the organization. They are ideally suited for this role because they act as gatekeepers for the executives, filtering demands of clients and constituencies that must be dealt with through the allocation of budgetary resources. This allows MLMs to determine what claims get considered by administrators and ultimately the legislators. MLMs thus critically influence what government does, because most of what administrators recommend is authorized.

It is important to understand the MLM personnel responsibility for the preparation of the budget. In the informal give-and-take between budget controllers and the budget makers (mainly line officials), a number of decision rules have been developed at the national and, especially, at the local levels. Rules for preparing and submitting a budget include the following:

1.   Avoid asking for sums smaller than the current appropriation.

2.   Use the basic budget for money needed to minimally carry on existing functions. Reserve new requests for highly desired or priority items whenever possible.
3.   Make all desired increases look small, appearing to grow out of existing operations. Never give the appearance of a fundamental change.
4.   Leave the reviewers something to cut.

RULES FOR BUDGET REVIEWS

1.   Decrease or cut out all requests for new personnel.
2.   Suggest repairs or renovations of facilities rather than their replacement.
3.   Avoid whenever possible cutting safety or health-related requests or programs that have high public support.
4.   Cut departments that have a poor image or a bad reputation.
5.   Decrease or cut all nonoperating costs by a fixed percentage.[29]

MLMs are responsible for maintaining and evaluating the financial process to see that the planned objectives are achieved. In day-to-day activity, it is the line MLMs who exercise the critical role of seeing that administrative objectives are implemented. They are the ones who must keep abreast of variances from budget standards. They are the ones who must communicate what the budget ultimately says. They are the ones who must motivate personnel to achieve administrators' goals, who must prepare and implement all budgets, and who must explain to personnel why the budget allocated only 2 percent for salary increases rather than 10 percent. It is therefore obvious that the financial administration function cannot be effectively carried out without the aid of MLMs. They exercise a critical and influential role that cannot be discharged in the public interest if they are not continuously mindful of the mutuality of individual interests and those of the public.

The quest for accountability is endemic in financial management systems. The establishment of line-item budgets and the creation of purchasing and auditing routines were prompted by the need to prevent the manipulation of government resources for personal gain. It should also be noted that financial management systems now extend beyond fiscal monitoring to include analysis of program activities and the assessment of the impact of government programs on society. PPBS and ZBB, in particular, look more at effectiveness (outcomes) than at securing resources through sophisticated record keeping. Despite this extension, however, it should also be clear from this chapter that the operation of all financial management systems is in the hands of an increasing army of middle- and lower-level officials who actually collect the information, keep the ledgers, and explain what that data mean to their superiors. In short, it is increasingly clear that much power still operates outside the surveillance of superiors, making accountability dependent on the value systems of individual MLMs. On a larger stage, moreover, increasingly accountability means not just honesty but also a capacity to increase the effectiveness of the government in the exercise of programs undertaken.

DISCUSSION QUESTIONS

1.   Why is financial management intimately related to an organization's structure?
2.   In the modern democratic state, why was the development of the budget so closely tied to questions of accountability?
3.   Discuss why revenue raising, though critical in determining who will bear the burden of taxes, tends to be less political than budget making.
4.   Discuss why the budget can be viewed as a political, economic, and social document.
5.   Why does ZBB face some of the same problems that plagued the implementation of PPBS?
6.   Obtain a budget from your local government and identify and discuss its social, political, and economic implications.
7.   What are the implications of the increasing national debt?
8.   What are the role and function of the federal CFOs?

NOTES

1.   John M. Pfiffner and Robert Presthus, *Public Administration*, 5th edn. (New York: Ronald Press, 1967), p. 351.
2.   Lennox L. Moak and Albert M. Hillhouse, *Local Government Finance* (Chicago: Municipal Finance Officers Association, 1975), p. 26.
3.   Jerome B. McKinney, *Effective Financial Management in Public and Nonprofit Agencies*, 2nd edn. (Westport, Conn.: Quorum Books, 1995), pp. 4–7.
4.   International City Managers Association, *Municipal Administration*, 6th edn. (Chicago: International City Managers Association, 1962).
5.   Moak and Hillhouse, *Local Government Finance*, pp. 29–30.
6.   Quoted in William F. Willoughby et al., *Financial Administration* (New York: D. Appleton, 1922), p. 29.
7.   E. L. Normanton, *The Accountability and Audit of Governments* (New York: Frederick A. Praeger, 1966), p. 4.
8.   William F. Willoughby, *Encyclopedia of Social Sciences* (New York: Macmillan, 1930), p. 39.
9.   Aaron Wildavsky, *The New Politics of the Budgeting Process* (Glenview, Ill.: Scott Foresman and Company, 1987), pp. 1–3.
10.   Public Law 93-344 (July 12, 1974). Quoted in Albert C. Hyde and Jay M. Shafritz, eds., *Government Budgeting: Theory, Process, Politics* (Oak Park, Ill.: Moore Publishing, 1978), pp. 344–372.
11.   Committee on Economic Development, *The New Congressional Budget Process and the Economy* (New York: Committee on Economic Development, 1975), p. 2.
12.   Allen Schick, *Budget Innovations in the States* (Washington, D.C.: Brookings Institution, 1971), p. 47.
13.   Marshall E. Dimock and Gladys Ogden Dimock, *Public Administration*, 4th edn. (New York: Holt, Reinhart, and Winston, 1969), p. 534.
14.   Jerome B. McKinney, *ZBB Promise and Reality* (Chicago, Ill.: Public Policy Press, 1979), pp. 111–12.

15. Thomas W. Wenz and Ann P. Nolan, "Budgeting for the Future: Target Base Budgeting," *Public Budgeting and Finance*, 2, No. 2 (Summer 1982): 80.

16. Robert K. Goetz, "Target-Based Budgeting and Adaptations to Fiscal Uncertainty," *Public Productivity and Management Review*, 16, No. 4 (Summer 1993): 426.

17. Irene S. Rubin, "Budgeting for our Times: Target Base Budgeting," *Public Budgeting and Finance* 3, (Fall 1991): 5.

18. Ibid.

19. McKinney, *Effective Financial Management*, Chap. 12.

20. Paul Masson and Michael Mussa, "Long-Term Tendencies in Budget Deficits and Debt," Symposium sponsored by the Federal Bank of Kansas City, Jackson Hole, Wyoming, August 31-September 2, 1995.

21. Benjamin Friedman, *Day of Reckoning: The Consequences of American Economic Policy Under Reagan and After* (New York: Random House, 1988), p. 272.

22. Ibid.

23. Frederick Thayer, "Do Balanced Budgets Cause Depression?," *Social Policy* 25, No. 3 (Summer, 1995): 49–55.

24. Robert Heilbroner and Peter Bernstein, *The Debt and the Deficit: False Alarm/Real Possibilities* (New York: Norton, 1989), Chap. 1–4.

25. Moak and Hillhouse, *Local Government Finance*, p. 343.

26. While post-auditing traditionally monitors the legal regularity of expenditures, more recent developments emphasize judgments about what the public received for the resources expended.

27. Statement of Elmer B. Staats, comptroller general of the United States, to the Joint Committee on Congressional Operations on Efforts to Strengthen Congressional Information and Analysis Capabilities, 92nd Congress, First Session, June 19, 1974, (Washington, D.C.: Government Printing Office), p. 4.

28. McKinney, *Effective Financial Management*, pp. 227–29.

29. Thomas J. Anton, *The Politics of State Expenditure in Illinois* (Urban, Ill.: University of Illinois Press, 1966), pp. 6–51; and Aaron Wildavsky, *Budgeting* (Boston: Little, Brown, 1975), p. 124.

15

Productivity and Evaluation

This chapter provides a brief overview of the practices and methods employed in evaluating public programs. Six main sections have been included. The first examines the meaning, process, and distinguishing characteristics of evaluation. The second discusses the context in which program evaluation takes place. The next demonstrates the links between program evaluation and productivity. The fourth section examines some of the problems that evaluators must recognize if they hope to minimize the pitfalls in public program evaluation. The fifth discusses the role of top administrators and shows the kind of leadership that they need to exercise. Finally, we examine the critical role of MLMs in facilitating or impeding evaluation.

LEARNING OBJECTIVES

On completing this chapter, the reader should be able to:

- Define evaluation and productivity.
- Outline the evaluation process.
- Understand how evaluation improves the quality of public decision-making.
- Appreciate the difficulties inherent in conducting public-program evaluation.
- Link evaluation and productivity.
- Distinguish the roles of participants in the evaluation process.
- Design a simple program evaluation model.
- Understand how evaluation can be used to maintain power and achieve accountability.

Evaluation has emerged as a logical progression of public organization theory associated with productivity. From the 1880s to the 1950s, reformers and writers in the field of public administration concentrated on questions of efficiency, which they saw as a means for reducing taxes (due to retrenchment in expenditures) and "boss rule," countering graft and corruption, and promoting more responsible government. Writers such as Gulick and Urwick viewed efficiency as the greatest good in administration, a view that conforms closely to basic American mores.[1] Behavior that wastes resources is generally thought irrational, if not immoral.[2]

The reformers at first naively believed that the path to efficiency lay in electing "good men to office." The election of the good men, however, has failed to produce that result. The emphasis on simply changing politicians shifted in the latter part of the 1880s to reforming structures, methods, and procedures. According to William H. Allen: "Inefficiency of government is primarily due to badness of methods of men. Efforts to correct misgovernment have too frequently failed, or have had only passing success, because men not methods were changed or attacked."[3] This new concern was instrumental in getting governmental jurisdictions to set up commissions on economy, efficiency, and reorganizations to improve government operations. The major effort at the national level took place in 1910, with the establishment of the Taft Economy and Efficiency Commission. After this came the first (1945) and second Hoover commissions (1955), as well as many little Hoover commissions at the state and local levels.

It was early accepted that efficiency meant spending less to gain more—a definition based on an economic criterion. Thus, efficiency was obtained by minimizing inputs while maximizing outputs. It was also assumed that there was one best way to carry out a given task or activity. This preoccupation with the internal aspects of administration paid virtually no attention to the negative and positive impacts of programs but emphasized only rules, procedures, and compliance.

Today, clients, constituents, and the public at large are concerned not only with how much government spends (inputs), what it buys, how much service it provides (outputs), or how well or productively (efficiently) it implements a program; they are also concerned with what impact was achieved (effectiveness, including sustainability). This orientation contrasts sharply with traditional thinking, which emphasized inputs (labor, materials, and equipment), and not outputs (things produced or service provided).

The stress on inputs, a carryover from traditional thinking that is still widely practiced, has created an unfortunate and pervasive outlook on government spending, especially at the state and local levels. It has assumed what has come to be called the spending service cliché, which equates increased service expenditure with automatic increases in services/goods output. For example, as the per pupil expenditure on education increases, it is assumed that the quality and effectiveness of the educational system are automatically improved. This reasoning has been called into question because citizens have seen vast sums of money spent on programs that simply do not work, such as the Great Society programs in education and health, President Nixon's massive expenditure on anti-crime programs administered by the Law Enforcement Assistance Administration, and the large Clinton administration expenditures on crime. It is not enough for administrators to simply say that they have built X number of miles of highway. Citizens demand that they speak about comparative impacts on community residents and the environment that the building of the road created.

The cry everywhere today is to have a government that provides "more for less. " The implied belief is that "Big Government" can be responsible and accountable only if efficacy and efficiency are improved. This is one of the guiding principles of the tax revolt advocates. To achieve greater public sector effectiveness and productivity, government has been following the lead of private business by downsizing, decentralizing, adopting total quality management (TQM), and reengineering (see Chapter 3).

As this chapter later shows, productivity and program evaluation or evaluative research are intertwined in public sector management. Productivity may be viewed as a way of achieving efficiency. It means using resources (inputs such as labor, supplies, etc.) to produce specific goods or services (outputs such as client service, loans processed, miles of road paved). In summary, productivity is the achievement of the highest performance with the least utilization of resources. Productivity is linked into the management operating system as shown in Fig. 15.1. Efficiency is achieved only when the cost and/or units of resources used are reduced. Thus, the greater the number of outputs compared with inputs, the greater is the efficiency. Since productivity is a comparative indicator, to determine how productive we have been we compare one period's output with that of a succeeding one.

Fig. 15.1. Linking Inputs with Outputs

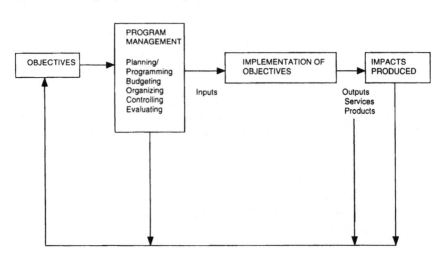

In 1970, because of the expressed interest in measuring public sector productivity, President Nixon appointed a task force that led to the creation of the National Commission on Productivity, evolving later into the National Center for Productivity and Quality of Working Life. The federal effort was instrumental in providing incentives that fostered the development of twelve productivity centers or institutes in the states. Because of lack of political support, the National Center for Productivity and Quality of Working Life folded in 1978. The functions of the center were transferred to the Center for Productive Management, which later because the National Center for Public Productivity, and currently serves as a national clearinghouse for public productivity studies for all levels of government.

Prior to and during the dismantling of the National Center for Productivity and Quality of Working Life, efforts were being made to integrate productivity and program evaluation into federal agencies. The 1974 Congressional Budget and Impoundment Control Act required the General Accounting Office to "develop and recommend to Congress methods of reviewing and evaluating of Government programs."[4] The program evaluation function is carried out in GAO's Division of Program Evaluation and Methodology.[5]

Evaluation is inextricably linked to productivity. While productivity emphasizes the matching of units of inputs to units of outputs, evaluation typically stresses qualitative dimensions—impact, effectiveness, timeliness, satisfaction, and possibly sustainability (extended time period over which impact lasts in producing desired change). The General Accounting Office describes program evaluation as "a way of bringing to public decisionmakers the available knowledge about a problem, about the relative effectiveness of past strategies for addressing or reducing that problem, and about the observed effectiveness of particular programs."[6]

PRIVATIZATION AND PRODUCTIVITY

Both Presidents Reagan (1982) and Clinton (1993) appointed commissions to examine how best government can perform its functions to enhance the effective delivery of public goods and services. In both instances the leading figures, J. Peter Grace, former head of the G. W. R. Grace company, and Vice President Al Gore focused attention on the methods and techniques that the public sector could adapt from private business. Peter Grace headed President Reagan's Private Sector Survey on Cost Control (known as the Grace Commission), focusing attention on minimizing fraud, waste, and abuse in government. Al Gore directed the efforts of the National Performance Review Commission (known as the NPR or the Gore Commission on Reinventing Government) producing a document, *Creating a Government that Works Better and Costs Less*. Gore's efforts were subsequently complemented by a Congressional Government Performance Act of 1993.

The Grace Commission was highly critical of federal government performance. It recommended a number of actions that, if implemented, would save the federal government approximately $424.4 billion.[7] The NPR report (see Chapter 3) echoed the view that government was too costly and that better systems, measurements, evaluations, prioritizations, delegations, and decentralizations could bring about a transformed and responsive government.[8]

Since the demise of Zero-Based Budgeting (ZBB) and the Planning, Programming, and Budgeting System (PPBS), there has been little emphasis linking goals and objectives with program results. The GPRA's purpose is to "provide for the establishment, testing and evaluation of strategic planning and performance measurements in the federal government and for other purposes."[9] By 1999, the act requires explicit links between stated expected results and achieved and budgeted expenditure results. All federal programs must develop systems to show how planned results and outcome measures are linked.[10]

Privatization

The momentum for privatization, or contracting out public services, was given renewed life with the election of President Reagan. Chief motivating factors behind the privatization movement have been a conservative ideological orientation and the belief that it is a potent means for enhancing productivity. The underlying view is that privatization allows government to achieve efficiency while permitting private businesses to benefit handsomely with lucrative contracts in delivering public goods and services. The efficiency generated by privatization would produce savings that could be directed toward the reducing the deficit.

The effort to make government productive during the Reagan presidency began in 1982 with Reform 88, which was initiated by the president's Council on Management Improvement. The initiative attempted to incorporate productivity goals within the basic functions of government as a means of making "the bureaucracy perform like the corporation."[11] To speed privatization efforts, OMB modified its circular A-76 on "Performance of Commercial Activities." The Grace Commission, which published its report in 1984, provided an extensive rationale to support its recommendations to discontinue many federal programs while strongly suggesting that greater use be made of private sector companies to more efficiently deliver many public sector services.

While the zeal for privatization abated somewhat under President Bill Clinton, the privatization movement is alive and well. *Creating A Government That Works Better and Costs Less*, known as the Gore Report, embraced the Gaebler and Osborne reinventing movement, which calls for significant privatization in an effort to promote efficiency and customer satisfaction. The reinventing theme has been gaining converts at state and local levels of government.

The public is concerned about the efficacy and cost of government programs but they are unwilling to pay more taxes to realize the best outcome. Citizens are saying that the tradition of carrying on services or programs simply because they have been initiated no longer provides a justification for continuance. Stress is now put on both the quantitative and qualitative aspects; the public wants to know if the program is worth the cost and if administrators are doing what they are supposed to do, producing identifiable and acceptable results. Legislative and executive officials want to know how priorities should be established and revenues allocated and the potential pay-off they can expect. It is generally believed that evaluation can provide information that can improve management decisions and performance because it makes us mindful of the past and aware of the present and provides us with insights into future decisions.

Three modes of analysis have typically been used to assess social programs. The first consists of an individual or group evaluation based on personal objectives and values. This has been and still is the most widely used approach to analysis, though it is being replaced gradually by more formal ones. In the second mode, programs are evaluated on the basis of a consultant's expert knowledge. The third mode employs the scientific approach, using canons and values established by rational methods.

DEFINING PROGRAM EVALUATION

Program evaluation aims to obtain valid, verifiable data on the structures, processes, outputs, and impacts of programs. Such information enables managers to initiate program improvement and achieve accountability.[12] Program evaluation is capable of responding to concerns such as the desired level of a particular objective to be achieved, alternative ways of achieving the objective, the resources required to realize the objective, potential obstacles to the implementation of the objective, and associated costs of eliminating the obstacles to the objective. This definition allows for the assessment of impact and attention to internal operations such as procedures and staffing.

Evaluation attempts to assess program accomplishments (outputs) in terms of planned accomplishments (objectives or standards). The focus is on results: Program performance is measured in terms of its impact on citizens and clients. Evaluation seeks to tell us the extent to which a particular program has changed the condition of targeted population groups and the community. Information is gathered, and what the program was supposed to do (objectives) is compared with what it did in fact achieve (output and impact). In essence, program evaluation serves as a learning device: Past performance is used as an aid for improving future performance. The positive or negative information generated assists managers in making resource allocation decisions.[13] In addition, it should permit policy officials to determine whether a program is continued as is, expanded, reduced, or eliminated.

Fig. 15.1 also shows that those responsible for program management play a significant role in the success or failure of most program evaluation. Assume the objective was to reduce assaults in public parks and streets. The following steps would be involved:

1.   Program managers accept a reduction in assaults of 40 percent as a realistic figure, if greater enforcement of the crime code is achieved.

2.   Budgets are prepared and funds are authorized to hire more security officers (inputs) to assist enforcement of the crime code.
3.   Security officers are trained and assigned (implementation).
4.   Because of the program, 1,800 additional arrests are made (program performance).
5.   A reduction of 35 percent of assaults (impact) is recorded following the program implementation.

Different Types of Program Evaluation

A distinction is made between two basic types: the summative and formative approached. Summative evaluations are attempts to assess the impact of a program after the program has been implemented. In the formative approach, the program assessment is made while the program is being implemented, allowing for adjustments and improvements to occur on an ongoing basis.

EVALUATION PROCESS

The evaluation process includes four main phases: selection, execution, reporting and communication of results, and recommendation and implementation of findings.[14]   Among the reasons a program may be selected for evaluation are the following: (1) poor operating results compared with expectations; (2) information needed for improvement; (3) interest in transferring a successful program elsewhere; (4) a new technology; (5) evaluation as a routine; (6) funding source requirement; (7) to determine if program needs are being satisfied; (8) to gain program support; (9) to justify past and projected expenditures; and (10) to provide accountability to clients and the community.

The execution phase requires that the evaluation be conducted in accordance with the canons, values, and guidelines established by the scientific community. In program evaluation, this normally involves (1) determination of explicit measurable objectives, clearly setting forth the level of planned program performance; and (2) establishment and design of procedures to organize and analyze data.

Reporting and communication of results provide feedback to decision-makers. This phase is critical because it contains an assessment or critique of the procedures and evaluation process. The way the information and critique are presented may spell the difference between acceptance and rejection by program managers (MLMs). Additionally, as James Coleman has noted, many evaluations are not accepted because of the differing orientations and perspectives of practitioners and evaluators.[15] Often, the MLM criterion for acceptance is usefulness, while the evaluator is concerned with symmetry and validity in this context. Evaluators tend to minimize the fact that evaluation has political implications, and it is only one of many inputs that enter the MLM decision-making process.[16]

Although recommendation and implementation is a crucial stage, there is little guidance to assist evaluators in their recommendations. Because this stage deals with suggestions for alternative policy responses, it requires political acumen. This skill is indispensable because the evaluation of social programs is inherently political. There are proponents and opponents of the programs. Program managers are by no means neutral observers; thus, when evaluation results diverge or fail to mesh with the political motives of MLMs, the chances for rejection are greatly increased.

USEFUL DISTINCTIONS IN EVALUATION

There are a number of concepts and types of analysis useful to management in evaluating public programs.

Program impact indicators are directly expressed or implied in program objectives. Program impact relates directly to public social needs or policies by indicating what the program is supposed to accomplish in terms of public policies (for example, an irrigation dam is intended to increase earnings).

Output efficiency relates to a level of economic performance in which resource inputs (skills, money, and materials) are measured and directly compared with of resource outputs (things produced and/or benefits provided) achieved.

Operations indicators are measures of output activities. Most often they are nonfinancial expressions of an agency's products or services. These may include miles of highway built during a given period, number of automobile licenses issued, or the number of clients visited by a welfare worker. Generally these figures are merely statistics and indicate neither efficiency nor effectiveness.

Effectiveness measures achievement against social or performance goals. Because it is normally difficult to quantify this measure, it is often expressed in qualitative terms. For example, a recreation program may use effectiveness criteria such as citizens' attitude about worth or measures of crowding in a facility.

Compliance control emphasizes the monitoring that is carried out to determine how well administrative regulations and legislative intent are being achieved.

Strategy evaluation assesses the strength and efficacy of the strategies employed in delivering particular goods and services.

Factor analysis assesses options prior to any decision being made about undertaking a new program.

Sustainability analysis, while somewhat akin to front-end analysis, tends to be more encompassing. Sustainability evaluation is prospective. It seeks to determine not only the cost and benefit of each policy or program undertaking, but how the proposed impact of the proposed action will change or enable the target individuals or groups, making them independent over an extended period.

Meta-evaluation is a retrospective approach that involves reanalysis of past evaluation findings to determine what lessons were learned from the past. It integrates and synthesizes a number of findings aimed at highlighting the aspects contributing to the problem and the factors enhancing the effectiveness of the program in achieving the objective.

Productivity auditing consists of monitoring and evaluating organizational practices to determine whether functional units, programs, or organizations are applying their resources efficiently and effectively to accomplish articulated or implied objectives. Where objectives are not being realized, productivity auditing pinpoints and recommends actions to correct or eliminate the identified shortcomings and system deficiencies. Productivity auditing is typically used to: (1) continue or discontinue an organization, a function, or a program; (2) allocate resources among competing organizations, functions, and programs; and (3) improve practices and procedures among competing organizations, functions, and programs.

Productivity studies traditionally focus more on implementation and efficiency as opposed to accomplishment and effectiveness (see the discussion on linking evaluation and productivity below for a more recent and broader focus). Examples include increasing the number of clients visited by a social worker (without examining the impact that increased visits have on clients) or increasing the number of miles of highway roads built (without examining the impact on residents).

Policy issue or program analysis attempts to identify important problems being faced by an agency or government. It is a systematic examination of alternative ways of reaching specified public objectives. It is prospective (as opposed to evaluation, which is done after the fact) in that it estimates future cost, effectiveness, and all relevant impacts associated with each alternative. This approach helps legislative and executive officials allocate limited resources to continue or modify an existing program or adopt new ones.

Monitoring is an ongoing control mechanism that assesses the ability of a system to run as planned. At the federal level, this function is usually carried out by audit agencies and includes site visits, checking expenditure documentation, examining indicators such as staff–client ratios, unit cost for a given activity, and so on.

Financial auditing is often referred to as regularity or compliance accountability. It is primarily concerned with fiscal operations to see if expenditures were properly made, correctly recorded, and reported, and whether program operations were efficiently conducted. Since the late 1960s, financial auditing has also begun to report on program measures and accomplishments. It should be a significant aid to program evaluation in the future.

Policy research is initiated most often by executives, administrators, and legislative officials and seldom by program managers. It is concerned not with correct programs, but with the options for future actions. Like evaluation, it is initiated because of the inadequacy of existing programs. Additionally, it requires an assessment of need. Policy research aims at a major change of direction, such as in an energy program or health insurance.

THE ENVIRONMENT OF PROGRAM EVALUATION

Social programs are enacted to meet particular demands and needs articulated by individuals and groups. Thus, every social program can be traced to an interplay of forces attempting to further particular interests. The community or government policy that initiates social programs indicates who will have needs attended to and who will have to wait. These decisions involve value choices; they confer, enhance, or modify power relationships.

A major objective of evaluation is to determine whether to maintain, modify, expand, or discontinue programs. Because these programs were set up to confer advantages, evaluation may be used to change existing power relationships by increasing or decreasing resources (funds, money, positions, and staff) supporting the programs.

We must be aware of the motives and the values of those requesting evaluation. Administrators and MLMs sometimes wish to have programs evaluated for personal reasons, to improve their chances of organizational survival. For example, as Andie L. Knutson has shown: (1) evaluation may be the "in thing to do;" (2) it may be a means of attracting favorable attention in order to obtain bigger budgets; or (3) it may be a way to obtain a promotion.[17] Additionally, it is not uncommon to find specific groups or persons requesting evaluation because they have particular objectives.

The motives held by those seeking the evaluation will often influence (1) the kind of program selected for evaluation; (2) the kind of assumptions presented to the evaluator; and (3) the judgment that will be made in measuring the degree of program effectiveness.[18] If the motives of the administrators or MLMs are ignored, this may hinder their acceptance of the results.

When program evaluation has the ultimate effect of redistributing resources, it also changes the power equation among groups and individuals. This conclusion has been amply demonstrated in school district consolidations.[19] Where proposed consolidation shows that existing power relations will be left in place, the chance for change is greatly increased. However, in cases such as the Braddock School District of Allegheny County, Pennsylvania, where unification meant a change in power relations, it became extremely difficult to effect consolidation.

LINKING EVALUATION AND PRODUCTIVITY

Measurement and Productivity

Productivity can be effectively managed only when productivity measurements are carefully identified for each process in the primary goal of the organization. When a medical intern is forced to deal with a profusely bleeding accident victim he or she needs to know the highest measured productivity within seconds to stop the bleeding and to save a life. Budget officials analyzing contract vendors' performance require productivity measurements in order to have standards or indicators to assess responsiveness to correct or avoid cost overruns. If performance and resources cannot be measured, the organization's process must be changed or redesigned to enable measurement. Productivity consists of two critical components: a ratio of some measure of input to output.

The productivity index or ratio measures how well expended resources accomplish articulated and agreed objectives. The goals of the MLM involve mobilizing resources and knowledge to encourage productivity and growth. This means establishing standards or measurement ratios that can be used to assess and compare progress and achievement. The following guidelines are suggested in developing ratios:

1.   Use only ratios that have demonstrated validity for the organization or the responsibility center.
2.   Develop ratios at the designing stage of the work processes.
3.   Always quantify measures and objectives to tell how much and what is needed.
4.   Always focus measures on output of the process.
5.   Use ratios that are organization-specific (not macro-economy level) to ensure maximum usefulness.

When developing productivity indexes, it is useful to use fully established categories. The first may be referred to as the overall indexes that measure the final outputs of the organization as a whole. The second consists of the objective ratios that measure the accomplishments of individual MLMs, responsibility centers, or departments. Third are cost ratios that measure performance output in terms of costs. The fourth emphasizes work standards that measure work units or the work produced by individual responsibility centers compared with typical standards in similar organizations. Fifth, time standard ratios measure performance output as compared with expected required time. The formula that is to be used is:

$$Productivity = \frac{Productivity,\ current\ year\ x\ 100}{Productivity,\ cost\ year}$$

At the basis of the valuation is the concern for increasing the productivity of public programs. Productivity may be understood as a ratio of outputs (goods and services produced) to inputs (money, materials, and labor). To improve productivity requires that outputs increase while using equal or fewer units of inputs. Productivity is not a synonym for working harder but working smarter. Thus, productivity is a measure of how wisely limited resources are used. It encompasses quality as well as quantity and effectiveness as well as efficiency.

By the latter we mean carrying out a program at minimal costs as represented by the formula:

$$Efficiency = \frac{Outputs \; (narrow \; view \; of \; productivity)}{Inputs}$$

But the narrow concept of efficiency in public sector programs is often inadequate to signify the output produced (for example, miles of street paved or number of inspections made) because the factor of effectiveness is not addressed. Effectiveness emphasizes impact, adequacy, and performance. By emphasizing the result or impact factor, productivity is seen as a ratio of outputs to inputs compared to or matched with standards or goals (desired results). This may be represented by the formula:

$$Productivity = \frac{Outputs \; obtained}{Inputs \; expended} + \frac{Performance \; achieved}{Resources \; consumed} = \frac{Effectiveness}{Efficiency}$$

Both efficiency and effectiveness may be examined more closely. Efficiency focuses on unit cost, work measurement, and productivity measurement (increases or decreases between a prior period and the present). Efficiency leads to resource utilizations (minimizing the use of input resources). Effectiveness stresses performance—the congruence between planned and achieved goals and objectives—and may ideally, include service quality, indicating timeliness and convenience of delivery and adequacy (to what extent an identified need is met). Effectiveness leads to performance (results and possibly to sustainability). Fig. 15.2 shows how productivity systems operate in an organization.

An understanding of the relationship between evaluation and productivity has much to offer those interested in assessing program performance. When data about social programs are hard to obtain or questions of measurement are difficult to resolve, we are obliged to settle for operations indicators (statistics about work completed) or surrogates (something in place of the final outcome or effectiveness). For example, it may not be possible for a health officer to determine a specific relationship between an immunization program and the subsequent incidence of children's communicable diseases. It would, however, be possible to count the number of children vaccinated. Because vaccination is a significant contribution to children's health, "we can use the number of vaccinations or percentage of children vaccinated as a surrogate or proxy measure for the change in health conditions."[20]

When we examine the different types of program evaluation, as suggested by Edward Suchman, the link between program evaluation and productivity becomes clear.[21] In attempting to say something about program operations, we need two broad kinds of information, the first in inputs or efforts that a program expends (known as evaluation of efforts). The inputs/efforts are composed of

Fig. 15.2. University Department of Security (Police)

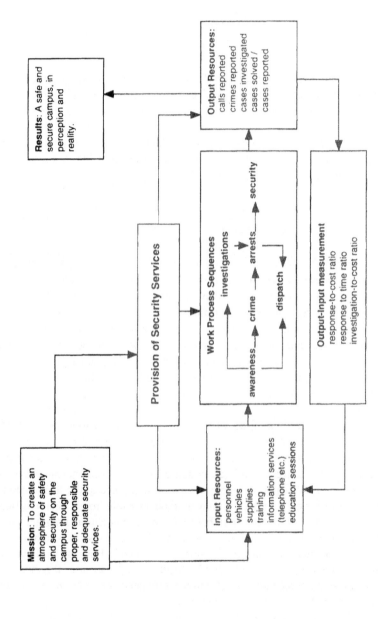

Source: Adapted from Karen Lee Jewell in Jerome McKinney's *Class in Public Sector Productivity*. University of Pittsburgh, PA. September 1992.

operating expenses (also known as applied cost). The second requires that we know something about accomplishment. This requires that we measure the benefits or results of the efforts expended, which permits us to match effort and accomplishment and shows their complementary nature. The effort generated is schematically shown in Fig. 15.3.

Fig. 15.3. Effort as Input

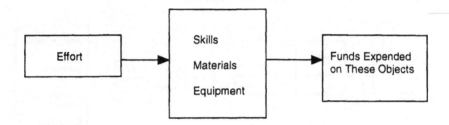

Evaluation of performance (work completed/products produced, or outputs) shows the amount or level of activity that the efforts generated. Indicators would include the number of tickets issued, number of students taught, number of meals prepared, or number of miles of highway constructed. This schema would resemble Fig. 15.4.

Fig. 15.4. Linking Effort to Work Completed

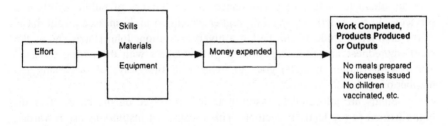

Evaluation of impact is the degree to which performance (effectiveness) is sufficient to meet the total need. It attempts to assess the extent to which clients have changed as a result of a program. Examples include the number of clients successfully treated, the impact that students have on the society as a result of their education, the number of cases cleared and successfully prosecuted. The schema would resemble Fig. 15.5.

Evaluation of efficiency is concerned with the alternative methods of achieving a specified result. It is concerned with whether the same result can be achieved at a lower cost. It examines the ratio between the efforts expended (inputs) and the impact achieved (effectiveness). The smaller the ratio of resources expended (effort) to results achieved (effectiveness), the greater is the productivity (less effort for more results). Such ratios could be cost per mile of streets built or resurfaced, student-teacher ratios, patient-nurse ratios, and so on. By examining these indicators, we can get an idea of "the efficiency with which resources are being used as well as an indication of workload."[22]

Fig. 15.5. Linking Effort to Impact/Sustainability

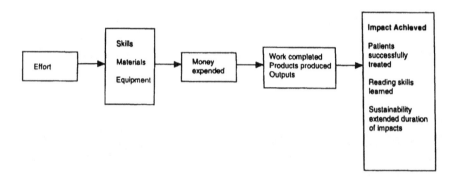

Evaluation of process, though not "an inherent part of evaluative research," permits management to analyze the "whys" of the success or failure of a program and allows a program to be modified "so that it will work instead of being discarded."[23]

It should now be obvious that no single type of evaluation will typically give an adequate picture of performance in the delivery of public goods and services. In the practice of funding higher education in Tennessee on the basis of the number of students enrolled at a given institution, John Harris shows the short-sightedness and preoccupation of policymakers with the wrong things.[24] The reward (larger budgets) goes to those who find ways of increasing the number of students.

Funds are allocated to institutions in Tennessee on the basis of credit hours earned (a productivity factor). This means that institutions are rewarded for the quantity of efforts and not necessarily for quality in achieving the institution's mission or goal. The pressure to obtain earned credit hours creates laxity in admissions and academic standards (especially where there are no restrictions on entering college). The criterion for successful funding, based on earned credit hours, provides the incentive to set up as many degree programs as possible to attract a wide range of students. Thus, there is a proliferation of new programs rather than improvement of existing ones. The result of all of this is increasing mediocrity, the institution's failure to achieve its mission or goal.

Instructors are not rewarded for student achievement, for it is accepted that high-quality achievement is produced in every program. Yet Harris points out: "Studies show that the major differences in the accomplishment of graduates of institutions is due more to the type of student an institution admits than to what it does to or with the student."[25]

The above discussion clearly shows how emphasis can be misplaced and goals distorted when the interrelationships among efforts (inputs), work completed (outputs), and impact (effectiveness) are misunderstood. In this case, an institution's budget is determined by the credit hours earned (work completed), which is equated both with productivity and effectiveness with no analysis to determine if the criterion is the appropriate one.   The process produces maldistribution of available resources and distorts the policy objectives of the state, agency, and community.

The link between productivity and evaluation should now be clear. Effort is the one element that provides the common denominator in all levels of evaluation. Effort (inputs) is compared with work completed (outputs) and with effectiveness (impact).

IMPEDIMENTS TO EVALUATION

Conflict in Perspective

Too often the evaluator and practitioners (administrators and MLMs) operate under entirely different assumptions and orientations, which inevitably creates tension and pressure. Barriers to communication are created, making it difficult for practitioners to accept suggestions.[26]   Evaluators are generally trained too narrowly in psychology instead of having a broad background in a number of fields, such as anthropology, cost accounting, philosophy, and the content area for which the evaluation is being conducted.

The evaluator sees the job as conducting an objective study according to his or her discipline and the canons of scientific inquiry. The practitioners, however (usually MLMs), often refuse to accept the evaluators' suggestions unless they are of practical use.

Purpose of Programs Unclear

Typically, the evaluator of the effectiveness of social programs encounters:

- The absence of a statement of objectives.
- Objectives that are too broadly stated.
- Unrealistic or unachievable objectives.
- Partial or inaccurate statements of objectives.[27]

Joseph Wholey has indicated that, at the federal level, objectives of social programs are not normally set forth and the criteria for measuring them (effectiveness) are seldom fully considered.[28]

Lack of Political Perception

Many evaluators do not recognize that evaluations are essentially political acts. The fact that programs are hammered out through a political process means that compromises are inevitably made before many programs are given life. The ideal or the best possible program seldom emerges. Many programs are never initiated to cure problems in their entirety but to have only incremental effects. The federal act to provide equal treatment for the disabled provides a good example.

The law granted sweeping rights and benefits, requiring virtually every place or program receiving federal funds to make special dispensations to accommodate the disabled. The officials (MLMs) who have been responsible for administering the law call it a nightmare. One MLM in the Pittsburgh area said: "This law is so frustrating; it promises so much yet there is little or no enforcement authority to implement it and really help the handicapped." One congressman who voted for the law commented off the record: "It was a great thing that the law was enacted the way it was because it would have been a bigger nightmare if it were given strict enforcement power."

Unclear Roles and Problems of Measuring

The evaluator and managers seldom attempt to clarify each other's purposes and objectives. Many managers believe that the uniqueness of their programs makes them resistant to measurement. But, say Harry Hatry et al., although there are substantial limitations to what can be measured, "at least partial and practical means are available for measuring impact (of almost any program) and new methods are being developed."[29]

The Problems of Skill and Motivation

Especially at the state and local levels of government, the skills and resources required to undertake evaluation are often not available. Business and public administration schools are now beginning to offer courses on productivity and evaluation.

Research Methodology

Two methods are normally employed in conducting evaluation research—experimental and quasi-experimental. The classic method is experimental; it employs a projection of what should have been the outcome based on a theory about normal performance. Actual results are then compared with expected results. Typically, the experiment includes comparing the performance of an unknown group with a group whose performance is known in advance (see Fig. 15.6).

The program is said to have an effect on the experimental group (B_2-B_1) and not be responsible for any effect on the control group (A_1-A_2). The total effect due to the program is the difference between the experimental group and the control group or $(B_2-B_1) - (A_2-A_1)$.   Before any conclusion is drawn, attention should be directed to certain problems.

Fig. 15.6. Experimental and Control Group in Randomized Allocation of Participants

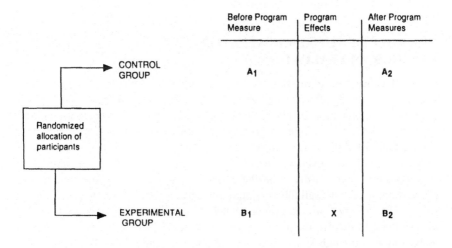

The fact that some individuals are given treatment and some are not creates questions of ethics and accountability for administrators and MLMs. Many believe their evaluation actions may be depriving individuals of important and proper services. This type of conduct runs counter to the public service philosophy, which espouses the view that services should be available to all. For example, a welfare department may wish to test the nutritive value of certain prepared meals for shut-ins. To include some and leave others out may create agonizing concerns.

Concern about experimental designs have not been confined to administrators and MLMs. Congress felt so strongly about the experimental use of schoolchildren that it prohibited the use of randomization as a basis of determining who will participate in the Secondary Education and Assistance Act of 1965. Parents, especially of schoolchildren, do not want their offspring to be used as guinea pigs.

When experimental designs are not possible, quasi-experimental designs may be tried. Here, repeated measurements are taken over a period of time before and after the introduction of a program to two similar groups. This approach has its problems, too. Where equivalent groups are used, the closer their characteristics, the greater is the likelihood that the effects of the program may not be identifiable.[30]

The reverse, or nonequivalent group, approach may also be attempted where both pre- and post-tests are given. In this application, the differing characteristics may be so great that the impact due to the program may not be distinguishable. The comparison made between police traffic-ticket writing in Boston and Dallas in Chapter 2 provides a good example of the problem of attempting to employ nonequivalent groups. In that comparison it was seen that although Dallas had the same approximate population as Boston, Dallas issued about two and a half times more tickets.

THE ROLE OF TOP ADMINISTRATORS
IN PROGRAM EVALUATION

Because top administrators play an important role in initiating broad agency policy and influence budgeting, they can be an important force in the acceptance or rejection of innovations such as evaluation. Administrators are concerned with such major budgetary questions as whether the government should fund 800,000 or 1.5 million new jobs; whether 70 percent or 80 percent of parity should be given to farmers to maintain a given level of purchasing power vis-à-vis other workers in the country. Additionally, administrators are responsible for the overall functioning of the agency.

The administrator is accountable for the failures of the agency and is always there to receive the accolades for its success. He or she is the goodwill ambassador to the public and provides the political leadership. This means that he or she sets the environment in which evaluation will take place. To ensure success, he or she must give the support of his or her office to new evaluation units and see to it that the evaluation staff has ready access to his or her office.

Administrators have the responsibility to:

- Evaluate the progress of the agency periodically.[31]
- Promote the climate in which evaluation takes place.
- Encourage efforts by providing sufficient resources and seeking the cooperation of various groups in this endeavor.
- Discuss and use the evaluation findings.

Because of evaluation, the relative newness of its political context, and its potential for creating change, especially at the MLM level, top-management support is crucial to its survival. Where MLMs can use their power of implementation to scuttle or frustrate evaluation recommendations, administrative power and influence can be a positive force to make evaluation work.

THE ROLE OF MLMS AND ACCOUNTABILITY IN EVALUATION

Perhaps the greatest need for accountability in evaluating public programs is required at the MLM level, because managers are expected to implement recommendations that affect their programs directly. MLMs also have the opportunity to select program results that reflect favorably on their programs. This means that MLMs exercise considerable influence in program evaluation. They can decide what portion of an evaluator's report they like and have the power to determine how and to what degree the recommendations will be implemented.

As noted in Fig. 15.1, program evaluation is a management function. Thus from the inception of a program to the determination of its impact, MLMs play an important role. They are responsible for developing program objectives and performance indicators that will be important inputs in guiding evaluators. Additionally, they are expected to monitor the activities of evaluators as the evaluation progresses.

MLMs therefore exercise strategic if not determining control over the ultimate success of program evaluation. This means that MLMs exercise considerable power in public program evaluation. For evaluation to be successful, it must provide something that enhances the role and job of MLMs while informing the public as to how well programs are succeeding.

Thus, MLMs must see evaluation not only as checking up on them but as enhancing their role as managers and their need for survival. The double-edged political role of evaluation must be recognized. Evaluation cannot seek to change resource allocations without obtaining the understanding of MLMs, for where the budget is affected, so also is the basis for a program's survival. Successful evaluation requires that the interest and concern of MLMs be recognized along with the need to obtain accountability for public programs.

DISCUSSION QUESTIONS

1. Why has the pursuit of efficiency dominated the history of American public administration?
2. Why is it important to recognize that politics plays a big part in public program evaluation?
3. Why is the success of program evaluation so highly dependent on MLMs?
4. How can we defend the statement that productivity and evaluation go hand in hand?

NOTES

1. Luther Gulick and L. Urwick, eds., *Papers on the Science of Administration* (New York: National Institute of Public Administration, 1937); and Luther Gulick, *The National Institute of Public Administration: A Progress Report* (New York: National Institute of Public Administration, 1928).

2. Herbert Simon, et al., *Public Administration* (New York: Alfred A. Knopf, 1958), p. 71.

3. Quoted in *Proceedings of the Pittsburgh Conference on Good City Government* and the Fourteenth Annual Meeting of the National Municipal League (San Francisco, Calif.: National Municipal League, 1908), p. 127.

4. U.S. General Accounting Office, *Evaluation and Analysis to Support Decisionmaking*, PAD-75-9 (Washington, D.C.: U.S. Government Printing Office, 1976), pp. 1–2.

5. Susan Solasin and Lawrence Kevins, "Fostering Federal Program Evaluation: OMB Initiatives," *Evaluation* 2 (August 19, 1975): 37–41.

6. Eleanor Chelinsky, "Evaluating Public Programs," in *Handbook of Public Administration*, James L. Perry, ed. (San Francisco: Josey-Bass, 1989), p. 259.

7. Carole Dineen, "Productivity Improvement: It's Our Turn," *The Bureaucrat* Volume 14, No. 4 (Winter 1985): 10–14.

8. Despite Grace's harsh criticism of the government's inefficiency, in his own organization there were problems of inefficiency and bad decision-making. In one such example, Frace was forced to sell his company, Mr. Gasket Company in Brooklyn, Ohio, to stem the losses. The former owner who purchased the business from Grace for $57 million, at a significant loss to Grace, saw its value rise $151 million in three years. See Jerome B. McKinney, *Effective Financial Management in Public Nonprofit Agencies* (Westport, Conn.: Quorum Books, 1995).

9. U.S. Senate, *Report of the Committee on Governmental Affairs 103-58* (Washington, D.C.: U.S. Government Printing Office, June 16, 1993).

10. Ibid., pp. 18–19.

11. Graeme Browning, "Quest for Quality," *National Journal* (December 21, 1991): 1496.

12. Jack Franklin and Jean H. Thrasher, *An Introduction to Program Evaluation* (New York: John Wiley & Sons, 1976), p. 23.

13. Harry P. Hatry, Richard Winnie, Donald Fisk, and Louis Blair, *Practical Program Evaluation for State and Local Government* (Washington, D.C.: Urban Institute, 1974), p. 28.

14. Franklin and Thrasher, *Introduction*, p. 72.

15. James Coleman, *Policy Research in Social Sciences* (Morristown, N.J.: General Learning Press, 1972).

16. Franklin and Thrasher, *Introduction*, p. 111.

17. Andie L. Knutson, "Evaluation for What?" in *Program Evaluation in Health Fields*, Herbert C. Schulbert, Alan Sheldron, Frank Baker, eds. (New York: Bexanomical Publications, 1969), pp. 43–44.

18. Ibid., p. 45.

19. David B. Cohen, "Politics and Research: Evaluation of Social Action Programs," in *Evaluation Actions Programs*, Carol Weiss, ed. (Boston: Allyn Bacon, 1972), p. 139.

20. Lennis M. Knighton, "Accounting for Benefits of Public Programs," *Federal Accountant* (March 1972): 13.

21. Edward Suchman, *Evaluative Research* (New York: Russell Sage Foundation, 1967), pp. 60–71.

22. Hatry et al., *Practical Program Evaluation*, p. 9.

23. Suchman, *Evaluative Research*, p. 66.

24. John Harris, "Program Evaluation Funding: An Alternative to Funding

Public Higher Education by Number of Students," *Southern Review of Public Administration* (December 1977): 232–33.

25. Ibid.

26. Michael Scriven, "The Methodology of Evaluation," in *Perspectives of Curriculum Evaluation*, Ralph W. Taylor et al., eds. (Chicago: Rand McNally, 1967), pp. 39–83.

27. George H. Johnson, ed., "The Purpose of Evaluation and the Role of the Evaluator," in *Evaluative Research* (Pittsburgh: American Institute of Research, 1970), p. 5.

28. Joseph S. Wholey, John W. Scanlon, Hugh G. Duffy, James S. Fukumoto and Leona M. Vogt, *Federal Evaluation Policy* (Washington, D.C.: Urban Institute, 1973), p. 22.

29. Hatry et al., *Practical Program Evaluation*, p. 20.

30. Carol H. Weiss, *Evaluation Research: Research Methods for Assessing Program Effectiveness* (Englewood Cliffs, N.J.: Prentice-Hall, 1973), p. 72.

31. Hatry et al., *Practical Program Evaluation*, p. 113.

Part V

Policy Areas

16

Intergovernmental Relations and Administration

If MLMs are to function optimally, they must understand federalism or, as we describe it here, the system of intergovernmental relations. This chapter illustrates the dynamic intergovernmental setting in which the typical government unit operates. Five sections are included. The first examines the development, characteristics, problems, and advantages of the U.S. federal systems. The second explores the powerful role that finance plays in determining the policy direction of different levels of government. In the third section, the role of the federal government in urban America is briefly examined. The fourth section discusses the role of top administrators in intergovernmental administration. The last section describes the critical role that MLMs play in influencing intergovernmental policy.

LEARNING OBJECTIVES

On completing this chapter, the reader should be able to:

- Understand the many complementary parts involved in managing an agency in the federal system.
- Understand the need for cooperation.
- Be aware of the continuous bargaining that goes on among the government units.
- Identify the different types of financial operations and administrative arrangements.
- Understand the powerful role of finance in the intergovernmental system.
- Appreciate the critical role that MLMs play in intergovernmental management.

The U.S. federal system was created by people who wanted the fruits of a centrally coordinated government but feared the power that such a system might exercise. The Constitution authorized governmental power that is fragmented, conditioned, and prohibited. On the federal level, fragmentation results from the separation of powers and the system of checks and balances. Each branch (Congress in the form of two houses representing different interests, the presidency with a separate constituency, and an independent judiciary) was given some independence but also some overlapping powers enabling it to be a check to the others in some matters. All 50 states also operate on this principle of horizontal fragmentation (government branches at the same level check and balance each other).[1]

The Constitution specifically prohibits *ex post facto* laws (regulations of past behavior) and bills of attainder (legislative punishment for specific persons) in the federal system. It makes contracts inviolable and prohibits governments at the national and state levels from depriving any person of "life, liberty, or property without due process of law."[2] While the national government is supreme in several spheres of power (e.g., foreign commerce and foreign relations), the selection of members of Congress and the president and the ratification of proposed constitutional amendments are powers reserved for the states.

Federalism is the cornerstone of the U.S. government system. Under federalism, powers are divided between a semi-autonomous national government and semi-autonomous states. The Constitution specifies how each level is related and where it is "supreme in the areas of powers assigned to it."[3] Each level of government has the right to act directly on the people: "The distinctive feature of federal political systems is that decision-making is divided between two 'government' entities neither of which can dictate the decisions of the other."[4]

The federal system provides for two divisions of functions: (1) those having primarily national importance and (2) those of mainly local concern. In the case of the former, functions that have importance for the country as a whole are assigned to the national government. These include defense, foreign relations, foreign commerce, and the monetary system. The primary local functions include such matters as public education, police protection, roads and highways, and health. These latter powers, unlike those of the central government, were not outlined. For this reason, the powers of the national government are known as the delegated powers and those of the states as reserved powers. Any unstated powers, often called residual powers, are also assumed to rest with the states.

During the past 225 years of the federal union, there have been differing interpretations about the extent and scope of the division of powers. Federal systems generally find it difficult to distribute power on a permanently satisfactory basis due to constantly changing conditions in the environments in which government actions take place. The distribution of power is affected by crises, the popular mood, and demands that the people make on government—what we have described earlier as the external environment. The amount of power is not constant; it may increase at the national, state, and local levels simultaneously: "The amount used depends not on the calculus of a mathematical equation but on the needs of a people and how they determine to satisfy them."[5]

ADMINISTRATIVE FEDERALISM

Since World War II, the U.S. federal system has undergone significant changes. The growth pattern in government functions and activities has moved from the federal to state and local levels. As Table 16.1 shows, between 1954 and 1992, state and local employment grew more than three times as much as that of the federal government or the private sector.

Barring an unforeseen national crisis, the federal bureaucracy, in terms of employment, may never have future growth rates comparable to those of the private and state and local government sectors. Federal agencies created since the 1940s are overwhelmingly "pass-through agencies." These agencies receive congressional appropriations and pass them on to state and local spending (implementing) agencies and private contractors. The federal agency thus acts as a policy initiator and goal setter and not as a direct instrument for the delivery of goods and services.[6]

Table 16.1.   Government and Private Employment in the United States, 1954–92 (000,000s*)

	1954	1992	% Increase
Federal government	2.2	3.05	38.6
State and local government	4.6	15.69	241.1
Private sector	42.3	92.80	119.4
Total non-agricultural employment	49.1	111.54	399.1

*Refers to wage and salary workers in non-agricultural establishments and includes postal workers.

Source: U.S. Bureau of Census, *Statistical Abstract of the United States, The National Data Book. 1995* (Washington, D.C.: U.S. Government Printing Office, 1995). Table 542.

The units of government functioning at state and local levels now number about 80,000. Within this large number of governmental units, there are diversities that bring many problems and offer many opportunities.

Diversity with autonomy inevitably generates problems: (1) It tends to produce jurisdictional conflicts and overlapping functions; (2) it creates confusion and bewilderment for citizens in their attempts to determine who is responsible for the delivery of what services; (3) it fosters inefficient and uneconomic management; (4) it provides the opportunity for powerful minorities to capture and dominate government; and (5) it allows for the development of inequality in the standards of public service throughout the country. The endless swirl of government units, agencies, functions, and individuals with differing standards and loyalties operating with no apparent overall goal makes us wonder who is minding the public's interest.

Far from being inimical to a democratic and pluralistic society, however, diversity also provides unique opportunities for citizens to work with each other and do those things that they would not be able to do in larger homogenized units of governments. Diversity (1) helps to promote a sense of neighborhood responsibility and spirit of self-reliance and facilitates adjustment to changing conditions and outlook in the community and in society as a whole; (2) promotes adaptation of public services to local needs; (3) engenders socially beneficial intercommunity competition; and (4) provides the opportunity for experimentation with innovative methods of governmental organizations. For example, local units have been instrumental in providing novel experiments in job rotation, "flexitime," productivity-costing systems, and public bargaining and negotiating systems.

CHARACTERIZING INTERGOVERNMENTAL RELATIONSHIPS

Since the republic's creation, three terms have been used to describe the interactions among different levels of government. The first has been referred to as *dual federalism*. This pattern began at the early stages of the new nation. During this period federal and state governments competed with each other to carve out policy space or spheres of influence. Observers viewed the relationship as a "layer cake." Government was seen as a server of layers. Localities were at the bottom, the state in the middle and the federal government at the top. Each level defended its autonomy.

Conflict more than cooperation characterized the early period. There was one major notable exception, the Morill Act of 1862, which gave land to universities to establish agricultural programs. This effort led to the development of land grant colleges and agricultural extension agencies, leading to phenomenal success of U.S. agriculture.[7]

Cooperative federalism describes the period following dual federalism. This period was marked by increased complexity and interdependence and was notable more for its cooperation and sharing than for its conflict. Roles and responsibilities were intermixed, overlapping, and parallel, like a marble cake. President Franklin D. Roosevelt was a significant force in promoting cooperative federalism through the programs initiated to stimulate economic recovery following the Great Depression. While the president's programs were national in scope, the programs were operated through the state and local governments. The cooperative federalism produced a kind of win-win situation in which federal power was greatly expanded but by greater sharing of responsibilities among the three levels of government.

Picket-Fence Federalism ushered in a new phase of competition among the various government jurisdictions. In this phase of federalism, many problems surfaced, such as the need for coordination, program effectiveness and competence of the delivery systems and the opportunity for citizens to participate in policymaking. To meet the new situation the federal government replaced its reliance on project grants with block grants, revenue sharing and the reordering of its categorical grants. Because of the creation of numerous categorical grants, and the competition and fragmentation that this generated among the multitude of interest groups, intergovernmental relations during this period were referred to as picket-fence federalism.

CONFLICT AND COOPERATION

It is not unusual to pick up the daily newspaper and read that county X and city Y are engaged in a bitter dispute or that state B is taking the federal government to court. In August 1977, the federal Environmental Protection Agency (EPA) issued an order to U.S. Steel to bring two of its manufacturing plants in Allegheny County, Pennsylvania, into compliance with U.S. air quality standards by 1980. Two weeks of intense negotiation began in which the county, state, and cities participated. The Allegheny County commissioners were adamant that the EPA change its timetable to permit the steel companies to make the changes over a longer period. When the EPA refused to extend the time, the commissioners demanded that the issues be put to a referendum in the city and county, asking the voters to decide between jobs and regulations, and then threatened a suit against the EPA. Beginning in late 1992, Governor Robert Casey expressed mild concern about the new car-emissions standard that the federal government required the state to adopt. In the governor's race that followed in 1994, the Republican candidate and later Governor Ridge vehemently opposed the measures. To minimize conflict between the federal EPA and local government, the timetable and the standards were modified to allow the program to begin in 1997.

In 1975, Pennsylvania, along with a number of states, cities, and civil rights organizations, brought suit against the secretary of the Department of Agriculture to prevent him from enforcing his proposed reorganization and resulting cutback of food stamp programs for the poor and needy. An injunction stopping the secretary from putting his proposal into effect was obtained.

The vast number of cooperative acts that take place among the different levels of government far outweighs the conflicts that usually capture the headlines. Local police and the FBI constantly exchange information to the mutual interest of all concerned. Airports are typically run by the local governments in which the facility is situated, but no flight or airline could operate without numerous acts of cooperation between federal and state officials. Every major snowstorm or flood brings a number of government units into cooperative action. During the 1977 flood in Johnstown, Pennsylvania, a host of federal agencies moved into the city. The governor flew over the city, inspecting damage and deciding what help the state could render. The following day the secretary of HUD, Patricia Harris, inspected the area on behalf of President Jimmy Carter. Later, the commissioners from Allegheny County visited Johnstown to see how the county could best help. The response from numerous federal agencies such as HUD, HEW (now the Department of Health and Human Services, DHHS), the Department of Labor, and the Army Corps of Engineers, the state, and numerous cities and counties was overwhelming. When Hurricane Andrew devastated south Florida in 1991, the same pattern of assistance and cooperation was repeated, though on a larger scale. So great was the damage that the U.S. military participated in the relief and restoration.

The federal government and states have been known to cooperate even in the area of foreign relations. President John F. Kennedy was instrumental in persuading the state of California to subcontract with the Agency for International Development to provide direct technical assistance to Chile. In the course of the activity, California assisted in such areas as education, highway transportation, planning, budgeting, water resources, management, and agricultural marketing.[8]

LAYERS OF GOVERNANCE

As indicated earlier, the typical citizen must contend with myriad government units. Though cooperation eases the difficulty, it does not obviate the necessity of the citizen dealing individually with each unit of government if he or she wishes to take advantage of the service provided.

Fig. 16.1 provides an excellent example of the layers of governance of Whitehall, a small suburban community in Allegheny County, Pennsylvania, in 1996.[9] The citizens obtained services and benefits from and paid taxes or user charges to 17 different government or quasi-government units.

The Whitehall resident—beyond financial concerns—is also affected by the planning programs of the criminal justice commission and by the regulatory activities of the air-quality control agency. In addition, areawide organizations for comprehensive health and personnel planning, community action, and economic development have a direct impact on Whitehall Borough.[10]

REGIONALISM

Layers of government such as that shown in Fig. 16.1 have provoked considerable thought about the adequacy of the existing local and state jurisdictions in responding effectively to the needs of citizens in the federal system. As Martha Derthick puts it, there are some things that simply "do not fit neatly into fixed geographic jurisdictions."[11] The acceptance of regionalism has increased because citizens have found that government units within traditional boundaries often cannot solve problems. Regional organizations can respond to problems of scale that exceed a single jurisdiction (for example, when New York City's "withdrawal of water from the Delaware River in Upper New York State threatened cities down river in Pennsylvania").[12] Many problems are beyond the scope of the individual state (for example, organized crime or air and water pollution), but are not an appropriate function for the national government. Such problems call forth some kind of subnational (including two or more states) authority or arrangement.

Fig. 16.1. Layers of Governance, Whitehall, Pennsylvania, 1996

17. United States of America
16. Commonwealth of Pennsylvania
15. Air Quality Control Region
14. Southwestern Pennsylvania Regional Planning Commission
13. Western Pennsylvania Water Company
12. Allegheny County
11. Allegheny County Port Authority
10. Allegheny County Criminal Justice Commission
9.   Allegheny County Soil and Water Conservation District
8.   Allegheny County Sanitary Authority
7.   City of Pittsburgh
6.   South Hills Area Council of Government
5.   South Hills Regional Planning Commission
4.   Pleasant Hills Sanitary Authority
3.   Baldwin-Whitehall School Authority
2   Baldwin-Whitehall School District
1.   Borough of Whitehall (Population 14,451)

We can imagine the difficulties that would be involved if we were to attempt to coordinate the diverging interests in the six-county Pittsburgh Metropolitan Standard Area (MSA).[13] In 1996, there were over 800 government units in these counties, many having taxing authority, including 54 municipalities. Allegheny County alone has 131 municipalities, 43 school districts, and numerous special districts.[14] The point is that regionalism must seek some way to coordinate the interests of governments.

The creation of subnational regional arrangements has both positive and negative aspects. Any kind of regional government will still require intergovernmental cooperation. When permanent regional commissions or authorities are created, such as the New York Port Authority or the Appalachian Regional Council, they themselves become governments creating bureaucracies that must be maintained and coordinated. Most tend to have low visibility and no direct accountability to the people. According to Derthick, "There has never been a sustained movement for regional organization that left its impression across the United States. . . . Perhaps because the fashion has never gripped political scientists, the regional idea has not taken shape as a specific set of proposals for regional organizations."[15]

There are several important contributions, however, that a regional organization can make. It may be an important instrument for settling disputes that arise when the actions of one jurisdiction adversely affect a neighboring areas. It may be the mitigating instrument to decentralize federal functions, thus achieving greater responsiveness. The Appalachian Regional Council (ARC) provides a good example. The council argues that federal highway programs cannot respond to local needs because they are intended to promote a policy—control of traffic congestion—that is opposed to the wishes of the people in the area. The ARC seeks to increase traffic growth to encourage more rapid economic growth and development.[16]

The regional organizations initiated at the state level typically attempt to centralize activities as a means of achieving greater responsiveness to citizen demands. Examples are the New York Port Authority and the multistate tax compacts, which have operated very successfully.

Substate regional arrangements are created to bring coordination and grouping of functions within a state boundary "to meet the need for effective areawide solutions to problems resulting from rapid population growth and technological change."[17] The federal government initiates and provides leadership for such organizations through its financial and administrative support, as expressed in the Office of Management and Budget's Circular A-95. This federal action came in response to the lack of interest shown by state and local governments in the face of evident need for some sort of regional council or areawide planning agency. The responsibilities envisioned for these "were planning, communications, coordination and grants-in-aid administration."[18]

Areawide substate agencies, however, have been the subject of criticism. They have produced fragmentation and proliferation of single and multipurpose areawide bodies, due in major part to the lack of a clear and consistent substate regional policy by federal or state governments. Thus, the number of areawide districts has mushroomed, but they have failed to deal successfully with the problems they were created to solve. Additionally, they have diverted attention from the "traditional ways of dealing cooperatively with interjurisdictional problems. The principal local options include intergovernmental service agreements, special districts, annexation, city-county consolidation and federation."[19] The state can exercise a more forceful role in overcoming fragmentation by adjusting boundaries, requiring mandatory performance of functions, and assessing local political, economic, and social viability.[20]

RETHINKING GOVERNMENT STRUCTURES

Constructive intergovernmental relations requires that functional responsibility be clearly defined and aided by policy that promotes cooperation and facilitates maximum cooperation. This requires that different units of government "be brought into play to meet area-wide, community and individual service needs without any of them being hamstrung by jurisdictional isolationism of other units."[21]

The Advisory Commission on Intergovernmental Relations (a government created entity which studies, collects, and coordinates data on state and local governments) has suggested four criteria—economic efficiency, equity, political accountability, and administrative effectiveness—that should provide the basic guidelines in reassigning functions to government units (because of marked differences in tax base and wealth) to permit maximum efficiency and effectiveness in the delivery of public goods and services.[22]

Economic Efficiency

Efficiency requires that jurisdictions (1) be optimally organized and large enough to achieve economy of scale, maximize use of technology, use specialization of labor, and effect greater savings (e.g., purchasing in large quantities to reduce unit cost) but small enough to avoid diseconomics (overly large units increase coordination costs; e.g., most human resource services); (2) be willing to provide alternative high-quality services to citizens at reasonable prices; and (3) use market-type pricing in delivery of goods and services when feasible.

Equity

Equity requires that jurisdictions (1) be large enough to bear the cost and receive the benefits or have the capacity and willingness to compensate other units that provide them benefits (this would mean that a declining community that pays for educating individuals who move to a developing community should be compensated in some way); and (2) possess adequate fiscal capacity to pay for public service undertakings and willingness to implement measures to effect fiscal equalization "to insure that a jurisdiction or individual can buy a level of public service at a price that is not more burdensome than the price that most other jurisdictions or individuals would pay for that service."[23]

Political Accountability

This requires that jurisdictions (1) be responsive to their citizens in the performance and the delivery of public goods and services; and (2) provide maximum opportunities for citizen participation in the performance and delivery of such goods and services.

Administrative Effectiveness

This requires that jurisdictions (1) balance competing interests; (2) have a geographic area adequate for effective performance of a function; (3) identify objectives and means for implementing and reassessing program goals and objectives in light of planned performance; (4) promote means for facilitating cooperation and minimizing local conflict; and (5) provide adequate legal authority for the effective performance and administration of the function.

FISCAL FEDERALISM

Fiscal relations in federal systems have created the greatest challenge to the stability and unity of these systems. The wealth and size of government units tend to have the most strategic impact on intergovernmental relations because they permit a unit to bargain with the central government and/or other units. In other words, wealth or a large population gives power and the potential to use influence.

Generally, "a wealthy unit can exercise influence more than proportionate to its relative size if it is able to use its superior wealth to buy political influence or if, because of its wealth, it is able to produce an influential elite at the national level."[24] In a democratic state, areas that are poor but large (as to both geography and, especially, population) carry the same potential to dominate due to superior voting strength. It would also follow that in the same country, a poor and small unit will have little influence. These are factors that create continuing strain and tension in federal systems unless there is a mechanism to continually compromise and adjust interests. In the United States, the Constitution is the most fundamental means for establishing the bargaining rules of the game. (Due to the seniority rules of committees of elected representatives, small states may exercise significant or disproportionate influence.) Where no recognized rules are accepted, open conflict and dissolution of the federal system may occur.

Fiscal relations between the governmental levels have had a long history. For example, under the Articles of Confederation, Congress passed the Northwest Ordinances of 1785 and 1787, which provided every township with land on which it could build public schools. The surplus that built up in the U.S. Treasury in 1836 during the presidency of Andrew Jackson was distributed to the states with no repayment requirement. The vast majority of all early federal aid to states for building and construction of roads, canals, railroads, and flood control projects carried no federal strings or payback provisions.

Under the Articles of Confederation, the weakest link in the union of the states was the central government's inability to levy and collect taxes and regulate interstate commerce. Delegates at the Constitutional Convention felt that this situation had to be corrected. Thus, Article 1, Section 8 of the Constitution gives the federal government (Congress) very broad powers "to levy and collect taxes, duties, imposts, and excises." Unlike the Articles, the Constitution grants both the central and state governments the power to tax (known as concurrent power). No specific direction was given as to how this power should be shared.[25]

Acceptance of the fiscal role for the state and federal government was achieved soon after the implementation of the Constitution. Under the principles enunciated under Chief Justice John Marshall (a proponent of national supremacy), the immunity of federal instrumentalities from state taxation was established. Later, this doctrine was reciprocally extended to the states.[26]

The fiscal balance of the 19th century eventually gave way to the dominance of the federal government in fiscal matters. Among the causes were the following:

- The passage of the Sixteenth Amendment in 1913, giving the national government wide power "to levy and collect taxes from whatever sources derived."
- The development of the categorical grant-in-aid system.
- The catastrophic effects of the Great Depression and the inadequate fiscal resources of state and local governments to meet the exigencies.
- State and local imposition of many constitutional restrictions on the power to borrow and tax.
- The federal government's need to centralize fiscal policy to promote stability.[27]

Fiscal aspects play a major role in determining the character and scope of intergovernmental relations. Government units have traditionally been faced with geometrically increasing public demands for goods and services while revenue to meet these demands has been increasing only arithmetically. Citizens have been asking for more things than governments can reasonably provide, creating a satisfaction gap (the difference between expectations and the actual response made to satisfy them). The problem has been exacerbated by the unequal distribution of wealth (the basis on which to tax) and the disproportionate share of responsibilities among governments for the aged, the unemployed, and so on. These problems have produced both vertical differences (between states and the federal government) and horizontal differences (between the same level of local governments) and have created keen competition, frustration, and even conflict between state and local governments that strive to obtain federal revenue to help satisfy their citizens' many demands.

NATIONAL PREEMPTIONS MANDATES AND INTERGOVERNMENTAL ADMINISTRATION

Preemptions

This action allows the federal government to take precedence over areas traditionally thought to be the province of state or local governments. The mandates often seek to promote social and national goals and standards. In some mandates, specific financial, criminal or civil penalties for violating the stipulations are set forth.[28]

Mandates

These typically involve "conditions-of-aid" and "direct order," typically requiring the government to do something that it might otherwise not do. Direct order by the federal government relates to areas such as clean air standards, or the requirements to pay a welfare program. Conditions are often tied to grants-in-aid; the federal government may also require environmental impact statements before initiating capital improvements or that construction projects be accessible to the disabled. Mandates have become controversial because the federal government may dictate the requirements but not the necessary funds to implement them. It is estimated that mandates cost about $100 billion a year.[29] Generally, most mandates attempt to promote financial accountability and the achievement of particular intergovernment program objectives. Many others use the instrument of local governments to enforce national government policy objectives in their jurisdictions.

Federal mandates fall into four categories:

- *Crosscutting* requirements stipulate the compliance of all governments receiving the grant. Nondiscrimination clauses are an example.
- In *partial exemption* mandates, Washington requires that the state adopt and administer the program standards. This approach denies subnational units their traditional prerogative of overseeing their enforcement of the grants' requirements.
- *Crossover sanctions* allow the mandate to punish the state by reducing or withdrawing the federal aid in other programs if federal standards are not being adhered to in another program.
- *Direct order* tell the states and local governments that specified penalties will be imposed if instructions are not followed.

Between 1960 to 1990 the four types of mandates have increased greatly.[30]

The federal Constitution enumerates certain powers that the national government exercises and reserve powers that the states may control. Precisely what specific powers each level commands has long been a point of controversy. The Fair Labor Standards Act of 1938 (FLSA) set minimum wages and maximum hours that were to be worked before overtime must be given to employees.

Initially the law applied to the private sector, but in 1974 it was extended to state and local governments. When the law was challenged in 1976 in the case of *National League of Cities vs. Userg*, the Supreme Court ruled that the Tenth Amendment interpretation of the functions of "general government" were part of the powers reserved for the states and could not be regulated by the federal government. Thus the FLSA was not applicable to the states.

Uncertainty about the federal government's power over general government functions continued until 1985, when the Supreme Court ruled in *Garcia vs. San Antonio Metropolitan Transit Authority* that the right to act in areas reserved for the states was a political question to be settled by legislation and not by judicial inquiry.[31] Subsequently, in the case of *South Carolina vs. Baker* (1988), South Carolina tried to determine whether the federal government had the authority to tell the states what form of bond they could issue. The court decided in the affirmative; it also ruled that the federal government could tax income earned on tax-exempt bonds.

The preemption issue is not a point of contention in the relations of state and local government: The local governments are creatures of the state. The Dillion Rule, rendered in 1911 by Judge John Dillion, states that local governments have only those powers specifically granted in their charters, and those reasonably implied by expressed powers, those deemed essential to the purposes granted in their charter.

GRANT-IN-AID: AN OVERVIEW

Because the grant-in-aid system still constitutes the cornerstone of fiscal federalism, a brief overview (state or federal) would be helpful. A grant-in-aid is the payment of funds by a higher level of government to a lower level (state or local) in order to accomplish a specific purpose. Normally, grant funds require that the money provided be matched according to some required standard. The grant-in-aid system became important with the adoption of the Sixteenth Amendment in 1913, giving the federal government vast power to raise money. Major expansion of the grant-in-aid system occurred during the 1930s as a result of the Great Depression. Since this time, the system has been growing steadily.[32]

Types of Grants

There are three main types of grants:

- *Categorical grants* are transfers of money that are to be spent within identified categories and do not require repayment.
- *Conditional* or *matching grants* are a special type of categorical grant that requires the recipient government to spend the money according to specific guidelines or administrative regulations and often includes a provision for matching. A matching grant requires that the local unit contribute some of its own resources (constituting of a percentage of the total cost of the program).
- *Block grants* were devised in the 1970s. These bring together a wide range of activities within a broad functional area. Examples include:

in the health field, partnership (PHA) grants; in the welfare field, social services (SSA) grants; in the personnel field, comprehensive employment and training (CETA) grants; and in the community development field, community development (CDBG) grants. The block grant allows wide discretion in identifying problems and developing solutions to them; cuts down on administrative red tape and fiscal reporting; distributes on a formula basis, thus providing greater certainty to grantees; and provides for clear eligibility, making grants more understandable to elected officials and the administrative generalists.

The purpose of grants is to assist various units to find solutions to their problems within the existing political framework. There are many grant programs serving multiple objectives and needs. Deil S. Wright has listed a wide array of objectives:

- To stimulate state or local activity deemed desirable, such as public housing.
- To provide a minimum level of service where local resources may not be adequate.
- To equalize services where fiscal capacity of the state or locality is taken into consideration in distributing or allocating funds, such as for CETA programs.
- To provide economic stabilization and development by providing money for employment security and public works to increase employment, thus keeping up consumer spending in the government unit.
- To take care of special hardships such as floods, major snow storms, and other disasters.
- To initiate experimental or demonstration programs to test the feasibility of an approach to problems.
- To provide for planning and coordination to allow the grantees to achieve their objectives in a more consistent and rational manner. [33]

Advantages and Disadvantages of Grants

A summary of the pros and cons of grants may help to give us a more balanced perspective.[34] Among their advantages, grants:

- Represent a desirable means of joining different levels of government in pursuing common enterprises and solving mutual problems.
- Provide the avenue to finance important services that are beyond the capacity of state and local governments.
- Enhance state and local standards of administration.
- Facilitate the redistribution of income and promote progressive taxation.

- Assist in preserving the institutional framework of state and local government.
- Serve as a useful device for stimulating local government to enter neglected fields in which there is a special national interest.
- Promote the maintenance of minimum service and performance.

Some of the disadvantages of grants are that they:

- Permit the federal government to enter fields of activity denied to it by the Constitution.
- Carry the risk of centralizing too much power in the national government, contrary to the letter and spirit of the Constitution.
- Create excessive competition for funds, leading to sectional jealousies and jockeying for benefits.
- Induce waste and minimize the need for strict accountability in the spending of funds because the taxing and spending authorities are separated.
- Distort state budgets due to matching provisions for some programs, changing the state and local priorities.
- Weaken the initiative of state and local governments to solve their problems.
- Create a self-perpetuating cycle of dependency on the part of recipient governments and political interest groups.
- Foster federal control of local activities.

EMERGING PATTERNS OF INTERGOVERNMENTAL FINANCE

Federal assistance to state and local governments grew significantly during the 1970s in terms of amounts, functions, and programs. Federal grants and shared revenue to state and local governments totaled nearly $50 billion in 1975. Between 1950 and 1975, federal assistance grew an average of $2 billion a year. Since the late 1970s, federal revenue to states and local governments has been falling.

As Table 16.2 shows, the five-year period between 1970 and 1975 saw the biggest growth taking place in four categories: health; education; employment training, social services and national resources; environment and energy.[35]

The functional character of the grants was also changing. While income security (expenditures) was the largest grant in 1970, by 1995 health, education, training, employment, and social services had taken this lead.

Expenditure Impact

In discussing federal assistance to state and local government, we often neglect the significance of direct expenditure within the recipient jurisdictions.

Parks, highways, and hospitals are often very important because they provide services and economic advantages (for example, increased jobs). This is why selecting the location of a proposed facility engenders intense lobbying.

Writing in 1969, R. J. May indicated that "there has always been strong opposition to any move to introduce a needs element into federal grants to states; in fact until quite recently per capita income and federal grants received per capita in the states seem to have been positively correlated."[36] This view is supported when we compare the per capita personal income in the states with the per capita federal aid provided in 1974, a comparison that reveals no clear patterns. Programs do not redistribute income to the rich or poor states. The numerous uncoordinated federal grants overlap, offset, and neutralize each other.[37]

Table 16.2. Selected Federal Aid Distribution by Function,
Fiscal Years 1970 and 1995

Function	FY 1970	FY 1995
	($ Billions)	
Natural resources, environment and energy	.43	4,573
Health	3,849	93,244
Administration of justice	.42	1,300
Education, employment, training, and social services	6.471	36.138

Source: U.S. Bureau of Census, *Statistical Abstract of the United States, The National Data Book 1995* (Washington, D.C.: U.S. Government Printing Office, 1995), Table 479.

State Aid to Local Governments

Comparatively speaking, state aid to local governments is far more significant. In fiscal year 1990–92, federal aid to states totaled $155 billion and to local governments $19.2 billion. During this same period, state aid to local governments amounted to $182.7 billion, more than nine and one-half times greater than the federal aid, as shown in Fig. 16.2. With the exception of special districts, state aid to local governments exceeded federal aid in every function.

It should be made clear that the aggregate figures presented in Fig. 16.2 provide us with only general averages and overlook specific cases in which the averages sharply diverge. For example, New Hampshire provides 14 percent of local revenue, while New Mexico provides 51 percent.[38]

The largest portion of state aid goes to elementary education. Fig. 16.2 shows that states give school districts 51.4 percent of their total revenue. Typically, distribution of state aid to schools is made on the basis of per pupil or per classroom attendance. Usually, formulas for distributing aid consider real estate property assessments so that low-assessment districts can receive a greater portion of the funds. In some instances, pre-school, disadvantaged, and disabled children are included in the distribution criteria.[39]

Fig. 16.2. Intergovernmental Sources of Revenue for Types of Local Government, 1990–91

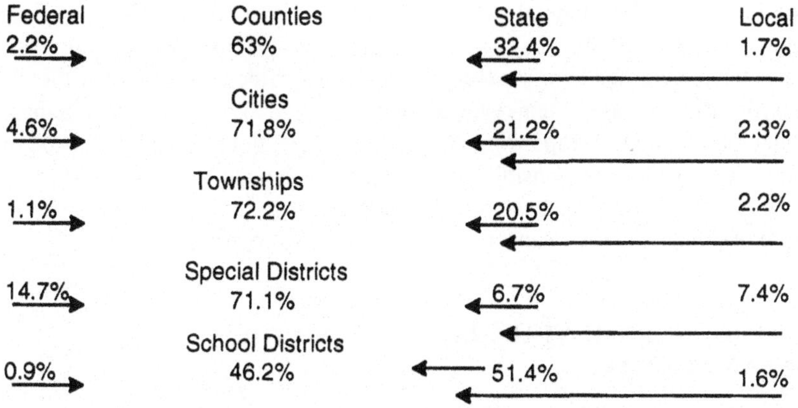

Federal	Counties	State	Local
2.2% →	63%	← 32.4%	1.7%
	Cities		
4.6% →	71.8%	← 21.2%	2.3%
	Townships		
1.1% →	72.2%	← 20.5%	2.2%
	Special Districts		
14.7% →	71.1%	← 6.7%	7.4%
	School Districts		
0.9% →	46.2%	← 51.4%	1.6%

Source: Governmental Finances in 1990-91 (Washington, D.C.: Government Printing Office, 1992, p. 7, Table 6).

Because of the wide diversity in the distribution of wealth and the resulting different tax bases among communities within a state, many groups have opposed the formula distribution. The general view is that the formulas do not sufficiently address the question of equal educational opportunities guaranteed by the Fourteenth Amendment to the Constitution. In a Texas case, the U.S. Supreme Court set this view aside, ruling that education was a state responsibility that is not controlled by the Constitution.[40]

The categorical grant system has been undergoing intense criticism for many years. Grants proliferated in the 1970s (there were 1,100 at the federal level in 1976) and generally focused on narrow, specific types of projects. As noted above, grants tend to distort priorities because government units are tempted to apply for funds that are available even though they may have more desirable alternatives that would provide greater benefits to their citizens. Furthermore, "grantsmanship" carries a premium. Often a community loses out simply because it lacks the technical staff to put an acceptable proposal together. Lack of coordination between grants and little feedback about the status of a proposal creates considerable uncertainty as to budgeting (though the initiation of the Federal Assistance Act in 1969 has speeded up this process). All of these factors were instrumental in helping President Nixon to win support for revenue sharing, which remained a significant source of revenue of small cities under 10,000 in population until the Reagan administration dropped it in 1981.

DECLINE IN FEDERAL AID TO STATE
AND LOCAL GOVERNMENTS

The year 1978 marks the peak period for federal fund transfers to state and local governments. In 1991 federal aid declined to 20 percent for states and 3 percent for local governments from 22 percent and 9 percent, respectively, in 1978. The fall in 1991 would have been significantly greater if Medicaid grants (federal health assistance to the poor) had not been increased by approximately one-fourth. In 1996, federal aid to state and local governments approximated the level of the late 1950s. To help fill the gap occasioned by the federal cuts, the states have increased their support.[41] To meet this added responsibility they have significantly increased their revenue-raising efforts. When the states demanded greater devolution of responsibility from the federal government, they had hoped that, with the added responsibility, increased revenue would follow. This has not been the case, and it has been an important factor in influencing the states to be more responsive to the financial needs of local governments.[42]

INTERGOVERNMENTAL RELATION AND THE
URBAN AGENDA

The United States is an urban nation. Since 1960, most of the population has been moving into metropolitan standard areas, creating what has come to be known as the "metropolitan problem" and compounding the difficulties of governing: "The concentration of the American people in metropolitan areas is evident from the fact that 113 million persons, nearly two-thirds of the entire population, lived in 212 areas classified as metropolitan in 1960, and these areas accounted for 80 percent of the nation's total population increase during the 1950–60 decade."[43] This trend has continued through the 1990s.

The movement of people to urban areas has brought with it industrial and commercial development and the concentration of social, cultural, and educational resources, so much so that cities have become the "focal point of American life in the mid-twentieth century."[44] The major problems of modern America—racial conflict, crime, pollution, traffic congestion, and unemployment—are found in its cities. Most domestic and social legislation focuses on the city. President Ford's message to Congress in 1975 exemplifies the emphasis of national policy on the urban area: "In the remainder of this century—in less than forty years—urban population will double, city land will double, and we will have to build our cities as much as all that we have built since the first colonist arrived on these shores. It is as if we had 40 years to rebuild the entire United States." These predictions have been materializing. Perhaps lack of sufficient attention and investment in urban areas has allowed crime (especially by gangs), poverty, a decline in education and general decay to rise significantly. The urban areas, which people romanticized as the best opportunity to practice civility and to experience the flowering of civilization's achievements, have in many instances become scary places that must, in the 1990s, be avoided to preserve personal safety.

INTERSTATE METROPOLITAN AREAS

These areas have been a growing problem, but the administrative measures advanced to meet it have been unfeasible and unimaginative. This failure is evidence of the division of power that typifies the U.S. federal system and presents the "sharpest challenge to continued development and progress of the American people."[45] The problem has been exacerbated because political and administrative officials have been unable to understand and deal with the interdependence that links residents and communities in metropolitan areas: "As urban settlements [expand] across lines of local jurisdictions, the cities and suburbs together come to comprise a single, integrated area for living and working. People look for housing and employment within a broad region circumscribed more by the convenience of commuting and by personal preferences than by local boundaries."[46]

Today, 33 of the 267 Metropolitan Standard Areas (MSA) in the nation are interstate, containing 45 million people, or 22 percent of the total U.S. population. Transportation has been the most successful joint activity of the interstate metropolitan areas. Perhaps the New York and New Jersey Port Authority provides the best example. The Port Authority builds bridges and tunnels and coordinates people and goods with "other modes of transportation, including highways, railways, airports, and truck terminals."[47]

The fiscal problem remains, due in large part to the mobility of people working and commuting in interstate jurisdictions. If there is no commuter tax, individuals can escape paying their fair share of taxes to the central business district. This can be a particularly burdensome problem in those areas where the wealth in the different districts is unequally distributed. In such a case, one area controls the resources while the other ends up with the problems, like New York City.

CITY-COUNTY CONSOLIDATION

Though some consolidations have taken place among metropolitan units of government, the number in terms of the potential has been insignificant. For example, only three of the 127 single-county MSA areas in the United States had city-county consolidation in 1970. Despite the small number of such metropolitan consolidations, the ones that have been successful, such as Indianapolis-Marion County, Nashville-Davidson County, and Jacksonville-Duval County, provide comparative examples.[48]

Dramatic changes in the urban areas are occurring, for better or worse. The central city is increasingly black, poor, and crime-ridden. Business and political leaders who once controlled the central city power structure and cultural life are moving to the suburbs, taking with them industries, jobs, and skills. Industries that once had to cluster in the central area because of the need for ready communication now rely on computer technology. Because services are the fastest-growing area of the economy, businesses can easily adapt to suburbia. All of this exacerbates the problems of survival for the central city.

INTERGOVERNMENTAL RELATIONS:
THE REAGAN AND BUSH YEARS

These years were marked by the strong desire of the administrations to reduce the role of the federal government in state and local governments. President Reagan's reductions in regulations and federal funding in a variety of programs were one important way to achieve ideological and budgeting objectives. The president's massive tax cut to promote his supply side economics called for continued military expenditures. This meant that cuts had to be made elsewhere in the spending program if his tax and budgetary goals were to be realized. Thus, in 1981 he reduced federal grants to state and local government from $95 billion to $88 billion for fiscal year 1982, the largest cut occurring in employment and training programs.[49] Cuts were also made to Aid to Families With Dependent Children (AFDC) payments.

Since the public viewed the level of expenditures in such areas as social welfare, environmental protection, and infrastructure maintenance as unacceptable, the second Reagan administration was forced to reverse some of his earlier policies. The AFDC cut was restored, and the Superfund to clean up toxic wastes was funded at higher levels than the president requested. Both Superfund and the Highway Trust Fund received higher levels of authorization over the president's veto. However, General Revenue Sharing (money to state and local governments to spend essentially at their discretion), which was initiated during the Nixon administration and continued during the Carter years, was eliminated. As noted previously, this action caused significant loss to communities, especially those with populations of 10,000 and under. In many of these communities police and fire departments and agencies such as parks and recreation had to lay off personnel to maintain budget stability.

TOP ADMINISTRATORS IN INTERGOVERNMENTAL
MANAGEMENT

In the intergovernmental environment, the role and political skills of top administrators are very important. They are the ambassadors who build bridges and explore opportunities for cooperation with other agencies. They are the generalists who have the overall view of the agency. Most top administrators at all levels gain their positions through politics, not merit. As a result, they tend to have little understanding of the technical operations of their agencies. Typically, these administrators have the constant aid of technical specialists (MLMs) who answer questions and explain details about specific programs. Because of top administrators' heavy reliance on specialists for information on intergovernmental programs and grants, considerable decision-making discretion is left to MLMs.[50]

Keeping on top of intergovernmental relations is not an easy task because of the fickle nature of Congress in appropriating funds for ongoing programs. Often the expected amount is cut, as was the case in three successive years in Hill Burton appropriations, or new programs are imposed with no warning, so that state and local long-range planning is made extremely difficult.[51]

MLMS: POWER AND ACCOUNTABILITY IN INTERGOVERNMENTAL MANAGEMENT

Many people tend to believe that MLMs exercise little or no influence on intergovernmental administration, but this is not the case. The late Senator Edmund Muskie observed in 1966: "Many federal officials, particularly in the middle management level, were not interested in, and in fact, were hostile to coordinating programs within their agency and between their departments, and were reluctant to encourage coordination and planning among state and local counterparts."[52]

MLMs exercise wide discretion in intergovernmental administration because of their professional status and monopoly of the technical details of intergovernmental programs. MLMs represent continuity from one administration to another, and they outlast the many changes that take place among the top administrators. Constantly changing programs, with their attendant rules and criteria for application and entitlements, allow MLMs to gain a high degree of technical expertise.

MLMs at all levels are the individuals who write the rules and procedures, and they are the ones who implement them. As noted above, they are the technical persons who advise top administrators about the nature, scope, and details of programs. Thus, when mistakes are made in the applications of procedure, it is left to MLMs to correct them.

The Public Works Act of 1975 provides a good example. The act was designed to provide aid to communities that had high unemployment and relatively low per capita income. In one case, a wealthy suburb of Philadelphia used the unemployment figure of the city of Philadelphia as its base and was top-ranked, allowing it to obtain huge sums of money. Mount Lebanon, Pennsylvania, got more than a million dollars because it used the unemployment figures of Allegheny County, while the city of Pittsburgh received no money (the initial distribution of the funds known as Rounds 1 and 2). In another case, one community that never applied got a hefty sum because its zip code was similar to that of a neighborhood community with high poverty and unemployment (which applied for and received no funds). Because MLMs did not check carefully, the policy was subverted.

On a daily basis, MLMs make many decisions that have far-reaching consequences. For example, if we pick up any *Federal Register* (a document publishing proposed rules and regulations in federal agencies) or the *Commerce Business Daily* (which publishes proposed federal works or projects to be contracted), numerous proposal specifications, rules, and procedures are outlined. In many instances, a simple change in eligibility from one level of income to another will affect thousands or even millions of recipients.

When President Carter took office, he issued an order requiring that all administrators read the *Federal Register* and sign off on what was said. Soon after the order was issued, it was allowed to go unenforced, due to the impossibility of getting top administrators to review and understand the materials, and thus leaving the way open for continued dominance by the MLM. Vice President Al Gore expressed the view that regulations that administrations are required to follow are too burdensome. In the *National Performance Review* report he suggested cutting 50 percent of the rules to free up the administration to pursue higher priorities.[53]

This section demonstrates that MLMs do exercise power, not only on internal policy but decisively in intergovernmental administration. It also shows that formal accountability has real limitations.

DISCUSSION QUESTIONS

1. Define the characteristics of the federal system.
2. Why have regional governments appeared in the American federal system?
3. Discuss the criteria that have been proposed in reassigning the government functions among government units.
4. Why have alternatives to the categorical grant systems come into operation?
5. Why has the federal government's attention been focused more and more on urban America?
6. Why do MLMs exercise great influence in intergovernmental administration?

NOTES

1. U.S. Constitution, Article 1, Sections 9–11.
2. U.S. Constitution, Amendments 5 and 14.
3. Richard Leach, *American Federalism* (New York: W.W. Norton, 1970), p. 1.
4. R. J. May, *Federalism and Fiscal Adjustment* (Oxford, England: The Clarendon Press, 1969), p. 1.
5. Leach, *American Federalism*, p. 26.
6. Bruce L. R. Smith and D. C. Hague, *The Dilemma of Accountability in Modern Government* (New York: Saint Martin's Press, 1971), p. 21.

7. Richard P. Nathan, Fred C. Doolittle, and Associates, *Reagan and the States* (Princeton, N.J.: Princeton University Press, 1987).

8. P. Dvorin, "Foreign Aid by States," *National Civic Review* (December 1964): 585–622.

9. Advisory Commission on Intergovernmental Relations (ACIR), *Regional Decision-Making: New Strategies for Substate Districts*, Vol. IA-43 (Washington, D.C.: Government Printing Office, October 1973), p. 3.

10. U.S. 1990 Census and conversations with borough officials in the *National Performance Review* report, which suggested cutting 50% of the rules to free up adminis-tration to pursue higher priorities; see p. 47.

11. Martha Derthick, *Between State and Nation* (Washington, D.C.: Brookings Institution, 1974), p. 1.

12. Ibid., p. 6.

13. An MSA is defined by the Bureau of Census as a central city having a population of at least 50,000 and whose county is contiguous with other counties of a metropolitan, character having a number of local units of governments.

14. Derthick, *Between State*, p. 3. Updated from data provided by the South-western Pennsylvania Regional Planning Commission (SPRPC) in Pittsburgh, May 2, 1996.

15. Ibid., p. 3.

16. Ibid., p. 12.

17. ACIR, *The Challenge of Local Governmental Reorganization*, Vol. 2 (Washington, D.C.: ACIR, February 1974), p. 2.

18. Ibid.

19. Ibid.

20. Ibid.

21. Ibid., p. 14.

22. Ibid., pp. 10–15.

23. Ibid., p. 12.

24. May, *Federalism*, p. 8.

25. Leach, *American Federalism*, p. 195.

26. *McCulloch vs. Maryland*, 4 Wheaton 316 (1819); *Osborn vs. Bank of the United States*, Wheaton 738 (1824); and *Weston vs. Charleston*, 2 Peters 449 (1829).

27. Leach, *American Federalism*, p. 175.

28. ACIR, *Regulatory Federalism: Policy, Process, Impact and Reform A-95* (Washington, D.C.: U.S. Government Printing Office, 1984), pp. 7-10; also Academy for State and Local Government, *Preemptions: Drawing the Line* (Washington, D.C.: Academy for Local Government, 1986).

29. David Berman, "State/Local Relations," in *Municipal Yearbook* (Washing-ton, D.C.: International City Management Association, 1992).

30. ACIR, *Federal Regulations of State and Local Governments: The Mixed Record of the 1980s*, A-126 (Washington, D.C.: Government Printing Office, July 1993), p. 46.

31. Kenneth S. Howard, "A Message from Garcia," *Public Adminstration Review* 45, Special Issue (November 1995): 738–41.

32. Deil S. Wright, *Federal Grants-in-Aid: Perspectives and Alternatives* (Washington, D.C.: American Enterprise Institute, 1968), p. 6.

33. Ibid., pp. 3, 5–77.

34. Condensed from Council of State Government, *Federal Grant and Aid* (Chicago: Council of State Government, 1949), pp. 41–42; ACIR, *Impact of Federal Urban Development Programs on Local Government Organizations and Planning*, *Committee on Government Operations*, U.S. Senate, 58th Congress, 2nd Session (1964), p. 22.

35. David B. Walker, "The Changing Patterns of Federal Assistance to State and Local Governments," in *Public Administration and Public Policy*, H. George Frederickson and Charles Wise, eds. (Lexington, Mass.: D. C. Heath, 1977), p. 82.

36. May, *Federalism*, p. 21.

37. U.S. Bureau of Census, *Governmental Finances in 1973–1974* (Washington, D.C.: Government Printing Office, November 1975), p. 47; U.S. Bureau of Census, *State Government Finances in 1974* (Washington, D.C.: Government Printing Office, August 1975), p. 59.

38. Bureau of Census, *Governmental Finances in 1973–1974*, pp. 31–32.

39. Jesse Burkhead, *Public School Finance: Economic and Politics* (Syracuse, New York: Syracuse University Press, 1964).

40. *San Antonio School District vs. Rodriguez*, 411 U.S. 1 (1973).

41. Richard P. Nathan and John K. Lago, "Intergovernmental Relations in the Reagan Era," *Public Budgeting and Finance* 8 (Autumn 1988): 27.

42. Steven D. Gold, "The Federal Role in State Fiscal Stress," *Publius* (Summer 1992): 33–47.

43. *Metropolitan America: Challenge to Federalism*, report of the Advisory Commission on Intergovernmental Relations, Committee on Government Operations, House of Representatives Committee Print, 89th Congress, 2nd Session (1966), p. 2.

44. Leach, *American Federalism*, p. 144.

45. Ibid., p. 146.

46. Ibid., p. 5.

47. ACIR, *Regional Decision-Making*, p. 8.

48. Ibid., p. 9.

49. David R. Bean, "New Federalism, Old Realities," in *The Reagan Presidency and the Governing of America*, Lester M. Salamon and Michael Lund, eds. (Washington, D.C.: Urban Institute, 1984), p. 420.

50. Observations obtained from interviews with intergovernmental administrators.

51. Leach, *American Federalism*, p. 174.

52. Senator Edmund Muskie, "The Challenge of Creative Federalism," *Saturday Review* (June 25, 1966), pp. 12–15.

53. Al Gore, *Creating A Government that Works Better and Costs Less* (Washington, D.C.: Government Printing Office, 1993).

17

International Administration
and Development

This chapter provides a very brief overview of the theory, setting, and conduct of international and development administration. The chapter begins with a brief overview of the underlying theories and principles on which international organizations generally operate. The United Nations is used as a case in point. In section two, again using the U.N. as an example, we attempt to show how personnel policies are determined and administered. The third section examines staffing in U.S. overseas programs. In the fourth section, we examine the problems and concerns that overseas personnel face. Section five briefly explores development administration theory, discussing approaches and practices found in the U.N. Development Program and the U.S. Agency for International Development. Section six discusses the role of top administrators. Section seven examines the role of MLMs in exercising power and accountability.

LEARNING OBJECTIVES

Upon completing this chapter, the reader should be able to:

- Understand the political context governing the administrative principles operating in international organizations.
- See how personnel policies are practiced in the United Nations.
- Appreciate the problems and concerns of overseas personnel.
- Recognize how national interests and objectives affect international organizations.
- Become aware of the evolving nature of development theory.
- Understand the role of MLMs in exercising power and accountability in international organizations and development administration.

Increasingly, we are coming to accept the reality that we live in a highly interdependent world in which domestic and foreign affairs are continually affected by many international cooperative agreements. For example, the Universal Postal Union makes it possible for us to exchange letters with individuals from the most remote places on the globe, and the International Telecommunication Union helps us to directly communicate with people virtually wherever modern technology has been introduced.

International organizations continue to come into being to satisfy the needs and desires of individual nations that wish to cooperatively carry out varying activities. These may range from the eradication of smallpox, to the monitoring of weather conditions, to the provision of a police force, or to maintaining peace in such areas as Lebanon or Bosnia.

From as few as 80 international bodies in the 1930s, there are now more than 200. The International Red Cross and the United Nations are two of the most prominent.[1] The 29 member states of the United Nations when it was formed in 1945 have now grown to 151, and they provide a U.N. staff of just over 35,000 employees.[2] The vast increase in U.N. member states and staff has increased the magnitude and complexity of obtaining international cooperation.

The growth of U.S. involvement in overseas problems parallels or even surpasses the growth of international agencies. Before World War II, the U.S. was represented abroad by only a small number of employees, the vast majority of whom came from the State Department. Now there are nearly 40,000 U.S. public servants representing many professions and government agencies. The emergence of the U.S. as the major world power following World War II significantly increased the number of U.S. personnel in overseas programs and international organizations. As John Macy Jr. observed: "During this quarter century of accelerated change, the American civil servant has taken up residence, usually for a short period of time, in virtually every country on the globe to perform the overseas tasks of the United States Government."[3]

Despite periods of disenchantment with U.S. policies abroad and the critical attitudes that are sometimes shown toward international organizations such as the United Nations, Americans of all ages are still excited about working overseas.[4] Similarly, many people elsewhere in the world are attracted to international organizations. One U.N. observer noted: "Many things that happen in the UN are history making, and if only in a small way, many people believe that it is an opportunity worth pursuing because it will permit them to participate in a positive way in the unfolding drama of history such as when a new nation is born under the auspices of the U.N."[5]

OPERATING THEORIES AND PRINCIPLES
OF INTERNATIONAL ORGANIZATION

The theories that undergird the administration of international organizations are seldom articulated at the birth of those organizations. Instead, theory is typically discerned from observing practice, as exhibited in the process of administration. The participants with the greatest power tend to incorporate the prevailing norms and practices of their countries.[6] According to Herbert

Lehman, this is an inevitable result and an accepted model for international administration.[7]

In retrospect, most international organizations employ classical or conventional organization theory, as set forth by Max Weber, Woodrow Wilson, and advocates of the administrative management schools. The structure of the United Nations, it is said, was a compromise between the views of Prime Minister Winston Churchill and President Franklin Roosevelt. Churchill wanted the U.N. to be based on a comprehensive system in which every activity could be related to others. This would have required decision-makers to continually keep in mind how their particular decisions related to or were affected by actions taken by other U.N. units. Roosevelt, on the other hand, held out for (and won) a functional organization based more on specialized activities, similar to the division-of-labor approaches practiced in the U.S. at all levels of government. While functionalization has the potential for bringing superior skills to bear on a problem, this approach tends to minimize the exchange of information and to create problems in achieving coordination.[8]

FINANCING INTERNATIONAL ORGANIZATIONS

The way an international organization is financed reflects an underlying concern about the way its members exercise power or political leverage. This view follows directly the basic theory underlying public budgeting. The more secure an agency's source of funding, the less opportunity external interests have to influence a particular policy. Thus, we note that the U.N. operates on two types of budgets—one based on specific assessment and the other on voluntary contributions.[9] Under the assessment type, there is little opportunity for nations to exercise policy influence over the agency's budget because each nation has only one vote. Voluntary contributions to international agencies, on the other hand, because there are no fixed limits, give the contributing nation maximum opportunity to influence policy direction, while at the same time protecting its national interest. This is perhaps one of the major reasons that the voluntary budget is the largest single U.N. budget. The U.N. Development Program (discussed at greater length in another section of this chapter) is a case in point. The voluntary contribution allows each member to contribute, or to refuse to do so, depending on the nature and direction of the U.N. policy being pursued. Indeed, M. Elmanjara feels that it is mainly through the financial structure that the issues and behavior in international organizations take on meaning: "If one were forced to choose, one should opt to read the membership of the organization and its series of annual budgets rather than its charter, for the charter has not proved to be the decisive determinant of the development of the U.N."[10]

STRUCTURE OF THE UNITED NATIONS

In examining the structure of the U.N. at its formation, we can glimpse its operating theory and principles. The dominant organizational idea in the U.N.

structure is the commitment to achieving efficiency. It reflects Weberian approaches of (1) strict hierarchical control; (2) merit and professionalism; (3) division of labor; and (4) loyalty and adherence to rules.

The reading of the U.N. Charter gives the impression of a strong executive. Unlike the heads of nation-states, the secretary-general appears to have unlimited power with respect to hiring, promotion, and dismissal of employees. As Lehman indicates, this internal power is indispensable because the leader must be given leverage in dealing with sovereign states.[11] It must be recognized, however, that the U.N. executive does not have power to act directly on member citizens. He or she must employ moral suasion to obtain agreement from member nations, and lacks the power to penalize constituents who fail to conform.

Powers of the Secretary-General

Article 97 of the U.N. Charter makes the secretary-general the chief executive officer of the organization, and Article 99 confers special political power on him or her. In 1945, the Preparatory Commission, which was concerned with putting the U.N. Charter into operation, gave the secretary-general powers to go beyond any authority previously accorded to the head of an international organization.[12] The secretary-general is empowered in Article 99 to bring to the attention of the U.N. Security Council any matter that may threaten the maintenance of international peace or security.[13] In appointing or deploying staff, the secretary-general does not have to obtain the consent of member governments from which staff are being drawn.[14] According to Sidney Bailey, "Since 1954, the policymaking organs (the General Assembly and the Security Council) have increasingly . . . [empowered] the Secretary-General with diplomatic and operational functions."[15]

Trygve Lie, the first secretary-general, viewed the discretionary political power in Article 99 broadly. Perhaps due to this interpretation, Lie has been described as a forceful initiator and doer: "Lie was never simply an administrator. He concerned himself with political questions and took definite positions when he considered that the principles of the Charter were at stake even when this seemed likely to bring him into conflict with one or the other great powers."[16]

Dag Hammarskjold, the second chief executive of the U.N. continued this broad interpretation. At the outset of his administration, in 1953, he asserted responsibility for all the actions that were explicitly or could be reasonably interpreted as being attached to the secretary-general's office.[17] In 1955, he acted as an intermediary in notifying Greece that Albania was interested in diplomatic relations and exchanged views with Beijing regarding the release of captured American personnel.[18] Reiterating his views upon his reappointment in 1957, Hammarskjold told the General Assembly that he would act if guidance could be found in the Charter or in decisions of the United Nations' main organs. He also said he would act without guidance where a vacuum existed or where the

U.N. Charter and traditional diplomacy provide no means of safeguarding international peace and security.[19]

In a speech in Chicago in 1960, Hammarskjold attempted to explain his responsibilities in constitutional terms. The Charter clearly set up a one-member "executive," he said, with explicit authority in administrative matters "supplementary to but not overlapping the authority of either the [Security] Council or Assembly."[20]

The way they perceived the power of their office and the way they used it brought both Lie and Hammarskjold into conflict with the former Soviet Union. The Soviets viewed Hammarskjold's handling of the Congo situation, in which the U.N. closed the airport and the radio stations, as being partial to that country's pro-Western president and detrimental to the Soviet-supported prime minister. This, among other concerns about the exercise of power by the secretary-general, generated a Soviet call in 1961 for a change from the singular U.N. executive. The Soviets argued that accountability to and protection of the interest of the major blocs could only be guaranteed by a plural executive known as the Troika, comprising representatives from the nonaligned, socialist, and capitalist blocs. This arrangement would ensure that the U.N. would not carry out actions detrimental to any of the component groups.[21]

The U.N. has many characteristics reminiscent of the U.S. government under the Articles of Confederation: (1) the inability to tax or deal directly with member nations' populations; (2) the apportionment of revenue needed for operations among the states; and (3) reliance on the state to equip and supply the resources for police or military action. A main difference, however, is the international civil service.

Merit and Professionalism

Commitment to the idea of an independent civil service can be traced back to the League of Nations and the 1920 Balfour Report.[22] The framers of the U.N. Charter clearly established the merit principle as a major criterion, with due recognition given to geography for the selection, hiring, and promotion of personnel. Recruitment of staff was to be an internal U.N. matter and states were prohibited from pressuring for their nationals to be hired for specific jobs: "The Secretariat was to be international in the sense of being staffed by appointees of the organization, paid exclusively by the organization, and responsible solely to it."[23] The Charter attempted to ensure that personnel would be independent and free from bias toward special interest groups or ideologies.[24] To foster independence, impartiality, and freedom from external pressures, positions are secured by tenure so that they can be professionalized and made careers.[25] As the U.N. Preparatory Commission observed in 1945:

Unless members of the staff can be offered some assurance of being able to make their careers in the Secretariat, many of the best candidates from all countries will inevitably be kept away. Nor can members of the staff be expected to subordinate the special interests of their countries to the international interest from national administrators and remain dependent on them for their future.[26]

In 1954, the International Civil Service Advisory Board (ICSAB) established four standards for the international civil servant to follow in the daily execution of his or her duties: (1) integrity, including such traits as honesty, trustworthiness, and freedom from corruption; (2) loyalty and willingness to be tolerant of different points of view, different work habits, and cultural patterns; (3) independence from authority external to the internal organization; and (4) impartiality, attempting to be objective and free from bias.[27]

Division of Labor

The division of labor is one of the important cornerstones of mechanistic or traditional organization theory. Though modern organization theorists have attacked extreme application of division of labor when it leads to boredom and lack of control of one's destiny, this basic principle has never been a point of contention in international organizations. Functional specialization, in which work, as, for example, in a personnel department, is broken down into such components as position classification, record keeping, salary administration, and performance evaluation, is an accepted norm.

Loyalty and Adherence to Rules and Procedures

The requirement for organizational loyalty is clearly spelled out in U.N. rules and regulations. Prior to taking a U.N. position, prospective members must swear their loyalty to the organization as follows:

I solemnly swear . . . to exercise in all loyalty, discretion and conscience the functions entrusted to me as an international civil servant of the United Nations, to discharge those functions and regulate my conduct with the interest of the United Nations only in view and not to seek or accept instructions to the performance of my duties from any other authority external to the organization.[28]

ADMINISTERING PERSONNEL POLICIES AT THE UNITED NATIONS: BRIEF OVERVIEW

Since Article 100 of the U.N. Charter gives the secretary-general sole discretion for the recruitment, selection, and management of personnel, it might naturally be assumed that the responsibility can be discharged as a routine administrative activity. However, multiple factors come into play to render this notion untenable. Some nations look at their nationals' work at the U.N. as a potential source of leverage, and others view their nationals' work for the U.N. as a brain drain. Still other countries see U.N. employment as a training ground for administrators to gain valued experience. Indeed, some governments may view working with the U.N. as a source of employment for their educated intelligentsia or radicals who may be a source of trouble at home. These, among other considerations, create a complex set of dynamics that makes the administration of personnel policies critically important.

Filling Vacancies

As vacancies occur in operating departments, the central Personnel Services makes the information available throughout the U.N. system, including its specialized agencies, such as the World Health Organization (WHO) and the Food and Agriculture Organization (FAO). Initially, the system attempts to fill vacancies from within. Only when the vacancy cannot be filled internally does the U.N. advertise in national publications in member nations. Whenever recruitment is sought externally, geography must be considered. As noted above, competence is not enough. Ideally, the competent individual must also be from the appropriate (underrepresented) geographical areas. To help fulfill the organization's mandate to obtain geographical distribution, U.N. policy permits the training of talented individuals from underrepresented countries, subject to budgetary constraint.

Controversies over geography and tenure. At the heart of the personnel controversy is disagreement over the relative weight to be given merit and geography. The large and economically developed countries have extensive cadres of trained professionals, but some less developed countries (LDCs) have only limited numbers of such trained persons. The idea behind the geographical principle is that professionals at the U.N. should be drawn from as diverse a geographical base as possible. Because there are only a few professional positions available, keen competition ensues, resulting in professionals from a few countries—usually the large ones—topping the merit assessments made. This result is contrary to the geographical distribution objective.

Nevertheless, it is argued that the criterion of equitable geographical distribution, given secondary status to merit in the U.N. Charter, has now become the central determinant of U.N. hiring policy.[29] Theodore Meron believes that geography tends to take precedence when merit and geography are not congruent: "The United Nations Secretariat has not developed as yet, a complete sophisticated system of comparing various national university degrees, system of education, types of practical and professional experience acquired in different states."[30] With the lack of definitive criteria, external pressure for greater geographical distribution allows the administrator to exercise considerable subjective judgment in selecting candidates. In Meron's view, this practice has resulted in the overrepresentation of some developing states.[31]

Of the major powers, the former Soviet Union has been the most consistent critic of U.N. Secretariat staffing. In the 1966 General Assembly Fifth Committee, the Soviet representative stated that a permanent contract permits "staff to pursue a life-long career in the United Nations, prevents underrepresented countries from gaining access to the Secretariat, and cuts off the flow of fresh talent, experience, and knowledge."[32] With the independent and assertive role of the secretary-general in the early 1960s, the Soviets began to maintain that the career concept practiced in the U.N. was inimical to their interests. In the Soviet view, impartial international civil servants are not possible.[33] Russia, which succeeded the Soviet Union in the U.N., has taken a more supportive stance of U.N. operating systems.

The traditional positions of the various nations and blocs are often exchanged regarding the criteria for selection and promotion.

1.   North Atlantic Treaty Organization (NATO) countries uphold the career principle as the major personnel grouping, with some temporary staff appointments.

2.   Countries making up the former Warsaw Pact group take varying positions or selective criteria. Generally, most are supportive of the status quo.

3.   Delegates from African and Asian countries continue to push for a greater share of posts in the Secretariat and support increasing the number of fixed-term appointments.[34]

When their interests have converged, as in the demand for more equitable geographical representation, developing countries have teamed up to pursue these interests collectively. A good example of this occurred in 1966 when Iran, Cameroon, and Hungary put forth a resolution in the General Assembly asking the secretary-general to relax recruitment on the basis of permanent contracts and to give greater preference to candidates from under-represented countries.[35]

Appointment outside the career system. Most U.N. agencies employ temporary personnel in the field for technical assistance projects in developing countries.[36] David A. Kay would like to see far more staffing take place by fixed-term contracts, which would increase the present ratio of 25 percent temporary (fixed-term) contracts to 75 percent permanent contracts. He believes that permanent appointments in international organizations are not conducive to effectiveness and that fixed-term contracts should be more the rule than the exception.[37] Henry Raymond, on the other hand, feels that most U.N. employees should have permanent status.[38] His view is that permanency will encourage highly qualified people to make their careers in the Secretariat. To do otherwise, he argues, will keep away the talented and have a detrimental effect on the agency.

Seymour Finger and John Mugno agree with Raymond and take sharp exception to Kay, noting that the political pressures applied to "geographical balance" have had harmful effects on the quality of the U.N. staff.[39] They ask for a redoubling of U.N. resolve to uphold Article 101, which seeks "the highest standards of efficiency, competence, and integrity." Finally, John Macy believed that many problems have occurred with geographical balance, but that on the whole it has worked reasonably well.[40]

Loyalty

The issue of loyalty is especially difficult in an international organization. Do simply taking an oath and receiving the prescribed standards set forth by the ICSAB transform individuals into neutral civil servants? A number of U.N. members, particularly the former Soviet Union and other Warsaw Pact nations, think not. According to Tien Cheng Young, simply changing location and meeting people from different cultures may not be enough to dissipate one's prejudices and transform one's dislikes into love and harmony.[41] Expressing a somewhat similar view, David Owens has observed: "It may well be asked, is it really possible that men and women, conditioned by their own particular national and social inheritance and upbringing, and governed by normal human possessions and frailties, can exhibit such loyalty in continuous practice?"[42]

We must come to grips with some practical realities that can fundamentally test the loyalty of international civil servants. Young believes that there are several models of loyalty, depending on the home country's pattern, that staff members bring with them to the U.N. Secretariat:

1. Those coming from countries that have a tradition of impartiality can serve any master with little mental adjustment.
2. Those coming from countries where the civil servants are part of the political regime are likely to change when the regime does.
3. For those from countries with no civil service tradition, a position with the Secretariat may be a matter of personal prestige and means for securing political leverage at home, and international loyalty may be no more than lip service.
4. For some the position in the Secretariat amounts to nothing more than a place for employment. Indeed, some participants from the Third World believe that members of the Secretariat should be allowed to take public positions on any important and controversial issues in the world.[43]

Salary

In 1945, the U.N. Preparatory Commission incorporated the 1921 Noblemaire Report, which enunciated the basic principle on which the League of Nations pay structure would be based.[44] The principle required salary to be based on "the highest home civil service of any member state."[45] To this the U.N. has added two other basic principles: (1) salaries for internationally recruited staff should be the same, regardless of an individual's nationality; and (2) the salary system should give due cognizance of the individual's purchasing power at home. These three principles constitute what is called the common system. The basic objective behind this common system was to make international civil service pay attractive enough to personnel in all member countries. Initially, the pay scale was based on the British system. Later, it was patterned on the U.S. system in an effort to attract U.S. citizens. The ICSAB has made attempts to devise a global "market rate" that would determine pay on a "composite of salaries paid by various public and private international organizations but statistical, and political difficulties conspired against it."[46]

Despite these three clear-cut criteria for salary determination, problems remain. In the first place, it is often difficult to find a counterpart job in a member country to serve as a guide for the international rate. Making periodic adjustments is another problem, because increments in some countries are determined through collective bargaining. In these cases, the rates arrived at reflect many other factors: conditions of work, fringe benefits, and comparable work performed by similarly situated workers. The result is that international organizations are forced to peg salaries on the basis of conditions that do not obtain at the international level.[47]

The pay scales that have been set, particularly those that were designed to attract Americans to international organizations, have come under sharp criticism. More than 100 positions in the U.N. now pay in excess of $70,000. In addition, there are fringe benefits, particularly of travel and education for dependents, that are more favorable than those available in member states. A further example is that all professional employees, whether stationed in the U.S. or elsewhere, receive a post adjustment in addition to regular salary. Only the European Union bureaucracy has a higher pay scale than the U.N. [48]

In a 1976 congressional report, the U.S. Senate Committee on Government Operations complained about the salary levels at the U.N., the World Bank, and the International Monetary Fund. It was found that the fringe benefits for U.N. employees average about 45 percent to 73 percent above the U.S. civil service level.[49] Ten years later in 1986, a member of the International Civil Service Commission estimated that compensation margins between the U.S. and U.N. civil service ranged between 17 percent and 24 percent. The U.N. has expressed the view that its pay system is based on two operating principles: "(1) that international civil servants should receive equal pay for equal work (referred to as the common system of salaries and allowances); and (2) that professionals-and-above employees should receive compensation high enough to attract nationals from the highest paid national civil service. . . . "[50]

The State Department has said it can get little collective action on questions of U.N. salaries because the other members' contributions to the budget are not significant enough to cause them concern. U.S. officials also point out that competition with the European Union has pushed costs up in international organizations.[51]

STAFFING FOR U.S. OVERSEAS PROGRAMS

In examining staffing policies for a single nation, we encounter many of the same kinds of problems that are experienced in an international organization. The U.S. State Department's educational requirement presents social and geographical biases not unlike those faced in the U.N. The three major areas of the State Department dealing with foreign affairs are the U.S. Foreign Service,

U.S. Agency of International Development (AID), and the U.S. Information Agency (USIA). These agencies are concerned respectively with career diplomatic services, provision of technical aid in development projects, and dissemination of information about the U.S. throughout the world.

The Foreign Service recruitment patterns contrast sharply with those of AID. Where the latter puts emphasis on obtaining trained and experienced individuals, the Foreign Service seeks young college graduates recruited by annual examinations, whom it trains and molds to become the elite.[52] USIA, on the other hand, basically follows the Foreign Service model but obtains more middle- and top-level personnel by lateral entry (personnel coming from other agencies or units at approximately the same level).[53] Emphasizing more the USIA model of recruitment, the Secretary of State Committee on Foreign Affairs Personnel (1962) recommended that the State Department recruit fewer young generalists and more older recruits with special skills and management experience, many of whom would be women and minorities from graduate programs and law schools.[54]

Though a joint board of examiners has been suggested to replace the State Department Board of Examiners for the Foreign Service and include the representation of the Civil Service Commission (now Office of Personnel Management), it was not approved by Congress. The USIA and the State Department have, however, resumed the practice of giving joint junior officers' examinations.

In their styles and approaches, AID and the Foreign Service provide interesting contrasts.[55] The Foreign Service officer cannot afford to spend much time with host country nationals without impeding his or her chances for promotion. Interaction with Americans in the Foreign Service is viewed as a positive factor in promotion; without it, the officer abroad would be isolated from changes going on in the organization as a whole.[56] The reverse is true for the AID official, who must be intimately associated with host nationals.[57] Finally, AID has operated under a continuing state of uncertainty since 1962 due to its temporary mandate. AID can not promise any long-term career opportunities for its personnel because Congress could terminate it at any time. The Foreign Service, however, has a long-standing career tradition.[58]

PROBLEMS AND CONCERNS OF OVERSEAS PERSONNEL

In working in our local environments, we are able to use family, business, and government contacts to help us to adapt. When living overseas we are likely to face much that is unfamiliar—language, customs, laws, governmental structure, and patterns and modes of living. Working for an international agency is not like working for one's own government.

The number and degree of problems that will be faced depend on the individual's background, training, personality, and ability to adapt to new environments. Although adjustment may be difficult, many seek overseas assignments because they believe the rewards outweigh the costs and discomfort. These rewards include: (1) respect earned by being an international civil servant; (2) a higher standard of living, particularly for a native of a less developed country living in a developed country; and (3) the ability to mute career failures if they occur.[59] Of the drawbacks, lack of language skills and isolation are the most serious. This section will briefly examine overseas personnel concerns relating to language and isolation.

Language

The lack of language facility is perhaps the most serious problem encountered in overseas assignments. The frustration of being unable to properly speak the local language exacerbates the problem of adjustment. It keeps reminding the individual that he or she is in a foreign country but not part of it, creating a lack of understanding toward the host country and its people. The State Department now promotes language study among its personnel, recognizing that few Americans recruited for overseas jobs have fluency in other languages. In 1970, the department's Task Force on Personnel Training urged that "in a country in which language and knowledge is essential to the effective conduct of specific jobs, one or more of the officers in a mission should have a competence in the principle language and in related dialects as well." Additionally, the report suggested that an inventory be made of the language fluency and that important positions (administrative, political, and economic) be staffed with individuals who have demonstrated language facility. The same task force also recommended that continued advanced training be given when feasible and that spouses also be given the opportunity for language training.[60] To meet its responsibility in this area, the Foreign Service Institute has upgraded and expanded its language programs.[61]

Language proficiency is as important in international organizations as it is in national overseas commitments. In monitoring committee meetings in international bodies, considerable advantage goes to those who have complete command of the official languages. Alexander Lovejoy has observed that "those who possess [language fluency] are likely to advance more rapidly than those who do not."[62]

The U.N., like the State Department, has recognized the critical need to upgrade language fluency. In 1968, the U.N. General Assembly adopted a plan to permit salary bonuses when employees obtain a certificate of competence in a second of the official languages (English and French). While this plan was not adopted at the time (due to the opposition of the ICSAB), it has since been adopted on an expanded basis. For facility in two languages beyond one's native tongue, additional bonuses are awarded.[63] At the U.N. headquarters in New York, it is possible for staff members to learn up to six languages free of charge. Officials have expressed satisfaction concerning the progress in language proficiency that has been made.[64]

Isolation

At the U.N., one observer pointed out a number of other problems that arise from being separate from one's home country:

- There is a feeling of isolation.
- There are internal stresses in the family when the young make cross-cultural adaptations more easily than the old.
- There is concern about the Americanizing of children at U.N. headquarters.
- When children are sent back to the home country for education, husbands and wives are forced together who might have led more separate lives at home.
- There is a feeling of civic impotence (especially in the U.S.) due to the prohibitions on U.N. personnel participating in U.S. electoral processes.
- Death or divorce usually means that the family must leave the host country.[65]

In AID, for example, isolation from the host country culture (the creation of American ghetto communities abroad) fosters social cohesion that helps U.S. personnel cope with an unfamiliar environment. At the same time, however, this cohesiveness weakens the ability of AID personnel to sensitively understand the local culture.[66] This is especially disturbing when it is realized that only maximum personal interaction with the host country nationals can compensate for past "big stick" approaches and "dollar diplomacy." Similarly, the European powers' colonial domination of Asia and Africa is still remembered with resentment. Thus, actions that call to mind the past will make it difficult for the U.S. to dispel apprehensions about direct U.S. foreign aid, as opposed to aid coming from an international body such as the U.N.

HISTORICAL MODELS OF ADMINISTRATION AND DEVELOPMENT

This section is concerned with the meaning of development administration, problems with existing theory, and a brief examination of development administration models in AID and the United Nations Development Program (UNDP).

Development of Administration Systems

Differing administrative models have flourished for long periods. Around 1500 BC, the Chinese practiced the Mandarin system based on elites who dominated the decision-making process. The system was characterized by three main features: (1) functional specialization of the state in specific areas such as agriculture; (2) a well-defined hierarchy; and (3) selection by merit and competition as a condition for holding a government position.

Around 1000 BC, the Egyptians practiced the technician model, including architects and engineers who were then Egypt's bureaucratic elite. Emphasis was put on technical and physical aspects. During the period between 27 BC and AD 476,. the Roman model emerged, stressing financial administration and control exercised through taxation and collection of levies. The Roman system drew distinctions between private and public responsibilities of the head of state and the separation of personal property of the head of state. Additionally, the Roman model included civil servants and citizens who had particular rights and obligations.

The history of these administrative systems shows that as these bureaucracies grew, they gained increasing prominence. The fast growth of these systems produced excessively centralized bureaucracies, corruption, and the abuse of power.

From AD 300 to 1500, the European Model rose to prominence. When the Roman empire collapsed, the European system reverted to the fused system in which there was no hierarchy or layers, only loyalty to the apex of the administrative system. The monarchs, clothed in divine right, became the absolute rulers. The bureaucracy emerged as an important institution based on the classic administrative system in Prussia. The Prussian bureaucracy was legalistic and highly elitist. Membership required university education. In time the Prussian administrative model became the dominant model throughout Europe.

Max Weber's writings provided the main source of knowledge of the Prussian bureaucracy.[67] He set forth three main types of authority:

1.   The *traditional model* incorporated the fused system of the Chinese and Roman empires that demanded loyalty to the hereditary rulers of the state.
2.   The *charismatic ruler* obtained the support of his followers because of his special captivating qualities.
3.   The *legal rational model* shifted loyalty to the state, its political leadership and the supporting bureaucracy, which had specifically defined characteristics such as a chain of command, division of labor, merit selection, specialization, and defined rules (see Chapter 7).

Scholars such as Fred Riggs criticized the legal-rational model as irrelevant as a practical guide for developing countries. Riggs put forward his own models: (1) the *traditional fused model* in which the ruler exercises authority, directs all functions, and commands total loyalty; (2) the *defracted model*, which in a modern society typically applies rational rules and process in implementing laws and regulations; and (3) the *prismatic model*, which has attributes of both the fused and the defracted on modern society—that is, the system has the appearance of rational rules for operating the government.[68] However, the rules are never uniformly enforced, and bribes and tributes distort the implementation of the laws.

DEVELOPMENT ADMINISTRATION: WHAT DOES IT MEAN?

Traditionally, development administration has been studied in the political science subarea of comparative government. Woodrow Wilson's classic essay, "The Study of Public Administration," drew attention to the need for more rigorous study of different types of regimes so that we may find universal principles to assist in improving the mechanics for carrying on the public's business. Other writers reinterpreted, re-emphasized, and gave new meaning to Wilson's statement of the need to examine other societies and culture.[69]

Despite recognition of the value of comparative studies, there has been little change from orthodox principles of public administration—the emphasis on structure, the maintenance of the status quo, and continuing concern for efficiency and performance. The theories that have been developed tend to be broad extrapolations of existing practices and are only minimally based on empirical findings.[70] Although these orthodox principles are useful for a general framework, they do not constitute a practical guide for the development administrator struggling to achieve specific goals abroad.

Development administration evolved in the 1950s from a merger of classical economics and public administration, and its adherents defined development from a strictly economic perspective. The organization designed to achieve economic objectives was structured on the Weberian model of bureaucracy, and development was measured in terms of per capita increases in the gross national product. In other words, development was equated with the amount of tangible resources produced in relation to the size of the population, expressed in such terms as industrial output, agricultural produce, and raw materials. The determinant of the growth of productive goods (output) was dependent on the inputs or factors of production of land, labor, and capital (with special attention being given to the efficient use of the last). Technology was considered neutral.

Consequently, most development plans created between the 1950s and 1960s indicated the extent of growth expected by showing how the per capita gross national product would be increased. This emphasis later gave way, in developing societies, to values and priorities on ways to achieve equitable distribution of wealth and income, full utilization of workers, better utilization of natural resources, and protection of the human environment."[71]

It is interesting to note that development, defined in the broader sense above, goes beyond a concern for the impact that increases in the gross national product have on other social and physical factors in a particular country. This broad definition views development as a state of mind, a psychological condition. For example, when a government creates jobs to make work in a society where work is necessary to give minimal subsistence and a sense of worth, productivity has very little meaning.

In defining development administration we need to recognize the dual nature of the term. First, we mean the political commitment and the enhancement or improvement of the techniques, processes, and systems that have been organized and effectively coordinated to increase the administrative capacity. Second, we also mean the state of readiness and the degree and extent to which organizational skills of government agencies, in the case of the public sector, can be mobilized and applied to realize development goals and objectives.[72]

Our emphasis on political commitment is crucial because it indicates the seriousness of the government's involvement and shows the priorities of the leaders and their willingness to provide legitimacy and to use their power and influence to generate popular and organizational support for the developmental objectives. Thus, administrative capability is viable and efficacious only to the extent that it is based on realistic congruence with the political and social context of each situation. In this context, power and accountability are brought together to achieve the common objective of development. The administrative capability, which is most concerned with how the developmental goals will be achieved, is meshed with the values as authoritatively set forth by the political leaders. This is very important because development is at the center of the politics of developing countries.

BASIC APPROACHES TO DEVELOPMENT

While the role of the state in productive economic policies is diminishing in developing countries, it still has a place on the agenda in developing countries. There are a number of basic approaches to development that may be pursued:

1. *Imperialism* suggests that the country is ruled by an external power. While this approach may not typically be idealized as a development approach, it has played a major role in many developing countries. Imperialist policies were concerned more with economic policies than the expansion of European culture, language, and administration. Yet the policies made major contributions to the developmental processes in the different colonies.

2. *Modernization* emerged after World War II. It emphasized foreign technical assistance programs and was led by the United States. These main components were emphasized:

    A. The *empathy concept* ensured that there were two distinct social stages that operated within the country. The traditional society is characterized by a value system that is not development-oriented, while the modern stage is.

    B. *Industrialization* focuses the country on the societal level as opposed to the individual level. Modernization is viewed from two polar perspectives, having a dual economy. The society is dichotomized as Western and non-Western or as traditional and industrial. From time to time the society moves from one approach to the other.[73] The traditional society is typically agrarian and committed to fixed rules, customs, and functions. The industrial approach employs rational, universalist rules, laws, merit, social mobility and division of duties. These societies tend to be rich, techno-logical, urban, literate, and democratic.

C. *Social mobilization* is a process in which the state is the chief initiator in bringing about modernization. This approach sees the state and the bureaucracy gradually transforming the society from a personalist orientation to commitment to universalist values. The state is a strong, main driver of actions. With the partnership of the bureaucracy, the state becomes the supreme agent of change.[74]

There have been a number of challenges to modernization. *Dependency theory* challenges the underlying assumptions of modernization and the idea of a dual economy. Unlike modernization, which holds that poverty is internally created, dependency theory holds that poverty is externally introduced based on the policies of the developed economies and their periphery (developing economies). To overcome the problems of dependency and to correct the problem of inherent modernization, three social dependency strategies have been proposed: (a) regional cooperation; (b) avoiding dependency by reducing economic transactions with developed countries; and (c) self-sufficiency.[75]

3. The *basic needs theory* rejects the view that development depends on the rural society's becoming urbanized. It says that focus must be put on improving the agricultural sector and its related infrastructure. The bureaucracy is given a prominent role to provide required support such as education and health to encourage rural development.[76]

4. *Neo-orthodoxy* was given prominence during President Reagan's tenure. The laissez-faire view of limited government was accepted as the preferred operating norm and government was expected to have no role in the productive process of the country. Neo-orthodoxy is based on three strategies: privatization, market exchange, and public sector reform. Government is expected to achieve greater results with fewer resources. President Clinton's "reinvention of government" subscribes to aspects of the neo-orthodoxy approach.

DEVELOPMENT ADMINISTRATION THEORY AND PRACTICE: SOME PROBLEMS

It is commonly said that the rise of the modern state came hand in hand with the development of the rational bureaucratic structure. According to Lucian Pye, "The fact remains that effective bureaucratic structures have made the modern nation-state possible."[77] Though there is little empirically based information to tell us how and to what extent this assumption is true, it has been widely accepted. The natural next step then has been the attempt to implement the rational bureaucratic machinery (as based on Max Weber, with its emphasis on a neutral competent civil service and professionalism) in developing countries. A number of concerns, however, must be recognized with the operation of the neutral, competent civil service:

- It accepts the dichotomy between policy and administration.
- It promotes individual and organizational survival.

- It routinizes activities in an attempt to preserve the status quo.
- Because of education and connections, it may be a source of elite power, generating awe and resentment.
- It may be the only instrument or organized machinery in a developing country.
- The Bureaucrats, because of the above, constitute a major power base and/or hindrance to political leaders.

In advocating the neutral, competent civil service for developing countries a number of problems must be faced. First, there is no guide to tell at what state in a country's history a neutral civil service is desirable. As a case in point, the modern neutral, competent civil service did not emerge in the U.S. until after the passage of the Pendleton Act in 1883. Second, and much more to the point, during its period of greatest modernization and development, the U.S. had a spoils system. Corruption in both the public and private sectors was largely overlooked precisely because corruption seems to be a means for accelerating the pace of development. Third, neutral competence has been a mixed blessing. In recent decades it has brought unresponsiveness, and Franklin Roosevelt had to establish competing agencies to get around it. President Nixon complained about the same problem and attempted to reorganize the government strategically by placing loyal supporters in administrative positions in an effort to gain greater responsiveness. It would seem, therefore, that neutral competence may be a "blessing" that some developing countries can ill afford.

The assumption of the universal applicability of the Weberian bureaucratic model tends to ignore the importance of the situational context. It is likely that such factors as leadership, resources, and needs will differ from place to place. In a country where farmers have little access to roads to get their commodities to local or export markets easily, it is counterproductive to build four-lane highways to accommodate fast-moving vehicles. Similarly, the attempt to transfer to developing countries new management styles with their lack of emphasis on hierarchy will likely find little acceptance.[78]

Enthusiasm for building up structural administrative development capability must be tempered by an understanding of the situational context of each country or community. Means to accommodate the political leadership must also be incorporated, so that policymaking is not separated from administration. Perhaps most important, greater attention should be given to the notion of an organic structure, one that is put together to meet existing needs, not built in anticipation of future ones.

The technology transfer efforts of the past two decades illustrate a basic feature of public administration that has been so extensively and expensively exported to developing countries: It has aimed more at maintenance needs than developmental needs. Moreover,

some western scholars have come to fear the possible effects of bureaucratic modernization in countries with feasible political institutions. The bureaucrats might take command of policy making as well as execution. The emergence of "technocrats" as key elements of policy leadership in a number of development countries suggests some basis for concern.[79]

Public Administration and the Academic Community

In most developing countries, public administration tends to operate outside the intellectual stream of regular disciplines. A number of reasons have been offered for this. It is said that public administration is more concerned with the practical side of getting things done, with little interest in the development of knowledge. Public administration has had difficulty in gaining respectability, especially because the leaders of the older disciplines (e.g., sociology and political science) do not see themselves as client-oriented.[80]

In many developing countries, the universities and the government tend to live in a state of continued tension, resulting in mutual distrust between those institutions. Academicians believe that the government will seek to influence the development of knowledge, while the government feels that the universities will subvert its policies. For this reason, leaders of developing countries often create new and competing institutions (e.g., institutes of public administration) outside the established institutional structures. By so doing, they believe that they can affect the development of knowledge.

The university-government conflict in developing countries contrasts sharply with their relationship in the U.S. Many reasons account for this, including the larger role that the public sector now plays, the greater concern for making government operations more efficient, and the availability of federal funds for research. Yet there is also concern in the U.S. about the way knowledge is developed and used. In many cases, when the government submits problems to the attention of scholars, it has already determined the solution, and scholarly intervention is intended mainly to marshal confirming data and information. Of particular interest is that most of the research findings that have government support are never utilized. Thus, there seems to be two levels of knowledge: (1) knowledge acquired to legitimize a solution already reached; and (2) knowledge obtained through rigorous and disinterested research. The competition of these two levels of knowledge has a built-in tension.

Definitional Problems

Literature on development administration, comparative politics, and economic development can be a source of confusion and frustration because of the imprecision and uncertainty in the use of words and concepts. Such words as decentralization, deconcentration, development administration, and civil service are used with varying meanings. In some cases the same writer uses terms differently. Additionally, there is no common source to which one can turn to find any degree of uniformity or codification. Writers rarely include glossaries.[81]

Geopolitical Factors: Resistance to Change

International organizations that are important potential contributors to development administration operate in the framework of each particular country's national interest.[82] As noted earlier, international organizations, such as those falling under the U.N. umbrella, are functionally rather than systematically structured. This functionalization (organizations structured on the basis of specialized knowledge) has created fragmented policymaking and isolated agencies, giving many of them the feeling of self-sufficiency. In many of the agencies, budgets are determined on the basis of voluntary contributions and are administered through decentralized boards or commissions. The chief executive (such as the secretary-general) cannot use the budget as an effective means of control. This has been the cause of much lack of coordination among agencies, such as the U.N. Conference on Trade and Development (UNCTAD), the United Nations Development Program (UNDP), the World Bank, and the International Monetary Fund.[83]

The functional division by which international organizations are generally structured is not accidental, as was noted earlier in this chapter. The nations that had the greatest influence in creating international organizations acted to maximize their national interests. For example, the requirement that certain technical reports or feasibility studies be produced and the required representation of specific skills on many international bodies mean that only a few technologically advanced nations have personnel eligible to assume such positions. The requirement that materials purchased with loans from a particular country be transported by ships of the financing country provides yet another example of the pursuit of national interest.

It is important to remember that international bodies do not act with a single mind for people everywhere. International interest is but a reflection of the segmented, enlightened, or unenlightened sum of individual nations' interests. International bodies are not a system of people but a system of governments. Thus, changes in the U.N. and other international agencies can only be realized if the individual nations view such changes as coinciding with their national interests.

MODELS FOR ADMINISTRATION FOR DEVELOPMENT AID

Many types of approaches have been used to encourage development. One means involved the establishment of some 70 institutions of public administration throughout the developing world. Among the institutions participating were the University of Southern California, Harvard University, and the University of Pittsburgh. The last-named worked for nearly a decade in institution-building at the University of Malaya and at Ahmadu Bello University in northern Nigeria. Such an undertaking involved bilateral and multilateral aid through the UNDP, the Ford Foundation, and AID.

AID

AID is a provider of "technical assistance, which may be defined as supplying of expert professional personnel [to] the developing countries, the training of nationals of the countries at home through fellowships and abroad, and research, scientific, and technical problems by aiding countries for developing" (as in research into tropical diseases or agricultural products).[84]

According to C. J. Dove, the objective of AID is to facilitate a two-way process of communication in bringing about change. The following steps are included:

1.   The prospective recipient country articulates a problem.
2.   That country and the U.S. (the resource-contributing country) exchange information regarding the problem.
3.   Mutual understanding as to whether the problem is to be partially or totally met is arrived at and the U.S. pledges resources, resulting in joint development objectives.
4.   Objectives are converted into plans, and the plans are executed with joint participation.[85]

Judith Tendler summarizes:

The country mission was based on the belief that development assistance involved more than mere routine cut-and-dried transfer of capital, and that such efforts could be successful only if institutional and experimental factors were brought to bear on the design of development projects. This could be done only by the technicians with a feel for the country under constant exposure to problems, and familiarity with—specifically, by having the technicians live in the assisted country.[86]

AID may thus be described as using the country-adjusted model designed to reduce alienation. This is in opposition to the International Bank for Reconstruction and Development (IBRD), which employs the briefcase approach: The expert stops over for few days, expresses his ideas, and leaves, having little feeling for the country's limitations and possibilities.

The philosophy of AID's model contrasts sharply with some of its practices. Encouraging of AID personnel to empathize with the nationals of their host country is virtually obliterated by the privileges given AID employees as added inducement to work abroad. These privileges include:

- access to the Army PX
- a housing allowance that covers rent and utilities (up to specified limits)
- an Army Post Office (APO) system that makes it possible to circumvent the host country's mail system
- the opportunity to import duty-free from around the world
- low or free maintenance of furniture and major appliances

- an organized liquor pool, allowing liquor to be purchased at one-third the U.S. retail cost
- government medical and accident care
- a one round trip per year (to and from the post) for each dependent attending a school outside the host country.

UNDP

While AID represents a single national effort—namely, that of the U.S. to promote development—the U.N. Development Program is an international effort toward development. The UNDP is funded through voluntary contributions by member nations, and "[t]he primary objectives of UNDP are to support the efforts of the developing countries, to accelerate their economic and their individual and collective self-reliance for such efforts through sustained assistance to them in the field of technical cooperation based upon their national development priorities."[87]

The UNDP, created to act as a central coordinating body for all U.N. programs dealing with development, serves two major functions: (1) as an instrument for allocating resources to development projects throughout the U.N. system; and (2) as a coordinating arm of the operating agencies engaged in carrying out development activities. The UNDP provides four basic services:

1. It surveys and assesses such things as farmland, forests, rivers, and subsurface.
2. It stimulates capital investment as needed.
3. It assists countries in selecting and applying suitable and environmentally sound technologies.
4. It provides training in various vocations and professions.
5. It assists in economic and social planning, giving particular attention to the least developed countries and the poorest segment of the population.

Geopolitics and UNDP Financing

Because the UNDP budget is determined by voluntary member contributions, it tends to be unpredictable, creating uncertainty not only for UNDP but especially for the operating agencies receiving its funds. The UNDP has experienced crises from time to time due to a shortfall in revenue, which forced it to drastically cut back its distribution of funds to executing agencies.

During the mid-1970s, a major cause of the fiscal crisis can be traced to the undersubscription of the U.S. The voluntary subscription on which the budget is based allows each member to withhold contributions or provide it only to the extent that UNDP policies coincide with member nations' national interests. Thus, the present voluntary financial arrangement for the UNDP allows maximum maneuvering aimed at enhancing individual member's national objectives.

Changing Emphasis in Development Administration

The traditional emphasis in development administration has been on building techniques and administrative structures as the critical means for development. Institutions for building development capability were introduced without a thorough understanding of the environmental factors (cultural, social, economic, political, etc.) of the particular country. This orientation allowed public administration to be viewed as an end in itself. Public administration became more an instrument to allow elites to perpetuate their interests and to dominate and oppress the people. The controllers of the administrative apparatus neglected to search for solutions to problems and confined themselves to territorial maintenance, never venturing beyond a given jurisdiction. The pursuit of these objectives has resulted in continuing goal displacement—too expensive and burdensome for the typical developing country. These concerns, among others, have forced a rethinking in development administration. The earlier emphasis on building up administrative tools and techniques and equating them with development has been repudiated. Some important reasons for this turn of events are: the rigid adherence to procedures, the inability to see administration as an instrumental means and not an end in itself, and failure to link inputs (the resources required to undertake a program) with outputs and, ultimately, with impact or effectiveness. These factors made it difficult to obtain support for public administration. Administration has been forced to change in order to take due cognizance of the economic, political, social, and cultural forces operating in its environment.

Now (unlike before) public administration structures and developed to accommodate specific functional activities. Indeed, training in areas such as project planning management, financial management, local revenue and tax policy, and labor-intensive public works has taken on renewed interest. But it is no longer viewed as desirable apart from the sector or specific area where it can be used to assist in achieving the development objectives sought. Development training capacities are initiated only as they are related to a specific need in agriculture or health and not because a particular profession or interest demands it. The new focus aims at building capacity in those sectors and countries where they are needed.

The operating emphasis seeks to bring the development efforts in harmony with the organic conditions taking place in the environment. (In developing countries, the environment may be the most critical element in the development process. In Bolivia, for example, the health minister changes virtually every year.) There is a conscious effort to deliver goods and services that people want. Administration is no longer seen as a separate and compartmentalized instrument, but, more particularly, as it serves development efforts to enable people. There is greater effort to promote more meaningful participation in development efforts both by the individual donor countries and international organizations such as the U.N., the World Bank, and the International Monetary Fund.

Finally, administrative development emphasis in the international arena is focused on rural development. Some of the administrative concerns are not unlike those in the U.S. In developing countries, people in rural areas demand decentralization and greater attention to their problems. Similarly, in the U.S., there is a continuous cry to move Washington and the state capitals to the field or community. Additionally, many labor unions, as in developing countries, support labor-intensive public works.

THE U.N.: IS ITS SURVIVAL AT STAKE?

Once a proud organization that became an instrument of U.S. and Western policy during the Cold War, the United Nations is now struggling for its independence and existence. With the Cold War gone, there are still many problem areas such as Somalia and Bosnia that tax its efficiency and ability to keep the peace. Everyone expects more of the U.N. but few are willing to advance the required resources. Unlike the heyday of the Cold War, the U.S. is now the largest delinquent dues payer ($1.2 billion) of the U.N. The U.N. has had to cancel meetings because of leaking roofs that it has no money to repair.[88]

Despite the United Nations' plight, Congress will not be mollified if the U.N. reduces its dues. Congress' distrust of the organization is implacable. The U.N. is viewed as unreliable, arrogant, and extravagant. The U.N. past is littered with stories of its wastefulness and incompetence.

If Congress began paying its arrears, it demands that the U.N. be massively reformed. The U.N. budget must show zero growth. But this is a "catch 22": Reform and cutback measures cannot succeed, given the existing financial concerns: "Financial underpinning is essential to radical restructuring; even so relatively straightforward a task, for instance, as getting rid of the worst of the human deadwood is impossible if there is no money to pay people off."[89] If members, especially the U.S., do not pay their arrears, there will never be enough money to carry out fundamental reforms. This reality creates great uncertainty for the future viability of the U.N. To show its resolve to reduce its monetary commitment to international organizations, Congress urged the U.S. State Department to prioritize its funding requirements to the U.N. and other international organizations. The State Department criteria "included the extent to which the United States directly benefits from the organizations' activities, how much the organizations' budgets are devoted to activities benefiting the United States, the scope and depth of the organization constituencies, and their responsiveness to management improvement efforts."[90] Perhaps the one billion dollars pledged by Ted Turner to the U.N. for non-administrative costs will induce other donors and influence the U.S. to be more receptive toward paying its dues.

THE ROLE OF MLMS

Because of the decentralized nature of international agencies and national overseas programs, MLMs can exercise considerable power and influence. AID missions provide a good example. Because these missions are far-flung, officials in the field must constantly serve as transmitters of good, bad, or neutral information on the status of each program or project falling under their jurisdiction. This places AID MLMs in a position to exercise discretion in determining how policies are implemented in the field.[91] Decentralization and the difficulty of developing standardized evaluation methods all keep the top management in AID headquarters from exercising more than minimal control. What gets done is heavily dependent on what MLMs choose to do or not to do. Since recommendations to continue funding or terminate projects become a responsibility of MLMs, they play a relatively important role in designing loan programs and are responsible for most of the adaptive and innovative actions that take place.[92] As an effective guide to behavior, whenever the Congress or Treasury expresses disapproval of actions, MLMs will avoid such actions in the future, even if they are the most economic strategies to achieve objectives at hand.

MLMs in international agencies are delegated the power to apply geographical factors in the hiring of professional staff for the U.N. Secretariat. Because the precise guidelines for employing this criterion have never been clearly and specifically set forth, MLMs have broad discretion.

The power that decentralized MLMs wield was vividly demonstrates in the Congo (now Zaire). U.N. representatives temporarily closed down the radio station and the airport in the capital city in an effort to prevent the outbreak of violence. They believed their action was a neutral one in the political conflict between the prime minister and the president. However, the action turned out to be inimical to the prime minister, and this action created a dilemma for Secretary-General Hammarskjold.[93] The actions by representatives in the field were strongly protested by Communist countries. Hammarskjold felt obliged, nonetheless, to support the action of his subordinates. In doing so, he risked an open conflict with the Communist nations.[94]

One official indicated that it may be more appropriate to look at the power of MLMs not so much as a positive one but as negative, in the sense that they prevent the implementation of the intended policy. In international bodies MLMs have only limited opportunity to directly influence the initiation of policy, but they are able to make important contributions by supplying advice and information (produced and exchanged).[95]

Finally, the question of accountability may appear to present especially difficult problems for international civil servants, particularly where traditional hierarchical concepts of accountability continue. Simply moving a civil servant from his native social milieu to the U.N. Secretariat probably will not transform him into an internationally accountable individual with unswerving devotion to U.N. objectives. The internalized concept of accountability we propose in this volume requires that an international civil servant be socialized to be responsive to the needs of clients, constituents, and the public, wherever they may be. This emphasis transcends political and local boundaries; the goal is to be responsive to the legitimately articulated needs of the people.

DISCUSSION QUESTIONS

1.   What is meant by development administration?
2.   Why is the U.N. secretary-general said to have considerable power in operating the internal structures of the U.N. but minimal power in dealing with member states?
3.   Why has recognition of geography as a basis for U.N. recruitment become a source of power to developing nations?
4.   Discuss the reasons that national interests play a significant role in international organizations.
5.   What are the similarities between AID and the UNDP?
6.   What accounts for the differences in perspective between the U.S. Foreign Service and AID?
7.   Why is it said that the two types of budgets found at the U.N. tell more about its policies and operation than perhaps any other factor?
8.   Why ought it be said that the conflict in the U.N. is but a manifestation of multinational pluralism?
9.   Why has the U.S. failed to pay its assessed U.N. dues?

NOTES

1.   Robert W. Cox and Harold Jacobson, et al., *The Anatomy of Influence in International Organization* (New Haven, Conn.: Yale University Press, 1974), p. 1; some additional examples are the Organization of American States (OAS), European Economic Union, and World Bank.

2.   Sidney Mialeck, "Toward an International Civil Service," *Public Administration Review* (May-June 1970): 206.

3.   John Macy Jr., *Public Service, The Human Side of Government* (New York: Harper & Row, 1971), p. 233.

4.   Ibid., p. 245.

5.   Interview No. 2, United Nations, September 1978.

6.   Ibid.

7.   Herbert Lehman, "Some Problems in International Organizations," *Public Administration Review* (Summer 1945): 93; see also Interview No. 2, United Nations, September 1978.

8.   Interview No. 2, United Nations, September 1978.

9.   The U.N. biannual budget for 1976–77 was $745.8 million. During the same two years voluntary budgets for economic development projects alone exceeded $950 million.

10. M. Elmandjara, *The United Nations System: An Analysis* (Hamden, Conn.: Anchor Books, 1973), p. 210.

11. Lehman, "Some Problems in International Organizations," p. 97.

12. *Report of the Preparatory Commission of the United Nations* (Document PC/20, December 23, 1945), Chap. 7, Section 2, Para. 16, pp. 86–87.

13. Sidney D. Bailey, *The Secretariat of the United Nations* (New York: Carnegie Endowment, 1962), p. 21.

14. Ibid., p. 24.

15. Ibid., p. 34.

16. Ibid., p. 35.

17. Ibid., p. 38.

18. Ibid.

19. Foreign Agricultural Organization, 12th Session, 69th Planning Management (Sept. 26, 1957), paras. 72–73.

20. U.N. Document SG/910 (May 1, 1960), p. 6.

21. Bailey, *Secretariat of the United Nations*, p. 40; see also Foreign Agricultural Organization 5th Session, 869th Planning Management (September 23, 1960), paras. 283–85.

22. Henry Raymond, "Some Unresolved Problems of the International Civil Service," *Public Administration Review* (May-June 1970): 225.

23. Theodore Meron, *The United Nations Secretariat* (Lexington, Mass.: Lexington Books, 1977), pp. 82–83.

24. Ibid., p. 83.

25. Ibid., p. 226.

26. *Report of the Preparatory Commission of the United Nations* (Document PC/20, December 23, 1945), p. 92.

27. John Macy Jr., "Towards an International Civil Service," *Public Administration Review* (May-June 1970): 259.

28. Staff Regulation 1-9, U.N. Document ST/SGT/Staff Rules/1, 16 (March 1962).

29. See Article 101, para. 3 of the United Nations Charter.

30. Meron, *United Nations Secretariat*, p. 48.

31. Ibid.

32. Quoted in Henri Raymond, "Staffing of the United Nations Secretariat: A Continuing Discussion," *International Organization* (Autumn 1967): 759.

33. Seymour Maxwell Finger and John Mugno, *The Politics of Staff: The United Nations Secretariat* (New York: Ralph Bunche Institute of the United Nations, 1974), p. 20.

34. Raymond, "Staffing of the United Nations Secretariat," p. 751.

35. Ibid.

36. Ibid., p. 756.

37. David A. Kay, "Secondment in the United Nations Secretariat: An Alternative View," *International Organizations* (Winter 1966): 63–75.

38. Raymond, "Some Unresolved Problems," p. 225.

39. Finger and Mugno, *Politics of Staff*, p. 27.

40. Macy, "Towards an International Civil Service," p. 260.

41. Tien Cheng Young, *International Civil Service and Problems* (Brussels: International Institute of Administrative Sciences, 1958), pp. 141–40.

42. David Owens, "Reflection of an International Civil Servant," *Public Administration Review* (May-June 1970): 208.

43. Young, *International Civil Service and Problems*, pp. 140–1.

44. Richard M. Swift, "International Salary Administration in Search of Principles," *Public Administration Review* (May-June 1970): 237.

45. *Report of the Preparatory Commission of the United Nations* (Document PC/20, December 23, 1945), pp. 94–99; *Report of Committee of Experts on Salary, Allowance, and Review System*, ORGAV (1950), Supp. 7A.

46. Meron, *United Nations Secretariat*, p. 123.

47. Ibid., p. 239.

48. "High Pay at the U.N.: It's Drawing Fire," *U.S. News and World Report* (August 29, 1977), p. 61.

49. "Bloated Bureaucracy of Geneva U.N. Officers Comes Under Criticism," *Wall Street Journal* (August 11, 1976), p. 1.

50. U.S. General Accounting Office, *United Nations Personnel Compensation and Pension Issues* (Washington, D.C.: General Accounting Office/NSIAD-87-53, February 1987), p. 12

51. "High Pay at the U.N.: Its Drawing Fire," p. 62.

52. *Personnel for the New Diplomacy, Report of the Committee on Foreign Affairs Personnel* (Washington, D.C.: Carnegie Endowment for International Peace, December 1962), p. 28.

53. Elizabeth A. Bea and Herbert J. Horwitz, "Is the Foreign Service Losing Its Best Young Officers?" *Foreign Service Journal* Vol. 45 No. 2 (February 1968), pp. 30–32 and 44–45; Judith Tendler, *Inside Foreign Aid* (Baltimore: Johns Hopkins University Press, 1975), p. 16.

54. *Diplomacy for the 70's, A Program of Management Reform for the Department of State* (Washington, D.C.: Government Printing Office, 1970), pp. 265–69.

55. *Personnel for the New Diplomacy*, pp. 22–71.

56. Tendler, *Inside Foreign Aid*, p. 19.

57. Ibid., p. 20.

58. *Personnel for New Diplomacy*, pp. 25–26; in 1962, the Herter Report suggested that AID has the nucleus for a career personnel system.

59. Robert S. Jordan, *International Administration* (New York: Oxford University Press, 1971), p. 9.

60. *Diplomacy for the 70's*, pp. 42–45.

61. U.S. Department of State, "Reform" Bulletin No. 23 (June 22, 1971); Department of State, Bulletin No. 30 (December 8, 1971).

62. Alexander Lovejoy, *Reflections in International Administration* (Oxford, England: Clarendon Press, 1956), p. 77.

63. International Civil Service Advisory Board, Report of the 18 Series of the Board (New York: United Nations, ICSAB, xviii, 1, July 1970), pp. 35–36.

64. Interview No. 2, United Nations (September 1978).

65. Jordan, *International Administration*, p. 9.

66. Tendler, *Inside Foreign Aid*, p. 28.

67. Max Weber, "Essays in Sociology," edited and translated by H. H. Gerth and C. Wright Miller (New York: Oxford University Press, 1946).

68. Fred Riggs, "The Sales Model: An Ecological Approach to the Study of Comparative Administration," *Philippine Journal of Administration* 6, No. 1 (June 1962): 3–16.

69. David E. Apter, *The Gold Coast in Transition* (Princeton, N.J.: Princeton University Press, 1961).

70. Gabriel A. Almond and James S. Coleman, *The Politics of Developing Areas* (Princeton, N.J.: Princeton University Press, 1960); Robert T. Holt and John E. Turner, *The Political Basis of Economic Development* (Princeton, N.J.: D. Van Nostrand, 1966); Fred W. Riggs, *Administration in Developing Countries: The Theory of Prismatic Society* (Boston: Houghton Mifflin, 1964); Gabriel Almond and G. Bingham Powell, *Comparative Politics: A Developmental Approach* (Boston: Little, Brown, 1966); Robert Dahl, "The Service of Public Administration," *Public Administration Review* (Winter 1947): 1–11; Dwight Waldo, "Public Administration," in *Political Science: Advance of the Discipline*, Marian D. Irish, ed. (Englewood Cliffs, N.J.: Prentice-Hall, 1968), pp. 153–89; and Dwight Waldo, *The Administration State* (New York: Roland Press, 1948).

71. *Development Administration: Current Approaches and Trends in Public Administration for National Development* (New York: United Nations, 1975), p. 8; and Ferrell Heady, *Public Administration: A Comparative Perspective* (Englewood Cliffs, N.J.: Prentice-Hall, 1966).

72. United Nations, Development Administration., p. 32; our definition incorporates many of the ideas of the U.N. definition.

73. Bert F. Hoselity and Wilbert More, eds., *Industrialization and Society* (New York: UNESCO, 1973), pp. 159–73.

74. Gary Peters, *The Politics of Bureaucracy*, 4th edn., (New York: Longman, 1995), pp. 337–45.

75. R. S. Miling, "Bureaucracy and Development Administration," *Public Administration* 51 (Winter 1973): 411–15.

76. Louis Picard, "Rural Development in Botswana, Administrative Structure and Public Policy," *Journal of Developing Areas* B No. 3 (April 1979): 286–92.

77. Lucian Pey, *New Approaches to Personnel Policy for Development* (New York: United Nations, 1975), p. 2.

78. Interview No. 4, United Nations (April 1978).

79. William J. Siffin, "Two Decades of Public Administration in Developing Countries," *Public Administration Review* (January-February 1976): 68.

80. Interview No. 2, United Nations (September 1978).

81. Ibid.

82. Ibid.

83. "Bloated Bureaucracy of Geneva," *Wall Street Journal* (1976), p. 1.

84. Francis Sutton, "Technical Assistance," *Encyclopedia of the Social Sciences* (New York: Free Press, 1968), p. 565.

85. C. J. Dove, *International Training for Foreign Assistance* (Ann Arbor, Mich.: University of Michigan Microfilms, 1968), p. 13.

86. Tendler, *Inside Foreign Aid*, p. 30.

87. *A Fact Sheet on the Operational Activities of the U.N. System* (New York: United Nations, 1976), p. 3.

88. "United Nations Head for Bankruptcy," *The Economist* (February 10, 1996), p. 41.

89. Ibid.

90. U.S. General Accounting Office, *State Department: U.S. Participation in Special Purpose International Organization* (Washington, D.C.: General Accounting Office, March 1997, NSIAD-97-35).

91. Tendler, *Inside Foreign Aid*, p. 24.

92. Ibid.

93. Bailey, *Secretariat of the United Nations*, p. 40.

94. Ibid.

95. Interview No. 3, United Nations (September 1978).

18

Balancing Power
and Accountability

There should now be no doubt that MLMs exercise considerable power in public organizations. In this chapter, we attempt to promote a commitment to greater accountability by demonstrating how MLMs have the power to change public organizations. The chapter begins with an analysis of the problem of administrative power. We next turn to the question of accountability. Finally, we discuss the interdependency of power and accountability as providing a way to restore public confidence in government.

LEARNING OBJECTIVES

On completing this chapter, the reader should be able to:

- Identify the importance of power in organizations.
- Show how the unrestrained use of power impedes responsible management.
- Demonstrate the interdependence of power and accountability.
- Present a case for increasing public accountability by empowering recipients of public goods and services.

Throughout the text, we have emphasized two themes: the strategic role of MLMs in converting publicly determined objectives into programs and projects, and the interdependence of power and accountability.

The focus of both themes has been on management. We have stressed that public administration is mainly the daily activities of implementing programs carried out by MLMs. Those sections of the book dealing with processes, functions, and structures have stressed the necessity of mastering management skills if the aim is to have effective administration.

Because MLMs monopolize power in program implementation, they play a key role in any strategy to enhance accountability. Thus, the first step in increasing accountability is to recognize the utility of power. Power is needed to execute programs, and accountability cannot result from simply reducing power.

While the conflicts that the struggle for power entails cannot be eliminated, they can be turned to an advantage. Accountability, properly understood, is a far more complex undertaking than curbing abuses; it is the composite of all that is needed to bring theory and practice together in the achievement of public goals. Evidence of greater accountability is demonstrated in more people being able to do things better for themselves as a result of public programs.

The exercise of power by MLMs has been highlighted in every aspect of the administrative process.

1. *The context.* The lesson of Watergate is that power exercised in secret leads to abuse. The effort to correct abuses by circumscribing elected officials has only strengthened the hold on government by administrators and managers, thereby further weakening democratic control of government.

    Public administration is best defined by examining how it is practiced. This investigation reveals that much of government is carried out through private business and the third sector, through contracting out. MLMs in government are the major links between the sectors.

    The study of policy documents why particular programs are authorized and what happens to them in the process of implementation. Policy is what gets done, and MLMs play strategic roles in this process.

2. *Organization theory.* The dominant theory in government is derived from Weber and focuses on the bureaucracy (i.e., the interests of managers and the survival of organizations). Modifications of this theory, even though it stresses the adjustment of the organization to the individual, still emphasize power and productivity. In practice, government operates largely without the utilization of theory, and the norms come largely from the internal struggle for power.

    The required re-evaluation of theory must focus on conceptions that balance this power with accountability. This can be achieved by supplementing interests of economy, efficiency, and effectiveness with concerns for social equity through the creative use of conflict.

3. *The internal functions of management.* The substance of management is planning, organizing, coordinating, and controlling in order to achieve predetermined objectives. If desired outcomes are to be achieved, communication and decision making must be improved.

    In all of these functions of management, MLMs use their superior knowledge of detail and their position (proximity) between top administrators and operators to control the internal environment.

4. *Processes of implementation.* In personnel, the insistence by civil servants on their rights through court action, unionization, and professionalization and the demands by top administrators for greater productivity have fostered a human resource development approach.

    In the management of finances, promising reforms like PPBS, ZBB, and now TQM have had only limited success because they have not been institutionalized in the ongoing decision-making and budgetary allocations systems. The detailed control information that is now used to achieve regularity or narrow control accountability does not require accountability in terms of outcome, impact, and sustainability. The federal Government Performance Result Act of 1993 (GPRA) is a step in the right direction. To succeed, it must become part of the MLMs operating routines, a commitment to sustainability.

In each of these processes, MLMs occupy the key organizational points between program objectives and outcomes.

5.   *Policy areas.* Regardless of the governmental level—urban, national, international, or intergovernmental—and irrespective of the subject area—personnel development, energy conservation, or urban renewal—MLMs largely control the delivery of services.

THE PROBLEM OF ADMINISTRATIVE POWER

Administrative power expands relentlessly. The fear is growing that the nation is headed toward an administrative state. "The essence of the administrative state," in the view of Emmette S. Redford, "is that men are born and live not merely . . . in subordination of power, but under a regime in which they are both served and controlled by an institutional complex composed of organizations."[1] Within this organized existence, top administrators perpetrate abuses, partly by what they do and partly by what they prevent government from doing. In the middle and lower levels, the problem of administrative power appears to be individual corruption, but more pervasive is the condition where "wrongdoing has become the norm, and the standard accepted behavior necessary to accomplish organizational goals."[2] The power that permeates the public bureaucracy grows out of the discretion public servants exercise and the inadequacy of present controls (especially internalized ones). The central problem is how to legitimize this power and bring it under more democratic control. As we noted in Chapter 1, we offer a commitment to the public service philosophy as an answer.

THE ADMINISTRATIVE STATE

The emergence of a state run by administrators, not by elected officials, resulted from the increasing complexity of government, which has made the delegation of vast discretionary power to administrators inevitable. From a theoretical perspective, it reflects the failure to bring together the ideal of representative democracy and the need for a highly professionalized bureaucracy. The politics–administration dichotomy that would have promoted accountability has been abandoned as no longer possible in big government. The separation of powers between the executive and the legislature or between levels of government is no longer effective. Administrators and managers, who were not mentioned when the Constitution was written, have now formed a fourth branch of government that towers over both elected officials and the general public they are to serve.

Redford has charted the rise of the administrative state:

1.   We give power to public organizations.
2.   Specialized structures carry out that power.
3.   These structures multiply.
4.   Administrative staff of these structures make most of the policy decisions.
5.   Managers dominate increasingly complex delivery systems.
6.   Key decisions are made by a small group of administrator-managers, powerful interests, opinion makers (media), and selected consumers.
7.   Administration satisfies the few who have the power to bring about change.
8.   The general population is frustrated and sees no alternative.
9.   The system increases in complexity and consolidates.
10.   Disillusionment deepens as the democratic state appears to evolve into the administrative state. [3]

Redford does not despair of this development but instead directs us to search for a "workable democracy," which he defines as getting the most democracy available under the conditions that have produced the administrative state. We agree with that search but believe better guidelines to operationalize workable democracy are necessary.

There is a generally accepted view that a universal model of bureaucracy is equally applicable to any regime or ideological setting.[4] We question the view that bureaucracy is a universal norm. The use of the bureaucratic form by totalitarian countries should alert us to the need for an administrative model that is in keeping with or uniquely fits the practice of democratic governance. We believe a modification of bureaucratic structure must go hand in hand in the long-term training of public personnel to internalize a public service philosophy.

ABUSES OF POWER AT UPPER LEVELS

The most common administrative abuse of power of which the public is aware is illegal or unethical acts. We are upset when an administrator acts to satisfy personal wishes. The newspapers almost daily detail abuses in high places: personal misconduct, conflicts of interest, violation of procedural due process, gross inefficiency, attempts to cover up mistakes, or the hazing of lower-level employees.

An increasing array of surveillance systems is now employed to counter these abuses. Legislatures have made efforts to reassert their control. A number of states have passed "sunset legislation" providing an automatic termination for programs (usually after four years) unless they are reauthorized. Budget analysts scrutinize executive plans during the appropriation process, and administrators who abuse their power are likely to find their budgets cut. Legislatures have also employed other controls, such as committee hearings at which administrators are called to testify about their actions, special investigating committees to uncover undesired behavior, and the confirmation process (for major appointments). Increasing attention has been given to legislative oversight as a means to control administrative behavior. Routine program-evaluation reviews have been instituted to determine if administrators have accomplished the objectives for which they have been charged. At the federal level, additional controls include the following:

1. The Administrative Procedures Act of 1946 allows for a review of agency action where abuse of discretion, exceeding statutory authority, the abridgement of constitutional rights, or improper proceedings is charged.

2. Executive agencies are now required to give full publicity to their proceedings and provide notice and the opportunity for public comment on rule changes; to list the name of the person responsible for initiating a new rule; and to carry out administrative adjudications (of administrative rules and regulations) only after hearings in which impartial procedures have been followed.

3. Through the Freedom of Information Act of 1966, most of the files of public agencies are open for public inspection, and through federal "sunshine legislation," the meetings at which commissions and boards make their decisions must be open to the public.

4. The Civil Service Reform Act of 1978 encourages and provides for the protection of "whistle-blowers" who publicize abuses of authority; authorizes a general counsel in the Merit System Protection Board (MSPB) to conduct investigations inside the bureaucracy when charges of mismanagement are made; and authorizes the removal of members of the Senior Executive Service following two unsatisfactory evaluations.

5. Massive regulations, especially at the federal bureaucracy, have been cut. Many procedures instituted mainly to control unacceptable acts (of scandal) have been eliminated. As the controls have been diminished, oversight for accountability has gone to frontline MLMs, making them even more critical in the pursuit of accountability.

While these are powerful tools, they still are inadequate to control the acts of upper-level administrators. The main weakness of these measures is that they are ineffective as deterrents; they tend to be used after abuses have occurred. Also, surveillance requires the expenditure of resources and the availability of technical personnel. Though Congress has the capacity to thoroughly check the expenditures of administrators or to evaluate the quality of their output, it has been slow in developing criteria for assessment. Where such standards have been developed, they are seldom used to redirect policy.

Most states and local governments have no counterparts to the U.S. Comptroller General or Congressional Budget Office and no built-in and reliable performance appraisal system. At all levels of government, controls are inadequate because they tend to focus on detailed acts and not on organizational processes and their outcome; they are threats rather than a pursuit of available alternatives to achieve or produce the best. Surveillance occurs without a rational plan for making change. Disclosures are usually no more than inputs into the next law-making cycle. Top administrators can be prosecuted for taking bribes or for fraudulent behavior, but the process is lengthy, difficult, and often has spillover effects injurious to the agency. Typically, agencies allow an administrator to resign rather than subject her or him to prosecution for infractions.

The most important form of abusive action occurs when administrators simply fail to carry out the responsibilities entrusted to them. These refusals to carry out legislated intentions often surface on a grand scale, as when the American Indian population rises up against the Bureau of Indian Affairs, when universities attack the Office of Education, or minorities speak negatively of affirmative action officers. Failures ranging from the inadequacies of correctional and educational institutions to unsatisfactory road maintenance further illustrate the abuses associated with grossly inefficient, untimely, or simply undelivered services. This generalized dissatisfaction was alluded to centuries ago by Shakespeare in response to the "law's delay" and "insolence of office."[5] In short, controls must extend beyond what administration does to include what it fails to do. Most government programs are intended to improve conditions— to make the streets safe, to collect taxes, to provide education, or to enhance a community's health. The primary complaint is that these promised results are not being achieved despite ever-rising taxes and expanding bureaucracies. Yet devices for protecting the public from what administrators fail to do are all but nonexistent.

In some places, an ombudsman system has been tried. Usually a person in an organization is specifically assigned the task of receiving complaints directly from clients and of investigating the complaints from inside the organization. Ombudsmen are usually authorized to criticize the wisdom of administrators' decisions. While this procedure has gained some acceptance in Europe, it has very limited use in the United States, due in great part to people's lack of understanding and resulting lack of popular support. It does bring out, however, that effective controls will have to be instituted inside the organization itself.

ABUSES OF POWER AT MIDDLE AND LOWER LEVELS

MLMs commit abuses quite similar to those ascribed to their administrative superiors. Because they operate in a more limited area of the organization, the abuses tend to be more limited in scope (see Table 18.1). There are ample opportunities for dishonest acts at the MLM range, as when a transit driver pockets a fare rather than putting it in the fare box or an IRS auditor accepts kickback payments for overlooking fraud. James S. Bowman surveyed a sample of federal managers concerning abuses and how the behavior of middle-level managers compared with that of top-level administrators.[6] The questionnaires required respondents to indicate: (1) whether they considered specific behaviors to be unethical; (2) whether their peers would consider them to be unethical; and (3) whether top management would believe them to be unethical.

Table 18.1 suggests that individual managers have a fairly good ethical set of beliefs:

1. Nearly all of the 17 items were regarded as unethical.
2. Generally, managers see their peers as holding similar values, although at a slightly lower ethical level.
3. Managers perceived their own ethical standards as higher than those of their superiors.

Despite these observations, it has become evident that many managers engage in many practices that run counter to the public interest.

Table 18.1. Comparison of Managers' Beliefs with Perceived Peer and Top Management Beliefs (n = 343, percent agree)

	Behavior	Managers	Peers	Top Management
1.	Passing blame for errors to an innocent co-worker	96.4	86.1	75.7
2.	Divulging confidential information	87.5	83.1	84.6
3.	Falsifying time/quality/quantity reports	94.4	81.0	78.3
4.	Claiming credit for someone else's work	94.7	71.8	57.6
5.	Padding expenses over 10 percent	95.0	81.9	82.5
6.	Pilfering agency materials and supplies	83.4	69.7	82.2
7.	Accepting gifts/favors in exchange for preferential treatment	94.7	85.8	75.1
8.	Giving favors in exchange for preferential treatment	88.1	76.0	63.5
9.	Padding expenses up to 10 percent	84.0	61.4	69.1
10.	Authorizing a subordinate to violate agency rules	74.8	69.4	61.4
11.	Calling in sick to take a day off	70.0	48.4	67.4
12.	Concealing one's errors	68.0	48.2	46.3
13.	Taking longer than necessary to do a job	69.7	49.6	63.5
14.	Using agency services for personal use	78.9	62.3	58.5
15.	Doing personal business on agency time	58.5	42.7	46.9
16.	Taking extra personal time (lunch hour, breaks, early departure)	50.1	35.0	42.7
17.	Not reporting others' violations of agency policies and rules	43.0	33.2	52.2

Source: Adapted from John W. Newstrom and William A. Rich, "The Ethics of Management and the Management of Ethics," *MSU Business Topics* (Winter 1975): 29–37.

In probing the increased visibility of corruption in government, Gerald E. Caiden and Naomi J. Caiden offered the concept of "systemic corruption." Corruption has traditionally been viewed as deviant or exceptional behavior by a dishonest individual, but systemic corruption generalizes these acts to the organization as a whole. The primacy of the goal of organizational survival becomes regularized and institutionalized. In systemic corruption:

1.   The organization professes an external code of ethics that is contradicted by internal practices.
2.   Internal practices encourage, abet, and hide violations of the external code.
3.   Nonviolators are penalized by forgoing the rewards of violation and offending violators.
4.   Violators are protected and, when exposed, treated leniently while their accusers are victimized for exposing organizational hypocrisy and are treated harshly.
5.   Nonviolators suffocate in the venal atmosphere, finding no internal relief and much external disbelief.
6.   Prospective whistle-blowers are intimidated and terrorized into silence.
7.   Courageous whistle-blowers have to be protected from organizational retaliation.
8.   Violators become so accustomed to their practices and the protection given them that, on exposure, they evidence surprise and claim innocence and unfair discrimination against them.
9.   Collective guilt finds expression in rationalizations of the internal practices, and without strong external supports there is no serious intention of ending them.
10. Those formally responsible for rooting out corruption rarely act and, when forced by external pressure to do so, excuse any incidents as isolated rare occurrences.[7]

Systemic corruption is evidence of collusion at MLM levels of organizations. Knowledge of wrongdoing is widespread. "In contemporary public administration," conclude the Caidens, "the issue is not so much individual misconduct in public office, serious though it is, but the institutional subversion of the public interest through systemic corruption."[8]

Efforts to bring about reform have been unsuccessful. Investigations by prosecutors, requirements of public disclosure of private holdings, and the tightening of regulations seem to have made little change in behavior. Procedural and structural changes have generally not been successful; neither have advisory committees or public interest groups. The search for accountability in the middle levels of organization must thus be instituted based on a different set of assumptions.

THE QUEST FOR ACCOUNTABILITY

The ideal of a neutral bureaucracy, one that favors no particular societal group, was an attractive one but it failed to take into account the danger that the bureaucracy could become partial to itself. This now seems to have occurred, and public trust in government is at an all-time low. We need therefore a greater accountability generated from within organizations. In this quest for account-ability, MLMs can be major agents for change.

What Is Accountability?

Amitai Etzioni has called attention to three popular meanings associated with the term "accountability": (1) greater responsibility to elected superiors; (2) greater responsiveness to community groups (usually meaning minorities); and (3) greater commitment to "values and higher standards of morality."[9] In prac-tice, however, efforts in all three directions are seldom accompanied by specific arrangements for implementation, making accountability difficult to realize.

We have defined accountability as any situation in which individuals who exercise power are expected to be constrained and in fact are reasonably con-strained by external means, and to a degree by internal norms. We shall now explore the imposition of external constraints and the internalization of norms and the problems associated with each of these dimensions of accountability.

ACCOUNTABILITY THROUGH EXTERNAL MEANS

Accountability as responsibility means being held to account for steward-ship of a resource or authority. Typically, administrators have several account-abilities to discharge:

- Fiscal accountability—responsibility for public funds.
- Legal accountability—responsibility for obeying laws.
- Program accountability—responsibility for carrying out a program to achieve specific results.
- Process accountability—responsibility for carrying out agreed pro-cedures.
- Outcome accountability—responsibility for results.
- Sustainability accountability—making clients better off and indepen-dent for an extended time horizon.

Accountability, in the external sense as defined by Frederick Mosher, is the objective responsibility for actions of a person or an organization to something outside of one's self.[10] The following questions can be asked: (1) How well did the results conform to the given task? (2) How efficient were the means employed? (3) Was the operation carried out in accordance with the legal mandate? (4) Are the people satisfied with the results? (5) Did results produce enablement and sustainability?

This type of accountability remains elusive mainly because of the complexity of public affairs but also because goods and objectives are not clearly articulated. As we have seen, ideas and interests that stimulate legislative action have to be converted into programs and projects and then carried out by managers in an environment in which key conditions cannot be anticipated. Bargaining and compromise characterize the authorization phase. Second, legislative intentions are often difficult to convert into operational programs, resulting in goal displacement. In many public programs, it is difficult to determine who is accountable for what and frequently impossible to determine the results of the implemented programs. The information links between what was intended and what is accomplished are not usually provided.

ACCOUNTABILITY AS AN INNER CHECK

The second dimension of accountability refers to internal norms. Here we turn to certain professional, ethical, and pragmatic guides for the manager in daily work. Given the complexity of governmental programs, it is important to emphasize that these internal checks are probably the major means of controlling large public bureaucracies. If the abuse of government power is to be checked, these means must be strengthened.

In a 1936 essay, John M. Gaus discussed "the responsibility of public administration" by addressing "the inner check."[11] He argued that managers could find many guides to responsibility by following the standards and ideals of the profession. The American Society for Public Administration (ASPA) and its companion organization, the National Association of Schools of Public Affairs and Administration (NASPAA), see themselves as guides, thus reflecting the old traditions of crafts and guilds and of municipal leagues and civil service associations before the turn of the century.

But professional guidelines, as inner checks, have limits. Professional public administration associations are now accused of supplanting broad public interests with their own agenda: the building of large and influential professional organizations that could influence the flow of money from federal and state governments into training and thus ultimately limit the number of trained professional administrators in the marketplace in order to keep their salaries high. ASPA resisted mounting its own equal employment opportunity program for women and minorities and has remained at the fringes of equal employment opportunity programming, thus making it necessary for minorities and women to form their own competing professional organization.

The search for internalized checks of abuses has taken the recurring form of establishing codes of ethics for elected officials and public employees. Such codes contain a list of moral judgments offered as a standard to be followed even when behavior is not monitored. Typically, these codes provide for dismissal as a penalty for infractions rather than criminal prosecution. Congress promulgated such a code in 1958, and in 1962 President Kennedy issued Executive Order 10939, which was a set of ethical standards. Many departments and agencies of state and local government have also set up comparable codes of conduct. The International City Managers Association's widely known code is commonly cited as a guide because of its use of a board of ethics.

In the wake of the Watergate scandal, the National Academy of Public Administration (NAPA) issued for discussion a threefold guide on ethical behavior. An abbreviated version is shown in Table 18.2.

Table 18.2. NAPA Code of Ethics

Outputs to Decisions	Limits of Compromise	Implementing Decisions
1. Inform others participating in the decision of significant information.	1. Resist decisions before they are final, even by going to the legislature if the pending mistake warrants this action and the risk of losing future usefulness in the agency is a price worth paying.	1. Ask no subordinate to take any illegal action.
2. Interpret data not only unbaised by conflict of interest, but also with one's value base revealed.	2. While one may be required to prepare a disputed document on an objectionable subject, one is not required to sign it.	2. Do not suppress significant public information.
3. Be guided in advocacy by the importance of the issue, one's competence, and by one's place in the hierarchy.	3. Uphold the law in one's sphere of responsibility and discretion.	3. Carry out legal decisions in good faith despite one's disagreement with their merit.
4. Accept decisions made within the rules even if one regards them as unwise.	4. Resign if interpretations of the law by superiors are unacceptable.	4. Underlying all guidelines is that all administrators are bound by the law of the land and are obligated to use their power in the public interest.
5. Defend decisions that have been properly made, even though personally objectionable.		

Source: Adapted from George A. Graham, "Ethical Guidelines for Public Administrators: Observations on Rules of the Game," *Public Administration Review* (January-February 1974): 90–92.

Generally speaking, codes of ethics have failed to curtail administrative abuses. They project a double standard between administrative behavior and the behavior of the larger society. Corruption by business, the buying of influence by large corporations, cynicism about the church, white-collar crime, and a general respect accorded to money irrespective of its source are omnipresent.

Moral standards also vary among ethnic and income groups and are dependent on circumstances. A widespread American value is pragmatism, the view that permits moral behavior to be guided by practicality and experimentation. Closely related is the popular endorsement of competitive struggle, in which felicity consists of getting ahead of one's neighbor by pursuing self-interest. Undertones of pragmatism come through in the NAPA guidelines.

A second problem is that words in any code are subject to varying interpretation In the NAPA example, it is not clear what is meant by "significant information" or how one reveals a "value bias" or operationalizes "competence," "legality," or the "public interest." Most codes offer little more than moral exhortations, for they are generally devoid of practical means of enforcement.

EDUCATION AND TRAINING FOR ACCOUNTABILITY

For accountability to be a an effective guide to action, it must be internalized to become an operating philosophy and habit in the daily decisions of MLMs. Public interest values must occupy a premier position in the education and training of public servants. We believe that this can begin with the recognition that MLMs—that is, most public servants—exercise significant power and discretion. Accountable public servants must internalize norms to work against what we have labeled goal displacement (i.e., the pursuit of personal gain and preoccupation with the survival of the bureaucracy).

Public servants must obtain the knowledge and skills necessary to meet the ever increasing demands being placed on government. This duty cannot be neglected, but a more crucial aspect of the preparation goes beyond technique toward wisdom. The pursuit of what ought to be done begins with self-reflection; MLMs must consciously confront their own values and take responsibility for the acts they take or fail to take. Former Harvard University President Derek Bok has suggested some critical topics that would be appropriate in building a greater sense of ethics:

1. A sense of the constitutional system and the limitations it places on the administrative discretion of public executives.
2. A well-rounded background drawing on liberal arts curricula, ranging from anthropology to psychology, introducing students to a wide range of values held by different groups in society.
3. Studies of history and biographies to deepen understanding of human experience and give judgmental tools about recurring dilemmas.
4. The study of political philosophy to provide a basis for understanding fundamental values.
5. The use of the case method to help develop more rigorous analytical tools for resolving conflict.[12]

Some have suggested the systematic study of Supreme Court decisions in order to locate values within the context of contested issues. Still others suggest that briefing sessions be held on ethical conduct and accountability as part of regular in-service training. All of these suggestions point in the right direction and bring out how woefully deficient the public administration curriculum has been in the recent past. Any new approach to the study of public administration should based on a disciplined and internalized public service philosophy. Alternatively, the Japanese system of administrative inspection might be considered. Japan's Administrative Management Agency (AMA) is located in the prime minister's office and carries out administrative inspections primarily "concerned with improving the operation of government agencies."[13]   It determines the appropriateness of policies and government agencies' implementation of policies and their impact. Each year twenty topics for the year are identified based in part, on consultations with experts outside of government. In selecting the agencies to be inspected, emphasis is given to:

1.   Government programs requiring implementation.
2.   Priority areas targeted for financial improvements.
3.   Malfunctioning interagency problems due to poor coordination.
4.   Reviewing obsolete programs.
5.   Reports from local AMA agencies identifying the need for policy review.
6.   Matters brought to light by the media.[14]

While administrative inspection has some similarity to the federal General Accounting Office (GAO), there are significant differences. Evaluations are predominantly nonfinancial and priorities are determined by a carefully defined process based on criteria established by the executive branch and not the legislative branch, as is generally the case with the GAO.

The accountability report card is another option to be considered. Each administrator or official participating in the delivery loop (providing goods and services to target populations) is held accountable for the program goals and objectives. Program statements require identification of outputs, inpacts, and sustainable changes that are being sought. Achievement of 100 percent of the targeted goals and objectives would produce complete congruence between intentions and achievements; however, this seldom occurs.

Thus, to avoid a moving target regarding the degree of accountability achieved, an accountability continuum system that incorporates the gap concept could be instituted. At any given point in time in the stage of program implementation, an accountability assessment gap can be agreed upon. . . . At the inception of each program or undertaking, a threshold should be identified regarding the level of the accountability gap that will be reasonably tolerable and acceptable. This would allow citizens to predict and know when and at what level of achievement will be the acceptable accountability.[15]

THE INTERDEPENDENCE OF POWER AND ACCOUNTABILITY

Accountability in the middle levels must have a foundation in power as well as a moral base. In simplest terms, effective accountability reflects what Robert T. Golembiewski has called "the more and more hypothesis," in which greater accountability yields additional increments of power (and vice versa) and where the lack of accountability diminishes available resources.[16] Accountability and the empowerment of people are mutually supportive. Accountability must be redefined to show its interdependency with power and operationalized so that abuses of power can be minimized.

The major abuses of power are the failure of government to deliver the programs and services that have been authorized and funded, and the displacement of publicly determined program goals with organizational aggrandizement and personal objectives (job security and promotion). Thus, to enhance accountability we must improve the capacity of government to achieve publicly articulated goals. This inevitably focuses attention on MLMs because they are the major translators of publicly determined intentions into outcomes. Accountability thus must rest on a facilitation of MLM capacity to act.

We need not lament the need for granting greater power to MLMs so long as they are monitored by external controls and internal checks. However, much greater attention must first be given to assessing the impact of goods and services and developing a public interest philosophy that shows the congruence of personal and public interests in the pursuit of publicly determined objectives.

ACCOUNTABILITY REDEFINED

The traditional view of accountability placed emphasis on holding officials "answerable" to superiors for their acts. It was as though the "account" in "accountable" was the primary concern. Implied is a hierarchical view in which top administrators check the performance of MLMs. Such a posture paid little attention to program outcomes but accepted the view that power operates as a zero-sum game. When subordinates gained power, it meant a loss of power by superiors. Accountability was imposed from the top with the conscious intent of circumscribing the exercise of power at each successive level down the hierarchy. Mary Parker Follett labeled this tendency the "domination view of power."[17]

A redefined concept of accountability must take into account the many topics we have taken up in this volume—the cultural setting, internal processes, and the behavior of administrators. This redefinition will not be easy but it will emphasize the "able" in "accountable" by stressing the acts of MLMs that have been enabling for consumers and the community. This point has been stressed in one way or another in virtually every chapter in the text. In Chapter 6, for example, it is at the heart of security maximization in the discussion of political economy. In Chapter 7, it comes out in what Follett describes as power seen as integration.[18] Enablement must be the essence of the way MLMs exercise influence in the internal environment, because they provide the link between the old approaches to personnel administration and newer themes of human resource development. When administrators discharge their jobs effectively, they aid clients and simultaneously increase the agency resource base, giving administrators greater rewards and recognition for a job well done. In other words, accountability must be seen as the congruence between personal and public interests.

The new accountability must give power to both those delivering goods and services and those receiving then. This brings theory and practice together—the basic test of a good organization. It shows us how inputs or desires are initiated and converted, producing outputs and impacts that are compared with intended goals. All parts of the organization are thus woven into a working functional whole; in a word, they are integrated. No one part dominates, and the increasing power of one element translates into the strengthening of all other parts.

Let us use order-giving to illustrate an integrative view of accountability. Order-giving is not complete until the receiver implements the intentions of the person giving the order. In an integrated process, not only do the administrators issuing the order and the managers implementing it gain but, more important, the publicly determined objectives—the outcomes and impacts—are given priority.

Operationalizing accountability thus stresses satisfying the people's needs. As managers look toward outcomes, it becomes clearer that the conditions that have led to the administrative state can be countered significantly by greater participation in administration. This view pragmatically recognizes that many programs require consumer acceptance, which helps to promote greater accountability.

All of these changes will require the fostering of a new philosophy of administration. As Etzioni has put it:

The objective is *not* to fly in the face of reality or power groups, nor to widely pursue Utopian notions of social justice or accountability–such an administrator is all too likely to be quickly expelled—but to help shape, mobilize, and combine the vectors which determine the unit's direction and accountability model so as to bring them close to the desired system. To shape these forces requires educating the various groups to definitions and demands which are close to what is equal and ethical and just. This is probably the most difficult part of creating the administrator's job.[19]

With this book, we hope we have made a start by directly addressing MLMs as the key agents of organizational change. They have the power to bring about a "workable democracy" by balancing power with accountability to enhance people's quality of life. The balancing of power and accountability is an arduous task that requires that power be subservient to the kind of accountability that improves the quality of governance in a democratic state.

ACCOUNTABILITY IN A CHANGING ENVIRONMENT

We have shown that we are moving into a new era in which the strict Weberian or the Taylor or Gulick and Urwick modified mechanistic approaches no longer apply in many, if not in most, cases to produce the best outcomes in the delivery of goods and services. The team approach, with its emphasis on maximizing customer and clientele satisfaction, is becoming the accepted norm in organization. This does not mean that strategic planning has been thrown out. It has simply been moved from the top of the hierarchy to each responsibility center.

Strategic planning is inescapable for organizations. It is critical for all major decision-making levels and points in the organization. Chairman Jack Welch of General Electric says that all responsibility managers (especially in large divisions) should view themselves as chief executive officers. The function of hiring and selecting personnel is to obtain the best people in terms of skill and philosophy. These individuals will typically find the optimum ways to produce the best results consistent with expectations. Once charged with responsibilities, these highly qualified, motivated and committed individuals will achieve the ideal accountability or at least minimize the accountability gap. In the public sector, committed MLMs are driven to realize maximum sustainable accountability in the delivery of goods and service.

DISCUSSION QUESTIONS

1. Discuss why the administrative state has developed in American society.
2. What is meant by internal and external checks on accountability? Indicate the advantages and disadvantages of each.
3. What is administrative corruption, and why has it taken such strong hold in the bureaucracy?
4. Discuss the reasons that power and accountability are inseparably linked.
5. Discuss the Japanese practice of administrative inspection.
6. What is the accountability report card concept? Is it consistent with democratic governance?

NOTES

1. Emmette S. Redford, *Democracy in the Administrative State* (New York: Oxford University Press, 1969), pp. 38–39.
2. Gerald E. Caiden and Naomi J. Caiden, "Administrative Corruption," *Public Administration Review* (May-June 1977): 306.
3. Redford, *Democracy in the Administrative State*, pp. 179–204.
4. John M. Pfiffner and R. Vance Presthus, *Public Administration,* 3rd edn. (New York: Ronald Press, 1953), p. 521.
5. For more details see Alan L. Pean, "Re-establishing Confidence in Government," *Public Administration Review* (January-February 1977): 83–88.

6.   James S. Bowman, "Ethics in the Federal Service: A Post-Watergate View," presented at ASPA Convention, Atlanta, Georgia (March 10-April 2, 1977).

7.   Caiden and Caiden, "Administrative Corruption," pp. 306–307.

8.   Ibid., p. 308.

9.   Amitai Etzioni, "Alternative Conceptions of Accountability: The Example of Health Administration," *Public Administration Review* (May-June 1975) 279–285.

10.   Frederick C. Mosher, *Democracy and the Public Service* (New York: Oxford University Press, 1968), pp. 7–9.

11.   John M. Gaus, *The Frontiers of Public Administration* (Chicago: University of Chicago Press, 1936), pp. 26–44. Reprinted in Dwight Waldo, ed., *Ideas and Issues in Public Administration* (New York: McGraw-Hill, 1953), pp. 432–440.

12.   Derek C. Bok, *The President's Report, 1973–74* (Cambridge, Mass.: Harvard University, 1974), pp. 13–14.

13.   Kiyoak Tsuji, ed., *Public Administration in Japan* (Tokyo: University of Tokyo Press, 1984), p. 176.

14.   Ibid., p. 177

15.   Jerome B. McKinney, *Understanding ZBB and TQM: Promise and Reality* (Clinton, Maryland: Public Policy Press, 1995).

16.   Robert T. Golembiewski, *Men, Management, and Morality* (New York: McGraw-Hill, 1965), pp. 211–12.

17.   Henry C. Metcalfe and L. Urwick, eds., *Dynamic Administration: The Collected Papers of Mary Parker Follett* (New York: Harper and Brothers, 1940), pp. 36–49.

18.   Ibid.

19.   Etzioni, "Alternative Conceptions of Accountability," p. 284.

Appendix: Public Administration Research Aids

KEEPING UP TO DATE AND DOING RESEARCH IN PUBLIC ADMINISTRATION

There are literally hundreds of publications and sources serving as reference guides and information providers for the fields of government and public administration.

This Appendix provides suggestions on ways to conduct research in the field and locate sources to keep those interested in public administration up-to-date. The ease of access provided by the Internet, World Wide Web, gopher servers and online databases makes research easier, thereby providing incentives for administrators to obtain the latest information more frequently.

The availability of the fax machine, e-mail, and direct links with agencies for online questioning and answering has facilitated and shortened the time line for communication and information. Most of the information sources available to public administrators can be easily and quickly found online. Most sources provide the complete bibliographical reference and an abstract, and many retrieve the actual work itself. For this reason, the following reference guide to these sources is representative, rather than comprehensive (a nearly impossible task due to continual change). The intent is to provide the reader with a guide to finding appropriate information, recognizing that the Information Age is rapidly bringing more timely, useful information to the citizenry continuously through more sophisticated and user-friendly formats.

RESEARCH MAP TO PUBLIC ADMINISTRATION INFORMATION SOURCES

Electronic searching is the key to modern research techniques and is a frequently used entry path into libraries, the Internet, indexing systems, and publications.

Once the search terminology is decided (it is usually preferable for the user to experiment with a variety of key words), there are several sources for finding data. The following section provides information on both online and printed data in the public administration field.

COMMON SEARCH TERMS FOR SUBJECT
AND KEY WORD SEARCHES

Major search terms, used individually or as a prefix, encompassing the field of public administration include:

administration, administrative agency, bureau
budget, public finances, tax, taxation
census
executive, legislative, judicial
foreign policy, United Nations, international, comparative government
government (federal, state, local, city, municipal, borough, township, SMSA, county, intergovernmental, international)
grants
law, justice, courts
political parties
public, public sector, public policy
public opinion, voting, citizen, election, electoral, interest group, lobbying, politics, political
regulation, regulatory
urban, urban affairs

These search terms are often combined with the general or specific topic of interest, such as various management topics (e.g., human resources, leadership), individual agency names, citizen concerns and interests (e.g., environmental, automobile registration, safety and health issues), geographical location, and so on, to locate relevant information.

ELECTRONIC SEARCH TOOLS AVAILABLE
TO THE RESEARCHER

As more data become electronically accessible, the boundaries among the various sources for finding information become more blurred. The following discusses various search tools available to the researcher. Our caveat, however, is that over time, as search tools become more sophisticated and interwoven, the sources will become less distinct.

The Catalog Goes Electronic

A typical and historical entry point for library research has been the general catalog, which is automated in most libraries and is rapidly becoming accessible from offices connected through the Internet. A subject and/or keyword search of the catalog using search terminology geared toward the public sector (illustrated above) coupled with the specific topic of interest will result in a list of available sources (books, newspapers, journals, etc.) and locations. Specific author, title, and call number searches can also be undertaken.

THE INTERNET, ONLINE DATABASES, AND INDEXES

The Internet

The Internet, commonly referred to as the information superhighway, has quickly become a multipurpose vehicle for all sectors to provide and receive information. Government units at all levels utilize the Internet to communicate with the public, to provide both new and traditional information, and to link with other information providers.

The government information and home pages are accessible, both through specific addresses (typically called a URL) and using the search techniques discussed above. At the time of the publishing of this book, there were over 250 search services of which approximately 25 are frequently used. These services are often called search engines. Some of the services have a specific government category (for example, *Yahoo, InfoSeek Guide,* and *Excite*), but most of the general search engines also will retrieve government Web sites and connect the user to the desired information. The analogy to the superhighway is relevant; a user can get to the same information by taking a variety of roads. For example, searching with *Yahoo, Lycos, Webcrawler*, and several other search services will all get the searcher to the White House home page.

Government and other information relevant to public administrators available through the Internet spans a multitude of content and formats. Examples of content include: information on government agencies and personnel (all levels of government), listings of available government opportunities (jobs, grants, research), U.S. bills, laws and regulations (searchable for easy access), *Monthly Catalog,* government reports and budgets, key statistics (e.g., census or labor), research projects and findings, bibliographic information and summaries of available data, access to online indexes, speeches, press releases, announcements, and news stories.

Data formats also vary, as do readability and accessibility. Many government agencies are utilizing the World Wide Web home pages to present information and links to further material. Home page locations are accessed by specific URL addresses, and typically referred to as Web sites. In addition to knowing a URL address, researchers can easily locate Web sites through search engines. When accessing by URL, the user must ensure the address is typed exactly or an error will occur. Search engines allow less exact keyword entries, employing algorithms to retrieve near matches. Examples of Web sites include: the White House, Senate and House of Representatives, which link to individual elected member sites, government agencies, important government reports, and so on.

Web sites are typically organized in visually appealing and easy-to-use formats that provide several information choices to the user. Each choice is linked to other sources of information on the Internet, making searches convenient and quick.

For example, a recent visit to the U.S. Department of Education Web site (http://www.ed.gov/) provided a well-designed menu with graphics and subsequent link points to: *Welcome* (an introduction to the department); *News; Guides; Money Matters* (grant, contracts, student financial assistance, etc.); *Secretary's Initiatives; People and Offices; Programs and Services; Publications and Products; Other Sites* (links to educational resources); *Search* (retrieval tools to find documents within the Department or elsewhere on the Internet); and *Picks o' the Month.*

The U.S. House of Representatives' home page (http://www.house.gov/) presented the following categories and selection choices: *What's New; The Legislative Process* (information on latest floor action, bills, resolutions, and members' votes); *Schedules* (for legislative activity); *Who's Who and How To Contact Them; Organization and Operations; Member, Committee, and House Organizations' Published Information; Laws; Visitor Information; Educational Resources; Empowering the Citizen; Listing of All Information; Other Government Information Resources;* and *Your Comments Please!*

Government reports available on the Internet are retrieved through file servers, called gopher servers, which are accessed through links on Web sites, search engines, or specific URL addresses. Gopher servers, accessed through the Internet search tools (such as *Veronica, World Wide Web*, etc.), store files containing text or binary data, directory information, images, and sound, and provide gateways to other information systems.

Typical gopher access is through the network service, Telnet, which connects the user to data located in libraries throughout the world. There are thousands of government documents retrievable online, many with search capabilities, such as the U.S. budget, census data, government job listings, audit reports, guides and handbooks, tax forms, agency publications and reports, U.S. codes and regulations, and so on. Users can download many of these documents electronically via File Transfer Protocol (FTP).

Some examples of frequently accessed Web sites include:

> http://www.fedworld.gov (major government site)
> http://www.irs.ustreas.gov/prod/ (IRS)
> http://www.business.gov (U.S. Business Advisor)
> http://www.census.gov/ (U.S. Census home page)
> http://www.sbaonline.sba.gov/ (U.S. Small Business Administration)
> http://www.usps.gov/ncsc (U.S. Postal Service)
> http://www.whitehouse.gov/ (White House)
> http://www.state.gov/ (Department of State)
> http://www.un.org/ (United Nations)
> http://www.loc.gov. (Library of Congress)
> http://www.lib.umich.edu/libhome/documentcenter (University of Michigan)
> http://www.elibrary.com (Electronic Library)
> http://www.lexis-nexis.com (Lexis-Nexis - legal information)
> http://nasire.org/ss/index.html (state search - links to all states)
> http://www.law.vill.edu/fed-agency/fedwebloc.html (federal web locator)
> http://www.business.gov (U.S. Business Advisor)
> http://www.nttc.edu/nttc.html (National Technology Center)
> http://www.iso.ch (International Standards Organization)

http://www.loc.gov/copyright (Copyright Office)
http://www.enviro-net.com/regulations (Enviro-Net - federal and state regulatory information)

Online Access Systems and Tools for Government Documents

The *Federal Web Locator*, (http://www.law.vill.edu/Fed-Agency/fedwebloc.html) a service provided and continually updated by the Villanova Center for Information Law and Policy, contains a large list of federal government Web sites. The *FedWorld Home Page*, provided and maintained by the National Technical Information Service (NTIS), accesses federally produced scientific, technical, engineering, and business information. Seven thousand new documents are sent monthly by over 200 agencies.

GPO Access, (http://www.access.gpo.gov/su_docs/aces/aaces001.html) a service of the U.S. Government Printing Office, provides links to the *Federal Register, Congressional Record, Congressional Bills, General Accounting Reports, United States Code, U.S. Budget, Economic Report of the President* and various other documents. At the time of printing of this book, there were thirteen libraries providing links with free connection to GPO Access through the Internet.

MOCAT, (gopher://www.access.gpo.gov:80/hGET%20/su_docs/dpos/adpos400.html) the online version of *Monthly Catalog*, is also on the Internet.

The National Trade Data Bank, (http://www.stat-usa.gov/BEN/Services/ntdbhome.html) contains online information on international trade statistics and data on countries.

Electronic Indexes and Databases

Prior to the development of user-friendly and easily accessible link to the Internet, online searches concentrated on specific indexes and databases provided and updated by vendors and institutions. With the advent of the Information Age, databases are proliferating, and users are beginning to identify more with search tools than with specific databases and indexes. For example, a search using *Infoseek, Lycos,* or *Yahoo* will obtain the same information that is available by searching a specifically requested database.

Several databases serve as indexes to publications and reports, searchable through the same methods. Most of the databases provide an abstract of the reference, and some provide and print the reference in its entirety on request. Although indexes are also available in print form, electronic search capabilities are converting most researchers to the electronic media, and publishers are rapidly making online and CD-ROM versions available. Although the Internet links to many abstracts, titles and tables of contents of copyrighted materials from private vendors and publishers, fee-based databases and CD-ROMs still play a large role in research.

Access through Internet to Telnet connections, indexes and databases housed in libraries is rapidly expanding, and undoubtedly over time, more of the databases will be accessible through Internet gopher and web site connections to specific vendors, libraries, university centers and document providers (although fees may be applied to content retrieved). For those that are not yet available on the Internet, many libraries subscribe to on-line databases and the CD-ROM versions, which also provide search capabilities. Additionally, there are on-line search systems which perform searches into a multitude of databases simultaneously.

Indexes remain very useful research sources, because they are very focused and are typically not available on public access links. Because not all sources are indexed in the Internet, a search of a specialized index is very useful. (Internet search engines index only those materials that are published and/or referenced on the Internet). Indexes that are useful to the public administrator include: *PAIS, Social Science Citation Index, INFOTRAC, The Newsbank, and the National Newspaper Index, Uncover Index to over 17,000 periodicals)*.

In addition to *GPO Access, MOCAT,* and the Web search engines, database systems providing access to multiple databases simultaneously include: *National Trade Data Bank, CARL, FirstSearch, and EPIC*.

ASSOCIATIONS

Associations collect and provide useful information and updates on topics relevant to their members' interests; they also publish newsletters and periodicals. A search of the *Encyclopedia of Associations* under "government" yielded approximately 100 associations whose service areas involve one or more aspects of government. This search did not include civic interest organizations.

Associations are indexed in the *Encyclopedia of Associations*. Associations that may be useful to those interested in public administration include:

Academy for State and Local Government, Washington, D.C.
Advisory Commission on Intergovernmental Relations, Washington, D.C.
American Management Association, New York, N.Y.
American Planning Association, Washington, D.C.
American Political Science Association, Washington, D.C.
American Public Welfare Association, Washington, D.C.
American Public Works Association, Washington, D.C.
American Society for Public Administration, Washington, D.C.
Council of State Governments, Lexington, Ky.
Government Finance Officers Association, Chicago, Ill.
International City Managers Association, Washington, D.C.
International Personnel Association, Alexandria, Va.
National Association of Counties, Washington, D.C.
National Association of Schools of Public Affairs and Administration, Washington, D.C.
National League of Cities, Washington, D.C.
U.S. Conference of Mayors, Washington, D.C.

Some selected institutes and foundations include:

American Productivity Center, Houston, Texas
Brookings Institution, Washington, D.C.
Center for Science in the Public Interest, Washington, D.C.
Common Cause, Washington, D.C.
Conference on Minority Public Administrators, Washington, D.C.
Congressional Quarterly Service, Washington, D.C.
Institute of Public Administration, New York, N.Y.
National Center for Productivity, New York, N.Y.
Policy Studies Organization, University of Illinois, Urbana, Ill.
Public Administration Service, McLean, Va.
Rand Corporation, Santa Monica, Calif.
Tax Foundation, Washington, D.C.
Urban Institute, Washington, D.C.

FREQUENTLY ACCESSED GOVERNMENT REPORTS AND PUBLIC ADMINISTRATION LITERATURE

The following are citations of frequently accessed government documents. The majority are accessible through the Internet and the search vehicles described earlier, as well as in printed versions. They are listed here because of their centrality to government research:

1990 Census of Housing Reports
1990 Census of Population Reports
Commerce Business Daily
Congressional Quarterly
Healthcare Financing Review
Historical Statistics of the United States: Colonial Times to 1970
Monthly Catalog
U.S. Government Manual
U.S. Statistical Abstract

JOURNALS

The following are some journals that contain public affairs information:

Academy of Management Review, Ohio Northern University
Administration and Society, Virginia Polytechnic Institute and State University
Administrative Science Quarterly, Cornell University
American Review of Public Administration, University of Missouri, Kansas City
California Management Review, University of California, Berkeley
Canadian Public Administration, Institute of Public Administration, Canada
GAO Journal, U.S. General Accounting Office
Governing, Congressional Quarterly Inc.
International Journal of Public Administration, Pennsylvania State University, Harrisburg

Journal of Policy Analysis and Management, University of California, Berkeley
Journal of State Government, Council of State Governments
New Directions in Public Administration Research, Florida Atlantic University
Organizational Dynamics, American Management Association
Public Administration, Royal Institute of Public Administration, Oxford, England
Public Administration and Development, London, England
Public Budgeting and Financial Management, Pennsylvania State University, Harrisburg
Public Manager, The Bureaucrat Inc.
Public Productivity and Management Review, Jossey-Bass Publishers
State and Local Government Review, University of Georgia

Selected Bibliography

Anton, Thomas J. *Administered Politics: Elite Political Culture in Sweden.* Boston: Martinus Nijhoff, 1980.

Appleby, Paul. *Policy and Administration.* Tuscaloosa: University of Alabama Press, 1949.

Archibald, Samuel J. "The Freedom of Information Act Revisited." *Public Administration Review* 39, No. 3 (July–August 1979): 311–17.

Argyis, Chris. *Intervention Theory and Method.* Reading, Mass.: Addison-Wesley, 1970.

Ban, Carolyn. *How Do Public Managers Manage.* San Francisco, Calif.: Jossey-Bass Publishers, 1995.

Barbour, George, P. Jr., Thomas W. Fletcher, and George A. Sipel. *Handbook: Excellence in Local Government Management.* Washington, D.C.: International City Management Association, 1984.

Bartolome, Fernando. "Teaching About Whether to Give Negative Feedback," *The Organizational Behavior Teaching Book for Human Relations Training.* Bethel, Maine: NTL Institute for Applied Behavioral Science, 1976.

Bass, Bernard M. *Stogdill's Handbook of Leadership: A Survey of Theory and Research,* rev. edn. New York: Free Press, 1981.

Beam, David R. "New Federalism, Old Realities." In *The Reagan Presidency and the Governing of America,* Lester M. Salamon and Michael S. Lund, eds. Washington, D.C.: The Urban Institute, 1984.

Bennis, Warren. "The Artform of Leadership." In *The Executive Mind,* Suresh Srivastya, ed. San Francisco: Jossey-Bass, 1983.

Bennis, Warren and Bert Nanus. *Leaders: The Strategies for Taking Charge.* New York: Harper & Row, 1985.

Berlu, David K. *The Process of Communication.* New York: Holt, Rinehart & Winston, 1960.

Bernard, Chester. *The Functions of the Executive* Cambridge, Mass.: Harvard University Press, 1938.

Blake, Robert R. and Jane S. Mouton, *The Managerial Grid III.* Houston: Gulf Publishing, 1984.

Brett, E. A. "The Participatory Principle in Development Projects: The Costs and Benefits of Cooperation." *Public Administration and Development* 16, No. 1 (February 1996): 5–20.

Burns, Nancy. *The Formation of American Local Governments: Private Values in Public Institutions.* New York: Oxford University Press, 1994.

Caiden, Gerald E. and Naomi J. Caiden. "Administrative Corruption." *Public Administration Review* (May–June, 1977): 306.

Caldwell, Lynton. *Administrative Theories of Hamilton and Jefferson.* Chicago: University of Chicago Press, 1944.

Carnegie, Dale. *How to Win Friends and Influence People.* New York: Simon & Schuster, 1936.

Carroll, James D. "The Rhetoric of Reform and Political Reality in the National Performance Review." *Public Administration Review* 55, No. 3 (May–June 1995): 302–12.

Carroll, James D. and Dahlia Bradshaw Lynn. "The Future of Federal Reinvention: Congressional Perspective." *Public Administration Review* 56, No. 3 (May–June 1996): 299–304.

Carroll, Stephen J. and Dennis A. Gillen. "Are the Classical Management Functions Useful in Describing Managerial Work?" *Academy of Management Review* (January 1987): 38–51.

Coe, Charles K. *Public Financial Management.* Englewood Cliffs, N.J.: Prentice-Hall, 1989.

Denhardt, Robert B. *The Pursuit of Significance: Strategies for Managerial Success in Public Organizations.* Belmont, Calif.: Wadsworth, 1993.

Dimock, Marshall E. "The Criteria and Objectives of Public Administration." In *The Frontiers of Public Administration,* John M. Gaus, Leonard D. White, and Marshall E. Dimock, eds. Chicago: University of Chicago Press, 1936.

Dimock, Marshall Edward and Gladys O. Dimock. *Public Administration.* New York: Holt Rinehart and Winston, 1964.

Doig, A. "Good Government and Sustainable Anti-Corruption Strategies: A Role for Independent Anti-Corruption Agencies." *Public Administration and Development* 15, No. 2 (May 1955): 151–66.

Douglas, Morgan, Kelly G. Bacon, Ron Bunch, Charles D. Cameron, Robert Deis. "What Middle Managers Do in Local Government: Stewardship of the Public Trust and the Limits of Reinventing Government." *Public Administration Review* 56, No. 4 (July/August, 1996): 359–66.

Downs, Anthony. *Inside Bureaucracy.* Little, Brown, 1967.

Drucker, Peter. Innovation and Entrepreneurship. *New York: Harper & Row, 1983.*

Dubrin, Andrew J. *Reengineering Survival Guide.* Cincinnati, Ohio: Executive Press, 1995.

Dye, Thomas and Virginia Gray, eds. *The Determinants of Public Policy.* Lexington, Mass.: Lexington Books, 1980.

Eggers, William D. and John O'Leary. *Revolution at the Roots: Making Our Government Smaller, Better and Closer at Home.* New York: Free Press, 1995.

Espy, Siri N. *Handbook of Strategic Planning for Non-Profit Organizations.* New York: Praeger, 1986.

Fallows, James. *Looking at the Sun: The Rise of the New East Asian Economic and Political System.* New York: Pantheon Books, 1994.

Fayol, Henri. *General and Industrial Management,* trans. by C. Storrs. London: Isaac Pitman and Sons, 1949.

Fiedler, Fred E. *A Theory of Leadership Effectiveness.* New York: McGraw-Hill, 1967.

Fiedler, Fred E. and M. Charmer. *Leadership and Effective Management.* Glenview, Ill.: Scott Foresman, 1974.

Finer, Herman. "Administrative Responsibility in Democratic Government." *Public Administration Review* 1 (Summer 1941): 335–50.

Fischer, Frank and John Forester, eds. *Confronting Values in Policy Analysis: The Politics of Criteria.* Newbury Park, CA: Sage Publications, 1987.

Fisher, Louis. *Congressional Conflicts between Congress and the President,* 3rd edn. Lawrence, Kan.: University Press of Kansas, 1991.

Flanders, Loretta R. and Dennis Utterback. "The Management Excellence Inventory." *Public Administration Review* 45 (May–June 1985): 405–10.

Fleishman, Joel. L., Lance Leibman, and Mark H. Moore, eds. *Public Duties: The Moral Obligations of Government Officials.* Cambridge, Mass.: Harvard University Press, 1981.

Freeman, J. Lieper. *The Political Process: Executive Bureau Legislative Committee Relations.* New York: Random House, 1965.

French, Wendell L. and Cecil H. Bell Jr. *Organization Development: Behavioral Science Interventions for Organization Improvement,* 4th edn., Englewood Cliffs, N.J.: Prentice-Hall, 1990.

Friedrich, Carl J. "Public Policy and the Nature of Administrative Responsibility." In *Public Policy,* Carl J. Friedrich and Edward S. Mason, eds. Cambridge, Mass.: Harvard University Press, 1940.

Gabor, Andrea. *The Man Who Discovered Quality.* New York: Times Book-Random House, 1992.

Gardner, James R., Robert Rattlin, and H. W. Allen Sweeny, eds. *Handbook of Strategic Planning.* New York: John Wiley, 1986.

Gardner, John. *On Leadership.* New York: Free Press, 1990.

Gardner, Neely. *Group Leadership.* Washington, D.C.: National Training and Development Service, 1974.

Gaus, John M. *The Frontiers of Public Administration.* Chicago: University of Chicago Press, 1936.

Gellerman, Saul W. "Why 'Good' Managers Make Bad Ethical Choices." *Harvard Business Review* (July–August 1986): 85–90.

Gerge, H. Frederickson. "Comparing the Reinventing Government Movement with the New Public Administration." *Public Administration Review* 56, No. 3 (May–June 1966): 233–70.

Golembiewski, Robert T. *Humanizing Public Organizations.* Mount Airy, Md.: Lomond, 1985.

Golembiewski, Robert T. *Man, Management and Morality.* New Brunswick, N.J.: Transaction Books, 1993.

Goodsell, Charles T. *The Case for Bureaucracy,* 2nd edn. Chatham, N.J.: Chatham House, 1985.

Gore, Albert. *Creating A Government That Works Better and Costs Less: Report of the National Performance Review.* Washington D.C.: U.S. Government Printing Office, 1993.

Gruber, Judith E. *Controlling Bureaucracies.* Berkeley, Calif.: University of California Press, 1987.

Gulick, Luther. "Notes on the Theory of Organizations." In *Papers on the Science of Administration,* Luther Gulick and L. Urwick, eds. New York: Institute of Public Administration, 1937a, pp. 1–46.

Gulick, Luther. "Science, Values, and Public Administration." In *Papers on the Science of Administration,* Luther Gulick and L. Urwick, eds. New York: Institute of Public Administration, 1937b, pp. 189–95.

Gulick, Luther, and L. Urwick, eds. *Papers on the Science of Administration.* New York: Institute of Public Administration.

Gurstein, M. and J. Klee. "Towards a Management Renewal of the United Nations, Part I." *Public Administration and Development* 16, No. 1 (February 1996): 43–56.

Gurstein, M. and J. Klee. "Towards a Management Renewal of the United Nations, Part II." *Public Administration and Development* 16, No. 2 (May 1996): 111–22.

Habermas, Jurgen. *Knowledge and Human Interests.* Boston: Beacon Press, 1972.

Hale, Mary M. "Learning Organizations and Mentoring." *Public Productivity and Management Review* 19, No. 4 (June 1996): 422–33.

Hatry, Harry P. *A Review of Private Approaches for Delivery of Public Services.* Washington, D.C.: The Urban Institute, 1983.

Henry, William. *In Defense of Elitism.*

Herzberg, Frederick, Bernard Mausner and Barbra Snyderman. *The Motivations to Work.* New York: John Wiley and Sons, 1959.

Ingraham, Patricia W., Barbara S. Romzek and Associates, eds. *New Paradigms for Government.* San Francisco: Jossey-Bass Publishers, 1994.

Jreisat, Jamil E. *Managing Public Organizations: A Developmental Perspective on Theory and Practice.* New York: Paragon House, 1992.

Jummel, Ralph P. *The Bureaucratic Experience,* 3rd edn. New York: St. Martin's Press, 1987.

Jun, Jong S. *Management by Objectives in Government.* Beverly Hills, Calif.: Sage Publications, 1976.

Kanter, Rosabeth Moss. *The Change Masters: Innovation for Productivity in the American Corporation.* New York: Simon & Schuster, 1983.

Kanter, Rosabeth Moss. *Men and Women of the Corporation.* New York: Basic Books, 1977.

Kastenbaum, Martin I. and Ronald Straight. "Paperless Grants Via the Internet." *Public Administration Review* 56, No. 1 (January–February 1996): 114–20.

Kaufman, Herbert. *The Forest Ranger.* Baltimore, Md.: Johns Hopkins University Press, 1960.

Kaul, M. "Civil Service Reforms: Learning From Commonwealth Experiences." *Public Administration and Development* 56, No. 2 (May 1996): 123–30.

Kettl, Donald F. *Sharing Power.* Washington, D.C.: The Brookings Institution, 1993.

Kettl, Donald F. *Government by Proxy.* Washington, D.C.: CQ Press, 1988.

Khan, Robert L., B. N. Wolfe, R. P. Quinn, and J. D. Snock. *Organizational Stress Studies in Role Conflict and Ambiguity.* New York: John Wiley, 1964.

Kincaid, John. "Reinventing Federalism." *PA Times* 16, No. 2 (February 1, 1993): 3.

Koontz, Harold. "The Management Theory Jungle." *Journal of the Academy of Management* 4, No. 3 (December 1961): 174–88.

Kravchuk, Robert and Ronald W. Schack. "Designing Effective Measurement Systems Under the Government Performance Results Act of 1993." *Public Administration Review* 56, No. 4 (July/August 1996): 348–58.

Krislov, Samuel. *Representative Bureaucracy.* Englewood Cliffs, N.J.: Prentice-Hall, 1974.

Kuhn, Thomas. *Structures of Scientific Revolution.* (Chicago: University of Chicago Press, 1962.

Latane, Henry A. "The Rationality Model in Organizational Decision Making." In *The Social Science of Organizations,* Harold J. Leavitt, ed. Englewood Cliffs, N.J.: Prentice-Hall, 1963.

Lee, Young S. *Constitutional Values and Public Service.* Westport, Conn.: Quorum Books, 1996.

Likert, Rensis. *New Patterns of Management.* New York: McGraw-Hill, 1961.

Lowi, Theodore. "Four Systems of Policy, Politics, and Choice." *Public Administration Review* 32 (July–August 1972): 298–310.

Marini, Frank. *Toward the New Public Administration.* Scranton, Pa.: Chandler Publishing, 1971.

Maslow, Abraham. *Motivation and Personality.* New York: Harper & Brothers, 1954.

McGregor, Douglass. *The Human Side of Enterprise.* New York: McGraw-Hill, 1960.

McKinney, Jerome B. *Effective Financial Management in Public and Nonprofit Agencies.* Westport, Conn.: Quorum Books, 1995.

McKinney, Jerome B. *Risking a Nation.* Lanham, Md.: University Press of America, 1995.

McLaughlin, Curtis. *The Management of Nonprofit Organizations.* New York: Wiley, 1986.

Meltsner, Arnold J. *Policy Analysts in the Bureaucracy.* Berkeley: University of California Press, 1976.

Mooney, James and Alan C. Reiley. *The Principles of Organization.* New York: Harper & Row, 1939.

Morgan, Douglas, Kelly G. Bacon, Ron Bunch, Charles D. Cameron, and Robert Deis. "What Middle Managers Do in Local Government: Stewardship of the Public Trust and the Limits of Reinventing Government." *Public Administration Review* 56, No. 4 (July–August 1996): 359–66.

Morgan, Gareth. *Creative Organization Theory.* New York: Sage Publications, 1989.

Morley, Elaine. *A Practitioner's Guide to Public Sector Productivity Improvement.* New York: Van Nostrand Reinhold, 1986.

Murray, Sylvester. "Privatization: Myth and Potential." *Urban Resources* 2 (Summer 1985): 3–5.

Myers, F. Scott. *Every Employee a Manager.* New York: McGraw Hill, 1970.

National Commission on the Public Service. *Leadership for America.* Washington, D.C.: National Commission on the Public Service, 1989.

Nolbandian, John. "The U.S. Supreme Court's Consensus on Affirmative Action." *Public Administration Review* 49 (January–February 1989): 39.

Nutt, Paul C. and Robert W. Backoff. "Fashioning and Sustaining Strategic Change in Organizations." *Public Productivity and Management Review* 19, No. 3 (March 1996): 313–37.

Oleszek, Walter J. *Congressional Procedures and the Policy Process,* 3rd edn. Washington, D.C.: Congressional Quarterly, 1989.

Organ, Dennis H. "A Review of Management and the Worker." *Academy of Management Review* 11, No. 2 (April 1986): 459–64.

Osborne, David and Ted Gaebler. *Reinventing Government.* New York: Addison-Wesley, 1992.

Ostrom, Vincent. *The Intellectual Crisis in Public Administration.* Tuscaloosa: University of Alabama Press, 1971.

Ouchi, William G. *Theory Z: How American Business Can Meet the Japanese Challenge.* Reading, Mass.: Addison-Wesley, 1981.

Perrow, Charles. *Complex Organizations,* 3rd edn. Glenview, Ill.: Scott Foresman, 1986.

Peters, Thomas and Robert Waterman. *In Search of Excellence.* New York: Harper & Row, 1982.

Peters, Tom. *Thriving on Chaos.* New York: Alfred A. Knopf, 1988.

Posner, Barry Z. and William H. Schmidt. "Values and the American Manager: An Update." *California Management Review* (Spring 1984): 202–16.

Pressman, Jeffrey and Aaron Wildavsky. *Implementation.* Berkeley: University of California Press, 1973.

Quade, E. S. *Analysis for Public Decisions,* 2nd edn. New York: North-Holland, 1989.

Ragu, V. William. "Struggles in Transformation: A Study in TQM Leadership and Organizational Culture in a Government Agency." *Public Administration Review* 56, No. 3 (May–June 1996): 227–34.

Rawls, John. *A Theory of Justice.* Cambridge, Mass.: Belknap Press of Harvard University Press, 1971.

Redford, Emmette S. *Democracy in the Administrative State.* New York: Oxford University Press, 1969.

Reich, Robert B. "Public Administration and Public Deliberation: An Interpretive Essay." *Yale Law Review* 94 (1985): 1617–41.

Riggs, Fred W. *Administration in Developing Countries—The Theory of Prismatic Society.* Boston: Houghton Mifflin, 1964.

Ripley, Randall B. and Grace A. Franklin. *Congress, the Bureaucracy, and Public Policy,* 4th edn. Pacific Grove, Calif.: Brooks/Cole, 1987.

Rogers, Carl R. and Richard E. Farson. *Active Listening.* Chicago: Industrial Relations Center of the University of Chicago, 1976.

Rohr, John A. *Ethics for Bureaucrats.* New York: Marcel Dekker, 1978.

Rubin, Barry M. "Information Systems for Public Management." *Public Administration Review* 46 (November–December 1986): 540–52.

Savas, E. S. *Privatization: The Key to Better Government.* Chatham, N.J.: Chatham House Publishers, 1987.

Schachter, Hindy Lauer. *Fred Taylor, The Public Administration Community: Reevaluation.* Albany, New York, 1989.

Schachter, Hindy Lauer. "Reinventing Government or Reinventing Ourselves: Two Models of Improving Government Performance." *Public Administration Review* 55, No. 6 (November–December 1995): 530–37.

Schachter, Hindy Lauer. *Reinventing Government or Reinventing Ourselves,* Albany, New York, 1997.

Schein, Edgar H. *Organizational Culture and Leadership.* San Francisco: Jossey-Bass, 1987.

Schein, Edgar H. *Process Consultation: Its Role in Organizational Development.* Reading, Mass.: Addison-Wesley, 1969.

Selznick, Philip. *TVA and the Grass Roots.* Berkeley: University of California Press, 1949.

Sherwood, Frank P. "An Academician's Response: The Thinking, Learning Bureaucracy." *Public Administration Review* 56, No. 2 (March–April 1996): 154–56.

Siegel, Gilbert B. and Robert C. Myrtle. *Public Personnel Administration: Concepts and Realties.* Boston: Houghton Mifflin, 1985.

Simon, Herbert. *Administration Behavior,* 3rd. edn. New York: Free Press, 1976.

Simon, Herbert A., Donald W. Smithburg, and Victor A. Thompson. *Public Administration.* New York: Alfred A. Knopf, 1950.

Simpson, Anthony E. *Information-Finding and the Research Process: A Guide to Sources and Methods for Public Administration.* Westport, Conn.: Greenwood Press, 1993.

Smith, Hedrick. *Rethinking America.* New York: Random House, 1995.

Steil, Lyman D., Larry L. Barker, and Kittie W. Watson. *Effective Listening.* Reading, Mass.: Addison-Wesley, 1983.

Stokey, Edith and Richard Zechuaser. *A Primer for Policy Analysis.* New York: Norton, 1978.

Swieringa, Joop and André Wierdsman. *Becoming a Learning Organization: Beyond the Learning Curve.* Reading, Mass.: Addison-Wesley, 1992.

Sylvia, Ronald D., Kenneth J. Meier, and Elizabeth M. Gunn. *Program Planning and Evaluation for the Public Manager,* Pacific Grove, Calif.: Brooks/Cole, 1985.

Taylor, Frederick W. *Scientific Management.* New York: Harper & Row, 1923.

Tender, Glen. *Political Ranking.* Boston: Little Brown, 1970.

Thompson, Dennis F. *Political Ethics and Public Office.* Cambridge, Mass.: Harvard University Press, 1987.

Thompson, James D. *Organizations in Action.* New York: McGraw-Hill, 1967.

Thompson, Victor A. *The Development of Modern Bureaucracy: Tools Out of People.* Morrison, N.J.: General Learning Press, 1974.

Tucker, Robert C. *Politics as Leadership,* rev. edn. Columbia, Missouri: University of Missouri Press, 1995.

Tullock, Gordon. *The Politics of Bureaucracy.* Washington, D.C.: Public Affairs Press, 1967.

Vroom, Victor H. and Phillip W. Yetton. *Leadership and Decision-Making.* Pittsburgh, Pa.: University of Pittsburgh Press, 1973.

Walker, David B. "The Advent of Ambiguous Federalism and the Emergency of New Federalism III." *Public Administration Review* 36, No. 3 (May–June 1966): 271–80.

Wamsley, Gary I., and Mayer N. Zald. *The Political Economy of Public Organization.* Lexington, Mass.: Lexington Books, 1976.

Weber, Max. *The Theory of Social and Economic Organization,* Talcott Parson. ed., A. M. Henderson and Talcott Parson, trans. New York: Free Press, 1947.

West, Jonathan P. *Quality Management Today.* Washington, D.C.: International City Managers Association, 1995.

White, Leonard D. *The Federalists.* New York: Macmillan, 1948.

White, Leonard D. *The Study of Public Administration.* New York: Macmillan, 1948.

Wholey, Joseph S. et al. *Federal Evaluation Policy.* Washington, D.C.: Urban Institute, 1973.

Wilson, Woodrow. "The Study of Public Administration." *Political Science Quarterly* 2 (June 1887): 197–222.

Wort, Montgomery Van. "'Reinventing' in the Public Sector: The Critical Role of Value Restructuring." *Public Administration Quarterly* 19, No. 4 (Winter 1996): 456–78.

Wren, Daniel A. *The Evolution of Management Thought,* 3rd edn. New York: John Wiley & Sons, 1987.

Yates, Douglas. *Bureaucratic Democracy.* Cambridge, Mass.: Harvard University Press, 1982.

Yin, Robert K. and Douglas Yates. *Street Level Government.* Santa Monica, Calif.: Rand Corporation, 1974.

Young, Dennis R. *If Not for Profit, for What?* Lexington, Mass.: Lexington Books, 1983.

Zaltman, Gerald and Robert Duncan. *Strategies for Planned Change.* New York: Harper & Row, 1977.

Zuck, Alfred M. "Education of Political Appointees." *The Bureaucrat* 13 (Fall 1984: 15–18.

Index

About the Authors

JEROME B. McKINNEY is Professor of Public Management and Policy at the University of Pittsburgh. He has held government positions at state and local levels, and acted as a consultant to all levels of government. He is the author of *Effective Financial Management in Public and Nonprofit Agencies, Second Edition* (Quorum, 1995).

LAWRENCE C. HOWARD is currently Distinguished Professor at Chatham College. He is a former Dean of the Graduate School of Public and International Affairs at the University of Pittsburgh.

CPSIA information can be obtained
at www.ICGtesting.com
Printed in the USA
BVOW06s1016061117
499654BV00012B/489/P